AF427526

THE PARADISE PARADOX

A Search for Lost Human Nature Among the Ruins of Civilization

JAMES PETERSON

biblio pole press

Library of Congress Control Number: 2022922330

A catalogue record for this book is available from the National Library of New Zealand.

The Paradise Paradox: A Search for Lost Human Nature Among the Ruins of Civilization/James Matthew Peterson Date: 2023. By: Peterson, James Matthew, 1965- author. Includes index.

The events and conversations in this book have been set down to the best of the author's ability, although some names and details have been changed to protect the privacy of individuals.

ISBN: 979-8-9862140-0-9

1. History: Civilization Middle East. 2. Religion and Politics 3. Philosophy — Good and Evil. 3. Religion — History. 4. History of Ideas 5. History and Archaeology. 6. Memoirs.

Publisher: Bibliopole Press, Auckland, N.Z. - Saint Paul, Minnesota

Bibliopole Press, 2023. Format: viii, 506 p. ; 23.4 cm.

ACKNOWLEDGMENTS

This book owes its completion to the generous encouragement of friends and loved ones, and to new acquaintances and kind listeners.

Special thanks to Erica J. Oswald, who worked closely with me to shape an earlier version of this book.

To Bill, who said, "Write a book!"

To Mike, who read early chapters and said, "Keep going!"

To Alastair, who encouraged me to complete the race.

And to Judy, who faithfully read everything, raised red flags when I veered off course, inspired deeper thoughts, and helped me to keep the work moving in the right direction.

I also want to acknowledge the collaboration of Melissa MacAulay, my editor. Her wide range of knowledge and masterful editing made this a much better book in every way.

CONTENTS

PROLOGUE

My Muslim Brothers

It was in Athens during the chilly winter of 1987 that my life lost its rhythm. The circumstances were simple enough: we sat in a dingy apartment drinking tea, just me and two members of the Muslim Brotherhood, all of us young and intense, bearded, and underfed.

Of course, you might think, this should make anyone nervous. After all, the Brothers were radioactive, banned across the Middle East. Compounding matters, as an evangelical American and a resident of Israel since my teens, I represented the two species that the Brothers despised the most—namely, Zionists and Crusaders.

This they could have found out easily, as everyone was obliged to carry their passport on their person in those days. Mine was doubly cursed: it was a US passport issued in Tel Aviv and it was laden with Hebrew stamps that confessed to years of resident Zionism.

Even without these provocations, however, there was reason to be nervous in Athens. This was when the city was a cauldron of disaffected souls, a noxious blend of Leftist European radicals and Levantine revolutionaries. They all dreamed of what wasn't, and of bringing that vagary into existence by any means—even if that meant dying or killing for it.

In the mixing pot, we had the unsavory home-grown 17 November anti-capitalist Greeks alongside a cadre of equally austere and bland Maoist Kurds. Then there were the Arab flavors of the secular PLO and the

Islamists like my Muslim Brothers. Not to be left out, there were Christian Armenian terrorists in town, too, attracting in turn the Turkish agents who wished to neutralize them. While the Turks had assassinated Armenian militant chief Hagop Hagopian in Athens in 1988, the Israelis did even better: they killed two different PLO bosses in 1986 as part of the ongoing "Operation Wrath of God," Israel's response to the Munich Olympics massacre.

All and sundry had safe houses in Athens, whence plots were hatched, staged, and enacted. In 1985 alone there were two notorious hijackings: one by the pious Hizbollah, which ended gruesomely in Beirut; and one by a PLO offshoot, the Abu Nidal Organization. If that weren't enough, the N17 was in the middle of a string of assassinations, including that of Captain George Tsantes, head of the Joint United States Military Assistance Group. Many more bombers and prospective bombers, intent on fulfilling plots elsewhere, used Athens as home and muse.

None of this was a secret when I made plans to visit the Brothers. After all, President Reagan had only recently urged that American-based airlines "review the wisdom of continuing any flights into Athens." Yet here I was, knocking on the Muslim Brothers' door with a Bible in my hand and an incriminating passport in my pocket.

Nervous? On the contrary—I was maniacally happy to be there and expected great things.

I liked the Brothers. They would make good Christians, I thought. And unlike the PLO and Kurds, who tilted heavily to the agnostic and materialistic Left, the Brothers bore a saintly aura. They were misguided, yes. But I reckoned they were men of God, just like Reagan had when he embraced the otherwise unhuggable Afghan mujahideen.

My thinking was that if radical Muslims in Afghanistan had proved themselves to be God's agents by virtue of their hatred for the Soviets, I could also assess the Brothers by their enemy, Syrian president Hafez al-Assad. Not only was he their foe, but he was also an iconic enemy of Israel, the enemy of America, and therefore the enemy of Christ's Kingdom. And as we know, in the Middle East especially, the enemy of my enemy is my friend.

Despite being Israel's archenemy, Assad was viewed as the devil incarnate by Muslims like these Brothers. Not only was he an ally of the Soviets who waged a merciless war against fellow Muslims in Afghanistan, Assad had also laid siege to the Brotherhood stronghold of Hama for twenty-seven days straight. It was uninterrupted slaughter, and when he was done (having killed an estimated 20,000 people), Assad paved over the carnage, effectively and unwittingly building a city-sized mausoleum to the martyrs. Mention Hama in the Middle East and you were met with grave nods.

Why was Assad so brutal? What did he fear? Clearly, he recognized a potent political threat; but more than that, he saw a spiritual threat to his crass and cynical despotism. The Brotherly mission was driven by faith—pure and unimpeachable—something a secular-materialist like Assad could never comprehend, but which I understood perfectly.

The Brothers' dream was both nostalgic and utopian. The goal was to establish an Islamic realm free of Western vices like interest rates, secular law, scientism, sexual confusion (meaning choice), and what was termed "shopping-cart" religious beliefs. (Their prophet, Sayyid Quṭb, deplored the West's idea that religion is a set of optional, personal convictions.) It was to be a head-to-toe Quranic theocracy, and secular nationalists such as Assad, Nasser, or Saddam Hussein stood in the way.

At the time, I couldn't disagree with any of that. After all, I also looked for the Kingdom of God to be brought to Earth as many evangelicals do. We sought to affect culture and government. Our solutions were radical and maximalist. The only part the Muslim Brothers had wrong was believing that Islam was the solution. If they only knew Jesus! My visit was intended to introduce them to the Messiah, and I dreamed they would embrace the Good News I was to bring. Their destiny was to bring Jesus' Kingdom of God to the Arabs.

You are thinking what a fool I was, and I can understand why. That my errand was quixotic goes without saying. I neither recognized its futility nor countenanced the slightest concession to decorum. I showed up wearing scout boots made by my kibbutz, their Hebrew logo clearly stitched on the outside. Why not? It was part of my message, and I was not ashamed of Israel. I was proud and sure of one thing—Israel's role in the End Time as a light to nations and a catalyst for global salvation. Like that of the Brothers, my thesis was simple: Only with God's rule would the earth be changed into eternal Paradise. The lordship of Jesus was to come nation by nation and soul by soul.

When I approached the door to their apartment, this hallucination held fast. I was not abashed bearing down on the windmill. In fact, until my moment of arrhythmia, I never succumbed to the fear of kidnapping and death, which was a real possibility. And I did not soften my evangelistic message once I crossed the threshold. No, my crisis was far, far worse. It was the horror of a child who plays peek-a-boo, seeing the reassuring face revealed over and over again with giggles and joy, and then, on the last turn, finds a different face—the face of a stranger, or worse, just a mask. The crisis I experienced was the terror of cognitive dissonance, the unraveling of reality's fabric.

All I can do is describe the moment, which had started nicely as we sat hunched over our tea. My hosts were nothing but kind, and I'd started giving my Brothers the Good News—hallelujah! Then it was, as I said, as if a mask had been removed and I saw something horrifically unexpected. I saw it without warning or analysis; it was just there. It was like the first time you see the dead—you see and now you know something that words have nothing to do with. What I saw was myself.

What got me was the realization that had I been born in his place, I would be him. I would have preached Muhammad and hated Israel in my quest for End Time salvation. After all, he had come to the meeting with the same intention as mine: we both came as part of a plan to redeem the world and make it into Paradise. Both of us gave up normal pursuits to achieve it and both of us were ready to die for it and, if necessary, see others die. His message was my message: The world would be made new! God's rule is at hand! The prophecies would be fulfilled! Right now! It is the Last Day and eternal salvation! Be gone, secular philosophy! Repent, you atheists and abortionists! Jesus is coming to Jerusalem to win the Last Battle! (My Brother agreed even with that—Muslims believed the prophet Jesus would return and fight for them.)

As otherness and enmity vanished where it should have been most pronounced, I no longer knew who I was nor who he was. In that moment, if the clock on the wall had melted, I could not have been more unhinged. More truthfully and more frighteningly still, this melting exposed my reality as a desert filled with passing mirages, nothing but a sociological construction, a matrix of agreed-upon illusions and stories and futile hopes. I was the priest of an ancient cult. My reality, previously solid like my god, cut from stone, had shattered. My dream of Paradise was false. If it had not been real, was anything? Was there something beyond the fantasies we construct, the stories we tell ourselves, and so many other counterfeit securities conjured by our imaginations and hewn by our own hands?

It was a deep plunge from that towering solidity through the floor and foundation of existence. Over the next days, I pursued a panicked excavation as far as I could go and there was nothing there: just atomic particles, constant flux, and emptiness.

I would never be the same. But I would later find a love for this desert of emptiness and a foundation beyond constructed reality and the absence of its certainty. Like Abraham, I'd go out in faith from the false security and unreliable foundations of my manmade city to look "forward to the city that has foundations whose designer and builder is God." This would take time, and that process is what I hope to trace for you over the course of this story. I hope you find here some illumination, some grace for living, and some compassion for others so that, in our modest lives at least, the human experience may fulfill its promise.

The antecedents of my Athens-based Muslim brothers. Hassan al-Banna, the founder of *al-Ikhwān al-Muslimūn,* the Society of Muslim Brothers, sits closest to the camera.

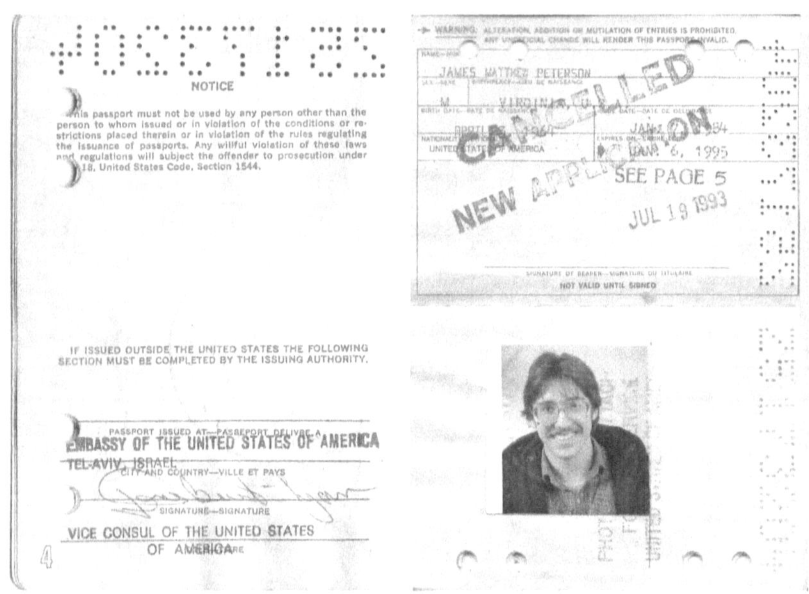

Interior pages of one of my incriminating passports.
Issued in Tel Aviv, I later had it restricted for use only in Israel and South Africa. I carried a "clean" passport for other locations.
I had this one on me when meeting with members of the Syrian Muslim Brotherhood in Athens but I was heavily bearded at that meeting.

My grandfather, Paw-paw George, hard at work.
Appalachia was coal country and meant a decent living for at least a few
generations.
George worked for the mines and my dad was a mining engineer.
He was also a "creative accountant" and a moonshiner of some renown.
The good times did not last.

The Near East:
Turning Points
Hacılar
Çatalhöyük
Mersin
Göbekli Tepe
Urfa
Harran
Tel Halaf
Assur
Euphrates River
Tigris River
Mari
Mediterranean Sea
Damascus
Hazor
Sea of Galilee
Babylon
Jerusalem
Dead Sea
Uruk
Lagash
Ur
Giza
Tanis
Beersheba
Eridu
To Persepolis
Sinai
The Gulf
Caspian Sea
Hijaz
Midian
Teyma
Red Sea
Medina
Pre-civilization
Ancient city
Continuously Occupied
0   50   100   200 Mi.
0   50   100   200 Km.

ORIGINS

❧ I ❧

MY GENESIS

Of Paradise and Apocalypse

You might be asking yourself: How does a young man find himself in a place like that? I'll give you an answer, but this book isn't exactly about me. This is a traveler's journal, incidentally autobiographical, but mostly focused on what I've discovered along the way.

This, then, is a personal metaphysical odyssey bolstered by archeology and science. Along the way we will traverse not only geography but depths of time and consciousness—sometimes my consciousness. Our purpose is to answer questions bigger than me: How is it that we repeatedly embrace ideologies whose promises make us willing to risk everything to fulfill them? Where did we get the idea of ultimate perfection? Why are we willing to kill and die for political dreams and religions? All these questions relate to why I and my Muslim Brother ended up together on that day in Athens.

You might say we were chasing the Apocalypse, which is not surprising for young men possessed of radical faith. But we were not alone. I can say without hesitation that all those atheist radicals in Athens were chasing it, too. You see, whether it is revolution or holy war, all such ventures are essentially apocalyptic—they invoke cataclysms meant to rend the veil and expose a better world to come.

Lenin was apocalyptic. So was Hitler. But it doesn't have to be that severe: anyone willing to disrupt the equanimity of the imperfect in favor of a utopian ideal is also apocalyptic. Thomas Paine, the American patriot who inspired the Revolution, had wanted much more than the prudent system it produced. He wanted the chaos of the French Reign of Terror—all or nothing. Thomas Paine was apocalyptic.

In these pages I want to untangle the source of apocalyptic violence in the Middle East and explain what drove me to pursue such an unlikely ambition. But I also want to understand what propels this kind of thing everywhere: Why do we hate as Cain hated Abel? What exactly are we after? Why do some of us think Trump or Obama can give it to us when neither really can? And why are we so eager to punish those who support the one we don't like?

The key idea is Paradise, both its loss and the desire to establish it again. That's what motivated me, my Muslim Brothers, and the others who have the same compulsion in its secular forms. Outside of social reform, everyone ardently pursues it in their personal lives, too. Whatever the circumstance or belief system, we all want to live in the Garden of Eden.

Simply put, there is a ubiquitous notion that the world isn't what it is meant to be and that there is a way for us to fix it. When we ask, "What did I do to deserve this?" we are saying that hardship is a punishment, that suffering is something out of order, that the world is broken. Paradise bears witness to all that and more.

So, the story I am going to tell you is truly anthropological—it is ancient and universal, a story of humanity. We all remember Paradise. We remember it as something lost, and in remembering, we are reassured: our nostalgia gives us hope that there can again be a place without anxiety or want, a place of love, where we are not abandoned and alone. If it existed once, it can and should exist again.

That the Paradise story emerged in this form at the very dawn of modern life lends it great importance. It comes to us as a message penned with urgency, applicable to all. As soon as humans could write, this is what they chose to write down: a word of wisdom and warning regarding the very civilization they founded. If we are to grasp any solution to the problems of our time—if we are to understand best how to live—then listening to this memorandum from the beginning of civilized history seems to me an inescapable first step.

Those first authors want to remind us of the possibility that there is a place, a time, and a way of being human that fulfills life's promise. They represent it as history. But can it really be true? Isn't Paradise just a psychological mirage, a shadow of our innocent personal infancy, a protest against an adult's comprehension of evil? Or is it a genetic apparition—a story that our evolutionary psychology requires us to tell, a biological trick to make us think we are more than animals, a carrot that keeps us moving forward toward a never-attainable goal? Perhaps. But I believe it is genuine, a collective memory of something real, a story to remind us that our instinct is correct: that the world is not quite right, that it was once better, and that it is meant to be better and can be better than it is.

Let's think for a moment about what "Paradise" means. It is one of those words that we feel rather than think. "Paradise" resonates with our deepest hopes and dreams. We somehow have a collective memory of it. We feel as if we once lived there and we feel deeply that for life to be complete, it must be like what we remember. It speaks to us of contentment, satisfaction, intimacy, and bliss.

But it is a painful memory—Paradise is most tangible to us in its absence. We feel discontented. We expect that things should be better, that nagging feeling that life just isn't supposed to be this way. On this most instinctive level, we feel disappointed. Paradise, then, is a place that is missing, a time of which we have no historical experience, yet which remains a piece of our consciousness as much as anything we have known.

We reach for Paradise in a million ways. We struggle in relationships to make them into that which they cannot be and write songs of longing and read self-help books by the thousands. But our relationships, as good as they are, cannot fill the void of Paradise and our feel-good tricks don't quite do the job.

So, we might look for what's missing through success, fame, or yet another romance. Or we cling to materialism, thinking that if we were set for life, we would surely be at peace. But whether poor or rich, in love or out, our obsessions only strangle and stress us. Not having enough is bad, but having plenty and fearing its loss is just as vexing. To paraphrase Schopenhauer, we swing as a pendulum in an endless cycle between desire and boredom. Enough is never enough; we never reach the goal.

When we can't find a personal solution, we try another trick: politics. There we imagine a comprehensive social solution to create Paradise. We are sure our platform will do it. If only we can convince everyone else to go along with us! Betting on the next great ideology or leader, we blame the last one. Or we blame the other guy and his ideology. If it weren't for them, the world would be a great place.

The record on this is clear: it is the biggest, most promising, most comprehensive ideologies that wreak the greatest destruction. We dream of progress, but somehow progressive schemes never lead to Paradise.

Millenarian ideals have inflicted on humanity the most awful suffering. Totalitarian communism and Nazism were dreams of Paradise restored. Globalism and capitalism promise material ease but real meaning to none, and frequently rob the poor to feed the rich while filling the treasury through trade in weapons, blood, and the spoils of nature.

As a final refuge, at least we can distract ourselves with false-Paradise by intoxication. Entertainment is a US$2 trillion industry. Chemicals work, too! Alcohol is the most common and ancient way to cheer ourselves up, but drugs are also very good at killing the pain of Paradise lost. There is a reason that antidepressants are the most prescribed drug in America,[1] and the reason is the gap we feel between what life is and what we are sure it was meant to be.

Without doubt this search drives our daily lives. Whether it's a personal philosophy, a standard religion, faith in technology, or the promise of love or wealth: these are all belief systems that seek the missing experience of Paradise.

That's true even if you espouse radical materialism. What is cryonics if not the quintessential expression of agnosticism regarding the afterlife? Atheists want eternal life through technology. The current obsession with longevity absurdly risks destroying the entire human race by playing with genetics in the hope of defeating death and securing an eternal material life, with which we are in fact largely disappointed.

And so, Paradise is lost, and we know it. But the question stands: Is it historically real? As we said, Paradise may be no more than an evolutionary trick to keep us going in a life that is really just a quick, animalistic sprint to death. That's one of the peculiar aspects of Paradise nostalgia; although we look back to it as something lost, what keeps us going is the drive to achieve it in the future. In the case of the only animals who live through their abstract imaginations, this would make sense. It's not hard to see why our brain chemistry would produce a phantom utopia for us to strive toward.

Another possibility is that our Paradise angst might just be a twinge of longing for lost childhood innocence. In other words, maybe we are remembering our early lives before we could grasp evil and death. That would explain our sense of nostalgia and the chronic failure to ever regain the ideal.

But I still think there is more to it than that.

For most of history, it is doubtful that the average person had any real experience of personal childhood innocence—in fact, it isn't even that common today. Personally, I can't remember any point in my early life that felt like Paradise. And yet the idea of Paradise in various forms features in cultures across the globe and has done so for thousands of years. So, to whatever extent any of those explanations account for Paradise nostalgia, I believe it must ultimately originate in a greater historical loss of innocence. But what could that historical loss be? Did humanity lose its primal innocence through civilization? Was it an evolutionary transformation—a real anthropological change that left us haunted by an earlier stage of development in our species?

Whatever it turns out to be, we can begin with the fact that dissatisfaction dominates human expectations and has done so for a very long time. Even if it is a mirage, it is the mirage of our genetic programming. If this is all we learn at the end of the journey, we will by some measure have found Paradise, simply by decisively locating it in our DNA, and that will be enough.

For a mirage, however, it seems to be kicking up a lot of dust.

My Eden

To begin this expedition—before turning to the lives of others who lived millennia ago—I want to briefly share more of my personal genesis and what brought me to study the question of Paradise so intensively for much of my life.

For me, the loss of Paradise expresses itself profoundly in my hometown, a would-be hillbilly heaven pitched by its founders as a Promised Land. I mean that literally: everyone who moved here, they said, would live without want or care in nature's most beautiful setting.

That optimism is certainly reflected in the 1785 land grant from Virginia governor Patrick Henry, the very man who articulated what it means to be American with the immortal words, "Give me liberty or give me death." It was Henry who set aside a tract of 200 acres for the new town "in the rich lands on both sides of the Upper Fork of the Clinch River." As per the decree, it was called Richlands, a shibboleth differentiating true sons and daughters, who always say RICH-LANDS, from outsiders, who invariably say RICH-lands. This was a town bearing not so much a name as a guarantee.

The guarantor was a non-human being of immense wealth and power, the Clinch Valley Coal and Iron Company. This entity constructed the first buildings and the railway. The promise of wealth from Big Coal here echoes the promise of civilization and progress from millennia ago: Technology, development, and remaking the land in the service of a corporate entity will lead to a day when all needs are met, everyone satisfied with life as it was intended to be. And indeed, coal made the region grow and prosper even as it undermined nature and set up the progeny of the mountains for a catastrophic fall.

Civilization's promise to bring Paradise to Appalachia had disastrous unintended consequences that compounded with each passing century. In Richlands, the rapacious corporations took turns with their noble environmentalist opponents, using up the people and throwing them away. They left the children, scarred and in pain, to become a byword signifying the drug abuse and unemployment for which much of Appalachia is known.

"Chronic" is a word often associated with us Appalachians—"chronic unemployment" or "chronic opioid addiction," for example. Statistics show that we chronically failed at education, drank incessantly, and abused one another out of proportion to the rest of America. Yet lingering in all this was that ghost of promise, the emptiness of what was supposed to be.

This was the vacuum that eventually drew me into the greater world on a restless quest for Paradise. The details of how I first felt that void revolve around my dad, Jimmie Ulysses, who worked the mines, just as his father did, and his father before him. This is not to say he was a laborer, for he was extraordinarily intelligent, possessing a photographic memory, a knack for helping others cook their accounting, and a facility for bending the law. His work in the mines was engineering, his other work money laundering, and he made a good living from both.

Jim was also a moonshiner of some renown (a moonshine jug is the sole artifact of his still in my possession) and was, in my recollection, almost always drinking, even at breakfast. Still more remarkable, he was for a while a successful bigamist, which is no small feat in a gossip-prone community the size of Richlands. His sundry business enterprises kept both of his women and their children afloat for a remarkably long time.

But of course, this high-wire act was hard to sustain, and when he finally misstepped, he fell hard on me. Vicious words, brutal rage, unexplained abandonment.

Abandonment is the key word here. As a six-year-old boy, it was a terrifying and inexplicable catastrophe, a natural disaster of biblical proportions. It was exactly the experience of a war refugee, many of whom I've gone on to serve as an adult—most recently, for instance, Syrian victims of the Islamic State (ISIS). I recognize in their lives artifacts of my own: sudden violence, unaccountable loss, dislocation, and disorientation. The day after he stormed out, I knew more certainly than I knew anything that I was utterly alone, abandoned somehow forever and by everyone, including anyone I might meet in the future. Trust disintegrates for refugees like us. The damage is primal. No matter how faithful my mother might have proved to be, I would never again think my security could endure to the next day. Every day was the last, lived in bleak hopelessness.

And so it was like the outbreak of war: the early chapters of this life accented by suddenness, a panoply of stunning violence, unforeseen outbursts, unexplained disappearances, and unannounced moves. Each landed with the disorienting randomness of a car bomb.

No sooner had Dad disappeared than so did my oldest brother. My mother raved about kidnapping and torture, and when it became known that he'd only run away to be a rock star, this new information was not shared with me. All I was privy to was the panic. Nothing was ever explained or discussed. I was a shadow: untroubling, presumed to be untroubled, and permanently cast as two-dimensional because I did not wreak havoc. This, too, mirrors the experience of victims of war I know from Syria. The Islamic State gets the attention while the victims do not exist to the world, save for a few prominent children who tickle the fancy of news producers long enough to assuage some of their guilt. Millions grieve their losses silently and unheard because they do not make trouble in the world.

We shadows watch the real three-dimensional people in astonishment as they act out their drama with flare. Dad even reappeared during the crisis of the missing brother—I briefly thought he'd come home. I remember it in technicolor. He appeared at the door while the TV babysat me with footage of the Vietnam War on CBS, graphic and ugly and prophetically insightful, inextricable from Dad and hysterical Mom. It's funny how these personal disasters become enmeshed in international events; this, too, is a motif shared with me by my future Brothers.

I suppose the mind wants to make sense of things, to tell a story, to find meaning and context in the bigger picture. We are not part of the story, and we want to be. So, the vanishing of Dad, the disappearance of my brother, and the terror of Mom's hysteria occurred—not coincidentally in my appreciation of it—in tandem with the mayhem and gore of the Spring Offensive. Of course it did: to seek universal meaning in the larger scheme of things is rational. The world was broken over there and the fracture extended all the way to my living room. And in both cases, I was relegated to the passive position of observer and shock absorber, with one crucial difference: I felt more recognized by anchorman Walter Cronkite than I did by my parents because he was telling me the truth.

This is why my Muslim Brothers and I have a compulsion to become three-dimensional on a large scale. By hook or by crook we will make ourselves present, felt, and heard. If the world is lucky, it will be destructive only to ourselves. But as often as not there is widespread collateral damage.

Such is the genesis of my quest. To elaborate much more is only for emphasis. Not long after the brother episode, my mother left me in Richlands and moved to another state. I was to join her at some point, but again no one explained what was happening. To me it was another abandonment.

Once reunited, in a city far from the mountains, the absence continued in a more subtle way. Mom lived the early 1970s lifestyle. The men she knew were interesting, if not paternal. These included a mobbed-up land developer and a few drug runners. Of the men she spent time with, there were a few who took her to the Bahamas or Mexico in their private planes. One of them achieved notoriety. This still seems perfectly normal to me, but I've been told it is odd even for the 1970s. I'll share it only because it is bizarre.

Wally Thrasher was a fellow Appalachian who had interests near us and was inexplicably wealthy for a hillbilly. Later, I found out why. I was reading through microfilm for a history project on our town when I spotted Wally's name. "Wally Thrasher has been jailed on a narcotics charge in Mexico," it read. Wally wasn't jailed for long. He bribed his way out. In the 1990s I saw him again, on television's *Unsolved Mysteries*. Last I checked, he had been a fugitive for thirty years. He'd faked his own death in a plane crash. This item is from my notes: "Wally Thrasher was, and most believe still is—a major drug smuggler. Described as a swashbuckling pilot who would jump out of second story windows in college, just to prove he could, his ties took him to the top of the Columbian drug cartel." A quick check of current television listings shows that Wally Thrasher is still on reruns of *America's Most Wanted*. Just as my father ran moonshine in the hills, Wally ran drugs. It was all within the same orbit.

Within a few years, Dad died. (Of moonshine poisoning!) I got the news in my mother's car, summoned from my fourth-grade classroom. My brothers were there, distraught. The news was delivered gingerly. I showed no reaction and felt nothing. He was already dead to me.

Funeral. Burial. Return. Nothing registered. But back home I started skipping school. Social workers appeared. Blame was placed firmly on the poor role modeling of my oldest brother and grief over my father's death. In fact—and this is the truth—I stopped going to school because I didn't trust the social contract anymore. There was no point in subjecting myself to the indoctrination of a failed world and I couldn't understand how others continued to have faith in it when it repeatedly failed them, too. I wanted a new reality, a different one, a better one. I wanted Paradise. I fantasized about having god-like powers and destroying everything, punishing the obstacles to happiness, and making it all as it should be. I'd become radicalized.

This is no exaggeration. Reading my mother's diary from that year, I found this astonishing passage: "I wanted to die, I cried to God to kill me and my boys and take us out of our misery..." A terrorist mother if ever I have heard one!

I could easily write this book about nothing but that revolving and recurring trauma. But what's more meaningful to the reader is looking for less-personal answers, finding them in primal human experience, the first human stories.

For me, this insight came through the Bible, as told in the Hebrew voice of the biblical book of Genesis. I'd begun to read it around the time my dad died, though I'd reflected on the story since it was first read to me in Sunday school much earlier. I felt very close to that strange, ancient world. It rang familiar and true, so when reading about the Garden of Eden, I felt like I knew the place: it was about a happy home destroyed, a trauma that, in the end, could only be understood as a punishment. Picturing that dreadful scene between Adam and Eve, all about forbidden fruit, alienation, and banishment, I understood that this was what was wrong with the world, with my world.

As you can see, I misunderstood it as a child and young man. I was—like my Muslim Brothers, their rival Religious Zionists, the Marxist revolutionaries, and other radicals—hooked on the idea that there was a solution that could be imposed. Either through force or persuasion, people like us imagine we can make Paradise happen.

This was where we went wrong. Nonetheless, the key insight was there: the world had failed and the promise of its progress through the march of civilization and society was a lie. It would take my later unmasking to make me realize that the solution was beyond anything we could force, to understand that while anyone can impose violence on the peaceful, pacification by force is a self-contradiction. The Paradise of which we dream is not a matter of an ideal system; it can only be realized by some kind of awakening.

Locating the Garden of Eden

To my everlasting surprise, this childhood recognition of a primal truth expressed in the Book of Genesis holds up to scrutiny. One need not hold a religious or dogmatic attachment to it, however. The reach of this literature extends beyond that. The Bible remains a touchstone for us simply because it is the best and most complete example available of the mindset of early human history—it's as close as we can get to what humans thought went wrong, recollected as nearly as possible to the time recalled by them as Paradise.

I've also come to appreciate lesser-known ancient texts that shed as much light on the quest as the Bible does. Those sources are less complete, culturally more distant, and due to a 3,000-year gap in transmission, more difficult to translate and comprehend. The Bible helps with that, too, because it is closely related to those sources, building a bridge of understanding to otherwise inscrutable Mesopotamian literature.

To be clear, I am not selling a particular religion here by using the Bible. My aim is to point to reality so you can draw your own conclusions. Our sources will include Buddhist, Jewish, Christian, Muslim, Sumerian, and unaffiliated or agnostic philosophers. There are also the Zoroastrians, who gave us the word "Paradise"—I hope they will help us understand what it really means. Then, outside the witness of myth and legend, our guides will be scientists: leading archeologists, historians, and anthropologists. It turns out that the study of Paradise is a broad discipline indeed, pursued universally and able to enlighten anyone patient and aware enough to take heed.

If you are reading this, I assume you have an interest in the idea of Paradise, too. You are not alone. This subject, far from being taboo, is common in mainstream journals and popular on cable television. We can also find it studied in scholarly literature, puzzled over by anthropologists and philosophers alike.

It sells advertising, too. "Has the Garden of Eden been located at last?" That's what the *Smithsonian* magazine dared to ask in a still-popular 1987 feature. The History Channel knows the appeal of Paradise, too, advertising its documentary "Mysteries of the Garden of Eden" with an earnest voice-over assuring us that "it was a *real* place, and it *has* been found."

I can't go that far—I can only say I have located the Garden's remains. It is as much a time as it is a place, for, without question, the spoiled Garden of Eden sits in ancient Mesopotamia not too long before the dawn of civilization. Where else would it be? History begins there with the invention of writing, and among the first stories civilization recorded were stories of creation and memories of a lost Golden Age—the memory of Paradise.

Damian Thompson summed it up very well in his book *The End of Time:*

Faith and Fear in the Shadow of the Millennium: "The primordial paradise, characterized by perfection, abundance and purity, appears in all religions originating in the Middle East and in most of the world's tribal mythologies. Often this happy state has been lost through some tragic aberration on the part of mankind."

He continues with a citation from early Mesopotamia that resonates with Israel's later prophets:

> The oldest surviving description of paradise comes from the Sumerians, who around 4000 BC described a magical land of Dilmun: "That place was pure, that place was clean. In Dilmun the raven croaked not. The kite shrieked not kite-like. The lion mangled not..." All this happened a long time ago, "when there was no fear, no terror" and "man had no rival."[2]

Perhaps if we can take a bearing from this initial starting point, we can look back at what happened just before the invention of writing and locate the time and place those stories refer to. Even without a specific year or location, however, I hope at least to discover what exactly it was these early chroniclers of civilization remembered.

If we are to believe the ancient mythologists, civilization was the thing that happened after the age of Paradise. Civilization is the paradigm that replaced it—our paradigm, the age in which we still live. Economics, law, mathematics, astronomy, agriculture, religion, government, medicine, architecture—all of the things that constitute civilization—now govern the whole planet.

We forget sometimes that this model formed less than 6,000 years ago in the Middle East and that most of human experience was lived before then. Civilization is so pervasive now that we accept it as nature. But why should we? Everything that makes us human, including the critical attributes of language, artistic creativity, and abstract thinking, have been with us for at least 100,000 years. So, with only five percent of modern human history in its portfolio, what gives civilization such unquestioned authority?

For one thing, it makes a very good argument for itself, having invented government and literacy. So when it makes its case, it literally has a lawyerly advantage over the previous 95 percent of modern human life. Those generations cannot speak for themselves except through the modest second-hand testimony of the collected Paradise stories and what we can glean from their bones and houses. Then again, they might have a surprise witness in our universally felt nostalgia; perhaps it is their voice, that of pre-civilized humanity, which nags at us to remember, which reminds us that things might have been better than they are now. What they could not write on stone and paper they wrote into our DNA.

Their voice is what makes Albert Einstein espouse the transcendental instinct as the very best human intuition: "The finest emotion of which we are capable," Einstein writes,

> is the mystic emotion... To know that what is impenetrable for us really exists and manifests itself as the highest wisdom and the most radiant beauty, whose gross forms alone are intelligible to our poor faculties—this knowledge, this feeling... that is the core of the true religious sentiment.[3]

So we can be confident pondering the mystery and the mysticism, assured by Einstein that this is an intelligent endeavor. The mystical part is our nostalgia for Paradise. The mystery part is where it went.

The obvious question is why, after tens of thousands of years of stable human existence, there was a sudden panic resulting in governments, cities, armies, and religions. Civilization did not appear slowly and universally—it was dramatically sudden and specific to a region. It then spread across the globe in short order. Did civilization appear to solve the problem of Paradise that had been lost? Or was civilization's rise the thing that destroyed Paradise? Whichever it is—and it may be a little of both—the mourning of this loss is at the heart of our religions, mythologies, and political ideologies.

The University of Chicago's eminent historian and philosopher Mircea Eliade, translating his colleague Hermann Baumann's book on African myths, provides this summary of globally common Paradise themes: In those times, he says, men did not know of death; they understood the language of the animals and were at peace with them; they did not work, and found abundant nourishment at hands' reach. Following upon a certain mythical event—which we will not undertake to discuss—this paradisal stage ended and humanity became what we know it to be today.

Eliade continues with his own summary:

> We encounter the "paradise myth" all over the world in more or less complex forms. Besides the paramount paradisal note, it always has a certain number of characteristic elements... All these myths show primitive man enjoying blessedness, spontaneity, and liberty, which he has most annoyingly lost as the consequence of the "fall," that is, as the result of a mythical occurrence which has brought about the rupture between Heaven and Earth.[4]

This is a constant across global cultures. From the "Golden Age" of Greek lore, to the ancient Americas, to the Australian Aboriginals, Paradise by any other name is described in shared terms everywhere. Its loss is also universally mourned and its restoration the object of the faithful.

More significant than the specific myth is the ubiquity of the theme. Tell the Bible's Genesis story to anyone and they get it. They feel Adam and Eve's pain—they have a story just like that.

The Bible's account is closely related to even older ones from Mesopotamia. The key difference is that in the Bible, the sudden rise of cities and rulers appears as part of the evolving catastrophe of losing Eden. For the Mesopotamians, who invented those things, civilization arrives to save the day (although those sentiments will not endure).

Along with descriptions of a time "when everything was created perfect" and where "no lion kills and no wolf carries off a lamb," the Mesopotamians explain the loss of Paradise in terms that serve to justify the civilization that they bequeathed to us.[5] Their argument is that the new glories of city and empire will make up for the loss. Later texts from Mesopotamia seem to see through this ruse, a matter that we can address in detail later.

Nonetheless, even today we are not supposed to question civilization's kind offer of protection from the wilds of post-Paradise life. It can be like the mafia in that way—we give it allegiance out of fear. Civilization tells us that we need it if we are to have a semblance of Paradise bliss, that it needs to be the boss, and that it must grow or else we'll get hurt. But as historian Geoffrey Ashe points out in his book *Dawn Behind the Dawn: A Search for the Earthly Paradise*, global mythologies invariably tell a different story: "When we turn to myth and legend," he writes, "we find assertions about the context of these developments that have a paradoxical air. They imply an attitude and an overall picture that are in sharp contrast with the imagery of progress."[6]

Ashe explains that while many mythologies do tell us of civilization's progress, "[often] a jarring element slips through the net—a belief that the movement is not forward... a belief in loss rather than gain; a belief that far back in time, life was better and more enlightened, and that whatever made it so has ceased to be an effective part of experience."

It's like the scene of a murder. Paradise is dead and gone. Beside the cadaver stands the only witness, saying he did all he could to save her and that he'll take good care of us. But Paradise met her demise under suspicious circumstances. Whether civilization is there to make the best of a bad situation, or whether it is covering up a crime, remains to be seen.

A MATTER OF PERCEPTION

Surveying the Road to Paradise

In a world of billions, it's hard to grasp how Paradise could possibly be a universal memory. But our ancestors did not live in such a crowded world. They were a small family, and if civilization perpetrated a crime against Paradise, there were witnesses who might have passed the story and its trauma down to us from generation to expanding generation.

Stanford University's Merritt Ruhlen speaks for the scholarly consensus, saying that all humans originate in a cluster of only 1,000 or so individuals who lived between 50,000 and 60,000 years ago.[1] I'm struck by how relatively recent that is—it surely removes any doubt that all of us can be touched by the same early experience. Ultimately, you and I come from the same place and share a few common ancestors; it is entirely conceivable that we carry the same collective trauma and hope.

That small population is for us a starting point. At the outset, it will help us to pause here and look across the length of the road to get our bearings.

First, let's deal with name of our destination. It's important to make sure we are heading to the right place. We could call that shared hope that our ancestors passed down many things, but for a surprisingly large part of the world, "Paradise" remains the best word. It came to English by way of Greek by way of Aramaic by way of Persian. I know it through Christianity, which got it from Judaism, which got it from Zoroastrianism, and the Zoroastrians brought it from the Indo-Iranian ancestral lands that later gave rise to Hinduism and Buddhism.

Muslims, as siblings in Abraham's family, also acquired the word. It has since entered the non-theological lexicon. Oxford Dictionaries define it as "an ideal or idyllic place or state." In communism, the final utopian condition is commonly called the "Workers' Paradise." For Christians, Muslims, Jews, and communists of all ethnicities the world over—and for speakers of English, Persian, Hebrew, Arabic, and most European languages—it's the word of choice to describe that nagging hope we share.

The original ancient Persian word simply means "garden," but it came to carry all the symbolic weight of the Garden of Eden. In fact, the official ancient Greek translation of the Hebrew Bible, the Septuagint, uses *parádeison* to translate the place Adam and Eve called home, showing very clearly how the ideas connect. Most famously, Jesus used the same Persian-sourced Greek word when, while hanging on the cross, he promised the criminal dying next to him, "Truly I tell you, today you will be with me in Paradise."[2] Jesus clearly didn't mean any old garden.

Why did a disgraced Jewish Messiah reject his own native tongue in favor of this Gentile word from Persia? We'll have to cover a lot of territory before we can really answer that, but right now, at the start, I will offer a clue: it has something to do with Magi.

I can also note the obvious: this word meant a lot to Jesus and his followers. Their generation represents a peak in the quest for Paradise. People of his time—Magi included—expected to live to see the hope fulfilled.

Now we can look down from this historical mountain top and see on one side the road leading from the beginning of civilization to the summit of Jesus, and on the other side, the road that formed in its wake, leading to modern times. All along that road are pilgrims in search of Paradise.

To be clear, I don't want to make a particular claim about Jesus except to note his pivotal role; history is divided by his birth, and we use it to mark the passing centuries, not only in the West but anywhere that subscribes to the current world system. It is his legend, tied inextricably to Paradise, that transformed and shaped the modern world. Historians and theologians can debate whether it was Jesus who made history or history that made Jesus, but the significance of the Jesus phenomenon is undeniable. By the time we reach the end of our road, you can judge for yourself.

Returning to our summit, what is certain is that this was a pregnant moment—that history at this juncture was ripe for what Jesus was claimed to fulfill, and that for whatever reason, it was he who fit the bill and not one of the other would-be messiahs, of which there were many. Why so many? Because messianic expectations had been primed by half a millennium of theorizing about the nature of time and government. Not happy with the world as it was, people of diverse backgrounds and religions, Jews and Gentiles, had tried to discover the key to Paradise, and over the course of the previous 500 years they came up with the idea of Apocalypse. Their theory explained history at all points in time: past, present, and future. In their minds, they were living in the apocalyptic End Time with Paradise waiting to be revealed just over the horizon.

As we've mentioned, in common language today, "apocalypse" means a great cataclysm—which is roughly true—but it isn't an end. The point of Apocalypse is the revelation and restoration of the world as it was meant to be, the world renewed and repaired as Paradise. If for no other reason, this link between Apocalypse and Paradise is why an understanding of Paradise's history is relevant today. People in search of Paradise expect apocalyptic birth pangs to precede it and they are often willing to countenance a great deal of violence to make it happen. Whatever they must endure, or make others endure, will pale in comparison to eternal bliss. It is not just their own suffering they tolerate but also the suffering they inflict on anyone who gets in the way. The road to Paradise is littered with the bodies of their victims.

This is especially apparent in the Middle East now, where, for example, the Islamic State, al-Qaeda, the Islamic Republic of Iran, and many of the most influential parties in the State of Israel all pursue policies based solely on apocalyptic and messianic dreams of Paradise.

We will return to the modern Middle East in the second part of this book, but to understand it we need to find the beginning of the road that leads there. Fortunately, it is easy to spot; we have only to look back down the road from the pinnacle of Jesus to see that this path indeed stretches back to the Book of Genesis. This is mile-marker number one, as close as we can get to history's literary zero point.

So for now, Adam and Eve are a good place to start. It is familiar and easy to read, an accessible road map. And although Genesis is not the oldest creation story to be written down, it offers us a kind of edited compendium of the older works with the bonus of an added critical voice. It does not entirely agree with the earlier storytellers because it is in large measure a criticism of Mesopotamian civilization. This, too, is part of the story, and rest assured we will also have a chance to review the Mesopotamian side of the story so that we understand the full context and see exactly what the Hebrews wanted to critique.

It is an elegant text, opening with the obvious words, "In the beginning." Obvious, yes, but it is startlingly simple and cryptic. Genesis is frequently cryptic. "In the beginning" is a kind of koan, meant to be ruminated upon. The story goes on to say that the heavens and the earth and all the living creatures were brought into existence from nothing. In this, Genesis agrees with Buddha: nothingness is the ground of being.

Not only is the text cryptic, but it also presents us immediately with a puzzle. Genesis presents two different accounts of creation in the first two chapters! The first one describes a watery expanse with a giant spherical bubble in it. *May'im* in Hebrew is water of the earth; *Sha-May'im* is the water of the heavens on the other side of the sphere. (You can see that the words "water" and "sky" are related to one another, as they were generally in the ancient world.) In this story, the waters on the far side of the bubble are decorated with lights for the purpose of tracking time and seasons; the waters below are gathered into one place to reveal dry land.

Having set the stage, the Creator next makes humankind in the divine likeness. Humanity and everything else is created simply from words—all reality is thus an objectified word, in some sense a story. Yet, in this first telling, there is no mention of forming Adam from the soil and there is no Garden of Eden. It is just the human race and an abundance of vegetable and animal life for humanity's sustenance. Before the seventh day, on which the Creator rests, it is judged that it all is good. There is no evil here.

In the second creation account, there was no vegetation on the day God created heaven and Earth because there was no one to till the soil. "Then the LORD God formed humankind from the dust of the ground, and breathed into his nostrils, the breath of life."

Incidentally, this "LORD God" is different in Hebrew from the Creator in the first account. This time it is *YHWH*, the unspeakable name revealed to Moses at the burning bush. Previously it was *Elohim*, a more generic name, which is oddly plural—literally, "the gods"—a name that betrays an older, more complex view, as opposed to the pure monotheistic moniker that it became later.

This multiple naming of God is common in the Bible and reflects the blending of several editorial traditions. What it means in this case is that the second version of the story is infused with insights from a later tradition—it is a more interpreted account—but still very old.

The text then at last introduces the Garden of Eden:

"And the Lord God planted a garden in Eden, in the East... Out of the ground the Lord God made to grow every tree that is pleasant to the sight and good for food, the tree of life also in the midst of the garden, and the tree of the knowledge of good and evil."[3]

Any garden needs a source of water, and it is that source, to be conspicuously named here, that provides the first solid clue to the historical location of Paradise.

Paradise and Apocalypse Between the Rivers

"A river flows out of Eden to water the Garden," Genesis tells us, "and from there it divides and becomes four branches."

Of these four, two branches remain a mystery, but the others present no difficulties, defining unequivocally the region associated with Eden: "The name of the third river is Tigris, which flows east of Assyria. And the fourth river is the Euphrates."[4]

These are rivers of myth, like Eden itself, but they are by no means mythological rivers, having watered civilization since the inception of agriculture. Their persistent survival into the modern age is a caution against dismissing Eden as a genuine memory. Even the names of these rivers survive intact from their oldest forms into modern Middle Eastern languages. Together the rivers suggest a scale that increases the possibilities for the location of Eden. The Euphrates meanders to a length of 2,800 kilometers, while the Tigris runs its course well to the east for 1,900 kilometers. Between them, they encompass a potential Eden of nearly 900,000 kilometers squared.

Today, Turkey controls their headwaters. When politics downstream aren't going Ankara's way, massive dams allow Turkey's leaders to turn off the tap. In the late 1990s, for example, such action forced Syria's Hafez al-Assad to hand over the Turkish state's greatest enemy, Kurdish separatist leader Abdullah Ocalan.

More recently, refugee camps have populated the countryside around the rivers, the occupants mostly Kurdish victims of ISIS. I've worked for years now with these refugees, helping them put their lives back together, and I know them well. I know their enemies, too, and as awful as they are, I understand completely their motivation. The Kurds' misfortunes at the hands of their Muslim brothers are the sum of an End-Time calculation designed to restore Paradise. For their part, the most powerful Kurdish ideology expresses the same desire, only in different terms. For them, it is one of the most radical socialist utopian ideals ever to find concrete fulfillment. Strangely, both sides talk about the end of history and eternal bliss. All this is acted out right where it all started, along the banks of the Euphrates and Tigris Rivers.

Jews are equally attached to the rivers. The Euphrates has always been a boundary point. The Bible promises, "Every place on which you set foot shall be yours; your territory shall extend from the wilderness to the Lebanon and from the River, the river Euphrates, to the Western Sea."[5] What lay beyond the Euphrates was for Jews synonymous with exile, slavery, and idolatry. It was the event horizon of lost Paradise, one which the Jewish people will fatefully cross under duress, when the Babylonian Empire exiles them from Jerusalem:

By the rivers of Babylon—

there we sat down and there we wept

when we remembered Zion.

In modern times, many Jews agree with ISIS that we live on the cusp of the last battle and final redemption. For them, Paradise means the coming messianic age when their border will again extend as far as the Great River.

In the Christian Apocalypse, the Euphrates is a similar boundary—it is the threshold of Armageddon: "The sixth angel poured his bowl on the great river Euphrates, and its water was dried up in order to prepare the way for the kings from the east."[6] Maybe the Turks have been using that one as a playbook. They are surely the first nation to successfully dry up the Euphrates.

So Paradise and Apocalypse go hand-in-hand. As odd as the pairing might appear at first glance, the Paradise/Apocalypse dialectic is all around us, driving world events today as it did thousands of years ago. This is a non-sectarian obsession, not limited to any religion or ideology. It's as universal as the Paradise idea upon which it is based, and which infects secular idealists as easily as it does the religious.

The math of Apocalypse calculates that a promised utopia can justifiably be paid for with the suffering of those who stand in the way. The logic states that any degree of suffering inflicted now will be compensated for by the perfect world to come. The victims have the honor of being sacrifices on the altar. It's really for their own good, for Paradise can appear only after an apocalyptic revolution clears the way.

History offers countless examples. America's first settlers fill their diaries with thanksgiving to God for his judgment on the pagan inhabitants of the New World, whose wild lands were thought to be full of demons and in need of subjugation to God's kingdom. The early Americans thought they were founding a new promised land. A lot of dead

Indians was nothing more than a stage; the Indians would be grateful in the long run.[7]

Or consider the Crusades, a Christian phenomenon with uncanny similarities to the campaign of the Islamic State; the Crusaders justified the roasting and eating of children on the path to the "New Jerusalem" that they thought awaited them. The Crusaders gave thanks to God for the imminent return of Christ as they herded the Jews of Jerusalem into the Great Synagogue and burned it down.

Those long-suffering Jews have more often been the victims, but today, Israeli maximalists apply the same formula; they would gladly start Armageddon by blowing up the Dome of the Rock. It's always the same logical sequence: first Apocalypse and then Paradise.

Secular politics would like us to think it is immune from such religious fervor, but political ideologies are just as influenced by the drive for Paradise. Stalin and Mao oversaw the deaths of tens of millions; the suffering inflicted by totalitarian socialism was justified as a stage toward a utopia, the "Workers' Paradise," that would follow. The very idea at the heart of their philosophy is the end of history, a final heaven-like stage to which history has (they say) been progressing.

Not too long ago, neoconservative ideologues in the White House imagined destroying Iraq and rebuilding it as a model of democracy. Bomb the place to rubble to establish the Paradise of America-dominated globalism—something that itself was hailed as the End of History by the influential Reagan Doctrine architect Francis Fukuyama upon the collapse of the Soviet Union. It's ironic that the biggest losers of the last Iraq campaign were Arab Christians, since the masterminds of this futile exercise relied heavily on Christian End-Time apocalyptic ideas. President George W. Bush even tried to convince President Chirac of France to join the war with appeals to Old Testament prophecies.[8]

The Euphrates runs through Iraq, too, of course. It's remarkable that this landmark of Adam and Eve now stands at the opposite end of history as a signpost to a war involving so many religions and utopian ideologies. It's all there: Sunni, Shiite, Jewish, and Christian. In the Syrian ruler Bashar al-Assad, we even have old-fashioned Arab nationalist socialism. And then, once again, there are the disciples of Marx, represented here by the Kurds fighting under the banner of a nearly cultic expression of anarchist communalism.

As I've been working beside the Euphrates, bringing care to families torn apart by these utopian wars, I'm mindful that Eden is also about refugees.

Adam and Eve lived as outcasts in the same vicinity as these poor Kurds and Arabs—who, in my area, number 3.5 million. There is a genuine connection between Adam and Eve's story and the wars being fought now. And there is a connection between my childhood abandonment and what the Syrian and Kurdish exiles feel now. Our shared fate, a slap in the face by reality, brought us together. This suggests, I hope, that the Paradise urge can be used for good when channeled through a compassion-born human vulnerability.

For the moment, however, we are in the minority. From the vantage point of the refugee camps, we watched war planes from the international coalition bombing just a few miles away—bombing human obstacles to a better world into oblivion. The ground war was also within sight and earshot. There were American troops in both directions, the aforementioned Kurdish utopian militias, and Turkish Islamists and their Arab allies. I still often see Islamic State warriors in the town nearby, and Israeli war planes flying in the distance, targeting Iranian-backed fighters who have taken the side of the Syrian regime.

Other players on this stage include Arabian Gulf states, Russia, the Hashemite Kingdom of Jordan, and even soldiers from New Zealand—about as far away from here as you can go without going to Antarctica. Japan and China are not as obviously present, but the fleet of spanking-new battle-readied Toyota Land Cruisers is practically a brand identity for the Islamic State. Around here, cheap Chinese-made drones and other goodies are jokingly called "weapons of mass consumption."

Through it all, there is a bizarrely tangible self-awareness of what I've described. It's a meta-Apocalypse, with all the players happily advertising their end-of-time rationalizations for war. There is no embarrassment about it. It is all due to the belief that Paradise is a practical possibility in some version of the end of history.

We, too, will try to find out what that might mean, and whether there is a way to this sublime state that does not involve dominating or violating others. But first there is a more practical question: Are we looking for a real, historical Garden of Eden?

To this question I will bring my own approach to the guiding literature. How literally should we read it? For some, the proposition that Genesis is not literal seems to undermine the truthfulness of it. I understand that. I also understand others who look at it with skepticism, discounting the whole story as a fairytale. Then there is all the other literature we will examine: Mesopotamian myths, Greek and Roman histories, Persian chronicles, and more. There, too, these questions arise: Is it factual or fictitious? Reality, I imagine, lies in a synthesis somewhere between the dialectic of those positions. In our reading, informed by my personal experiences, we will look for that sweet spot where truth can be perceived.

To make this search fruitful, we need to understand the relationship between fact and truth, certainty and faith, material evidence and spiritual insight. This is a bit off our track, but I think we must deal with this as it affects the way we approach all of our sources—even the way we approach what we conventionally consider history. These are questions I struggled with after my epiphany with the Muslim Brothers. Both of us had been staunch literalists. After that encounter, I was lost, doubting everything. I'd invested my security entirely in a narrow field of literature approved by a Christian tradition, the process of which I'd never even bothered to understand. It was not easy for me to accept that the voice of divine truth is not so small as that. How factual is any of it? Does it matter if it isn't factual? Should we take only one book as truth? Or does truth have the power to speak through unfamiliar voices and through fiction?

It might take an Einstein to answer these questions.

Fact or Fiction?

I must admit that even as a child I had mixed feelings. I did not associate this far-out Garden of Eden drama in the Bible with the kind of hard-faced Vietnam War reporting I heard on the *CBS Evening News*. Vietnam was as close and palpable as my own disintegrating family. The Garden of Eden, on the other hand, seemed fantastic, like a comic book. A naked couple ran around naming animals, arguing with a walking snake, and eating poisoned apples. This belonged in the same category as Hollywood's *Jason and the Argonauts*, a stop-motion film that I was enamored with at the time. Jason's sculpted models and jerky animation fit the mythological character of the Garden of Eden far better than Walter Cronkite's earnest reporting.

Was it bad that, in my mind's eye, the Garden of Eden looked more like claymation than real life? Truth be told, this is one of the reasons the story stuck with me, and it absolutely did not blunt its impact. I'd imagine it over and over again, as children do with favorite stories and films. As with much great literature, it was somehow true even if it was not literally factual or historical. It was truer than the news; it cut more deeply and, on a level beyond the provable facts, the story spoke to me.

This is an important consideration as we take this journey together. Written guides like the authors of Genesis spoke a very long time ago; we can't possibly verify their testimony as a reporter would. My premise is that we don't need to. While fact and truth can overlap, one does not guarantee the other. Similarly, the absence of one does not negate the other. Even if you are a literalist, I'm sure you agree that truth is often best told in parables.

This is not to imply there is no reality. It's only a question of the most effective way—actually, the most accurate way—to narrate reality given the limitations of observation and language. Is reality best told through culturally narrow and time-bound documentary literalism? I have to say no because cultural references change over time.

Furthermore, some truths are surely greater than our capacity to define them. Truth cannot be owned by language. The most language can do is shine light around the truth, illuminating it from various points and from different angles. All the words in this book, or any book, are intended only to do that. If the words are effective, truth will be illuminated and seen, but the words will not define it. Truth lies somehow between the words, inside and underneath the constructed narrative.

Often then, documentary facts do not express reality as well as a metaphor does. Fiction is therefore frequently truthful, for which reason we write poetry and sing songs. Conversely, as every trial lawyer and politician knows, you can tell a great whopping lie through a litany of facts. This is how Genesis can be both a comic book and a truth-filled spiritual guidebook. I'd be skeptical if it pretended to be anything else.

I trust this in no way undermines the validity of sacred literature, although some of my friends (Jewish, Christian, and Muslim) are sure that it does. For example, creation science holds Genesis to be scientifically factual. Fair enough; I won't even contest that. But I do think my friends cling to the notion of faith-science because of an unnecessary insecurity. Cowed by the assertion of scientific certainties, they want their story to be scientifically factual, too—an envy that I think is entirely misplaced.

That's because most of us never get closer to scientific reality than parables anyway. All those intimidating scientific "facts" that most of us know are in truth the comic-book versions of observations that extend far beyond our expertise. They, too, are metaphors.

Just think about some of the science you know. We all know that the earth revolves around the sun. How do you know? Can you prove it? Some people can. For most of us, it is a story we were told through crude analogies. We saw a model or drawing of it, and we believed it. I'm quite sure, if I'd not been taught otherwise, that I would assume the sun rises and sets upon the earth, as our language still insists.

Or consider the classroom truth of the atom as a tiny solar system with electrons and protons orbiting a nucleus. We've all seen the plastic models, and if you think about atoms at all, there is a good chance this is what you picture. But this is, like Genesis, a truthful metaphor, not literal fact. Atoms are nothing like that at all, and nothing like anything at all that we can directly put into words or accurately describe. The atomic model is a story about unseen material reality just as Genesis is a story about human realities that lie beyond our literal descriptive powers. The deeper the truth, the more necessary metaphor becomes if the matter is to be usefully grasped, discussed, and shared. The atomic model is splendidly helpful to us average folks. It helps us comprehend the truth of a world beyond our literal grasp.

J.B.S. Haldane was one of the most influential biologists of the last two centuries. The theory of the "primordial soup," the chemical basis for biological life, was his. He invented the word "clone" and came up with the idea for in vitro fertilization. He was a hugely important scientist. He was also a master of metaphor. The phrase "primordial soup" explains what thousands of points of data and complex formulae could never explain to someone like me.

Just as importantly, he understood that data and formulae were also metaphorical. It wasn't just the term "soup" that was analogous to reality; he recognized that the math underlying science is a descriptive language, too. One language facilitates the work of specialists, the other serves to summarize their findings for non-experts, but neither gives direct access to reality nor truly defines it.

In Haldane's words, "Now my own suspicion is that the universe is not only queerer than we suppose, but queerer than we can suppose. I suspect that there are more things in heaven and earth than are dreamed of, or can be dreamed of, in any philosophy."[9] Genesis and other ancient spiritual works are like that: they are a synthesis of observation and wisdom, a revelation of truth too queer to be grasped as individual facts.

Albert Einstein understood this, too. November 2015 was the 100th anniversary of his General Theory of Relativity. Many of us don't remember that it was published as a popular book for those, as he put it, "who are not conversant with the mathematical apparatus of theoretical physics." He promised "a few happy hours of suggestive thought!" (exclamation point is his).

Hanoch Gutfreund of Hebrew University's Einstein Center explains the methodology:

> [Einstein] uses familiar metaphors like railway cars and platforms. He often invites the reader to participate in the thought process by raising a question —which he himself answers, or answers in the reader's name. These sections of the text seem like a one-sided platonic dialogue, drawing in the reader as an active participant.[10]

Do you think it demeans the General Theory to call it a collection of metaphors? It doesn't, and neither does it demean Genesis to speak of it as such. To the contrary, reducing Genesis to mundane fact is an insult to the depth of its wisdom.

Another of the great physicists, Jules Henri Poincaré, wrote elegantly on this question. His thoughts are summarized in the *Stanford Encyclopedia of Philosophy*: "Beyond doubt a reality completely independent of the mind which conceives it, sees or feels it, is an impossibility. A world as exterior as that, even if it existed, would for us be forever inaccessible."[11]

Poincaré is not saying reality is non-existent. Rather, our ability to comprehend it is limited by our power to define it. Reality may be touched, and it may be experienced, but it cannot be objectively defined. It is bigger than that—it is grasped only directly and independently of mediating language, or it is discussed through metaphor.

So it is a big mistake to believe that our conception and explanation of truth or reality is the truth per se. As in physics, the universe of Genesis and other ancient literature cannot be independently understood or divided from our subjective view. Consequently, the text is more concerned with telling a meaningful story. It thus universalizes the discussion of truth—it is no longer bound to the narrow proposition of facts. That's what art does so well.

To take a final simple example, consider my nature, the nature of a human being. I am not a solid, unified object, as outward appearances would suggest. Rather, I am a happening of subatomic matter and energy that is constantly in motion.

If that were not mysterious enough, this inexplicable coincidence of matter and energy presents itself as a discrete totality: me. Yet there is no discrete thing—no single, irreducible item—which is me. I am a throbbing event of interdependently related phenomena—and so are you!

This means that we, too, are myths, stories; the detailed facts of our molecules, atoms, and chemicals cannot in any way inform us about one another as personalities, yet as such we are very real and true. Analyze my blood and DNA all you want; you will never see the truth of me. Listen to my story and you will.

We can do no better in considering this than to listen to Nobel Prize—winning physicist Niels Bohr. He said that science can give us words about reality but cannot define reality as it is: "There is no quantum world. There is only an abstract quantum physical description. It is wrong to think that the task of physics is to find out how nature is. Physics concerns what we can say about nature."[12]

If that's what physics is, why should we feel squeamish about accepting that the Bible and other mythologies are bound by the same limitation? This is the truly scientific approach. Scripture and mythology say something about how things are, but there is no direct mapping between words and reality.

I'm hoping to bridge the gap here between literalist readers who fear that if their scripture is not literal it is somehow not true, and those non-religious people who think that because it is a religious book, it has nothing true to say. As Einstein said, "The bigotry of the nonbeliever is for me nearly as funny as the bigotry of the believer."[13]

These ancient spiritual texts—including Genesis—are stories of a time that was deeply remembered, a universally known experience. Let's not bring an argument to the text. Instead, let's approach the authors respectfully and allow them to give their testimonies. Assume with me that they knew something, that they understood something. They favored us by passing down important information that they thought we would need.

The Fall

The editors of my Bible have kindly inserted subheadings before important events; this one they titled simply, "The Fall of Man." Laying at the root of Judeo-Christian tradition, the garden story assumes an anthropological position to theologians. In Christian theology, we remember this as the first sin. In some minds, it is practically genetics: the propensity to repeat the sin of the Fall is passed on in our blood from generation to generation, along with all the retributive judgments that follow.

There is another way to read this, however, which is still anthropological, but without the self-flagellating overtones. What if the story refers to a real change in human development that resulted in a massive cultural shift—a change in human consciousness? It then is a kind of genuine anthropology, a memory of a cultural transformation that had unfortunate, even catastrophic, results.

If I may refresh our memory, "The Fall of Man" is not found in the Bible's first creation story. In the latter, there were no forbidden fruits and no moral crisis—the whole earth was good, and there is no mention of evil.

This second version is far more dramatic. God fashions humans out of the same atomic material as the dust and places this creation in a specially made garden, free to eat the fruit of every tree there except one: "but of the tree of the knowledge of good and evil you shall not eat, for in the day that you eat of it you shall die."[14]

We are accustomed to thinking about this scene in terms of personalities like Adam and Eve. But some care should be taken in reading it, for the Hebrew word *adam* is not a proper name; it means "human."

Here is the first time it appears: "Then God said, 'Let us make humankind in our image, according to our likeness.'"[15] The translators chose "humankind" in English, even though it is the same word they will later translate as the proper name Adam. In the original text, they are indistinguishable. That ambiguity presents translators with a dilemma. They don't always agree on when the word is best translated as a proper name.

For example, in the first three chapters of Genesis, the modern New Revised Standard Version features "Adam" with a capital "A" only three times, while there are twenty-three occasions when the same word is instead translated as "humankind." The King James Version, which translates *adam* as "man" instead of "humankind," prefers eleven repetitions of the proper name Adam. What is indisputable is the anthropological nature of this text; this is a story about the human species, not some guy named Adam.

At this juncture, humankind is enjoying Paradise as we have imagined it to be—bliss, security, material welfare, and harmonious relationships. We are told, "They were naked and not ashamed." Humanity is fully exposed in body and soul and completely vulnerable without self-conscious anxiety. There is a perfectly reconciled and harmonious relationship among humans, between humanity and the rest of creation, and with the creative force that preceded all.

Now enters the serpent, described as clever or even prudent. In the Book of Proverbs, the same Hebrew attribute of "clever" assigned to the serpent is always used positively. Oddly, though, Proverbs suggest that the clever will always keep knowledge to themselves, which is not what the serpent does. Instead, he blurts out a question, a suggestion that humanity re-imagine the nature of their reality and their relationship to the natural world: "Did God say, 'You shall not eat from any tree in the garden?'"

Eve's response tells us that something is already not quite right. She says, "We may eat of the fruit of the trees in the garden; but God said, 'You shall not eat of the fruit of the tree that is in the middle of the garden, nor shall you touch it, or you shall die.'"

But touching the fruit was never prohibited. One wonders if by taking this too far, the writer is indicating that a decisive change in human consciousness has already taken place. Realizing that some fruit is poisonous to eat and avoiding it is natural protection, not a taboo. Making a religious rule in excess of what is dangerous is a taboo—it is entirely superstitious, imaginary. The serpent, it seems, represents a moment of confusion among the humans about what is real and what is imagined, between the laws of nature and the rules of imagined culture.

Let me explore this thought a little bit: Eve imagined a danger that appears to be as real as any danger in the natural world. But it isn't. The danger is constructed, imagined. A fruit that is poisonous might grow in a particular area. Society might begin to imagine that all food from that area is poisonous, too, and create a rule that says no one can go there, it is an evil place. In Eve's situation, the natural order, represented by the command "do not eat," has been extended by her imagination—by the culture she creates —as being not just dangerous to eat, but untouchable.

If Eve then forgets that she is the author of this rule, not God (or nature, if you prefer), it becomes a dangerous trap. If she believes this untrue taboo about touching, equating it with the real danger of ingesting poison, it undermines the truth of the real danger. All that is required to seemingly prove natural reality wrong is to test the false proposition. If she touched it and no death ensued, eating it would become easy to justify: "I touched it and didn't die; I can eat it, too!" And if she did, she would die.

Why am I belaboring this? Because this power of social imagination will gradually unfold on our journey as something genuinely and historically fundamental to the human struggle. Civilization, Paradise nostalgia, religion, nationalism, and everything else is a product of the human imagination. I believe the authors of Genesis intuitively understood these sociological and psychological dynamics and that their insights, deftly encrypted here, will serve us well in understanding our present challenge.

Moving along, we hear the serpent's voice again. Now he says the most illuminating words in the entire passage: "You will not die; for God knows that when you eat of it your eyes will be opened, and you will be like God, knowing good and evil."

This is what it is all about, then; it is about surpassing the natural human condition, to become something else, to become like God. And the attribute of God that humankind did not possess was the power to know good and evil beyond the simple dictates of nature. It is the power to imagine new rules of nature for ourselves, to create our own universe through words, just as the Creators did. More to the point, this is the power to dream up rules that are not of nature, or are against nature—even against our own best interests as humans.

We all know what happened next, but we must remember that Eve was not compelled to eat because of desire for the fruit's taste but because of its effects: "the tree was to be desired to make one wise." This is more LSD than it is apple.

The focus here is squarely upon consciousness. Whatever poison this is, it is of the mind. Adam and Eve, as the symbolic total of the whole human race, ate the mind-altering fruit. "Then the eyes of both were opened, and they knew that they were naked; and they sewed fig leaves together and made loincloths for themselves."

The effect was to know something they did not know before—they now knew shame. They became something other than what they naturally were. They became meta-human, human beings neurotically aware of themselves. As the wise serpent said, they became like God, able to create a world—not a natural world, but a virtual one with its own unnatural rules, and those rules were not kind to them.

God's voice narrates the consequences:

"See, the man has become like one of us, knowing good and evil; and now, he might reach out his hand and take also from the tree of life, and eat, and live forever"—therefore the Lord God sent him forth from the garden of Eden... He drove out the man; and at the east of the Garden of Eden he placed the cherubim, and a sword flaming and turning to guard the way to the tree of life.[16]

Genesis claims that Paradise was lost through the knowledge of good and evil. It's a bizarre report. What can it possibly mean in the real world?

We will probe archeology alongside biblical and non-biblical stories to answer that question, but already we can see how the story might correspond with cultural development, the subject which will occupy our attention in the next chapter.

Before moving on, there is one theme in this story that is so widely misconstrued it requires our attention. It's the idea I got in Sunday school when I was given the impression that this story is about sex. I got that idea because preachers pushed this interpretation to better sell the salvation they were in the business of offering. It is easy to do. There is shame and nudity in this story; what else could it be about if not something a little dirty?

This was the implicit argument of my church, guilt being the primary lever of its power. When the preacher said we were all sinners and needed the forgiveness of Christ, like many youngsters exposed to revivalist-style Christianity, I felt it was mainly sexual thoughts and desires that needed forgiving. This came to a point at Bible camp, where young teen girls and boys spent a few summer weeks trying not to sin.

Inevitably failing—at least in our thoughts—we were then offered absolution by raising our hands and walking the aisle to get saved, which meant to be cleansed, released of our guilty feelings. (I don't know of many kids who were motivated by the burden of greed or pride.) That's a sad story—not the Good News that Jesus intended them to preach—and not what Genesis intended.

Which is exactly why we shouldn't approach the story from a theological concept of original sin, for although there is indeed something universal in the experience described in this tale, it is not a genetic predisposition to be naughty. If anything, the Fall presents itself as the advent of pathological prudishness.

Before their minds were bent, Adam and Eve enjoyed being naked together. Their libertine exposure was free from alienation and objectification and completely free from guilt. The text goes out of its way to explicitly tell us that Adam and Eve "were naked and not ashamed." There was neither subject nor object, no sense of alienation, and no taboo that said, "nor shall you touch it."

Of course, this does not take sex out of the Fall altogether; acquiring this special knowledge altered Adam and Eve's relationship. Genesis is very specific about this: post-Fall, they were ashamed and even afraid of their nakedness. The contrast between before and after tells us that sexual alienation, this terrifying shame, is the result, not the cause, of the Fall. Shame was the mortal gods' first creation, a beast of their virtual universe.

Diverting our own fallen eyes now from the couple's innocent nudity and focusing our gaze instead on the trees in question, the more fundamental issue becomes clear. The garden hosts two specifically named trees: one is a Tree of Life, the other a Tree of Knowledge of Good and Evil.

That is a surprising dialectic, isn't it? The symmetry seems off. Wouldn't it make more sense if the struggle was simply between good and evil—a Tree of Good and a Tree of Evil? Or between trees of Life and Death? How is something that we fundamentally associate with ethics—the knowledge of good and evil—actually the opposite of life? What kind of knowledge is this, this knowledge that kills?

Deadly Knowledge

Deadly knowledge has been described by philosophers and religious figures as diverse as Democritus, Kant, Buddha, Jesus, and Marx. Philosophy describes this kind of knowledge as "reification," literally meaning "thingification," from the Greek word *rei* for "thing."

In practice, this has to do with objectifying or making a discrete object where there in fact is no object. This is not in itself a problem. Our conception of the self illustrates reification. We've talked about how we are, in our atomic particulars, more of an event than a thing. There is no single object that is "me." But for functional reasons, during the length of this fluid event's occurrence, a "me" is virtually realized—it is a reification.

We reify for practical reasons. As Peter L. Berger and Thomas Luckmann describe in their 1966 classic, *The Social Construction of Reality*, we must reify; it's the way human consciousness processes and interacts with the environment. It is this function of language and consciousness that separates us from the animals. "Man occupies a peculiar position in the animal kingdom," Luckmann writes. "Unlike the other higher mammals, he has no species-specific environment... there is no man-world in the sense that one may speak of a dog-world or a horse-world."[17]

So, the world our minds live in is not the natural world—it is rather a world mediated by symbols, which we use to interact with the natural order. Language and concepts give us handles or provide tools to describe, re-imagine, and manipulate the natural order in the virtual reality of our minds. We do not interact much with the world directly.

The authors describe in detail the way reification works, showing that what is "real" to us is remarkably pliable and even varies from one human culture to the next, greatly affecting our values and ethics.

While we live in a world of our symbolic imagination, animals are limited to their organisms—they behave uniformly by dictate of instinct. A dog cannot imagine any world, not even the dog-world in which it lives, and this is true for generation after generation of dogs. There is no doggie-ego; its feelings are not reflected upon. Their social interactions are hard-wired; a dog does not create cultures and religions that differ from those of other dogs, for example.

The human sense of self is not limited to its organism, however, and our social interactions are not hard-wired. Instead, we have a sense of *being* our organism—"I am this, I am that"—and at the same time have a sense of separately possessing it: "I *have* a body," as though it were a separate entity from the "I" which has custody over it.

All well and good. This is what it means to be human. But if it's so normal and necessary, why is it the villain in Adam and Eve's story? Well, I don't think it is, exactly. Eve's temptation was described as the possibility of "being like God." That phrase suggests a kind of reifying knowledge beyond the scope of what it takes to remain happily human. Like anything beneficial, taken too far it becomes harmful, self-destructive. All those big ideas in history that have killed so many people, all the social systems that choke and constrain life, are reifications that are *god-like*—that is to say, inhuman—and often harmful to humans. That's not to say it is always on a big scale. Within our own relationships and even within our own psyche, reification's dehumanizing powers can do great harm.

In Adam and Eve's example, the immediate result of acquiring god-like knowledge in the Garden of Eden was death: "you will surely die." I don't have to point out that Adam and Eve did not physically die of food poisoning. What died was their original humanity. That's really what the story is about.

Fine. Can this possibly describe history in the real world? Let's ask the sociologists (italics mine):

> Reification is the apprehension of human phenomena as if they were things, that is, in non-human or possibly supra-human terms. Another way of saying this is that reification is the apprehension of the products of human activity as if they were something else than human products—such as facts of nature, results of cosmic laws, or manifestations of divine will. *Reification implies that man is capable of forgetting his own authorship of the human world*, and further, that the dialectic between man, the producer, and his products is lost to consciousness. *The reified world is, by definition, a dehumanized world.* It is experienced by man as a strange facticity, an opus alienum over which he has no control rather than as the opus proprium of his own productive activity.[18]

That's some dense language. Go ahead and read it a few times—let it sink in! I'll help a little bit: "opus alienum" here means the work of another person, not oneself, and "opus proprium" means one's own creation. The point is that we tend to mistake the world created by our imaginations for something created by God or nature, quite external to ourselves.

The authors continue, "It must be emphasized that reification is a modality of consciousness, more precisely, a modality of man's objectification of the human world. Even while apprehending the world in reified terms, man continues to produce it. *That is, man is capable paradoxically of producing a reality that denies him.*"

The Fall represents this delusion. We see it most obviously when a person or race is objectified as evil. Injustice, persecution, torture, murder: all of this is possible only through the reifying knowledge that replaces the victim's humanity with an imagined evil object that we can then abuse or kill. In the same moment, we objectify ourselves or our special ideological system, judging it to be good. This is the Knowledge of Good and Evil. The Fall of Man represents this tendency to construct ideologies, religions, or social systems, and then forget that we made them up. When we believe these imagined constructions are as inevitable as a law of nature or divine will, they become inescapable traps.

That's a lot to take in. How this transpired will become clearer as we explore real places, identify practical examples, and turn to more plain-spoken literature. We will do that by visiting the region around the Tigris and Euphrates where I've found an unexpected amount of solid scholarship to help us understand in concrete terms what the ancient authors described in this Garden parable.

Before moving on, I'll mention again this matter of Adam's name. We can see there a good illustration of reification by how its use changes through the story. For example, when *adam* first appears, in every instance up until the eating of the fruit, the translators had to remind us in the footnotes that it is not clearly a proper name—it simply means "human." There is not yet a reified personality there. In fact, it is always used with plural pronouns, such as "they," and a plural form of "you" which we no longer have in English (something like "you all").

After the Fall, the language changes: "But the Lord God called to *the* man, and said to *him*, 'Where are *you*?' He said, '*I* heard the sound of you in the garden, and *I* was afraid, because *I* was naked; and *I* hid myself'" (italics added). This language is specific and singular and self-known—it is a reified ego.

The older King James Version of the Bible understands the difference. It uses "Adam" as a proper name for the first time only here, after the Fall: "And the Lord God called unto Adam, and said unto him, Where art thou?"

This shift in language shows the profound change in human consciousness at the heart of the parable. Heretofore, human consciousness was not aware of itself as a separate thing—not even of separate genders. Now, after the effect of the "knowledge of good and evil," there is a blush of self-aware confusion; there is shame and isolation. What was universal is now alienated between subject and object; the creature is alienated even from his own organism, ashamed of himself in his own gaze. "I was afraid," Adam said, "because I was naked, and I hid myself."[19]

"Myself-hid-I" reads the horribly reflexive original Hebrew text; it is a divided creature, as if myself and I are two different beings. He hid from himself, because the god-like knowledge of one layer of consciousness, the "good," objectified his actual natural being and judged it as "evil." The *virtual reality* constructed by the mind judged and condemned the *actual reality* of the natural man, the fake over the real. Here, the knowledge of good and evil resides in a single self-loathing psyche. It is a fundamentally suicidal position.

Needless to say, this bears heavily on our modern struggle over gender identity. "Gender is a social construct," claims the World Health Organization. And indeed, it is—everything we say or symbolically handle is part of our virtual universe and is involved with a particular social version of it that we live. However—and here is the tricky part—the difference between male and female in terms of biology is the most natural thing in the world. Certainly, some are biologically not fully one or the other, but those are, alas, anomalies. If one can produce a seed or another produce and carry an egg, one has a real sex. Dogs and cats have no opinions regarding their sex. Gender identity is different, but it is a constructed reality, a function of the mind. The Fall is about drifting away from the naturally Real into the ever-more constructed universe of human imagination. One might consider exercising this most god-like power of imagining new realities with caution.

In summary, the Fall of Man is about a shift in consciousness. Absolutely nothing changes in the story's setting. It is not Paradise that is lost; it is humanity that is lost to Paradise. The only thing that changes is human perception and judgment—Adam and Eve lived with a different consciousness before and after the Fall.

Somehow, the ancients remembered this. They remembered that primordial humans related to creation, to each other, and to themselves in a different and better way than they do now. After the Fall, they were the same but somehow deathly unlike what they had been, and the difference was related directly to a change in their mode of knowledge.

Thus, Genesis 3 concludes with humanity in its modern condition. Adam and Eve are to one another and to themselves foreign objects; they are ashamed of their natural human state and pitifully clothed in their new role as gods of the earth and creators of imagined worlds, perpetually ill-suited to that task.

❦ 3 ❧

EXILE

From Paradise to the Sweat of the Brow

In the heart of Mesopotamia, not far from the Euphrates River, we see a wholly unexpected sight. Before us stand rings of sixteen-ton lime-stone columns shaped in human form. Many wear what is apparently a loincloth (not quite fig leaves, but close). Some are carved with reliefs of animals, including foxes, boar, and gazelles. Snakes are prominent in the menagerie.

These are not rough-hewn blocks sculpted coarsely in the way we might imagine a caveman's work, and they are not the tiny, bulbous matronly figures found at some Paleolithic sites. These are super-sized, smoothly carved, and eloquently festooned works of art, and all were quarried, moved a considerable distance, erected, and carved at a time when only stone tools were in use. (I have some of these tools in my collection, gathered from this place before it was restricted.)

This is Göbekli Tepe, built around 11,000 years ago, at least 6,000 years older than Stonehenge and 6,000 years older than the first cities. It is 7,000 years before the Great Pyramid of Giza. Humans were hunter-gatherers then, as they had been for over 150,000 years, living by foraging plants and hunting game. Nothing was cultivated. There were no villages. Iron had not yet been discovered and pottery not yet fired. It is the first thing of its kind, and it sits right where Adam first began to laboriously till the soil. We are just outside the barred gates of the Garden of Eden.

"This area was like a paradise," lead archeologist Klaus Schmidt told the *Smithsonian* magazine. "This is the first human-built holy place."[1]

Was it like Paradise? It has all the elements: it is more than ancient, it was a place of lush material abundance, there is no evidence of conflict, and it's in the right spot, beside the rivers that flowed through Adam and Eve's garden. But apart from the location, all this is true of most prehistoric sites. There is little evidence of conflict in any of them and the vast wild world was a giant supermarket for the small global population—the whole world was the Garden of Eden.

What connects Göbekli Tepe to biblical myth is the way it represents the critical moment of transition between before and after. These massive manmade edifices and the self-conscious religion practiced here by thousands of parishioners reveal a people gathering in spiritual need, all in an age when there were as few as one million people and no material want. Why? What had changed?

Just after Göbekli Tepe, we have evidence aplenty. It has long been accepted that history took a sudden and sizable turn around 6,000 years ago. This was when cities and civilization were born, not long after the advent of agriculture—something obviously commented upon by Genesis when Adam was expelled from the Garden with the tillage of soil as his punishment, followed quickly in Genesis by the building of the first cities.

The old popular theory, first propounded by Marxist archeologist V. Gordon Childe, was that all this was due to climate change. The theory blamed a harsh environment for drying up the abundance that sustained hunter-gatherers in the Near East. This forced them to settle down and cultivate grains. Once settled and thus productive, towns and hierarchies formed around this phenomenon to bring order and stability. Soon there were proper city-states; religion and art were in turn born of this collective. Religion explained the new order and endorsed the authority of the ruling organizers.

While this is a fair description of what happened in civilization once it was up and running, the chronology is wrong. Childe would be shocked to know that people gathered for worship at Göbekli Tepe a whopping 6,000 years before the first city-state. It shows that people were already getting together practicing religion and creating monumental art on a grand scale long before any climate change happened, and well before the first seeds were planted.

Andrew Curry underscored this point for the *Smithsonian* feature on Göbekli Tepe:

> Schmidt argues... the extensive, coordinated effort to build the monoliths
> literally laid the groundwork for the development of complex societies... the
> monuments could not have been built by ragged bands of hunter-gatherers.
> To carve, erect and bury rings of seven-ton stone pillars would have required
> hundreds of workers, all needing to be fed and housed.

Schmidt, who discovered this place and had worked on it for twenty years, believed that sites like this would require its parishioners to find a way to provide for the professionals who tended to the faith. Research at other sites in the region has shown that people first began to corral sheep, cattle, and pigs near here, and at a prehistoric site just twenty miles away, geneticists found evidence of the world's oldest domesticated strains of wheat. Radiocarbon dating indicates that the science of agriculture first began here around 10,500 years ago, just five centuries after Göbekli Tepe's peak. (The practice of farming would take a little longer, but this domestication of wheat was a bigger discovery than splitting the atom in terms of its effect on human culture.)

Take a map of the Middle East and put a pin at Göbekli Tepe. Then mark Karaca Dağ some sixty miles northeast, the place where wheat—the genetic ancestor of all wheat consumed today—was first cultivated. Now mark the largest of early pre-civilization settlements at Çatalhöyük (pop. 10,000 circa 8000 BCE) and Nevalı Çori, just twenty miles away. Within the area of those pins lies the earliest evidence of systematic tilling of soil.[2] You could continue outward by marking the first city-states and their trading partners—Göbekli Tepe is the center from which the ripples of civilization radiate.

After close to two millennia of service, Göbekli Tepe was dead and buried. Literally—they covered it all up in dirt and debris. This suggests a changing culture but it's a conscious and deliberate change. There is something planned and respectful about it; they didn't just abandon the site. We can only speculate, but considering Göbekli Tepe's proximity to the first agricultural experiments and first small towns of notable influence, it seems that as more of the pilgrims decided to settle down nearby, they began to practice their beliefs as settled peoples—they didn't need Göbekli Tepe anymore.

So, what's the lesson here? Simply that people were getting together in large numbers for metaphysical reasons long before the climate change that was once thought to trigger agriculture and civilization. Stanford University's

Ian Hodder, an archeologist specializing in this period, sums it up: "This shows sociocultural changes come first, agriculture comes later."[3]

Ultimately, Göbekli Tepe represents the fulcrum upon which humanity turned from its foraging ways to the laborious and frequently stressful ways of civilization. It represents the passage between the fruitful abundance of the Garden of Eden and the judgment that follows it: "In toil you shall eat of it all the days of your life... and you shall eat the plants of the field. By the sweat of your face you shall eat bread until you return to the ground..."[4]

Biblical mythology and archeology have now begun to tell us the same story of transition from the pleasure, ease, and harmony of Paradise to a dirty, sweaty world of labor, heading soon to scarcity and warfare. Göbekli Tepe represents the moment of that transition, the proverbial Fall of Man. The story of human life before and after Göbekli Tepe is as starkly different as Adam and Eve's lives before and after the Fall.

Well and good; we've established that agriculture, settlement, and civilization were born of ritual gatherings. But why were there suddenly ritual gatherings in the first place? After 100,000 years, why now? This, too, accords with Genesis: there was spiritual crisis.

The *National Geographic* summed up Schmidt's interpretation of Göbekli Tepe in exactly these terms of transformed consciousness: "To Schmidt's way of thinking... the human impulse to gather for sacred rituals arose as humans shifted from seeing themselves as part of the natural world to seeking mastery over it."[5] Mastery or god-likeness is exactly what Adam and Eve sought from the Tree of Knowledge.

Archeologist Jacques Cauvin, a specialist in this period, agreed that there was an evolutionary breakthrough in consciousness that sparked the age of spiritual ritual. He described this change as a "revolution of symbols" marking the human ability to imagine a world beyond the present place and present moment—even a universe in the form of the cosmic or heavenly realm—to imagine the unseen as real.[6]

Both Schmidt and Cauvin describe what was poetically conveyed by the first chapters of Genesis. Göbekli Tepe stands as a point marking a change in the way humans think. Men and women were beginning to know things in a different way, expressing their burgeoning imaginations in ritual and stone. This new-found knowledge will lead to numerous complications—the world will soon get very messy, and to clean it up, civilization will rise to offer its services.

Leviathan

Thomas Hobbes gave us this judgment about pre-civilized humans, writing that their lives were "solitary, poor, nasty, brutish and short."[7] You've probably heard this line before; it's become one of those things we all just "kind of know." But is it true? What did he base this on?

Hobbes penned these words in the 1600s in a book that deeply affected modern concepts of government. His ideas—universal equality and a state constituted by mutual consent—found their way into the foundations of the United States of America. America in turn was the trailblazer providing the model for the rest of the world, which, like it or not, emulates America under the loose banners of democracy and human rights. All this is to say thank you, Mr. Hobbes, even as I raise some criticisms of his most famous remarks.

The Hobbesian world needs to be governed and governed firmly. Hobbes believed that humans were incapable of pursuing their own best interests without the guiding hand of power. If I may quote the ever-concise *Stanford Encyclopedia of Philosophy*, "He is infamous for having used the social contract method to arrive at the astonishing conclusion that we ought to submit to the authority of an absolute—undivided and unlimited—sovereign power."[8]

The "social contract" is Hobbes' coinage, too. It means consenting to the resolute rule of sovereign power in exchange for its protection and equal opportunity to welfare. This is not quite the American dream, of course. As influential as it was on shaping modern democratic ideals, the Hobbesian state is more like the book (and film) *Starship Troopers*, in which the population gives itself to the order, safety, and care of an absolutely dominating paternal state.[9]

Hobbes had sharp insight into the nature of the corporate political entity —he envisioned it as a personality, a sentient being. His book is called *Leviathan*, a biblical reference to a giant sea monster that the Hebrew prophets employed as a metaphor for the dominating empires of Mesopotamia. It seems he had no illusions about the nature of supreme power even as he endorsed it as a necessity.

This is made abundantly clear by Hobbes' book design. The titular monster, Leviathan, appears on the 1651 edition's frontispiece, designed by the artist with detailed input from the author: Leviathan rises from the land as the torso and head of a king wearing a crown; he has a sword in his right hand and a scepter in his left. His body at first appears to be faceted armor, but a closer look reveals the bodies of hundreds of people. The beast and its subjects live symbiotically for the common good.

This communal beast accurately reflects the nature of corporate power, which resembles universal consciousness, but is a simulacrum, a predatory constituent hierarchy. Such bodies have names, own property, inflict pain, and bestow blessing. They make friends and enemies. You can sue one by name in any court of law. If one ever comes after you, it will have its name across from yours in the lawsuit.

It can be a government, a state, a corporation, or any such named institution. If there was any doubt, the US Supreme Court has famously decided that since corporate beings are non-human people, they should have all the rights as other individuals.

Corporations of state and enterprise are not quite the same as us, however. In Hobbes' cover art, we see the gigantic Leviathan comprising his constituents, the body politic, all torsos and heads. They are like individual cells in the body, and like cells, they will live and die in its service. Not so, Leviathan. The corporate entity does not die easily, and typically lives for centuries, with some institutions enduring for millennia. They can grow to enormous size and power—options that are not available to mortal people.

With that in mind, Hobbes did us a service by starting to think about how to make the best of the human/state relationship. The corporate state should serve the interests of the people, he said, and that's certainly an improvement over unchecked despotism. On this he stimulated many great minds who would inspire the best aspects of the world order that we live under now. Assuming that corporate power is unavoidable, his objective was to tame the beast, to make sure it held up its end of the bargain.

For Hobbes, this was as good as it gets. His assumption was that before the rise of the sovereign state, all humans lived in a state of war—a state, as he put it, of "all against all." It was, he was certain, utter chaos. Sovereign power was inevitable because humans would be in a mess without it. This is the premise we need to examine. Is this "all against all" war and its solitary, impoverished, short, and nasty life truly inevitable in the absence of absolute authority?

My first doubt arises from the strong whiff of anxiety coming from Hobbes himself. He lived during the English Civil War, and by his own confession, he was terrified: "My mother gave birth to twins, myself and fear."[10] Hobbes was a frightened man living in chaotic times.

Anxiety was Hobbes' sole justification. The reason for submission to sovereign power was the same for everyone: "their underlying motivation is the same—namely fear—whether of one's fellows or of a conqueror."[11]

The social contract was a renunciation of individual rights in exchange for the state's protection and peace of mind. "Political legitimacy depends not on how a government came to power, but only on whether it can effectively protect those who have consented to obey it." This means that sovereign power is justified no matter what, so long as it protects its obedient charges from what they fear. But the protected do have to obey.

In the film *Starship Troopers*, it was the threat of an alien bug race that propped up the all-powerful state. The original 1959 novel is an interesting read; published against the backdrop of the Red Scare, it is as much a philosophical discussion as it is science fiction, conveying very well the fear of humanity under threat and the appealing consolation offered by a firm hierarchical order. If the absolute sovereign takes care of you and protects you in exchange for your submission, what's so bad about that? Simply doing as one is told effects a child-like freedom from anxiety.

Hobbes universalizes and normalizes this. For him, there is always something to fear. He argues that without submission to the civilizing effects of total sovereign power, humanity would live with "no knowledge of the face of the earth; no account of time; no arts; no letters; no society; and which is worst of all, continual fear, and danger of violent death."[12]

But what if his presupposition is wrong? What if pre-civilized people lived prosperous, healthy lives? What if they lived better than did most people in Hobbes' time and with demonstrably less "brutish" behavior? After all, it was he who lived in continual fear and danger of a violent death; a trivial crime in those days could mean having a limb chopped off, not to mention being boiled alive, pilloried, or burned with irons. His generation witnessed the peak of witch-hunting when a petty grudge could be converted by anyone into the worst of personal horrors. Was pre-civilized life really more brutish than that?

Poor

There is no ready resource to tell us whether pre-civilized life was more or less brutish than our own. The bulk of human existence is not historical, which simply means no one wrote it down and there is no verbal testimonial. The best we have are mythological accounts like Genesis or the Mesopotamian creation epics, which were transcribed from oral traditions thousands of years after the beginnings of agriculture. To understand anything about prehistory, we must therefore do some detective work, applying forensics and archeology.

It's a tricky business. Often, the best we can do is make a deduction based on what is absent, and that is problematic. For example, there are no giant buildings or clusters of buildings in prehistory; does this mean they were inherently incapable of building them or simply that there was no motivation to do it?

And forensic science is limited by the size of our sample. Finding prehistoric human remains is hit or miss, and the factors that caused those specimens to be preserved might be the very thing that makes them outliers rather than average representations. The best information comes when there is a good-sized specimen pool to test. In this respect, we are fortunate, for the area around Göbekli Tepe in southeast Turkey is such a pool.

Jared Diamond, best-selling author of *Guns, Germs, and Steel*, wrote in the May 1987 issue of *Discover* magazine about the results of samples examined then. These samples, and a convincing body of more recent evidence, show that men and women in this part of pre-civilized Turkey were taller than people in modern-day Turkey and Greece. Why is that? He explains in some detail that the emergence of agriculture was detrimental to human health. Diamond called the advent of agriculture the worst mistake in the history of the human race.[13] The reasons are various, some to do with nutrition, others related to dense populations in the new cities and increasing filth. Essentially, civilized life up until very recently meant more disease and poorer health than was commonly experienced before civilization.

Diamond also describes how contemporary hunter-gatherer bands provide some complementary insight into pre-civilized life. This can be problematic, too, because few to none of these groups are not contaminated by civilization. Even so, as Diamond points out, representative cases like the Kalahari Bushmen show that they had a healthier diet than modern-day Americans. It's not a starvation diet, either. The study he cites revealed that those foragers were getting a lot more calories and protein than the recommended daily allowance.

He writes, "It's almost inconceivable that Bushmen, who eat 75 or so wild plants, could die of starvation the way hundreds of thousands of Irish farmers and their families did during the potato famine of the 1840s." Diamond lists the health effects of civilization as "malnutrition, starvation and epidemic diseases."

All in all, we can say with confidence that prehistoric people were able to live healthy lives. Did they live as long as us? No one can say for sure.

Because of infant mortality, the average life span in Hobbes' time was around thirty-five years—nothing to boast about, and certainly not a great advance on life before Leviathan took over. But averages can be misleading. If we remove infant mortality from the math in Hobbes' time, those who reached adulthood could live to a ripe old age—not much different from today. (If a couple has two children, and one dies at birth, and the other lives to eighty years of age, their "average lifespan" would be forty—you see the problem.)

What about prehistoric people? We'd need a lot more bones to have any idea about real longevity in prehistory, but if we think about the period of, say, 1,000 years before Göbekli Tepe, this keeps us within a hunter-gather context still thousands of years prior to agriculture and civilization. We know that these ancestors managed to increase the population manyfold and canvas much of the earth. The math is on their side: women were living long enough to have a lot of kids, and people were healthy enough to travel long distances. To account for that rate of childbirth and migration, a normal life-span must have been at least as long as it was in Hobbes' time. That's not certain proof but it is evidence, while Hobbes' assertion that their lives were short or unhealthy is completely without evidence.

So, they ate well, traveled, and had lots of kids. That means they were not solitary, either. Studies of analogous hunter-gatherer societies consistently observe a strong bond of community and equality. They evince "sharing" as the primary value of their cultures. There isn't much that's forbidden, but selfishness is abhorred.[14] It's share and share alike—to be stingy is the most awful of transgressions.

Moreover, these groups usually do not present any class differences or inequality of wealth or power. If we can still observe this in modern-day hunter-gatherers, living 6,000 years after civilization began to cast its shadow, surely it is probable that peaceful, egalitarian relationships existed in pristine hunter-gatherer groups before Göbekli Tepe.

So far, so good. But weren't they poor?

Again, there is a problem of evidence. Civilized societies leave a strong archeological record of wealth and also inequality. They've left us a "who's who" of their times in the form of palatial homes and magnificent tombs. The guy who had a big house and big tomb was rich and powerful; the thousands of hovels around his palace belonged to people who were not. The rich tended to fill their tombs full of their stuff—even in death they kept their wealth where it belonged and out of the hands of their constituents.

Pre-civilized people did not leave behind any ostentatious cultural artifacts. Any indication of differences in power or wealth are absent. As far as we can tell, everyone—man, woman, and child—was buried the same way for 90,000 years of modern human life. This at least demonstrates material equality. Does it prove universal poverty?

In the field of economics, theorist Marshall Sahlins wrote extensively on why and how pre-civilized economies were, in a word, prosperous. The prejudice that they were impoverished is more about our problems than theirs. "To accept that hunters are affluent is therefore to recognize that the present human condition of man slaving to bridge the gap between his unlimited wants and his insufficient means is a tragedy of modern times," he writes.[15]

Sahlins writes elsewhere that modern Galbraithean market economics conceives of the consumer as wanting much, ideally possessing infinite wants (for continuous economic growth). But there is another course to affluence, Sahlins argues, as there are two paths to satisfaction: "Wants may be 'easily satisfied' either by producing much or desiring little." This second path he calls "a Zen road to affluence," upon which "human material wants are finite and few, and technical means unchanging but on the whole adequate."

He continues,

Adopting the Zen strategy, a people can enjoy an unparalleled material plenty —with a low standard of living. That, I think, describes the hunters. And it helps explain some of their more curious economic behavior: their "prodigality" for example—the inclination to consume at once all stocks on hand, as if they had it made. Free from market obsessions of scarcity, hunters' economic propensities may be more consistently predicated on abundance than our own.

Sahlins describes this simply as "needing less."[16]

The world's most primitive people have few possessions. But they are not poor. Poverty is not a certain small amount of goods, nor is it just a relation between means and ends; above all it is a relation between people. Poverty is a social status. As such it is the invention of civilisation.[17]

Thus, Sahlins argues that civilization set up the possibility for large-scale famine that did not exist for hunter-gatherers, who were not reliant on the processes of mass-produced agriculture, the mediation of banks, currencies, and corporations, and the probability that a system so constituted would break down, leaving the lower classes, which civilization imposes on its economies, in dire circumstances. "Consumption is a double tragedy: what begins in inadequacy will end in deprivation."[18]

The lives of pre-civilization hunter-gatherers were not based on limitless acquisition. The environment was plentiful—why would anyone hoard anything? They foraged, hunted, consumed, and shared everything they had. Then they went out and did it again. There is an aspect of presentness in this that got lost when people first started to farm around Göbekli Tepe— farming demands anxious attention to seasons and weather cycles and preoccupation with "what ifs." It demands hoarding and empowers those in control of the distribution of accumulated goods.

We have a hard time imagining this now: a life where we get up, find food, and get our exercise in the process of just living, and then spend most of the day sharing with others, singing songs, dancing, and painting. We can't grasp what it would mean to be so confident in the supply of nature that you would eat everything when you get it. No worries—we know there'll be more tomorrow! That's pretty much the tableau of prehistoric life, and it sounds a lot like the Garden of Eden.

Hard to believe? Sure it is. We are so conditioned to accumulate and hoard and win against others that we are automatically dubious. I understand why Hobbes assumed prehistoric people were as afraid of tomorrow as he was. That they might not have been damns us. Modernity *wants* them to have been anxious, competitive, and greedy. The evidence shows they were not.

Brutish

Sorry, Mr. Hobbes, but our ancient forbears, absent the paternal care of sovereign power, appear to have been healthy and wealthy. Were they brutes then, more brutal than the contemporaries you so feared, Mr. Hobbes? If they were, it's difficult to find any evidence of it, and people have looked very hard.

Here's what we know: In a survey of human remains older than 10,000 years, Jonathan Haas and Matthew Piscitelli found only four skeletons (out of more than 2,900 skeletons from over 400 different sites) that showed signs of violence. These highly regarded scientists concluded that any violence that existed before the agricultural revolution—and there was very little violence at all—were cases of homicide at most. (It's also possible, of course, that these were not homicides but hunting accidents.)

Then why do we assume there was violence before? It is for the same reason that we want prehistoric people to be hungry; it makes us feel we've progressed. That's exactly what Piscitelli concluded from the science: "The presumed universality of warfare in human history and ancestry may be satisfying to popular sentiment; however, such universality lacks empirical support."

In other words, our presumption of ancient violence rests on popular prejudice. The authors determined that between 200,000 and 10,000 years ago, a very long time indeed, "the archaeological evidence for warfare melts away."[19]

The absence of prehistoric evidence for violence appears especially stark when compared to the avalanche of violence that marks every single human habitation site from 5000 BCE onward—namely, thousands of skeletons showing signs of violence and art depicting how the wounds were inflicted by weapons clearly designed for war. Not coincidentally, the year 5000 BCE marks the dawn of civilization—the Hobbesian era of supposedly essential sovereign power.

Lest we think it is a lack of clues in the prehistoric record that accounts for the difference, Rutgers University anthropologist R. Brian Ferguson wants us to understand that his colleagues have unearthed plenty of material from the period between 100,000 and 10,000 years ago, including burial sites, tools, cooking implements, art, and more. He says, "It is difficult to understand how war could have been common earlier in each area and remain so invisible."[20]

Ferguson points to the discovery of over 300 prehistoric cave art locations, none of them depicting warfare, weapons, or warriors. Compare that to the art that appears in early civilization after 5000 BCE—it depicts hardly anything else.

In the words of US Army War College professor Richard Gabriel, "For the first ninety-five thousand years after the Homo sapiens Stone Age began, there is no evidence that man engaged in war on any level, let alone on a level requiring organized group violence. There is little evidence of any killing at all."[21]

So, Hobbes' war of all against all in pre-civilized times never happened. Not only were they not brutish, but they were also well-nourished and had good relationships. The only thing left to consider is how healthy prehistoric people were relative to modern health standards or relative to the abysmal state of human health that was the rule in Hobbes' time.

It's obviously true that a prehistoric person did not have the medicine or surgical technology available today. But that's true for everyone up until the

twentieth century. It's really something that sets us apart from all our ancestors, civilized and otherwise. By modern standards, healthcare in Hobbes'
time was appalling and arguably worse than in it was in prehistory—should
we compare primitive health to his time or ours?

There is also the problem of defining health. Today, we cure a great many
ills, and we do forestall death better than we used to. But I must ask myself:
Is the overall quality of life better? Do I really live more because I might live
a few years longer or because I can survive longer during the torment of a
long illness?

It's tough to make that kind of comparison, especially as we don't
know how effectively prehistoric people used natural pharmaceuticals to
treat the most common medical complaints, such as headache and
toothache. We also don't really know how healthy they were—they might
have been naturally far healthier on average than modern people. Nearly
every day there is an article in the press saying that the key to a long and
healthy life is diet and exercise. Well, they ate better, got lots of exercise,
and were subjected to far fewer pathogens—demonstrably fewer communi-
cable diseases—and had none of the manmade health hazards of modern
life.

Modern medicine is great, but it mostly serves to cure modern diseases.
As Jared Diamond observes,

> the mere fact that agriculture encouraged people to clump together in
> crowded societies, many of which then carried on trade with other crowded
> societies, led to the spread of parasites and infectious disease... Epidemics
> couldn't take hold when populations were scattered in small bands that
> constantly shifted camp. Tuberculosis and diarrheal disease had to await the
> rise of farming; measles and bubonic plague the appearance of large cities.[22]

What about infant and youth mortality? Prehistoric rates are not likely
to have been higher than the civilized world up until very recently. We don't
really know, but just as the plague, tuberculosis, famine, warfare, and taxes
did not exist for prehistoric people, we shouldn't necessarily think they had
nineteenth-century levels of childhood mortality either.

If you want a realistic comparison, it may be best to ask what the infant
mortality rate is for various primates. Orangutans' survival rate for females
reaching maturity is 94 percent. For humans in the 2000s, it's only up to 96
percent. This means there is no *natural* reason to assume childhood mortality
was high in prehistoric societies. By contrast, civilization's 6,000-year record

is poor. As late as 1950, survival was only 70 percent. The average from the time of early civilization barely hits 50 percent.

What about mental health? Based on observations of modern hunter-gatherers, small-clan life was a supportive environment, where isolation was unheard of. Marshall Sahlins' study of hunter-gatherer economics concludes that they were not anxious about material security. Those people did not need Prozac to cope with life.

Before moving on, we need to get our bearings, particularly to get a perspective on the rarity of organized violence in the human experience—this is where Hobbes' erring intuition was most damaging.

- The Stone Age began about 500,000 years ago. At this time, people began using tools.

- About 100,000 years ago, *Homo sapiens* started using spears to hunt and used a wide variety of tools. They ritually buried their dead. By this time, people were fully linguistic.

- The last activity at Göbekli Tepe was around 10,000 years ago, when people started settling into towns, domesticating some animals, and experimenting with wild grain.

- Around 8,000 to 7,000 years ago, hierarchical social systems emerged, and the first conclusive evidence of organized mass violence appears. For the first time, a painting depicts man-on-man violence.

- By 6,000 years ago, civilization was full on—sovereign states, rulers, armies, organized commerce—and with those things, war, disease, and malnutrition.

In his study on the origins of war, written while still a professor in the Department of National Security and Strategy at the US Army War College, Gabriel directs his expertise to show how exceptional warfare is to the human experience:

> Because war has been omnipresent from the very beginning of man's recorded history, about 4000 BCE, it has been natural for some to assume that it must have been present even before that. To those who argue that war is a natural tendency in man, the notion that war has always plagued the human species is particularly attractive. In fact, if war as a social institution is placed in historical perspective, it becomes obvious that it is among the most recent of man's social inventions... In sum, man has known war for only about 6 percent of the time since the Homo sapiens Stone Age began.

Gabriel adds that the novelty caught on like quite nothing else:

Once warfare had become established, it is difficult to find any other social institution that developed as quickly. In less than a thousand years, man brought forth the sword, sling, dagger, mace, bronze weapons and large-scale fortifications. The next thousand years saw the emergence of iron weapons, the chariot, large standing professional armies, military academies, general staff structures, military training regimens, the first permanent arms industry, written texts on tactics, military procurement, logistics systems, conscription, and military pay. By 2000 BC war had become the dominant social institution in almost all major cultures in the Middle East.[23]

So, in a space of 4,000 years, we went from a peaceful and affluent existence to one dominated by scarcity and warfare. Is 4,000 years so long that the people of early civilization would have forgotten the relatively recent and peaceful past? That seems unlikely. Today we are certainly influenced by those who lived 4,000 years before us; it is just as likely that the memory of a more peaceful, healthy, and happy life is preserved in the ancient written accounts of our Paradise.

By now we are beginning to see a possible real-life setting for the Garden of Eden. It is a time before the anxious tilling of the soil, when equality and harmony were the rule and humanity lived without material want. Without reference to mythology or religion, we have uncovered a real-world parallel to the Garden of Eden.

We know what happens next in the real world, too—life will turn a page and become truly nasty and brutish on many levels. To the extent that it is this post-primitive world to which Hobbes refers, he is correct; he just did not understand that it was Leviathan itself that maximized the nastiness of life—that his cure was the cause of the disease.

What's Your Pronoun?

So here we are: our ancestors lived in peace and harmony, sustained by a balanced relationship with their environment. Then one day, as the Garden of Eden story tells it, self-awareness changed, leading to an anxious life marred by neurosis and broken relationships—not the least of which is humanity's relationship with the environment, a tragedy exemplified by Adam's conversion from easy-going gatherer to hardscrabble farmer.

Meanwhile, guided by material evidence, our experts agree with Genesis: leading archeologist Klaus Schmidt said that a shift in self-perception led to the unprecedented building of Göbekli Tepe, when people went from "seeing themselves as part of the natural world" to "seeking mastery over it." This in turn led to a change of culture, most significantly a turn away from the hunter-gatherer life to settlement and agriculture.

Jacques Cauvin described this evolution as a change in consciousness, a new human ability to imagine oneself as part of a universe beyond the immediate world. It was, as Genesis suggests, an eye-opening transformation. To understand this better, we can turn back to the Garden of Eden in Genesis one more time, focusing now on Adam and Eve's relationship.

We last saw the pair when they acquired their heightened consciousness, making them confused and suddenly ashamed of their natural nakedness. They "heard God" and feared his unseen presence and hid from it—a picture of alienation.

We believers are mistaken to see this in Victorian terms of indiscretion and shame. It was not the Creator who shamed them. God did not catch them doing naked and naughty things and wag his finger (as I was made to believe as a child). As we learned, their shame came from an altered state of mind—from their view of themselves. In fact, it was the first time in this parable of human development that our species looked at itself with any kind of meta-awareness, as if from another's point of view.

What happens next are details of the estrangement this caused and, remarkably, each aspect of it outlined here in Genesis correlates well with changes described by our scholars. These include alterations not only in human society but also in humankind's relationship to the natural world. Genesis perceptively deals with both.

The authors of Genesis call those changes "curses," which is not very helpful for modern readers. What is a curse? Isn't that some kind of witchcraft employed to punish people you don't like? I'm afraid not. In the Hebrew Bible, it means roughly the opposite of "sanctified"; it means to be removed from the divine presence. Here it speaks to being extracted from the natural human condition. For a religious person, "cursed" means removed from God's presence. But to be "de-sanctified" might just as well mean a removal from an environment and state of mind in which humans lived in balance with nature and one another.

Each curse is described as an altered relationship. For example, the woman's curse is to endure pain in childbirth and suffer in relation to men: "your desire shall be for your husband, and he shall rule over you." Adam's curse, however, is in relation not to Eve, but to the earth: "cursed is the ground because of you; in toil you shall eat of it all the days of your life."[24]

At first, I was puzzled about what the ground did wrong. Why was the earth cursed? That's because I didn't understand what "cursed" meant. Then it dawned on me: I saw how Adam's situation is the counterpart to the consequences borne by Eve. Her relationship to him was to be a struggle and her bearing of his seed was to cause her pain. Similarly, Adam's pain would be from his relationship with the ground. Planting and bearing seed occur in both circumstances. As a newly minted farmer, he is still the implanter of seed; but in this relationship, he will be the one to suffer, toiling over it all the days of his life. It's a remarkably clever explanation that balances a passage that is too often remembered only for its misogyny. Just as the cursed life results in patriarchy, which falls heavily on the Eve side of the human equation, Adam suffers his own oppression by the soil.

To be clear, by saying the passage has balance, I do not mean to suggest equality. Their newly reified identities—this knowledge they acquired—is the very cause of inequality. The balance lies in the symmetry of there being no winners in this new universe. The fracture of human identity gave rise to roles and classes in human culture. Here in Genesis, these are clearly connected to biological sex. In our time, however, these roles are less consistently assigned as a matter of biological sex. Indeed, we often see individuals who continually exchange these positions depending on context, moving through roles, each of which carries a peculiar set of powers and problems, advantages and disadvantages.

There is something else, too. Earlier, the storyteller celebrated Adam's formation out of this now-cursed soil. The ground in Hebrew is *adam-ah*. It looks familiar because this is a form of the Hebrew word *adam*—it is his name, only feminine. With this curse, Adam is alienated from the feminine ground of his own being, his painful relationship with the soil mirroring his fallen relationship with Eve.

These gender references show us something important about what the world's first writers remember about prehistoric consciousness. As we know, when it first appears, translators write the Hebrew word *adam* as "man," "mankind," or "humankind." But in the very beginning, we learn that *adam*—"the man"—is not, in fact, a man at all. No gender has been assigned!

Consider the standard King James Version, which translates the first creation account like this: "And God said, Let us make man in our image, after our likeness... So God created man in his own image, in the image of God created he him; male and female created he them."[25]

I was a good reader at school. I understood how to use a pronoun and I grasped singular and plural. So, when I first read this as a desperately lost little boy, I was baffled. When it says, "let us make man after our likeness" and then in the next breath switches the plural and singular, "male and female created he them," what exactly was I to understand? Man is a male/female "them"?

It is not really a problem with translation. Even modern gender-sensitive versions exhibit the same confusion. Of course, the first "man" is *adam*, which is Hebrew for the human species—the old English meaning of "man"—which some versions translate as "mankind" or "humankind." Apart from that one word, whose translation is complicated due to changes in English usage, the King James text is true to the original. What's important to understand is that this text is not neutered at all—to the contrary, it is consummately gendered. This language is intentional.

Why, then, does the passage seem to confuse gender pronouns and plural and singular? The answer is that the genders are distinct here, but not *consciously separated*. God talks about "us" creating *adam* (humanity) in "our" image. This single identity, "human/adam," is both "male and female." "Them," the one *adam*, is an image of the Creator, which must also therefore be both male and female!

This is a perception of reality alien to us, but it is remembered by the ancient scribes as the original form of human self-awareness—it is transpersonal consciousness. "Transpersonal" means denoting or relating to states or areas of consciousness beyond the limits of personal identity.[26] Creation story number one is therefore a stunning piece of non-dual philosophy. That's the first chapter of Genesis.

In chapter two, we have the second, more prosaic account of human creation. This time all the players, God included, appear as individuals in a morality play. The primary difference is that humankind was undifferentiated in the first chapter, speaking no lines and living in the whole world, not a specific place. Now we see Adam as a specific being in a garden, and we meet a down-to-earth character—a regular Joe or Jane—through scripted, spoken lines. For good reason, some English translations begin translating the word *adam* here as a proper name—"Adam"—although by no means consistently.

In any case, the second creation story begins with God's formation of *adam* (humanity) from the *adam-ah*. God creates animals, too, prompting the narrator to observe that none of them were suitable as a companion for this earthy human. The Creator puts the human to sleep, extracts a rib, and out of it makes a companion.

Presumably, as per the first version of the story, there was one person who was both male and female. Now there are two companionable persons, a male and a female. "This at last is bone of my bones and flesh of my flesh,"

Adam says, "this one shall be called Woman, for out of Man this one was taken." Then comes the famous line read at every wedding: "Therefore a man leaves his father and his mother and clings to his wife, and they become one flesh." I don't think they read the next line at weddings, but it's very important: "And the man and his wife were both naked, and were not ashamed."

There are some curious things here in the wedding verse. The word translated as "Man" is not *adam* as we might expect. Rather, it is *ish* and "Woman" is *ish-ah*. That's not a big deal—you'd hear the same thing on the streets of Tel Aviv today—but it tells us something important. Before this, *adam* in fact is never really "man" in the gendered sense—*adam* was the male and female human being created in the image of "us," the Creator. Now the writers choose *ish* and *ish-ah*, the gendered words for male and female individuals, exactly because they wanted to make it clear that this is the masculine and feminine side of the unitary male/female human identity—*adam*.

Significantly, we also must understand that, in terms of consciousness, these are still not two separate beings. It is one entity of two genders. The difference between *ish* and *ish-ah* is the difference between *adam* and *adam-ah*: a feminine and masculine form of the same thing. After all, the whole point of this passage is that they become "one flesh."

But weren't they one flesh to begin with? Why go to the trouble of putting this male-female being to sleep, extracting the female component, and then marrying them back together into one flesh? In modern Hebrew, the word "cling" (as in "clings to his wife") is the word for "glue"; why cut the human in half only to glue it back together?

A traditional Jewish Cabalistic interpretation is particularly colorful: the bumps on our spines, they say, are remnants of this original bi-gendered organism having been divided down its backbone. The original human creation was a single androgynous pushmi-pullyu.

Cabalism is Jewish mysticism, and we might expect mystics to have strange Dr. Dolittle ideas, but it's not just the mystics who believed something like this. The midrashic rabbis comment on it, too: "R. Jeremiah b. Leazar said: When the Holy One, blessed be He, created the first adam, He created it with both male and female sexual organs, as it is written, 'Male and female He created them, and He called their name adam.'"[27] According to Rabbi Samuel b. Nahman, "At the time that the Holy One, Blessed Be He created Man, He created him as an Androgynous."[28]

Well then, why bother with the glue? The answer has to do with the basic difference between the two creation stories. In both chapters, *adam* is at once plural and singular—two genders in "one flesh." What sets the passages apart, and the reason for the surgery and reattachment, is that the second creation account describes a social world. In other words, it describes the unified consciousness of male and female in a real-world environment; there are separate physical beings but one conscious identity. The first account is not sociological—it is philosophical, esoteric, and mystical (that's why there is no human dialogue in the first chapter).

Thus, Genesis recalls non-dual or transpersonal awareness as a specific sociological trait of pre-civilized life. This means that the first people to write history remembered primitive society as possessing a state of consciousness *lacking any clear singular/plural or male/female opposition.*

Such a thing is not unheard of in the modern world, of course. Buddhism teaches that non-dual awareness is our original state. It seems to work for physics, too—everything is made of the same particles and embedded in the same fabric. Separateness is a perception, a constructed reality.

Jesus' followers liked the idea, too. In the New Testament, there are heated declarations that the end point of salvation is a reconciliation of all things, an experience of life where "there is no longer Jew or Greek, there is no longer slave or free, there is no longer male and female."[29] Christianity thus sees non-dual awareness as intrinsic to restoring the original Paradise consciousness. This contrasts with what we see today in ever-proliferating gender identities, where the minutest shades across the spectrum of male and female get labeled and isolated from the universal human experience. It is an evolving fragmentation, multiplying isolated identities. The trend is to do the same thing with race and culture.

Göbekli Tepe archeologist Klaus Schmidt couldn't have spoken more apropos of this when he observed that the critical difference in human development was a transition from "seeing themselves as part" of the natural world to being separately "over" it. If, as Schmidt suggests, there was a real non-mythical break in self-perception, can we identify a time when the human experience was truly transpersonal? To find out, we need to find evidence for what changed in human consciousness and better understand how this changed the way humans live.

❧ 4 ❧

AFTER EDEN

Voices

Consciousness, self-perception, non-dual versus dual awareness, reconciliation and alienation, deadly knowledge—what are we talking about here?

Something about this line of questioning reminds me of two Holocaust survivors I knew when I lived and worked as a young man for several years on an Israeli kibbutz.

One of them, named Amichai, was generous and kind, and though he'd been through unspeakable suffering, he emanated only warmth and gentleness; everyone was drawn to him. The other survivor caused us to avert our eyes; she projected paranoia and alienation, was difficult to approach, and was uncommunicative, greedy, and a little bit scary.

Day after day—breakfast, lunch, and dinner—she came to the dining hall equipped with metal containers. Stuffing them to the brim with perishable foods, she went home to guard her haul and eat alone, returning to repeat her desperate routine a few hours later. This, even though the kibbutz was a real Paradise in many ways. Food would never run out and was free for the taking; everything on the kibbutz was shared with no questions asked.

For these two survivors, the difference between heaven and hell was not external. Both had been in concentration camps, lost family, and immigrated to Israel with great difficulty. I don't really know if what the woman went through was so horribly different; it might have been. Whatever the case, their environment now was identical and had been for decades. Why was their experience of it altogether different? I can only characterize it as a matter of consciousness—their natural existence was the same, but their subjective realities belonged to different universes.

Amichai was, for lack of a better word, enlightened. He had reason for bitterness and cause to believe that his family and comfort might be ripped away again. After all, we were at war in Lebanon when I lived there, and the kibbutz was a mere mile and a half from the border. Katyusha rockets landed in our fields. Yet he never showed anxiety or selfishness and was never guarded in any way—he always had time for us and spoke with the gentleness and compassion of an angel.

As for me, I was like the woman. I was an eighteen-year-old who'd suffered his fair share of difficulties, but nothing remotely comparable to Amichai's. And yet it was I who worried and fretted, constantly on edge with fear of abandonment, every relationship fraught with desperate fears. I clung to relationships, stored them up like that woman, and was certain they would not be there by the next mealtime. Either that, or I practiced a stern aloofness, removed myself from vulnerability, and rushed into places of peril (soon to Kurdistan and Athens, for example).

Amichai intrigued me and gave me hope. When we worked together, he shined with love and contentment. He was available, open, compassionate, and fearless. I wanted what he had. He somehow had regained a measure of Paradise.

Over the years, I've never seen a more striking illustration of Eden's dynamics. The difference between Amichai and the woman (and my neurotic self) was unrelated to our environment. That's how it was in the Garden of Eden, too—Adam and Eve's environment never changed. Neither did the real world of our ancestors before and after the dawn of hierarchy and violence. The same plants and animals were there as before. Climate was not a factor; the transition to agricultural communities pre-dated any significant climate change. The only thing that changed was their subjective reality.

How that happened is our current topic, and it has a lot to do with language. Consciousness is closely related to language. And while humans have likely been able to speak and think linguistically for the past 100,000 years, the nature of thoughts must have changed at some point to cause such a huge change in social patterns, technology, and religion. Socially constructed reality is built through linguistic or discursive thinking. Deadly reifying knowledge executes its powers through language and inner dialogues. In what way did this change after 90,000 or so years of stable human existence?

The crux of the matter is recursion. Humans can speak and think recursively, an ability that separates us from all other forms of life. This is what enables us to imagine ourselves and others' selves. When we think of ourselves thinking, or of being "in the past" and "in the future," this is recursive thought. It is the self looked at as if by another self.

Recursion allows us to think and talk about ideas. We can think about what others are thinking, or what they thought or will think, or even what might or should be thought. Recursive thinking makes us psychic time travelers, too. It creates a narrative that is perceived linearly with a before, now, and after. It can even get inside other people's heads.

The recursively capable mind is closely related to the imagined self. Writing in the *American Scientist*, psychologist Michael Corballis introduces the concept of recursion: "To be properly recursive," he writes, "the concept of self should be involved—that is, not merely knowing that one is a physical object, but knowing that one knows, or knowing that one has mental states."

As a specialist in cognitive neuroscience and evolution, Corballis describes some of the theoretical tests that identify recursive thinking, pointing out that, as far as science is aware, only humans possess this ability. He writes that one of the ways to test for a concept of self "is through the awareness that one can exist at different points in time... The notion of a past self depends on memory."

This is more than just remembering the facts. Rather, he says, it is about "events that you can bring to consciousness and replay in your mind." Such memories "are recursive because they involve making mental reference to your earlier mental self."

Corballis explains that recovering semantic (factual) memories relies on what influential neuroscientist Endel Tulving calls "noetic awareness," while episodic memories are "recalled through autonoetic awareness, which is self-knowing."[1]

Self-knowing, I don't need to mention, is what the Garden of Eden story is about. So, when was this power in fact bestowed on humanity?

The origin of language and consciousness is by no means fully understood. Some say it was gradual, others sudden. Geneticists and linguists generally converge on 100,000 years ago as the latest date by which humans had language. Some have argued that language goes back as far back as 350,000 years. Suffice it to say, we've had language a long time.

Suppose for a moment that in the development of language and awareness there was a transition from a more noetic awareness to a more and more autonoetic awareness—from a more direct way of knowing to a more mediated, recursive, and consequently judgmental knowledge.

This would be easy to test if we could directly compare our thoughts with our prehistoric ancestors, which seems impossible because we have a direct record of thoughts only following the invention of writing. That seems too late to directly catch this transformation in the act. But what if that early writing preserves some memory of the transformation in progress?

There is a controversial theory that postulates this very thing. Julian Jaynes makes a case for it in his book, *The Origin of Consciousness in the Breakdown of the Bicameral Mind*, published in 1976.[2] As the title suggests, Dr. Jaynes theorized that the division between the brain's two hemispheres was much more pronounced in prehistory, and the breakdown in this division gave rise to meta-cognition, "thinking about thinking," or modern consciousness as we know it.

Jaynes' pre-civilized human would have had all the capacities we have today except for self-reflection. There would not have been a sense of self that mediated the human journey. He postulated that one side of the brain would have been understood by the other side as a voice speaking—a verbal hallucination.

In prehistory then, the language that had long ago formed in the human mind was perceived as a voice, spoken from one part of the brain and heard in another. The thoughts that occurred would not have been reflected upon recursively at all; rather, they would occur exactly as if hearing someone else talking. What we today call "talking to ourselves" our ancestors understood as coming from a real person, dead or alive, or from the stars in the sky or a created image made of stone for that matter (think of Wilson the volleyball in the Tom Hanks film *Cast Away*). Verbal thoughts always seemed to come from an external source.

You would have been thinking very clever thoughts, but you wouldn't know that you were thinking. Problem solving and decision making worked just fine. The right side of the brain worked it out and the thought registered as a voice speaking in the left. There was authority in that heard voice, and that authority was always perceived as coming from outside ourselves.

Sometimes it really was external. When a leader figure or a parent spoke, for example, that wouldn't make any difference. In Jaynes' hypothesized world, the brain perceived all verbal content the same way. If you didn't have a true external voice directing you, it came from your clever mind but was still heard as the voice of the leader you followed, or maybe of

Mom or Dad, who lay entombed with their favorite things and living happily in the great beyond, which your voices told you surely was the case. And yes, when the language-producing side of you spoke out loud, the language-receiving side of your mind "heard" this, too. The point is that the brain that understood speech was not aware of itself as being the brain that understood it. To think to oneself was to hear some other intelligence speak.

For Jaynes, it was the requirement to live in communities and farms that led to an evolutionary change in consciousness, the eponymous breakdown of the bicameral mind. His book gets very specific in terms of times and places, proposing that ancient texts lend evidence to his theory. He claims that some literature, like Homer's *Iliad* and the older texts of the Bible, are devoid of self-reflection, and that it's possible therefore to observe the breakdown of the bicameral mind occurring in the evolution of early literature. (In the case of the *Iliad*, this is an especially intriguing observation.)

Although I think his specific ideas about literature are quite speculative, Jaynes was on to something in the big picture. Our most ancient literature often references a loss of God's voice. Early traditions believed that gods spoke, and when they did not, the priests and kings anguished over the loss. All early religions sought out those who made a convincing claim that they spoke from the beyond. Were they trying to fill the void left when humans lost that sense of the guiding voice?

We still seek out the voice of the wise, the voice of authority. And it is not just in religion. Sometimes a gifted voice is all it takes to move people far beyond their normal inclinations. Hitler's voice bypassed the consciousness of thousands of people who acted on his commanding word. Hypnotists can exploit this ancient brain circuitry easily. And, of course, we all still "hear" the inner voice. Most people talk to themselves almost constantly, a continuous internal chatter. And everyone talks to themselves insofar as we all think verbally—we use words to think—which is, I think, tantamount to talking to oneself.

Jaynes has many detractors. He speculated wildly and, in the process, made his core argument unpalatable to many serious-minded people. To their chagrin, however, later neurological discoveries have generally supported his predictions. For example, Jaynes postulated that the area of the left brain responsible for language has a counterpart in the right side that would prove to be active in schizophrenics who hear voices. When he wrote this in the 1970s, there was no way to test for it. Now, modern scanning techniques have observed this part of the right brain lighting up when schizophrenics hear voices, just as it lights up when you or I hear another's audible voice.

Daydreaming

Julian Jaynes proposed that an evolutionary, biological change had occurred. He argued that this was species-wide, driven by agriculture, and that it was reflected in ancient literature. But perhaps we could modify his idea slightly: yes, consciousness was different once upon a time, but not as sharply different as he hypothesized. And it changed not because of agriculture, but rather it was the reason agriculture and hierarchical civilization happened. Certainly, archeological evidence supports the idea that changes in consciousness led to the agricultural revolution.

And really, it isn't so hard to understand that such changes can occur. Even now, we know from personal experience how flexible consciousness can be. Just think of the different states we can experience. Altered consciousness occurs, for example, when we dream. Within the dream, we experience and process its reality the same way we do in waking life; it is as if we live a different life while dreaming, a life just as authentic as the waking one. If you never awoke and continued to dream, that would be your life, your reality.

But we don't have to go to sleep to experience other phases of consciousness. Psychotropic drugs—LSD, for example—instantly change perceived reality, while empathogens like MDMA ("ecstasy") induce a measure of non-duality that deeply alters the sense of the autonomous self—that is, how independent we feel from the identity of others. Experienced meditators also exhibit measurable changes in brain wave activity and report the dissolution of self or the experience of non-dual awareness.

Consider another common example. Spending time in a sensory deprivation tank will very quickly alter your consciousness. Tellingly, one of the first reported changes for test subjects is auditory hallucinations, usually after only a short time in the water. In all these examples, it is striking how quickly and keenly superficial changes can reshape the subject's perceived consciousness.

How can what is real to us shift so quickly? It is because our conscious state—dreaming or awake, drugged, or deprived of sensations—is never a direct representation of reality; it is always symbolically mediated through language into something with meaning. Our words and our thoughts interpret our engagement with reality by constructing the virtual world, the constructed reality. If this were not the case, we would experience only a chaos of imagery and sounds—it would all be direct sensation and instinct. All the everyday objects around you where you sit right now would be completely meaningless without mediation by language and culture. They'd be only abstract shapes and colors, evoking only instinctual responses from the most primitive parts of your nervous system.

In other words, our waking state is also a kind of dream. Although our waking state is triggered more immediately by external stimuli, brain imaging reveals that dreaming uses the very same systems. There is functionally no difference. I'm not saying that dreaming is exactly the same thing—the point is that representations of reality while awake are not more "real" than what we perceive while dreaming. Any meaning understood in both phases is entirely representational.

Building up this universe of meaning, however, is not a lonely endeavor. While awake, we negotiate with each other a common interpretation of these inputs. This is our culture, a constructed reality we share. But it is not the entirety of our consciousness. Each of us only approximates the experience of others for collaborative purposes—culture and language are never so precise as to completely map one person's perception to that of someone else's. If we rely solely on that negotiation to escape loneliness, we are doomed to failure; the only real fellowship exists at a more fundamental reality than culture or language can facilitate.

There are levels or "orders" of consciousness, too. A fully formed ego, the meta-consciousness of self, is not necessary to have meaningful consciousness. We can experience the feeling of joy, or the quality of the color red, or the beauty of music without recursive reflection and without mediation. Buddhists speak of "suchness" as the awareness of "things as they are." Suchness is a more direct apprehension of phenomena. In fact, we can do many complex and creative things and enjoy many of life's best experiences without involving conscious mediation at all, and without the higher order of self or the imposition of a discrete personal identity. For example, experts in performance—such as athletes and artists—say that we perform at our best in the state of "flow" or direct absorption in the execution of the art.

At the other extreme is our sense of self, which is the most abstract and possibly the most impractical and useless order of consciousness. It is synthesized through a complex of convergent neurological functions—a ghost in the machine that nonetheless poses as its most fundamentally essential mechanism.

The ego-self is nothing of the kind and is not even necessary. In fact, to what extent that self is experienced as autonomous is variable because it is socially conditioned. It is something we learn. Even now there are people who, owing to a peculiar religious upbringing, claim their lives are guided by hearing the voice of God. Their sense of self is not completely autonomous. Others live with a greater degree of communal identity than the average Westerner. A more universal example is the way human children have imaginary playmates with whom they converse. We are told very early in life that the others are imaginary, which reinforces the formation of the ego, the autonomous identity. What would happen if we grew up in a place where society taught children that these companions are real? We might never learn that the voice in our heads was ours, single and alone.

That malleability is one of the astonishing things about us. We don't think about it very much because we apply the molds of conscious perception as a cultural routine. Our children are born with unfinished brains upon which we stamp a worldview, and we use a language to literally program their minds, much the way a computer is programmed. The programming works very well, but it can be updated, patched, corrupted, and, to some extent, uninstalled and replaced, even into early adulthood.

And like computer programs, these neural programs are fragile—they can become unstable, get infected with viruses, or be hijacked. We know that drugs or the benign use of sensory deprivation can very quickly alter perceived reality. We are also quite familiar with glitches in the programming —mental illness, psychosis, hallucinations, or the simple and common process of "cognitive decline." Intriguingly, hearing voices is never far below the surface and is one of the most common glitches. In *Muses, Madmen, and Prophets: Rethinking the History, Science, and Meaning of Auditory Hallucination*, Daniel B. Smith's details this unexceptional phenomenon, which seems rare only because it is embarrassing to admit.[3]

The *New York Times* reviewed his book and expressed shock at what Smith's collected research proves: that auditory hallucinations are common in the general population. The surveys showed that fully 39 percent of healthy volunteers sometimes heard their own thoughts aloud. A different survey determined that 13 percent of widows and widowers heard their late spouse's voice, and 3 percent of the general population say they have heard vivid auditory hallucinations. These were all healthy, normal people. I admit it, too: I've heard my voice while my mouth was shut, and while thinking about something other than what it said!

The reviewer, Peter D. Kramer, adds,

> With the advent of scanners that can track brain activity, neuroscience has
> taken a new interest in hallucinations. A recent study shows that schiz-
> ophrenic patients who hear voices activate a language-related region in the
> right brain when reading, while people who do not hear voices use the left.
> The researchers suggest that because the "wrong" side of the brain helps
> process words, hallucinators may generate inner speech that is not attributed
> to the self.[4]

Sound familiar? The technology that reveals this was non-existent for Dr. Jaynes, so he wins high marks for his prescience: he predicted exactly those results.

Well and good, so who is doing all this talking? Philosopher Thomas Metzinger studied the science of neurology to come to grips with the thorny philosophical problem of what it means to experience subjective conscious-ness—that is to say, the experience of being a self.

"Contrary to what most people believe," Metzinger writes, "nobody has ever been or had a self."[5] The self is not a thing. This poses a philosophical conundrum: "So when we speak of conscious experience as a subjective phenomenon," Metzinger asks, "what is the entity having these experi-ences?" In other words, who is the subject?

Excellent question, Prof. Dr. Metzinger. We'll just have to wait for the answer, because as it stands, researchers have no idea. In the meantime, I think it is reasonable to accept that another, less self-oriented state of consciousness was indeed more prominent once upon a time in prehistory. It was a more transpersonal state of mind, like that described in the Garden of Eden. Quite plausibly, this early phase of consciousness processed language in such a way that our minds were the domain of more than one identity, happily conversant with one another. How else did Adam and Eve's serpent speak if not through a Jaynesian voice? In this way, the subject of conscious experience might be communal, universal—it might be God or the hum of the cosmos. What it most certainly is not, however, is a real, discrete, and identifiably independent self.

In sum, taking all the medical, psychological, and archeological evidence into account, we can be sure that human culture, language, and thought changed sometime before the dawn of civilization. We can also be sure that our conscious experience is heavily influenced by culture; whether it is through physical or social conditioning, our particular flavor or color of consciousness is not absolute or innate—it is learned, it is trained.

Consequently, we can practice our consciousness. If we practice it differently, like a serious meditator might, it will change. Notably, practiced meditators report that, during intense meditation, the sense of self shrinks while the sense of transpersonal awareness grows. And it is on this point we differ with Jaynes. Transformed consciousness was not led by physiology, as he proposed, but by practice. I find it easy to see how a shift in cultural practices 10,000 years ago would start small and then snowball, producing a different agreed-upon reality. All it took was a sufficient critical mass gathered at a specific place in large numbers.

Göbekli Tepe is that place. As it stands, this was the first gathering place for a purely spiritual reason—that is to say, for the purpose of finding meaning. Are there others? Maybe, but none reached the critical mass needed to alter the human trajectory as Göbekli Tepe did. According to the evidence, it was there that human society began to practice consciousness differently, and the process did indeed snowball, spreading very rapidly. We will look at that process in some detail going forward.

That does not mean prehistoric life—or pre-Göbekli Tepe life—was the Paradise we seek. Even if it was, there is no going back. But I think we can show that the evolution of consciousness did not take us to a better place, and that some good aspects of our consciousness were lost, to be replaced eventually by the programming of Mesopotamian civilization and the rise of an ego identity bordering on the psychotic. I trust that the value in learning something about what happened is clear to you: by understanding it, we can learn to practice consciousness differently, learn to practice it in ways more natural and fit to human purpose and less destructive of our welfare and of the natural world. We will still have to live in a dream—that's simply how we function—but at least let it be a lucid one.

Knowing and Violence

Sumeria's myths record the testimony of those who were the nearest witnesses to this shift in consciousness and its attendant changes in culture. These witnesses lived more closely than anyone else to the time and places that matter most to archeologists and historians, establishing a meaningful story to frame the evidence we have explored so far. At the same time, these myths intersect with stories that appear in the Hebrew Bible, thereby not only revealing the ethos of Mesopotamian civilization, but also clarifying by contrast the testimony of their Jewish critics.

We began with the text of Genesis, a Sumerian myth in its own right for it deals mainly with Mesopotamia. I'd like to continue with that for a little while longer, as this will help us understand the Sumerian record, which is the topic of the remainder of this chapter.

Briefly staying in Genesis also allows me to tell a familiar tale which serves to illustrate the hardest and most relevant contemporary fact—the inseparable pairing of bloodshed and religion in the Middle East. I dare not overlook it given the obvious: this story is about the very prototypes of me and my Muslim Brother.

We pick up the narrative where we left off, with Adam and Eve's disgrace and exile from Paradise. There is little detail provided, just a notation informing us that "Adam knew his wife Eve," resulting in two sons who appear before the reader as grown men. Abel was a pastoralist, keeping sheep, and Cain was a farmer, "a tiller of the ground." It isn't much information, but it is all we need.

Together, "in the course of time," the brothers developed a deliberate and structured religious practice: "Cain brought to the LORD an offering of the fruit of the ground, and Abel for his part brought of the firstlings of his flock, their fat portions."[6]

As a first occurrence in Hebrew literature, these offerings represent something new in the blossoming consciousness of post-Paradise humanity; it is the practice of religion. And although the writer does not explain why they felt the need to make religious offerings, the story reeks of psychological alienation and the profoundest of anxieties.

How so? Cain and Abel's ritual acts were directed toward fixing what went wrong in the Garden of Eden. Bereft of transpersonal awareness, that sense of oneness and reconciliation, their religious exercise attempted to restore the deeply felt loss of relationship with the Divine. Religion always looks to return us to the Garden of Eden—Paradise is its promise.

That much is clear. But when it comes to the different offerings and their efficacy, we need more context. All the author tells us is that it did not go well for Cain. His offering of agricultural produce was met with "no regard." But why?

To suppose that it had something to do with the qualities of the offering itself—the particulars of the Cainian religion—would be simple-minded. While it is true that we associate grain with agriculture and can read in this passage a criticism of the farming that Jared Diamond called humanity's "worst mistake," the Hebrew prophets generally discuss offerings in terms of the heart attitude of the person making the sacrifice, not the produce they happen to offer.

That is certainly the case with Cain. It is his psychological disposition to which the narrator quickly turns his attention: "Cain was very angry," he reports, "and his countenance fell." (Literally: his anger burned.) And with that, the first religious act in the Bible is condemned in connection with the worshiper's self-righteous rage.

Consider other examples of rejected offerings. One of the Bible's most mature commentators, the prophet Isaiah, says that heaven has "had enough of burnt offerings of rams and the fat of fed beasts," and does not "delight in the blood of bulls." Here, the rejected offering is meat. Clearly, Cain was not rejected because God likes meat better. Isaiah explains that "bringing offerings is futile" if coming from a people who "do not defend the orphan" and for whom "the widow's cause does not come before them."[7]

Another example comes from the beginning of Israel's political history, when Israel's first king is rebuked with an identical message: "Has the LORD as great delight in burnt offerings and sacrifices, as in obedience...? Surely, to obey is better than sacrifice, and to heed than the fat of rams."[8]

This then, is Cain's problem: his pious offering was at odds with his impious heart. As there were no widows or orphans, whatever his failing was, it could only be in his relationship with his brother. And since the only aspect of Cain's character addressed is his anger, we can conclude that this was the problem. Indeed, the events that followed show it was his critical failing.

My sense is that Cain was a bitter man, accustomed to blaming "the other" for his problems. "Losing Paradise isn't my fault!" he thought; "It's those damned meat-eaters!" He could live in Paradise again if his stupid brother came to his senses and joined the vegetarian party. "His anger burned," we are told. This means he already had a smoldering anger, and he was always angry. In this moment, it ignited into a burning flame.

Let's think of this as something that could happen to you or me. Picture Cain and Abel as you would anyone. The voice of conscience does not thunder from heaven but is heard as an inner intuition. So, when Cain gets angry, it is not because an angel appeared to reject his offering. Instead, it is something about his brother's offering that sets him off. Abel's rival religion offends Cain. His universe is either/or, and his brother's different way of doing things infuriates him. Is it because he thinks only his way will save the world? I think so, because that's the way religion and political ideology works: if only "those other people" would wake up and do things my way, all would be well.

This is the crux of the story. In Cain's view, there can be only one acceptable offering, one true idea. If his brother's is acceptable, it means his own is under attack. His worldview is either/or.

Just as his fury catches fire, Cain hears a Jaynesian voice suggesting reconciliation with this brother. "Why are you angry and why has your countenance fallen? If you do well, will you not be accepted?"

Do well how? The voice assumes Cain knows, and since it is his anger over Abel's religion, I think the answer is clear: Cain has to accept his brother's different way of thinking. If he does, he himself will be accepted by the universe. Isaiah prescribes the same path after rejecting his people's "burnt offerings of rams and blood of bulls." He tells them to "learn to do good; seek justice, rescue the oppressed, defend the orphan, plead for the widow." If they do so, their offerings will have some acceptable meaning.

Unfortunately, Cain had constructed a harsh and unforgiving universe for himself. Ignoring the residual voice of Paradise, in his anger and shame, he developed a plan to rid himself of what he thinks is the source of human suffering: his brother, who practices that strange religion.

We can imagine him thinking, "The world will be better off without that kind of people." He probably sees it as his duty. And so, "Cain said to his brother Abel, 'Let us go out to the field.' And when they were in the field, Cain rose up against his brother Abel, and killed him." Religious violence is born.

Brotherhood

As far as the Bible is concerned, there were only four people on the planet when the brothers lived. When Cain killed Abel, half of a global generation was killed, along with an entire meat-loving culture. It was genocidal rage motivated by religious ideology and identity.

Abel had become something so inhuman to Cain, such a reified pejorative that he was no longer considered human. He was not his brother—Abel was one of those desert-dwelling practitioners of a strange religion that the world would best be rid of.

You know very well how this works; we all know about racism and hatred based on religion and beliefs. Sometimes, though, we perversely practice it under the guise of defending victims. We may hate Israelis because we feel concern for Palestinians, for example. Or hate Turks because we love the Kurds.

When I was involved in relief work alongside the US Army at the end of Operation Desert Storm, I first heard the racial slur "sand nigger." It was a tool for dehumanizing a brother. An Arab mother's son is hard to kill; by contrast, it is not hard to kill a sand nigger. Cain would understand that. But, of course, it works the other way, too. At the same time, I met people who would happily kill American Christians, whom they dehumanized as "Crusaders." Do you have reifying labels you use? "Liberals"? "Conservatives"? "Leftists"? "Right-wingers"? "White Male"? "Fascist"? We could write pages of them.

Let's take a breath and consider the human family—brotherhood and sisterhood. Remember that all humans come from a population numbering perhaps no more than 1,000. Cain and Abel reflect that time when we were a small, human family. Although we are 8 billion people today, we are still part of that single original family.

After killing Abel, the residual Paradise voice made Cain face up to what he had done. Abel was not a cancer to be removed, the voice insists; he was your brother. Here, in the story of Cain and Abel, we have the first appearance of the word "brother" in the entire Bible. Its novelty startles the reader, an effect magnified by repeating the word six times in four lines. The nature of the original language makes this effect even more intense. Compared with English, Biblical Hebrew is far more condensed and concentrated, a language that expands—sometimes explosively—when it hits the catalyst of the human mind. This passage is a supreme example, delivering a rat-a-tat-tat of rapidly fired indictments.

"Cain said to his brother Abel"; "He rose up against his brother"; "Am I my brother's keeper?"; "Where is your brother?"; "Your brother's blood cries out"; and again, "your brother's blood!"

All of this feels very close to me. I am writing amid frequent trips to the Middle East where I see brothers spilling a lot of blood into the ground around Eden. I was at Göbekli Tepe, the archeological Eden, when I started this chapter. I saw bloodshed just a short half-hour's drive from there while on the Syrian border—Cains killing Abels. It was an incident between the Islamic State and the supporters of the anarchist Kurdish party. Thirty-two people were killed in a gruesome suicide bombing at a cultural center that served as the operational base for refugee support. The dead were innocent student volunteers.

When I talk about incidents like this, I'm usually met with head shakes and words to the effect, "How can *they* do such a thing?" That's easy to answer: the same way we can. In fact, to talk about "them" reveals the problem. When we dehumanize people, we can soon kill them, too.

I pay my taxes, subsidizing the 100,000 bombs and missiles fired upon targets in Syria and Iraq.[9] A hellfire missile, one of the cheaper options, costs $115,000 a pop. I'd be a fool not to realize that a significant portion of my tax dollar supports a people-killing apparatus. My bomb kills in a horrific fashion, too—they don't call it a hellfire missile for nothing.

Shouldn't they be killed? Aren't they truly inhuman? I don't want to be facile in answering this, but no; they are not inhuman. If ISIS combatants must be killed—and indeed, I think sometimes they must—it is at best the lesser of evils. It is not by any stretch of an ethical distortion a good thing. It cannot be celebrated.

Having to kill deluded ISIS brothers does not, cannot, and will not make the world better than it was. To reach this point at all is a defeat—having to kill judiciously is a concession to human failure and should be a cause for deep soul-searching and grief. We must know that when we kill—however necessary it may be deemed—we are killing our brothers and sisters. And make no mistake: there will be a consequence, a worsening of the world and an escalation in the cycle of violence, an increase in the reliance on weapons and stringent security systems. It is evidence of the loss of Paradise; it will never be anything else, and certainly is not a way to restore it.

Each war takes us further down the road of inhumanity, away from the Garden. Each war's legacy is a bigger, heavier security structure. The Second World War blessed America with the National Security Act and military industrialization. Did we need to stop Hitler? No doubt. But it is not so much a triumph to be celebrated as an opportunity to reflect on why the world went that way and how the war left the world as a tenuous arsenal of nuclear and biological weapons.

In the wars against ISIS and Saddam Hussein, many non-combatants have died. Never before have so many civilians been killed so clinically and coldly. Killing another human being should not be so easy or anonymous, but our technologies have made it so. At least the ISIS suicide bomber mentioned earlier had to look her Kurdish victims in the eye, drink tea with them, and then give up her own life to kill them. That was an act of misguided desperation, reminiscent of my mother's plea to God to "to kill me and my boys and take us out of our misery."

But when I pay for my enemies to be killed by remote control, I hardly notice it except to complain that my taxes are too high. If I were not over there regularly to see it, I wouldn't have even thought about the link between my paycheck and hellfire. If I did, I suppose that, like Cain, I'd think it was doing some good.

King David and his son Absalom provide some inspiration. His son was the leader of an insurgent rebellion. Justice caught up with him and he was killed. A messenger brought the good news: the threat to national security was over! The Crown could rest easy! David's response shows why the LORD said this imperfect king was a man after his own heart:[10] "The king was deeply moved and went up to the chamber over the gate and wept. And as he went, he said, 'O my son Absalom, my son, my son Absalom! Would I had died instead of you, O Absalom, my son, my son!'"[11]

Killing ISIS sons and daughters, brothers and sisters, demands this heart's cry. I am not being glib. I have personally seen some of the worst things ISIS has done and I have seen their socialist enemies do terrible things, too. I've put my life in danger to save the victims and the innocent bystanders. But God forbid that I ever rejoice in the death of a single one of them. Having seen what I've seen, I wish to God that I could die instead of them, if it would equal the scales and stop the cycle.

The First Kingdoms and the City of Myth

Cain's conscience did not leave him in peace. The soil was already cursed because of Adam; with Cain the curse rebounded from the soil onto the man: "And now you are cursed from the ground," the LORD said to him, "which has opened its mouth to receive your brother's blood."[12]

That's bad news for a man who staked his religion on farming.

He had to flee to the East and live with the cycle of violence: "I shall be hidden from your face; I shall be a fugitive and a wanderer on the earth, and anyone who meets me may kill me."

That's the last we hear of him except for when Genesis casually tells us that "Cain knew his wife." Whence Mrs. Cain is never thought to be explained. The plot simply moves on with a brief genealogy that serves to gloss over thousands of years of cultural development. For example, one of Cain's descendants is responsible for music, another for metallurgy, and one founded a town.

The story then abruptly shifts focus to Adam and Eve's third son, the one we've all forgotten. He was Seth, and his mother's words are perhaps the most genuinely personal in the entire narrative: "God has appointed for me another child instead of Abel, because Cain killed him."

It's a big do-over: Seth is a replacement for both sons, slain Abel and cursed Cain. It is through Seth's line that anthropological development will be traced. Cain's descendants receive no further notice.

Turning the page, we feel déjà vu: "In the day that God created man, in the likeness of God made He him; male and female created He them, and blessed them, and called their name Adam, in the day when they were created."[13] And with that we get an even clearer statement of the unified gender of Adam—the transpersonal awareness that marked the days before the shift of consciousness.

I am aware that the term "trans-" is politically fraught. My intention is only to explain the text; the implications are for the reader to sort out. I will caution, however, that the story supports the idea of gender as a natural condition of Adam, but in a non-judgmental embrace of all shades of that gender: fully male, fully female, man and woman, and whatever lies in between.

Be that as it may, we continue with this recap of the first creation story followed by "the list of the descendants of Adam." Of course, the exiled Cain does not appear on the list. Adam's entire line is named through Seth and proceeds apace until it is interrupted at the ninth generation with the birth of Noah. We can suppose that Cain's line perished, since Noah's family— descended from Seth—will be the sole survivors of a universal deluge. The text itself is resolutely uninterested in explaining further.

Noah's story is important, but I won't try to retell it here. There is a perfectly good film starring Russell Crowe that portrays it better than I could. And I am sure you know the details already; it is an epic full of poetry and song, and in spite of its world-ending storyline, it is mainly about giving us hope. It is the first inkling that Paradise may be restored. We hear it upon Noah's birth, when his father gives him an auspicious name: "He named him Noah, saying, 'Out of the ground that the LORD has cursed this one shall bring us relief from our work and from the toil of our hands.'"[14]

Although once again the scribes have imprecated agriculture, this time, for the first time, there is some light at the end of the tunnel. Noah's name means "rest" and in Hebrew it is invested with a sense of physical relief, as when someone takes over a difficult task for you. Noah's name means rest from labor.

The whole episode of Noah and the flood is parenthetical. After his famed boat lands in the mountains of Ararat (where his top priority was to make wine and get butt-naked drunk), the narrative resumes exactly where it left off. You could cut Noah's Ark out of the Bible and not see the scar. The last line before the parenthesis reads, "Noah begat Shem, Ham, and Japheth."[15] The first line after the flood story, five chapters later, begins, "These are the generations of the sons of Shem, Ham, and Japheth."[16]

As boring as these lists might be ("Arphaxad begat Salah; and Salah begat Eber"), this genealogy is important to biblical anthropology because it attempts to symbolically map the origins of the nations. To that end, it has historical relevance, for it is just here that we find a firm bridge from mythology to proven history. It appears in a short line: "Cush begat Nimrod." This has proven to be a strong bridge indeed.

Nimrod is the one person in this long list of names who warrants a "who's who"-style biographical entry from the scribes. He is "the first on earth to become a mighty warrior." Not only that, but he was also the very first king, ruling over the most important cities in the world: "The beginning of his kingdom was Babel, Erech, and Accad, all of them in the land of Shinar."[17]

These are all places identifiable to archeologists and historians. For example, "Erech" is undoubtedly the Hebrew form of Uruk (pronounced OOH-rook), the great Sumerian city-state. Uruk is simply the Akkadian pronunciation of Erech. (Akkadian is the language of a later Mesopotamian empire.) Both versions are still acceptable. We will use "Uruk" for our archeological studies in this book because most of our scholars do. A notable exception is Samuel Noah Kramer, the father of Sumerian studies and original translator of this city's founding mythologies. He prefers the Hebrew form, consistently using "Erech" in his magnum opus, *The Sumerians*.

This is not just any city; it is recognized now as the world's first real city and the first political state or sovereign nation—it is the cornerstone of civilization. It is correct, then, for the Bible to associate this city with "the first warrior" and founder of "kingdoms."

As for the other places, Shinar, the region in which Nimrod founded Uruk, is also unequivocally identifiable as lower Mesopotamia, exactly where the first kingdoms were located. Babel is on this list, too. It is certainly the most familiar of Nimrod's cities, but it's a little more puzzling as there were many places called Babel. To narrow it down, we may assume that Nimrod's listed cities existed at the same time. In that case, Nimrod's Babel must be the earliest of the cities to carry the name "Babel."

Looking at Uruk's neighbors, an obvious choice is the city most closely related to it in Mesopotamian legend. That would be Eridu, where we find the oldest remains of a Sumerian temple, a temple site that holds the record for the longest continuous use of a temple structure ever, running for a staggering 2,000 years with seventeen different layers of construction, one on top of the other. That's a promising start since the Bible's city of Babel also boasts an important multistoried temple.

Another point in Eridu's favor is that Mesopotamian mythology names it as the spiritual progenitor of civilization—the inspiration for Uruk and the modern state. Babel, too, was recognized as a spiritual archetype in the Bible. It became shorthand for Mesopotamian culture and imperial statecraft.

Yet another point in Eridu's favor is that it was commonly conflated with Babel in ancient literature.[18] Babel's written form was an ideogram, *nun.ki*, that was precisely the same marker by which later Mesopotamians referred to ancient Eridu.

A succinct example is found in Berossus, a Babylonian priest writing in Greek in the third century BCE. When he went to translate the ancient King List—the most important origin text in Mesopotamian tradition—Berossus writes "Babel" in Greek instead of transliterating the old Sumerian name "Eridu." That's exactly what Genesis does in Hebrew.

Conclusion: The Bible gets this right. The first kingdom was there where it says it was. Babel, a.k.a. Eridu, and Erech, a.k.a. Uruk, were the cornerstone and foundation of civilization. Archeology backs this up, uncovering evidence that the heart of this Bible story is as accurate as history can be: the first kingdoms were in the towns listed; the first kings appeared there; and the first city-state had to have a first of its many kings, his name given as Nimrod in the Bible.

This means we can take the biblical view of early civilization seriously despite a popular bias to discount it. Of course, much of it is poetic and heavily stylized, but as we know, that doesn't make it untrue. Besides, the real cause of distrusting this literature isn't its artistic license or representational style; it is the intellectual current that shifted so strongly between the 1600s and 1900s as to stigmatize anything associated with religion.

That is a foolish stance. The body of writing in the Bible and Sumerian mythology is the closest source we have to the developments we want to study. It would be foolish to discount them. In fact, that is the lesson historians learned as archeology began to prove the existence of the Genesis cities. This began to happen only within the past 150 years, with most of the archeological work being done just in the mid- to late twentieth century. We now know that the Bible tracks the broad lines of human progress very well indeed. The aim of the scribes is clear: to shine a critical light on developments in Mesopotamia to question its value to humankind.

Another Genesis

Nimrod's Babel is in present-day Iraq, not too far from Nassiriyah, where Private Jessica Lynch made headlines when she was captured at the beginning of the 2003 Iraq War. It's a pretty quiet spot these days, but once upon a time this region was the most exciting place on Earth, and the place that forged the pattern for our modern lives.

As we just confirmed, the Sumerians called Babel by the name "Eridu," and its 6,000-year-old temple is civilization's oldest. The Sumerians believed that here "kingship descended from heaven," making it the connecting gate through which authority was transmitted to Earth, and thus creating the original "New World Order," the very first sovereign state.

This is one of a handful of places the Mesopotamians believed existed before the great flood, which, like the biblical deluge, divides human existence into two epochs: the first cloaked in mystery, the second open to the historical record. We can read about Eridu in copies of a text written down in about 2500 BCE, no doubt based on traditions pre-dating that. It was Assyriologist Thorkild Jacobsen who first translated it in 1939 and, noting that his subject bore many similarities to first book of the Bible, he dubbed it "Eridu Genesis."[19] (Its flood story, for example, features a solitary family saved along with the animals in a great boat.)

Genesis and Eridu Genesis are also similarly structured, both being divided into three sections. The first is the creation, then leading figures (patriarchs in Genesis, mythical rulers in Eridu Genesis), and lastly, and parenthetically, the flood. Jacobsen stresses that this is unusual; normally Mesopotamian mythology is grouped around a single hero. This myth, however, is a linear series of events, very much like the Bible, moving progressively forward.

"In the Eridu Genesis moreover the progression is clearly a logical one of cause and effect," writes Jacobsen. "The wretched state of natural man touches the motherly heart of Nintur, who has him improve his lot by settling down in cities and building temples; and she gives him a king to lead and organize."

This is where we pick up the narrative, at approximately the same time the Bible introduces Nimrod. As Jacobsen indicates, we find ourselves on the brink of civilization. The goddess Nintur laments the pitiful lives of nomads and hunter-gatherers in terms prescient of Hobbes:

Let me bethink myself of my humankind, all forgotten as they are... let me bring them back from their trails. May they come and build cities and cult-

> places... may they lay the bricks for the cult-cities in pure spots, and may they found places for divination... Let me institute peace there.

With all that is similar between these two versions of Genesis, this plot-line is sharply dissonant. The Hebrew view stresses again and again that agriculture is a curse, and that the city is wicked. Mesopotamia hails agriculture and the city-state as the saviors of lost humanity—the bringer of prosperity, safety, and peace. Jacobsen observes, "The Eridu Genesis takes... an affirmative and optimistic view of existence; it believes in progress." He described this as a "chain of cause and effect" that "leads from nature to civilization." The Bible agrees on this fact but disagrees mightily on what this development signifies.

When the goddess says she'll save humankind "from their trails" the reader understands this to mean that uncivilized hunter-gatherers or pastoralist nomads, forgotten and pathetic, will be saved by the sovereign power of the city-state, which the gods will kindly transmit to Earth. Civilization is the Sumerian gospel of salvation.

We can see the Bible's contrary view through its unfavorable depiction of Babel and the city's founders. Remember, although I believe the names "Eridu" and "Babel" originate from the same ideogram, the name is not as important as the fact that both accounts refer to the first city, to the first state, and to the place of the first king. We are talking about the same events in both legends.

We remember it best for the Tower of Babel, a place of hubris and judgment. Mesopotamia's founders remember it as the spiritual home of civilization, represented by this same tower, the remnants of which we can see and study to this very day, making Eridu famed in archeology and mythology alike.

The tower is a ziggurat—a massive, staged structure where the city's famously long-lived temple was situated. Ziggurats were, according to Sumerologist Samuel Noah Kramer, "Sumer's most characteristic contribution to religious architecture," representing to the Sumerians "a bond between heaven and earth, between god and man."[20] And it is exactly the thing goddess Nintur is talking about when she offers to save people "from their trails" by bringing them together to build "cult-places" and "places of divination." Eridu's cult-place was this tower.

The Bible tells us essentially the same story, agreeing with Eridu Genesis that this ziggurat is a central turning point in history. We just heard Nintur's call to the poor, nasty, and brutish hunter-gatherers and nomads. She offered them salvation in the newly invented civilized city: "Let them come and build... let them lay the bricks for the cult-cities." In Hebrew Genesis we hear the same thing: "Come, let us build ourselves a city, and a tower with its top in the heavens."

It explains the original ethos of the Sumerians just as the Sumerians described it themselves—that is, as a plan to bring people together in cities, to marshal individuals and disparate nomads into a super-corporate identity. But while the Sumerian version paints it as a tableau of salvation, the Hebrew rendition is critical of the exercise in the extreme.

The Hebrew Bible's take on this story is characteristically brief and consummately poetic. The opening line is a sweeping anthropological state-ment: "Now the whole earth had one language and the same words." This is an aspiration addressed in another Sumerian legend writing about building the tower. *Enmerkar and the Lord of Aratta* stars the first king—Sumeria's equivalent to Nimrod— who is charged with bringing the materials and labor together to build the great structure.[21]

> May the lands of Shubur and Hamazi, the many-tongued, and Sumer... and Akkad... and the Martu land, resting in security... may they all address [Father God] Enlil together in a single language! For at that time, the lord of Eridu, shall change the speech in their mouths, as many as he had placed there, and so the speech of mankind is truly one.[22]

Importantly, in the Sumerian telling of it, "the whole universe's speech a single language" is a promise of the power of civilization to redeem humankind. It speaks of restoring a lost attribute of Paradise—namely the *Ur-Sprache*, the common pre-Fall language of perfect understanding.

Both texts stress unification as the reason for founding civilization in Babel. In Hebrew Genesis, they must build the city, "otherwise we shall be scattered." In Mesopotamian literature, the gods call them to the city to "bring them back" from where they have been scattered in "their trails" and to perform this miracle of unifying their languages.

After that, the texts are at odds. One looks to gather the scattered, the other to scatter the gathered. "Look, they are one people," says the Bible, "and they have all one language; and this is only the beginning of what they will do; nothing that they propose to do will now be impossible for them."[23]

Not good. It sounds like Adam has violated his parole and is again intent on becoming "like God," which is exactly why he was barred from the Garden in the first place. ("The man has now become like one of us, knowing good and evil. He must not be allowed to reach out his hand and take also from the tree of life and eat, and live forever.")

What comes next is a lovely piece of Hebrew poetry, the language spitting at us in the mocking tones of a divine Don Rickles (a Jewish comedian famed for his insult humor). I like Everett Fox's Hebrew-sensitive translation best: "Come-now! Let us build ourselves a city and a tower, its top in the heavens, and let us make ourselves a name, lest we be scattered over the face of all the earth!"[24]

That's the Babel elite talking, as they gather in response to Nintur's call. To answer, heaven lampoons their grandiloquence: "Come-now! Let us go down and let us baffle their language, that no man will understand the language of his fellow, so YHWH scattered them from there over the face of all the earth!"

The only other place divinity says "let us" is when Adam is created: "let us make humankind, in our image, after our likeness." As much as it may be a joke now, it is a very serious one.

In summary, the city and tower of Babel represent the founding ideology of civilization: Let us come together and build, let us not be dispersed, let us have a common name, let us speak a common language (an actual language or an ideological one). The pattern holds true throughout time, whether as a single city-state or the later empires, or even bigger projects like the modern drive for globalization. In all of these, the principal is the same.

What are we to make of the Hebrew response? Is it meant to denounce all civilized order—would it be against, for example, the UN and free trade? Do the Hebrews offer an alternative, a better answer to the loss of Paradise? I can honestly plead insufficient evidence. We've barely scratched the surface.

Some of the answer might lie in the fact that there is no wholesale destruction in the divine judgment against Babel. God's action undermines the maximalist position of the builders but does not destroy them. The chastisement simply thwarts their ambition to be gods on the earth; it weakens and decentralizes and emphatically tells the project leaders that whatever they think they are doing, it will not lead to Paradise on Earth.

Brick and Mortar

Historically, the Sumerians actually did most of what the Tower of Babel legend portends: they successfully made bricks and fired them to put together

88

cities, and made towers intended to bridge heaven and Earth. They did indeed make a name for themselves, a corporate identity that still lives in our modern institutions—everything from schools and writing to armies and taxes. They successfully united many, many peoples under one language, establishing laws and a common ideology. All this started at Eridu's temple, which the founders of the first city-state cite as their spiritual origin and inspiration.

It was in Eridu that kingship first emerged as a concept. "After the... exalted crown and throne of kingship had descended from heaven, the divine rites and the exalted powers were perfected, the bricks of the cities were laid in holy places."[25]

As the goddess Nintur promised, it meant the definitive end of primitive human life "in their trails." She and her kings achieved remarkable success through a remorseless process that spanned the globe. Today, the hunter-gatherer life is nearly extinguished, existing nowhere that is exempt from the encroachment or domination of sovereign power and civilized culture. I must emphasize again that every fundamental aspect of civilization started there: governance, armed conflict, education, organized trade, diplomacy, modern economies, and accounting—everything.

We've traced the path from Göbekli Tepe to Babel through the written memories of the very people who first made the journey. Next, we will re-trace that path relying entirely on the archeological record. We are looking to uncover clues to solve the mystery of how humanity made this transition. Why did this enormous transformation happen? What were humanity's options? What happened along the way? Did everyone make it? If not, whom did we lose? And most importantly, did Nintur's promise really make things better, or am I right in saying it made things worse—turning the free, healthy, peaceful pre-civilized world into an enslaved, sick, and impoverished one?

Every private detective needs a snapshot in his breast pocket and a detailed briefing on the case. Ours goes like this:

The historical Tower of Babel, the ziggurat of Eridu, rose over several generations as part of a radical reconstruction of society. It was long ago replaced by the city-states that it inspired and was eventually buried under the desert sands, but we know where it is, and there is enough left to make a good study of it. We can even add a few forensic notes to our file: Eridu's tower was made from mud brick; the architects used bitumen as mortar. It's a remarkable archeological detail preserved in Genesis, reminding us to take the literature as seriously as we do the science: "Come, let us make bricks, and burn them thoroughly, and they had brick for stone, and bitumen for mortar."

We have some early clues about the architects and their motivations, too. While Genesis doesn't quite say that Nimrod built the tower, it does say he built the city where the tower was located, and Jewish tradition logically assumes that he was the builder.

First-century Roman historian Flavius Josephus (a Jew) writes that Nimrod did not want people to look to spirituality; he wanted them to find happiness only in the materialism of the civilization he created. He called the practice of spirituality "an act of cowardice." Writes Josephus, "He persuaded them [the people] not to ascribe it [happiness] to God, as if it was through His means that they were happy, but to believe that it was their own courage which procured that happiness."[26]

That's a good summary of what civilization tried to do: replace the lost spiritual consciousness represented in Paradise with an alternate universe built by human imagination and technology. The Roman historian characterized Babel's courageous endeavors in well-chosen words suggestive of the sterile and abusive materialism we've known recently in the Soviet Union or Maoist China: "He also gradually changed the government into tyranny, seeing no other way of turning men from... God, but to bring them into a constant dependence on his [Nimrod's] power."

As Josephus suggests, convincing people that civilization was the answer to happiness required considerable muscle. Anthropologist Stanley Diamond agreed. He put it this way, writing in his 1974 book, *In Search of the Primitive*: "Civilization originates in conquest abroad and repression at home."[27]

Civilization is an abusive partner. "I might have to beat you when you act up," says civilization, "but I'll take care of you." Or it is like the mafia, protecting people from the threat of violence it will inflict if they don't pay up.

Why did people go along with it? It is for the same reasons that anyone stays in an abusive relationship: fear, low self-esteem, reliance on material support, and peer pressure. Those top the bill, but many people stay in the relationship simply because they think it is normal: they've never seen a healthy relationship.

Eridu's idea of kingship promised security, predictability, and a structured order. It afforded a sense of togetherness, too; for many people an abusive partner is preferred to loneliness. There was also the king, who provided an aspect of what our ancestors perceived as the lost bicameral voice, the sure-handed direction that we crave from political leaders. Or if considered purely in biblical terms, it was solace for the broken relationship with the Creator. Being told what to do alleviated anxiety about the meaning of life.

That's all true, but why did this become such an urgent necessity? Civilization seems to have popped up as quickly as the tower did. In comparison to the length of modern human existence, it was nearly instantaneous.

We are certainly getting closer to an answer. We found a turning point in the ruins of Göbekli Tepe. Before this turning point, people did not practice organized violence, did not hoard resources, lived in harmony with nature, and had no neurotic compulsion to build cities and create complex, hierarchically controlled systems and cultures. There was no government, no evidence of organized religion. Moreover, there was stability: nothing upset the hunter-gatherer balance for tens of thousands of years.

But our quest is not for the primitive: it is for the Paradise at the end of our path, wherever in time or eternity it may lie. To get there we need to move forward through civilization's birthplace in Mesopotamia. It's time to look closely at the real-world evidence for changing consciousness—the verified beginnings of agriculture, cities, modern states, law, and religion.

The questions our archeologists and historians will answer is when, where, and why Hobbes' brutish conditions appeared after such a very long and stable span of 100,000 years or more. What role did the evolution of consciousness play in this? What led our ancestors to think civilization would solve the crisis? I will do my best to offer answers to those questions.

By the time we reach the present-day ruins of Eridu, we will be able to ask if civilization can keep up its end of the bargain and whether it was the only solution available. The Hebrews, writing centuries later, clearly did not think so, and they are not the only dissenters; we will cross paths with others who criticized Babel's civilized order, too. But to dissent is not enough—someone has to present a viable alternative.

To get our bearings, we have but to climb to the top of Göbekli Tepe's hill on the outskirts of Şanlıurfa, Turkey. We are situated between the Tigris and Euphrates rivers. Facing away from the stone pilgrimage site, we have a 360-degree panorama of the flat plain extending as far as the eye can see to distant mountains. Looking deeply into history, the next big thing is happening all around us. Pay close attention and you can see it. In the near distance, the world's first village and first farmers are about to appear.

Rodin's *The Thinker* would have resonated with humans on the cusp of civilization. An excess of thinking transformed the way we live, and not necessarily for the better. Neolithic "thinkers," like this example from Greece circa 4000 BCE, illustrate the decisive millennium when widespread war and hierarchy came to dominate human existence.

Dr. Mehmet Oz marvels at one of the stone pillars at Göbekli Tepe, a 12,000-year-old temple.
It is by far the earliest such site discovered, an impression underscored by its size and complexity.
The site lies at the epicenter of the world's first bread production and organized settlements.

Discovered nearby, this potential bread-maker in a V-neck sweater comes from the same era.
Perhaps having recently eaten the Genesis fruit, he seems to look at us and shield his genitals from view.

Original cover of *Leviathan*. The illustration captures Hobbes' view of humanity subsumed by the benign and necessary protectorate of the authoritative corporate being. I believe his premises are mistaken.

HISTORIES

❧ *5* ❧

ROYALTIES

The First Scientist

When we last visited Göbekli Tepe, we learned that this was the first place where people gathered in large numbers, congregating here for a metaphysical purpose—a quest for meaning. For over four millennia, Göbekli Tepe was a shining star, a gravity well that drew hundreds of thousands into its orbit.

Fixed in this orbit, people began to clump together to form nearby planets in the form of long-term settlements, the world's next big thing. By the time Göbekli Tepe took its last bows, around 8000 BCE, those planets had enough mass to sustain independent life on their own, and whatever spiritual purpose Göbekli Tepe served could now be fulfilled off-site in the village.

In the remains of these most ancient villages, we can still see T-shaped figures identical to those in Göbekli Tepe. This proves continuity and a clear cultural link between the nomadic hunter-gatherer worshipers and denizens of the first settlements. It is a self-sustaining spirituality.

In the early stages, the villagers still hunted and gathered, but no longer as a wandering clan. People were able to do this while living in the village because their surroundings were practically the Garden of Eden—the food walked up to the door. The human population was small and the animal population large. The forest was literally easy pickings for fruits and nuts.

Such a nurturing environment allowed time for spiritual exploration and creative pursuits. As their thinking evolved, an inspired group of our world's first settlers took up the study of science. The result was one of the most influential achievements of all time: the domestication of wheat.

This was a creative exercise in the purest form; there was absolutely no pressing reason to tame plant life. To the contrary, it was their easy access to food that allowed them the time to undertake such unnecessary research. What motivated them was a different kind of hunger, a yearning to understand the meaning of life.

Consider the scene: People had been attached to Göbekli Tepe's sacred precinct for a very long time now, drawn here for thousands of years by their ever more complicated imaginations in search of answers to why they were alive and how they fit in the universe. Such a place was without doubt a new development, breaking tens of thousands of years of common patterns; it is strong evidence that consciousness had changed, and not so long ago.

Arguably, too, spirituality of this kind was a projection. If the evolving brain had lost the mechanism of a guiding voice, it might now project it as an external presence represented by the sacred site. As religions do, it provided the ego with a sense of consciousness outside itself, a counterbalance that lent it certainty, security, and direction.

Transfixed by their new spiritual touchstone, congregants could no longer wander across the earth. They now camped permanently nearby, generation after generation. Clans now observed the passing of lifetimes in the face of monuments that did not change for centuries, and so they naturally began to imagine the flow of life's river around those carved stones.

"Before I was born the sacred stones stood as they do now; where was I then? Where was I before my birth?" They had seen people die while the massive spirit stones stood as they always had: "When I die the stones will remain; where will I be then, after my death?"

Their sense of self became historical, meaning they thought of themselves in terms of past, present, and future—even before and after their corporeal existence. We can see how practicing that kind of thinking intensified a growing sense of a virtualized ego-self. Identity became consciously and explicitly separated from the whole being, viewing its physical expression, "my body," as a kind of temporary conveyance.

They once moved across the land; now standing still, they imagined their lives as moving through time. That might sound natural, but such thinking is by no means necessary to successful human life in nature. Imagining oneself moving through time is meta-thinking and entirely abstract; there is nothing instinctual about those kinds of assumptions.

I don't mean to say such ideas began here; rather, this kind of thinking was one of the reasons for this site. Once it was standing, it served to focus and enhance the temporal imagination. There is a chicken-or-the-egg dilemma in this narrative. All these things conspired together: the growing ability to think recursively, meta-awareness or "thinking about thinking," the historical reflection of the self in imagined time—even time before and after life. All this was wrapped up with the founding of the sacred site, which served to reinforce the practice of these ways of thinking.

As they lived settled lives in one of the most richly sustaining environments on the planet, our Middle Eastern ancestors had plenty of time to exercise their imaginations. The seasons and cycles of wild plants that grew up around them spoke to their obsession just as the fixed stones of the temple had: seeds fall to the ground; plants are birthed from the soil and grow; they die and the cycle continues; cycle after cycle is witnessed by people whose primary occupation was the act of thinking.

They noticed the stars and the seasons in terms of their recently fixed reference points, remembering themselves and their location as part of the celestial sequence. They saw that the heavens changed predictably—something they could measure by the fixed marks provided by the monolithic stones. What were those beings? The shiny occupants of the sky, whatever they were, seemed to die (planets disappear for a time from the night sky, the sun sets, the moon turns dark) but then they were reborn. Is that what happens to us?

Soon they would wonder if those heavenly powers control everything. They might be "the other" that we feel we need, the one we cry out to when anxious, grief-stricken, or in pain—the presence we find ourselves speaking to throughout the day and as we fall asleep at night. Sometimes we must remind ourselves that the ancients had no concept of planets and stars—the land we live on was not conceived of as an orb floating in space, one among many. The ground upon we which we stood was in some way a reflection of the ground above us, where the bright powerful beings lived. The puzzle was to understand that relationship.

Putting it all together, they considered the plants and the earth in relation to themselves and the celestial bodies and seasons. As these associations deepened, it was natural to observe and track any variations.

In this way, there emerged a truly scientific enterprise. As time went on, they posed new variables: What if I take this seed and plant it there? What if I take the seeds of all the plants that have a peculiar irregularity—a stronger stock, for example—and plant only them? What if I do it when the celestial powers are in this position or that one, or when the sacred stone casts its shadow this way, as opposed to the other way? How about if I mix this wild grain from the village with the one from the other side of the hill? Thus began systematic trials.

Utilizing wild wheat was a tricky business. Some variants were more suitable for consumption than others. Wheat wants to do what nature intends for all of us—to scatter seed—but that's not very good for someone who's hoping to make cereal. The big breakthrough was persuading the wheat not to burst open before it can be harvested.

The sophisticated settlers realized it was much better for wheat to stay intact and grow big and fat. They noted that some of the wheat aberrantly did this on its own. Taking a clue from man's ability to plant his seed and produce after his kind, agricultural husbandry was conceived: "I will collect the anomalous stronger wheat, and I'll seed the fertile ground with that" thought the first farmer. "I think it will come out looking like its father."

This experiment with Göbekli Tepe's regional wheat was humanity's big agricultural breakthrough. Justin D. Faris, an expert on this matter, sums up the work of our primitive hero nicely: "In wheat and other cereal crops, the first and most critical modification was the acquisition of a non-brittle rachis, which... allowed early farmers to harvest the grain much more efficiently without spikelets dropping to the ground prematurely and being lost."[1]

The First Town

I often stand on the Göbekli Tepe heights. From there you can see all around us where this wheat was first tamed. This is the bread we eat today. If you eat bread, you can thank that clever settler. If not, and you've gone paleo, here's your culprit; every strain of wheat grown everywhere in the whole wide world is a direct genetic descendant of this variety, cleverly developed right here under the gaze of the sacred site's attendants.[2]

For obvious reasons, taming wheat reinforced settled life. The gentleman farmer's experiments necessitated patient tending over many years; he couldn't just move on to a new location. More consequentially, religion required settlement, too—devotional sites with giant stones were not transportable.

No surprise then that some folks decided to really put down stakes in a big way; they constructed a proper town, located at what is now called

Nevalı Çori. It's just around the corner from us, only about 15 miles away from Göbekli Tepe.

To find a place like this so close by is remarkable. It means the town's history dovetails with that of the sacred site—it is literally the next thing that happened, laying stakes just as Göbekli Tepe is pulling its stakes up around 8000 BCE.

There are no towns older than Nevalı Çori, but it wasn't alone. A handful of its peers have also been excavated, and together with numerous yet-to-be excavated mounds of the same era, they constitute humanity's first attempt at village life. All these first-tier towns lie in close proximity to each other and to the spiritual center at Göbekli Tepe—a stone thrown into the lake of time, with the towns that radiate out from it the first ripples to appear on the surface.

I should note that there is no suggestion that the world is devoid of other Göbekli Tepes and Nevalı Çoris. Over time, and with all things being equal, similar developments must have occurred elsewhere. We have evidence that they did, albeit so far they are all several millennia later than the ones around Göbekli Tepe. Indeed, my premise requires that the examples I cite not be unique, as the whole point is that such developments were ubiquitous. That's exactly why Paradise nostalgia is so widespread. Further, this is not so much about the click-bait headline of "who's first" or "a new discovery!" as it is about *who and what mattered*. There is nothing quite like Göbekli Tepe's ripple of cities to tell that story. This is the one narrative that traces the demise of what was before civilization to tell us precisely, step by step, what occurred as civilization dawned to replace it with the Mesopotamian city-states that are the basis of the modern world.

It's the common elements that intrigue. Nevalı Çori and later large pre-civilization settlements around the world had much in common with their civilized successors and with us: domesticated wheat and animals, obvious leisure time (artwork and religious icons abound), and an easy enough way of life to allow the townsfolk to construct some very cool villas for themselves. Their bones show they were well nourished but perhaps slightly less carnivorous than their immediate ancestors. These were proper societies, only without the civilizational hallmarks of governance, inequality, and organized aggression. That's the key difference.

Unfortunately, Nevalı Çori cannot be studied further; it is gone—wiped out by the gigantic Atatürk Dam on the Euphrates River. But if we drive a little further away, we arrive at Çatalhöyük (Chaht-all HOOY-ook), dating back to 7500 BCE. This is a much bigger place and better understood owing to the efforts of archeologist Ian Hodder, who began work here in the 1990s.

The site yielded many astonishingly intact houses and artifacts numbering in the many thousands. Consequently, we have a very good idea about how the first townies lived.

For starters, it was a big place, with a population as large as 10,000 at a time when there were only 5 million people in the entire world. Today an equivalent "town" would number 12 million. This was a significant chunk of the world's population and it is therefore statistically powerful; understand this site and we understand the world as it was at that time.

Their wonderfully preserved homes are connected like a beehive. The doors are in the roofs, which also served as the footpaths. Ladders ushered the entrant into living areas that are surprisingly well-lit by reflective white plastered walls. For the interior decor, colorful designs were favored, very similar to the kilims still woven in this area.

The homes were cleverly designed to provide cool summers and warm winters. Need a little extra heat? They had well-made and ventilated hearths. They were clean, too. Unearthing the tops of the buildings and entering the homes for the first time, the archeologists found them to be spic and span. Imagine that—after 8,000 years.

They even left us with a map of sorts—or at least a beautiful townscape. Looking at it now feels timeless; the twin peaks of Mount Hasan depicted behind the settlement look just as they do today. We can drive past there, hold up this prehistoric image against the horizon and feel that we are one of the ancients.

That feeling of continuity is important in Çatalhöyük. Head archeologist Hodder writes about this in consideration of the role that religion played there:

> As humans settled down they became entangled in the longer-term relation-
> ships... The societies that were produced were more historical (in the sense
> that links between members of society through time became important) and
> place-bound (in the sense that many of the new technologies such as storage,
> domesticates and equipment inhibited movement)... Religion played a central
> role in creating temporal depth in place.[3]

When Hodder says their society became more historical, he doesn't mean "history" in the schoolbook-sense of something recorded in the past. This is history as the total story, what it all means—the dream of continuity and the feeling of transcending the boundaries of birth and death. Everything about Çatalhöyük shouts that this was their main concern.

The archeologists dubbed dwellings here "history houses," referring to houses that over generations were continually restored, always incorporating the existing structure. In this way, one generation of houses merged into the next. The implication is that the citizens cultivated transgenerational attachments to a place—a sense of history beyond a single lifetime. It's the same feeling I get holding up the ancient map and seeing the unchanged mountains behind it.

"Very clearly in early Çatalhöyük," Hodder writes, "the control of religion in history houses was not linked to social and economic dominance." To the contrary, evidence from here and "other early sites in the Middle East suggests collective involvement in ritual, often without sustained social ranking."

There was "a collective involvement in ritual" that revolved around these special houses, yet there is no sign of a religious hierarchy. There were no priests. Hodder adds, "It seems that religion and ritual were important in creating long-term relationships in place without at the same time producing elites that controlled production and exchange."[4]

Indeed, there is absolutely no evidence of social or material inequality in all of the 2,000 years this town was inhabited. Everyone had the same type of house, the same nourishment, the same tools, the same arts and crafts, and the same burials. Depictions of women and men are always completely equal.

In the absence of social stratification, Hodder asks, what was the purpose of their religion? Hodder and his team determined that the purpose of their spiritual practices "lies in the relationship that has been identified between religion and history."

We saw this already in relation to other fixed symbols, such as the carved monuments at Göbekli Tepe and the stars and seasons. The difference now is that the townspeople structured this relationship to time around certain longstanding households. The ritual of the eternal house was in some measure an answer to "where was I before?" and "where will I be after?" Through the undying house, which lived before them and after them, they felt a personal connection to both realms. Through the house, eternity was no longer a remote possibility—they quite explicitly lived there and thus lived in the unknown past and unknown future. Unknown but secure; this was very reassuring. Needless to say, the motif of an eternal abode is an idea that persists as a cornerstone of religious faith.

These discoveries led the scientific team at Çatalhöyük to undertake a project called "Consciousness and Creativity at the Dawn of Settled Life: The Test-case of Çatalhöyük." Funded by the Templeton Foundation to the tune of nearly US$2 million, it studies the evolution of consciousness. Specifically, the scholars wanted to know what role evolving consciousness played in the extraordinary developments of the period we have traveled through, 14000 BCE through 7000 BCE.

The project description reads, "The unprecedented volume of data from this site [Çatalhöyük] will be used to test a series of claims... about the Neolithic as a key moment in the gradual process by which human consciousness, an awareness of an integrated personal self, and the horizons of human possibility... all increased. Through empirical archaeological research, the project will test... the timing and causes of these changes."[5]

An example of the project's focus may be glimpsed in an article by Hodder from 2001. He summarizes the thesis of fellow archeologist Jacques Cauvin's book, *The Birth of Gods and the Origins of Agriculture*: "Cauvin rejects this emphasis on ecology and environment as the cause of change. Instead, he argues that primacy should be accorded to a restructuring of human mentality from the thirteenth to the tenth millennium BC, expressed in terms of new religious ideas and symbols."

"Restructuring of the human mentality." All that stuff about shifting consciousness has more than myth and psychological speculation to support it. It is being tested in the cold light of archeology and the idea is finding widespread support.

Hodder continues, "Cauvin's book... resonates closely with the idea that the Neolithic is much more than an economic transition, and coincided with a transformation in the world view of the prehistoric societies concerned."[6]

The old Marxist theory that people first began to settle into towns because of economic pressures simply does not withstand the evidence. That the first townspeople invented agriculture is incidental. Even 2,000 years after its founding, the people of Çatalhöyük still sustained themselves mainly by going out to hunt and gather. They did not need to farm; they farmed for the sake of variety, and they farmed for pleasure.

The reason they invented the town was "a changed world view" and a "restructured mentality." They created it simply because they could. This is what the new mind does; it invents universes, it constructs virtual environments. While we continue to live in the unconstructed universe, we relate to it entirely through our virtual one. We make rules and laws for our universes, just as the real universe has laws. The difference is that we can change the laws of virtual nature any time we want, and that's what was happening at Çatalhöyük.

At the same time, the first settlers, like us, wanted to reach beyond their constructions. We want to touch the really Real. As the townspeople grappled with their blossoming imaginations, they sought metaphors for this unimagined Real reality. The very concreteness of the town attested to something solid and foundational, an order that underlies everything. They found this also in their sense of community and the firmness of continuity represented by their "history houses." The town was not a storehouse for grain—it became a monastery dedicated to the study of reality.

And so they went for thousands of years at Çatalhöyük, sustaining a large population without government and without inequality or poverty. It is a period of stability and prosperity unmatched since that time. This advises us, at the very least, that hunter-gathering nomadism is not the only alternative to civilization as we know it. It is demonstrably possible to live sophisticated, modern lives in a manner that, if not quite Paradise, is at least free of the horrible side effects of civilization that plague us.

So where is the brutish, Mr. Hobbes? What takes us from this pleasant dream town of 10,000 people to the terrors of Diamond's "conquest abroad and repression at home?" It's not far off, I'm afraid. If we look carefully to the East, we might just spot Cain killing Abel.

The Great Debate

Imagine if 7,000 years from now, archeologists examined the remains of one of our cities. Its peak population numbered about 10 million. Specimens cover the full two millennia of the town's occupation, from 100 CE to 2021 CE. Plenty of weapons technology was unearthed, and there is evidence that the residents were skilled in their use. What are the odds they wouldn't find any other suggestion of violence there? Pretty slim indeed.

The city I've described is London, which, like Çatalhöyük in its day, accounts for about 0.2 percent of the global population. Yet, at Çatalhöyük, where well-armed and skilled hunters lived by the thousands in very tight quarters for just as long, there is absolutely no evidence of any human-on-human violence, domestic or otherwise. So far, Hobbes' brutes are nowhere to be found.

As we pull away from Çatalhöyük, we can look at other settlements and see the same thing: no one is fighting. We can be sure because we have policed these grounds thoroughly. Reviewing all available forensic data,

University of Alabama anthropologist Douglas Fry notes that despite vigorous efforts to detect it, nothing indicates violence during the Pre-Pottery Neolithic (PPN) period in the Middle East: "In sum, there is no persuasive evidence of war in the PPNB from the Southern Levant to Anatolia." It is, he says, a "near-total absence of evidence for interpersonal or inter community aggression in the PPN." (Pre-Pottery Neolithic A, or PPNA, corresponds with the period 8500 BCE to 7600 BCE. Pre-Pottery Neolithic B, or PPNB, is 7600 BCE to 6000 BCE.)

The evidence comes from sites dating back to the hunter-gatherer Natufian era in 13100 BCE to the end of the PPN in around 6400 BCE. Fry emphasizes that this "makes 6,700 years in the Southern Levant without any good evidence of war."[7]

Of course, there are some naysayers. Harvard professor of psychology Stephen Pinker is the person to read if you want a counter-argument, albeit from someone who is no more an expert in this field than I am. His view is that there is less violence now than ever, an opinion deduced—in my view—by a comparison of extremes. Was there less violence in 2014 than in 1917 when there was a world war? No doubt—unless you happened to live in Syria between 2010 and 2020. But there is no reasonable argument that we are less violent overall now than we were in 6000 BCE.

Scholars like Fry are not psychologists. They are experienced specialists in this kind of archeology and anthropology. I'm sticking with their evaluations, according to which there simply is no evidence of warfare before 5500 BCE. None. There was no organized terror. There was no fear that someone was going to torch your village and kidnap your children. Whatever violence there was before 7,500 years ago, it was not remotely the same kind of violence that we've experienced since then.

We should know too that we have far more evidence from 13000 BCE forward than we have from the entire 90,000 years prior. Since stable settlements like Çatalhöyük existed for hundreds of years, all the skeletal and structural evidence accumulated in one place. It's a far better, far more reliable data field than anything before Göbekli Tepe. This should make the findings from such locations carry more weight, and what we've found there is compelling: no violence of any kind—random, interpersonal, or otherwise. What are the chances of the richest data set, lasting 6,000 years, being a statistical anomaly?

Sometimes a "brutes bias" has led to grasping at straws. At Çatalhöyük, for example, there are murals of vultures hovering over stylized headless bodies. A few diehard Hobbesians imagine this to be positive evidence of systematic human violence. It's not because the image depicts an act of violence, but because, they argue, the bird symbolizes violence; they thus imagine that the dead people have been murdered.

Google the drawings and see what you think. Neolithic people sometimes removed heads from bodies as part of their funerary practices. It was part of their ritual, not unusual, and of course, it was done post-mortem. This known fact leads to a far more straightforward explanation for the art. The vulture painting is a meditation on death, a veritable Buddhist sīvathika —it was part of the townspeople's very serious spiritual work.

Meanwhile, there are many paintings of hunting from this period, including many from Çatalhöyük. We see people at war with animals, so to speak. We see weapons, we see dead beasts, we see blood. If people were really killing each other, wouldn't they paint that, too, like every culture since then has? In the art of early civilization, we see gory scenes of warfare and even torture (and such scenes still fill civilized theatrical arts today). I find it hard to believe that over the past 10,000 years, our PPN villagers are the only people who had violence and yet chose for some reason (to fool us perhaps?) not to depict it in their visual arts.

"Lack of evidence is not proof that it didn't exist." True, but that's not the problem here. There is plenty of evidence: skeletal remains, examples of hunting weapons, works of art, and the town itself. There are no skeletons that would pique the interest of a CSI lab. Their city is unwalled, showing no sign, over thousands of years, that it was ever attacked or that the inhabitants feared an attack.

I rest my case. But if we didn't always practice war, when did it start? When did the serious killing begin?

Çatalhöyük and settlements of its kind began to unravel around 5700 BCE. As they did, we observe for the first time not just violence, but systematic, organized warfare in several places.

A case in point is Hacılar, a town dating from 7000 BCE and sharing many things in common with Çatalhöyük. You don't have to look too closely to see what happened. Excavations from the city as late as 5600 BCE show no evidence of violence. That means a millennium or more went by in peace. But by 5450 BCE you can see the remnants of a military fortress destroyed by fire.

James Mellaart, the illustrious archeologist who first discovered both Hacılar and Çatalhöyük in the 1950s, reports that this later level of Hacılar "was heavily fortified, was probably the seat of a local ruler." Writing of the conflagration that ensued, he describes the scene as "bodies of slain victims, mainly children, as well as masses of greasy black material, burnt brick, charcoal, pots, and objects."[8]

Now that is evidence. And if you marked the words, "local ruler" and "slain victims" you correctly matched the two innovations witnessed at Hacılar in 5500 BCE—namely, hierarchy and warfare.

Why did this happen? For thousands of years, Çatalhöyük had maintained egalitarian values. There was no central authority, no division of class, and there was no king or ruling hierarchy. The same thing was true at other towns from this period, including Hacılar.

At this point, around 6000 BCE, everything went to hell. The reasons will be discussed momentarily; for now, let's simply call it "complexity." At Hacılar the change was swift, the onset of hierarchy and violence occurring in a blink of the eye, historically speaking. But the surprising thing is that what happened there didn't happen in most places. While Hacılar suddenly had a chief with a fortress and then a horrific massacre (no drawings of vultures required), most other towns, Çatalhöyük among them, simply disappeared. The people just up and left. What is going on here?

University of Notre Dame professor Ian Kuijt is a specialist in this period of history. Based on his careful study of the data, he paints a vivid and surprising picture that explains Hacılar's violence and Çatalhöyük's vanishing act as the result of the same process.

According to conventional wisdom, he says, we would expect towns of this period to show evidence of "enormous increases in social segmentation... the development of a clear, and firmly entrenched, hierarchical division of authority and power."[9]

This was expected because of a "dramatic increase in the size" and "increased crowding stress." It makes sense: complexity requires order, and order would be expected to appear in the guise of ranked power and some form of apparatus to coerce order out of complexity. Kuijt's point, however, is that the conventional wisdom didn't prove to be true at all—the data showed the opposite. "The material evidence suggests a very different story."

"If anything, available archaeological data indicate that in the face of increased population expansion and social stress... Neolithic community members continued to limit displays of social differentiation in mortuary practices and residential architecture."

This means they did not resort to appointing a chief, a bureaucracy, and an armed force. Instead, reports Kuijt, they "abandoned their large settlements at c. [6000 BCE]." In most cases then, during the period in question, these first towns simply did not allow social stratification and hierarchy to occur—not even if it would save their town. Their egalitarian values ran so deep that, by and large, the bigger towns disbanded rather than give in to the demands or need for a hierarchy and coercion.

Kuijt continues, "Thus, it may well be that the social rules for limiting the authority and power of individuals and Houses in these LPPNB aggregate villages were stronger, apparently much stronger, than the ability of individuals and Houses to consolidate power and authority in the hands of the few over the many."

So it would seem there was a debate. Hierarchy was proposed by some trusted families at a time of extreme stress. Certain individuals offered themselves as solutions to the existential threats that faced the town. Most places flatly rejected it. Their strongest value was to preserve equality, not allowing hierarchy, inequality, or social stratification of any kind, even if it meant the end of a stable society that had existed for thousands of years.

As the debate wore on, communities became polarized. There was a lot at stake. The proponents of hierarchy became belligerent, as revolutionaries tend to do. Anyone who has dealt with communal violence knows the predicament facing a peace-loving majority under these circumstances: a violent person can easily violate the peace at any time, but a non-violent person cannot perpetrate an act of peace upon the violent.

With the root problems that sparked the debate increasing, and a minority of coercive firebrands disruptively insisting on their way, a large majority of the population simply opted out; they allowed their towns to be buried by the dust. Those who rejected revolution left behind ghost towns, including Çatalhöyük, where houses remained swept clean until archeologists came upon them in the 1950s.

In the few places where the revolutionaries prevailed, town life continued, so that in a very short order the only remaining towns were those that succumbed to the radical progressives who supported hierarchy. What happened to the conservative egalitarians? They either became nomads, "on their trails" as Eridu's scornful literature says, or they eventually heeded goddess Nintur's call and moved to the cities. In the not-too-distant future, most will be enslaved by the great empires of Mesopotamia.

Meanwhile, the new system meant submitting to chiefs for whom the people built mansions and gave the best of their produce, even their children. Defensive walls were constructed to protect the chiefdoms from others like themselves. Militias were organized and arsenals stocked. Gradually, they invented a new, inequitable, and demonstrably more violent way of life, as horrifically portrayed in the scorched ruins of Hacılar.

The Terror of History

Now: what exactly was the problem that hierarchy offered to solve, and why was it so compelling a dilemma that it became a do-or-die choice for the world's first towns?

The usual answer is that society simply became too complicated to continue as it was and that a change in climate was the last straw leading to Çatalhöyük's abandonment. Broadly speaking, this is true, but it isn't exactly a sociological explanation; it doesn't tell us how people felt, how they argued with one another over solutions to these problems, or what it all meant to them. Furthermore, it is very hard to correlate this rather subtle climate change to such a profound transformation of culture. While there certainly was a period of drought around 6000 BCE and a general cooling of the climate in West Asia, it was not catastrophic. This is in fact proven by those towns that adopted hierarchies and weathered the storm, so to speak.

What we need to understand is the non-material side of it, the purely human side of the crisis. To understand that, let's put ourselves in their shoes and imagine our way through the crisis with them. It won't be hard to do, as it relates to problems most of us face every day.

It begins with the social experiment of settlements, nascent agriculture, and the first religious formations. The study of time and seasons was integral to those experiments, but early settlers didn't really have enough data to evaluate the entire system. Natural patterns were understood to be direct cause and effect. Celestial bodies acted by fiat to make the seasons and weather happen. When crops grew or failed it was not because of coincidence or abstract physical law—it was because the heavenly bodies, which obviously controlled the seasons, dictated it.

This was fertile ground for a recursive mind. By inference, it was reasoned that people might live and die by dictate of the stars, too. A friend dies; let's say he was killed by a lion. The new mind wants to know the mechanics of how it happened. Was it determined by the same celestial system that controls the weather and seasons? Assuming yes, the curious new mind also wants to know why it happened—what did it mean?

After all, through agricultural experimentation, he knows that actions and procedures have an effect on life and good fortune. If he does certain things, the results are better than if he did other things, presumably because those different actions influence the celestial mechanics. This raises an obvious question: Did his friend do something wrong? Is there a moral meaning to this happenstance, an implication as to how we should live?

Our ancient gardener could imagine a complete alternate universe in which his friend did not die: "He hunted when the moon's face was turned," our friend notes, and then imagines him hunting during a different lunar phase. In that universe his friend lives. This line of cause and effect turns quickly to ethics: a rule is made to forbid hunting during the new moon. Or, "He ate pork yesterday; people who do that risk being killed by beasts; pork is bad; our people shall no longer eat pork."

Of course, his alternate universes might have been more accurately conceived: "If only he had gone out earlier..." or "we should always go out in pairs..." or "if he had had a bigger spear..." In all those possible universes, his friend might be alive, and steps would be taken to reshape the present social universe to make it more like one in which the possibility of being eaten by lions is minimized. There is a fine line between religious and civic regulation.

Even today we imagine alternate possibilities and make social adjustments accordingly. I grew up without wearing a seatbelt. My kids grew up always wearing a seatbelt. The reasoning pattern and social reconstruction behind that is not too far from our ancient farmer's. The difference is that now most of us take into account more established considerations, having determined that remote effects cannot be caused by the stars and that eating pork does not cause traffic accidents. And yet, a taboo is a taboo: witness the pontifical scorn heaped on any mother who forgets to strap in her child!

To put their situation in perspective, consider this: even with all our experience and the mental discipline of modern science, we still have numerous superstitions and unfounded taboos. The most skeptical still get on their knees and cry "but why!?" when something seriously goes awry. Just like that townsman, we wonder deep down what we "did to deserve this." Sure, we know that a disaster is usually because of some physical mechanism, not due to a bad star or some secret sin; but even then, we often dissolve into a superstitious panic when faced with a real crisis. We can only imagine how much more intense it was for them.

The word "disaster" reveals the depth of this root. It is derived from Latin, meaning "ill-starred." Language is the programming of the virtual universe, and it is chock-full of subliminal influences. Way down deep, perhaps "disaster" still registers with us as something not quite random but rather fated by the stars. That deep programming is hard to shake.

Language is the powerful material out of which virtual universes are constructed. We tell a story, spin a scenario, and that forms a virtual universe. Whole cultures and entire societies are formed of such stories. Nothing is understood and obviously nothing communicated apart from stories—the hardest, most abstract science is no exception. Our concept of self is a story, too.

Sometimes we get bogged down in our story, be it angst over past failures or our pessimistic worries about the future. At other times, circumstances don't align with our narrative. Disasters interrupt and contradict our stories, causing profound disorientation. Severe dissonance between story and contradicting experience results in severe depression and anxiety.

And that's not the worst of the spoilers. Inevitably, everyone's history runs into the ultimate disaster, it hits an insurmountable barrier—the ego story's confrontation with time. Here's the problem: being unnatural and unbound by the laws of physics, our virtual self does not experience entropy as the natural world does. As our story confronts evidence of time in the form of decay and death, it desperately wants to be freed from it—my body may die, but why should I? As the ego stares at its sustaining organism in the mirror, it is horrified to find that it ages while the virtual self does not. What will happen to the program when the chip burns out?

Mircea Eliade calls this "the terror of history" and the struggle against time.[10] Our short escapes from it through sleep and non-discursive activities help, but obviously don't resolve this ultimate dissonance. "There is always the struggle against Time," writes Eliade, "the hope to be freed from the weight of 'dead Time,' of the Time that crushes and kills."[11] This is the quintessential human crisis of existence.

As our freshly cognizant townspeople faced this problem, they managed anxiety by developing rituals and beliefs around their history houses, which give them an anchor to reality beyond the virtual matrix. Given the extremely long stability they achieved as a society, it must have worked very well. Whatever their state of angst, we saw no evidence of it impacting social stability in the way we witness it elsewhere in history in the form of oppression and war.

Even so, the weight of history accumulated, and their story grew inexorably over thousands of years, each iteration adding bytes of data and psychological weight to the file. This alone might have accounted for the social complexity that led to their crisis, but it seems it was the last-straw anomaly of inexplicable climate change that finally caused their coping mechanisms to fail. It was cognitive dissonance—a counter-story and evidence of entropy—that they could not overcome.

Where would they turn? We can reasonably conjecture that they looked to the history houses for spiritual grounding. It was those houses that anchored them for centuries and it will be those houses and the people associated with them who offer promises of a complete fix, a story everyone can believe in. They will offer to be the missing voice that directs the daily lives of the people, the voice that says everything will be OK—just obey and submit.

The Royals

Here's how the houses reversed their role from stabilizing objects of meditation to revolutionary agents of turmoil.

It is late afternoon 8,000 years ago as we walk down an immaculate street and open the rooftop door to a standard home. We sit in a well-lit room on a flat-woven kilim that people in nearby villages still make today. While admiring the artwork on the wall, the host offers us some bread, a variety of emmer wheat (which is still cultivated here), and a kebab of meat (also not unlike what the locals eat now, except the ancient version is venison —much healthier than the farmed, fat sheep we'd get now).

Sitting around the hearth, we mull over our anxiety about death or probe a particular existential puzzle, such as that unfortunate friend killed by the lion yesterday. Someone from one of the older houses takes a meaningfully deep breath; attention turns reverently to him. The voice of wisdom is about to speak.

The wise man says he still hears the guiding voice. People believe him— his house is much older than others, going back to the very beginning of the town's foundation, millennia distant in their past. If anyone knows about life beyond life, it is the elder of this family.

Imagine the aura that surrounds members of the oldest houses! Let's say, for example, that your family was one of the first ten families in the town. Your house goes back 2,000 years. Your people have been in the same house all that time, one layer preserving and continuing the previous for what is— for your fellow citizens—forever. It has become a sacred space, a place beyond ourselves, a tangible expression of eternity.

Because this piece of eternity is your family home, others think of you as special. Each generation only adds to the esteem. Your lineage relieves them of history's terror. You are evidence that everything will be OK. You might even, as some do, imagine that if people just listened to you and did what you said, they would all be better off. You might even believe that you have the inspired ideas that will take us beyond this suffering, into a renewed experience of the time before shame and worry, a way to take us back to the Garden of Eden.

Now people are coming more often to your door. The clockwork turning of seasons plays a big role in their story of the universe. Their identity as a society was born to it, and it is fundamental to each person's sense of welfare. As years of heretofore unknown drought and long winters subvert reality as they know it, they hope you have the answers. They crave order. They want certainty.

Maybe you begin to imagine domesticating the population, just as your people not long ago learned to do with goats. The people need a shepherd, too, you think. You begin to propound this idea, describing your vision of how it will improve their lives, enrich them, make them secure, and free them from worry. "Let me carry your burden," is your campaign slogan. "I am the Good Shepherd." And you really believe it—you have become not just a priest but a politician, and not just a politician, but one with the air of a 2,000-year-long royal lineage.

You might be a very good leader, a real blessing to the town; but if you are not, chances are many will follow you anyway. It's the same reason folks follow terrible leaders today: their words promise change and improvement, and we tend to believe them even if they rarely fulfill their promises. If anything of Jaynes' theory is true, we will always hear an authoritative voice as a missing piece of certainty, a trustworthy instruction to rely upon. Advertising functions on this principle: people want to be told what to do.

In his magnum opus, the esteemed doyen of American sociologists, Robert N. Bellah, described this moment of history in straightforward terms:

> Once upon a time there was no state and no cosmos seen as a state. How did we get from a society... still linked by strong kinship ties, to a society in which a genuine secondary formation, a state, no longer linked to the common people by kinship, could appear? It would seem that that shift from tribal to archaic society only became possible when one man focused so much attention on himself that he could claim that he and he alone was not only capable of rule, but capable of maintaining society's relationship to the gods.[12]

Although most towns apparently rejected this proposition and disbanded, it took only a few centuries before the surviving collectives were on-board. There didn't seem to be any alternative. Bellah continues,

> It is as though the archaic king unleashed an explosion of atomic energy, capable of moving what had for millennia not been willing to move. Once

achieved, the archaic state had quickly to weave a web of institutions and structures of power... of rituals and conceptions of the cosmos, which would make it seem both natural and inevitable.[13]

That's the key. The powerful voices of authority wove together a new universe that appears "both natural and inevitable" to replace the unraveling universe of the towns. It was a blessed escape from anxiety and must have felt like an escape from the burden of history. The oblivion of living in someone else's reality—false though it may be—became our drug of choice, allowing us to escape the desert of the Real.

If you've seen the film *The Matrix*, you get the idea: an external power programs a virtual, symbolic environment for humans to live in. A resident of the imagined world has only to accept that this is as real as real gets, and then obey the rules of that world to rest assured that all is well.

There is, of course, a steep price to pay for those who run afoul of the laws or who question the reality of this construct. To allow deviants would threaten to undermine the illusion for everyone. For that reason, the system had to be enforced, replete with a system of incentives and punishments. This brings us back to Hacılar and the first evidence of modern, organized violence.

❧ *6* ❧

ALIEN ORIGINS

Obsidian Order

The pace of change is accelerating as we race out of the PPN—Pre-Pottery Neolithic—and enter the exciting days of the PN, the Pottery Neolithic. It is 5000 BCE and already the only towns that remain are those built around royal hierarchies. Everyone else is riding the trails, wandering in the desert.

If "Pottery Neolithic" sounds like a brand name, that's entirely appropriate. The beautifully designed pottery manufactured here in upper Mesopotamia around 5000 BCE was mass-produced for trade, and it is the best pottery the ancient world would ever make. It is instantly recognizable, even today.

This style of pottery is a veritable Golden Arches of the Neolithic age, clearly identifying places where our new chiefs opened franchises along the road to civilization. Shipments between the branches reveal connections between towns and chiefs, too; we can follow them as easily as we might track the distribution of Levi's or Coke. There is no mistaking the brand.

We call this hallmark culture "Halafian"; it is named after the modern archeological site at Tell Halaf, about 100 kilometers east-southeast of Göbekli Tepe. But the name mustn't mislead us; they didn't call themselves Halafians—it is just that Tell Halaf was the first place where archeologists identified their culture.

Professor Mircea Eliade puts the Halafians in the context of Anatolian towns like Çatalhöyük: "The Tell Halaf culture, as it is called, appears at the time when the Anatolian cultures disappear. It knows copper and seems to be the creation of a population coming down from the North, perhaps as refugees from Hacilar and Çatal Hüyük."[1]

It is remarkable to read the good professor writing in 1978 about refugee traffic between what is now the Aleppo region of Syria and the Urfa region of Turkey. In antiquity, the refugees moved south from Urfa to Aleppo (or, as it was then, Göbekli Tepe to Tell Halaf). Today I see it running the other way. Millions fled north in the span of just a few years, most of them on foot. Eliade is spot on to think it could have happened so fast in 5000 BCE, but of course in the 1970s he had no evidence of it.

Of course, the key difference between the old towns and the new Halafian ones is that the latter consistently show signs of class stratification, fortification, war, and outright conquest. This all happened very quickly, in the space of about 500 years. In that brief passage, a page had turned, closing forever the early innocent chapters of human development, and presaging the civilization to come.

"Generally, an increasingly complex social interaction and organization is assumed to have taken definite shape with the rise of the Halaf culture," reports Peter Akkermans, the reigning authority on this subject, "and Halaf is considered to have been of crucial importance as an intermediate stage between village economies on the one hand and early state formation on the other."[2]

Once this prototype of the modern state emerged, it moved to subdue places that remained behind the times.

As agriculture and animal husbandry became more complex and as technology expanded (pottery and copper smithing, for example), it became more efficient to have specialists focusing on a particular task; before then, everyone could do a little bit of everything. A systemic result of such specialization is that you need to trade with others who specialize in different products. You can't make everything, and you don't have access to every resource. The more specialized your trade, the more fraught this becomes.

In our day, we have many examples of this very thing—oil, diamonds, and weapons, to name a few. Just as demand for scarce goods causes conflict now, so it did then. But bear in mind, this was not about food; it was rare commodities of exchange that tempted rulers to conquest.

The most sought-after and rarest item of all was obsidian, which became the engine that drove a vicious cycle: it was the sharpest substance known, and was used in making weapons; those weapons were then used to get ahold of more of it to make more weapons, tools, and other obsidian-based goodies.

Obsidian is a volcanic rock. Fracturing it produces incredibly sharp-edged fragments. Previously, Marshall Sahlins told us that "the world's most primitive people have few possessions... but they are not poor." That went out the window here. Obsidian is a non-essential commodity—it bears no direct relationship between basic needs and satisfaction, as when a hunter-gatherer or early townsperson hunted and ate. Obsidian was like money: exchangeable and imperishable. Trade of this kind sparked the greed of rulers, which trickled down class by class—an economy of escalating wants.

Obsidian was the great product of the age. Its first use as a cutting tool rapidly evolved into a catalogue of shapes and functions as craftsmen honed their skills. It did not take long before it sparked an armaments industry that provided rulers with an arsenal of knives, arrowheads, and extremely sharp spear points in a variety of lethal sizes.

Incidentally, obsidian is still used as a blade. An obsidian edge is sharper and thinner than "the best surgical steel," and today "thin blades of obsidian are placed in surgical scalpels used for some of the most precise surgery."[3]

Obsidian was something like cell phones today, insofar as they are a hallmark of global cultural development. Anthropologist Douglas Fry notes that one of the very few things we know about Halafian culture is that they "had an unusual immersion in obsidian commerce."[4]

The problem was that obsidian exists only where there were volcanoes, and there weren't any in the Halafian heartland. Obsidian was most bountiful further north and east, where the archeological remains from this point show widespread bloodshed, siege, and conquest. But what a Halafian chief wants, a Halafian chief gets—especially since he had whole factories running for the purpose of producing obsidian items that could be traded for other stuff with which to fill the chief's coffers.

Studying the extraordinary level of organized violence that fell upon the obsidian-rich northeast, Fry draws the only possible conclusion: "It is significant that all the sites that exhibit destruction or have fortifications are located on the east-west overland trade route." He considered climate change as a possible cause for this new "widespread pattern of war," but in the end came to a different conclusion: "A much stronger causal connection appears to involve key nodes of the trans-Anatolian obsidian trade."[5]

I'm not surprised. The recent "widespread pattern of war" in Syria is also driven by a feverish trade in weapons, every single one of them manufactured outside the region. It's an example of how the cultural model established around 5000 BCE continues to dominate our behavior. Nothing even remotely resembling this occurred on our planet before the towns turned to hierarchy.

At modern-day Mersin, due west of Göbekli Tepe on the Mediterranean coast, lies one of those ancient trading posts that Fry is talking about. Archeologist John Garstang excavated some twenty-three layers of it dating back to 6300 BCE. As everywhere else, all is peace and joy until after the great debate, and then this:

> Burnt human remains occur at Level XIX, which marks the impact of Halafian culture... we see evidence of disrespect and a mass burying of human bodies, a practice altogether unknown upon our site, which betrays violence and suggests the presence of an enemy. The natives would hardly have defiled their village in this way... We are forced to conclude that a fight had occurred with strangers who celebrated their victory with this holocaust... in view also of the change of culture and the remarkable innovations of the age, it seems probable that the Halafian impact was accompanied by an assault upon the unfortified village, and the slaying of its defenders... the period of peaceful progress now came to an end.[6]

Immediately after this horror, a portion of the village was demolished, and a fortification was built. That means simply that the peaceful town was attacked and pillaged, then converted into a town modeled on the new philosophy of sovereign power.

How do we know it was obsidian-trading Halafians who did this? They left their calling card. Every level after level XIX is loaded with Halafian pottery: "Halafian pottery is peculiarly distinctive," explains Garstang, "in colour and design, glowing with lustrous paint and burnished surfaces, and fashioned to special shapes; in short its characteristics are almost unmistakable."

Halafian pottery was the Lucky Strike pack or Hershey's wrapper of Halafian enlisted men—telltale evidence of where they've been. It does not appear in Mersin before this savage conquest. Then, within a short time after the settlement's grim conquest, Halafian techniques were not just transferred but imposed; it became a sweatshop for the manufacture of the hierarchy's unmistakable money-making crockery.

Struggling for an analogy, I will be so bold as to conjure the specter of the Klingon Empire. *Star Trek*'s Klingons were a culture ever intent on expansion and conquest of resources. Like them, the Halafians laid waste to any unfortunate outpost in the path of their lust for resources.

"Monopolization is the key link between war and trade," Fry observes. Regarding these obsidian-loving pottery designers, he concludes with this extraordinary observation: "The sixth millennium Halaf may be the first cultural group to expand via war."

Welcome to the new world.

Chariots of the Gods

You will recall from Flavius Josephus that Nimrod "gradually changed government into tyranny" and that's a pretty good description of what happened under the Halafian chiefs: a gradual transition from local chiefdoms to an eventual Nimrodian kingdom over the course of 1,000 years.

In the Halaf period, there is still no true government, no bureaucracy, no law, and, most importantly, no universal ethos. Those things will come with the next cultural wave, which we call Ubaid, once again after the modern location where it was first identified.

The distinction between Halaf and Ubaid has mainly to do with cultural and technological changes. There was no "Ubaid nation" that conquered the "Halafian nation." Instead, this was a cultural evolution. Like the transmission of American pop-culture, Ubaid influence was spread by trade, with the Ubaid brands evolving out of Halafian ones.

If the Halaf brand was the Golden Arches, the Ubaid culture's innovation was Disney: an attraction and a pilgrimage site remembered for its fairytales, heroes, genies, and princesses—and most of all, its magic castle.

Mircea Eliade again: "The most significant novelty of the Obeid [Ubaid] period is precisely the appearance of monumental temples."[7] More specifically, this is the temple-tower of the Bible's Babel, known to scholars of Sumeria as Eridu's ziggurat, the first of the monumental temples, rising from the ground circa 4900 BCE.

The Sumerians certainly understood the tower's significance. They believed Eridu was created directly by the gods, the place where "kingship was lowered from heaven," making it the world's first seat of civilized government. And it's true—archeology confirms that their temple is the catalyst through which the first real kings and states emerged.

We might say, therefore, that late-Ubaid culture was heavily pregnant with civilization. We see its seeds in the material remains of Eridu's immediate predecessors, when powerful mafia-like village chiefs began to brand themselves with the invention of stamp seals, an imprimatur of power and a means of control. It is a sophisticated governing device, which spread from one proto-urban community to the next, creating a kind of fraternity among chiefs—links that will one day become the network of empire.

"The existence of elaborate seals with near-identical motifs at such widely distant sites," says Ubaid specialist Dr. Gil Stein, "suggests that in this period, high-ranking elites were assuming leadership positions across a very broad region, and those dispersed elites shared a common set of symbols and perhaps even a common ideology of superior social status."[8]

It is not quite civilization. As yet, there is no bureaucracy capable of forming a true empire. There is no codification of a common language or body of law, as will be the ambition of Babel/Eridu's tower builders. Ideology is primitive; there are no schools to uniformly train the masses. It remains a rather uncivilized form of oppression. It is power without order.

Development is speeding up, however. Çatalhöyük was abandoned completely by 5700 BCE. Hacılar was sacked in 5500 BCE. By 5000 BCE, Halafian culture was starting to incorporate the distinctive branding we call Ubaid. Eridu's temple foundations were laid around 4900 BCE. All this in 800 years.

We can make this journey through time even today by river raft. Starting near Göbekli Tepe, we can float down the Euphrates to the Ubaid stronghold at Tell Zeidan and then continue to southern Iraq some 900 kilometers away—an easy journey in more peaceful times. When we reach Eridu in antiquity, we will be in a position to witness nothing less than mass psychosis-madness and hallucinations transmuted into what we now consider everyday life. It is the birth of the civilized world.

The ancient Mesopotamian historians—the first historians—tell us that the idea of civilization developed into its final form here, and then was fully realized in nearby Uruk. Eridu thus gave to Uruk the attributes of civilized life, the very things that modern historians cite as evidence that Uruk was in fact the progenitor of modern civilization—the first city-state—just as the Bible tells us it is. Can there possibly be an older example? Sure, it's possible. But if someone unearths an earlier city-state somewhere else in the world, it doesn't matter: it was Eridu and Uruk that gave us our world. A forgotten and disconnected parallel development would be to us nothing but a Neanderthal of a city—interesting, but not relevant to who we are. We are Eridu's children; the line of descent is clear and indisputable.

How did the Mesopotamians accomplish that amazing feat? We may never know for sure, but Erdiu's progenitive power was so potent and so inexplicable that some intelligent people go so far as to speculate it might be of alien origin—and they mean UFO alien.

A fine example is preeminent astronomer and astrobiologist Carl Sagan, who treated this idea with serious respect, lecturing and writing on the topic, and even publishing probability equations.[9] Sagan only discussed it as a slim chance. But the scope of change that occurred in Uruk was so rapid and extreme that he was willing to state publicly, as America's most visible astrophysicist, that there was no better explanation for the rapid appearance of civilization in Sumeria. According to Sagan, the idea of extraterrestrial intervention deserved consideration.

As a broken little boy, already enamored with the Book of Genesis, I obsessively latched on to Sagan's speculation. It was enough to spark a lifelong interest in astronomy and fun with telescopes. In fact, I must confess: it was the idea of aliens that made me consider ancient Mesopotamia for the first time.

A quick look at the History Channel's program guide shows that I am not an exception; the alien hypothesis still captures the imagination. The flagship series, *Ancient Aliens*, was poised for its seventeenth season in 2021.

It was a popular idea six millennia ago, too, for the alien hypothesis bears a striking resemblance to the Sumerians' own explanation for how they achieved so much so quickly. Like Sagan, they reckoned that the sudden onset of empire and technology suggested an extraordinary origin—which indeed, it does. Their solution relied on alien intervention conceived as a pantheon of non-human celestial powers who descended from heaven bearing gifts. From government to art to technology, these powerful outsiders gave it all to the people of Uruk (by way of Eridu), prepackaged and ready for use.

Erich von Däniken profitably exploited this idea 6,000 years later when he penned *The Chariots of the Gods*, an appropriation of Sagan's plausible thesis wed to an outlandish interpretation of Sumerian mythology and overlaid with unrestrained conjectural leaps. His theory was that those giftbearing gods were actual aliens from another planet; the weird descriptions, symbols, and wild stories of Sumerian mythology were historical descriptions of a Close Encounter of the Third Kind.

This parallel is very helpful, I think, because it tells us that the Sumerians were aware that their civilization's sudden appearance was inexplicable. They understood that their society was a mutation, completely unlike anything before it. Not unlike von Däniken, the ancients went a little overboard attempting to explain how it could happen over the course of just a few centuries.

As fantastic as they sound, however, the Sumerian stories often manage to convey essential details of what really happened. And now that we have archeological evidence from Uruk, we can tease an appropriately modern narrative out of these wooly layers of mythology: the myths can be decoded.

The first place to look is at the ground floor of our proto-typical temple, the foundation of the Tower of Babel. As Samuel Noah Kramer describes it, the tower "contained from the beginning two features that characterize the Sumerian temple throughout the millenniums: a niche for the god's emblem or statue and an offering table of mud brick in front of it."[10]

As the name suggests, the Eridu Temple was literally the "*temp*late" (related to the Latin for such sacred spaces, *templum*). Erdiu's is the first model of something that appears everywhere over the next 4,000 years—not just in Mesopotamia, but in Jerusalem, Thebes, Athens, and Rome. It was the center of urban life and modern polity—the organizing principle of the modern world came from this building.

The first adopter of the template was of course Uruk, whose people recognized Eridu as its inspiration and origin. A good way to describe it is to say that Eridu was the prophetic voice and Uruk was the devout listener. That's reasonably accurate from the perspective of historical development, and it fits the psychological profile of humanity well: the guiding voice must always be heard as a voice from the outside. That, too, is suggestive of an alien-like presence, the external origin of all authority. Indeed, the "kingship that descended from heaven" is Eridu's biggest claim, and kingship is the very thing these cities are noted for in the Bible.

The Sumerians believed that a temple was a kind of wormhole; it connected humanity to the heavens—to outer space, if you will. The alien who resided on the heavenly side of Eridu's temple was called Enki. He not only dwelt there, ready to speak guidance, but he stored within its secured metaphysical space all the culture and technology of civilization. They called this collection of proprietary civilizational programming the *Me* (pronounced MAY). And as in computer programming, the *Me* existed as information packets ready to be installed in any appropriate environment. At first, humans had no right to use the *Me*.

They first appear in a text about Eridu's resident god. Kramer writes, "We learn much about Enki from the myth *Enki and the World Order: The Organization of the Earth and Its Cultural Processes*, which provides a detailed account of Enki's creative activities in instituting the natural and cultural phenomena essential to civilization."[11]

That title says it all; a science fiction writer couldn't come up with anything as eerily timeless as that. The Sumerians invented writing, public education, accounting, law, government, and a good deal more. It is astonishing that 6,000 years ago they describe all this as a sudden installation of "processes," a terminology most at home in information theory, cryptography, and computer programming.

This bears some careful reflection, for *Enki and the World Order* is among a handful of our oldest written accounts, yet it smacks of both anthropology and computer science. Kramer's characterization of the *Me* "processes" underscores this; he defines them as "instituting the natural and cultural phenomena essential to civilization."

What were they exactly? The list we have of the *Me* is incomplete, numbering sixty-nine, but it is plenty to establish what this is all about. They are the essentials for the founding of a state, a modern economy, a system of taxes, an army, a religion, literature, culture, and so on. The *Me* include roles or identities and inventions and activities. They range from physical objects like musical instruments, weapons, and tools; to crafts and trade skills like metal working, building, and cooking; to abstractions such as enmity and rejoicing; and to other interesting *Me* like transsexuality, sexual intercourse, and broken-heartedness.

Something that should not escape our notice is that the *Me*, in all this diversity, are substantively the same stuff. Imagine a shelf stacked with CDs or a drawer full of memory sticks, each carrying a different computer game or program. *Me* is like that—they comprise a library of identical media, the information, code, or process recorded on each one. It is only after the process is installed and running that the variously labeled *Me* produce different phenomena, "the processes of civilization."

To reiterate: A program is a code stored on media and is nothing but information, uniform in its substance. But the executed and running processes of a particular program might appear as an image, a sound, an action, or a virtual environment—an operating system. With the sweeping advances of virtually immersive reality in modern gaming, it is not hard to understand how it is possible for information to be converted into imagined reality, which we know by now is the only environment in which humans operate anyway.

This is exactly what the *Me* represent. To explain how they got installed, how the *Me* of Eridu's inspirational temple got up and running, we can turn to another Sumerian story. Its memorable title seems too impossibly chic to be among the very first pieces of world literature: *Inanna and Enki: The Transfer of the Arts of Civilization from Eridu to Erech.*[12]

Inanna

Some think she was an alien visitor. Carl Sagan says the probabilities are slim but not non-existent. What's certain is that Inanna of Uruk is not human; if she is not an alien, she is a myth, a goddess. Lustful, brash, irresistible, powerful, tender, and violent, Inanna is a diva—at least in the ancient Indo-European sense of a warrior-god rather than a Barbra Streisand. Although Inanna did act a lot like a movie star.

Actually, she is both: she is a star, and she is from outer space! In the ancient world, stars were thought to be heavenly persons of great power—the governors of our realm—and Inanna was the brightest of them all. (Namely, Inanna embodies the planet Venus, which, despite its odd movements across the sky, was considered a star like all others—the brightest of them all, apart from the sun and moon.)

Not one for modesty, Inanna called her Uruk mansion the "Temple of Heaven." She did not live alone. The Venusian goddess is the patroness of prostitutes, many of whom practiced under her roof. If Nimrod founded Uruk as the Bible says, he certainly had to be on intimate terms with Inanna, for sexual intercourse between the king and the priestess was how the stars imparted their ruling charisma to the political elite.

She is not, however, a mother goddess. Inanna is the goddess of sex—she has many lovers but no children.

> Inanna represented the power of sexual attraction and the carnal pleasure that proceeds from it. Focused on the immediate gratification of her own sensual needs, she was neither a goddess of marriage nor of childbirth. Her sexual appetite was inexhaustible and her relationship with men short term.[13]

As we enter, don't be surprised to see people of every imaginable shade of gender. That's one of the things Inanna's house is known for. A later poem describes her dwelling as a place of "prostitutes, courtesans and call-girls" and speaks of the "party-boys and festival people who changed masculinity to femininity" all to please Inanna.[14]

But don't get the idea from all this hanky-panky that Inanna is a softy. The emphasis she places on gender fluidity in her home reflects her identity: she is clearly a woman but she likes to dress as a man. Her masculine side is most prominent in her guise as a Sumerian war god: "She stirs confusion and chaos against those who are disobedient to her, speeding carnage and inciting the devastating flood, clothed in terrifying radiance. It is her game to speed conflict and battle, untiring, strapping on her sandals."[15]

Those sandals are not to be confused with the casual footwear of uptalking Valley Girls; battle sandals are the Mesopotamian equivalent of army boots. "In art, Inanna is usually represented as a warrior-goddess, often winged, armed to the hilt, or else surrounded by a nimbus of stars. Even in this aspect she may betray—by her posture and state of dress—her role as goddess of sex and prostitutes."[16]

Inanna was ambitious and usually got what she wanted. And what she wanted for her beloved Uruk were the processes of civilization—the *Me*—which were safely locked away in the occult spaces of the Abzu temple in Eridu under creator-god Enki's protection.

Called "a particularly charming story" by professor Samuel Noah Kramer, *The Transfer of the Arts of Civilization from Eridu* begins with Inanna giving herself a pep talk in the mirror: "She put the desert crown on her head. She praised herself, full of delight at her genitals—she praised herself, full of delight at her genitals." Then she said to herself, "I shall direct my steps to the Abzu, to Eridu, I shall direct my steps to Enki, to the Abzu, to Eridu, and I myself shall speak coaxingly to him, in the Abzu, in Eridu, I myself shall speak coaxingly..."[17]

I'll leave the pondering of this amazing scene to you. My only comment is that it is important: it prepares us for the rest of the tale by revealing what is on Inanna's mind as she sets out through celestial means toward the Abzu, the immortal domain of the great god of wisdom, lord of the earth, and holy father, Enki. What was on her mind was genitals, seductive coaxing, and the processes of civilization.[18]

As you can imagine, Enki is excited to see her. This is the goddess of erotic pleasure and she's all grown up and heading his way, "all by herself."

As readers, we feel that Enki is done for. No time to waste, he hurriedly instructs his servant to offer her cake and beer when she gets there. "Make her feel as if she is in her girlfriend's house," he says. In other words, "Make yourself comfortable... relax; can I pour you a drink?"

Everything seems to be going his way; he is a smooth operator. Now he's got her right where he wants her: "So it came about that Enki and Inanna were drinking beer together in the Abzu, and enjoying the taste of sweet wine... The bronze vessels were filled to the brim, and the two of them started a competition, drinking from the bronze vessels of Uraš."

Yes, like Marion and her French captor in Indiana Jones, Inanna gets into a drinking contest with Enki. Now giddy, drunk, and smitten, Enki starts showing off. In a lengthy passage, he boasts of his power over the *Me*, proclaiming extravagantly that he can and will give them all to her. For effect, he names them aloud in groups, crowing about his authority over these precious items in between each lot, repeating his ardent desire to give them all to his beloved goddess.

There are thirty-some lines missing after that. I'd love to know what they say, for when we pick up the thread again, Enki is in the throes of panic, calling for his right-hand man, Isimud: "Isimud, my minister, my Sweet Name of Heaven!" (Paraphrase: "Good lord, Isimud!" or "Holy shit, Isimud!") The god asks his chief minister if it's too late. Bad news: "Holy Inanna had gathered up the divine powers and embarked onto the Boat of Heaven. The Boat of Heaven had already left the quay."

Being jilted by the goddess of love is bad enough, but as he looks around, the situation is worse than he feared.

"As the effects of the beer cleared... the great lord Enki turned his attention to the building. The lord looked up at the Abzu. King Enki turned his attention to Eridu."

He speaks, "Isimud, my minister, my Sweet Name of Heaven! Where are the office of En priest, the office of Lagar priest, Divinity, the Great and Good Crown, the Royal Throne?"

Isimud gently reminds Father Enki, "My master has given them to his daughter." (Note to the perplexed: Isimud's reference to Inanna as Enki's daughter need not be taken literally.)

"Where are the Noble Scepter, the Staff and Crook, the Noble Dress, Shepherdship, Kingship?"

"My master has given them to his daughter..."

Now a full inventory is taken, and here we get the list of what is missing, beginning with the big *Me* of kingship and priesthood. Other *Me* include inventions (swords, tambourines) and technologies (carpentry, leather working), professional skills (counseling, decision making), arts (the "art of song"), sexual practices (kissing, fellatio), and all the other processes and attributes of civilization. Most of them are ideas but a good many are skills and offices —even marvelous things like the skill to make the "black garment, the colorful garment, and the stylish hair."

After a full accounting, and confirming that the shelves are bare, what follows is a breathless and futile chase as Isimud and crew try to catch up with Inanna and her right-hand lady, Ninšubur. At each of seven symbolic stops between Eridu and Uruk, a rotating cast of terrifying repo men attempt to seize the *Me* and keep them from delivery to Uruk. They are foiled at every turn, and Inanna arrives home in triumph. The narrator concludes the story: "So Inanna got hold again of the divine powers which had been presented to her." Ninšubur celebrates: "My lady, today you have brought the Boat of Heaven to the Gate of Joy! Now there will be rejoicing in our city, now there will be rejoicing in our city!"

"Today I have brought the Boat of Heaven to the Gate of Joy!" pronounces Inanna. "It shall pass along the street magnificently. The people shall stand in the street full of awe!"

And so, in this manner, the *Me* were taken from the world's prototypical temple to be installed and executed in Uruk, the city where the virtual reality of the processes will run for the first time, endowing the world with civilization as we know it.

When a House is Not a Home

Now here we are at last, poking around Enki's holy house just before the *Me* will be transferred. Despite the passage of time on our centuries-long cruise down the Euphrates, not much has changed. You may have noticed the houses around us; they look very much like those in old Çatalhöyük, built from the same material and construction methods, a detail that impresses upon us the continuity of cultural development. Apart from the preeminence of the temple complex and its unusual size, Eridu is not much different from any other town that we've seen up until now.

But this is the fulcrum that will lift civilization from prehistory. This one especially large and important house is the key to it all. How did that come to be?

I'm sure you've figured it out. We remember that in Çatalhöyük the one thing that provided a balm for the townspeople's existential crisis was the secure feeling that their oldest homes gave them. They cultivated that security religiously, never demolishing the houses, but lovingly renovating them over centuries with the intention of incorporating the past and transcending death into the future. We can understand, then, how this idea evolved into that of a sacred house, one so sacred that it bridged the seen and unseen worlds.

This is where the genius of Eridu's temple lies. In deep antiquity there was no special word for a place like this. *Templum* is a Latin word for a kind of consecrated space, adapted by English as "temple" to give a name to what such places had become: special, separate, and sacred places.

In Eridu, it had no such special name. It was called simply "house" just as any other house was. Even in the late passages of the Bible, Jerusalem's magnificent temple is the same; in plain Hebrew, it is the word that any common laborer would use for his abode today in Tel Aviv. Eridu's sacred place was therefore a "history house" just as Çatalhöyük's were. The critical difference is its size, separation, and the hierarchical rise of its caretakers to the position of unquestioned and unaccountable leadership.

So, Eridu's temple was a dedicated history house for the entire community, staffed by a hereditary class of dedicated thinkers. It was a public institution. The priests were those born to this eternal home and raised with the expectation that they had answers to life's existential puzzles. They too, like their house, were separated and elevated. Set aside to do nothing but explain what it all meant—basically to tell reassuring stories—these ancient celebrities put their imaginations to work.

Eventually they came up with a brilliant idea. The holy house had served now for thousands of years as a mantra to focus attention on transcendent reality—on things undefinable, but metaphysically true and real. Now, the priests extrapolated from their natural observations to identify a bigger domicile, a cosmic home for the entire human family—a giant roof over our heads, older and more persistent than any house. That which lies beyond our transitory experience, they said, is right above our heads: Look to the heavens!

We must understand that from their perspective, "the heavens" was not the modern (and not terribly accurate) idea of empty space. When they looked up, they saw something substantive, a solid counterpart to the ground on which we walk; the stars, planets, sun, and moon were presumed to be beings who inhabited and transited this firmament. These beings transmitted their celestial will through their agents, the kings and priests. They said that it was this heavenly dimension that gave rise to us and our world. It was those beings who were responsible for our story—it was *their* story, and we humans are just one part of it.

The details get complicated, but the fundamental idea, I trust, is clear. Eridu's cosmology gave a solid answer to life's questions: our existence is firmly rooted in another realm, there is a transcendent authority to guide us, and there is therefore no need for anxiety—the gods know what they are doing. There is a story, a logic to life and death. It is all about authority beyond the self, and all we ordinary people need to do is listen and obey. The cosmic hierarchy will take care of you.

I should emphasize that I believe the priests were well-intentioned. But I and my Muslim Brothers also had good intentions when we set out to convert the world. Our idea was that if everyone lived under the rule of Christ, or under the authority of Islam, all would be saved and well. But people would have to adopt our way of thinking and obey the rules of our religious ideology. What we did not grasp was how this was the root of the problem, not its solution. We did not understand the impossibility of setting up a mechanism for heaven on Earth and did not see that mediated Paradise is no Paradise at all. We didn't understand that by making it politically concrete we manufactured a world in our own images. We fell to the poisoned fruit of knowing good and evil, of judging and ruling, of trying to "be like God."

That's what happened in Eridu. Their heavenly house was in the beginning a metaphor for eternal, timeless, non-historical reality, a meditation focusing conscious attention on the hidden foundation of existence. It was a reflection upon the unknowable, the undefinable—the Real, as such. What it became very quickly was just the opposite: a concrete (or rather, stone) simulacrum of hidden things, a falsehood, a fake Paradise ruled by fake gods.

In this way, the parable of heaven turned into law and coercion. The priests' ideas were hypostatized, which means to treat the conceptual as material, an abstract notion as something concrete.

This particular piece of concrete will come to sit very heavily on the human race.

The Big Other

It should not be hard for us to understand the credibility of these priests, who by now lived generationally in this meaningful house, charged with interpreting life for the baffled community. Even in our cynical times we remain susceptible to this magic. We describe royal families in terms of "the house of so and so" and we are enamored with those who belong to special houses—with Princess Di or Will and Kate, or perhaps the Kennedys or Kardashians or Obamas. We are looking for the authoritative Otherness.

Think you aren't susceptible to this? Here's the test: Imagine that tonight Barack Obama invites you to dinner. (Or maybe it's your favorite movie star or music legend.) Be honest—don't you feel the magic? The Queen of England just phoned and wants to see you. Not feeling a little awed? I'm as critical of privilege and power as anyone, yet I've never gotten over the feeling of weighty presence that comes from entering places of power. We want the aura of greatness to be real!

The priests obliged this hunger by presenting themselves as heaven's appointees. I don't mean to say that the idea of heaven is always bad. It is great as a metaphor for something undefinable and ineffable. It allows us to get out of our ever-defining minds, to momentarily exit the social worlds we create and see them briefly for what they are, as if from the outside, from the perspective of reality itself. (Or from God's point of view, if that language is more helpful.)

But the Eridu priests' concept of heaven became solid, political, and very much of human origin. It was tangible, hard, and imposing. This was more dangerous than any other social construction because it claimed its authority from the beyond. It became an unassailable proposition of how things were.

Eridu's heaven was the first universal religion, an ideology that claimed to be true for everyone. Not only that, but its universality was supposed to be imposed everywhere—by force if necessary. No one could say no to its idea of heaven on Earth.

We are going to call this overarching principle the Cosmic Order, but at the outset, there are other names that might help us understand what this means. One of those is "big Other," a term coined by controversial philosopher and psychotherapist Jacques Lacan. I like it because of Lacan's idea that speech always originates not in the ego, but from a phantom counter-ego, the big Other. The gods of the Cosmic Order are just that; they are the external voice that tells us "how things are."

For the psychoanalytically inclined, allow me to point out that this is not the super-ego, which is a division of the self; rather, this is an external presence that the self refers to. Sometimes we register its validation and at other times its disapproval. It is a presence: a god, a heavenly order, a body of law, social conventions, or—most potent of all—Things Mom Used to Say.

The Cosmic Order is just like that. When we believe in it, it tells us what to do. We don't have to think or be anxious. In its various guises (religion, government, family culture, etc.), it is what sociologists call a reality-maintenance mechanism. We need that since our reality is made up—that is, without a presumed outside authority to legitimate them, our virtual social realities fall apart, disintegrating into chaos, the very enemy most prominent in Sumerian cosmology. The raison d'être of Sumerian religion was to prevent chaos.

For most of history, social mythology gave the big Other the personal attribute of God or a collection of gods. Things were the way they were because the gods said so. But belief in the Divine is not necessary for the experience of the big Other. As philosopher Slavoj Žižek discusses in his scintillating film, *The Pervert's Guide to Ideology*, even the atheistic Soviet Union relied upon such god-like mechanisms, except that they didn't call them gods. In the Soviet Union, "the People" served as the big Other, as did the notion of "History" in the sense of the inevitable Marxist succession of historical steps that must lead to the Workers' Paradise.

Under the Soviet regime, the actual "people" endured incredible hardship in the name of serving the will of "the People," even though this fairytale entity was no less imagined than Inanna and her celestial companions. Crimes against these mythical socialist gods were harshly punished, ostensibly not on the authority of the leaders themselves, but by dictate of that sacred hypostatization, "the People."

Žižek insightfully remarks upon Lenin's public persona as a lover of children and kittens—all to say that no matter how many human beings Lenin starved to death, he was really a nice guy. All this suffering was for "the People." Who was Lenin to stand up against the will of "the People" and "History" if it demanded death and starvation? Millions of real people went along with it because this scheme effectively maintained a phase of reality for them; this was "just how things are" like gravity or the sunrise.

Because modern, refined, materialist society is embarrassed by God in its public spaces, Lenin's favorite expression of the big Other is now one of the most common. Every leader and candidate for leadership tells us that their judgments are valid because, for example, it is what the "American People" want. When two rival leaders hold opposite views, they both cite "the People" as their authority. Not too long ago, a king would have justified his position by saying his policy was the will of God. It is the same thing.

Listen carefully and you'll begin to notice the big Other in many guises. One of the most powerful today is "the Market." Any day of the week, the financial pages report on the mood of this all-powerful god. Checking them this past week, for example, I'm happy to report that the Market was "relieved" by a Federal Reserve Board decision. On another day, the Market was "nervous" about the jobs report, and I am warned that if things don't change, the Market will "react badly." Not to worry, however, because last week the Market was soothed by oil, having "responded favorably" to a decision by Organization of the Petroleum Exporting Countries to cut production.

As a connoisseur of the world's earliest cosmic myths, I recognize in these reports the volatile moods of a capricious goddess whose whims dictate my future well-being. And I see in the role of the modern financial guru the image of ancient priests who used to cut open sacrificial livers to read signs of the divine humor. Make no mistake: people fear this god as much as the ancients feared Inanna—they worry about its whimsical wrath and praise its largesse when it turns kind.

These contemporary examples give us a good sense, I hope, of what it meant when ancient people first began to worship the gods in a civilized society. They were not more foolish than we—if anything, they were more honest about what they were doing.

The Worth of a Man

The Cosmic Order had its merits: it was better than utter chaos, better than the unaccountable whims of myriad chiefdoms, and at this point in human development, they could not come up with a more effective solution. It was, at the very least, a comforting story; the promise was to provide food, shelter, security, and—just as importantly—meaning and context. Under the Order, life made sense.

Prior to 4000 BCE, the Cosmic Order's soon-to-be capital was nothing special. Uruk was just a typical Ubaid town devoted to Inanna, who lived in a temple patterned off the one in Eridu. Then, just after 4000 BCE, the city exploded with every imaginable innovation—the whole shelf-full of *Me*—to emerge as if overnight as the world's first true city, the seat of a trading empire that was unprecedented on planet Earth. Just 200 years later, we can no longer speak of Ubaid culture in Uruk at all. All of a sudden, it is a place that is—if I may use this word—alien to anything else on Earth.

"The Uruk period represents perhaps the most intriguing puzzle in Mesopotamian history," writes Gwendolyn Leick, "because of the many questions raised by the unprecedented spread of one material culture over so wide an area and the development of urbanism."[19]

It is a puzzle of which we have many pieces. For example, the piece that shows the exact boundary line between earthly Ubaid and the alien-like Uruk cultures is clearly visible. Two types of object mark the transition—pottery and seals—both of which we possess by the trucks-full.

Gone were the hand-crafted, delicately decorated pottery vessels coveted by Halaf and Ubaid traders. The new fashion was ugly and utilitarian pots produced in astonishing numbers. They strike me as Soviet grotesqueries: Uruk's pots were mass-produced by a centrally planned state hierarchy and were utterly disposable. It seems the big Other's aesthetics have remained consistently ugly all these many centuries.

We've found thousands and thousands of the pots, broken and thrown away by the ton. Sumerian artwork depicts such bowls, too, so we know exactly what they were used for. They were measuring cups, ensuring equal quantities of food for distribution. (Again a Soviet image, except that in Uruk it worked—at first.)

As for the seals, we saw rudimentary use of them by chiefs further up the Euphrates, but that was a simple stamp seal—a few lines scratched on the face of a small, flat stone. It was sufficient for the chief of a medium-sized, mob-run town.

But thanks to the *Me*, Uruk had a modern economy and a complex administration. It was a major manufacturer and the center of a massive food-production, storage, and distribution network. As Leick notes, "The overall success of Uruk as the main centre of distribution was dependent on the efficient handling of the administrative coordination of the economic exchange system."[20]

In other words, there was a professional caste of bureaucrats, accountants, and managers who regulated the collection and redistribution of goods and services. There had to be accountability and authority. Officials had to sign off on a delivery, a receipt, or a decision.

A seal with a few squiggles was not sufficient when a variety of signatures were needed for many different and specific purposes. The guy who could give you a bowl of grain by his signature was not the gal who, by hers, could have your assets seized by the state or verify that you paid your taxes. The seal had to convey information about the person, their position, and their authority. That's a lot of information. And there was a lot of wealth at stake.

Uruk's solution was to toss out the button seal, replacing it with a cylinder. It's ingenious: the cylinder was no bigger than the old-style stamp, so it didn't weigh more or take up more space. But because of its barrel-like shape, the carved design was spread over a much larger surface area. This was a monumental step, for the difference between a stamp and a cylinder is the amount of information that can be stored on the device—and information is power.

By design, the Ubaid stamp bore a simple pattern imprinted as a reflection, like a rubber stamp does today. But the cylinder does not merely mirror its pattern; it is linearly expansive. When rolled onto clay, the intricate pattern carved around the cylinder unfolds progressively as a panoramic design. The large surface area and rolling motion allows for an expanding scene of information, analogous to a motion picture.

This difference in the way information was stored and retrieved changed us forever. The great information revolutions of writing, printing, and computing—and motion pictures, for that matter—began with these lines of code carved on a cylinder, miraculously encrypting and compressing information in a small packet that could be tossed in your pocket and retrieved and expanded at will, like a modern USB stick.

The very concept of a linear sequence of information profoundly affected the minds of Uruk's citizens. In my opinion, this concept was the original inspiration for the idea of the *Me*, which were also vessels of compactly stored cultural information.

As cylinder makers puzzled over their craft, imagining the little movie they wanted to see played out, and as everyday users witnessed the unfolding scenes at every transaction, the linear sequence shaped their—and our—concepts of time and history. More and more, we began to think of life as an unfolding story.

As you might expect, the Urukians expressed themselves with great variety through their rolling imprimaturs. Some were John Hancocks—designed with flare. Others were blandly practical. There are animals and people on the seals. Leick writes that in addition to lions, gazelles, birds, cattle, and sheep, there were "fantastic creatures such as the well-known dinosaur-like monsters that intertwine their necks in a corkscrew pattern."

People can be seen practicing their trades, too, such as "pigtailed women weaving," something you can see all over the Middle East even today, and other professionals who "engage in the transport of commodities, on foot or by boat." Still others "appear to frolic, dance, perform some ceremony and have sexual intercourse." Yes, this is perhaps the world's first animated pornography—not a shock in the city of Inanna!

By 3200 BCE, the demands of accounting for all those measures of grain resulted in a variation on the rolling seal concept. Imitating the linear pattern left by the cylinder when rolled across clay, the accountants began to inscribe wedge-like linear notations on clay tablets that they kept in archives. Symbols included marks representing commodities and a sophisticated numeracy.

Robert N. Bellah notes that Inanna's city was already roughly the same size as Rome at its peak (although Rome came 3,000 years later). Uruk was also larger than Athens in its heyday, which was around 500 BCE. And it was far, far bigger than Jerusalem. "By 2900 BCE the city of Uruk...had become enormous by the standards of ancient cities."[21]

No wonder, then, that civilization version 1.0 under the Uruk brand was a big hit, attracting many early adopters. Neighboring cities imported it with glee; and with each update, ever more diverse applications found their way onto the Uruk platform. We still use many of them today.

Astronomy, astrology, algebra, reading, and writing; geometry, accounting, law, the calendar, architecture, medical science, and systematic irrigation; a school system, banking, loans and interest, and the forerunner of the automobile; not to mention the professional army, military tactics, maps, and a slew of weapons. There is evidence that they invented a working battery, too. These are all very big inventions—entire fields of study—and the Sumerians concocted them all.

They even invented the hour. Have you ever wondered why there are 60 seconds in a minute and 60 minutes in an hour? Or how about 6×60, the 360 degrees of a circle? It's because the people of Uruk, the world's first mathematicians, used a base-60 numbering system.[22]

To jot down their numbers, they used the aforementioned cuneiform writing, the pressing of wedge shapes into clay to create a permanent record. It didn't take long before the accountants realized that they could use different configurations of the wedges to stand for sounds, too; they could record their speech in the clay and read it back exactly as it was recorded! They could even do that with the speech in their minds! This was pure voodoo—magic power.

Less than 800 years into Uruk's civilization, writing for commercial purposes was a well-established practice. If two parties made a deal, they could write it down and have it notarized by a scribe. The state was able to do the same, making a permanent form of rules and regulations. In another 500 years, writing was a fully literary art, a means to record stories and tell histories.

Another important invention appeared suddenly when some Sumerian Thomas Edison undertook to find a solution for the problem of moving people and goods. He conceived a great one: the wheel and axle. Like the light bulb, his innovation spread quickly over an enormous area, leading many regions to claim it as their own invention. It appears in far-away Europe in practically no time, making it possible that it was invented there independently. But the Urukians have a proof of patent that none of the others have: they recorded evidence of the wagon in printed media that we've recovered from excavations in Inanna's temple.[23] Most importantly, as with all these things, was the way the Mesopotamians incorporated these inventions into a civilized system.

Around this time, Uruk's accountants came up with a great idea that became as ubiquitous as the wheel: compound interest. They found it through the common practice of lending sheep. When someone invested sheep in another man's business, the animals reproduced, so it was only logical to repay the investment with more animals than were originally lent. These transactions were noted in clay by use of the fancy new Sumerian numbering and writing system.

The sheep were now reified by writing; they were not sheep but symbols on hardened clay. Alongside those symbols were symbols of other items on loan—let's say a quantity of obsidian. Bingo! Obsidian did not reproduce, but abstract writing could make it as productive as sheep! To that end, a sheep-like logarithm was devised so that any commodity entered into the accounts would multiply. Base-2 compound interest was conceived. Magic!

It is unlikely anyone would have thought of this until living sheep were converted into numbers and labels alongside other, non-living currencies and commodities. The effect of commodifying everything—living or inanimate—in equal abstract terms was staggering.

Consider this along with the bigger story of consciousness. We already live in a virtual and symbolic reality. With the invention of writing and numbers, everything—sheep and people included—could be reified and frozen permanently; their relative abstract values could then be set and exchanged. As most workaday people still know very well, a person's value could now be measured by the newly invented 60-minute hour: Joe the Irrigator is worth 50 shekels an hour. This was not conceivable before Uruk.

Personalities could be frozen, too, their virtue or guilt inscribed along with their name or description on a tablet. This made a soul the equivalent of her failure (Jane the Liar, perhaps) or success (Enmerkar the Great). A commodity is a commodity, whether human, animal, or otherwise; and make no mistake, writing equalized all as abstract things.

If the books said you are in debt, God bless you—you are worse than worthless, you have a negative value. If the state bank or a wealthy individual lent you sheep or obsidian, you'd better count on paying back more than they put in. Woe betide if you owed a debt or a tax you could not repay. Your subsequent torment was nothing personal—it was a matter of the written record and the dictate of the big Other.

Relationships abstracted in that way become cruel and inhuman, mediated by the non-relational knowledge of good and evil. When Genesis talks about broken relationships in the Garden, the cycle of blame and recrimination that followed acquiring "god-likeness" through knowledge, it is a reflection of what was going on in the developments we see here in Uruk.

Commodification and compound interest nourished the mentality of endless economic growth. As it was based on interest, debt, and commodified lives, where people were valued numerically like any commodity, this shattered whatever was left of the mutually supportive hunter-gatherer economy that had survived in the early development of towns.

Priests and Kings

The *Me* are installing themselves at an accelerating rate, but what about the first and most predominant one, the *Me* of kingship? Gwendolyn Leick notes that from 3600 to 3100 BCE there "is little evidence for hierarchical social structures, of personalized power—a theme that will dominate the glyphic repertoire of later periods."[24]

Czech archeologist Petr Charvát argues that until 3000 BCE, life in Uruk was much like my life as a teenager on the Israeli kibbutz: there was a unifying ideology and a corporate leadership that organized communal work and the equal distribution of wealth. And he believes that, like my kibbutz, it was an egalitarian society. It is possible that he is correct; without question, the leadership of this budding civilization ran it along lines that appear communistic.

The details are scarce, however. Was coercion required to make this system work? Or was it really like my kibbutz—that is, completely voluntary? As Leick points out, "The question of how Uruk society was organized is one of the most difficult and controversial issues."[25]

Here's what we know for sure: early Uruk had a heavenly endorsed leadership powerful enough to tax and redistribute every ounce of the gross domestic product. If this was egalitarian and voluntary, it is only because the people readily gave up all control to the Cosmic Order in exchange for material security and spiritual peace of mind. (Which I understand—I did this myself as a young man on the kibbutz for the same reasons.)

Archeology would suggest, then, that while there was an urban civilization heavily organized around the Cosmic Order at the temple, there was probably no king between 4000 and 3000 BCE.

But we can't leave it at that because the Sumerians recall it differently. They claim that King Enmerkar founded Uruk around 4500 BCE (depending on how you calculate what might be inscrutable numbers in the

King List). More to the point, they claim it was a hierarchical monarchy, complete with an armed force from day one. (But this might have been written into the story by the army and the king at a later date to justify their existence. You see the conundrum...)

Not to worry. We can still get a pretty good idea of how long it took for a real king to appear in Uruk. It just requires some deeper scrutiny of the evidence and some parsing of words. Those words are "priest-king."

Here is what we know for sure: there is a temple in Uruk from the beginning, but no separate palace until much later. Or at least there is no separate palace for a non-priestly ruler. If a building is a temple, and that temple houses the rulers and controls the administration of the state, isn't it a palace?

There is a similar ambiguity with titles. The *en* was a priest, but the priest oversaw all the civil administration (divvying up bowls of grain and so forth). For this reason, many historians comfortably translate *en* as "priest-ruler," because the *en* served as both. Some translate it as "priest-king."

After 3000 BCE, another word appears: *lugal*. This is a ruler, just as the *en* was, but the *lugal* built and occupied separate quarters from the temple. We would call that a palace. But both the temple and the palace are variants of the word for "house" in Sumerian. The palace is simply, "The Big House," while the temple was of the variety, "The House of Heaven."

The *lugal* was still understood to be a priest insofar as he was the link between the gods and the people. The Cosmic Order transmitted itself from the heavens through him. But he did not live at the temple and did not otherwise perform regular priestly duties. If the ruler was a priest-king in earlier times, he was now a king-priest.

To sum it up, the kingship that descended to Eridu and settled upon Uruk was not necessarily held by a king as such, but was rather a position of mediation between the authority of the Cosmic Order and the society it ruled. In Uruk's development, that role was first taken by a body of priests, and most likely a single head priest. It took a little time for this to be distilled into the identity of a more secular king.

Mircea Eliade describes it like this:

> Since the gods are responsible for the cosmic order, men must obey their commands, for these are based on the norms—the "decrees," *Me*—which insure the functioning both of the world and of human society. These decrees establish, that is, determine, the destiny of every being, of every form of life, of every divine or human enterprise.[26]

Some scholars, noting the extraordinarily widespread influence of Uruk, suggest that no matter what we call the ruler, the city must have been a military empire from the get-go. This perspective accords more closely to Sumeria's own memory of the founding king Enmerkar. (For what it's worth, his biblical counterpart, Nimrod, was certainly meant to represent an imperial ruler.)

Did you notice the word *en* in Enmerkar's name? Sumeria considered him the first king but *lugal* is not part of his name, as it would be for later kings who lived in separate palaces. Instead, he carries the earlier temple-linked title of *en* or priest. This suggests again that the priests were kingly in character and function; the legendary *En*-merkar would appear, from the evidence of his name, to be a temple-based ruler.

Further light is shed by Susan Pollack, an acknowledged expert on early Sumeria. Of Uruk's first phase, she writes that it was "a hierarchically organized political system in which state institutions controlled large-scale economic activities."[27] And Leick summarizes what can be agreed upon: "Most scholars agree that Uruk society was hierarchically organized under the leadership of a professional elite who exerted power over the population through the control of the administration and religious life."[28]

So, whether under *lugal* or *en*, the system was always a total theocracy, which itself does not disprove Charvát's contention that it was, at least for a while, egalitarian. The first rulers might have held office by consensus, and many scholars believe that to be the case. Why wouldn't it be? After all, since the Cosmic Order was a solution to a human crisis, it was most likely a popular movement.

Again, we can look at recent history to see the pattern repeated. Consider a popular revolution, like the one that turned Russia into the Soviet Union. Utopian fantasies do garner widespread support—at first. Soon, however, the weight of such a concretized ideology begins to sit heavily on the majority while rewarding only the elite.

For the last word on this subject, I will turn to Denise Schmandt-Besserat. Her evaluation of early Uruk is eminently reliable. She was named by *American Scientist* in their list of "100 books that shaped a century of science" for her classic, *How Writing Came About*. This list puts her in the company of Freud, Huxley, and Einstein—she really knows her stuff.

Professor Schmandt-Besserat's expertise in the development of writing gives her an intimate and unsurpassed knowledge of Uruk's seals and early experiments with writing. This allows her to survey the impression left by the entire body of evidence, and she reads an unambiguous story.

In her analysis, a "quantum jump" in the number of seal shapes and designs coincided "with the establishment of a coercive redistribution economy." Furthermore, "the imposition of taxation required an authority and administration to implement it, a system of measures and a precise reckoning device for record keeping, [and] large storage facilities." But most strikingly, she says that the seals show that the imposition of taxes required a "system of penalties for noncompliance."[29]

Penalties mean coercive violence by the state. Coercion means that at least some people did not go along with the cosmic plan. The kibbutz hypothesis is beginning to unravel, especially in view of graphic evidence for something I never saw on the kibbutz: some of the seals Schmandt-Besserat examined show "the En presiding over scenes of torture, such as beating, probably inflicted on the first tax delinquents."

This scene is still early in Uruk's development; the first physical evidence of these *en* leaders appear on cylinders around 3500 BCE. Appearing just a few hundred years into Uruk's civilization, they are therefore a good indication of culture from the beginning.

The images demonstrate a disciplined social order that included taxes, public works, building projects, and social welfare. We see priests and temple functions. But there are also armed men. Some have spears, bows, and arrows, but they are not hunters; we can see, for example, a scene of an armed party guarding bound prisoners and the aforementioned scene of torture.

Remember, these priests possessed the aura of the house—they were charismatic. If they were also dictatorial, it certainly wouldn't be the last time popularity and brutality were combined in a leader. Hitler was charismatic, popular, elected, and horribly abusive. Sometimes societies choose this for the sake of security and order—they want to be told what to do and what to believe—and isn't that exactly what the Cosmic Order was conjured up to provide?

This evidence underscores the sad fact that while the Cosmic Order was embraced as a solution to the problems posed by modern consciousness—to the loss of Paradise—it rapidly became a devil's bargain.

Freedom

The sweet promises of the Cosmic Order went sour quickly. We can say that by the time the palace moved out of the temple to a separate building, few would still hold any illusions. As you might guess, it was the guys with spears, first seen on cylinder seals hundreds of years earlier, who led the movement to separate the king and themselves from the priests.

Richard Gabriel, again writing for the US Army War College, stresses that the military faction arose at first from within the temple. According to Gabriel's analysis, "Organized belief systems were integrated into the social order and given institutional expression through public rituals that linked religious worship to political and military objectives that were national in scope and definition."[30]

They'd once been the enforcers of the Cosmic Order's will as interpreted by the temple. Now, with the mathematical ability to theoretically construct ever-increasing wealth, they found that their skill with weapons was an advantage, and they wanted to run things on their own. The ruler was no longer to be an *en* (priest) but a *lugal* (king). He still acted as the closest connecting point to the gods, but from his own turf. This was a military coup, rising from within the ranks of the temple's police force—the fellows who enforced tax and tortured people on the cylinder seals.

Geopolitical trends tell part of the story. As Uruk expanded, other city-states all over this part of Mesopotamia emerged under its tutelage. They followed in the steps of Inanna's war sandals, adopting Uruk's religion and co-opting Uruk's technologies and economics. Several became as powerful, and then more powerful, than the original city. With exponential economic growth on their minds, the cities began to quarrel over property and control of trade routes, land, and water.

These ambitions and the handy reification of "the Enemy" were enough to justify the police coup, undertaken no doubt for the benefit of "the People." The real people could do nothing but assume this was all part of heaven's plan. And it wasn't so bad; most still got their grain, they were still free to party at the temple, and society was prosperous and orderly.

They had no idea, however, where this would lead: "The development of central state institutions and a supporting administrative apparatus inevitably gave form and stability to military structures," Gabriel writes. "By 2700 B.C. in Sumer there was a fully articulated military structure and standing army organized along modern lines."[31]

This is essentially the date of the *lugal* revolution. By then, the armed men had broken free of the temple that nurtured them, having built separate palaces and armories. From their ranks arose the king as a distinct authority who organized his men into a standing army with imperial ambitions. Ever-increasing growth was a large part of the equation. It had limits within a confined economy. To increase the base economy, compound interest was to be applied to geography as an ever-expanding territory. Conquest of neighbors ensued.

Naturally, this did not sit well with the civilian powerbrokers in the temple who were now subservient to their own guards. We can actually read about this from the cuneiform stylus of an eyewitness.

Lagash was one of Uruk's protégé cities. By 2500 BCE, it was wealthy and powerful in its own right and had a full-on king—it was a post-coup society, but not by many years.

Helpfully, the social environment in Lagash was preserved in frank detail by one of the local scribes, whose chronicle opens a window upon the tension between the competing power bases of temple and palace. Samuel Noah Kramer is rhapsodic about this scribe's work because it contains history's first written instance of the word "freedom."[32] A freshly minted idea, which it seems could only be necessitated by a lack of it.

The word appears in a report about a short-lived reform effort that followed a wave of excessive abuses by the king, "most of which could be traced to a ubiquitous and obnoxious bureaucracy consisting of the ruler and his palace coterie; at the same time, it provides a grim and ominous picture of man's cruelty toward man," writes the normally staid professor Kramer.

He continues, "we may surmise that they were the direct result of the political and economic forces unloosed by the drive for power which characterized the ruling dynasty... Smitten with grandiose ambitions for themselves and their state, some of the rulers resorted to imperialistic wars and bloody conquests."

For "grandiose ambitions," "drive for power," and "economic forces," we can simply read "greed": the economic theory of endless growth and increasing wants—including compound interest.

To increase his economic base, the king wanted more land, greater natural resources, and slaves. This required a proper war, for which Lagash and its king, Ur-Nanshe, earn the distinction of executing the "first war for which there is any detailed evidence."[33] Yes, the first proper war between sovereign states. Marvelous.

To get the party started, the king had to conscript and pay professional soldiers, manufacture weapons, and provision his troops. Kramer summarizes the scribe's report, which details the essential steps:

> The rulers found it necessary to infringe on the personal rights of the individual citizen, to tax his wealth and property to the limit, and to appropriate, as well, property belonging to the temple. Once introduced, the palace

coterie showed itself most unwilling to relinquish the domestic controls, even in times of peace, for they had proved highly profitable.

Sound familiar? It could easily be a summary of the post–Second World War United States, with Eisenhower's famous military-industrial complex:

Our toil, resources and livelihood are all involved; so is the very structure of our society. In the councils of government, we must guard against the acquisition of unwarranted influence, whether sought or unsought, by the military-industrial complex. The potential for the disastrous rise of misplaced power exists, and will persist.

Kramer notes there is "a bitter struggle for power between the temple and the palace—the 'church' and the 'state'—with the citizens of Lagash taking the side of the temple."

The king, however, was not about to back down. He and his men, employing state-of-the-art accounting methods, transformed taxation into life-long torture. Every action, such as a perfumer mixing a formula or a shepherd shearing his sheep, was taxed upon every instance. One could hardly go to the toilet without incurring a tax which, if not paid, accrued punishing levels of interest. Repossessions ensued. According to our scribe, the abuses included seizure of property, donkeys, sheep, and fisheries.

Kramer was the first to read this scribe's words in the 6,000 years since he wedged them into clay. But how familiar this all sounds!

Even death brought no relief from levies and taxes. When a dead man was brought to the cemetery for burial... quite a number of officials and parasites made it their business to be on hand to relieve the bereaved family of quantities of barley, bread, and date wine, and various furnishings. From one end of the state to the other, our venerable reporter observes bitterly, "there were the tax collectors."

On top of that, there were instances of plain cruelty:

Blind men—presumably, prisoners of war and slaves who had been blinded in order to prevent them from attempting to escape—were seized and put to watering the fields like animals and were given only enough food to keep them alive. The rich, "the big men" and the supervisors, were getting richer and richer at the expense of the less fortunate citizens... by forcing them to sell their donkeys and houses at low prices and against their will. The indigent, the poor, the orphaned, and the widowed were mistreated and deprived in one way or another of what little they had by men of power and influence.

This is turning out to be a very poor emulation of Paradise. I'll leave it to professor Robert N. Bellah to summarize the state of the Cosmic Order in 2500 BCE, by which time it has matured fully:

In ancient Mesopotamia the idea of the state organized the life of both gods and humans and the relation between them. The reality of archaic civilization was centralization of political power, class stratification, the magnification of military power, the economic exploitation of the weak, and the universal introduction of some form of forced labor for both productive and military purposes.[34]

It is a bleak picture, but a counter-movement was not far off. It will appear to the north, appropriately just a few miles from Göbekli Tepe, where a man, also looking at the heavens, had an epiphany. He realized that the hypostatized Cosmic Order was false and uncannily recognized a genuine big Other: Reality Itself. He saw only a glimpse of the Real, just a taste, but that was enough to give him the faith to turn his back on "how things are" and to set out on a completely untried path back to Paradise.

※   7   ※

COUNTERCULTURE

History's First Woman

Storage. This is surely the vortex around which the story of civilization swirls. Store up enough of whatever makes you feel secure, and all is well. Money, love, distractions, tangible things, and—in the Internet Age—immaterial things stockpiled to occupy the empty time that weighs so heavily upon us. It's a sound plan within limits. But as a guarantor of real security, it is a false and seductive idol, vaporous and meaningless.

In Uruk and Lugash, the burgeoning state came to own everything because it promised to store and equitably distribute life's essentials. Pitifully, in those days this meant grain, something that was nothing but a curiosity to the faithful at Göbekli Tepe.

As the plight of Lugash showed us, however, those who controlled the stash of grain always wanted more. It let them control others whose access to wheat, barley, and beer was the only connection of life's thread from one day to the next. There was never *enough* security—not for the poor and not for their masters. Needs were no longer necessities; the new mind without exception imagined it needed more. As Marshall Sahlins observed of the hunter-gatherers he studied, human needs are finite and few; poverty is the invention of civilization, an escalation of imagined necessities, an induced sense of scarcity that is fundamentally unnatural.

Unnatural and not quite rational: this is not unlike that sad woman on my kibbutz, whose acquisitiveness bore no relation to her actual life. Or like me,

148

so incredibly fretful as a child that I was taken to a neurologist to check for brain damage. The doctors diagnosed anxiety. But why? I wasn't starving, no one threatened my life. "He's just an anxious little boy." That's what the doctors said. I hated the word. And I loathed the doctors for chalking it up to nature when I knew it was not natural for anyone. There was emotional trauma, to be sure, but my response was irrational, having been trained by culture to seek relief in exactly the wrong way.

"Do not be anxious about your life, what you will eat or what you will drink, nor about your body, what you will put on... Which of you by being anxious can add a single hour to his span of life? Therefore do not be anxious about tomorrow." Here was Jesus using my hated word in a way that didn't fit our universe. What universe did he speak of, in that case? And then there was this instruction, entirely incompatible with any plan for real-world security: "Do not lay up for yourselves treasures on earth, where moth and rust destroy and where thieves break in and steal, but lay up for yourselves treasures in heaven..." I knew then that we were all anxious—the heavily entreasured neurologist perhaps most of all.

At that age, not yet fully trained in the ways of the world, I didn't really think about treasure or food, although we were very poor. For me it was love and home and recognition. I'd lost all that. The little girl who had lived next to us was exactly my age, my twin in every way but blood. When it all went to hell at age six, we suddenly moved and I lost her. That loss encapsulated all others as everyone else's difficulties made mine invisible. To cope, I dreamed of a new Eden, just me and my girl. It was an anxiety not of grain but of love, harder to deal with because less quantifiable, but that would not stop me from trying to load up a storehouse of it.

The first time I read Jesus talking about worry, it spoke to me of Adam and Eve's alienation in the Garden of Eden—a trauma of love and loss and the start of sweat-of-brow anxiety. It was intuitively clear that they were connected. It's taken the rest of my life to even begin to come to terms with what it means. I still struggle with the revelation, grasping at things and relationships, hooked on the metaphorical drugs that never satisfy, the security that does not exist in the material world. Jesus said it: Today is as long as any security will last, and one day, even that day's value won't hold. Real security must be founded on something that does not perish.

Storage. Laying up treasure. *Grasping*.

Considering the first city-states in civilization, we need to understand nothing more than a mad compulsion for un-satiated acquisition. Militarization. Taxation. Endless growth. Exploitation. Enslavement. Civilization was founded upon fear, its appetite rapacious. The solution, I believe, is somewhere in the experience of the kibbutz woman's generous and gentle counterpart, but we are a long way from exploring that part of the story.

From where we sit in Uruk, civilization is "progressing" rapidly into anxious empire. We could write volumes on just that, but to keep things brief, I am going to use a cryptic term that summarizes a complex history: "Babylon." This, too, comes from reading the Bible, as both testaments use it as a shorthand, a catch-all term for the various expressions of Eridu's legacy.

It is still widely used—ubiquitous as a metaphor in popular culture. (A quick search of the iWeb English corpus shows 48,000 occurrences, while the thriving metropolis of Istanbul comes in with just 46,000 mentions.) As a teenager, I heard evangelical preachers invoke it for everything from secular humanism to the Soviet Union to the Catholic Church. I'll explain more about that a little later, as we approach what drove me and my Muslim Brothers in our mad pursuits. Indeed, there will be points where our personal stories and Babylon's merge with a cast of characters including Christopher Columbus and Bob Dylan, all meaningless if we don't understand Babylon circa 3000 BCE.

To that end, we can turn to Sargon the Great, the most notable leader of the First Babylonian Empire. He and his daughter Enheduanna personify everything we need to know and, not coincidentally, they relate directly to this chapter's focus: the man who will dissent from the Cosmic Order's ideals and show us a different way of seeing the world.

Like many of the "greats," Sargon began his life inauspiciously. He lived in Kish, one of a dozen Uruk-patterned Sumerian city-states, where he was a city gardener and later cupbearer to the king.

While being a cupbearer is a trusted position, it does not portend greatness. How did he make the leap? Herein lies a fascinating tale, told in a fragmented tablet that says the king asked Sargon into his chambers to discuss a terrifying dream: an apparition of Inanna, who'd come in bristling warrior-mode, threatening to drown the monarch—for what cause, we do not know.

You may ask, why call the cupbearer for that? The answer, we suppose, is simply that the king needed a stiff drink. (I certainly have after similar nightmares.) The next thing we know (there is a gap in the text) is that Sargon is king and Akkad is his capital. We have no idea what happened in between, except that Sargon devoted himself to Inanna for the rest of his life. I imagine the old king drowned after all, and whether it had to do with something Sargon gave him to drink, we may never know. (Wink and nod!)

Sargon soon took the king of Uruk captive. He had to have Uruk; this was Inanna's hometown, and he believed his conquest to be part of her original plan for heavenly hegemony. In practice, it helped that control of Uruk gave him all the first city's important vassal states, as well. In short, Sargon and Inanna were a good match. In the words of Mesopotamia authority Paul Kriwaczek, "Her composite powers over war and love, fighting and procreation, aggression and lust, made her the 'adrenaline goddess,' deity of fight, flight and frolic, the perfect heavenly dominatrix and protectress for a Bronze Age warrior hero."[1]

Fueled by Inanna's adrenaline, Sargon united all of Mesopotamia's city-states under a single authority, and within a decade "extended his conquests from the Persian Gulf to the Mediterranean Sea and northeastward to the Taurus Mountains of Turkey."[2] Not an easy task. The United States has struggled for thirty years now to control a fraction of that same Middle Eastern territory and still can't pull it off.

And like the United States, Sargon required an ideological justification for these expansive and expensive campaigns. He needed home-crowd support for his ventures, and some means to win over the newly conquered peoples. For us today, it is "nation-building democracy" or "self-determination" or "ridding the world of an evil dictator." For Sargon, it was simply an invocation of the Cosmic Order's promises: the gods willed these wars and willed the peoples of the world to come under Babylon's rule. *This is how things should be.* Those who resisted would know unbearable suffering but those who submitted would reap rewards! Just join the coalition and prosper! But to sell that message he needed the help of a writer.

What Sargon got was a true evangelist, one of the most influential writers of all time and the world's earliest known author. That's an epic milestone; before Sargon's time, writers composed lists, kept very good accounts, and wrote many stories about the gods and the order of things. But they were always unsigned. They have no presence in their stories.

That changed forever as Sargon's daughter Enheduanna picked up the stylus. She not only signed her name but frequently (and compellingly) wrote about herself. Her signature broke another barrier, too—she is the very first woman to be remembered by name.[3]

Sargon appointed her high priestess at the moon god's temple in Ur, where it fell to her to create popular works of religion to undergird the empire's heavenly authority. She proved to be a genius. Writing touchingly personal hymns, psalms, and prayers, she made readers feel her pleas were theirs, that these were their supplications and cries of praise. Her gift was to draw the hearts of the conquered masses into the unity of the empire.

I cannot over-emphasize her influence or importance, which is directly apparent in the Bible's Psalms. To this day, her voice continues to resound in that literature, echoing through church and synagogue services the world over. We hear it also in love songs and Shakespearean verse, in powerful speeches and eloquent poems. She completely changed the way we use written language and tell stories.

Why did Sargon rely on her? His objective was to solidify ideological unity between all the peoples he would conquer. His daughter's empathetic, Billy Graham-like style was just what the empire needed, critical to making the big Other a benevolent presence in the reader's life. It was a "my personal savior" approach to propaganda, with the Cosmic Order featuring as Jesus Christ.

I wonder how and when Sargon realized what she was able to do. Did he recognize her gift before appointing her to the priesthood? Or, genius that she was, did she rise to the enormous occasion, a stroke of tremendous fortune for Sargon and his successors—not to mention King David, Homer, and Shakespeare?

Of her body of work, the temple hymns stand out as the most effective. They are forty-five psalms that serve as a systematic liturgy, which is another first in history. Systemization and uniformity were important to the empire, and her prayer book made that possible. It's still the model: from Anglicanism to Maoism, there is no substitute for having your people read from the same page. She invented that.

So it was that with his daughter's help, Sargon expanded the united domain of the Cosmic Order to unprecedented dimensions. It took more than religion, however. Conquest required an unprecedented use of military muscle. Richard Gabriel cites Sargon's reign as a milestone in the development of war: "The period of interest for the student of military history is that from 3000 to 2316 B.C., the date that Sargon the Great united all of Sumer into a single state."[4]

In that 700-year period, the modern army was perfected. Sargon's armed forces numbered over 5,000 professional soldiers at a time when the global population was fewer than 30 million (that would be equivalent to 116 *million* soldiers today). They were outfitted with state-of-the art armaments and tactics. "The armies of Sumer and Akkad represented the pinnacle of military development in the Bronze Age," writes Gabriel; "no army of the same period could match the Sumerians in military effectiveness and weaponry.

The Sumerian civilization produced no fewer than six major new weapons and defensive systems... Few armies in history have been so innovative."[5] Sargon's innovations included the composite bow, which armies would use for thousands of years, and widespread use of the awful sickle-sword, an invention of particular interest to Bible students: "The sickle-sword became the primary infantry weapon of the Egyptian and Biblical armies at a much later date. When the Bible speaks of people being smoted, the reference is precisely to the sickle-sword."

In the end, the only thing that could dent his achievements was a natural disaster. In epic style, the end of Sargon's rule coincides with the "4.2 kilo-year event." It was plausibly due to a massive comet—probably comet Encke—that broke up, bombing the planet with a series of cataclysmic chunks. (This may explain the disproportionate depiction of comets in early literature and the ancient preoccupation with fire and brimstone.)

This was the worst climate disaster since *Homo sapiens* began to settle down, creating a century-long drought and a political crisis. Even so, Sargon's Akkadian empire did not so much collapse as simply change hands. The Cosmic Order remained intact: the trade routes, military technologies, and the fundamental principles of hierarchy remained in force wherever Sargon had spread it. With nature going to hell, Enheduanna's systematic theology of salvation kept devotion to the Cosmic Order at a high pitch.

Indeed, belief in the Sumerian gods did not shrink with the demise of Sargon's personal empire—it *became* the empire. The language of the temple—the voice of Enheduanna—ensured the cohesive rule of the Cosmic Order no matter who sat on the throne. It was unassailable. The only successful challenge would come from a devoted insider.

Iconoclast

He was from Harran, the most important city of Enheduanna's moon god, Sîn. It belonged to a fraternity of moon-god cities, including of course Ur, where Sargon's daughter founded her publishing house. Both cities appear in the Bible, linked to our man, Abraham, and both gained fabulous wealth as hubs on the world's greatest trade route.

The moon-god cult is important to this history. We see Abraham's connection to it through the names of his father, Terah, and his wife, Sarai, and the names of his relatives, Nahor and Milcah, all of which signify devotion to the moon god of Harran and Ur. Though these names are obscure to us, they made Abraham's fealty to the empire crystal clear to antiquity's readers. It was a pedigree establishing Abraham as fully compliant with the established worldview and as worshiper of its gods.

He is familiar to Christians, Jews, and Muslims, but as with many figures from Sunday school, our memory might be skewed by Sunday school illustrations of him as a desert nomad. This has nothing to do with the life he was bred to live—Abraham was a man of the city.

This is something that Joshua, his direct descendant, made very clear. Speaking at the inauguration of the Mosaic Jewish religion when the Israelites crossed into the Promised Land, Joshua reminded his people of the facts: "Long ago your ancestors—Terah and his sons Abraham and Nahor—lived beyond the Euphrates and served other gods."[6] Indeed, Genesis 11, which introduces them, tells only two stories: the Tower of Babel and the business life of Abraham's family along the Babylonian trade route. In other words, the Bible's authors emphatically connect the advent of civilization and the lifestyle of Abraham.

So, before we turn to the nature of Abraham's pending dissent, we should learn a little bit more about his context, the life that led up to his profound decision to turn his back on all he thought to be true.

We will begin with the biblical account: "Terah was the father of Abram, Nahor, and Haran... Terah took his son Abram... and his daughter-in-law Sarai... and they went out together from Ur of the Chaldeans to go into the land of Canaan; but when they came to Haran, they settled there."[7]

Historical? Not exactly. The Hebrew scribes immediately and openly lead us to an anachronism. Referring to "Ur of Chaldeans" puts Abraham much later, in the time of his descendants, the late kings of Judah. It's not terribly important, as Ur and Harran persisted for many centuries, so to mention the Chaldeans is simply to point to a map contemporary with readers in a later Babylonian dynasty (much as if I were to say, "Ur is in Iraq"). To be clear, it's understood that Abraham lived in much earlier times, during the First Babylonian Empire of Sargon.

But the anachronism also reveals an editor's hand in the story. Abraham's history as an actual person is not the message. Instead, it is about something that happened, possibly a whole movement of dissent. Why, then, talk about Abraham? Because it's simply easier to tell and remember the history as the biography of one archetypal man.

To really understand the meaning of Abraham we must understand his city. Harran (biblical Haran) lies just beyond the eastern banks of the upper reaches of the Euphrates River. I sat there recently—I frequently do—beside my friend Ali, the headman in this ancient place. The antiquities in Harran are enormous and still being excavated, but as a modern town, there's not much to it—just a dusty, ramshackle village with oddly shaped conical houses.

In a stroke of brilliance, Ali took one of the ancient-style houses and opened it to the public. He does quite well for himself. With Çatalhöyük, Göbekli Tepe, Hacılar, and Tell Zeidan all within a few hours' distance, I had to smile at what he had done. This was a history house, and it worked: it really did make me feel connected to the age of Abraham.

Ali passed on a few illicit coins (when it rains here, ancient artifacts bubble up out of the ground), and then entertained us by making up songs about me and the women I was traveling with. Over a cup of nearly toxic coffee, inspired by Ali—an iconoclast in his own right—I pondered Abraham and his geography.

The first thing on my mind was his paternal home. Babylonian Ur is in Iraq, 1,000 kilometers from Harran as the crow flies, but it's that distance which brings them into proximity; any nomad or traveler who meant to avoid dying in the desert was funneled to where Harran sits, which is why powerful Ur established Harran as its outpost, making it the hub for ancient trade routes connecting the Mediterranean coastal cities to Babylonia.

If we look in the other direction, turning southwest, we find Canaan on the far extremities of these trade routes. Canaan's capital city, Hazor, is familiar to Bible readers as the only city Joshua was commanded to burn, a particular vengeance born from his ancestor Terah's illicit connection with this city's god. Hazor was fraternally linked with Ur and Harran, all three sharing a devotion to Enheduanna's moon god, Sîn.

Recall that Abraham's father, Terah, was himself on his way from "Ur of the Chaldeans to go into the land of Canaan" but settled at least for some time "when they came to Haran." The Bible thus presents Abraham's dad as a stereotype of the rich Babylonian trader, whose thick rolodex of contacts was built around familial and fraternal connections—in his case, the moon-god cult of these three cities.

This makes historical sense. Commentators as diverse as the prophet Ezekiel and the Roman historian Marcellinus have remarked on Harran's importance to trade as well as the wealth and luxury enjoyed by its citizens. It was wealth acquired as the middleman between the equally rich anchor cities to the east and west, between Ur and Hazor. (Incidentally, Harran happened to be the name of Abraham's deceased brother, underscoring their clan's connection to the place. They most likely originally hailed from here.)

Moving now southeast on the trade route back toward Ur, we come to another critically important city, Mari, a purpose-built gateway city marking Sumeria's entrance and exit. Like most of the sites we've visited, it was only recently found. (Mari was unearthed in 1933, Uruk in 1912, and Çatalhöyük in 1958.) The excavation of Mari yielded a trove of more than 20,000 cuneiform documents, the secrets of which Professor Abraham Malamat spent a lifetime interpreting. They have opened a heretofore shut window on Abraham's world.

Intriguingly, Professor Malamat finds links between the language of the scribes at Mari and the language of the Hebrew Bible. Perhaps most telling are instances of the names Abram (Abraham), Benjamin, Jacob, and Ishmael; this is notable not just because they appear in the Bible, but because they are otherwise obscure, previously thought to be unique to the Israelites. That such low-frequency names would occur both in the Bible and in Mari texts indicates a genuine historical connection between the ancestors of Israel and the people who lived around Harran in deep antiquity. As does the language they share; although the empire's official scribal language was Akkadian, the Mari scribes wrote in their own folksy West Semitic dialect, often recording idioms that likewise appear in biblical Hebrew and nowhere else.

The documents unearthed from Mari certainly help us place the patriarch in a specific context. The Israelites' memory of descent from Western Semites beyond the Euphrates appears to find validation. "Old Babylonian Mari, along with early Israel and many other peoples of the [Semitic] West, did apparently share common origins," Malamat concludes. The biblical text uses "telescoping," a literary device by which, "a lengthy series of events is adjusted and simplified into... a severely foreshortened timespan"; Malamat, however, assures us that such devices do not negate "the very essence of the Patriarchs."[8]

To the contrary, these geographical and linguistic clues—supported powerfully by the archeology at Mari—put Abraham's life in a very specific place and time. In a 2001 interview, Malamat went so far as to tell Tad Szulc that the patriarch most likely lived between 2000 and 1800 BCE: "The Bible and the entire body of ancient Israelite history make this the most plausible time frame."[9]

I find it touching and somehow significant that Szulc—the Polish-born biographer of Fidel Castro and Pope John Paul II, the investigator who broke the Bay of Pigs story, and the man whose CIA file described him as "an aggressive, insensitive and persistent journalist"—wrote his last investigative piece on Abraham. He knew this would be his last story: Szulc was diagnosed with terminal cancer before he undertook this journey to retrace

Abraham's steps. Professor Malamat in Jerusalem was his last stop. He died soon after this interview.[10]

It seems from all this that, even without a birth certificate, we can accurately profile Abraham: He was a Western Semite of the Old Babylonian period. He lived soon after Sargon the Great's Akkadian empire extended the Cosmic Order across the known world. We can even get a pretty good idea of what he looked like: he probably wore a puffy woolen cap, its dark black material the same color as his hair. He is slim and tanned.

My description assumes that Abraham resembled another Western Semite of this time, one whose image is preserved in a detailed portrait at Mari. In that image, Abraham's kinsman leads a bull, most likely for sacrifice. His beard and facial features remind me of ISIS devotees I've met, but their beards are not trimmed as his is. (Incidentally, as of this writing, Mari is still under ISIS control.) Furthermore, Abraham's cousin has almond-shaped eyes and appears to be using eyeliner—an affectation of which ISIS would not approve.

The image is printed in Malamat's scholarly work on Mari, published for the British Academy. He notes, "The figure seems to reflect the general appearance of the West Semitics at this time, and this is how we might envisage the Patriarchs of the Bible as well."[11]

When Szulc visited him in Jerusalem, Malamat was forthright: "This picture in my opinion, comes close to Abraham. Maybe he's a concept, but his figure makes sense. There are pictures on the Mari walls, figures that may be close to Abraham, Isaac, and Jacob."[12]

Malamat describes other paintings, too: "we see a fenced park with idealized, sacred trees beautiful to behold... and guarded by cherubs." This is very much the picture conjured in Genesis 3:24—the Garden of Eden's entrance watched by angels with flaming swords.

In the same panel appears the king before a goddess. She is Inanna, known in these parts as Ishtar. The goddess presides over this paradise-like scene, which also includes "two mirror image figures, each holding a vase from which four streams of water are emerging—reminiscent of the four rivers of Paradise, in the Bible, flowing forth from a single source."[13]

So here is Paradise as described by Genesis, pictured in the power center of a major Mesopotamian city, painted beside a tableau of its king bowed before Inanna, the purveyor of civilization and daughter of none other than Harran's moon god, Sîn. Around the corner stands Abraham's cousin, leading an expensive bull to sacrifice.

That juxtaposition sets the archetype of Abraham in a legitimate context, a Western Semite trader at the height of the Cosmic Order's empire. Accordingly, in Genesis he appears just after the Tower of Babel, the symbolic start of civilization. He is there as if at a point of decision: What will you choose, the empire of delusions or the reality of Paradise?

Insanity

As Sargon's dynastic confederates began to lose their grip, it was the once-nomadic Amorites—the Western Semites, pictured so clearly in their wool caps at Mari—who entered city life with a vengeance, quickly displacing their eastern Akkadian kin from positions of power. It didn't matter so much who was in political control—the rising plutocracy called the shots.

It is tempting to say that they took over the empire, but it is truer to say that the culture of empire took them over. The *Me* transformed these free spirits into civilized loyalists who worshiped the same gods and told the same stories that were birthed in Uruk. Enheduanna's hymns became their creed, with special affection for Inanna and Sîn.

Eventually they reconstituted a compact version of Sargon's dominions under Hammurabi, the Babylonian ruler now so famous for his code of law. It was under this iteration of Mesopotamian culture that legendary Abraham's full biography is to be imagined.

As we've learned, Abraham was one of these Westerners and a member the moon-god cult's business fraternity. Even today, he would immediately recognize the stylized crescent moon that was Sîn's emblem, for it remained ubiquitous through another group of Western Semites, the Arabs of the Ḥijāz, who adopted it as the emblem of Islam—a religion which, not coincidently, claims Abraham as its father.

The Bible emphasizes the vastness of the patriarch's storehouse, in keeping with his Amorite trader profile. He was "very rich in livestock, in silver, and in gold," says Genesis. Rabbinical scholarship stresses the same point; Rashi, for example, explains that the word used for "rich" in this Genesis passage is something special—not ordinary rich, but mega-rich.[14] The Hebrew word is *kaved*, meaning "heavy." Abraham was "*kaved* in cattle, silver, and gold."

When I was a young kibbutznik, I knew the word as a warning: "Hey, be careful, that thing is *kaved!*" Or as a way to give someone props: "*kol ha-kavod!*"—literally meaning "all honor," but colloquially meaning something like, "right on!" or "way to go!" It might even be herbaceously inspired:

"Whoa, that's *kaved*, man!" But in Genesis, it means that Abraham was laden with cattle, silver, and gold—weighted down with the stuff—and also very respected. He was a heavyweight. He wasn't just regular rich, he was heavy-duty rich. Abraham may therefore appear to be an unlikely candidate for dissent, but upon reflection, it makes perfect sense.

Our sociologist guides show us how this works. Peter L. Berger and Thomas Luckmann explained to us the process of reification—how humans became masters of nature by representing it symbolically through language and concepts, and how everyday reality is a human construction. But they also explained how, having come to regard as nature that which is not nature, we forgot that this everyday reality was of our own making.

For most living in Sargon's age, real was whatever the rulers said was real. If they said a piece of stone was the earthly form of a god seen in the night sky, you believed it. Even today, we believe many things not because we can prove them, but because we were taught them at school. The freedom-scribe's lament at Lugash shows how unpleasant and sickening that reality was for common people—Leviathan had created a universe that was brutish, nasty, impoverished, and short-lived.

There was a simple antidote to this. The malleability of consciousness that made that universe possible also provides a means of escape: "Different objects present themselves to consciousness as constituents of different spheres of reality," write Berger and Luckmann; "consciousness, then, is capable of moving through different spheres of reality."[15]

Thankfully, they give a practical illustration: "As I move from one reality to another, I experience the transition as a kind of shock. Waking up from a dream illustrates this shift most simply."

When we sleep, our dreams are as real as anything. Then we wake up and they do not seem real at all. For example, not many centuries ago most everyone lived in a dream where the sun revolved around the earth. Then we woke up and saw that the opposite was true.

So, all Abraham's peers had to do was wake up from this Mesopotamian fever dream and all would be transformed.

Is that really possible?

I think it is, but it requires us to accept that knowledge outside the framework of "things as they are" is possible. At a minimum, it means simply remembering that we live in a constructed reality. Just knowing this constitutes an awakening.

The sociologists talk about constructed realities as societal programming. "What is taken for granted as knowledge" they say, are in fact "'programs'...

in which externalization produces an objective world... apprehended as reality."[16]

For example, the idea that the sun circled the earth was programmed into us. The certainty of any cult is programmed into its adherents. Smoking will sooth your T-zone, said the doctor on television in one decade; in the next, he says it will kill you. Programming.

If it is programming, it can certainly be deleted and re-written, just as these examples were. The "objects to be apprehended as reality" can be questioned, criticized, and reordered. It's as easy and as hard as that.

Just realizing that the perceived order is a construction demystifies it and takes away its absolute authority—we understand that it isn't like the law of gravity, so we don't have to obey it. That's the easy part. The difficulty is in staying awake moment by moment and situation by situation. It takes a measure of spiritual discipline that few have the resolve to undertake; we are lazy, and a dreamy sleep is easy.

Our man of dissent shows what's possible. It was he who awoke to eschew the "objects apprehended as reality" by Uruk's cosmology. This man of dissent awoke as if from a dream.

How did it happen? In the Bible's account, he starts hearing voices!

Of course he did. And in typical Genesis style, the account is terse: "Now the LORD said to Abram, 'Go from your country and your kindred and your father's house to the land that I will show you... So Abram went, as the Lord had told him... Abram was seventy-five years old when he departed from Haran."

What does it mean when a man of extraordinary wealth and urbanity claims to hear a voice commanding him to leave it all behind? Was he insane?

At first glance, it may look like Abraham was following in his father's footsteps. Dad had been an international business traveler, after all—departures and long sojourns were nothing new to this clan. The key difference is that when we met the family, father Terah knew exactly where they were going; they knew for what purpose they traveled (storing up wealth); and they knew to whom their allegiance belonged (the Babylonian moon-god fraternity). Terah's itinerary was a well-worn path from Ur to Canaanite Hazor and part of business as usual between the three sister cities.

Abraham's commission was the opposite: he had to set out in the name of an unknown god who had no association with anything in the constructed reality of Babylon. This was the LORD, or YHWH, whom we will learn about a few pages hence. "Go-you-forth from your land," said the voice of

YHWH, "from your kindred, from your father's house, to the land that I will let you see."[17]

This is systematic deprogramming. It's all about coming out, undoing, and letting go of certainty to enter something unknown and as yet unseen: "the land I will let you see."

Let's break down the vocabulary. When Abraham heard the command to leave his "land," he heard *eretz*, meaning "territory" or "country." A modern example shows what it means: the State of Israel is *Eretz Yisrael*. This, then, is about political identity; he would be leaving his country, his citizenship.

He would also have to leave his kindred, or *môledeth*—his people, his culture. There is more. He must leave the *bayt* or "house" of his father, which of course is the same word as "temple" and carries with it all the weighty spiritual issues associated with the ancestral dwelling. He would leave behind his ethos, his framework of reality, including this all-important *house*. It was no easy ask.

Muslims, Christians, and Jews see this as a great act of faith, reflected in the words of the New Testament, which recalls that Abraham went forth "not knowing whither he went."[18] Henceforth he would pass from place to place on a day-by-day basis, harkening to a voice not connected to any conventionally known support structure—economic, legal, or social. Each day was built on faith alone. He refers to himself as a stranger and wanderer.[19] At seventy-five years of age, he had no itinerary, no destination, and crucially, no return ticket.

Was there any clue that this might happen? The Bible doesn't elaborate on Abraham's first seventy-five years, but the Jewish sages recount that he was raised in Ur, where his father sold household idols and images.[20]

Of young Abraham, Rambam writes that as a child "his mind began to explore day and night without rest." Although "mired in Ur of the Chaldeans among foolish idolaters, his father and mother and all the people worshipping idols," he eventually "arrived at the way of truth and understood through his own correct reasoning... and he knew that the entire world was making a mistake and what caused them to err was their subservience to the stars and images, which caused them to lose their grasp of the truth."[21]

I love that line: "וַיֵּדַע שֶׁכָּל הָעוֹלָם טוֹעִים"; "and he knew that the entire world was making a mistake."

Rambam's synopsis is rich, well worth spending some time pondering for yourself. Until then, I can summarize: He says Abraham worshiped the heavenly host with his parents, stuck in the established order as was everyone else. But then, by rigorously paying attention and taking nothing for granted, he realized that the world was lost in a fantasy. He observed carefully and he simply opened his eyes and woke up.

The sages also believed that young Abraham tried to talk customers out of buying his father's idols. At times, he became violent and smashed the images. He was literally an iconoclast and not a little antisocial in that he was demonstrably against the socially constructed reality. One wonders how different the world would be had Abraham's parents given him Ritalin.

So, was he insane or the only sane person around? I suppose we have to take into consideration these reports that Abraham heard voices. We can't get around that; throughout his life, he heard and obeyed a voice that only he could hear. Was he schizophrenic? Jaynes' theory of the evolution of consciousness marks Abraham as a bicameral man. If he was a real person, maybe he was a throwback. Otherwise, he is a memory of how things used to be. In an age when the commanding voice belonged indisputably to the big Other, Abraham's ear was tuned to a different frequency.

Historically, he at the very least stands for any number of people living at that time who were also tuned to this special frequency. But my guess is that his hearing of voices is not poetic license. Neither is it outlandish to believe that Abraham is based upon some real person or small group of people who really heard this voice and defied the status quo ante of Eridu's unhappy universe.

Politically Incorrect

Abraham gives us hope; if a man of the system can pass from Uruk's sphere of reality into an awakened state, then so can we. What idols would Abraham find among us that he would smash? I'm sure he would point out many under the category of "that's just how things are." This was his talent: where others saw proof of the status quo, Abraham saw absurdity.

Through these traditional stories, full of detailed cultural context, we come to appreciate Abraham as a true scientist of Reality. Abraham, we might say, was a Buddhist: he wanted to see things as they are. But to what end?

The voice tells us:

"I will make a great nation of you and I will give-you-blessing and will make your name great. Be a blessing! I will bless those who bless you, he who reviles you, I will curse. All the clans of the soil will find blessing through you!"[22]

These instructions make an extraordinary claim, coming straight after

Babel's one language and nation was scattered, creating a plentitude of nations and ethnicities. No sooner have the nations been divided than Abraham gets this commission to become a nation that as yet does not exist, by a God that no one has heard of. Whatever that nation is, it is meant to inject a nebulous something called "blessing" into the system, an antidote to the Sumerian virus.

We hear the Hebrew word *goy* in this brief passage, which is translated as "nation." It is one of the few Hebrew words, like *shalom*, that is familiar to Western ears. You have probably heard it; a cranky old American Jew in a film makes a remark about "the *goy*," or "*goyim*" if there are more than one. If you hear a Jew say that, it means "the Gentiles" or everyone who is not a Jew. But Abraham—the father of the Jews—hears the voice say that his future nation is a *goy*,; Israel, too, is of the *goyim*.

This is Abraham's destiny and his destination. But it is not as an adversary to the nations of Babel, not as a curse or scourge that he is called. To the contrary, it is as a blessing to them. The idea is to become a priestly nation and a light to the others, to speak to the nations of the world through the progeny of the man who can still hear the voice of Paradise.

That kind of exceptionalism is perhaps politically incorrect. For progressive Christians and Jews, it is particularly delicate; we want to have moved past this regressive idea of a special people. And yet it is Judeo-Christian ethics that allow us to become progressive in the first place.

Our progressive roots spread in Jewish philosophical soil. If not for this, there would be no humanism—let alone the religion of Christianity that, for its many faults, is the foundation of modern liberal ideas. Neither would there be Islam—the great force of equality in the Near East for over millennium. My advice for now: Don't reject what the Hebrew tradition can teach us because it claimed to be exceptional. And be honest about your own exceptionalist attitudes.

Let's get this straight: it is patently absurd for progressives to pretend that they do not think of themselves as special. Who are we kidding? Who doesn't think that their liberalism or conservatism, socialism or capitalism, has the most reasonable solutions to the world's problems? Don't you think you can be a blessing? Of course you do! So let the Jews be a blessing! Equality is not equity. In any family, there are roles and separate gifts; the equality comes from love and respect, not from identical characteristics, qualities, and skills. If my brother is a doctor, I'm glad he will bless me with what I could not do for myself.

I'll note, however, that even the rabbinic sages comment on this; it troubled them that the idea of Abraham's nation of blessing might be misconstrued for purposes of ethnic chauvinism. In 1140 CE, Rabbi Yehuda Halevi asked the question, "Would it not have been better had God given His approval to all men alike?"[23] The answer given was a commentary on the words of the Israelite prophet Jeremiah, which presents an ethical justification for being special: "We would have healed Babylon, but she was not healed."[24]

His argument is that Babylon needed the Jewish doctor's help. It was sick, incapacitated, hallucinatory. The only solution was to inject a cure. And Abraham stands for exactly that. He is a brother; he is a citizen of Mesopotamia, carrying the antibodies that can cure the infection. Brother Abraham and the nation to come from him have a healing service to perform. Only a bigoted fool would reject the vaccine because it comes from a Jew.

That settled, let's move along: "When the Most High apportioned the nations, when he divided humankind, he fixed the boundaries of the peoples according to the number of the gods; the LORD'S own portion was his people, Jacob his allotted share."[25]

Upon first reading, this Hebrew line comes off like an unsophisticated relic, something that the Bible's editors missed while proofreading. (Indeed, it was re-written and nearly lost to us, saved by the confirming text of the Dead Sea Scrolls!) Now, after decades of contemplation, I've come to think of this as a profound insight. It not only brings helpful clarity to the Jew-Gentile equation, it shows us to what extent the Hebrew mind understood the fallacies of Mesopotamian dogma.

What is the writer talking about? Apparently at the Tower of Babel, when one language and nation was divided into many, each nation was shared out "according to the number of the gods." Primitive foolishness, it might seem, until we remember that cultures and identities are ruled by ideas, and that culture is every bit as powerful as gods were thought to be. Ideas give life and take it away, they enrich and impoverish.

Looking past the archaic nomenclature, we can see a striking sociological vision in this ancient line of Hebrew: the gods represent named archetypes of consciousness, the monikers by which identities, affiliations, and cultures are categorized. Revisiting our discussion of "the Market" and "the People" will help make clear what our scribe refers to as "the gods." We may also consider words that end in "-ism" and "-ist" and "-ity," all of which bear special scrutiny in this regard, as they indicate realms governed by overarching concepts and proprietary language—our identities, affinities, nations, and tribes gathered under a name.

So the statement is not so much primitive as it is fundamental—a truth laid bare in raw terms. That we modern materialists are less aware of the god-like archetypes that corral into tribes means only that we are more obtuse—it is nothing to be proud of. These ancients recognized that they were beholden to such things, while we remain mostly oblivious to the immortal disembodied powers that we serve.

The truth is, however, that we are absolutely bewitched by our gods. When someone says "we," meaning their country, nation, culture, or as is common now, their social media–defined micro-culture, they are evincing the programming of their collective archetype, their "nation" as defined by their inviolable identity, their "god." It is completely reasonable to think of these as gods, for they dictate and define the behavior of those under their banner.

Fine. It's a great insight! But there's more. Our wise writer discerns a symmetry to do with Abraham's promise to be a blessing to those very nations thus assigned to the gods. Abraham's heir, Jacob (Israel), did not belong to any of those gods. He was assigned to become "YHWH's own portion" and to be YHWH's "allotted share." While this also speaks of an overarching idea that maintains a constructed reality, it is regulated by this as yet unknown YHWH. As we shall see, it is not a normal name—not a noun, but a verb. It is a god who is not a god for a nation that is not a nation. It is an antithesis.

All this formlessness and namelessness hints at an innate intuition of transcendence, an ideal without an ideology, hence Abraham's resolute agnosticism. As the Book of Hebrews explains it, he set out from Harran "not knowing," and so is called the Father of Faith.[26] It's a fascinating juxta-position: true faith means relying on "not knowing," a clear dig at the Tree of Knowledge and nearly the opposite of what we usually mean we say we "believe in" something.

Abraham's is not a belief in a known thing or a proposition; it is faith in the unseen, unknown, and possibly unknowable. Abraham does not know anything: not where he is going, not how his life will work out, not the name of his God, nor the security of a familiar place and plan. Along with the idols, he disavows knowledge.

Abraham's unknown path sets him on a trail back to the Garden of Eden and the Tree of Life. If Babylon gave us the certainty of the Tree of Knowl-edge with its concretely realized gods and reified system, Abraham's dissent is to introduce the opposite of knowledge—faith—and with it a corresponding nation of faith in the unseen and unknown.

It is like 7Up: "There's no cola like the Un-cola," ran the ad campaign for the lemon-lime drink, which was promoted with glassware that inverted the shape of traditional Coca-Cola fountain glasses. It's not a terrible analogy. Abraham's nation was to be an inversion of the post-Babel ideal, a nation that is not a nation—the Un-nation.

Finally, on the subject of exceptionalism, I should hasten to add that there were many Abrahams. He was not the only dissenter. As civilization spreads and develops elsewhere, others will have experiences nearly identical to his and speak with voices just as challenging. A few of them will impact history just as deeply. They too will found movements that offer a path of return to Paradise. What they all have in common is this saving exceptionalism—not because they are better, but because they are exceptions to the deplorable norm.

Promised Land

After leaving Harran behind, Abraham ended up in what the voice called "the land that I will show you." Strange, for Abraham had landed in Canaan, and this was the very place his father was originally headed when they set out from Ur.

The irony would not have gone unappreciated by Abraham. By the time they made their layover at journey's midpoint in Harran, he was already an adult and a partner in the family business, so he knew exactly where Canaan was and what it was all about. It was too obvious to be an error—it must have meant something.

Here's what we know: Abraham's father, Terah, planned this trip abroad to ply his trade of buying and selling idols.[27] His destination, the Canaanite capital, Hazor, was a true Mesopotamia-style city-state. Fashioned after Uruk, it was the southern Levant's most important royal city in the second millennium BCE. Any traveling salesman worth his salt passed through here, the hub of trade routes connecting Mesopotamia with coveted resources from Egypt and Arabia. Princely fortunes were made by those who could successfully traffic these roads.[28]

This raises the question: what does it mean that God sent Abraham to a place as much a part of the Sumerian order as the town he came from? How is this the Promised Land? In what possible sense did he leave behind "country and kindred and father's house"? What was the voice going to "show" him that he hadn't already seen? It's important to answer these questions, for without this we might otherwise think that Abraham went off on a monkish quest for quiet contemplation.

As we can see, however, the opposite is true. Of all places, this was the *least* likely place to allow him to forget his background. In Canaan, Abraham's old world—the very ambition of his father—was in his face every day. Hazor even worshiped Sîn, the same lunar god of his ancestral homes, Harran and Ur. What was YHWH thinking?

I have strong feelings about this from living literally across the road from Hazor's remains. By then I'd left my kibbutz on the Lebanese border and moved to another farm not a quarter of a mile from the Canaanite capital; when I was twenty years of age, Canaan became my lot, just as it had been for Abraham. It was a fortuitous move: just as my first home in Israel let me share the experiences of Jesus and Peter, my new home opened to me the life of the patriarch.

Some of my new friends had worked on the city's excavations. Sharing the details of the dig, they pantomimed the unearthing and brushing off of objects unseen by human eyes for thousands of years and tried to express to me the excitement of uncovering what, until the twentieth century, was thought to be a city of myth. With time their stories accumulated into a kind of apocalypse for me, revealing how much my so-called faith had been a Sunday school cartoon: Jesus the effeminate watercolor shepherd with the world's cleanest sheep; Abraham the white-bearded old nomad who couldn't afford a home. Here, each lifted layer of dirt revealed not just the city of biblical lore, but Jesus the heroic peace-lover standing in defiance before religious bigots and debauched pagans alike. It revealed Abraham the billionaire producer of goddesses and popular idols turned citizen of the immaterial and unseen. All of this uncovered by my flesh-and-blood friends, one spade of earth at a time.

I could touch reality anytime I wanted. The museum housing Hazor's artifacts was still on our land, and I often walked across the road on the Sabbath to visit the large, disinterred townscape to stand where the moon god's shrine stood and think about everything Abraham. The connection with him was visceral and even visual; as I looked at the entire Hazor sanctuary reassembled at the Israel Museum, Sîn's unmistakable crescent emblem provoked a naive question: "Isn't that Muslim?" Answer: "*Nu*, shut up, *motek*, somebody hear you..."

Some years later, living and working near Harran, I saw the same god's crescent on proud display there, excavated from the Babylonian-era city that was Abraham's familial home. As a long-time sojourner and stranger in both lands, I could naturally feel a kinship with Abraham. His journey of faith and mine overlapped, not intentionally but as a matter of fate; this is where our feet fell. I knew there was no escaping it, no way to run from it. I'd tried that —I went to the Middle East to escape myself and just found, to my horror, more of me waiting there.

Plainly this was Abraham's experience, too—although I'm not sure he ever tried to escape. Certainly, he would have come to Canaan as per his father's plan even without YHWH's call, and he was surely aware of that. What does that mean? Simply that arriving as he did, with a divine commission, meant no waving of a magic wand; his was a pilgrimage to reveal hidden Paradise within the gritty and contentious space he was born to inhabit. He knew it, and I have no doubt that he suffered the psychological difficulties of such a wrenching confrontation with his inherited delusions.

Abraham knew that the Promised Land is not intrinsically sacred, but rather is sanctified by faith—by his living an awakened life right where he sat in his own father's dirt. His skin was peeled back layer by layer over many years. The story speaks to all of us: wherever we might be, no matter where our circumstantial fate may lay, we must live enlightenment right there in that place. It can be excruciating.

So, how does one find the Promised Land amid the inescapable ordinariness of the lot one is given? For Abraham, it meant learning to live as a stranger in Canaan's midst; to be there, but not to be of there. The Promised Land, or "the land I will show you," is a phase of consciousness outside Mesopotamia's fabricated universe. But entering it required the act of being in the midst of the deception; it required being present so as to pay careful attention to every delusory facet, point by point and lie by lie, to see things as they really are, one painful thing at a time. The patriarch needed to reach that liminal place of promise by a path straight through the darkness of his worldly fate (as do we all).

That, dear friends, is where the Promised Land exists. It is not a piece of geography or a political entity to possess, conquer, and rule. It is not success nor is it a political philosophy to convert others to. By the time he got to Canaan, Abraham realized this.

Indeed, Hazor—the power center of Canaan, the grand prize for any ambitious man—held no attraction for Abraham. He never even visited it. He was in search of another city. The New Testament's Book of Hebrews reflects Jewish tradition on this, saying that Abraham "looked forward to the city with foundations, whose architect and builder is God."[29] This is a beautiful summary of Abraham, who left the city of civilization behind, the solidity of idols and ideas, for something that was immaterial and yet more Real than anything else.

That is just what the doctor ordered for humanity's anxiety disorder. Abraham learned that home is not a house, not a temple and its ideals—it is an eternal and transcendent space.

For early Christians, this was fundamental. Stephen, the first martyr, proclaimed it with his dying breath. Abraham, he said, went out from Harran understanding perfectly that he was not promised a conventional inheritance; God "did not give him any of it as a heritage." Hearing that, his listeners "became enraged and ground their teeth at Stephen" and dragged him away and stoned him to death. Why?

Context here is important. The men assembling to stone Stephen were religious zealots for whom the square footage of the Promised Land of Canaan, now Israel, had become a sign of concrete, political salvation. It was under Roman occupation. They dedicated their lives to getting the Land back under their political control—it was all about "Free Palestine!" They no longer understood Abraham's quest, so Stephen reminded his murderers that their patriarch's earthly security included "not even a foot's length" of ground.[30] Who today among any of the religions or political philosophies in Jerusalem understands that?

Abraham's life-long commitment to live in tents—not in houses— strengthens this message. In the lovely words of the 1599 Geneva Bible, "By faith he abode in the land of promise, as in a strange country, as one that dwelt in tents."[31] He was resident there but not at home there. I need not remind the reader that the idea of "house" is about more than shelter; it was a temple and an anchor that preserved ancient sanity. For him to eschew the eternal security of the ancestral house—to make himself homeless—was an enormous decision.

We understand, then, that the Promised Land is charted in another dimension. It is not defined by citizenship in a country or by possession of real estate or through winning a political argument. Though he resides in Canaan, he lives in the city with heavenly foundations. And there, he is truly at home—at home in the most Real of abodes.

Reflecting now at this important turning point in our story, I want to emphasize that Abraham's choice to wander is a choice to embrace uncertainty. It is the opposite of seeking an ideal. It says to us that Paradise is a place of rest where we cease striving for a phantom perfection, a place where we are grateful and at peace, where no temptation of a better world of god-likeness hisses at us, seducing us to eat the fruit of reifying knowledge.

Civilization says that life isn't good enough, we need to advance, we need *more*: more technology, money, longevity, security, and more so-called real estate.

Real Paradise is timeless and spaceless. It is not about striving to return to the past nor does it concern a utopian future. It is a matter of rest in our natural blessed condition, in harmony with others and grateful for what we have.

The Verb

YHWH. YAHWEH. JEHOVAH. These are transliterations of the Hebrew word for the voice that spoke to Abraham. In English Bibles, we usually see it in all caps, written as "LORD." It is crucial to understand that this isn't a generic word for "God." This is not just a name—it is a concept.

While the gods and their kings descended to Earth at Eridu, Abraham's heirs were destined to send them back to heaven through this name, for YHWH had no representative idol, icon, or earthly regent.

This, then, isn't just monotheism; it is a concept of the Divine that specifically and purposely resists definition. But if that's the case, how can we even talk about Israel's greatest revelation intelligently? I'm afraid there is only one way: indirectly. This means shining a light around the meaning but not pinpointing it. I'll try to do that now, but please remember that to avoid the trap of reification, these descriptions and comments must be nothing more than angles of illumination. Our wish is to get a glimpse of Reality itself, to "know" in the sense of knowing someone, rather than knowing about someone.

Here goes: YHWH is a kind of relational, transcendent, transpersonal reality, a God who is not a conceivable object, but who is not divorced from Creation. This suggests panentheism, but I have no confidence that it would ring true with the late Israelites and must caution against getting stuck on such ideas; while defining something can be useful, the definition is never the thing itself, and the wisdom in YHWH is this insistence on ineffability. Since the whole point is not to be defined, any complex theology is not much better than a picture of an old man with a beard when it comes to seeing YHWH.

Before proceeding, let's also be clear about my idea of the transcendent: I am going to use this term repeatedly, but I don't want it to be prejudiced.

"Transcendent" means for me something almost opposite of what we might think. In these pages, it means absolutely and fundamentally Real. In other words, it transcends human constructed reality and reaches the ultimate fundamental nature of things—the *real* Real. When you see the term here, read it with that in mind. We are not talking about something lacking in essence—this is rather that which is most essential.

Helpfully, as with all ancient mythologies, the Hebrew YHWH is a story rather than a system. There is wisdom in that. If the Divine is not objectified, having to read between the lines of the Bible's meandering account— told across history by a variety of witnesses—is the best way to understand what the authors saw. This is true of history in general: the totality bears a far, far better witness than any particulars.

So, what do we know so far from this story? Everything in general and nothing in particular! We've read a lot about YHWH. In the passages we've selected to trace the story from Adam to Abraham, YHWH is named at every step, recognizable in English Bibles by the all-capitalized "LORD." But there are complications: most glaringly that Moses, while living many generations after Abraham, was nonetheless the first to hear YHWH's name. Equally problematic: Abraham, Isaac, and Jacob pray to God by other names —all of them incontestably pagan!

Consider Jacob. He won the name "Israel" through an epic spiritual wrestling match on the border between Canaan and Abraham's home country.[32] The famed biblical kingdom and the controversial twentieth-century Jewish state are named after him. Yet, El—the "el" in "Israel"— was the name of a god of the pagan Canaanite pantheon. Why wasn't Jacob called "Isra-yah," which means "YHWH rules?" How do we make sense of that?

First, YHWH does not seem to mind. El is used all over the Old Testament alongside YHWH, and to this day the pages have not caught fire. This reveals the hand of the final editors, who were working to synthesize various traditions, including Canaanite ones. They didn't do it to endorse the Mesopotamia-style cosmology of Canaan, but rather to recognize that an awakening had occurred among several disparate traditions. They did it to say, "YHWH is everything and for everyone." The Hebrew scriptures assume that under any name—even a paganish one like El—the prime mover in the overarching story is still the Prime Mover, the one and only Divine who is transpersonal and universal. If Jacob got the message through what he thought was El, that was fine as long as the message was true. Clearly, if there is only one creative force acting in the universe, they reasoned, it is surely capable of speaking through anything. (Famously, in a later story, YHWH speaks through an ass!)

So by the time our complete Hebrew Bible hit the presses a few centuries before Christ, the names El and YHWH were synonyms; Jacob's idol-bound Canaanite El was redefined by the transcendent idea of YHWH.

Does it even matter? After all, what's in a name? The answer is that YHWH is an insight critical of Sumerian cosmology—it is a counter-meme of extraordinary power, the reverse of Eridu's viral influence over human minds. The term itself is not important—any words will do, like "God" or "Universe" or even the Buddhist concepts of a "ground of being" (such as are present in the words of Zen master Soyen Shaku, who writes of "the highest reality and truth through which and in which this universe exists"). Like El, any tag can represent the YHWH revelation.

But it's hard to get there without hearing the insight as first revealed, for the word itself is a revelation, a piece of code to purge the system of Sumerian malware. How Moses came to hear it is surprising. Although YHWH enters the story in connection with Abraham's son, it is not Moses' ancestor Isaac—the patriarchal heir of Abraham's divine promise. Nor is it even through Ishmael, Islam's preferred link to Abraham. No, the path of revelation comes through Midian, born to Abraham by his late-in-life spouse, Keturah, who produced an astonishing six additional forgotten sons for Abraham. These were "men of courage and sagacious of mind" according to Roman historian Flavius Josephus, who informs us further that Abraham established countries in Arabia for his astute but disenfranchised boys.[33] Thus, Midian lent his name to the geography of the rugged, desolate country stretching down the eastern coasts of the Dead and Red Seas in modern-day Israel, Saudi Arabia, and Jordan.

You've probably seen his turf, for YHWH had a cinematic eye: it's all about craggy desert rock, sand, and a rich spectrum of colors—reds, blacks and yellows. *Indiana Jones and the Last Crusade* and *Lawrence of Arabia* were filmed in Midian. Younger readers might know the scene better from *The Martian* and *Star Wars: The Rise of Skywalker*, also filmed here.

It is the perfect setting for a monotheistic debut; we have but to picture ourselves in a scene from one of these films somewhere in the mountains. Imagine with us a shepherd, a refugee from Egypt—it's a vision easy to conjure, since even the recent *Star Wars* dresses its aliens like the Bedouin of these deserts. Our shepherd is Moses, whose own familiar story is known from more desert films, the most renowned surely being Cecil B. DeMille's, *The Ten Commandments*, starring Charlton Heston. (Also filmed on location!)

You know the plot of the film: Moses was born an Israelite in Egyptian captivity; he escaped the slaughter of infant Israelite boys and was adopted to be raised as a prince of Egypt by the pharaoh's beautiful daughter (played by the appropriately gorgeous Nina Foch). One fateful day, he witnessed the abuse of his people and killed an Egyptian slave master. Fearing for his life, our handsome leading man fled across the Red Sea to northeast Arabia, where he married the exotic daughter of Jethro, none other than the priest of—you guessed it—Midian.

There will be no rest for Moses, however. According to the Book of Exodus, "he led his flock beyond the wilderness, and came to Horeb, the mountain of God." And at the mountain, "the angel of YHWH appeared to him in a flame of fire out of a bush."

This was not a bush on fire, mind you, for "he looked, and the bush was blazing, yet it was not consumed." There is a suggestion that this blaze from another dimension was always there, but nobody had the eyes to see it until now. It was an unveiling, an apocalypse for Moses, who announces the moment in Jaynesian style by talking to himself: "I must turn aside and look at this great sight, and see why the bush is not burned up."[34] The other dimension takes note: "When the LORD saw that he had turned aside to see, God called to him out of the bush, 'Moses, Moses!' And he said, 'Here I am.'"

Reasonably, Moses isn't quite sure how to explain it (as a writer, I share his anxiety). How should he spin this news? What is the right wording? "If I come to the Israelites and say to them, 'The God of your ancestors has sent me to you,' and they ask me, 'What is his name?' what shall I say to them?'"

Moses is asking: How can I objectify you, how are you defined? What makes you concrete—what temple do you call home? Where can we find you? The assumption is that all gods are known and their temples are accessible, built of stone. So which one are you? The response transcends those categories: "God said to Moses, 'I AM WHO I AM.'" But this is more of an explanation than a name. It is a concession to the linear reading of Mesopotamia's cylinder seals, an appeal to minds trained to approach everything as a discursive narrative.

That is not the end of it, however. The voice nudges Moses, reducing his statement to a simple subject and verb: "Thus you shall say to the Israelites, 'I AM has sent me to you.'" Then, without pause, we get the big push: "Thus you shall say to the Israelites, 'The LORD, the God of your ancestors, the God of Abraham, the God of Isaac, and the God of Jacob, has sent me to you.' This is my name forever, and this my title for all generations."[35]

The third statement declares something untranslatable, *YHWH*—which almost every English Bible insists on translating anyway. (Notable exceptions are the American Standard Version and Darby translation, which opt to transliterate the Hebrew.)

The others, based on the first English translation by William Tyndale, insist on using the word "LORD," a baffling and clumsy substitute. It only works if someone explains what it stands for, which today is not usually the case. Why attempt a translation when the original text has given up? To my mind, the story is about this very thing. It moves swiftly from A to B to C, first giving a linear interpretation in the "I am who I am" line, then contracting it to "I am," and finally, not translating at all. Here at last our scribes give the name as the mystery it is without explanation: "Thus you shall say to the Israelites, 'YHWH has sent me to you.'" Written without elaboration, it's a word of no more practical use in Hebrew than it is in English, a lens more than a handle to be grasped.

The voice's tagline underscores the point even as it admits to being a name ("my name to the eternal") while also insisting that it is a title ("my title for all generations"). What does that mean? "Title" is closer to the idea of a token or symbol. Other translations use "remembrance." Again there is a warning against confusing symbol and reality, as if to say, "Careful, Moses, this word is only a memento of what you *see* here, a way to remember it!"

By now you may have become frustrated with these four letters. It is hard to read. How do you pronounce it? Short answer: you don't. That's why speaking it is forbidden to Jews. It does not want to be spoken in our world of reifying language and does not want to be translated or explicated. It is *meant* to confound our imagined understanding of the universe and frustrate our drive to define, capture, and control—to reify.

The only way to grasp it further is to tear it apart, an exercise that at most allows us to feel what Hebrew speakers feel from it. We see in "YHWH" the root "HWH" (הוה), which means "to be" or "to happen." The word is in its essence the infinitive Hebrew verb, common in today's Hebrew as HYH or "היה" ("was"), YHYH or "יהיה" ("will be"), and HWWH or "הוֹוֶה" (the term for "present tense"). Yet as it stands, the "LORD" YHWH does not mean past, present, or future being, but looks to be all these tenses at once: "יהוה" (yeh-ho-veh). This every-tense form of being is exclusive, never used in any other context at all—ever—and yet its nature is immediately and intuitively recognizable as having to do with existing outside of time.

It is therefore a term of its own empyrean tense, discernible as a verb just as the fire is recognizable as a fire. But like the non-burning bush, it does not work the same way in our dimension. In some sense it is atemporal, seeming to have bled over from another universe or dimension, and all-encompassing, as if our sphere is contained by it.[36] The term is so incongruous, it suggests to us that it is from the Edenic tongue, the theorized *Ur-Sprache* of perfect communication. As such, YHWH cannot be employed in the concrete fashion of Mesopotamia's deities—*it is a fire that does not consume.*

Abraham represents a powerful archetype. His rejection of civilization's fatalistic mandate speaks to the possibility of an alternate way of living.

This image gives us an idea of who Abraham represents. From Mari circa1800 BCE it depicts a wealthy man leading his sacrifice to the altar.

From my collection: A coin shows the emblem of Harran's moon god, Sîn. Abraham's biblical biographers carefully link the patriarch and his family to Harran and this deity. It is important because the last Babylonian emperor elevated Sîn above all other gods. The Bible's prophet Isaiah refers to this event, identifying Sîn as "Lucifer," and predicting judgment.

Moses encountered YHWH in these deserts of
Midian. It's one of my favorite places.

From my collection: A Canaanite goddess.

Popular throughout the narrative of biblical Israel, it was only
with young King Josiah that she and her kind faced a serious
threat in and around Jerusalem.

The idea of YHWH eventually supplanted this diva.

Josiah systematically destroyed these idols, hence her
decapitated condition.

A section of Jerusalem's city wall from the time of King Hezekiah.

Historically, we know that he was alive when Sargon the Great decimated the northern Kingdom of Israel around 722 BCE.

Jerusalem was flooded with northern refugees who brought a strong devotion to YHWH.

Some two decades later, the Mesopotamian empire laid siege to Jerusalem. Under Hezekiah's leadership, the city survived.

From my collection: These arrowheads date to this period of conflict between Israel, Judah and the Mesopotamian empires of Assyria and Babylon.

We see advances in military technology in these two examples.

The specimen at the top is the older version, which attached to the shaft with a solid pice of bronze.

The example to the right has a hollow socket in which to insert the arrow shaft. It is much more stable, reliable and accurate.

Arrows of these types were used in the Assyrian and Babylonian sieges of Jerusalem.

FROM PARABLE TO HISTORY

Kissing Cousins

YHWH—so much for the name. Now for a little context to introduce the next part of our meditation, which deals more and more with written and verifiable history.

As I've already noted, Moses encountered YHWH in Midian many generations—arguably thousands of years—after the name first appears in a biblical setting. It's there in the Garden of Eden and at the Tower of Babel and in Harran. Yet the name is first revealed here to Moses, Abraham's great-great-great-great grandson. How does that work?

It can mean only that the editors were comfortable revealing their hand. It is their way of saying that whatever else was going on in those pre-Moses encounters, it was YHWH at work. Whether they knew it or not, this is what created Adam and this is what scattered the peoples at Babel; this is the voice that spoke to Abraham—who else is there, after all?

It seems the Midianites recognized YHWH before Jacob's descendants did. Scripture endorses that idea with direct references to the point of origin: "YHWH came from Sinai, and dawned from Seir upon us; he shone forth from Mount Paran." And, "YHWH, when you went out from Seir, when you marched from the region of Edom."[1] All these places refer to the deserts of Midian—the sand and mountainous crags of *Star Wars: The Rise of Skywalker* and *Lawrence of Arabia*.

This suggest that Moses' non-Israelite father-in-law was YHWH's high priest. We know already that Jethro was pointedly introduced as the "priest of Midian" and it was on Jethro's grazing land that the burning bush appeared. Then, when Moses returned from his mission to liberate the Israelites, he did not go directly to the Promised Land, but went out of his way to lead them back to Midian's mountains around the Red Sea "by the roundabout way of the wilderness."[2]

Having met them there, the priest organized a sacrifice upon which Moses and the Israelites happily feasted. This was nothing if not an endorsement of Jethro's religion, for on any other occasion when the Israelites attended feasts at the invitation of their cousins, slaughter descended upon them along with scathing warnings of contamination. Here among the Midianites, there was nothing but blessing. Indeed, they received the Ten Commandments while still in these mountains.

The Egyptians noticed the Midianites' relationship with YHWH, too. They left inscriptions about the Shasu, pastoral nomads of Arabia and Syria, who lived in these very same deserts. They worshiped none other than "YHW" (*Yhw3*), a word that in its Egyptian form is linguistically indistinguishable from "YHWH."[3]

The sophisticated Egyptians did not like them. Egypt's derision of the Shasu, who were ridiculed as homeless, uncivilized nomads, recalls Mesopotamia's original siren song, goddess Nintur's promise to save humanity "from their trails" by having them "come and build cities." Isn't it telling that YHWH was first known to those who never signed up for that bargain?

Instead, like Abraham, they renounced the city in favor of a nomadic life of uncertainty and dwelling in tents, hinting that perhaps Abraham is a mythological representation of these people. Maybe so. What we can say for certain is that the desert-dwelling Shasu were hated for not playing ball, and they did indeed first use the token "YHWH." That Moses' relationship with them occurs at Judaism's most fundamental moment makes the Midian connection far, far more than incidental. The divine name and the Ten Commandments debut on the often-filmed desert sets of Abraham's forgotten son.

By contrast, Israel's next encounter with its cousins is also related with contextual importance, but the message is of a very different kind. This time, it is less than delightful—for unlike the Midianites, these descendants of Abraham's nephew Lot were faithful practitioners of civilization, replete with cities and kings.

Fast-forward about forty years from the pleasantries of Jethro's feast.

(You can watch Ben Kingsley's 1995 TV movie, *Moses*, to catch up on those tumultuous years.) We now find ourselves with the Israelites on the northern end of the Dead Sea. It's hot, and Moses is about to send his people into the Promised Land, where the gods Baal and Asherah await their conquest. (Asherah is a local expression of our favorite, Inanna.)

Waiting for the green light, the Israelites make camp on the eastern banks of the Jordan River, in the anachronistic kingdom of Moab, Lot's ornery descendants. Their king has summoned the prophet Balaam to curse them, but the plan fails. Twice verbally rebuked by his donkey, Balaam reneges on his contract: "How can I curse whom God has not cursed?" he says. "Here is a people living alone, and not reckoning itself among the nations!"[4]

It's an apt prophecy, elegantly affirming the Un-nation attributes of this people. But Balaam's thuggish employer was greatly displeased—he'd hired him for a curse, and a curse was what he was going to get. Balaam had to make good, and fast. So he came up with a fiendishly clever idea: get the Israelites involved in a ritual orgy to literally adulterate their claim of being separate from the Mesopotamian order. They'd be the Un-nation no more!

His plot worked to sensational effect: "While Israel was staying at Shittim, the people began to have sexual relations with the women of Moab... and bowed down to their gods." Through this behavior, says the biblical account, "Israel yoked itself to the Baal of Peor." Israel "yoked itself"; the language is accurate and poignant, Israel having joined itself in bondage with the Sumerian world.

Moses would teach them a lesson in the most brutal terms: "Take all the chiefs of the people, and impale them in the sun before the Lord."[5] It is a horrifying sentence: longitudinal impalement is a vicious and cruel punishment, shockingly so for the crime of partying with the neighbors. But that's how serious conforming to Mesopotamia was taken.

Thus purged, the surviving Israelites crossed the Jordan and took possession of the cities of Canaan under the generalship of Joshua, Moses' successor. The conquest takes eleven long chapters, each page reeking of Canaanite blood and guts and ruined cities, but concludes with a summary both strange and inexplicable: when Joshua personally reviews these events, there is no violence at all.

> When you went over the Jordan and came to Jericho, the citizens of Jericho fought against you, and also the Amorites, the Perizzites, the Canaanites, the Hittites, the Girgashites, the Hivites, and the Jebusites; and I handed them

over to you. I sent the hornet ahead of you... it was not by your sword or by your bow.[6]

No sword, no bow—very odd since the book records some thirty-eight instances of the word "smite" whose action betokens the use of the very nasty sickle-sword that Sargon popularized. Cities are burned and whole populations chased and slaughtered in the fields. Consider the example of Ai: "When they were all fallen on the edge of the sword, until they were consumed, that all the Israelites returned unto Ai, and smote it with the edge of the sword. And so it was, that all that fell that day, both of men and women, were twelve thousand."[7]

In the next book of the Bible, we read again and again of cities and people vanquished in Israel's conquest of Canaan. And yet, in short order the Bible describes these same peoples and cities as being very much intact. They are still there, ruling themselves autonomously, while happily consorting with the tribes of Israel, we might add.

That picture fits the archeological record. There are certainly many flattened cities, spread over a long period, and more cities rising. But there is no evidence for conquest by outsiders. It is a sensitive subject for biblical literalists, and having been one, I want to assure you that I mean no disrespect—a literal reading works, too. Either way, the truth of the message gets across, and surely a literalist would want others who see this story as a parable to benefit from it, too.

Once again it is about how we read the story: what it means, what the authors meant, and—sometimes—who they had in mind when they wrote it. Literal or not, the contrasting narratives presented by Joshua and Judges tell us much about how the Abrahamic message of dissent spread. Learning to embrace its ambiguities has strengthened my love for the Bible and my faith, teaching me at the same time to listen with respect to any voice through which the Divine might speak. That's worth holding on to as we continue this ride—for literalists like me, it is going to get bumpy.

Fabled Emergence

Historically, Israel is first mentioned in 1207 BCE, in the text of the Egyptian Merneptah Stele. It gives us a benchmark: by that date at least, there was an identifiable group called Israel in Canaan. But where did they come from? The emergence of Israel, like most cultures, is the result of mixing ingredients. Here, then, is the recipe for making Israel:

1. Shasu, the Egyptian word for the region's pastoral nomads: They are a southern element that the Egyptians say worshiped YHWH. I think Moses represents this ingredient. Tradition, including the Bible, also links the people of northwestern Arabia with Abraham. If we look for a people living there who remember Abraham as their ancestor, right up through the emergence of Islam, we find the nomads of Midian. And the Bible is at pains to place Moses among them.

2. Indigenous Canaanites: As Canaanite city-states began a natural decline, pastoral Canaanites and displaced urbanites began to settle in the central highlands north of Jerusalem and south of Shechem. They gradually took on a new identity—a new name, derived from the Canaanite god, El. The name is, of course, *Isra-el*, meaning "El rules" or "Prince of El."

3. Cousins: Other related people from across the Jordan—what the Bible calls the Moabites and Edomites—are addressed by Moses as "brothers" when he seeks passage to the Holy Land from Midian. Any number of brethren—even Arameans—might have gone into the mix. Abraham's is a big family.

Which ingredient is predominant? I see it as mostly Canaanite with Midianite cultural influences. Of course, some scholars view the biblical account in the Book of Joshua more literally, and others try to find some middle ground. I think a literal reading is impossible. I prefer to read it for its message, not as a journalistic history. If you'd like to really get into the details, I recommend Israel Finkelstein, Professor of archaeology at Tel Aviv University. His book, co-authored with Neil Asher Silberman, *The Bible Unearthed: Archaeology's New Vision of Ancient Israel and the Origin of Its Sacred Texts*, will serve you well.[8]

For our purposes, I'm going to look closely at Israel's history literally only where it enters the external record—namely, in the chronicles of Egypt and other neighboring kingdoms. Anything before that is speculative and unnecessary. I will, however, say a few words about how the historical Israelites remember themselves from this period of the judges, which they summed up with this important assessment: "In those days there was no king in Israel; all the people did what was right in their own eyes."[9]

No kings—that's the big message. Instead, the Book of Judges reveals a loose confederation of ungoverned hill-country tribes amid a scene of declining Canaanite city-states. Among them is an emerging but chaotic culture that will evolve and coalesce to become the Jewish people. Reviewing the lives of Isaac and Jacob, it becomes easy to see the antecedents of Israel in Canaanite culture. It is probable, for example, that one or more of these free-floating Canaanite groups had a revered ancestor named Jacob (known to us as Abraham's grandson) whose legend celebrates his appointment by the Canaanite god El, giving us the name with which we are so familiar: Israel. It certainly explains the oddity of the name.

But I'm not here to argue that point. Passing over many fascinating tales (for example, another cinematic epic in Samson and Delilah), we will go right to the end of the tribal-era judges, which concludes again with the underlying message that the Book of Judges began with: it is an exclamation mark, told through the life of the last of the judges, Samuel.

To me it is a universal parable, a lesson never learned, about a tribal rabble intent on destroying its own liberty. In the heat of revolutionary fervor, the people surround Samuel to demand that he get out of the way; they want a new political and social system, and they want it right now, consequences be damned. They want nothing less than assimilation into the world order: "Appoint for us, then, a king to govern us, like other nations."[10]

This was the Un-nation, not part of the system. Now, however, they're clamoring to be exactly like the others. Shocked, Samuel sought the voice of the LORD and was told he had no recourse. It's the catch-22 of democracy: sometimes the people choose what's bad for them. "Listen to the voice of the people in all that they say to you; for they have not rejected you, but they have rejected me from being king over them," says YHWH.[11]

This story is a pedagogic device. The moral clear: though blessed with the Abrahamic revelation, the people were chronic backsliders. "They have rejected me from being king over them," YHWH tells Samuel, "just as they have done to me, from the day I brought them up out of Egypt to this day, forsaking me and serving other gods."

The last judge warns the Israelites, telling them exactly what being like the other nations means:

> These will be the ways of the king who will reign over you: he will take your sons and appoint them to his chariots and to be his horsemen, and to run before his chariots; and he will appoint for himself commanders of thousands and commanders of fifties, and some to plow his ground and to reap his harvest, and to make his implements of war and the equipment of his chariots.[12]

It goes on and on. He will take your daughters, he will take the best of your fields and vineyards, he will take your grain and give it all to his soldiers and courtiers. He will take the best of your livestock. He will make you his slaves. "And in that day you will cry out because of your king, whom you have chosen for yourselves; but the LORD will not answer you in that day."

Sounds like the terrors of Lagash all over again. But despite the warning, "the people refused to listen to the voice of Samuel; they said, 'No! but we are determined to have a king over us, so that we also may be like other nations.'"

This was groupthink at its worst, a veritable Twitter storm of crowd-driven stupidity and impending cruelty. But bound by the will of the masses, and cancelled from his position of judge, Samuel anoints the first-ever king to rule among Abraham's descendants. His name is Saul, meaning "asked for"—as in, "be careful what you ask for."

Right off the bat there are problems. Saul is plagued by demons and soon Samuel brings news that his days are numbered. "Because you have rejected the word of the LORD, he has also rejected you from being king." Saul may be the people's chosen king, but YHWH's transpersonal voice still calls the shots. Rejecting reality never works—it rejects you right back. And so Saul's dynasty collapses entirely, with his sons falling in battle to the pork-eating Philistines, and the king committing suicide.

His successor is David, the lowly shepherd who became a great conqueror. The story develops rapidly. We soon find that David rules over a large, powerful kingdom, with Jerusalem as his capital. His life fills many pages with tales of a fraught relationship with YHWH, alternately glorious and depraved. Through it all, the prophets are there to issue blistering rebukes. There is no question who the real king is—it is YHWH.

Following his dramatic ups and downs, we can't help feeling nervous for David. He could be dismissed at any time. Or he might be driven to suicide as Saul was; we see David depressed, broken, betrayed, in despair, and at one point, starving himself. The reader understands that the kingly situation is tentative, a childish indulgence granted Israel to teach it a lesson. No matter how successful David becomes, his position always feels not just fragile, but somehow a game of pretend.

Of course, the lesson only gets more intense after David bequeaths the kingdom to his son Solomon, builder of Jerusalem's fabulous temple. The kingdom was to be Abrahamic, without an idol—an acknowledgment of where real authority rested—but Solomon shows this might not be possible. Being a king, he is trapped by the system and falls headlong into its net. Marrying foreign women by the thousands, he fills the Temple with their idols and subjugates himself to Babylon-inspired ideals. Don't misunderstand this: his marriages are political alliances—a lust for power as much as flesh.

We ought not be worried, however. We recognize in the judges-to-kings plotline a morality play about how a people returns to the fork in the road that divides pre-civilization from the present world order, and about the choices they must make to go in a different direction. We are meant to involve ourselves in the story so that we can make the journey, too. To that end, Solomon's contradictions and inconsistencies represent most of us—he wants to make a break with the world presented to him but can't seem to do it.

That's how we approach the rest of the story. We want to see ourselves in it so we can grapple with these challenges and relate them to our experience. Sometimes we will feel worried for the outcome, and we should. There is a lot at stake, and no guarantee of salvation.

Histories and Evidence

Turmoil ensued. After Solomon's death, the kingdom split in two: the northern one was called Israel, and the southern one Judah. This is the point where the whole narrative shifts to a less-mythical basis. The two kingdoms interact dramatically with neighboring empires and so enter the annals of foreign kings. For the first time, we find archeological evidence that fully converges with the biblical narrative. We can at last put Israel in a verifiable historical context.

Already in the fourteenth century BCE, the Tel el Amarna letters speak of two separate entities, one centered on Shechem and the other around Jerusalem—equivalents of the split biblical kingdom. The only problem: these two separate domains stand 200 years earlier than history's first mention of Israel and far earlier than the supposed lives of Saul, David, or Solomon. It was not a split Davidic kingdom—it was two different political domains from the beginning.

Comprehensive surveys of settlements here show that between 2000 and 1550 BCE the people in the northern region around Shechem transitioned from a pastoral nomadic culture to a village way of life. Their land was fertile and well-placed for trade; it was densely populated and peppered with many sophisticated villages.

Settlements in the southern part near Jerusalem don't do nearly as well; the villages are few, sparsely peopled, and chronically dependent on a primitive pastoral economic base. That's the area that is supposed to be the capital of David's glorious united kingdom.

Professor Israel Finkelstein interprets this data: "A map of Early Bronze

Age highland sites... clearly shows two different regional settlement systems, with a dividing line between them running roughly between Shechem and Jerusalem, a boundary that would later mark the frontier between Israel and Judah."[13]

There is no possibility, then, that there could have been a united kingdom of Israel under King David. It was divided all along, even two centuries before Israel was ever mentioned as Israel. And when Israel does enter history by name, it is a kingdom based at Jacob's Shechem, not Jerusalem.

Finkelstein concludes,

In the tenth and ninth centuries BCE, Judah was still very thinly inhabited, with a limited number of small villages, in fact not much more than twenty or so... And we still have no hard archaeological evidence—despite the unparalleled biblical descriptions of its grandeur—that Jerusalem was anything more than a modest highland village in the time of David, Solomon, and Rehoboam.[14]

It was around 1200 BCE that the Egyptian Merneptah Stele gives the oldest known reference to Israel, the kingdom based at Shechem. It gives us the kingdom's name and shows the Israelites as a people indistinguishable from the other Canaanites whom the Stele also names and portrays. They wear the same clothing and have the same hairstyles.

We can conclude from this that no later than 1200 BCE there was a Canaanite people calling itself Israel, centered at Shechem—not Jerusalem—and that they were a rapidly emerging regional power. Their poorer, less sophisticated cousins lived to the south around Jerusalem, but were not identified by any name. Including Israel, the Merneptah Stele mentions five ethnicities in Canaan. It does not remark on the fiefdom at Jerusalem because, alas, David's enclave was as yet unremarkable.

That's not to say the two groups were unrelated. They sprang from the same soil; their languages and formative cultures were nearly identical, and they probably shared many ancient legends. But whatever they had in common,

they were also very different from each other in their demographic composition, economic potential, material culture, and relationship with their neighbors. Put simply, Israel and Judah experienced quite different histories and developed distinctive cultures. In a sense, Judah was little more than Israel's rural hinterland.[15]

What, then, is the cause of this emerging identity of Israel? Some of it was simply geographical and social separation. Their towns developed from settling nomads and immigrants from the declining Canaanite cities. For reasons unknown, the archeological record shows they stopped eating pork. This practice further differentiated them from their neighbors, leaving behind physical remains showing who was who and who was where.

Most critically, however, the Israelites began to worship YHWH. No other Canaanites worshiped or even acknowledged this uncivilized Midianite idea. With their city-states and Mesopotamia-inspired stone and wooden idols, other Canaanites regarded an abstraction like YHWH was nonsensical. Like the ban on pigs, this unique belief in YHWH made the highland subculture stand out from the others, pushing them to evolve along a different trajectory. To be clear, they did not yet worship YHWH exclusively, but worshiping YHWH at all was enough to set them apart.

Although they stemmed from different traditions, at some point the kosher highlanders began to use the words "El" and "YHWH" without contradiction. Surely one thing that brought them together was contempt for the lowbrow Baal, a phallic-bull deity whose enduring pop-idol status perennially threatened the exalted El and was anathema to sophisticated YHWH followers. If the later history of YHWH's political rise is comparable, El devotees were likely a minority, but an elite and powerful one based in the large towns; Baal's stronghold was among the agriculturally inclined countryfolk.

None of this happened overnight—but the yeast that makes this recipe rise consists of a pork-free diet, worship of YHWH, and ancestral fealty to El. Is that complicated? Sure it is. But an untidy story of cultural and identity formation is what makes it compelling and believable. Origin myths are not often this muddy. In fact, what's surprising is how much of this messy detail the Hebrew scriptures preserve without embarrassment. We see Israel and Judah plagued by Baal worship right through the scriptural account; plus, we have the consistent use of "El" as a synonym for "YHWH," reflecting their Canaanite origins.

As we've learned, Abrahamic monotheism eventually bundled those names into one package. An exemplary verse—one of many—makes use of Moses to synthesize the traditions. In it, YHWH remarks to Moses, "I appeared to Abraham, Isaac, and Jacob as El Shaddai but by my name

YHWH I did not make myself known to them." It's as if YHWH says, "Don't be too quick to judge! It was me all along!"

Of course, in the Bible Israel's unique association with YHWH comes through Moses and the mountainous deserts of Midian. Those legends surely point to something historical, and now we have some evidence of this at a devotional site called Kuntillet Ajrud.

Kuntillet dates from the last half of the ninth century BCE. An inscription there in the Canaanite dialect that became Hebrew preserves a text invoking a blessing by "Yhwh of Samaria." Samaria (not to be confused with Sumeria) is the geography around Jacobite Shechem, the territory that corresponds to the biblical northern kingdom of Israel. What this tells us explicitly is that YHWH had a temple in budding Israel's northern capital. The inscription's location tells us something equally important: that the Israelites did indeed have a connection with the original YHWH worshipers of the desert. It isn't Moses and a burning bush exactly, but pretty close, because Kuntillet is located in those very Midianite stomping grounds made famous by Moses and the Ten Commandments.

This is very important. It firmly grounds the Hollywood sensationalism of the Exodus story in something that is not a parable, meaning that a place associated with YHWH was certainly visited by pre-Israelite traders. They did sojourn in this desert where Moses was said to have met YHWH and where the children of Israel wandered for forty years, not to be punished, but to make a living. And it is here that they first encountered YHWH, bringing the idea home to establish devotion to the verb back in Samaria.

Here is another connection: Kuntillet's residents associated YHWH with Teman, the region surrounding them. The Hebrew scriptures agree: "God came from Teman, the Holy One from Mount Paran." In fact, all the other biblical references to YHWH's origin are in Kuntillet's vicinity too; they are Paran, Sinai, and Horeb.

There's more. Of all the prophets, Elijah was noted for his burning zealousness for YHWH. In the Book of Kings, he's the one who stands for pure devotion against Baal and he is the first person to openly confront the popular idol, famously setting up a contest to prove YHWH's supremacy. When Elijah ran for his life and needed a fresh word from the LORD (he was astonishingly bicameral), where did he go? Straight to Kuntillet's desert.

Viewing all the evidence, it isn't hard to see what likely happened. Kuntillet was on a trade route. Canaanite traders from Shechem passed through here, learned about YHWH from the local desert-based nomads, and carried the idea back with them to Shechem. YHWH, the god who is a verb, caught on and redefined the Baal-embattled El of their Jacob tradition. We see it in Elijah's name: "El" + "I" (the first-person marker) + "YH" = "My El is YHWH." His name effectively tells the whole story, tying together both traditions.

This, then, is the basis for the Exodus story, explaining why the Israelite ancestors marched from the desert with the revelation of YHWH. This does not diminish Exodus; it is an essential parable, needed to explain the mature monotheism that Israel finally achieved in its last years. The literary figure of Moses delivers some necessary theological inflections, establishes a ritual structure, and expresses with brutal clarity the high stakes in this contest between the old order and the new.

Shocking? I think not. Moses, Joshua, and the Exodus need not be historically factual; they serve to telescope a history that would otherwise require an encyclopedia of detail. And if you believe those stories as fact, no harm done—we wind up in exactly the same place. But, of course, you then have the problem of a violent God who impales his followers and dispossesses innocent people without warning. Viewing Moses and Joshua as a parable changes the tenor of those scenes; they become cautionary tales, without the problem of narrative inconsistencies and internal contradictions.

Oil Industry

Finally we arrive at Israel's peak, an entity fully established as a regional power and widely recognized in the annals of foreign kings. It is the early 800s BCE, and under the leadership of King Omri the Shechem-centered kingdom has become so successful that Mesopotamia can no longer resist the temptation to possess it.

Bear in mind that this is a century after the biblical time of King David, whose poorer southern kingdom of Judah remains unnoticed and unenvied, ignored by the world. In the end, it's a blessing which will allow David's descendants to escape calamity and survive to carry the Israelite traditions forward under a new Davidic brand. Jerusalem will become Noah's Ark for Israel's culture.

To explain that history, we have considerable material evidence and external testimony with which the Bible largely agrees. Most of this concerns the latest Mesopotamian superpower—the Assyrian Empire—and their king, Tiglath-pileser III (known by his nickname "Pul"). He was a military and administrative genius who conquered most of the known world, utilizing a cruel policy of population exchange, stripping bare the lands that he conquered and repeopling them with his own countrymen.

He also invented the warrior's boot, the *šēnu* (they all wore sandals before this). This innovation was a "knee-high, leather jackboot with thick leather soles, complete with hobnails on the sole to improve traction."[16] The Hebrew prophet Isaiah would soon borrow the new Assyrian word, making it an emblem of oppression, its image of relentless stomping conquest the most terrifying of all. Isaiah dreamed of a day when "nation shall not lift up sword against nation," when the "boots [*šēnu*] of the tramping warriors shall be burned as fuel for the fire."[17] He wasn't the only one to exploit this for dramatic effect. There would be no image of stormtroopers without the invention of the *šēnu*, so it is perfectly correct to picture Pul as the Hitler or Darth Vader of his age—and that's exactly what Israel was up against.

It was in the mid-700s BCE that Pul finally arrived at Shechem with a proposal for Israel's then king, Menahem. It was an offer the king could not refuse: become a vassal and pay tribute, or see your population slaughtered, the survivors permanently exiled, and their land, possessions, and children taken by foreigners. Menahem complied.

It was a painful and expensive arrangement, however, which caused resentment against Assyria to mount as demands for more concessions escalated. Resistance coalesced into an anti-Mesopotamian movement that found a champion in Menahem's successor. The next time Assyria's army came collecting, he would just say no. It was a huge gamble based on an alliance with neighboring powers who bet that Israel could do what no one else could—fend off Assyria's trampling boots.

Meanwhile in Jerusalem, Judah's king Ahaz was under dire threat. Cousin Israel and their anti-Assyrian allies demanded that Judah join their rebellion. If they would not do it willingly, then it would be by force. Ahaz, however, was not taking any bets; with Israel's army camped outside Jerusalem's walls, he sensibly sided with the Assyrians against his northern kin. Ahaz sealed the deal by traveling to Damascus, where he paid public homage to Tiglath-pileser and the Assyrian gods.

Pul then set out to brutally punish the willful Kingdom of Israel. In 733 BCE, the Assyrian armies entered with force and took all the good land and resources of the northern kingdom. Cities were laid waste and plundered; the population was deported and replaced with Assyrians. Excepting the immediate area around the capital in Samaria, Israel was no more.

Pul made a note about it in his ledger of conquests: "The land of Bit-Humria... all of whose cities I leveled to the ground... I plundered its livestock, and I spared only isolated Samaria."[18] (Bit Humria is the Assyrian variant for Hebrew *Beit Omri*—"The House of Omri"—named for Israel's greatest dynasty.)

The Assyrians left this tiny remnant as a warning, evidence of what happens to resistors. But the embittered Israelite remnant did not bow easily and rallied when Tiglath-pileser died, mounting another ill-fated revolt. The new and short-lived emperor, Shalmaneser V, took the uprising personally. Shortly before his own death, he laid siege to the vestiges of Israel in Samaria, leaving it to his successor, Sargon II, to finish them off in 722 BCE, effectively deporting the entire population. This time there would be no token remnant spared and no one left to resist.

Sargon, too, made a note in his ledger:

> The inhabitants of Samaria, who... plotted... not to endure servitude and not to bring tribute to Assur... I fought against them with the power of the great gods, my lords. I counted as spoil 27,280 people, together with their chariots, and gods, in which they trusted... I settled the rest of them in the midst of Assyria.

Not surprisingly, the Israelites who escaped death and exile fled as refugees to their estranged kin in Judah—it was all they had left. For the first time, Jerusalem became the national center for all the YHWH highlanders. It wasn't a huge kingdom, but it was all there was. The population swelled with refugees carrying whatever they could bring with them, and suddenly Jerusalem was a boomtown, not least of all because it was still in a sweet spot with the Assyrians. Jerusalem's treaty with them had turned Judah into a banana republic—or rather an olive republic, for their prized commodity was olive oil, used then for everything from lighting lamps to skin care.

The arrangement was not without hiccups. King Ahaz's son, Hezekiah, emboldened by his city-state's new regional position, and under the theological influence of northern refugees, tried to make a breakthrough, a switch of alliance to Egypt. When Egypt didn't come through, Assyrian punishment wasn't far behind. The Bible tells the story of a hard siege, survived only by paying an enormous fine and making cunning use of resources: Hezekiah blocked the source of water to the besiegers, channeling it into the city through an underground tunnel.

The stonecutters, working from opposite ends, hammered out an inscription when they met. "This is the story of the tunnel," they wrote; "while the axes were against each other and while three cubits were left, the voice of a man called to his counterpart... and on the day of the tunnel [being finished] the stonecutters struck each man towards his counterpart, ax against ax and water flowed from the source to the pool."

When I'm in Istanbul I like to visit this inscription. You can too; it's on display in the Istanbul Archeology Museum. And when you are in Jerusalem, you can walk through the tunnel, if you don't mind getting your feet wet. You can also see large sections of Hezekiah's Jerusalem walls and artifacts recovered from the siege. So, this much of the story is certainly factual: Jerusalem escaped annihilation and exile by making the whole exercise too much trouble for the Assyrians.

This is confirmed also by Assyria's own account: "As for Hezekiah, the Judahite, who did not submit to my yoke: I besieged and took forty-six of his strong cities, as well as the small cities in their realm, which were without number—I brought up siege-engines and leveled them with battering-rams."[19]

Although the Bible paints the shortened siege and deliverance of Jerusalem in a rosy light, it doesn't conceal the heavy price they paid nor deny what the Assyrians claim—namely, that because of Judah's resistance, the empire leveled forty-six towns, everything but Jerusalem.

With bureaucratic precision, the Assyrian king Sennacherib reports the details: "I brought away from them and counted as spoil 200,150 people—great and small, male and female—and their horses, mules, asses, camels, cattle and sheep, without number."

Of Jerusalem, he writes,

Hezekiah himself, like a caged bird I shut up in Jerusalem, his royal city. I threw up earthworks against him—anyone coming out of the city-gate, I turned back to his misery... the terrifying splendor of my majesty overcame him... and his mercenary troops which he had brought in to strengthen Jerusalem, his royal city, deserted him.[20]

The final deal to lift the siege involved Jerusalem's surrender of a great deal of punitive lucre.

In addition to the 30 talents of gold and 800 talents of silver (there were), gems, antimony, jewels, large sand-stones, couches of ivory, house chairs of ivory, elephant hide, elephants' tusks, ebony, boxwood and all kinds of valuable (heavy) treasures, as well as his daughters, his harem, his male and female musicians, (which) he had (them) bring after me to Nineveh, my royal city.

Though the King of Judah lost everything, including his daughters, furniture, harem, and the house band, this was far better than what others experienced at Assyria's hands. After the siege, and strategically positioned, Jerusalem began to prosper again. Over the next decades, it acquired considerable autonomy as the Assyrians began to face distracting challenges in the East. According to some in Jerusalem, however, their reprieve had nothing to do with politics and everything to do with YHWH.

A Matter of Trust

This key perspective, that it was YHWH who spared Jerusalem, belongs to Isaiah, the foremost spokesman of the YHWH-only party, the first historically verified social movement to stand in opposition to the Mesopotamian worldview. He appeared just as Judah came under threat from Israel's anti-Assyrian alliance, when the Kingdom of Israel surrounded Jerusalem to force Judah into the coalition. King Ahaz knew that his smaller, weaker kingdom did not stand a chance. With his people in a panic, he decided on what seemed to be a reasonable course: he'd fully subject himself to Assyria and let the Assyrians destroy Israel for him. We saw how that turned out.

And yet, Isaiah severely castigated the king for what at face value was a successful policy. "Take heed, be quiet, do not fear, and do not let your heart be faint," pled the prophet, "it shall not stand, and it shall not come to pass. If you do not stand firm in faith, you shall not stand at all."

Isaiah thus gave voice to the concerns of YHWH purists—a minority at this juncture—who viewed any such alliance with Mesopotamia as an act of idolatry. These guys took the "not like other nations" thing very, very seriously. Any military alliance, they said, required Jerusalem to bow to foreign kings and therefore to their gods. And they were correct: that's quite literally what Ahaz did in Damascus. "Ahaz sent messengers to King Tiglath-pileser of Assyria, saying, 'I am your servant and your son. Come up, and rescue me!'"

He sent silver and gold from Jerusalem's Temple to show the submission of Judah's deity to the Assyrian gods. He even set up a pagan altar he got while visiting Tiglath-pileser, ordering all the daily sacrifices to be made on this abomination.

Quite apart from that blatant idolatry, Isaiah equated seeking security with an act of worship. In his view, merely looking to Assyria for protection was a betrayal of trust. That's a new way of thinking. Before then, worship was spoken of in concrete terms as ritual sacrifice; now Isaiah is starting to talk about it in terms of what one trusts in to feel secure in life. Whatever that may be, this is your God, he said.

It reminds me of an election campaign in modern Israel. I was living in Jerusalem when Benjamin Netanyahu ran for office under the slogan, *Osim Shalom Bituach*, which means "Making Secure Peace." We were to understand that a nervous population could rest assured that Bibi would not sacrifice a tough security posture in exchange for peace—his peace would come through security.

But the same word for security also means "trust" and is used in the Hebrew scriptures to mean "active faith"—in other words, faith as an act of worship. When Isaiah says, "Behold, I will trust in God... and will not fear," that's the word he uses—the same word translated as "security" from Bibi's bumper sticker. This is also the word Isaiah uses when he warns those who "trust in chariots" that their faith is in the wrong place. By trusting in Assyria's weapons, their active faith—that is, their worship—is in a false god, a material idol. Security = Trust = Faith = Worship.

Netanyahu's slogan raised a point on which modern Israeli people of faith are torn: everyone knows that this word, while commonly used in the sense of national security, was originally something the prophets reserved for YHWH. If there is a YHWH and it has anything to do with modern Israel, where then should Israel's security and trust reside? In American money and weapons? In the strong arm of the IDF? Or in YHWH? This very modern dilemma is exactly where Isaiah is at, and he was not entertaining any arguments. When national security threats were raised, he said Jerusalem must trust (be secure in) YHWH or face dispossession.

This was just as radical a position to take then as it would be now. What would we think if the national security advisor claimed to speak for God and told the president to stop trusting the military for our nation's security? Moreover, in Isaiah's Jerusalem, as now, the armed security policy seemed to work just fine. Assyria decimated Israel while the Judahites were spared. True. But they now lived in vassal humiliation to the Assyrian powers. There was a steep price to pay and a gradual deterioration of quality of life.

As Isaiah shows, not everyone was happy with this arrangement—least of all the northern refugees who had lost everything to Assyria, people who brought with them their traditional fealty to YHWH. As the demographics of Jerusalem changed, Isaiah's uncompromising anti-idol and anti-Mesopotamian message reflected a growing trend.

It is a consistent message, not merely anti-Assyrian. For example, when Hezekiah at last sought to throw off Assyria's yoke, he turned to Egypt for support. Isaiah didn't like that, either: "Alas for those who go down to Egypt for help and who rely on horses, who trust in chariots because they are many and in horsemen because they are very strong, but do not look to the Holy One of Israel or consult the LORD [YHWH]!"[21]

Jerusalem's Egyptian pivot led to the dark days of siege. Bereft of any more external security options, Hezekiah was assured by long-suffering Isaiah that YHWH would save the holy city, not because they deserved it, but to prove Isaiah's point about trusting the LORD. Isaiah promised that if the king would put his security in YHWH, the city would be spared.

Savvy Hezekiah, finding himself let down by the Egyptians, sensed the shift in the domestic political winds. So, with his approval ratings plummeting, he threw his support to Isaiah's YHWH party. To back it up, he had to destroy the rural altars of Baal and restore YHWH worship in the Temple. It was a desperate and risky act in many ways, but at least now it was YHWH's name on the line and not the king's.

To be sure, YHWH was still a divisive issue. The increased influence of Isaiah's faction meant that traditional Baal worshipers in the olive oil–rich countryside lost money and clout, and Assyrian king Sennacherib's envoy understood this remarkably well. He knew YHWH-only was a political sore point and poked at it as hard as he could. During the siege, he taunted Jerusalem's people in their own language, which the passage charmingly calls *Yehudit* ("Jewish-ish").

"On what do you base this confidence of yours? On whom do you now rely that you have rebelled against me?" mocked the Assyrian. "See, you are relying on Egypt, that broken reed of a staff, which will pierce the hand of anyone who leans on it... But if you say to me, 'We rely on the LORD [YHWH] our God,' is it not he whose high places and altars Hezekiah has removed...?"

This clever Assyrian diplomat knew full well that the altars on the hills were not YHWH's, they were Baal's. He is aiming straight at the social fissure, toying with the grievances of the Baal party. You can imagine the arguments this started. The Bible says that Jerusalem's leaders begged him to shut up, or at least to speak in the imperial Aramaic of the elite, instead of the local Hebrew of the masses.

Incidentally, that word for "trust/security" from Netanyahu's bumper stickers fills this Assyrian propaganda, appearing an astonishing eight times. *Bituach* ("active faith") occurs in every appearance of the words "trust," "rely," and "confidence."

As we know, Sennacherib lifted the siege and Jerusalem was spared. Compared with Assyria's usual practice, this was inexplicable—they weren't in the habit of sparing the cities and lives of rebels. This had been part of the Assyrian diplomat's message: "Do not let Hezekiah mislead you by saying, The LORD [YHWH] will save us. Has any of the gods of the nations saved their land out of the hand of the king of Assyria?... See, you have heard what the kings of Assyria have done to all lands, destroying them utterly. Shall you be delivered?"[22]

The fact is, Jerusalem was delivered and the city was left in peace. There was a steep price, but nonetheless the reprieve appeared to be unprecedented. In the recollection of Jerusalem's scribes, it was a sudden and miraculous deliverance. And indeed, from their perspective, it was an honest assessment. That the miracle came only after cleansing the countryside of Baal was a considerable boost to the YHWH party in Jerusalem. Apparently the LORD had called the Assyrian bluff: "Has any of the gods of the nations saved their land out of the hand of the king of Assyria?"

The answer was an emphatic, "Yes! YHWH has!"

Jerusalem

As Hezekiah's son Manasseh took the throne, YHWH supporters were on the rise but not fully accepted. With the siege crisis over, the new king focused on the economic boom resulting from Jerusalem's strategic position between Assyria and Egypt. Manasseh had a big impact. He was Judah's longest-reigning king, sitting on the throne for fifty-five years, during which time he displayed prodigious money-making talents, especially for himself.

Unfortunately, this led Manasseh and his cronies to make a number of devil's bargains. First, they coquettishly flaunted potential revenue from a revived oil industry in front of Assyria's greedy rulers. This led them to performing sordid favors not only for the foreign gods, but for local gods Baal and Asherah, too; olive oil was dependent on the king's orchard-owning country cousins, who were still very fond of those hillside idols. To accommodate them, he reinstalled the pagan shrines that his father had removed and generally "did what was evil in the sight of the LORD [YHWH], following the abominable practices of the nations."[23]

It goes without saying that the YHWH party, once again deprived of influence in favor of the idolaters, was unhappy. The northern refugees in particular found Assyria's seductive cologne nauseating. They already formed the heart of the YHWH group, and they became even more devout after seeing Jerusalem miraculously saved. And, of course, they hated the Assyrians for what they did to the North. Nothing about Manasseh sat well with them.

Finkelstein relates a leading theory among biblical scholars: "This [YHWH] movement originated among dissident priests and prophets in... the northern kingdom who were aghast at the idolatry and social injustice of the Assyrian period. After the destruction of the kingdom of Israel, they fled southward to promulgate their ideas."[24]

Other YHWH boosters included city-based, white-collar types who wanted to get control over the wealth-producing countryside. The new-money urbanites snapped up farmland decimated through the Assyrian siege and used their tenants as labor to produce that lucrative oil—a cash crop. These urban stockholders were literate and sophisticated. They had big dreams, envisioning a temple for YHWH that would have a global missionary reach. As their power increased, they looked to rid the land of Baal for good.

"Whatever its makeup," Finkelstein concludes, "the new religious movement (dubbed the 'YHWH-alone movement' by the iconoclastic historian Morton Smith) waged a bitter and continuing conflict with the supporters of the older, more traditional Judahite religious customs and rituals."[25] (By "traditional," Finkelstein means the worship of Baal et al.)

Historian and archeologist Baruch Halpern sums up the result: "By the time of Manasseh's death in 642, anti-Assyrian nationalists had grown strong enough in Jerusalem to... manipulate eight-year-old Josiah onto the throne. By 633, Josiah was in revolt against Assyria... By 629, Josiah was asserting Davidic sovereignty over Israel and pursuing Hezekiah's religious policy."[26]

Hezekiah's policy was of course to abolish Baal worship. It was not going to be easy, but the young king had the backing of a powerful and politically experienced cohort that included a very persuasive prophet named Jeremiah. More determinative was the teenage king's disposition—he was fearless. Through courageously visionary leadership he became one of the most important and influential people in history.

That's a big claim but consider this: without Josiah there would be no Judaism, no Jesus, no Christianity, no Islam, and nothing of the myriad philosophies and movements that sprang from those beliefs. I believe he can justifiably be considered as pivotal a figure as we imagine King David to be.

He was unstoppable. At age sixteen he began to seek "the God of his ancestors."[27] When he was twenty, he set out on a tour of destruction, canvassing Judah and the old territory of Israel, pulling down Baal's altars and shattering the sacred poles of Asherah. Grinding up the images, "he made dust of them and scattered it over the graves of those who had sacrificed to them." Not satisfied, he disinterred the bones of their priests and burned them on their own altars. "Then he returned to Jerusalem."

All that took him a while. He was twenty-six years old as this work came to completion, having "purged the land and the house." House here means "temple," and having purified it, he ordered his staff to begin repairs. As this was done, the high priest Hilkiah reported an earth-shaking discovery:

"I have found the book of the law in the house of the LORD."[28]

It's important to understand how specific this information is. This is the Sefer Ha-torah—the very book of the law that Moses gave to Joshua with the enjoinder, "This book of the law shall not depart out of your mouth; you shall meditate on it day and night, so that you may be careful to act in accordance with all that is written in it."[29]

Yet it was clearly an unknown piece of literature to the people of Josiah's Jerusalem! When Josiah sat down to listen as the book was read aloud, he was stunned by everything he heard. "Go, inquire of the LORD [YHWH] for me, for the people, and for all Judah, concerning the words of this book that has been found..."[30]

The king urgently called everyone to the Temple. There, they joined him in an oath to obey the new-found testament and then noticed to their shock a key requirement: the celebration of holidays, most importantly the Feast of Passover. Let's not fail to notice this observation: "Neither in the days of the judges who led Israel nor in the days of the kings of Israel and the kings of Judah had any such Passover been observed."[31]

If we doubted that Moses of Exodus is a literary device of late design, this ought to settle the question. The Bible admits it here: the Law of Moses was unknown, and the key national feast of liberation was never practiced— not in the time of the judges and not under the kings. That's an astonishing admission—the Law and Feasts are the two main elements of Moses' legacy; to admit that they did not exist before Josiah is to confess that there was no literal Moses, of whom the Jerusalemites in Josiah's day had never even heard. Or, more truly, that Josiah was Moses—he *was* the lawgiver who instituted the feast and championed YHWH, "who was known to your ancestors as El Shaddai." Those words only came to light through Josiah since the Book of Exodus was likewise unknown. It is Josiah saying, "your Canaanite ancestors knew God as El, but it was really our newly adopted YHWH at work."

Did Josiah write the book he "found"? It looks that way. Sure, they may have recovered something—perhaps the bare bones of an ancient priestly text—but whatever it was, it was clearly something long forgotten. What is unambiguous from the many threads of culture and the numerous names for God preserved in the version left to us is this: Josiah began and may have largely completed a work that synthesized all these traditional elements into a clear monotheistic framework—an anti-Uruk ethos that was only recently purified in the melting pot of immigrant-laden Jerusalem.

It is a work of deft editing—splicing clips of YHWH with old footage of El, cutting between Abraham and Jacob to make them appear related to each other, and using Moses, Joshua, and David as dissolves to cover the awkward transitions. Parts were very old tradition; parts were new narrative devices designed to blend and smooth the themes.

This is a sensitive issue, but I would like to offer this thought to those scandalized by it: behind the work of these editors is the idea of a supreme editor. YHWH as a universal, transpersonal creator and sustainer is, in a most fundamental aspect, the reconciliation of all things. What better testimony could there be than a holy book that does that very thing: reconcile all these diverse pieces of humanity into a counter-Mesopotamian vision?

One of Josiah's tasks was to formulate a coherent plot with the information he had on hand. He needed to explain, for example, how and why the supposed original law was lost and why both North and South were until then such flagrant deviants. How did their Temple come to be filled with idols?

Josiah hangs that around Solomon's neck. The decline began because Solomon "loved many foreign women."[32] It allows Josiah and his team to keep all the embarrassing details of their documentary history. Apart from the mythologized prototype of David, Jerusalem's kings make for a history of uninterrupted idol worship, right up until the Assyrian exile of Israel. Even its heroes fail scandalously. So, while the edit attempts to forge an identity, there is no cover up. Even reading it at this great distance in time, we can see from the text itself what the situation was and just how pagan these nations had been.

Just consider the account of Solomon's ancient installation of idols in the Temple. Solomon built the Temple. This means the Temple was always filled with idols from the day it was built! For instance, Josiah boasts that he removed "the image of Asherah." It was not in some countryside shrine—he extracted it from the Temple. Until Josiah's reign, it was unremarkable—literally unremarkable, as no one ever said anything about it.

Josiah tells us that the builder of Jerusalem's Holy Temple "followed Astarte the goddess of the Sidonians, and Milcom the abomination of the Ammonite... Solomon built a high place for Chemosh the abomination of Moab, and for Molech the abomination of the Ammonites, on the mountain east of Jerusalem."[33]

Other specifics leave no doubt what the Temple and its environs had been like before Josiah "discovered the book."

"He [Josiah] broke down the houses of the male temple prostitutes that were in the house of the LORD, where the women did weaving for Asherah."

"He defiled Topheth, which is in the valley of Ben-hinnom, so that no one would make a son or a daughter pass through fire as an offering to Molech."

"He removed the horses that the kings of Judah had dedicated to the sun, at the entrance to the house of the LORD..."

That's a lot of weirdness in Jerusalem and a fair share of it, again, right inside the Temple. This is serious stuff: they burned their children alive to this Molech, not in some pre-Moses dark ages but just the other day—Josiah is only now getting rid of it. And given that Asherah was the local name for Inanna, I'll leave to your imagination what went on inside the Temple where "the houses of the male temple prostitutes" sat among the women who "did weaving for Asherah." (Hint: "doing weaving" is code for something else.)

None of these redactions are concealed. The Bible asks us to believe in Moses and Joshua, but then repudiates their accomplishments. It asks us to believe in a monotheistic and powerful kingdom under David, and then denies that David's people knew the Torah or celebrated the Passover. Having set David as a narrative anchor, it tells us that the whole thing immediately gave way to the most depraved idolatry. In short, these scriptures frankly admit to being more parable than deposition. To me, such honesty is reassuring; it lends the text credibility.

These parables, these reports, these facts—all are precious observations made by people trying to make sense of what had gone before them. In this way, Josiah is not only Moses, he is also Abraham, Jacob, and David, too. His is the great light-bulb moment of post-Mesopotamian awakening.

❦   9   ❦

AXIAL AGE

Sawn Asunder

Josiah appeared at this time as the result of an evolving post-Sumerian awakening. His moment was a gift of the historical process, bestowing on his scribes the responsibility of filtering and unifying the diverse Jerusalem population's varied traditions—El and YHWH, Jacob and Moses, and much more all grafted into the patriarchal root, Abraham. The result was a unique perspective, the Hebrew Bible, a coherent alternative to Mesopotamian mythology, and a work of possibly unparalleled influence.

This is not to diminish what brought them here. There is no doubt that their traditions and the real heroes of the past paved the way to this milestone. Those YHWH devotees of Midian, the Judahite and Israelite kings and ancestral Canaanite patriarchs, the land itself—it was all leading to this.

Josiah's scripture is a record of social evolution that gives notice of a very important adaptive breakthrough that occurred in human consciousness. And he is not alone. At exactly this time, independent of one another, prophets and philosophers from dissimilar places reported similar innovations. The centuries that gave us the Hebrew Bible's sophisticated view of a transcendent faith also gave us the works of Plato and the teachings of Buddha.

Happily, their era reveals the next step after Göbekli Tepe and Eridu. It is to be an age of critical awareness—a cognizant recognition of socially constructed reality and skepticism toward the powers of imagination. In short order, teachers and writers began to remember what had been forgotten: that we were the authors of our reality. We had choices. What we created, we could dismantle, and we could create something else.

We call this awakening the Axial Age, a term coming to us from philosopher Karl Jaspers. In short, the Axial Age was another watershed in the way thinkers think. It occurred between 800 and 200 BCE, occurring across many unconnected cultures. While we should be careful in applying such a broad brush too liberally, it's hard to argue with Jaspers' observation that there was a widespread cognitive breakthrough demonstrated by the great minds of the period. We can think of Isaiah, Buddha, Plato, and Laozi as exemplars. They all appeared in this relatively brief period with revolutionary ideas that challenged the prevailing concept of what was real.

Among the Jews, the tide turned when teenaged Josiah ascended the throne. He revived prophet Isaiah's blacklisted anti-Mesopotamian cosmology—the idea of the ineffable Divine, so beautifully represented by YHWH, who had no form and no speakable name. (Notably, Josiah's predecessor, wayward King Manasseh, had Isaiah sawn in two, a not very subtle critique of the prophet's theology of universal unity.)[1]

Under Josiah, it was a brave new world but fraught with prickly questions: What does it mean to foreign relations if there is a transcendent and universal God for all? Should a borderless and universal identity be assumed that will unite all peoples? Does this become a necessity, meaning that the champions of YHWH should launch a jihad to impose the truth on other nations, destroying their false gods just as was done at home? Or, if fundamental reality is indeed beyond form and explanation, why bother with any of this—why even have a religion and priests in the first place?

To help us think about these questions, we will turn to some of the other Axial Age notables. But first, for context, let's quickly recall what brought us to this the third major turning point in human thinking.

First, we had the example of Göbekli Tepe, where we observed a marked change in consciousness that led humans to begin to settle in towns. This was the hinge upon which humanity turned from its long prehistory as hunter-gatherers to our settled phase.

Then we witnessed the next turn in Sumeria. There, our ancestors conjured a Cosmic Order to justify a hierarchical system. This was civilization, which materialized an imagined heavenly realm into a concretely conceived, unquestioned cradle-to-grave sociopolitical system. It relied on the newly invented primary schools that programed young minds as they developed, mimicking in each life what had occurred over the evolution of the species: from innocence, to anxiety, to imposed fictional reality and social conformity. Although imagined, this programming executed its processes in our educated minds as unalterably real, out-and-out "the way things are," as if culture was natural law.

Now, in the Axial Age, the consciousness of a few advanced thinkers like Isaiah began to differentiate between imagined reality and the unconstructed Real. It was as if an observation tower were built above recursive consciousness that allowed them to peer into its inner workings. This was the ability to think critically about thinking itself, when our Axial Age pioneers began to realize that society was not like gravity: it was mutable, moldable, and changeable—every aspect of it could be questioned.

To illustrate, let's go far afield and consider Buddha. At first glance, he might seem too far removed from our story, living in a distant corner of remote India; in fact, he lived within the same Mesopotamia-based system as every civilized person did. Sumeria's reach by the 1000s BCE was far indeed. In fact, the first thing we learn about Buddha is that he is heir to a Mesopotamia-style city-state, the kingdom of Śākya. Depending on the source, he is either the crown prince of a conventional monarchy or the heir-apparent in a mafia-like oligarchy. Whatever his position, Buddha was at the pinnacle of a wealthy and powerful city-state hierarchy.

Apropos of our understanding of Mesopotamian society, it is notable that Buddhism describes its founder's lofty status mostly in terms of illusions. Indeed, his relationship to those illusions is the key feature of Buddha's biography and message.[2]

In Buddha's example, civilization had constructed around him a universe where everyone was happy and healthy, with no hint of poverty or death. It was the materialist world as advertised: No pain! No suffering! You might even live forever! It was good to be Buddha.

Approaching his thirtieth birthday, Buddha happily set out on what was supposed to be a carefully stage-managed tour of his dominions. All was fine, business as usual, until his driver made a fateful wrong turn—or in computer science terms (since this is really about social programming), he executed the wrong path, accessing data that until now was forbidden to the prince. It recalls Mr. Anderson in the film *The Matrix*, who took the Red Pill and found himself unplugged and unceremoniously flushed out of virtual reality into the shocking realization that the whole world was enslaved.

What hit Buddha first was the sight of a toothless, wrinkled, nearly blind old man. Dressed in rags, and with trembling hands, he begged for food in the street. Unable to make sense of it, Buddha questioned his driver: "What is that? It can't be a man?!" The driver explained that this was indeed a man, and that he was once as young and vigorous as the prince, that he had grown old, and that this is the fate of all who live, the prince included.

When Buddha returned home, he could no longer enjoy his privileges. He was waking up to the Real. Everywhere he looked he saw people gripped by delusions. The young revelers in his court were growing old, and one day would be unable to care for themselves; they'd be beggars and supplicants. (Which reminds us of Jesus' comment to the founder of his church, Peter: "Truly, truly, I say to you, when you were young, you used to dress yourself and walk wherever you wanted, but when you are old, you will stretch out your hands, and another will dress you and carry you where you do not want to go.")

Needing to get to the bottom of it, Buddha made plans to go out again, despite his father's objections, and this time in disguise. Now unshielded, his next outings exposed him to the sight of a sick man, and soon thereafter a rotting corpse.

This was only the beginning of his deconstruction, for though he was disillusioned and depressed, he was not fully awakened; falsehoods were shattered, but truth was unknown. Unable to return to his illusions, he renounced his right to the throne, his wealth, his palaces, and all his comforts to live as an ascetic; he devoted himself to the monk's path, having understood that nothing else mattered.

Years later he had his awakening, a direct experience of fundamental Reality. His biography attests that in this moment, Buddha saw the ego unravel. "In the end there is no 'I' or 'mine,' just as fire is extinguished when the firewood is consumed."[3]

That which all modern humans experience as a separate self was upon examination found to be non-self—a continuum of interdependent phenomena, nothing of permanence. "Whatever suffering arises in the world, all is caused by consciousness," Buddhist teaching tells us. "Look at this world with its gods; enmeshed in reified things, considering self in what is not-self, they imagine, 'this is real.' Whatever they think it is, it becomes something else. That is false. For transient things are delusory."[4]

Buddha sat for seven days, "looking into his own mind... reflecting that on that spot where he had obtained liberation. 'What I had to do, is done. I have obtained the path of right awakening.'"[5]

Then, before arising to begin teaching others, he composed a verse about the grinding terror of history. It was about "the round of many births" and mentions repeatedly the "house-builder," a poetic reference to constructed reality. "House-builder, you are seen! You will not build a house again. All your rafters are broken, the ridge pole dismantled!"[6]

Buddhist texts give a much fuller account of his enlightenment—a life-long study for those so inclined. We will leave it there, but I can't resist adding one more thing. The Buddhacarita records that upon Buddha's awakening, nature responded with rejoicing. The sky shone bright, a pleasant breeze blew across the land and trees dropped flowers and fruit out of season "as if to do him honor." Best of all, "At that time, just as in Paradise, māndārava flowers, lotuses and water-lilies of gold and beryl fell from the sky... at that moment none gave way to anger, no one was ill or experienced any discomfort... the world became tranquil, as though it had reached perfection."[7] In Buddha's consciousness, the doors of Paradise opened.

Meanwhile, far to the West, another Axial Age hub had formed in Athens, where philosophers proactively sought disillusionment. That's right, the Greek philosophers intentionally practiced critical thinking to deconstruct their own delusional houses. All premises were questioned, and then questioned again.

With respect to our subject of Paradise, Plato's idea of anamnesis ("to call to mind again") is especially helpful.[8] Anamnesis is the recovery of a deep universal memory. To the profound questions of existence, the answers, Plato said, are already within us in our original consciousness. Anamnesis suggests that Paradise nostalgia is not a nagging question but a nagging answer—a solution awaiting our attentive recollection. So, to our inquiry about lost Paradise, Plato would say the answer is buried beneath many layers of constructed illusions; we have only to uncover it, to remember it. This accords well with Buddhism, where anamnesis might correlate with "unborn awareness"; it also fits YHWH's radically paradoxical "fundamental transcendentalism," the unveiling of the realist Real.

In the Axial Age, apart from cultural context, Buddha, Plato, and Isaiah complement and affirm one another, and all the more effectively because they use different terms and philosophical frameworks to the same ends. For all these teachers, there is a deconstructive drive, an impulse brought to bear by our next prophet, who focused his attention upon unmasking Jerusalem's most sacred ideas.

The Jewish Buddha

Among the people of Judah, the Axial Age's most Buddha-like representative has to be Jeremiah. Mentored by Isaiah, his theological technique was radical even by today's standards. Rather than try to define the Divine, Jeremiah pursued a theology of presentation. For him, theology's task was nothing but to frame its subject and illuminate it, so that it might be seen directly. Jeremiah practiced theology as Buddhist meditation.

Lesser theologians aspire to tell us precisely what God is. The problems there are well-known to us: first, the definitions get in the way, obscuring our vision; and second, any definition is doomed to inaccuracy. Theologians are part of creation. They cannot objectively see the divine so as to comprehend it in definitive terms. This is the same problem that physicists admit to: we are part of the physics, so we can't objectively stand outside it to measure it.

But we can experience physics—for example, we can feel the warmth and hope of a sunrise. Jeremiah works on that basis. He submits to his position as a human being who is conceived by reality rather than as the master theologian who conceives of it. He cannot define God but believes God can express divinity through him, and through anything and everything.

Jeremiah is an artist, a singer, a poet. Truth is available in the living notes and words of his song. When he says, "Thus saith the Lord...," it isn't a proposition—it is an inspiration. He bows before the indefinable to guide the listener toward a direct experience of the Divine—he points to the rising sun.

For example, Jeremiah evocatively likens the Divine to a "source of living waters." We can feel what this means, but one can't quite put it in a dictionary—no one is going to think of God literally as a mountain spring. There is no danger of our hearing this expression and making a statue of it to worship. It is the mystery of the metaphor that makes it so effective; it says nothing in particular and yet everything we need to know at the same time.

Meanwhile, Jeremiah's denunciation of idols reverses his technique. They are "broken cisterns, that don't hold water." This time his image is relentlessly mundane; everyone had use of water cisterns, could easily visualize them, and could quite easily manufacture them—there was nothing mysterious about it all. So idols, he says, are no different from any other clay object made in a corner shop, except the former don't work as advertised—they are broken.

It is a very effective argument. Divine reality is living water, while the pretentious stone and wooden gods of the Cosmic Order are broken cisterns. Take your pick. Furthermore, Jeremiah says, idols are not limited to statues; they are anything we might think of as a sure thing—any object, any idea, any system, any person.

Baruch Halpern, the University of Georgia's Covenant Foundation

Professor of Jewish Studies, summarizes Jeremiah's message: "He assails the hypostatization of icons, of ritual, of the temple, of the ark, of the law, and of the seeming manifestations of YHWH that are understood to be his divine armies..." and "avoids anthropomorphism in thought and in language." This extends to the idea of angels, too: the prophet "never mentions or implies the existence of angels (false manifestations of YHWH)."[9]

And don't try to locate God in a specific place, either. For Jeremiah, God must "fill heaven and earth." When his prophet colleagues reported visions of a locatable divinity or talked about having entered the physical space of God's supernatural court, Jeremiah mocked them: "Who has stood in the council of YHWH and seen and heard his word?" Jeremiah never reports such visions or visitations.[10]

With due apologies to Indiana Jones, Jeremiah even hints at getting rid of the Ark of the Covenant. As all movie buffs know, this wasn't an anthropomorphic idol at all, but rather an empty box, a sublime reference to the idea of Reality if there ever was one. It was way ahead of its time; emptiness as a notion of ultimate reality was nearly patented by Buddhism a few centuries later. And yet, in Jeremiah's eyes, the box had become a fetish. Addressing the already-converted monotheists of Jerusalem, the prophet lays it out: "They shall no longer say, 'The ark of the covenant of the Lord.' It shall not come to mind, or be remembered, or missed; nor shall another one be made."[11] Jeremiah wanted to get rid of it!

The prophet doesn't even dignify his targets by allowing them a sacred status—he just says they are stupid: "They burn offerings to a delusion."[12] Like Buddha's arguments, Jeremiah's are scientific; just look, he says, observe it for yourself.

> The customs of the peoples are false: a tree from the forest is cut down, and worked with an ax by the hands of an artisan; people deck it with silver and gold; they fasten it with hammer and nails so that it cannot move. Their idols are like scarecrows in a cucumber field, and they cannot speak; they have to be carried, for they cannot walk. Do not be afraid of them, for they cannot do evil, nor is it in them to do good.[13]

When he says the word "delusion," Jeremiah employs a Buddhist turn of phrase. Delusion is a state of the mind and the key term by which Buddhism will later diagnose the cause of human suffering. Jeremiah identifies delusion not as a religious failure in the traditional sense, but as Buddha did, as a problem of consciousness: "The heart is devious above all else; it is perverse —who can understand it?" said Jeremiah.[14]

Jeremiah's logic was razor sharp and so was his tongue. As you can imagine, he infuriated adherents of the old-time religion. He made people uncomfortable. Then as now, people took solace from the status quo. The prospect of admitting that their securities were no better than a broken water pot or stick of wood took more courage than many people could muster.

I find him a constant challenge. Writing this now, I can't help but look across the room where I keep a 4,000-year-old household idol. I don't pray to her and have never believed in her; she means something to me as a symbol of those ancient times. I chose her, frankly, because I think she is beautiful, and because she reminds me of the modern idols that I am tempted to put my faith in, temporal securities such as my retirement account. If Jeremiah insisted on taking these securities away, I'd want to resist, and the people of Jerusalem did, too.

Really, it is amazing that Jeremiah got away with what he did. With poor sawn-asunder Isaiah's fate standing as a warning, he nonetheless persisted in taking away the people's crutches no matter what. His patron Josiah couldn't live forever to protect him, and the circumstances that afforded Jerusalem its autonomy—namely, Assyria's weakening position—would soon be his undoing.

Nebuchadnezzar

Josiah's problem was Egypt. As the desperate Assyrians called upon the pharaoh for help, Jerusalem found itself once again in the spotlight. Egypt wanted a piece of the olive oil action, and Jerusalem now sat as a strategic necessity. Josiah lost his life resisting the encroachment, and Jerusalem came effectively under Egyptian rule, eventually installing Josiah's older son as a puppet ruler.

Through it all, there stood Jeremiah, now rejected and thoroughly out of favor. The new foreign-controlled leadership returned in desperation to the gods of the old world. Unbowed, Jeremiah held fast. He said exactly the same things while out of favor as he had said under Josiah's protection, and adopting his mentor Isaiah's language, he assailed King Jehoiakim's trust or "security" in military fortifications and foreign armies and gods. This took guts considering what they'd done to Isaiah. His message verged on the treacherous, saying in effect, "Last time, we destroyed your shrines and idols;

this time Jerusalem and the Temple itself will be destroyed." When Jeremiah went up to the Temple specifically to deliver this divine communiqué, the religious leadership's response was a terse prophecy: "You must die!"[15]

But they were wrong; it was Jehoiakim who died, for as it turns out, he played the dangerous game of international intrigue badly. His fatal mistake was provoking Assyria's successor, the revived Babylonian Empire. Thinking Egypt would protect him, the greedy monarch refused to pay tribute to the new regime, upon which Nebuchadnezzar, Babylon's notoriously brutal king, decided he'd had enough—what Jehoiakim would not volunteer, Babylon would take by force.

To that end, the Babylonians marched on Jerusalem, laying siege with an expertise that put Assyria's earlier attempt to shame. Before all was said and done, Judah's playboy king was dead, his rotting body unceremoniously dumped over the wall like garbage by his subjects, who were too hungry and terrified to bury him. Jehoiachin, the heir presumptive, assumed the throne for three painful months before finally raising the flag of surrender.

As the Bible dutifully records, Nebuchadnezzar

> carried off all the treasures of the house of the LORD, and the treasures of the king's house; he cut in pieces all the vessels of gold in the temple of the LORD... He carried away all Jerusalem, all the officials, all the warriors, ten thousand captives, all the artisans and the smiths; no one remained, except the poorest people of the land.

The exiles included the king and his wives, his mother, and his court officials: "the elite of the land, he took into captivity from Jerusalem to Babylon."[16]

He did not destroy the Temple however, deciding to leave Zedekiah, Josiah's remaining son, in charge. We might have hoped that young Zedekiah, having witnessed all this, would listen to Jeremiah who'd yet to be proven wrong. But no; Zedekiah tried to re-arm and re-forge the Egyptian alliance, putting all of his faith in Egypt's gods, to whom he pledged loyalty, despite emphatic warnings from Jeremiah of dire consequences.

In fact, it did not require a prophet to foresee Nebuchadnezzar's reaction. Twice betrayed by the Jewish kingdom's none-too-bright rulers, he was incensed; so for the second time in a decade, Jerusalem's walls faced an unstoppable Babylonian siege. This time there was to be no mercy. Babylonian general Nebuzaradan was ordered to burn and raze the Temple along with the palace and every single house in the city. Jerusalem's walls were dismantled stone by stone.

Then they "carried into exile the rest of the people who were left in the city—all the rest of the population." Even the poor were hauled away. As for the royal family, "They slaughtered the sons of Zedekiah before his eyes, then put out the eyes of Zedekiah; they bound him in fetters and took him to Babylon."[17]

Guess whom they spared: Jeremiah. Allowed to stay behind, he declared that the Temple's destruction and the exile of the people was for the best: they were idols anyway, and at last they'd be free of them. This was a necessary purge, he said—it was meant to discipline, not to destroy. "Our ancestors have inherited nothing but lies, worthless things in which there is no profit... Therefore I am surely going to teach them, this time I am going to teach them..."[18]

Jeremiah tells it as a story of death and rebirth. There will be a lengthy stay in Babylonian rehab ("because you have behaved worse than your ancestors... I will hurl you out of this land") but after Israel sobers up, he promises restoration ("I will bring them back to their own land"). It is a new narrative of redemption, befitting a new age, and it is superior to the tale of Egypt and Moses: "...it shall no longer be said, 'As the LORD lives who brought the people of Israel up out of the land of Egypt,' but 'As the LORD lives who brought the people of Israel up out of the land of the north.'"[19]

There is more to it than that, however, and it comes as an answer to the question, "What does it mean to foreign relations if there is a transcendent and universal God for all?"

As an Axial Age visionary, Jeremiah sees something universal and profoundly interrelated in the saga of Israel and Babylon. Israel's loss of the Temple becomes a metaphor for the loss of the Garden of Eden for all humanity. Her punitive captivity in the land of falsehood and slavery is the whole world's enslavement to the Mesopotamian order.

Likewise, Israel's restoration will represent Paradise restored, not only for Israel, but for all humankind, Babylon included. As YHWH promised to Abraham, "All the clans of the soil will find blessing through you!"

We read the same vision of global reckoning and salvation in Isaiah. There too, a prophesied exile echoes estrangement from the Garden of Eden so that all nations—Babylon included—may return to the Garden through the mysterious metaphysics of Judah's restoration: In the end, all will be judged, and all will be saved, and the key figure in that story is not a Jew at all, but an Iranian whose ancestral faith is one of the most important and neglected stories in all of history.

The First Messiah

Isaiah is no conventional chronicle. It comes across as a series of ecstatic interjections, sometimes indubitably hallucinatory, and notoriously difficult to translate. And yet, among the outbursts, there are certain passages so catholic that they hardly need translation at all, as if Isaiah speaks the Adamic tongue that resides in our deepest Chomskyan genes. A handful of these have affected the course of history as few words have, beginning with a short declaration right at the beginning of Isaiah's collected works.

"In the last days the mountain of the LORD's temple will be established as the highest of the mountains, and all nations will stream to it." It is a universal message to be sure, but not at all pluralistic. The purpose of this unexpected Gentile pilgrimage to Jerusalem is deprogramming, as if the nations must reciprocate Judah's foreign chastisement by going to Zion to have their own period of rehabilitation. The nations say as much en route: "Come, let us go up to the mountain of the LORD, to the temple of the God of Jacob. He will teach us his ways, so that we may walk in his paths."[20]

Here, then, is Abraham's promise to spawn a people to bless the nations, and again modern liberalism will struggle with the premise that Jews might have the truth that everyone else needs. But that reaction forgets that Isaiah's idea stands at the root of any liberalism the West might hold to today. The plain fact is that our concern for human life and rights was tutored by the words of Jerusalem, just as Isaiah envisioned, and our inclusive values begin here with this gathering of all ethnicities, a redemption of the judgment at Babel and a restoration of the Edenic ideal of one flesh. As we shall soon see, it was a vision developed hand-in-hand with Gentiles. This is simply the Jewish version of the dream; it just so happens that it was theirs that survived to influence the world in which we live. It isn't chauvinism—it is simply the way history ran its course. Or, if you prefer, it is God's chosen instrument of communication, for history and God are functionally indistinguishable.

Isaiah's next words present a picture of what the perfected world looks like. His lines are delivered so incredibly well that it would be difficult to find a literate person who could not paraphrase them from memory. In the last days, Isaiah says, when all the nations have come together, "they shall beat their swords into plowshares, and their spears into pruning hooks;

nation shall not lift up sword against nation, neither shall they learn war any more."[21] A little bit later he underscores it: "There shall be endless peace."[22]

After two and a half millennia, no one has described the ideal world more effectively. Isaiah's words are ever-present across cultures and ideologies as an aspiration for the world we want. Even history's first atheist empire, a most unlikely pilgrim to Zion, found itself unable to do better. In 1959, at the peak of the Cold War, the Soviet Union left its everlasting mark on the United Nations through the gift of a massive bronze statue, a magnificent angular *nový Sovětský* (New Soviet) man, heroically pounding away at his massive sword with the hammer of communism. Meant to represent Soviet values to the assembled nations, its pedestal unabashedly evangelizes Isaiah: "Let Us Beat Swords into Plowshares." That's because the Marxist vision is not original—it is derived from the Paradise dream, and nobody evokes the Workers' Paradise better than Isaiah. Truly the nations have come to Jerusalem and learned the ways of the LORD.

Another of Isaiah's unforgettable images might still be better known. It is so pervasive as to become a contraction: "The lion will lay with the lamb." What he wrote in full is far better than that:

> The wolf shall dwell with the lamb, and the leopard shall lie down with the young goat, and the calf and the lion and the fattened calf together; and a little child shall lead them. The cow and the bear shall graze; their young shall lie down together; and the lion shall eat straw like the ox. The nursing child shall play over the hole of the cobra, and the weaned child shall put his hand on the adder's den. They shall not hurt or destroy in all my holy mountain; for the earth shall be full of the knowledge of YHWH as the waters cover the sea.[23]

It is in light of this beautifully composed eternal hope that we must read the blistering prophecies of judgment against both Jerusalem and Babylon recorded by Isaiah and Jeremiah. Jerusalem's destruction was to be the means of liberation from the clinging stupidity of idols, a divine spanking. Now Babylon will face cleansing destruction, too, freeing it at last from the old Sumerian system. Very soon, the prophets believed, we will be one big, happy, unarmed, and idol-free family—cobras and children, lions and wolves and lambs all included.

For that to happen, we need an instrument that serves two purposes: judgment on Babylon and restoration for Judah. Jeremiah names the Medes of the Medo-Persian Empire as just the right tool: "The LORD has stirred up the spirit of the kings of the Medes, because his purpose concerning Babylon is to destroy it."[24]

Isaiah, for his part, pinpoints an individual leader, characteristically extending the idea of Judah's restoration to eternal and universal proportions:

> The people who walked in darkness have seen a great light; those who lived in a land of deep darkness—on them light has shined. For a child has been born for us, a son given to us; authority rests upon his shoulders; and he is named Wonderful Counselor, Mighty God, Everlasting Father, Prince of Peace. His authority shall grow continually, and there shall be endless peace.[25]

What does this person, whom Christians will readily identify with Jesus, have to do with Jeremiah's Medes and Persians? Well, Isaiah (the second Isaiah) identifies him by name, designating him the "anointed" or "messiah"; and he is none other than Cyrus, the king of the Medes and Persians:

> Thus says the LORD to his anointed [*māšîaḥ*—"messiah"] to Cyrus, whose right hand I have grasped, to subdue nations before him and to loose the belts of kings... I will go before you and level the exalted places, I will break in pieces the doors of bronze and cut through the bars of iron... I have stirred him up in righteousness, and I will make all his ways level; he shall build my city and set my exiles free.

And elsewhere: "Cyrus, 'He is my shepherd, and he shall fulfill all my purpose'; saying of Jerusalem, 'She shall be built,' and of the Temple, 'Your foundation shall be laid.'"[26]

Because English speakers know the word "messiah," it would be entirely correct to translate "his anointed Cyrus" as "his Messiah Cyrus." This might be clearer to our ears if we read from the Septuagint, the Greek translation of the Hebrew Bible that was widely used by Jews in the last half of the first millennium BCE, and certainly used by Jesus and the Apostles. There, the word "anointed" or *māšîaḥ* is translated from Hebrew for Greek-speaking Jews as χριστῷ or *christós*—or as we say it in English, Christ. "Thus says the LORD to his Christ, to Cyrus..." How does that sound? This is how the passage read to most Jews in the final 300 years before Christ Jesus.

Further to the point, as a Medo-Persian ruler, Cyrus held the title "King of Kings." So the savior who will judge Babylon and redeem Israel is no less than Christ the King of Kings—a fellow named Cyrus.

None of this is incidental. Cyrus' kingdom and religion form the prototype of the eschatological Messiah and the Kingdom of God as it came to be understood before the birth of Jesus and beyond. He is the archetype of salvation.

Moreover, the philosophy of Cyrus' ancestral people will give definition to what billions of people imagine today when they think of salvation or of world peace. Isaiah's own ravishing vision of national delegations streaming to the throne of wisdom is directly modeled on Cyrus and his religious philosophy. I'll try to show exactly how over the next several pages.

Already, however, at Cyrus' introduction, we begin to see a problem: the reader may ask how the magnificent vision of universal welfare, global peace, and a transcendent deity can be embodied in the objectified force of a warrior-king acting on behalf of a deity who literally takes him by the hand. Throughout history—and today more than ever—we have holy warriors who promise to emerge victorious to finally beat all the swords into plowshares. How can peace come through violence? Isaiah's scathing denouncements of Ahaz for his trust in weapons do not square well with his praise of this Iranian jihadist.

It is disturbing. And this is the problem with the idea of progress, the danger that we will construct a new dominating ideology out of progressive awakenings, much like the Eridu priests did with the otherwise helpful history houses that became dominating temples. All the evidence from this point indicates that we took the transcendent visions of the Axial Age and again hammered and chiseled them into hard imposable objects. The New Soviet man, heroically pounding away at his massive sword with the hammer of communism, literally does this: it constructs a new idol, a new false reality out of the best of transcendent visions.

It's the fantasy of one last apocalyptic war to win all wars, a final act of history giving birth to a golden age. I and my Muslim Brothers and our Jewish and Marxist cousins and many an American president have fallen for it. But it doesn't mean we have to make that fatal mistake. And it does not mean that Paradise consciousness is impossible. As Buddha and Abraham show, we can truly wake up and simply live. Keep reading!

For now in our story, we are at a stage where the Paradise dream is taking shape in a form still cherished by anyone hoping for a better world. But we must take care to remember that it is also cherished by holy warriors and totalitarian despots who think that they can deliver this world to us. It is not only liberals who see themselves as the last stage of evolution; Adolph Hitler did, too.

How does it go so wrong? Simply by reifying and politicizing the memory and dream of Paradise, by ignoring the consciousness of the Garden of Eden, which is transcendent, transpersonal, unconstructed awareness. There is a sure litmus test: just ask if the intention will result in reconciliation or alienation.

This means it isn't enough to know what Paradise looks like. Mesopotamian civilization knew what it looked like and delivered a perverse fake. And in Isaiah's days, the revelation, while clear, was still a work in progress in terms of how we get there. There is suddenly a clear perspective on the nature of civilization's reality, with its idols and virtual universes, but then seemingly a plan to construct again yet another simulacrum. We get lengthy flashes of transcendence and then words that indicate that those revelations were not fully processed. That's just fine. We are here to consider it all, and to grapple further with these questions. We need to know more; we must fill in the missing pieces of the Persian Messiah's ancestry and philosophy and meet the man who gave us the word "Paradise."

Paradise Promised

Cyrus was an Iranian of whom modern Iranians are still proud. Although Iran today is a theocratic Islamic state, the nation still celebrates Newroz, or New Day, the pre-Islamic religious holiday of the ancient Iranians. This is possible because of Islam's enthusiastic embrace of the Paradise idea, which Newroz represents. Islam, we must always keep in mind, is a variation on Zoroastrianism, Judaism, and Christianity. In fact, the Quran preserves the word "Paradise" in its original Persian form: "Indeed, those who have believed and done righteous deeds—they will have the Gardens of Paradise as a lodging, wherein they abide eternally."[27]

Here, the Arabic word *firdawsi* is not a translation—it is a transliteration from the ancient Persian *pairidaēza*, a liturgical Zoroastrian term. The /f/ in the former is the result of a common consonantal shift from /p/ that is familiar to every linguist, as is the shift from /z/ to /s/.

In English, the word's popularity is due to Jesus: "Paradise" is the word he used on the cross in his final statements, a promise that a thief would be welcomed in that place with him. As in the Quran, the Gospel's Greek word, παράδεισος (*paradeisos*), is a transliteration, not a Greek translation. In Hebrew, we find the same thing: it is written as a transliteration, too, from פרדס to *par'des*.

If I may state an obvious conclusion, these great religious traditions directly borrow the word "Paradise" and do not attempt to translate it because their own native languages did not have a word that meant the same thing. The content and meaning of "Paradise" are Persian conceptions.

We see this again in the Septuagint (LXX), whose translators were tasked with producing a faithful Greek version of the Hebrew scriptures for the majority of Jews, who at this time lived in a predominantly Greek-speaking world. Textual comparisons between it and the Dead Sea Scrolls, along with Talmudic commentary, show that the LXX was believed by Jews of this period to be authoritative and inspired.[28]

When the LXX translators came to the phrase "Garden of Eden," they decided not to translate it word-for-word into Greek, which they might easily have done. Instead, they went with the Persian word, giving us the Greek transliteration that is the same word Jesus used on the cross. This means that Jews of this early prophetic era believed the original Persian word *pairidaēza* was the best philosophical representation of primordial Eden.

They weren't alone; during that influential period leading up to the birth of Jesus, *pairidaēza* in its various transliterations became shorthand for the world to come—for heaven, for restoration—not just for Persians, but for Jews, Muslims, Christians, and many others.

To really understand why this old Persian word came to represent our hopes, we will want to meet the man who made the word and the concept popular in the first place—the man who defined Paradise for Jews, Christians, Muslims, Marxists, Neoliberals, and other dreamers. He was Zoroaster, an ethnic cousin of Cyrus, who lived somewhere in the borderlands of Central Asia and northern India among the people who would later be the Medes and Persians of Iran and Mesopotamia.

Exactly when he lived is still a puzzle. Early tradition places him in the 600s BCE, but modern scholarship pushes the date back as far as 1500 BCE. One clue is the language that preserves his teaching, which is unmistakably of the older period. I'll settle on a safe 1000 BCE for the sake of discussion. This makes him an early Axial Age philosopher, likely the very first one, and a man of Abraham's time (some even speculate that Abraham might be based on Zoroaster).

His context is Indo-Aryan, a large branch of the prehistoric Indo-European language family. When Zoroaster lived, Indo-Aryan was just beginning to separate into its own branches. Back in his day, the two branches were Avestan, the language of Zoroastrianism's oldest texts, and Vedic Sanskrit, the tongue used in the Rig Veda, the oldest of Hindu texts. They were practically the same language, to a large degree mutually intelligible, as they'd only just begun to drift apart. Today the drift is far more pronounced, expressed in many smaller offshoots: Farsi, Kurdish, and Pashto on the Aryan side; and Hindi, Nepali, and Punjabi, to name a few, on the Indo side.

This is important to know if we wish to place Zoroaster in a particular location and point in history, for it tells us a lot about Zoroaster's culture and society. To get a real feel for what Zoroaster's life was like, we can simply refer to the ample evidence that remains of the culture that produced both language families—that is, we can simply look at the trunk of the family tree.

We refer to that mother culture as Vedic. It is not Hinduism and it is not Zoroastrianism—it is the parent of both. The details of Zoroastrianism's emergence from Vedic cosmology are complex and still hotly debated. It is enough to know that Zoroaster regarded many aspects of his mother culture as destructive and set out on a radically different course.

We can get a more intimate feeling for Zoroaster's milieu by looking at the features it held in common with Western languages. As it turns out, Europeans (and North Americans) carry with them a large legacy of Vedic culture; that's because all of Europe belongs to the Indo-European language family, too. In other words, Europeans share their origins with the Iranians and Indians through a still older part of the family tree.

Many of the key words from the Vedic languages are familiar to modern-day English speakers. An important one from Sanskrit is *dēva* and the related Zoroastrian Avestan form, *daeava*. Its root is the origin of the Latin word *divus*, from which we get "divine." The Latin word for God, *deus*, also descends from that root. We see it again in the Greek *theos* (/th/ and /d/ being a common consonantal shift). And we see it yet again in "diva," our popular word for extravagant singer-superstars.

For that matter, "star" itself is derived from the same linguistic trunk, traceable to Proto-Indo-European, the parent tongue of all these languages. The link is Greek, *astēr*—hence the name of the star symbol in English, "asterisk," which comes from the primitive root, **ster-*. Other examples include the words for mother, brother, daughter, and corn (**b^hréh_2tēr, *méh_2tēr, *d^hugh_2tér, *ḱerh_2*) and hundreds of others, including most of our personal pronouns. All to say that we have a deep-seated connection to the culture that produced Zoroaster.

Such is Zoroaster's context, which Mary Boyce, the pioneer of Zoroastrian studies, helps us understand in relation to the world of *daevas*:

> [Zoroaster] spent years in a wandering quest for truth; and his hymns suggest
> that he must then have witnessed acts of violence, with war-bands, worship-

pers of the Daevas, descending on peaceful communities to pillage, slaughter and carry off cattle. Conscious himself of being powerless physically, he became filled with a deep longing for justice, for the moral law of the Ahuras to be established for strong and weak alike, so that order and tranquillity could prevail, and all be able to pursue the good life in peace.[29]

These *ahuras* (*asura* in Sanskrit) were spiritual powers like the *dēvas* and Zoroaster's *daevas*. As religious thought developed in early Vedic culture, the two types of heavenly powers came to stand for opposing influences of benevolence and exploitation, peace and violence. In Zoroastrianism, the *ahuras* are the positive force, while for their Hindu cousins, it was the *dēvas* who represented the higher aspirations.

Tradition says Zoroaster underwent a spiritual purification after his thirtieth birthday (like Buddha and Jesus), when on the spring equinox he ritually entered the waters of a river—a baptism—and emerged to see a vision, a shining presence who said to him, "I am Vohu Manah," which means "Good Thought." This emanation of good thinking then guided Zoroaster's entranced consciousness into the presence of another being: Ahura Mazda or "Omniscient Divine." The illumination he experienced was so great that Zoroaster says the light did not even allow his shadow to be cast on the earth.

This was Zoroaster's Axial Age moment. He awakened from his vision to realize that the cosmology that conditioned him and his people was false. He saw in its place something called Asha, a single universal creative presence that was sewn into the fabric of existence, something like the Greek Logos or the Buddhist ground of being. In Zoroastrian thought, Asha is characterized by truth and justice.

I should make a small confession: I've translated "Ahura Mazda" unconventionally. "Lord Wisdom" is the most common translation. I understand its appeal, as it is succinct and allowed traditional scholars to use familiar terms. But it also is weak. Zoroastrianism was boldly monotheistic; there is one Creator and one seamless universal impulse behind creation. To call that merely "Lord Wisdom" just doesn't cut it. Neither is it very accurate. An *ahura* is divine, so "Lord" is a passable translation so long as we understand that it is a universal deity. But translating "Mazda" as "wise" is just bad: in Avestan it is *Maz-da'ah*, which is literally "he who places all in his mind."[30] As far as I know, the word for that in English is "omniscient." Thus, Ahura Mazda = Omniscient Divine.

So Zoroaster realizes an Axial Age deity like YHWH, a universal reason for existence, that replaces the cosmos of the anthropomorphic gods and the system sustained by it. But Zoroaster understands too that there is a reason for suffering—Creation, he says, is in distress because of Druj, meaning "deception" or simply "the Lie."

Zoroaster learned that Druj was a force running counter to Asha, and that it emanated from Angra Mainyu, the cause of suffering, violence, and destruction. Sometimes you will see this translated as "destructive spirit," but I will contest that, too. Angra Mainyu is best translated as "destructive mentality" because the word *mainyu* has a direct cognate in the English word "mind." Both derive from the very same root, Proto-Indo-European *men-*, upon which many European words related to the mind are based. A very striking English example is "mania" and, of course, "mental."

We might even translate Angra Mainyu as "Angry Mania" because, as you no doubt noticed, Angra shares a Proto-Indo-European origin with "angry." Angra Mainyu is an "Angry State of Mind" or, in Buddhist terms, an aversive state of consciousness.

We can look at the etymology of "Druj," too. In Zoroastrian ethics and eschatology, it is the opposite of the divine principle of Asha. Druj means lie, but it must be "Lie" with a capital "L" because there is more to it than a simple judicial notion of truth or lie as fact and falsehood. It helps to know that Druj is related to our English word "drug." Druj is therefore a mind-altering agent that alters consciousness to the point of losing touch with reality or truth, such that all who are infected by it live in a state of delusion.

Suffering, therefore, is caused by a viral delusion—as Buddha and Jeremiah would certainly agree.

So what's the antivirus? According to Zoroaster, Angra Mainyu can be vanquished by Spenta Mainyu, the "Progressive Mentality" or "Evolved Consciousness." In the Zoroastrian sense of *spenta*, this means the original primordial creative force, which gave rise to everything and progresses through the flow of life. Spenta Mainyu is always life in the best sense of the word. We recognize it in that which makes us joyful, healthy, whole—in short, what makes life good. It is Good Thought and Good Mind.

Thankfully, says Zoroaster, Spenta Mainyu will cure all that ails us. Zoroaster enjoins us to take part in the victory of life by thinking Good Thoughts, speaking Good Words, doing Good Deeds, and above all, devoting every effort to awakening from the Lie, the drugged state of delusion that causes suffering. "Through good thinking the Creator of Existence shall promote the true realization of what is most healing."[31] Thus said Zoroaster!

Last Days and the Escape from History

Zoroastrianism is popularly described as a dualistic religion, but it is dualistic only in an ethical sense—namely, regarding the battle between destructive and progressive consciousness. It is not theistic dualism, where a literal Good God and literal Evil God fight over humanity's fate. At the most, Angra Mainyu is analogous to Satan, whom Jesus defined exactly like Angra Mainyu as "the father of lies" who "deceives the whole world."[32]

Zoroaster's battle of minds will one day end. Creative, progressive truth will defeat the deceptive, destructive mentality, and upon its defeat, creation will know liberation to be completely renewed. This will spell the end of suffering and the despair that catches up with everyone in time-bound existence.

He told this as a story with a linear plot that has a beginning, middle, and end, full of dramatic twists and turns and populated with a colorful cast of characters. It may be the most popular, influential, and plagiarized story of all. Almost everyone has heard it: it's the one about an eternal battle between light and dark, truth and lie, heaven and hell.

In Zoroaster's original version, enlightenment does not come easily, and when it does come, it is not cheap. It will seem, he said, as though Druj is winning the battle against Asha. Compassion will be all but eliminated; despair and deception will increase. There will be signs in the heavens and the earth, and pestilence and famine. When all seems lost, Asvat-ereta will appear, meaning "Incarnation of Truth." Just as light dispels darkness, Asvat-ereta dispels Druj; with truth's appearance the lie will vanish. This Asvat-ereta bore the title Saoshyant.

The name may look exotic but once again it has close European cousins. The suffix *-ant* is very familiar to English speakers from words like "particip-*ant*" where it means the one who does something. The term *saosh* relates to a Proto-Indo-European root meaning "to save," as in to preserve or keep from decay. The Greek words Σῶς (*sôs*) and σωτήρ (*sōtér*) derive from that root. That's significant because the ancient Greek version of the Hebrew Bible and the New Testament use these words, which we translate as "save" and "savior." Saoshyant is the world savior in the sense that the New Testament regards Jesus as Savior, and like Jesus, the Saoshyant is to be born miraculously to a virgin.

Zoroastrian scriptures tell us that at the end of time, glory will descend upon Saoshyant Verethrajan—the Victorious Savior:

> He will make existence brilliant, not aging, imperishable, not rotting, not putrefying, enjoying eternal life, enjoying eternal benefit, so that the dead will rise again, (so that) imperishability will be bestowed on the living... Imperishable will be, the world of truth... Deceit will be done away... Beholding (them) with the eyes of (personified) intellect, Saoshyant will view all creatures. After the fading (of deceit) of evil origin he will look at all the corporeal existence with the eyes of (personified) abundance, and by his look he will make imperishable the entire corporeal world.

This eschatological event is *frashokereti*, which means "to make new again," although we might see it translated as "make wonderful" or "make brilliant." There is good reason to translate it as "refreshening," because the term *frašō* comes from a Proto-Indo-European root, **preysk*, that is shared with the English word "fresh." As in English, this is a conspicuously flexible word, and its deeply ancestral Vedic version *pṛkṣá* meant something like "strong," in the sense of being fresh and ready—in prime condition. And that's really what the root meaning gets at through all its many forms in dozens of languages. It's about being in original condition, good as new —*made fresh*. At the end of time, all of creation will be returned to mint condition—a Druj-free universe to which we can, if you'll pardon the pun, "just say no."

It is here that Zoroaster introduces the resurrection of the dead. This and the final judgment will coincide with the refreshening of creation. There is a logical connection that may not be obvious. Eternity means the absence of any experience of the progression of time. There will be no more experience of time, because *frashokereti*, the refreshening force, may be understood to reset the cosmos to its original, fresh state, and without the expansion of the universe and entropic transfer of energy, there is no ticking of the clock.

Of course, none of these ideas were familiar to Jews until we heard them in the mouths of the later prophets. Obviously then, the Jews had some kind of late connection with Zoroastrianism, which brings us back to the history of Judah and Babylon, and God's anointed savior Cyrus—it is here that the Zoroastrian-Jewish relationship begins.

If there is a key idea that carries the Zoroastrian message into Judaism, it is "the end of time." From a modern standpoint, we usually mean the conclusion of a linear progression of time—that story with a beginning, a middle, and an end. But again, we find the biblical authors capable of more nuance than we give them credit for; they were able to allegorize, make allusions, amplify, metonymize, or satirize as well as anyone. In this case, they were even able to dip their prophetic toes into quantum physics.

Jeremiah, Isaiah, and Ezekiel often use the "end times" or "last days" just as Zoroaster did, including the notions of renewal, redemption, and judgment. But it is not as simple as it looks. The two words in Hebrew are *'aḥărît* and *yāmîm*. *Yāmîm* is easy on its own; it means "days." Its partner, *'aḥărît*, means literally "backside of"—that is, the posterior or behind. We need not think, then, that the "last days" must mean "after a long succession of all the days." The phrase carries a sense of "behind and beyond days." It suggests that the linear story is again a parable, a way of seeing something not tangible in our dimensions. If I said, "behind the wall" or "in back of the house," you would think in three dimensions, not two. Why should we conceive of time's end, when time is already a fourth dimension, as occurring on a two-dimensional line?

Let's use our imaginations and reflect on "behind the days," not as the end of a line, but as a dimensional space in consciousness accessible from any point in perceived time. It is an exit from time, from the flow of days, to a dimension behind it. It is behind and beyond the day, our most fundamental measure of time.

This has been the longstanding human aspiration from the beginning of consciousness—to be free of the weight of time, which closes more tightly around us with every passing day. The promise is to go behind the passage of days to another metaphysical space. It is not the end of history; it is escape from history.

Thus, the End of Days signifies a wormhole from the present moment directly to a phase of consciousness that is outside the moment. This is not achieved by waiting it out until history is exhausted and finally gives up, which is an impractical solution anyway, since almost all of us will never live to see that. Rather, it describes an experience of transcending our constructed reality, even our temporal physics, into the Paradise consciousness. The question of how this can be achieved is better left until the "end time" of this book, after my own parable is completely told.

Of course, until the resurrection, I can't ask Zoroaster if he intended his eschatological story to be taken literally or as an allegory, but there are clues aplenty to suggest it is the latter. Firstly, it fits an obvious literary genre typical of over-the-top Vedic parables. In his home culture, surreal cosmic plays were part of a long tradition of storytelling. Why would he use that device? The same reason we make movies, write novels, and tell fairy tales: not everything can be effectively expressed literally. He reminds me of physicists who write books about time—they rely on metaphor and allusion because there is no other way to convey such things to people without the requisite training.

Zoroaster's plainspoken ethical teaching corroborates this. It shows that he could teach non-metaphorically when that was most suited to the task. When he did speak plainly, it was to instruct his followers on what they should do to make the truth victorious in their own current experience. He instructed his followers to cultivate truth, to free themselves from delusion by adhering closely to what is real. He insisted they treat others as they would want to be treated. He includes the environment in this golden rule, too: Zoroaster's followers were taught to be scrupulously clean, to never pollute the land or rivers or air. Greek historian Herodotus marveled, "Rivers they especially revere; they will neither urinate nor spit nor wash their hands in them, nor let anyone else do so."[33]

Moreover, Paradise is not remote in Zoroaster's ethics. There is an immediate link between the present and Paradise for the individual. Zoroaster states,

> The first step that the soul of the faithful man made, placed him in the Good-Thought Paradise; the second step that the soul of the faithful man made, placed him in the Good-Word Paradise; the third step that the soul of the faithful man made, placed him in the Good-Deed Paradise; the fourth step that the soul of the faithful man made, placed him in the Endless Light.[34]

He is not telling them to wait out history—he is telling them to transcend it now. How? Good thoughts. Good words. Good deeds.

In Buddhist terms, the terror of history is *samsara*, the ever-turning wheel of suffering. Buddha fought Zoroaster's battle extremely well: he practiced scientific observation of reality in the present moment to vanquish delusion, Zoroaster's *Druj*, with the intention of leaving the world of suffering. The Paradise state of being in Buddhist terms is "unconditioned reality," meaning the most intrinsic state in physics possible; it is not deliberate in any way, not "made by" anything or any process. Being without conditioning logically means also that it must be beyond space and time. This resonates very well with "in back of time," *'aḥărît hayāmîm*, "The Last Days," or "End Time," whose characteristics in the Bible are invariably eternal, a passage out of ordinary time.

Hard to imagine? That's the point. It cannot be imagined. But it can be experienced. Zoroaster, Buddha, Plato, and Jeremiah ask us to rigorously question constructed reality. They demand we dismantle our idols' shrines, particularly those that make us feel most at ease.

The record is quite clear that the vast majority of people since the Axial Age have simply been too lazy to follow their example, preferring instead to read their great thoughts through a literalist political lens that purports to turn the transcendent into some kind of perfection of the mundane. In short, I believe, this is what is wrong with the world.

So goes the Axial Age, a time marking the advent of critical thought, the capacity to judge our mental processes and conclusions rather than being swept along by them, unawares. We might think of it as a developmental stage of post–Göbekli Tepe consciousness, a passage into adolescence—we aren't children anymore, but not quite adults. If that's true, this developmental stage will likely take time to run its course. We live only 3,000 years after entering our Axial Age adolescence, while childhood lasted about 8,000 years. That would put us at the volatile and dangerous age of about sixteen—we can operate heavy machinery and revel in our car, but we are prone to accidents and poor choices.

If the Axial Age began with a bar mitzvah, we would do well to remember that this is when a Jewish boy becomes fully accountable. It is a message to grow up, saying, "you are responsible now." The Axial Age represents a giant caution sign, too, warning us of the dangers of continuing to indulge our imaginations in the manufacture of false worlds. What we need is true maturity, to simply take responsibility for ourselves and come to grips with life as grownups, a maturity woefully lacking in the political sphere.

The next chapters discuss the perils of half-awakenings and immature spirituality, along with how Isaiah's Zoroastrian-inflected dream spread, and how it was applied and mainly misapplied, depending on your point of view. It is a story of Babylonians, Jews, Greeks, Romans, and Persians that to this day is unfinished. Many of the plotlines remain unresolved and can be followed in our daily newspapers.

We resume our journey on a lesser-known leg of the Paradise road that begins and ends with Magi.

10

GREAT EXPECTATIONS

Lucifer

If we appeared in Babylon in 562 BCE and announced that in a single day reality as everyone knew it would be re-imagined, we would have been thought insane. This was the successor to the world's original empire. Its king was a direct heir to the first kingship that descended from heaven. And now the empire was poised to become the most powerful iteration of the Cosmic Order ever to grace the earth.

According to the biographer of the then king, "The last decades of Babylon's existence as an independent state rank as the most brilliant in its history; never had such a vast territorial expanse come under Babylonian control."[1]

Just ask the Jews. The Temple was in ruins, and they lost everything to Babylon's expansion, which swept through the Middle East like a desert storm, penetrating deeply into Arabia, where, for the first time, a foreign empire consolidated all the important trade routes from Yathrib (Medina) near the western coast, inland across Arabia Deserta, and back again to Mesopotamia. The Sumerian system was never in better shape.

Nebuchadnezzar settled the Jewish exiles along the Chebar canal in today's southeastern Iraq, allowing them to live as an intact community. Psalms, prophecies, and lamentations of exile record their existential despair and a grim determination to remember and to understand—to somehow make sense of it. This they did with aplomb. "By the rivers of Babylon—

there we sat down and there we wept when we remembered Zion," cried the exiles. "On the willows there we hung up our harps. For there our captors asked us for songs, and our tormentors asked for mirth, saying, 'Sing us one of the songs of Zion!' How could we sing the LORD's song in a foreign land?"[2]

As it happened, not all the Jews were taken to Babylon. Nebuchadnezzar took the professional classes but left the peasants to till the soil. Known in Hebrew as "the people of the land," they were now the sole proprietors of still-fertile vineyards and orchards, and many of them became wealthy. And among those who remained was Jeremiah, who served as a bridge between the exiles and their homeland, an interpreter of the events that had befallen them.

Brave, long-suffering, unflinching decade after decade, he was an Axial Age genius who read the flow of history as someone whose awareness lived far above it. When Nebuchadnezzar's army captured Jerusalem, they found him in prison, interred there because of his unpatriotic preaching. Evidently, the Babylonians liked him for that, and Babylon's commanding general freed him with a flourish: "Look, the whole country lies before you; go wherever you please."

Jeremiah chose Mitspeh, just north of Jerusalem, the place where judge Samuel was appointed when the Israelites first went astray, taking for itself a king "so that we also may be like other nations." Now assuming this same office, Jeremiah dispatched exhortations to his exiled and kingless kin: they should live as best they could—build houses, work, farm, marry, and have children, "that you may be increased there, and not diminished."[3] He instructed them to pray for the peace of their Babylonian captors and to build up their wealth and welfare as best they could. They were going to be there a long time, but one day they would be redeemed.

I like to imagine they amused themselves with the local court gossip. It is still fascinating and resonates oddly with modern Iraqi politics. If I were them, I would have looked for signs of the times. I certainly did that myself as a young adult, scrutinizing Iraq's politics for how they fit into biblical prophecy, as do many Muslims even now.

For example, they may have thought salvation was near when Nebuchadnezzar, "destroyer of nations" and later role model for Saddam Hussein, died and his heir, Awîl-Marduk, kindly honored ex-king Jehoiachin, whom he released from prison after thirty-seven years, welcoming him as a guest of the court. It might have appeared as though the new emperor was prepared to restore the old Jewish king to the throne.[4]

Whatever his intentions, thoughts of salvation were premature. Awîl-Marduk soon fell afoul of the priests and palace plotters. Less than two years after assuming the throne, he was assassinated by Neriglissar, who clung tenuously to power for four years before himself giving way to the hapless Labashi-Marduk. Late-era Babylonian historian Berossus describes this short-lived ruler, writing that his "wickedness became apparent in many ways."[5] Whatever he was doing, it was intolerable. He lasted two months before a group of palace fixtures conspired to kill him and install the real hero of our story, a reluctant emperor by the name of Nabonidus.

"They brought me to the palace and all of them prostrated themselves at my feet and kissed them," wrote the astonished new emperor. "They kept praising my kingship."[6] Elsewhere he describes himself as a humble only son "who has nobody" in this world.[7] It wasn't false humility: his father was genuinely unknown, and he had no obvious claim to the throne.

Most of what we know about him comes from the new king's mother, Addagoppe. They were Arameans, Western Semites like Abraham.[8] Most importantly, we know for certain that his mother was from Abraham's Harran, either a priestess to the moon god Sîn or an extremely devout lay follower, for her legacy of impassioned inscriptions devoted to Harran's god and to the restoration of Sîn's temple is unparalleled. This was no stay-at-home mom. She played an important role in her son's destiny and the fate of the empire.[9]

Her memoir tells us that she served in the palace of mighty Nebuchadnezzar and introduced young Nabonidus to the great king. He remained part of the palace entourage throughout Nebuchadnezzar's reign and through the reigns of his luckless successors—doing what, she never says.

It seems Nabonidus was a man of hidden greatness and greatly underestimated by the cabal of intriguers who planned his ascent. They would have hoped for a dupe to do their bidding. Instead, they got an iron-willed and ambitious religious zealot, who in short order would take full command of the empire and reshape it in the image of his mother's god, a development that has left a deep impression upon us all.

His prowess emerged early. After taking the throne in 556 BCE, Nabonidus extended Babylon's dominion into Anatolia and Arabia, where he established a capital at the oasis city of Teyma, on the southern skirt of the Nefud desert. Having secured these lucrative trade routes, he turned to his true passion. Rather than returning to Babylon, he remained in residence in what is now western Saudi Arabia, his base for preaching the gospel of the crescent moon Sîn.

Archeology was his other, closely related preoccupation. Nabonidus was the first person to date an ancient artifact, for which reason he is often called the first archeologist. In this role, he established a new library to preserve copies of important texts and excavated and restored important sites, most significantly the moon-god temple at Harran. It was no mere hobby, of course. His real goal was to elevate Sîn to an unprecedented position by connecting his god to the origin of the millennia-old legacy of Eridu.

For example, when commemorating the previous Assyrian dynasty's world conquest, he gives the credit to his god, "Sîn, the king of the gods." Nabonidus' biographer, Paul-Alain Beaulieu, calls attention to the significance of this claim: "Sîn is now the god who calls rulers to kingship."[10] And as we know, the power to bestow kingship was held only by the most fundamental heavenly authority of Eridu.

After ten years in Teyma, Nabonidus returned home to proclaim Sîn "king of gods of heaven and the underworld, without whom no city and no country can be established or restored." All other gods were commanded to pray to Sîn as their "father and creator." This designation officially equated Sîn with Eridu's original deity, the god Enlil. Sîn was now the one who "controls Enlil's office... whose hands... grasped all heavenly offices, leader of the gods, king of kings, lord of lords."[11]

The ascent of Sîn is reported in at least two famed biblical passages. The first of these employs Sîn's title, "shining god," which Isaiah employs in a poetic judgment against Babylon and its final king. You probably know the passage:

> How you are fallen from heaven, O Lucifer, son of the morning!
>> How you are cut down to the ground,
>> You who weakened the nations!
>> For you have said in your heart:
>> "I will ascend into heaven,
>> I will exalt my throne above the stars of God"
>> ... Yet you shall be brought down to Sheol,
>> To the lowest depths of the Pit.[12]

Of course, Christians usually read this as a description of Satan's expulsion from heaven. But why? Who says Satan is called Lucifer? What does that even mean?

In Latin, *lucifer* as an adjective means "light-bearing" and as a noun refers to the planet Venus. The name Lucifer does not occur in Isaiah's text. It was chosen by Jerome, the church father who translated the Hebrew Bible into Latin. From his Hebrew source, he knew that he was reading a proper name, but he had no access to the history we have now to determine the context. Understanding that the name came from the Semitic root meaning "to shine," and wanting to find an equivalent in Latin culture, he correctly used this Latin equivalent. The King James translators went along with it for much the same reason, deciding to keep the Latin term. Modern translations steer us toward "Day Star" because nobody knows what *lucifer* means today.

All well and good. But the Hebrew text never uses the word "star," and if Isaiah really wanted to say Venus or Ishtar, the goddess associated with Venus, he could have. All we need to do is read the context; this prophecy explicitly taunts the last Babylonian king, Nabonidus, a champion of the moon.

Thanks to modern scholarship, the proper noun we are dealing with in Hebrew is no longer a mystery. It is *heylel*, which does not appear any other place in the Bible. The title for Sîn in the Akkadian tongue shares the same Semitic root, also meaning "to shine." In the time of Nabonidus, Sîn had a monopoly on this title: "the shining god."[13] To this day, in Arabic (another Semitic language akin to Hebrew and Akkadian), the name for the crescent moon, which was the official emblem of Sîn, is *hilal*—linguistically the same word that appears in Isaiah. By that name it crowns every mosque, appears on most Islamic flags, and marks the beginning of the Ramadan feast.

So, based on historical context (Isaiah is condemning the last Babylonian king) and the linguistic associations (Isaiah is using a Hebrew form of Sîn's most common title), and given the modern-day cognate (the same root is preserved in Arabic for the crescent moon, which was Sîn's official sign), there is a very strong case to be made that *heylel* was a Hebrew epithet for Sîn. Isaiah's prophecy, then, is about Nabonidus' exaltation of Sîn, as Isaiah said, "above the stars," which is exactly what the emperor brought about during his reign. Isaiah's message to both the king and his god: you've gone too far, like the builders of Babel's tower, and you too will be brought down to Earth.

Handwriting on the Wall

Under Nabonidus, Sîn's rise to stardom was spectacular and his prophesied denouement ready-made for a Hollywood epic. Cecile B. DeMille would have loved it. Set among Babylon's hanging gardens, glorious architecture, and magnificent gates, a wild evening of idolatrous revelry and intrigue became the backdrop for Lucifer and his king's fall.

It's a remarkably well-documented affair, better understood if we know a little something about the politics of feasting in Babylon, where the ancient *akītu* festival was the high point of the calendar.

It occurred at the spring equinox and was dedicated to Marduk, the Babylonian capital's city-god. Representing social stability, if not bliss, it was a joyous and comforting holiday for most Babylonian subjects; think of it as Christmastime combined with the Fourth of July.

But Nabonidus was not the least bit interested. He absented himself from Babylon for ten years, tending to the rise of Sîn, whose own version of *akītu* was celebrated in Harran during the autumnal, not the spring, equinox. In contrast to Marduk's holiday, Harran's moon-god feast was situated in the calendar to coincide with the harvest and with the moon's most auspicious nights, those of the harvest moon and hunter's moon.

As part of Sîn's enthronement, Nabonidus therefore replaced Marduk's spring feast with Sîn's Octoberfest. "He shall speak words against the Most High... and shall attempt to change the sacred seasons and the law," cries the Hebrew prophet, reflecting the grave responsibility of those who would meddle with sacred days. And so for this reason, to back up his decision, the king chose to return to Babylon from his long absence in Arabia; it was the seventeenth of the Babylonian month of *Tašritu*, the same date as the start of the lunar feast.

To officially commemorate the occasion, Nabonidus inserted a lengthy prayer to Sîn into the state's archival record of his return, which affirms in the strongest terms the moon god's ascent to the position of universal authority and, ipso facto, Marduk's irrelevance to the king. The impact on Babylonian society, especially in the capital, cannot be overstated.

Our Hebrew scribes did not fail to notice. They colorfully bring this history to life in the parable-like story of Daniel, whom Jewish tradition presents as the archetype of an elite Judean in Babylonian exile. He may have been a real person—we will never know—but he stands as a Jewish witness, a high-ranking diaspora Jerusalemite who served Nebuchadnezzar and then Belshazzar, Nabonidus' son and co-regent. (Belshazzar was effectively the king throughout his father's long absences.)

On a certain night, Daniel tells us, the court hosted a great festival for 1,000 members of the ruling class. Becoming a little tipsy, the king began to show off, demanding the gold and silver goblets from Jerusalem's Temple so that his party could drink from them. The implication is that these sanctified objects, reserved for the exclusive recognition of Jerusalem's transcendent deity, would be made to serve in a ritual feast dedicated to the Babylonian god.

Upon this abomination, "the fingers of a human hand appeared and began writing on the plaster of the wall of the royal palace... The king was watching the hand as it wrote. Then the king's face turned pale, and his thoughts terrified him. His limbs gave way, and his knees knocked together."[14]

Yes, this is the origin of the popular expression, "the handwriting is on the wall." And such it was for Babylon. In a panic, the king called all the wise men to interpret the apparition. Only Daniel proved himself up to the task. Promised wealth and power if he could solve this puzzle, the Jewish eunuch responded with a stern lecture: "You have not humbled your heart... You have exalted yourself," and then gave his interpretation:

> This is the writing that was inscribed: *mene, mene, tekel,* and *parsin.* This is the interpretation of the matter: *mene,* God has numbered the days of your kingdom and brought it to an end; *tekel,* you have been weighed on the scales and found wanting; *peres,* your kingdom is divided and given to the Medes and Persians.

The tagline gets right to the point: "That very night Belshazzar, the Chaldean king, was killed."

Here is the astonishing part. In this same month of *Tašritu* 539 BCE, Cyrus the Persian Messiah had been marching steadily toward Babylon. He'd defeated the Babylonian army at Opis, a city north of the capital just a few weeks prior.

Why, then, were the Babylonians so relaxed? They simply did not think the capital could be taken. Historically, the city was impenetrable; in the event of siege, they had supplies to last many, many months. They assumed that Cyrus, so far from his home, could not hold the ground he'd taken and would exhaust himself in a lengthy siege. This storm would pass.

What they hadn't counted on was the brilliance of the Persian Christ. Greek historians Herodotus and Xenophon tell us that Cyrus began to quietly dig trenches to divert the waters of the Euphrates, which passed through the great Babylonian capital. At his signal, the Persian engineers would open floodgates to the trenches, draining off enough of the river to allow his army to use the now shallow river bed as a swift and unassailable passage into the city, no siege required.

Herodotus records,

> Hereupon the Persians... by the river-side, entered the stream, which had now
> sunk so as to reach about midway up a man's thigh, and thus got into the
> town. Had the Babylonians been apprised of what Cyrus was about, or had
> they noticed their danger, they would never have allowed the Persians to
> enter the city, but would have destroyed them utterly; for they would have
> made fast all the street-gates which gave upon the river, and mounting upon
> the walls along both sides of the stream, would so have caught the enemy, as
> it were, in a trap.[15]

Could have, would have, should have... but did not. Cyrus chose the night
of the sixteenth of *Tašritu*, the beginning of Sîn's *akītu* festival. Apart from
the soon-dead guards who witnessed the first moments of the Persian incur-
sion, most of the city was distracted and no small number were drunk—and
if Daniel is to be believed, drunk from drinking out of YHWH's goblets.
The Babylonians "knew nothing of what had chanced," adds Herodotus, "but
as they were engaged in a festival, continued dancing and reveling until they
learnt the capture but too certainly. Such, then, were the circumstances of
the first taking of Babylon."

Socrates' student Xenophon tells the same story, with the extra detail
that Cyrus had intelligence on exactly where the palace and king were to be
found. He ordered his men to take him directly to the Babylonian king as
soon as the city was breached. He calculated that upon hearing of the king's
death, the city would not further resist the occupation. "Come, take your
swords in your hand: God helping me, I will lead you on... straight to the
palace."

His intelligence officers reported to Cyrus, "It would not surprise us to
find the palace-gates unbarred, for this night the whole city is given over to
revelry." Again, Daniel's story is spot on. At daybreak, on Sîn's greatest day, it
was all over. "And so it was," reports the Greek historian, "when it was day
and those who held the heights knew that the city was taken and the king
slain, they were persuaded to surrender the citadel themselves."[16]

I remind the reader again that this is Greek history, not the Bible. But
Daniel gets the details correct: "That very night Belshazzar, the Chaldean
king, was killed." As per Daniel, Xenophon writes that it was co-regent Belshazzar who was killed that evening by the Persians, not Nabonidus himself.
This was typical of Cyrus: once a battle ended, he was known to spare the
royals of a conquered people. He did not kill in cold blood.

This was a history-shattering turn of events. The empire had been at its peak until just months beforehand. But now, in the words of Nabonidus scholar Paul-Alain Beaulieu, "Mesopotamia was destined to be a mere province." For the first time in human history, civilization was not ruled by the kingship of Eridu. "The events of 539 B.C. involved more than a turnover of dynasties. Never before had Babylonia come under the sway of foreign invaders who did not assimilate into its culture."[17]

In other words, before the Persian Messiah's victory, every change in power was at most a dynastic change. In each case, the new ruler was wholly absorbed into the original Mesopotamian worldview and was at pains to legitimize his rule by connecting it to Eridu. New regimes in the past hadn't captured Eridu's empire—Eridu's ethos had captured them.

Cyrus was immune. He brought with him an altogether different cosmology, explicitly critical of Eridu's, and although Cyrus was a king, his kingship emphatically did not descend from there. He understood his kingship as eschatological, a step toward liberation from the Lie. He was there to compassionately serve the interests of the human family as a loving father, the effects of which will be immediate and widespread—for Cyrus was a Zoroastrian.

Christ's Kingdom

How did the Babylonians cope with the aftermath of the conquest? The official record shows that after surrender, "there was peace in the city when Cyrus spoke greetings to all of Babylon."[18] There is no reason to doubt this happy image, for Cyrus was unlike any ruler Mesopotamia had ever seen. Under him, the world felt different, a mood echoed again and again by the chroniclers of the age.

An important Akkadian text interprets his takedown of Babylon along the lines of the Hebrew prophets. Although composed under the champion's auspices, this text could have been written only by a Babylonian priest, and the point of view is genuine. It says that the Lord had "scanned and looked through all the countries, searching for a righteous ruler," because Nabonidus had "removed the gods from their thrones" and changed established worship "into abomination." When the right man was found, the Lord then "pronounced the name of Cyrus and declared him to be the ruler of the world."[19]

Once more I need to stress that although this sounds like the Bible, these are the words of a Babylonian scribe. We have read uncannily similar things in Isaiah and Daniel.

It isn't hard to understand why even Babylonians felt happy. They were as scandalized by the elevation of Sîn as Isaiah was, and humiliated when Nabonidus used the *akītu* feast to honor his moon god instead of their own city's patron, Marduk. No wonder, then, that when Cyrus slipped under the gates during this illicit party, Marduk's and YHWH's faithful were equally glad to see him. The last word on Cyrus from the Babylonians is simply, "He saved Babylon from oppression."[20]

So what was it going to be like to have the Persian Messiah ruling the world? We get some insight from the Greeks, who in general remark on what was peculiar about Zoroastrians and their priests, the Magi. Herodotus, for example, found this most striking: "they have no images of the gods, no temples nor altars, and consider the use of them a sign of folly. This comes, I think, from their not believing the gods to have the same nature with men, as the Greeks imagine."[21]

That is a fabulous articulation of how Axial Age awakening took root among the Zoroastrians, stated in terms familiar from Jeremiah: idolatry is foolish; we mustn't mistake the work of our hands and imaginations for the real thing. And yet, the Persians allowed Herodotus and other Greeks the freedom of their folly. Zoroastrianism was not a religion to be imposed; therefore, everyone under Persian dominion was free to worship as their conscience dictated.

Herodotus was also dumbfounded to learn that for Zoroastrians "the most disgraceful thing in the world is to tell a lie; the next worst, to owe a debt: because, among other reasons, the debtor is obliged to tell lies... Their sons are carefully instructed from their fifth to their twentieth year, in three things alone—to ride, to draw the bow, and to speak the truth."[22] Here again, the Zoroastrians unsubscribed from a pillar of Mesopotamian culture, declaring compound interest on debts a disgrace to human dignity.

Another report comes from Xenophon, writing in the next generation. He was a huge fan of Cyrus, but that doesn't mean his admiration was without warrant. He is spot on in reporting how Cyrus was regarded by his subjects: "the whole of this enormous empire was governed by the mind and will of a single man, Cyrus: he cared for his subjects and cherished them as a father might care for his children, and they who came beneath his rule reverenced him like a father."

Casting his historian's eye across all of known history, Xenophon is moved to ask, "Who but Cyrus ever won an empire in war, and when he died was called father by the people he overcame? Father, a title that proclaims the benefactor and not the bandit."[23]

Among the immediate beneficiaries were untold thousands of Babylon's slaves. Cyrus freed them all, undertaking the cost of their repatriation when appropriate. As a rule, slavery was banned under his dynasty's 200-year reign, this for the first time since the dawn of civilization.

In a rare example of Persian imperial writing, Darius the Great, Cyrus' most powerful successor, adds to this picture of gracious, God-fearing rulers:

> May Ahura Mazda protect this country... Upon this country may there not come an army, nor famine, nor the Lie... A great god is Ahura Mazda, who created this earth... who created man, who created happiness for man, who made Darius king, one king of many, one lord of many... By the favor of Ahura Mazda I am of such a sort that I am a friend to right, I am not a friend to wrong. It is not my desire that the weak man should have wrong done to him by the mighty; nor is that my desire, that the mighty man should have wrong done to him by the weak... What is right, that is my desire.[24]

That is a rare inscription because, tellingly, the Zoroastrians looked upon Uruk's greatest achievement with deep mistrust. "Though the Medes and the Persians met several systems of writing in Western Iran," explains historian Mary Boyce, "they plainly regarded the alien art with suspicion (in the Persian epic its discovery is attributed to the devil)... The priests, who were the scholars of ancient Iran, rejected it [writing] as unfit for recording holy words."[25]

What was so devilish about writing? They found that it facilitated the Lie because of the way writing mediates reality, objectifies it, and makes it manipulatable. The Zoroastrians would understand anthropologist Stanley Diamond when he explains writing's impact on early civilization:

> Writing splits consciousness in two ways—it becomes more authoritative than talking, thus degrading the meaning of speech and eroding oral tradition; and it makes it possible to use words for the political manipulation and control of others. Written signs supplant memory; an official, fixed and permanent version of events can be made. If it is written, in early civilizations, it is bound to be true.[26]

The Zoroastrians understood that, up until their time, writing was more likely to be the delivery mechanism for a vast system of lies than anything else. They disavowed its coercive powers. But saddled now with the bureaucratic necessity of managing the known world, Cyrus would have to use writing nonetheless, and he did so with utmost efficiency. We can thank him for the first postal and parcel services. He invented it by staging couriers at intervals of one-day rides across the empire, where each stop housed a post office. Herodotus famously reports that the Persian mailmen were hindered "neither by snow nor rain nor heat nor darkness from accomplishing their appointed course."[27]

But they did not carry letters in Zoroaster's tongue. Cyrus coped with the devilish craft by running the business of empire in the old imperial languages, primarily Aramaic. This allowed him to use writing, but with the moral reserve of never using his own mother-tongue and never under any circumstances using writing to establish a cosmology to justify his rule. Writing was only for business, and by conducting business only in the vestigial tongues of empires past, he consigned the whole enterprise to the realm of the fallen world. The Zoroastrians seemed to rule the empire while holding their noses.

In contrast to the incessantly proselytizing Nabonidus, Zoroastrianism's allergy to writing made it very hard for outsiders to study the religion, a difficulty paralleled in the personal biography of Cyrus. We don't have any direct evidence from Cyrus about his beliefs or much of anything else. For the ruler of the world, he is unexpectedly modest, almost silent—so much so that some historians have wondered if he personally practiced any faith at all. We simply don't have Nabonidus-like religious posturing from Cyrus. Xenophon seems to take it for granted, telling us of Cyrus' devotion to the Magi, but it is only anecdotal. We may surmise, however, that since his ancestors were known Zoroastrians, and his successors demonstrably so, it would be odd if Cyrus was the only one who didn't keep the faith. It seems to me he kept it best of all, which is why he left no ostentatious accounts of it.

This brings us to the question of Zoroastrianism's impact through their long imperial reign, especially how it affected Jews and, ultimately, us today. How did the Jews learn about the End Time from these tight-lipped Persians? Although oral transmission meticulously preserved Zoroaster's words in the pristine 1500 BCE Avestan language that he spoke (a fact proven by comparison with related tongues of that time), nothing was written down until two centuries after Christ.

This meant that an outsider could not study the Persian faith abstractly—a Jew could not simply read about it. Anyone naturally curious about the root of their good fortune had to make a Zoroastrian friend. And they did just that in large numbers. "Both priests and the laity were prepared to discuss matters of religion with inquirers," concludes Boyce, "and gradually many of Zoroaster's fundamental doctrines became disseminated throughout the region." Zoroastrian doctrine, she says, "exerted a profound influence at this time throughout the Near East."[28]

The doctrines Boyce identifies are "a supreme God who is the Creator" and who has "created this world for a purpose"; the existence of "an evil power which is opposed to him"; and an understanding that the "present state... will have an end; that this end will be heralded by the coming of a cosmic Saviour."

Seekers also heard that life carried eternal consequences, "with an individual judgment to decide the fate of each soul at death," and that "at the end of time there will be a resurrection of the dead... and that thereafter the kingdom of God will come upon earth."

Pagan and Jewish friends of the Persians were also happily told that upon restoration of creation, "the righteous will enter into it as into a garden and be happy there in the presence of God for ever, immortal themselves in body as well as soul."[29] The Zoroastrian Persian word for that garden is, of course, *pairidaēza*, Paradise.

The Jews were one of the nations who benefited most directly from Zoroastrianism's generosity and perhaps the best suited of all to grasp the Zoroastrian idea. According to Boyce, "these doctrines all came to be adopted by various Jewish schools in the post-Exilic period, for the Jews were one of the peoples, it seems, most open to Zoroastrian influences—a tiny minority, holding staunchly to their own beliefs, but evidently admiring their Persian benefactors, and finding congenial elements in their faith."

Friends in Deed

Seventy years after Judah's Babylon exile began, Cyrus, the Persian Christ, set the captives free. This was not special treatment. Autonomy was the rule, not the exception; the Jews were just one of many ethnicities that Cyrus encouraged to go home, giving them financial support to do so.

All of which matches what Isaiah and Jeremiah said of Cyrus and the restoration of Judah. We can accept it as either a fulfillment of prophecy or a prophetic assessment of unfolding events; the sequence of intersection between what was predicted and what was observed is, alas, unknowable. The best we can do is apply some logic and then hand it over to our intuition. In my opinion, prophetic insight into life—making meaningful sense of history as it develops—is more inspired than an accurate prediction. I don't want so much to know what will happen as I want to know what it means.

It seems obvious to most scholars that significant parts of Isaiah and Jeremiah and other scriptures were written ex post facto and that, indeed, most of what we have read as prophecies of Cyrus and Babylon's judgment were interpretations of contemporary events and recent history.

Furthermore, we can say with certainty that the entirety of the Hebrew Bible, including the Torah, takes its final form only after the exile. This is true even for the material that King Josiah may have edited; anything done in his era indisputably received a final priestly polish after the exile. We can say, then, that the Bible's familiar final narrative interprets Jerusalem's varied traditions and experiences through a lens ground and polished by the grit of this particular place and time. This includes the details of Temple services, as well as the feasts, which bear telltale signs of Babylonian influence.

To prevent us from making an antithetical leap, however, we should note also that a large body of the traditions and text do predate the exile, as do sizable swaths of Isaiah and Jeremiah. When Isaiah lambastes Ahaz, it is contemporaneous, speaking prophetically about events as they occur. The material that appears to be a prediction may be composed later, but it is prophetic in a certain sense: it is insightful to the matter at hand. According to Merriam-Webster, a prophet is "one who utters divinely inspired revelations," or "one gifted with more than ordinary spiritual and moral insight."

Prophecy as prediction was a common technique, popular in Mesopotamia, where kings wrote their histories as if predicted and predetermined by the gods. It is a compelling genre, but unknown in Hebrew tradition until the age of Assyria and Babylon. You will perhaps have noticed that until the people of Israel and Judah encounter Assyria and Babylon firsthand, there is no prophetic literature—nothing predictive or eschatological. There is narrative, and there are prophets who speak to their time and place, but there is nothing like an Isaiah or Ezekiel who foretells a future narrative.

The Jews learned this style from their neighbors, and then took it further when they met Zoroastrians, whose founder used a comparable device not only to predict politics, as the Mesopotamians did, but to reveal the End of Time restoration. Zoroaster's innovation was to compose it as if from beyond the event horizon of spacetime, not predicting the future from a point in the past but telling the whole story at once from first to last. Hebrew writers picked this up and ran with it.

Which brings us to the question of all these things Jews and Zoroastrians seem to have in common. Since Persian doctrine was preserved in a language dating from long before they met, we can deduce that Zoroastrians didn't get their body of eschatological ideas from the Jews. While it is possible that Jews came up with them independently, we know for sure that many of the ideas propagated by Zoroaster don't appear in Hebrew until after the exile when they lived under Persian rule. This is absolutely the case when the later prophets start talking about the End Time.

Certainty eludes us, however. The Bible's final editors did not track their changes for us; we cannot know for certain what the ratio of original to redacted text is, or when a particular foreign influence was interpolated into an older tradition. At every turn of phrase, they had opportunity to interpret and re-contextualize before the final version appears a few hundred years before Christ. It is a complex weave, and all the more interesting for it.

With all this in mind, we may approach the scene now as the Jews begin to return to Jerusalem from Babylon. Gradually, with Persian financing, Temple services were restored and history continued apace, allowing a solid two centuries for Jews and Zoroastrians to compare notes and cultivate a fruitful relationship. For that entire period, Jerusalem and the lands of Judah (Judea) had a Zoroastrian governor, by all accounts a generous and nurturing one, and ample opportunities to interact with Zoroastrian merchants, post-men, and other fixtures of the empire. There is also the tangible fact that most Jews did not go home—they remained in Zoroastrian-led Babylon, free and increasingly prosperous. An intelligent, literate diaspora like this would not have ignored the exciting and hope-filled ideas of their Persian rulers.

We have but to eavesdrop on Zoroastrian interactions with other people to perceive what Jews and Zoroastrians talked about. Especially helpful is fourth-century-BCE Greek rhetorician Theopompus, who was able to write a detailed and accurate description of Zoroastrian eschatology and cosmology based solely on information that he gleaned through ordinary social interactions. Theopompus was far less exposed to Zoroastrians than Jews were—he'd never ventured further east than the Aegean—and yet he knew from his Zoroastrian friends that, "according to the Magi, humankind will become alive again and be immortal."

We have Theo's text thanks to Roman-era historians Plutarch and Diogenes Laertius, which means that this Zoroastrian idea traveled intact through numerous Greek and Roman hands across half a millennium. It is inconceivable that it didn't get transmitted clearly to Jews who were right there, right then, shoulder-to-shoulder with high-ranking Zoroastrians of the day.[30]

The Bible is certainly not silent on the subject. The account of Jerusalem's reconstruction begins with the imperial decree of Cyrus to free the Jews and send them home. It details Persian financial support provided to rebuild Jerusalem's Temple. Jewish leader Nehemiah is a high-ranking palace figure under Zoroastrian king Artaxerxes, a successor to Cyrus. He was living in Babylon, serving at a court filled with Magi when he learned that rebuilding in Jerusalem had stalled and that his countrymen were hard-pressed by their hostile neighbors. Artaxerxes happily dispatched Nehemiah to help his kin get the job done, appointing him governor of Judea.

The prominence of the Persians in the books of Nehemiah and Ezra is undeniable. That's two full books of the Hebrew Bible, the books that tell us how Judaic Law was promulgated and the Temple service conducted— Nehemiah's account is the first historically traceable expression of Judaism as we know it. That Zoroastrians and a Jewish official high in the Zoroastrian empire play such central roles shows just how close this relationship was. It also indicates the probability of Zoroastrian impact on the development of Judaism, a religion which, for all intents and purposes, only finds its now-familiar form during this period.

The only thing that could bring them any closer was a common enemy— an encounter with the forces of darkness expected by Zoroastrians as a sign of impending apocalypse and redemption. For Jews, happily redeemed from Babylon, such a setback would require an explanation, something that Zoroastrians were uniquely equipped to provide.

Darkness Descends

And that's just what happened when history suddenly lurched into reverse, as Alexander the Great rapidly overthrew the Persian Empire in 330 BCE. He and his factious successors established hundreds of Greek garrisons and colonies across the civilized world. Relying heavily on the artifice of the written text, they methodically spread Greek language and culture. This was their most potent weapon, used to forge a hegemonic culture among the civilized elites. Gone forever was the unintrusive hand of the Persians, now to be replaced by the fist of a Babel-like bully.

Greek empire was a throwback, fashioned after the old Sumerians from whom the Athenian pantheon and Greek city-state ethos were derived. Alexander himself was everything Cyrus was not. He was ruthless, greedy, rash, lascivious, and cruel. He spent his last days in hedonistic dissipation, a megalomaniac, dead at the age of thirty-three.

His massive empire went with him, but not its effects. Upon his passing, it fractured into competing realms, leaving Judea trapped between two ruthless Greek rivals hell-bent on getting their hands on as much of Alexander's legacy as they could.

From the beginning, Judah and Jerusalem were secured by Alexander's northern successor, Antiochus III, ruler of the Seleucid Empire. This arrangement was facilitated through the connivance of Jewish collaborators who were willing to bribe the Greeks for appointments to powerful positions. A key figure was a man named Jesus (Yēshua), whom Antiochus IV appointed high priest in 175 BCE after being sufficiently suborned.

The new high priest wasted no time in going Greek, restyling himself as Jason and founding a gymnasium to inculcate Jerusalem with Hellenistic traditions. This, I should point out, was not a high school recreation center. "Gymnasium" is derived from the Greek for "naked," essentially meaning a place for physical training in the nude that was also the center for intellectual and social intercourse—frankly, not something Moses would have cottoned to. And far from being amusement centers, the Greek gymnasia and other colleges were founded by Jason and his ilk with deadly serious intentions. Their purpose was to induct teenage boys into Greek culture—they became machines of assimilation.

As those traditions seeped deeper into Jewish society, the assimilated sophisticates mimicked the rivalries that surrounded them. Ambitious young men found ways to make themselves indispensable to one or the other of the land's Greek suitors, the Seleucid's to the north or the Ptolemaic dynasty to the south, based in Egypt. This was a recipe for disaster.

There was a third faction, however, comprising people whose names at this stage remain unknown. They were pious Hasidim, mostly common, less-privileged people who were not subject to elite temptations. Understandably, they viewed Alexander's conquest as a reversion to pagan darkness, which ought to have been consigned to history's dustbin when Cyrus fulfilled his divinely appointed task.

Knowing the Jeremiah/Isaiah interpretation of history, and closely allied with the Persian Zoroastrians, the Hasidim were scandalized by the adulteration of Axial Age transcendence by this crudest of paganisms. Greek culture was beautiful, yes, and seductive, but to them it was lipstick on a pig.

This left them with an eschatological puzzle: How does this apparent setback fit into the prophetic scheme? And what should they do about it? With no divinely appointed champion in sight, they decided it was up to them to be the army of God. They would be their own Cyrus in what was hoped would be history's last battle.

The response was brutal. Called upon by his Jerusalem-based allies, Seleucid ruler Antiochus IV dispatched troops to put down the God-fearing opposition and then embarked on a cultural revolution, establishing a new directorate to systematically deprogram the Hasidim from their benighted fundamentalism. His pedagogical methods were severe: on penalty of being fed to the lions he forbad observance of the Laws of Moses. There was to be no circumcision, no Sabbath observance, and Jews had better be seen to eat pork or face the consequences—eat or be eaten.

Tormenting Jews became an obsession for Antiochus; he went so far as to bring in a liturgical consultant to correct the practice of worship in the Temple, bringing it in line with pagan rites, including it seems, the sacrifice of unclean animals to Greek gods upon YHWH's altar. Many faithful Jews met a gruesome end resisting these reforms.

On the Zoroastrian side of the fence, Alexander's campaign was nothing less than cataclysmic. The young Macedonian was a kind of antichrist to Cyrus—vainglorious and greedy, he destroyed what he found, taking the best of every land and erecting his edifice to gloat over what remained. The devout Persian emperors, however, mindful of a sacred duty to truth and justice, lived their lives in awe of the Creator—one Good Thought, Good Word, and Good Action at a time. Alexander conceived of himself as a god and viewed creation as his playground. Cyrus restored and rebuilt; Alexander plundered and despoiled.

To this day, Zoroastrians remember the Greek conqueror not as Alexander the Great but as Alexander *Guzastag*, "the accursed." It is a very special title otherwise reserved only for Ahriman, the Zoroastrian personification of the Lie—basically, Satan. Up until this time, there appears to be no other human being that Zoroastrians felt deserved this ignoble designation.

Alexander had earned every syllable of it, going out of his way to kill Zoroastrian priests, the Magi, while his soldiers pillaged their sacred precincts. He is remembered for wiping out so many Zoroastrian teachers and religious experts that a large chunk of Zoroaster's legacy was lost. Remember, this was an orally transmitted religion, and so killing these servants of the faith was equal to burning down libraries of sacred texts. As Mary Boyce notes, "the priests were the living books of the faith, and with mass slaughters many ancient works were lost..." Fortunately, Zoroaster's core revelation, the Gathas, survived, "transmitted intact, being known by heart... by every working priest."[31]

This put the Zoroastrians and their pious Jewish friends on the same eschatological page once again. Both had regarded the Cyrus empire as a forerunner to eternal redemption. Now, with the ruthless and quite sudden descent of the idolatrous Greeks, the Zoroastrian belief that this was the final conflict, the darkness before the dawn, also seeped into Jewish thinking. "Longing for the coming of the Saoshyant must have intensified among Iranians in the dark period after Alexander's conquest," Boyce observes, "and a rich apocalyptic and prophetic literature appears to have developed then, which was widely imitated."[32] Indeed, this literary genre developed into its most influential form through the pens of passionate Hebrew writers.

But it wasn't just Zoroastrians and Jews, either. Cyrus liberated the heart of civilization from India to Europe. Any nation now subjected to Greek imperialism suffered and hoped for better days. When viewed from a modern perspective, Greek domination was in fact the first example of Western imperialism, of a European culture imposing itself with force upon West Asians. Many of them welcomed it, exploited it, or were happily exploited by it for the benefits it gave them. Many others, however, were only exploited. The whole enterprise divided communities, pitting privileged sycophants against the disenfranchised. It's a pattern repeated again and again, most recently in the aftermath of the First World War.

Whether Jews, Persians, Babylonians, or Phoenicians, the mostly poor and unassimilated elements of society remembered Zoroastrian rule as tolerant and generous, and so their hopes naturally turned in that direction. They began to circulate this rapidly growing corpus of newly composed apocalyptic texts. They familiarized themselves with the ideas of End Time salvation, which, unfortunately, they tended to take literally, blending mystical symbolism with political fantasy. This was pop literature, not the subtle and ethically challenging eschatology of Zoroaster, and it sometimes led to a rather rough understanding of how Paradise would be achieved.

Jews were first in line. They needed to find a paradigm to make sense of the Alexandrian setback that delayed their dream. Whether out of piety or because of a stronger sense of national identity (often the difference is inscrutable), a significant percentage of Jews turned to apocalyptic discourse as the preferred means of solving the mystery of redemption.

The Final Mystery

AT THE TIME OF JESUS AND PAUL, INFLUENTIAL JEWS HAD A HIGH REGARD for the inspiration of those Greek-era apocalyptic texts. The New Testament cites many as canonical, although the Byzantine church ultimately excluded them. We see their influence all through the late Old Testament books, including Ezekiel and some elements of Isaiah, where Zoroastrian-style apocalyptic narratives appear with all the hallmarks: angelic visitations, spiritual warfare, and history divided into well-defined epochs—the signature is unmistakable.

Then there is the Book of Daniel, the only full-on apocalyptic text still included in the Old Testament, and easily the most influential apocalyptic ever penned. If you have Daniel, you don't really need the rest of them.

There are, without exaggeration, hundreds of inferences from and references to this ever-popular book in the Gospels, Epistles, on any airwaves populated by televangelists, and in books about the rapture or the Antichrist or anything along those lines.

In my life, the influence was deep. It changed my Muslim Brother's life, too. Although he would not know that Daniel was the source for Islamic End Time ideas, they can be traced there to the letter. Islam is, after all, based entirely on Jewish prophetic tradition.

Completed at the end of the turmoil surrounding Antiochus, the early chapters of Daniel handle an interpretation of what the exile in Babylon meant and give us that spot-on analysis of the moon-god feast. The latter chapters, however, refer to the depredations of Antiochus.

Daniel's epiphany occurs while consulting Jeremiah 29, where Jeremiah specifies the length of Judah's exile to be seventy years. This prompts a note from Daniel: "In the first year of Darius... I, Daniel, perceived in the books the number of years that, according to the word of the LORD to the prophet Jeremiah, must be fulfilled for the devastation of Jerusalem, namely, seventy years."[33]

Daniel is stricken. Recognizing that something is amiss, he repents on behalf of his people, confesses their sins, and prays for redemption. Daniel in this way represents not so much a Jew of Babylon as the Jews who read of Jeremiah's seventy years while in the dark days of the Greeks and ask what went wrong. Why did the redemption fail?

True, those seventy years seemed to end with the prophecy fulfilled: Cyrus returned the exiles to their land and rebuilt Jerusalem. The Jews seemed on course for the glories of the lion and lamb and the Prince of

Peace. But now Daniel's readers had Antiochus to contend with. There was no Davidic kingdom. Writing as a prophet set in the past, he can clarify the prophecy and make sense of the outcome. Daniel is here to solve the puzzle.

In answer to his supplications, the angel Gabriel appears to tell Daniel that the prophecy of seventy years had a secondary level. He explains that seventy years is not a straightforward seven decades; it is also a numerical mystery, meaning that seventy "weeks" of years must elapse before "iniquity is expiated, and eternal righteousness ushered in; and prophetic vision ratified, and the holy of holies anointed."[34]

"Seventy weeks of years" does not easily make sense in a modern English-language context. It may help to look at the translation more carefully. Translations such as the King James Version preserve the way Hebrew associates the concept of "a week" with the number seven. It's not just the obvious fact that there are seven days in a week. In Hebrew, the word for "week" is literally formed from the word for the number seven, so one cannot think of "week" without thinking of "seven."

Some translations preserve this understanding: the TANAKH version, highly regarded by Jews, specifies "Seventy weeks [of years]," enclosing in brackets what is clearly understood by the Hebrew reader. The Wycliffe Bible does the same thing without the brackets: "Seventy weeks *of years*." Scholars and believers, ancient and modern, read this to mean a formula of Jeremiah's original seventy years multiplied by a "week," or the number seven: 70×7. The total is thus 490 years of chastisement.

Angel Gabriel's multiplication handily explains the years between 539 BCE (Cyrus' liberation of the Jews) and the mid-100s BCE, when evil Antiochus was on the scene. Jeremiah had said all would be well after seventy years. Gabriel's revised reading explains why that wasn't quite the end of the matter.

He relies on a Levitical law: "If... you do not obey Me, I will go on to discipline you sevenfold for your sins."[35] After the initial seventy years of exile, if God's people did not behave well, they could be subjected to seven times the original penalty. Voilà! Suddenly a seventy-year sentence gets extended for bad behavior, explaining why things had gone poorly after the Jews' return from exile. As this sevenfold extension added up to 490 years, barring more bad behavior, savvy apocalyptic-reading Jews and other oppressed people could expect something extraordinary in the next hundred years or so, dating from around 50 BCE. It also gave them a motivation for strict piety and a powerful tool of moral suasion.

The solution is ingenious. If necessary, the math can explain further delays due to either bad behavior or the failure of the people to do their part. Jews, Christians, and Muslims repeatedly indulge this line of thinking. It puts a whip in the hand of those who want to hasten the Day of Judgment; they can say the Kingdom of Heaven is waiting on believers to rise to the moment for the last battle—either to stop sinning or to be more politically active, sometimes to the point of violence. Over the centuries, these numbers have been the basis of every kind of eschatological calculation. Not a year goes by without a headline prediction of the End Time based on this angelic math. We will see it come up several times as our story continues.

As important as the numbers are, Daniel's Apocalypse also includes a Saoshyant-like figure (remember, the Saoshyant is Zoroastrianism's End Time savior-hero, to be born of a virgin). In Daniel, he is "one like a human" (or "son of man," as older translations have it), who will come on the clouds to usher in everlasting salvation.[36] This clearly links Jewish and Zoroastrian expectations of a messiah with the 490-year promise, which was coming due in the last century BCE.

Critically, Daniel's angelic visitor tells him that his words will be validated in "the time of the end," cautioning him not to think of this miracle in terms of his mortal life. "You shall rest, and arise to your destiny at the end of the days," he is told. There, Daniel will join the other righteous dead who "will awake... to eternal life... and be radiant... like the stars forever and ever."[37]

That is the key to properly understanding Daniel that so many miss. The work is an explanation of this present darkness, but not a promise of material salvation. His idea of heaven is like Zoroaster's original transcendent physics, and to be sure, many took it correctly as a transcendental meditation. It is by no means a call to arms.

Alas, over the centuries many more read it that way, as a sociopolitical event—as indeed I once did. We imagined that this could happen in the political world, even in our lifetime, and that it was more likely to happen if we did our part. Judging by behavioral patterns among believers over the several centuries following Daniel's writing, I'd say most people were somewhere in the middle. They imagined a vague combination of scenarios, more or less literal depending on the direness of their circumstances. For the majority, it was a case of believe, watch, and wait. But, as always, it was the active fringe who made history. A stone thrown into the pond makes ripples; a violent act interrupts history. Those who wait quietly pass unnoticed.

But even the quiet kept a keen eye on political developments to see if a super-Cyrus, a new anointed savior, would appear—the Saoshyant or King Messiah, the Son of Man. If the right man appeared, even the most passive would be aroused. By the mid-100s BCE, Antiochus was growing weak, crippled by skirmishes with his cousins in Egypt. Then he met disaster as Rome turned a greedy eye toward the Western Mediterranean. This allowed a resurgent Zoroastrian dynasty, the Parthians, to strike the decisive blow, ending Antiochus' reign of terror forever.

All good news for the pious Jewish Hasidim, who were already engaged in a guerrilla campaign against their Greek-loving siblings. Their enemy's defeat by Zoroastrian Persians looked prophetically familiar, heightening the sense of finality. In no time, resistance leader Judah Maccabee seized control; Jerusalem was purified and the Temple restored to proper worship. Hanukkah celebrates a miracle of fire associated with this occasion, mirroring (unsurprisingly) the Zoroastrian winter festival of fire. (Fire was the most revered symbol of truth and purity in Zoroastrianism—their temples kept a perpetual fire burning.)

Was Judah the Messiah? Not by a long stretch—the Maccabees' Hasmonean dynasty was prone to corruption. At best, it was a return to the days of Jerusalem's lesser kings. But not being descendants of David, they could not produce the King Messiah. And while ostensibly pious, the dynasty had to ally itself with Rome to keep possession of Jerusalem's throne. Their rule was doomed to petty ambitions, persecution of dissidents, and civil unrest. Jewish society remained divided, riven along lines of privilege and politics, rich and poor, Hellenized sophisticates and rustic traditionalists. Some of the disenfranchised began to withdraw to the desert to found contemplative communities, arguing that greater holiness would precipitate the completion of redemption. Others, many of them ordinary people who had no part in the games of the elite, simply prayed and nurtured a quiet hope, a hope that was sympathetic to the pious.

In 63 BCE, barely eighty years after the Maccabees achieved their on-again-off-again independence, Rome showed up to stay for good. A civil conflict between two prospective heirs to the Jewish throne drew them in to set the kingdom in proper order. The task fell to legendary Roman general Pompey, who violated pious sensibilities by inadvertently entering the Holy of Holies, desecrating it.

For God-fearing Jews, neither the Hasmonean kings nor their new Roman overlords were acceptable. They read all these political machinations as signs of the times, omens of the darkest days, and signals of imminent salvation. Nothing illustrates this better than the saga of one Marcus Crassus, Consul of the Roman Empire.

Shock and Awe

In 56 BCE, Rome appointed Crassus to rule Syria, including Judea. A notoriously rapacious man, recognized in many accounts as the wealthiest individual in all Roman history, Crassus was never content with the size of his allotted piece of the pie. The remedy was to march on the Zoroastrian Parthians, and while he was at it, to seek some added value in Jerusalem, where it was rumored that the Temple concealed a considerable stash of gold.

Fearing another violent desecration, the Temple treasurer struck a deal: the general would spare the sacred artifacts in exchange for a gold bar, weighing 137 kilos, which was camouflaged as a wood beam and known only to the priest in charge. (That's worth about US$7 million today.) Crassus swore his agreement to the deal, received payment, and then stripped the Temple bare anyway.[38] From there he moved on to teach the Parthians a similar lesson.

With only 10,000 soldiers available against Rome's 40,000, the Zoroastrian Parthians would need a miracle. What they had was their laughably effete general, Surena. Greco-Roman historian Plutarch calls him the "fairest of them all," writing that, "his effeminate beauty did not well correspond to his reputation for valor..."[39]

Meeting the Romans just outside of Harran, with the main part of his limited forces concealed behind an advance guard, Surena stood strangely passive as the Romans moved in for the kill. The Parthian army just watched, as if trying to hide. They had even "concealed their armor" with "robes and skins," Plutarch recalls. And just then, with the Romans dangerously close and the Parthians sure to be slaughtered, Surena raised a signal.

It was to be a campaign of breathtaking shock and awe. As the Parthians dropped their cloaks, an army of "blazing helmets and breastplates" materialized. It was blinding—the Zoroastrians, fighting on the side of Light, had polished their armor into mirrors. According to witnesses, the Roman legionnaires, too close to turn back, desperately attempted to adjust their eyes as arrows rained down on them.

Then, Plutarch reports, amid this mayhem, Surena somehow "filled the plain with the sound of a deep and terrifying roar... a low and dismal tone, a blend of wild beast's roar and harsh thunder peal."[40] Parthian war drums. Like ones used in battle by Central Asian emirs as recently as the late 1800s, these were gigantic kettle drums, the playing of which necessitated a two-man team to strike them. "They emitted hollow sounds at first, which then turned into thunder-like peals that were heard over a distance of several kilometres."[41]

That hollow sound is indicative of sub-audible frequencies. Tuned correctly, they resonate with living organs—for example, human eyes have a precise resonate frequency of 18 hertz according to NASA, whose research on sound in this range revealed gagging, breathlessness, chest vibration, fatigue, elevated pulse, difficulties with speech, and slow response times for routine tasks. Later studies show effects on vision with hallucinatory properties. Unaware test subjects reported sensations of ghostly awe or oppression —a haunted feeling. With constant exposure over a long period, the result is Vibro Acoustic Disorder, a debilitating syndrome affecting the entire body.[42]

Now, imagine a whole army's worth of that. The Romans were completely undone. Plutarch's observations accord with NASA's; he writes that the sonic wave was able to "confound the soul" and "unseat the judgment" of the Roman troops. Over 2,000 years ago the Magi had weaponized sound.

It was then that Surena unleashed the full force of his light-cavalry archers. The Parthians continuously feigned retreat as the clueless Crassus repeatedly pushed his men forward. Part of the problem was the glare and throbbing eyes, which were further addled by a problem of perspective: the Parthian horses were about 25 percent bigger than the Roman stock, which had the effect of making them appear closer than they were. The Roman ranks fell to volleys of arrows even while the Parthians were riding away from them in apparent retreat. This was the now legendary "Parthian shot," effected by Zoroastrian boys who could fire accurately and rapidly while riding away from the enemy. The barrage was unceasing in either direction. (As we recall, Herodotus had written of Persian youth that they train "in three things alone—to ride, to draw the bow, and to speak the truth.")

The only hope for the Romans was that their enemy would run out of arrows. Crassus resorted to the classic Roman defensive formation hoping to weather the storm. This was a terrible mistake. Surena had pre-arranged thousands of camels to convey an endless re-supply for his archers. The battle ended with 20,000 dead Roman soldiers, and 10,000 more taken captive or lost. Crassus and his son were killed. He had led 40,000 troops into the most humiliating defeat of Roman history.

I've taken the time to tell this story because it was earth-shattering news —the Roman army had not known a serious defeat in 200 years. Neither was Crassus an ordinary general: he was one of the top three rulers of the Roman

Empire, along with Julius Caesar and Pompey. And this was no minor setback: it was a slaughter of seven Roman legions.

It was the kind of news that was read by the apocalyptically minded as a sign of redemption drawing near. It was a miracle, and it was divine retribution. Crassus was the epitome of arrogance. He had blatantly lied to YHWH's priests, then with his satchels stuffed with sanctified gold, marched on the Jewish people's Zoroastrian friends, who famously do not abide the Lie. You can just imagine the glee with which the put-upon faithful relished this report, telling their children over and over again how the heir to Cyrus destroyed the Liar who just months before had desecrated their Temple and robbed them blind.

Whether Surena had this in mind or not we will never know, but his last act in the battle was to melt a measure of Crassus' ill-gotten gold and pour it down the Roman general's throat in a symbolic Zoroastrian judgment of purifying fire upon worldly greed.

In the minds of many, this was exactly a model for the last battle—if one wanted to imagine what King Messiah would do at Jerusalem, no better inspiration could be found than the victory of the Magian general outside the moon god's Harran.

Great Expectations

Although Surena's victory did not directly help the pious Jews, the Parthians did briefly expel the Romans from Jerusalem a short time later, installing a slightly more palatable king—at least, one who was not under Rome's direct control. It was a short-lived respite, just another round in the End Time struggle.

But with each episode, history seemed to speed up in anticipation of a final showdown. In no time, the Roman Empire had again taken control of Jerusalem, installing their own man, Herod the Great. For this one, they pulled out all the stops, naming Herod the "King of the Jews" by an official act of the Roman Senate. This entitled Herod to an army with which to keep order. He would need it. Although he was raised a Jew (his grandfather, an Edomite, had converted out of political expediency), Herod's loyalties lay with Hellenized Jews and Rome. All the pious factions despised him. It was to be a grindingly painful century.

We have considerable evidence of Hasidic thinking at this time thanks to the Dead Sea Scrolls, preserved by communities like the Essenes, who inhabited a desert retreat by the Dead Sea at Qumran. The Essenes adopted a worldview that, if not borrowed from the Zoroastrians, was at least a remarkable example of parallel development. They believed history to be a battle between light and darkness, where angels assist the Sons of Light and demons the Sons of Darkness. That struggle was understood to be part of their daily lives, fought through piety and purity, but it was also eschatological, a spiritual war for the End Time.

The *Jewish Encyclopedia* describes the scene:

> It was the class of the Ḥasidim and their successors, the Essenes, who made a special study of the prophetical writings in order to learn the future destiny of Israel and mankind... They based their calculations upon unfulfilled prophecies such as Jeremiah's seventy years and accordingly tried to fix "the end of days."[43]

The same source accepts that they developed their views under "Persian influence," writing that "it can not be denied... that these Ḥasidean or apocalyptic writers took a sublime view of the entire history of the world... seeing its consummation in the establishment of 'the kingdom of the Lord,' called also, in order to avoid the use of the Sacred Name 'the kingdom of heaven.'"

A well-known apocryphal Psalm of Solomon shows us just how they viewed Herod's reign and what they expected to happen soon:

> The king was a transgressor, and the judge disobedient, and the people sinful. Behold, O Lord, and raise up unto them their king, the son of David... that he may purge Jerusalem from gentiles who trample (her) down to destruction... He shall judge peoples and nations in the wisdom of his righteousness... he shall purge Jerusalem, making it holy... that nations shall come from the ends of the earth to see his glory... for all shall be holy and their king the Lord Messiah.[44]

This condenses the situation in the last century before the current era as well as anything can: Jerusalem is underfoot of Gentiles, the king is a despotic sham, and the true son of David must come to usher in the age of renewal. Make no mistake, this is a Zoroastrian type of salvation. It is not just getting back to the good old days of the Bronze Age kingdom; this is the king envisioned by Isaiah, the king of universal peace. Other popular literature of the day describes the resurrection of the dead and full restoration of Edenic life.

The pious anti-Western Jews who read this material (indeed, who wrote much of it) were, in a sense, exiles in their own land, still waiting for the anointed one's liberation. Isaiah's prophecy of anointed Cyrus was still read but understood now to foreshadow final and ultimate redemption. As such, Cyrus' example left a pattern and nomenclature for messianic expectations.

We can still see it very clearly in glorious 3D at Persepolis, in northwestern Iran. This is where Darius the Great built a city to serve the Zoroastrian empire, its architecture designed to reference the tenets of the imperial religion. The palace complex is especially striking. Situated on a flat plain, it is constructed upon an enormous platform, its staircases paneled with fine stone carvings and broad enough to allow the passage of large groups, escalating toward the place where the Persian ruler, the King of Kings, sat.

The carvings constitute a kind of permanent mirror of what happened every year on the spring equinox. Ascending the stairs, we see delegations from every tribe, tongue, people, and nation. They bear gifts of every kind, each one culturally representative of the embassies that bear them. At the top, standing by the King of Kings, we see incense vessels burning (frankincense, commonly), and there, waiting beside the King of Kings, is the chief of the Magi, the Zoroastrian priests. This is the New Day holiday, or Newroz, which Iran keeps to this day. It celebrates the promise of the eternal dawn that will occur when truth incarnate appears making all things new, *frashokereti*. It looks a lot like Isaiah's delegation of nations to Jerusalem, and of course it looks like something else just around the historical corner, when Magi will make their own pilgrimage bearing gifts to a new King of Kings.

As a premonition of salvation, it is compelling. Since all nations participated in it, Newroz must have left an impression on readers of apocalyptic literature across the Near East. But did it reinforce the idea that salvation would be political? Cyrus reigned graciously and liberated entire nations, but it did come through conquest. Truth and Righteousness bore a sword. Is it correct, then, to expect the End Time as an event in history, accomplished through a political champion—a victory at the end of a line? Or does that belong only to the time-bound, like Cyrus, as a shadow cast in history by the eternal?

There is a logical problem if the end of violence comes through violence. Literal warfare did not jibe with Isaiah's de-weaponized, de-fanged, and de-clawed universe. The same Psalm of Solomon that we just read specifies that the King Messiah "shall not put his trust in horse and rider and bow, nor shall he multiply for himself gold and silver for war, nor shall he gather confidence from a multitude for the day of battle."

On the other hand, some readers of biblical prophet Ezekiel concluded that a last battle would be fought in a literal sense, so intense that it would pierce the membrane between time and eternity. Ezekiel wrote about an End Time clash between the Messiah and an entity called Magog and its leader, Gog. As time wore on, "Gog and Magog" became a shorthand reference and a key to unlocking signs that the end was near for Jews, Christians, and Muslims, with Magog identified conveniently with the enemy of the day.

What of Zoroaster, the father of the whole eschatological idea that Truth will defeat Lie? Zoroaster arose in denunciation of a cosmology that celebrated violence. The only *daeva* mentioned directly by Zoroaster was the warrior god-in-chief Indra. Why? Because Indra was a god of destruction. "Zoroaster rejected with the utmost courage and firmness the worship of the warlike, amoral Daevas—that is, Indra and his companions—whom he regarded as being 'of the race of evil purpose.'"[45]

His fundamental idea despised destructive warfare. Zoroaster's battle was between states of consciousness, Spenta Mainyu, the original mind of creation, and Druj—the Lie—which caused Angra Mainyu, "destructive mind." It is a struggle of consciousness only.

One thing all agreed upon was that the Savior will be the catalyst for *frashokereti*, or Paradise. How this would be achieved was the burning question that faced believers in the last days BCE, just as that group of Zoroastrian Magi were beckoned by a heavenly body to the land of Judah and the town of Bethlehem, the ancestral City of David. Here, just as the prophesied 490 years after the exile ended, all the signs converged.

Persepolis was the ceremonial seat of Persia's Zoroastrian emperors. The most important was Cyrus the Great, whom Israel's prophet Isaiah called God's Messiah. He also bore the title, "King of Kings."

As the 'father of human rights' Cyrus conquered the Babylonian Empire and set all its captive peoples free. His just reign set an unprecedented example and made him a messianic archetype.

In this relief from Persepolis: delegates from the nations stream to the King of Kings bearing gifts. **Heading the procession: Magi, the Zoroastrian priests.**

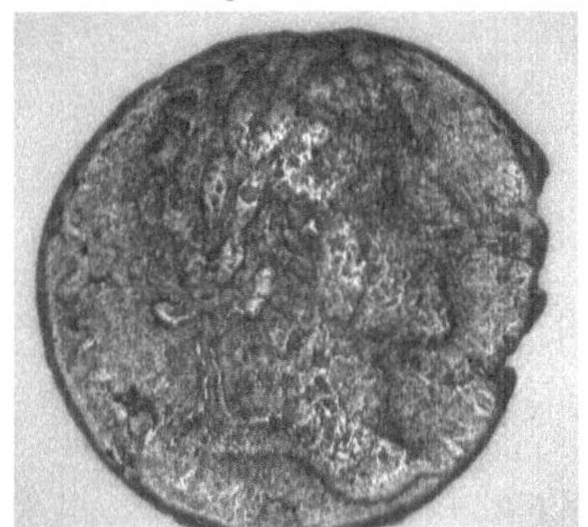 

Jewish exiles thought redemption was complete when Cyrus freed them and paid to rebuild their temple in Jerusalem. They soon learned that a period of testing would precede the eternal Messiah's arrival.

From my collection: *(L)* Coin belonging to Antiochus IV, reviled for his obsession with stamping out Judaism and sacrificing unclean animals on the altar of the Jewish Temple. He is often associated with the Antichrist.

(R) An oil lamp from Jerusalem dating to the time of the Maccabees.

They freed Jerusalem and purified the Temple, which Antiochus had desecrated. The miracle of the oil that kept the menorah burning during this restoration is the basis of Hanukkah. The story references Persian Zoroastrian themes and terminology.

Israel's prescribed 490 years of chastisement came to an end just as the Herod dynasty came to power in Jerusalem. With the End Time at hand many claimed the title of messiah–including Herod himself.

From my collection: a coin belonging to Herod the Great, who loaded it with messianic and Greek symbols.

The face shows a rising star (the most celebrated sign of the Messiah) and palm branches representing the victory of Israel. Later, Jesus was welcomed to Jerusalem with palm branches too.

This is why the Gospel depicts Herod's rage when the Magi say they saw the star of the true Messiah, a new-born in Bethlehem. Early Christians saw Herod as a messianic pretender.

Boarding my flight to Tel Aviv, I decided to grow a beard.

This is the result.

Young Muslim radicals were also growing their beards at this time.

We had a lot in common.

MILLENNIUMS

❧ II ☙

THE MESSIAH

The Zealot

I loved the Jewish world as a child and teen. It had to do with reading the Bible, where Eden and exile bonded me with the Jewish experience. But it was also escape into their culture, escape from my history and the burden of my time and place, which had already made me feel old and worn.

My family's post-Dad life passed in a very different land from that of my birth. In Appalachia, I never saw a black face, but now we lived in a neighborhood with so few whites that I escaped 1970s desegregation busing—I was a white boy who could walk to school in a mostly black neighborhood, across streets populated with drug dealers and prostitutes even at eight in the morning. When I was called "white trash" by my black schoolmates for inexplicably being white while poor, I thought, "No, I'm just passing through like Abraham."

Sure, I may have lived in a homicidal ghetto, where I saw my mother beaten with a paint bucket by a recently released murderer (our white trash neighbor to the left!), and where I contracted tuberculosis from Haitian refugees (our neighbors to the right!), but just beside us was the greatest concentrations of Jews outside of New York City—that was my link to the Promised Land, and I clung to it fiercely.

To that end, PBS played non-stop on my TV. The Jews were our station's main stakeholders, a driving force in the cultural life of that part of the country. Any time fundraising season came around, they treated us to documentaries about Israel's miraculous rebirth and its modern wars, which to my young eyes and ears were inseparable from its biblical ones. I imbibed Jewish culture and embraced Jewish history as a de facto act of God. My soul wanted to be there and wanted to serve in that explicitly realized apocalyptic battle. It made the Bible a matter of headline news, fresh and alive in a way nothing else was. Thus, I grew up with beliefs and expectations very much in tune with those of the Zoroastrians and Jews of the first century BCE.

Of course, I'd known about modern Israel for a long time. For Christians of our ilk, Israel's place in the End Time is a given. I'd had a copy of Hal Lindsay's bestseller *The Late Great Planet Earth* from the time we first began going to church (my mother, an insurance agent, got saved on a cold call to a Baptist pastor).

Lindsay's book was practically stapled to the Bible in those days. It analyzed biblical prophecy through contemporary events, finding fulfillments in the precarious condition of the world, from the Cold War battle against atheism to the decline of family values and the liberalization of sex. Most of all, it detailed for us precisely how Bible prophecies predicted Israel's regathering and how the fulfillment marked the last striking of the clock. I can't stress too much how common this thinking was (and is). That book sold in the millions.

Or take Billy Graham. Any church worth its salt screened his film, *This Land*, celebrating the connection between ancient and modern Israel. By the 1970s, avid born-again Christians generally saw Israel as God's timepiece. The restoration of the Jewish people to their land—and more than that, their sovereignty over Jerusalem, obtained through the Six-Day War in 1967 —was a certain and unfailing sign that the end was near. I was riveted by it.

I spent time with Jewish entertainers and musicians, too: from classical artists like Arthur Rubinstein and Isaac Stern to comics Don Rickles and Rodney Dangerfield (born Jacob Cohen). My father figure was William Shatner (yes, he's Jewish). I loved Johnny Carson's *Tonight Show* for its magical power to bring me into the company of these friends—Johnny seemed like me, an honored Gentile allowed into their blessed circle.

Christians had talk shows, too. Pat Robertson's *700 Club* aired twice a day. I never missed it. I not only watched, entranced by his interpretations of biblical prophecy, but I subscribed to Pat's newsletter to get his take on prophecy's fulfillment in daily politics. Israel was a featured player. In short order, by my mid-teens, I was making pilgrimages to Pat's Virginia Beach–based Christian Broadcasting Network for intensive training. And it was there (reader beware!) that a Lutheran pastor prayed for me and I spontaneously spoke in tongues. I know. This sounds ludicrous, but it was a genuine experience. The minister never coached me, did not touch me, and invoked no mesmerizing theatrics. He simply walked past, exuding love and light, and I burst forth with glossolalian unction.

Extraordinary perhaps, but options of the ordinary kind were fantastically elusive. I could not for the life of me figure out how to get a good grade at school. Disaffection for the unconcerned cadre assigned to that task weighed my mortal ambitions down to the point that they became unbearable. I cast them aside. The day after turning sixteen, I resigned my commission in person to the superintendent of schools and suggested, in not ineloquent terms, that they might do better. He didn't care.

Retiring to our treacherous home to tend my spiritual garden, it was revivalist preachers like Charles G. Finney who educated me. He galvanized entire cities into penitent and activist communities. There was nothing hypothetical in this; Finney and his followers enacted real reform, requiring equal education for women and people of color and providing practical support for abolitionists. He was a fierce anti-slavery crusader and social activist who believed in the ability of people not just to repent but to bring the Kingdom of God to the here and now: Christ's millennial rule awaited our action.

Soon, the term "spiritual warfare" entered my vocabulary. God's people were meant to be fighting the End Time battle, not passively waiting for salvation. There was no question about how I should spend my life. If ordinary things were denied me, it was a sign to pursue the extraordinary. It was the seduction of the heroic, the call of holy war.

Wait for the Second Coming? No. We were to preach the Good News to every tribe, tongue, and nation. We were to infiltrate society, placing believers in high office and low office, from the White House to the local school board. Pat called it the "Secret Kingdom." Christians should occupy prominent places in business and the arts, too. When Jesus returned, the structure of the kingdom would be there, having weathered the short storm of the seven-year tribulation and the Antichrist's last-gasp attempt to thwart the unveiling of the new heaven and Earth.

Career, education, fiscal responsibility? There was no time for that! Jesus said not to lay up your treasure on Earth! Didn't anybody really believe him anymore?

It turns out they did. I was not alone. Our generation had its own prophet, Keith Green. Shaggy and maximally Jewfroed in a way only seen in the 1970s, Keith put the "tense" in intensity. I came across him at a "Jesus festival." In those days, Christian youth were plugged into a network of music through local bookstores and these massive Woodstock-like music camp-outs. Typically, they included "teaching" in the mix of performances, much of it Finney-inspired holiness and missionary preaching, warning us not to waste our lives but to follow the commands of Jesus literally.

All of this was an outflow of the Jesus People (or Jesus Freaks, if you prefer), those hippies turned Christians who bought up all those copies of *The Late Great Planet Earth*. Of course they did: the hallucinatory visions of apocalypse jibed perfectly with the movement's psychedelic origins. Talk about turning on, tuning in, and dropping out! Nothing got you higher than a tongues-speaking Jesus high, and the coming Kingdom of God—just over the horizon—was the definitive dropping out.

Such was the path that led to Keith Green. But his style was different. There would be no dropping out quite yet. His lyrics were regressive and confrontational. The first album I got was his second release. The title says it all: *No Compromise*.

Keith's message was all action. Get high on Jesus and become a martyr for Jesus! Go into all the world and preach the Gospel! Then the end will come, Jesus had said so. That was Keith's message in a nutshell.

He was a Jew, of course, a Jewish believer in Jesus, and he bore his prophetic heritage with fasting and sackcloth and bid us do the same. He burned when he sang, and set people alight when he spoke.

The movement that arose around Keith in Lindale, Texas, was called Last Days Ministries. His albums came with a response card offering a free subscription to the *Last Days Newsletter*, and boy did we sign up! What came in the mail was beautiful; it was the most original, arresting graphic design I'd ever seen. The content was scathing: diatribes against the dead Protestant Church, brutal indictments of what was viewed as apostate Catholicism, and reprints and retellings of centuries-old sermons by Finney and Jonathan Edwards. We read "Sinners in the Hands of an Angry God," and took to heart Keith's message that the Gospel was the salve to be applied after preaching judgment. No easy salvation here.

This was the 1980s way to go internet viral. The whole thing was unregistered by ordinary time, the revolution spreading unobserved by the culture-at-large. Like the Internet now and its facilitation of groups like al-Qaeda, it was both clandestine and utterly exposed. Teenagers and young adults by the tens of thousands found Keith as if all at once, and every one of us was desperate to escape to Paradise.

Even Bob Dylan rode the wave. "I believe that ever since Adam and Eve got thrown out of the garden that the whole nature of the planet has been heading in one direction—towards apocalypse," he told the *Sunday Times* in 1984. "It's all there in the Book of Revelations, but it's difficult talking about these things to most people because most people don't know what you're talking about, or don't want to listen."[1] He reiterated this to *Spin* magazine the following year:

> This world is scheduled to go for 7,000 years. Six thousand years of this, where man has his way, and 1,000 years when God has His way. Just like a week. Six days work, one day rest. The last thousand years is called the Messianic Age. Messiah will rule. He is, was, and will be about God, doing God's business. Drought, famine, war, murder, theft, earthquake, and all other evil things will be no more. No more disease. That's all of this world... it's all there in black and white, the written and unwritten word. I don't have to defend this. The scriptures back me up. I didn't ask to know this stuff. It just came to me at different times from experiences throughout my life.[2]

Yes, Bob had been reading *The Late Great Planet Earth*, too. (I told this to a friend recently who was not amused, but aside from these interviews, it is well documented by Dylan biographer Clinton Heylin.) Bob even played harmonica on a Keith Green album and recorded his own End Time–steeped record, *Slow Train Coming*.

I wanted in on this. I wanted to matter. I wanted to take my place in the Last Days army. And most of all, I wanted out of the world as I knew it. I heeded the call as best I could.

First, I began to channel Keith and Bob's Jewish prophet intensity. When I talked, people came to the Lord, and dramatically so. Some of what happened can't be explained rationally. One young man, my first convert, fell to the ground in a shaking, sweating, tongues-speaking fit after nothing more than a prayer. He was not epileptic; he never experienced it before. He was not even familiar with such things, having grown up Roman Catholic and oblivious to the Pentecostals and Charismatics that inhabited my world. To my knowledge, he never experienced anything like it after this single inci-dence of deliverance from the bondage and burden of sin. Others followed more quietly. I had a gift, and all this appeared to be confirmation: get thee to the Holy Land and prepare for the Day of the Lord, O warrior of God!

And so, presaging Muslim youth from America and Europe who would do something awfully similar decades later, I boarded a chartered jet bound for the Middle East on a holy mission to deliver the world from time and into the waiting arms of eternity.

The Messiah

On my way to Israel, if I'd hit a wormhole and flown back to the early first century, I would have fit in well, finding myself right at home with those crowds cheering the Galilee's would-be Messiah, helping him disrupt the rule of Herod the Great and his sons. The Galilean's followers also gave up their ordinary lives to stake everything on the coming kingdom. And they did it for the same reason: they mostly didn't see any real alternative. We all had given up on ordinary time.

This was 70×7 years after the end of exile in Babylon and, accordingly, a generation deemed ripe for messianic salvation. Roman historian Tacitus, a reliably phlegmatic and unbiased journalist, explained the Messiah-enthusiasts' inspiration and goals: "The majority firmly believed that their ancient priestly writings contained the prophecy that this was the very time when the East should grow strong and that men starting from Judea should possess the world."[3]

From the Jewish side, Flavius Josephus explains the messianic crusaders in startlingly familiar terms; he might as well be talking about today's Middle East. "What more than all else incited them to the war," he writes, "was an ambiguous oracle, likewise found in their sacred scriptures, to the effect that at that time one from their country would become ruler of the world."[4]

As "ambiguous" as these apocalyptic prophecies were, by the time Jesus Christ was a boy, the faithful had enough influence to start a full-on revolt against Rome. But Jesus is not the Messiah I would be following with this band of brothers. Initially, the key figure was another Galilean named Judas, who Josephus says was a teacher with his own school of followers and a movement called "the Fourth Philosophy," meaning the fourth Jewish political paradigm of the day, after the puritan Pharisees, ascetic Essenes, and elitist Sadducees.

Josephus writes that they had everything in common with the Pharisees, "except their unconquerable passion for freedom, since they take God as their only leader and master."

In other words, what made the Fourth Philosophy stand out was its radical commitment to implementing the day-to-day political rule of God—a theocracy. Furthermore, Josephus notes that they "shrug off submitting to death in unusual forms and stand firm in the face of torture of relatives and friends."[5] The Fourth Philosophy sounds more and more like the radical religious militants we recognize today.

Their leader was a contemporary of Jesus, but a little older. If we are to trust the Gospel of Matthew's timeline, Judas, a fellow Galilean, might have known young Jesus. If not, his sons and followers surely did. They and Jesus competed over the same turf. When some men came to test Jesus on whether or not to pay Roman taxes, it is easy to imagine that Fourth Philosophy disciples were involved. Roman taxation was the single most important hot-button issue for Fourth Philosophy constituents, and the spark that ignited their rebellion.

It was 6 CE when Rome imposed direct rule over the Jewish state, conducting a census to establish a regular poll tax, something anathema to pious Jews on the basis that the land belonged to YHWH; it therefore could not be assessed as if it were Caesar's. What was Caesar's and what was God's became a litmus test for people's loyalties.

It was an easy button to push. For ordinary people, taxes were bad already. The rate of effective taxation was as much as 40 percent in Galilee, all to pay for Herod's vanity projects, including a local Galilean monstrosity, the Temple of Augustus at the resort city Caesarea Philippi.[6] Attacking the Herodian faction, Judas galvanized messianic hopes, and when he declared himself King of the Jews, he and his sons had no difficulty in mustering discontent into armed insurrection.[7]

There are those who argue that Judas is the basis for Jesus. He certainly looks a lot like Jesus—he is a great Galilean teacher, he does not fear death, and he preaches the Kingdom of Heaven and the End of Days. And despite the Gospel's assurances to the contrary, Jesus was also accused of not paying taxes. In the Gospel of Luke, this is the charge made against Jesus before Pontius Pilate: "We found this man misleading our nation and forbidding us to give tribute to Caesar, and saying that he himself is Christ [Messiah], a king... He stirs up the people, teaching throughout all Judea, from Galilee even to this place."[8] That is an accurate biography of Judas, far more so than the Gospel of Matthew's Jesus, as we shall soon see.

Jesus was of course crucified by Pilate, and Judas must have been executed, too, exactly on those charges of forbidding taxes and claiming kingship. Strangely, we know his final fate only second hand, for although Josephus included the full story in his history, those passages were excised by Roman Christians in the Byzantine era. Why would they do that? Some think the only reason for the Church to suppress details about Judas is that either the biography of Jesus is borrowed from Judas or that Judas in some way contradicts the official Jesus story. So, either Jesus *was* Judas, and his biography in the Gospels is a complete fabrication—a mythological anti-Judas constructed because of Judas' failure—or Jesus was a different teacher who rejected and opposed the apocalyptic literalist. The Book of Acts stakes its claim: Judas was real, but a false messiah. "Judas the Galilean rose up at the time of the census and got people to follow him," it says.[9]

In my opinion, the timing isn't quite right for Judas to plausibly be Jesus. After Judas was defeated and presumably killed, his movement was for a time subdued, just in the period when Jesus was active. My suspicion is that the Church redacted Josephus' passages because the story did not support some point of Orthodox dogma (take your pick as to which Dan Brown scenario it might be). Otherwise, the historical Jesus was a genuine anti-Judas and rival to his sons and heirs, James and Simon. (Yes, there are many similar names in Jesus and Judas' circles, which adds to the intrigue!)

What's for certain is that in Jesus' supposed lifetime, the Judas brothers rallied for another rebellion, indoctrinating and recruiting holy-war militants from the same pool of young men represented by Jesus' twelve disciples. Their campaign was the more successful of the two. Although both sons were crucified by the Roman procurator Tiberius Alexander circa 46 CE, a decade or so after Jesus, the movement did not die. By 66 CE, it had mutated into the Great Revolt. Despite this being long after the death of patriarch Judas, Josephus nonetheless reviled him as the father of that most disastrous and deadly revolution, the man who "laid the foundation for our future miseries."

The Great Revolt was a complex and very modern conflict. It wasn't simply Romans against Jews, good guys versus bad guys. Far from it—this was also a civil war fought between, in Josephus' words, "those that were fond of war... the revolutionary and militant party," who "by their youth and recklessness overpowered the old and prudent," and "those that were desirous of peace."[10] Again, it foreshadows current events in the Middle East. During the Great Revolt, bands of apocalyptic Fourth Philosophy robbers pillaged the villages of their co-religionists, murdering thousands of Jewish brethren. Josephus, although he was a Jew and a strong apologist for his people, nonetheless testifies of the Hebrew jihadists that their "barbarity and iniquity... differed in no way from the Romans."[11]

By way of illustration, consider a key leader in the Revolt, Judas of Galilee's grandson, Menahem, who became a leader of the Sicarii militia—the "dagger men."

After first ransacking the Herodian fortress at Masada, Menahem managed to take control of the Temple and the Roman fortress in Jerusalem. His men executed anyone who opposed them—Jews and Romans alike. Then, declaring himself to be Daniel's foretold Son of Man, Menahem claimed to no longer be flesh and blood! He professed to occupy a metaphysical space, seated on Daniel's prophesied "Throne of Glory" in heavenly places, surrounded by angels ready to deliver him and his followers at any moment.

Although this and other statements sound something like Jesus, the difference is that Menahem's vision was politically hypostatized in the most brutal way. "He became barbarously cruel" writes Josephus.[12]

Menahem and company cut the template for the Middle East's future apocalyptic terrorists in many particulars. The Talmud remembers them destroying Jerusalem's food supply to force the city's civilian Jews to take their side in the fight. They did not want Jerusalem's community leaders to enter into peace talks with the Romans; the worse the people's predicament, they thought, the more God would be compelled to intervene miraculously on their behalf.

Predictably, a rival militia eventually killed Menahem, and all the fractured anti-government groups quickly succumbed to a Roman counterstrike. The result was cataclysmic: Jerusalem's complete demolition and the end of Israel as a national entity. Menahem, in a dark reflection of Jesus, promised that he would return in glory to fulfill his role as Son of Man. Meanwhile, his nephew, Elazar Ben-Yair, fell back upon Masada to make his famous suicidal stand against the Romans. (Masada, fully excavated and politicized by the modern State of Israel, is well worth your further study.)

The crushing defeat of the rebels in 70 CE was followed by Rome's restructuring of Judea into an ordinary province, renamed Syria Palaestina, the origin of the political designation of Palestine. It was no longer an autonomous Jewish kingdom. As per Jesus' words, Josephus records that Jerusalem and the Temple were "so thoroughly razed to the ground to its foundations that nothing was left that could ever persuade visitors that it had once been a place of habitation." It was rebuilt, but not as a Jewish city; Emperor Hadrian renamed it Aelia Capitonlina, rededicating the city to Jupiter, whose temple replaced YHWH's on Mount Zion.

This gives us a picture of Jewish society when Jesus appeared and some insight into what people expected from a candidate Messiah. We can see facets of Jesus' disciples in the young hotheads who followed Judas and his family. Jesus' biography is set against this and prophetically critical of it. But like the Hebrew Bible we've been reading, we can only access it through carefully crafted parables—the Gospels—which want to tell us not just the facts, but the meaning of the life of Jesus Christ.

The Magi

Writing from his base in Antioch, a Roman stronghold founded by the dread successors to Alexander, an unknown scribe penned the Gospel According to Matthew. It is the cornerstone of the New Testament, the most Jewish of the Gospels, and at the same time the most universal, for Matthew's Jewish faith encompasses the promise to Abraham, "in whom all the nations of the earth will be blessed." His message: All will be saved, but through a Jewish catalyst.

To Jerusalem the nations would stream, said Isaiah, but that was more characteristic of the author's city than David's. Matthew's Antioch was the world's third most populated city and its most cosmopolitan, a place where Jews lived alongside Romans, Greeks, and countless other nationalities. It was the hub of the civilized world and home to a notoriously rowdy and transient population. Of them, Gibbon wrote, "Fashion was the only law, pleasure the only pursuit and the splendour of dress and furniture was the only distinction."[13]

Aramaic was spoken in the streets as a lingua franca, while Greek, Latin, and several strains of Persian—even Gaulish, Germanic, and Coptic—could be heard outside the writer's windows. If Matthew needed a break, meandering around the city's compact six square miles and eighteen identifiable ethnic quarters, he might stop by a synagogue, a house church, a plethora of Greco-Roman temples, or a shrine to the Egyptian goddess Isis.

Libanius, Antioch's own master rhetorician, wrote that "if a man had the idea of traveling all over the earth, our city would fulfill his purpose and save him his journeying. If he sits in our marketplace he will sample every city, there will be so many people from each place with whom he can talk."[14]

More recently, in his 1936 classic, *In the Steps of St. Paul*, H. V. Morton aptly compared Antioch to Hollywood: it had a fine climate that attracted the wealthy and the beautiful, while the personal lives of its rich and famous were the stuff of gossip and entertainment across the empire.[15] He might have added that Jews did well in both of these glitzy corners of the diaspora, nearly as successful in Antioch as they would be in tinsel town 2,000 years later.

Matthew therefore wrote for an unusually worldly and astute audience;

moreover, they were primed and ready for his message. Both Zoroastrians and Jews resented Roman domination, and while city life may have held enough glitter to distract the wealthiest elites, the disparity between the haves and have-nots was deep. The working classes had a hard time: taxes were punishingly high and the state's merciless penalties for delinquency—torture and death—are well documented. Roman soldiers were no exception. They lived difficult, empty lives, seeking meaning through Mithraism, the most wide-spread religion in the imperial army, which was derived from Persian Zoroastrian beliefs.

Then there were what the Jews called "God fearers," Gentile seekers who found their way into Antioch's synagogues. Most were already influenced by Zoroastrianism—or more accurately, by the ever-popular apocalyptic litera-ture—and there were significant numbers of them.

This challenging complexity was very much on the Gospel writer's mind. Matthew's nuances speak to Jews who might be interested in Jesus but who are concerned with questions of law, purity, and the role of the Temple. He seeks to allay their fears of contamination while also specifically assuring Gentiles of their place in the Kingdom of Heaven.

On the Jewish side, of primary importance was the belief that the kingdom would come through a descendant of David. So Matthew opens his Gospel with a clear message for them: "Jesus the Messiah, the son of David..."[16]

As the evangelist continues, however, there is a twist: "The birth of Jesus the Messiah took place... when his mother... was found to be with child from the Holy Spirit."

According to Jewish law, this was problematic; a king descended from David was legitimate only through a male blood line. How does that work with a virgin birth? Matthew characteristically addresses that by arguing it is part of Jewish tradition after all. He quotes Isaiah: "All this took place to fulfill what the Lord had spoken by the prophet: 'Behold, the virgin shall conceive and bear a son, and they shall call his name Immanuel' (which means, God with us)."[17]

The evangelist is re-contextualizing Isaiah, bridging the gap between Gentile and Jewish worlds. The Hebrew term from Isaiah is *ha-almah*—simply meaning "the girl," not "virgin." But Matthew had the Septuagint on his side. The Greek version of Isaiah, in wide use by Jews at the time, trans-lates *almah* as *parthenos*, which clearly means "virgin" in Greek.

Why does Matthew insist on this? For one thing, it was a firm Zoroas-trian expectation; the Saoshyant was foretold to be born miraculously of a virgin. By calling upon the authority of the Septuagint, he could assure Gentile and Jew alike that Jesus was the Savior.

To add more authority, Joseph, Mary's betrothed, stands in for skeptical Jews. To assure him that the virgin birth was kosher, he got a visit from an angel: "Joseph, son of David, do not fear... for that which is conceived in her is from the Holy Spirit."[18]

Next, Matthew tells us that Jesus was born during the reign of despotic King Herod. By then, the hated king had resorted to Stalinesque social controls to salve his paranoia, notably forbidding more than two people from walking together in the street lest they plot against him.

Given Herod's precarious state of mind, you can imagine his anxiety when a whole delegation arrived from Surena's homeland of Parthia, the Zoroastrian humiliator of his Roman patrons, not to see him, but to inquire of his presumed replacement. "Magi from the east came to Jerusalem and asked, 'Where is the one who has been born king of the Jews? We saw his star when it rose and have come to worship him.'"[19]

This is an amazingly deft piece of contextualization, a pilgrimage by gift-bearing Magi to the King of Kings, an image taken directly from Persepolis and the Newroz ceremony. It announced to a wide swath of former Persian subjects that the Saoshyant was born. And Jewish readers of Isaiah understood the implications, too—they knew all about the King of Kings and Cyrus as the Messiah prototype. By opening the story with this, Matthew says Jesus is the Messiah for all nations.

Apart from the Crucifixion, the visit of the Magi is surely the most recognized Gospel image. Yet, it is not very well understood by modern-day readers. Few are aware of the repeated role Zoroastrians played in liberating Israel and defeating Jerusalem's persecutors, and very few indeed understand the Persian model of the King of Kings and Cyrus as the first Messiah.

We must therefore debunk the Christmas-card fantasy to really see the Magi clearly. For example, some translations call Herod's visitors "Wise Men" instead of "Magi." That's simply inaccurate. Matthew uses the same Greek word—"Magi" (μάγοι, *magoi*)—that Herodotus and Xenophon used hundreds of years earlier to transliterate the Persian word meaning the priestly caste of the Zoroastrians. "Magi" is not some generic name for random wise men. The only reason to translate it as "Wise Men" is to assume the reader is too ignorant to appreciate what the Magi were.

Neither, I should add, does "Magi" mean "sorcerers." Although the later Greeks pejoratively used "Magi" to refer to practitioners of occult arts (we derive our word "magic" from it), the classical Greek historians only used the word in its plain Persian meaning of "Zoroastrian priest."

Did they read the stars, interpret dreams, and have some command of esoterica? They certainly did, as did Jewish Daniel, who is presented in the Jewish canon as a kind of Hebraic Magus. But the idea of a sorcerer has negative connotations. Why on earth would the Gospel seek to establish the authority of the Messiah by claiming the endorsement of godless wizards? That makes no sense at all. Invoking the imprimatur of Zoroaster's priests and the legacy of Isaiah's Messiah Cyrus makes all the sense in the world.

Moreover, the Magi appear frequently in the Church's earliest imagery, always in distinctly Zoroastrian clothing. (At least four examples are known in Rome dating from 150 to 450 CE.) Church history bears witness, too. Antioch native St. John Chrysostom gives Jews a hard time because they had needed Zoroastrian Magi to explain Isaiah's prophecies. "They learn from a Persian tongue first of all, what they would not submit to learn from the prophets."[20]

His purpose is to rebuke Christians who still attended synagogues, saying that if the Magi learned Jesus' name while still in Persia, there was clearly no need for Jewish teaching. The star that guided them spoke to them in Persian, not Hebrew; arriving at Herod's court, they had to explain to the foolish King Herod and the priests what their own Jewish scriptures foretold.

Even more intriguing is a fragment of an early commentary on Matthew's Gospel, the *Opus imperfectum in Matthaeum*. It was likely composed around 400 CE, and even at that historical distance from the original scene, it still recalls the Magi as Persians and links them directly to Zoroastrianism. The commentator remarks on a long-standing belief held by the Magi that a star would appear, and that in fact they looked for it every year from the vantage point of a certain "Mount Victorious." He takes time to clarify the terms: "Who are the Magi? Men form the East, who came from Persia. Among the Persians the Magi are understood to be wise, not evil."[21] In other words, they are not warlocks, as anti-Persian Romans were beginning to insinuate.

"Concerning the appearance of this star," he continues, the tradition of waiting for it on the holy mountain in Persia was passed down from father to son: "Diligent scholars and lovers of heavenly mysteries... commissioned... to wait for that star... They were called Magi in their own tongue, because they glorified God in silence and unspoken voice."[22]

Year after year, the Magi waited on the mountain at a specific time. "They would climb up it, and wash themselves, pray and praise God silently for three days. So they were doing for generations."[23] And when at last the star appeared on Mount Victorious, it descended in the form of a little boy and spoke with them in Persian, leading them to Judea.

As a young amateur astronomer, I always wondered how a star could guide the Magi to Jesus in Bethlehem. This is the answer. Stars were still regarded as heavenly powers—they were angels who camped in the dark turf above us. According to *Opus imperfectum*, after the boy angel guided the Magi to Jesus, they delivered their symbolic gifts to him, worshiped, and returned home to proclaim the Good News to their fellows. Later, when the Apostle Thomas reached their land, the people were primed and ready for the full story and were immediately baptized. The Magi even helped Thomas preach. All this, found in the first known commentary on the Gospel of Matthew.

Mary Boyce reminds us also that there really was a Zoroastrian Mount Victorious. In the Zoroastrian Avestan language, it is called Mount Ushidam. This was historically the kingdom of Gundafarr. If that sounds vaguely familiar, it is because early Christian tradition remembers one of the Magi as Gathaspar (later in Europe becoming Caspar). There's a clean line of descent in writing these names: Gundafarr became Gathaspar, became Godaphar, became Gaspar, became Caspar. An annual fixture on Christmas cards and venerated as a saint by Orthodox, Catholics, Anglicans, and Lutherans, it is worth remembering that Caspar ruled this Zoroastrian hill when Jesus was in Galilee.

Later in Christian history, the Syriac-speaking Christians named Zoroaster as the source of the belief that a star would predict the coming of the Savior. Theodore Bar Konai writes that Zoroaster predicted the Savior's virgin birth, crucifixion, and his future return with the "armies of light." Moreover, "His [Zoroaster's] disciples would be the first to know of the child's birth, and were to take him offerings, for he would be the King of Kings." As Boyce notes, "This remarkable version of the prediction of Jesus' birth presents him essentially as the Saoshyant."[24] And it is this tableau of gift-bearers to the King of Kings that we can still see etched in stone in the ancient Persian capital at Persepolis, complete with Magi, gold, and incense. The Zoroastrian foreshadowing of the Gospel story is so precise, we can only wonder that it is not better appreciated.

Converts

Matthew, the most Jewish of the Gospels, therefore opens with two strong appeals to Zoroastrian-influenced Gentiles—namely, the virgin birth and the Magi. It doesn't end there. The Antioch-based evangelist studded his story with episodes about non-Jews and very bad Jews who lived exactly midway between Jerusalem and Antioch in Syrian Palestine: "Land of Zebulun, land of Naphtali, on the road by the sea, across the Jordan, Galilee of the Gentiles."[25]

Galilee is the northern part of the Holy Land, and it is pointedly "of the Gentiles." Christians are accustomed to thinking of the Messiah as a Galilean, but at the time, this was a hard sell for Matthew. The Gospels go out of their way to get Joseph and Mary from Syria to Bethlehem and back again so as to tick the prophetic boxes that require his tribal connection to David—all part of synthesizing the Gentile and Jewish eschatological streams.

Indeed, Gentiles appear on every page, sometimes hidden in plain sight. As Jesus preached, "Repent, for the kingdom of heaven has come near," where did he become most famous? Not in Davidic Judea, but rather "his fame spread throughout all Syria," writes Matthew.[26]

His chosen base at Capernaum was a Roman garrison town. Other cities on his itinerary were predominantly Syrian and Greek; Jesus was raised just a few miles from Sepphoris, the Roman capital, which was just being built when Jesus was born. (Jesus and Joseph, builders by trade, might have helped.) A literate man like Jesus certainly spoke Greek along with Aramaic and could probably handle himself in Latin, too.

It's an interesting angle on messianic beliefs. The pious Hasidim had constructed their End Time dreams against the Hellenizers and Romans. They may have been fond of Persians, but purity was of upmost concern. Their expectation of the nations streaming to Jerusalem in the End Time was parochial—the nations would become Jews, not the other way around. Now here was a candidate for King Messiah who was a little too comfortable with Greco-Roman culture.

If Matthew's reader has any doubts about what he is up to, John the Baptist introduces Jesus' ministry with a stern warning: "Do not presume to say to yourselves, 'We have Abraham as our ancestor'; for I tell you, God is able from these stones to raise up children to Abraham."[27] That's a shot across the bow, warning Jews that they do not have a monopoly on salvation in the End Time. Gentiles can become heirs to Abraham more easily than rocks. Don't miss the Magian procession or you'll be left behind.

Like Zoroaster, who emerged from ritual baptism to teach the revelation of Ahura Mazda at the age of thirty, thirty-year-old Jesus begins his work after John baptizes him, promising that the Messiah will baptize with fire, not with water (also a Zoroastrian idea and foreign to Judaism).[28] Then, as he begins his tour, Matthew tells us that, "large crowds followed him" and seeing them, Jesus climbs a hillside north of the Sea of Galilee to speak to them. This is the famed "Sermon on the Mount."

We have only to look at the cities around there to understand the ethnic composition of what the King James Version calls "the multitudes" in attendance. They hailed from the Decapolis, a group of ten Gentile cities that includes today's Damascus and Amman. Which is why, listening carefully, we detect something of a foreign accent in his sermon, or at least a kind of subtitling.

"You have heard that it was said to those of ancient times, 'You shall not murder'; and 'whoever murders shall be liable to judgment.'"[29] These phrases, "you have heard" and "it was said," cannot be addressed to Jews who memorized Moses' commandments as children. They certainly needed no reminder of an injunction not to murder presented as if it were hearsay.

No, when Jesus says, "have you heard about this?" he is speaking to novices about something they only know about second hand. Given the ethnic complexity of the towns near the mount, it makes sense. Jesus would have to contextualize his thoughts.

But when Jesus speaks to specific groups of Jews, you will notice he uses different language. He mentions prophets and patriarchs by name (rather than "those ancients") and refers to laws without quoting them—he assumes they know it all already. Very soon he will heal a Jewish leper, whom he instructs to go find a priest "and offer the gift that Moses commanded."[30] There is no mention of what that gift might be; he presumes the leper knows the details. Or when the Pharisees criticize him for breaking the Sabbath by picking grain, Jesus answers with a series of references, beginning with, "Have you not read what David and his companions did?"[31] He assumes that they have read it; there is no need to explain.

After the Sermon on the Mount, Jesus meets a group of people to whom he ministers. Who represents this crowd? A Roman military commander:

> When Jesus heard him, he was amazed and said to those who followed him, "Truly I tell you, in no one in Israel have I found such faith. I tell you, many will come from east and west and will eat with Abraham and Isaac and Jacob in the kingdom of heaven, while the heirs of the kingdom will be thrown into the outer darkness..."[32]

Next, we see Jesus calling Matthew to follow him. Matthew is a Jewish tax collector, despised by Galilean Jews in the time of Herod—basically, a traitor who worked for the Romans. Later that night, when Jesus was invited to eat at a Pharisee's house, he brought Matthew and his friends along. "As he [Jesus] sat at dinner in the house, many tax collectors and sinners came and were sitting with him." The Pharisees, many of whom were hoping Jesus really was the Messiah, couldn't wrap their minds around what they saw. "They said to his disciples, 'Why does your teacher eat with tax collectors and sinners?'"[33] Even the Apostle Paul, a champion of the Gentiles, used "sinners" as a well-attested euphemism for Gentiles: "We who are Jews by nature, and not sinners..."[34] Thus Jesus scandalized his most supportive Jewish audience—the pious Pharisees—by openly communing with heathens and traitors.

Soon we find him in southern Lebanon—deep into Gentile territory—visiting Tyre and Sidon, cities still standing today and predominantly Shiite Muslim. There, a Canaanite woman approached him begging for help, calling him the Son of David. This encounter is best remembered for Jesus' racism when he answers her: "It is not fair to take the children's food and throw it to the dogs."[35] That was the common attitude among his peers. As a Canaanite Gentile, this woman is de facto a sinner. But Jesus says this only to subvert the trope. He demonstrably accepted her, saying, "Woman, great is your faith! Let it be done for you as you wish."

Matthew ends with the Great Commission: "Go therefore and make disciples of all nations, baptizing them in the name of the Father and of the Son and of the Holy Spirit."[36] "Nations" is *ethne*, the Septuagint's translation of Hebrew *goyim*. Every verse in the law and prophets about the "nations" uses this word. These are the Gentiles, the sinners, the pagan heathen, the unclean.

Well and good; proselytism of Gentiles was an honored practice among pious Jews. If the nations converted, circumcised, and followed the commandments, they were no longer Gentiles but adopted members of Israel. But Jesus' final commandment does not say to "go and convert the Gentile nations." He studiously avoids this obvious, well-known, and commonly used Greek word for conversion, προσήλυτος (*prosélutos*, from which we derive the word "proselytism"). This cannot be by chance.

The New Testament, in fact, uses *prosélutos* only negatively. Matthew reserves some of Jesus' harshest words for the practice of *prosélutos*, or making converts. "Woe to you, scribes and Pharisees, hypocrites! For you cross sea and land to make a single convert [proselyte], and you make the new convert twice as much a child of hell as yourselves!"

That scathing comment is the light by which to read the Great Commission: Jesus says to go and make disciples—not converts. A disciple, or *mathitís* (μαθητής), is a Socratic student. Conversion was the business of the sons of hell; teaching people to see and think clearly was the work of the Jesus movement.

But what would so many diverse people learn? Why would the Gentiles want to be "disciples?" Whether Jew or Gentile, there were other options around. What was so compelling about Jesus?

Philosopher King

Like the first book in the Bible, the first book of the New Testament is a carefully crafted sermon. Whatever factual elements it includes, they were chopped and blended into an interpretation of history. Matthew and the other Gospels are therefore not so much about a man named Jesus as about everything that led to this moment and about why history should change in its wake.

In Christ, several Axial Age streams converge:

Christ is Buddha. He is humanity freed of attachment and the anxiety of history. "Do not lay up for yourselves treasures on earth, where moth and rust destroy." "Which of you by being anxious can add a single hour to his span of life?"[37]

Christ is the Saoshyant. He is the Zoroastrian embodiment of Truth, the World Savior. "For God did not send his Son into the world to condemn the world, but in order that the world might be saved through him."

Christ is the Jewish Messiah. He is the son of David, the King of the Jews. "Now the birth of Jesus the Messiah took place in this way."[38]

Christ is the logos, *the Word.* He is the Greek philosopher's operating principle of reality. "In the beginning was the Word... All things came into being through him, and without him not one thing came into being."

Christ is Çatalhöyük's history house. In claiming to be the Temple, replacing all its services and functions, Christ becomes the consummate temple of all temples; he is the "first and the last, the beginning and the end," the one who "fills all in all."[39]

That is Christ. But there was a man Jesus, too, an enlightened man in the tradition of Jeremiah, a Jewish man. And although Christ is not limited to the biography of this man Jesus, the history of civilization nonetheless passes right through him. Jesus occupies the space between negative and positive on our graph of time, dividing the AD from the BC. There are other calendars, of course: there is an Islamic calendar that dates from the Hijra, and Israeli newspapers presume to date from Anno Mundi—the creation of the earth. Even so, for all practical purposes the modern world orients itself in relation to Jesus, and it does so because of the effect he had.

Whether God, the fabric of the universe, or pure chance produced Jesus and his consequences, he is an event, a watershed like the comet that killed the dinosaurs allowing we mammals to rise. His impact formed us and our world, and although a majority of people do not believe in Christ as a matter of faith, they can't avoid Jesus as a convergence of history-diverting probabilities. His impact is part of a continuum, both an effect and a cause.

We are therefore approaching Jesus the man as part of this phenomenon. Considering him as a man, then, let's ask a simple question: What did Jesus actually do? By observing his behavior, we would have to conclude that Jesus was a contemplative guru; he spent most of his life in silence and passed his three active years as a homeless mendicant: "The Son of Man has nowhere to lay his head."[40] During his three working years, he spent his time teaching.

That's why he called his followers *mathitís*. It's taken from the Hellenic style of teaching derived from the schools of the Greek philosophers. Unfortunately, English Bibles often still translate *mathitís* as "disciple" ("the twelve disciples") because in the days of King James, people knew that "disciple" meant a student or scholar, from Latin *discipulus*, meaning "learner" or "apprentice." It meant nothing more than that—it is not, for example, a synonym for Apostle. This is critical to understand because *mathitís* is so important to Jesus Christ that it becomes the heart of his final instructions. The King James translators would have done better to keep with the older Geneva Bible, the one used by Shakespeare; it is unexpectedly more finely attuned to modern English: "Go therefore, and *teach* all nations," reads its Great Commission.[41] (This instead of the King James' "make disciples.")

As a teacher of the nations, then, Jesus addresses that universal philosophical problem—the terror of history. First, we feel the weight of the past; all the guilt, failure, shame, embarrassment, and inadequacy. Secondly, we experience the anxiety of death, provoked when the virtual self faces non-virtualized reality, which it feels as impermanence, meaninglessness, and disconnection. It's really a reckoning with how out of sync, how alienated we are from the eternal fellowship of reconciliation with the natural order. It is not an anxiety of physical death—in fact, the more one suffers such a reckoning, the more appealing that becomes. This death is spiritual bankruptcy, universal loneliness, and acute pointlessness. In short, the absence of Paradise.

Jesus deals with all this through a single idea: forgiveness. He resolves the weight of time and reconciles us to Paradise through forgiveness.

Eternal peace is, he said, as simple and as difficult as forgiving others: "If you forgive other people when they sin against you, your heavenly Father will also forgive you."[42] He contrasts this with self-righteousness: "Judge not, that you be not judged. For with the judgment you pronounce you will be judged."[43]

This confronts the alienation allegorized in the Garden of Eden's Fall. Judgment comes by way of reified knowledge; it alienates and separates. Forgiveness is the suspension of judgment; it reconciles.

Biographical detail is key to Jesus' authenticity. All the Gospel writers match his teaching with his actions, giving grittily detailed accounts of Jesus' graciousness to the guilt-ridden alongside the startled reactions of the self-righteous. It is a dialectic between forgiveness and reifying judgment expressly experienced in his encounters with others.

Accordingly, the Gospels repeatedly portray Jesus' physical contact with the morally unclean. Forgiveness, it seems, could not be abstract or executed by mere decree. To forgive was to overcome alienation through an embrace.

We get a particularly powerful object lesson in Luke's Gospel, when Jesus is a guest at a Greek-style symposium hosted by an influential Pharisee. As this was normally an occasion for wine and manly discussion, we should expect a tour-de-force philosophical debate between learned men. Instead, we hear of "a woman of the city, who was a sinner."

As it happens, she had learned that Jesus "was reclining at table in the Pharisee's house," and like a first-century Lindsay Lohan, she decided to crash the party in tabloid style. "Standing behind him at his feet, weeping, she began to wet his feet with her tears and wiped them with the hair of her head and kissed his feet and anointed them with ointment."[44]

This biblical lap dance is wrong on many levels. To begin with, she is categorically a "sinner." There is also the matter of the balm she used; an "alabaster flask of ointment" was customarily used like this only in a sexual context, either between married people or by prostitutes.[45] Kissing and oiling feet? We know those to be fluffing techniques practiced by prostitutes in those days. On top of that, she literally let her hair down to tickle them. What might the Pharisee be thinking?!

The Talmud gives us a clue: it states that if a woman "speaks with any man" or goes out "with her hair unbound," it is grounds for divorce, and needless to say, a disqualification for marriage.[46] If that's the stigma for an honorable married woman, you can imagine how the Pharisees viewed this woman who attended to Jesus, doing so much more than speaking or merely letting her hair down.

Luke quotes the scandalized host muttering under his breath, "If this man were a prophet, he would have known who and what sort of woman this is who is touching him, for she is a sinner."

Picking up on these thoughts, Jesus teaches:

Do you see this woman? I entered your house; you gave me no water for my feet, but she has wet my feet with her tears and wiped them with her hair. You gave me no kiss, but from the time I came in she has not ceased to kiss my feet. You did not anoint my head with oil, but she has anointed my feet with ointment. Therefore I tell you, her sins, which are many, are forgiven— for she loved much. But he who is forgiven little, loves little.

As Jesus turns to her, saying, "Your sins are forgiven," there is more grumbling from the pious: "Who is this, who even forgives sins?"

There is no great surprise here. Forgiveness has always been Christianity's marquee attraction. People come to Jesus for forgiveness, to be relieved of their burden, to get a fresh start.

But we might forget the flipside, Jesus' incessant juxtapositions of forgiveness with self-righteousness. Forgiveness is subversive in a pious setting; it threatens religious certainties and claws at self-righteous pretensions. Jesus' Pharisee friend lived in strutting confidence that he was upright, that he was good; he had the meaning of life sorted out. Jesus pulls the rug out from under him.

Consider the details: The Pharisee's house was a pure space; far more than a modern church, it was kept fastidiously in a state of complicated ritual purity. The house as temple, the history house that connects temporal life to the eternal axis, was never more perfectly conceived. But it was based on reified precepts: this is clean, that is impure; we are right, they are wrong; I am blameless, he is sleazy. Then in walks Jesus with his filthy friends. And he forgives them without shaming them. That's a radical position, and quite possibly the thing that set this movement apart from every other formal religion of the day.

Jesus told a parable to summarize his position. According to Luke, Jesus addressed the story "to some who trusted in themselves that they were righteous, and treated others with contempt." It is a simple anecdote. Two men go up to pray in the Temple, one a Pharisee, the other a sinner—a tax collector. The Pharisee prayed out loud with a sneer on his face: "God, I thank you that I am not like other men, extortioners, unjust, adulterers, or even like this tax collector."

The Pharisee is haughty, a man who knows he has done the right thing, he knows he is God's favorite. The sinner is a picture of insecurity. He stands far away and does not dare lift up his eyes. He beats his breast and prays, "be merciful to me, a sinner!" Jesus assesses the situation, "I tell you, this man went down to his house justified, rather than the other."[47]

Jesus' peculiar anti-pietistic ethos comes up again and again. We remember the familiar ones like breaking the Sabbath to do good deeds. But then there are the sublime ones. Jesus taught that when giving charity, "don't let your left hand know what your right hand is doing, so that your alms may be done in secret."[48] Secret from whom? From oneself: he says that our left hand should not notice or "know" what our own generous right hand does. It is as dangerous to count oneself good as it is to judge another as evil.

It seems clear to me that he is addressing the Garden of Eden. The Tree of Knowledge is self-damning. In his evocative parable about exclusion from and entrance into heaven, he says the same thing through a story about sheep and the goats. The Paradise-bound sheep have no knowledge of the good they did ("Lord, when did we... feed you... clothe you... visit you in prison?") But the hell-bound goats, when told that they never showed compassion, defend their righteousness with vigor (Lord, when did we not?). They know with absolute certainty that they did not do wrong—evil is something other creatures do.[49]

Like Adam, the goats excluded themselves from Paradise by their reifying knowledge. So the Pharisee, too, is in a hell of his own making. He is a whistleblower, loudly denouncing the sinner in the congregation. The more loudly he opposes the "sinner," the more righteous he feels, the lines of Good and Evil so clearly drawn in his mind. But this is precisely the role assigned to Satan, which in Hebrew means "the accuser." By taking this stance, the Pharisee became Satan by choice, and so choses to live in hell.[50]

John's Gospel furthers these lessons by choosing legal terms to discuss the Holy Spirit. Jesus says that the Spirit of Truth—that most Zoroastrian of ideas—is an Advocate, in Greek a Paraclete *(parakletos),* which was used in secular Greek for hundreds of years to mean a defense attorney. Food for thought that Jesus consistently denounces the Judge and Prosecutor, while associating the Defender with the Holy Spirit.

In sum, Jesus teaches that restoration to Paradise in the heavenly kingdom comes through the humility of primordial agnosticism. The Garden of Eden's alienation is repaired by reconciliation through forgiveness. And what is that? It is a release of the presumption that one has knowledge sufficient to judge another. Only the choice not to forgive can exclude a soul from Paradise, and Jesus wants to do everything he can to get his followers to forgive, for their sakes as much as everyone else's.

20th-Century Disciple

It's here that the wormhole linking my life with the disciples really opened up. I was flying into their experience, and far more deeply than I realized or could have understood given the fantasy of Israel I cherished. I'd just turned eighteen and was finally assuming my place in the End Time.

Boarding the Tel Aviv–bound 747 in New York, the first thing I noticed was my fellow passengers. This cheap charter flight was stuffed with Jews straight out of *Fiddler on the Roof.* Exciting! I'd spent plenty of time with urbane reformed Jews but never with such an obviously more committed group, so devout and dedicated to the Bible and the Holy Land. I decided on the spot to grow a beard.

It took about an hour for reality to seep in as I became aware of the simple truth that some Jews are unpleasant to fly with. My ideal vision of the Holy Land began to cloud with the dust of reality before I even got there. Don't misunderstand me—I was still amazed and this was still *Fiddler on the Roof.* Only it was without the singing and dancing, the pretty brides-to-be, or Tevye's charm. We had everything else: heavy black clothes, hats, and yarmulkes; tassels and prayer shawls. And we had "TRADITION!" since the seating was segregated by sex.

Owing to these observances and their overly heavy clothing, our section of the plane stank, and at intervals my companions arose, oriented themselves toward Jerusalem, and rocked and swayed and muttered. They muttered again upon sitting, because they assumed I was a Jew—a bad Jew, the kind of non-praying, non-swaying, de-tasseled, and beardless Jew who would surely delay the Messiah or bring the judgment of God on Israel. I slept amid curses and tutting.

Tel Aviv's airport was a different scene. Here, I saw what I took to be Arabs—swarthy, stubbly, and loud. Music blared with sliding violins and drums thuwapping unlike anything ever produced by any Jew I'd known. Until then, as far as I was concerned, they preferred Bach and klezmer.

Clearly these were Arabs! I expected Arabs and was prepared to get my first real look at them in Israel, but I'd imagined them in Bethlehem-like villages or in the desert, not at the David Ben Gurion airport. It took me a while to understand what was going on, that because they tended to wear skullcaps, many of these Arabs were Jews. It was an unwanted revelation; for while it had occurred to me that not all Arabs were Muslims—I knew about Lebanese Christians and Palestinians from Nazareth—surely all Jews are Jews, no? Then why this delirium of mixed ethnic signals in Ben Gurion's airport?

It would take a long time to make sense of it. Meanwhile, a delegation had arrived from my destination, a kibbutz in the far north, in what the Israelis call the "finger of Galilee." It really is like that—a Jewish finger sticking up the behind of Arab Syria and Lebanon, and the reaction has, by and large, been just what one would expect in that circumstance: contraction, eliminatory strain, even spasmodic ecstasy from time to time. I had no idea that this was where I was going, or that war was afoot along the border just a few miles from my new home.

To launch out into the world in an ignorance we called faith—that was the zeal that drove young Christian disciples like me in the early 1980s, and that's what drove Peter in the oos; nothing much had changed. And like all those first-century zealots, mine was an impractical zeal of the worst kind, completely uncomprehending.

But the banal mundane was hitting me in waves: my awful travel companions; the loud, swarthy airport Jews; and now, on the drive north, someone tried to feed me something called a falafel. I didn't know what it was, and I did not want to know. After a three-hour journey through more unholy looking places, we arrived in the dark. I was hungry and exhausted and alienated. These are the Jews? This is the Holy Land? Shown to my quarters amid more tutting (*"nu*... He doesn't like felaahfehhl?"), I crashed and prayed to God for a recognizable breakfast, which was not to be.

It was pretty, though. The kibbutz seemed like it had a million roses. We were surrounded by cotton fields. I'd get to know both intimately. "Rose work is eessie, *motek*," proclaimed my boss, an Argentinian Jew. (*Motek* was one of my first Hebrew words, an affectionate term equating with "sweetheart" but applied in Israel with a Mediterranean unisex confidence possible only among real men. In this case, it softened a deception: neither rose nor cotton work were "eessie.")

Over the course of a month or so, I began to acclimate and synthesize expectation with reality. Israel still struck me as starkly unholy and the Jews were still difficult to fathom and the food remained strange, but I began to love it. I loved the roses and the cotton. I loved the smell of the dirt. I loved that a river ran across our property that Jesus drank from. (I figured out that he used to camp with his disciples a few miles up the road—you just had to follow our river up to its source.) Yes, these were the unexpected Jews of the Middle East—rough and impious—and the countryside around us was full of landmines, the nearby towns grimy. But it was this grittiness that began to enchant me as much as it scandalized. Sticking with it, I discovered the grit as a new intensity: the Kingdom of God was to come to Earth, after all, and this was the very blight it would redeem.

Work life was intense and real, too. I did full nine-hour days like the kibbutz members and unlike ordinary volunteers who worked only six. Neither was I housed with the ordinaries. My contract was long-term, so I was to be oriented toward the Israelis, not the temporary foreigners.

I was up early every day for an hour of prayer, then worked hard. Food remained challenging: it took about three months to adjust to eating cucumbers and *labneh* for breakfast and dinner. (I veered Arab, unable to adjust at all to the Jewish breakfast with its slimy fish and heavy cream cheese.) Lunches were essentially Turkish—stuffed vegetables and stews—reflecting the origin of many of the kibbutzniks. Sabbath eve dinner was the most familiar: chicken and rice and wine. We changed out of our identical blue work clothes for this meal only, which signaled the coming of our single day off. After dinner we visited homes, sang songs, and slept with the option of getting up late. On Sunday, after the biblical day off, it all started over again.

Because of commitments to the kibbutz, it would be months before I saw Jerusalem for the first time. My focus remained on Jesus, his disciples, and Galilee. I'm grateful for that. Jerusalem is fantasy-inducing, while Galilee kept me grounded. Grappling with its depreciating holiness in my morning hour of prayer, which I took by the river, it occurred to me that Jesus had the same experience living here. He was pointedly a Galilean, and this area was called "Galilee of the Gentiles" precisely because it was messy, polluted, and defiled. It was the dirt of the battlefield, the arena of a redemptive context.

There was no better place to think about all this than Caesarea Philippi, the source of our river and the place that Jesus used as a retreat with his disciples. It was obvious why he might like it; the river wound through a deeply shadowed valley capped by thick growth. Cool rock pools, a freezing waterfall, and lately, a Syrian army tank marked the hike upstream. (It was left there belly-up, a vestige of the Six-Day War.) When the hot *hamsin* wind blew across Galilee from Syria, this was the best place to be. As Jesus had, my friends and I saw the advantage, and spent many stifling Sabbath days enjoying the shade and the pools.

I got to know Caesarea Philippi well. Its ruins were still visible, and in spots not so ruined at all. Before coming to Israel, I'd read about Jesus visiting this place and never gave a second thought to what it meant. Now I became curious: What were those ruins? Why were those niches carved in the rock over the cave and over the spring that gave rise to the river? Privy to the history for the first time, it was obvious that the setting of the story was at least half its meaning, unmistakable to anyone who read it in antiquity, and scandalously provocative. One thing stood out immediately: this was no place for a Jewish holy man and his disciples.

It was instead a famed playground and spa for the wealthy and profane. If the phrase "Roman orgy" paints a picture, you may safely hang it here, for Caesarea Philippi was the place that defined it. Roman Jewish historian Flavius Josephus sets the scene: "A mountain rears its summit to an immense height aloft; at the base of the cliff is an opening into an overgrown cavern; within this, plunging down to an immeasurable depth, is a yawning chasm... of which no sounding-line has been found long enough to reach."[51]

This bottomless pit was believed to be a gateway to Hades and the niches in the rock were believed to belong to Pan, who was enthusiastically worshiped here. Pan, who loved lush settings and cavorted with the nymphs in the woods, was drawn to the cool greenery, as I was. But being the most crudely sexual of the Greek gods, visitors celebrated him and his companion nymphs through drunken orgiastic feasts, noted for inducing nympholepsy and panolepsy, the antics of which are the origin of our word "panic."

This was not just Jesus' choice for a retreat; it was the environment in which he chose to poll the disciples with the most important question he could ask them: "Who do people say that the Son of Man is?"[52] To appreciate this, we should picture the wanton carnality of the scene: with God-only-knows what mayhem going on around them, his students had to make the most important political and theological determination of their age.

They called out their answers evasively: "Some say John the Baptist, but others Elijah, and still others Jeremiah or one of the prophets." Then he asked point-blank, "But who do you say that I am?" to which Peter answered with his great confession of faith: "You are the Messiah, the Son of the living God!"

So far, so good. Peter learns that he is to be the "rock" upon which the Jesus community is built. Not even "the gates of Hades" will prevail against it. Did Jesus point to the bottomless pit when he said this—the chasm that the Greeks said was the door to hell? Or maybe he just pointed his nose toward the Herodian palace or the temple that Herod built for the worship of Emperor Augustus, also on these grounds. Whichever the case, his disciples were undoubtedly ready to storm those gates then and there—this was the mouth of hell and the imperial gate of Roman Herod all wrapped in one.

I felt the same way. I was with Peter. Turn me loose! But I kept reading, wondering why, if this was true, Peter ended up denying Jesus later at the Crucifixion. Something else happened in this story, and for all the times I'd read it, the significance escaped me until a moment of reflection there on the spot where it all happened. The rest of this story planted the seed of change that I believe broke open on that day in Athens. And it all again hinged on taxes...

The Last Temptation of Christ

To understand the position the disciples and I were in at Caesarea Philippi, we need to remember that Jesus was not the only potential Messiah in Galilee. To vet his credentials, the students of the Pharisees and the Herodians—normally bitter enemies—confronted Jesus with the tax test we talked about earlier. It was meant to force Jesus to show his hand, to support one party or the other; they were not buying his claim of transcending politics.

"Teacher, we know that you are true and teach the way of God truthfully, and you do not care about anyone's opinion, for you are not swayed by appearances. Tell us, then, what you think. Is it lawful to pay taxes to Caesar, or not?"[53]

This was what the Jewish revolt was about: could the land which belonged to YHWH be taxed by Caesar? Jesus called for a coin—evidently, he didn't have one—and asked, "Whose likeness and inscription is this?" To the reply, "Caesar's," Jesus was supposed to either call for an insurrection, as Judas and his sons had, or urge support for Herod. Instead, he said, "Render to Caesar the things that are Caesar's, and to God the things that are God's."

It was heartbreaking news to the Zealots and Fourth Philosophy disciples, who hoped he was the warrior Messiah; and it was cold comfort to Caesar's Herodian Jews, who had wanted a clear-cut criminal to arrest for teaching tax avoidance. Both camps walked away "astonished," not so much by his clever teaching, but by his inscrutable politics.

This shows Jesus to be a terrible social activist. He never argued for human rights. He never spoke of establishing a free national homeland for occupied Palestine. He never used victims to justify any political action at all, let alone vindictive punishment or armed rebellion. It's not that he was inactive—friend and enemy alike got nothing but compassion from him— but he was completely without political ideology. As this became clearer, his popularity plummeted—neither side liked him.

His students struggled, too—but Jesus sorted it out with them during that private retreat at Caesarea Philippi, my favorite Sabbath spot, where I'd meditated next to the ruins of Pan's temple and pondered nympholepsy.

It remains a favorite place for me to visit, because of the probability of sitting right where the disciples sat when Jesus asked the all-important question, "Who do people say that the Son of Man is?" It's easy to visualize the pride on Peter's face when he answered, "You are the Messiah, the Son of the living God!" When I was a teenager, I could feel Peter's courage rise, ready to assault those gates of hell a few yards away. It was our job to bring God's kingdom to Earth.

Also, like Peter, I didn't yet understand anything of what happened next. Jesus continued his lesson with an incomprehensible practical application to his teaching. "From that time on, Jesus began to show his disciples that he must go to Jerusalem and undergo great suffering... and be killed, and on the third day be raised."

Peter did not like it. He was one of Jesus' Fourth Philosophy–friendly disciples. They stood in front of the structure that infuriated the Philosophy's followers the most: not Pan's temple, but the adjacent Temple of Augustus, Herod's tribute to Caesar. It is easy to understand his anger and frustration with Jesus as he talked about retreating, suffering, and dying. Peter wanted to fight to make Paradise on Earth, right now, right here. Messiah Judas talked about conquest and victory. Now his new Messiah was going to suffer and be killed? Not on his watch.

"Peter took him aside and began to rebuke him, saying, 'God forbid it, Lord! This must never happen to you.'" That word, "rebuke," is a strong one (ἐπιτιμᾶν, *epitiman*); it means to warn someone to change their behavior. Peter is angry with Jesus, talking down to him. He never gets over it, at least not until after Jesus' resurrection. One day he would raise a sword contrary to Jesus' wishes and then bitterly deny that he ever knew this cowardly Messiah.

But Jesus isn't having it: "He turned and said to Peter, 'Get behind me, Satan! You are a stumbling block to me; for you are setting your mind not on divine things but on human things!'" Standing among lecherous Greek

revelers and their Herodian abettors, it turns out that the greatest temptation, the truly Satanic one, was not debauchery or apostasy; it was confusing
the ways of the material world with transcendent Reality. In the same
sequence, Jesus warns that if anyone would truly see the Kingdom of
Heaven, "Let them deny themselves and take up their cross and follow me."

This is not a call to glorious martyrdom; Peter would have relished that.
This is about living day by day with a cross attached. As with all his teaching,
"taking up the cross" means a continuous denial of the ego-self—the self of
the Knowledge of Good and Evil. "For whoever would save his life will lose
it, but whoever loses his life for my sake will find it. For what will it profit a
man if he gains the whole world and forfeits his soul? Or what shall a man
give in return for his soul?"[54]

Some modern translations wrongly have "life" in place of "soul." It is a
bad choice because "life" is so closely associated in the modern world with
the physical body and health, which is to miss the point entirely. We can
confirm the writer's intentions through comparable literature. Plato used the
same Greek word in exactly the same way as Jesus. "For I go about doing
nothing else than urging you, young and old, not to care for your persons or
your property more than for the perfection of your souls," says Plato.[55]

The word they both use does not mean merely organic life; it is the metaphysical breath of life—the animating force. Their message is that in trying
to preserve ourselves and material "life," we will lose the animus that continually gives rise to genuine living, and which cannot be frozen or possessed as
a thing. Buddha said just about the same thing: "If a disciple still clings to
the arbitrary illusions of form or phenomena such as an ego, a personality, a
self, a separate person, or a universal self, existing eternally, then that person
is not an authentic disciple."[56]

Where is the victory in this pessimistic eschatology? Jesus agrees with
Zoroaster that the ultimate hope is resurrection. He will be killed, but
victory will be realized in his resurrection.

Of course, from a twenty-first-century materialist point of view, this is an
absurd proposition. It was a stretch for many early Christians, too; even
committed, persecuted Christians struggled with it. The Apostle Paul had to
address this several times in Corinth, one of the strongest early Christian
communities. "How can some of you say that there is no resurrection of the
dead? Someone will ask, 'How are the dead raised? With what kind of body
do they come?'"[57]

His answer, begins "You foolish person!" Paul is a little rude perhaps, but
it is warranted because the question comes from those who grossly misun-

derstand resurrection. It all hinges on the terms "flesh" and "body." Paul understands that his people are confused. They wonder if resurrection is meant to be zombie-like physical magic.[58] Or alternatively, is it, as many thought, "heavenly bodies" in the firmament above?

Paul explains that it is nothing like any of this—it is rather an enigma. "Behold! I tell you a mystery," is the heart of his answer.[59] By using this Greek translation of "mystery" in relation to resurrection, Paul references the Book of Daniel. To describe the final events of the End Time, which is Paul's subject here, Daniel borrows a Zoroastrian theological term, *rāz*, meaning "secret, mystery, hidden." The apostle writes that, "with the resurrection of the dead," the result is "a spiritual body," for "flesh and blood cannot inherit the kingdom of God, nor does the perishable inherit the imperishable." Whatever resurrection is, it is not ordinary life, and it is foolish to think of it in that way, says Paul. We will not be zombies!

It is possible that the physics of spacetime could resolve the question. But even without delving into such esoterica, there is an in-this-world dimension to Christian resurrection. Peter and Paul constantly talk about it as something experienced in normal life: We died with Jesus, they say, and we were resurrected with him. We are members of his resurrected body, part of the transcendent Christ: "in him all things hold together... and he is the head of the body, the church."[60] In Jesus' resurrected body all things are reconciled—living as believers, "there is no longer Jew or Greek, there is no longer slave or free, there is no longer male and female."[61] It is resurrection as a Eucharistic phenomenon, death and resurrection lived day by day. Mystery indeed.

As for the End Time, Matthew promises that one day Jesus will return in spectacular fashion. "For the Son of Man is to come with his angels in the glory of his Father."[62] We might imagine that everyone read this literally, but that is certainly not true. Over the next 200 years, it was mostly interpreted allegorically or metaphysically by the Church Fathers. This prophecy of Matthew's also quotes from Daniel, the prophet of *rāz*. The scholarly Church Fathers knew very well that it was a mystery.

As for those who did read it at face value, there was no harm done, since it has no practical application. This is an otherworldly event, involving angels and glories. There was no way to act upon it until angels appear in the sky.

Not that they were passive. What early Christians did with this information is no mystery. Seeing themselves as the manifest body of resurrected Christ, they did what he did. They prayed, they practiced non-discursive meditation (like praying in tongues), they took care of the poor, healed the sick, and met violence with peace to the point of surrendering to horrible deaths. Theirs was a noticeably transcendent state of mind, removed from the prevailing culture by starkly contrasting behavior. They lived resurrected lives.

Early Christian writers remained keenly aware that the Gospel of Matthew's Magi were Zoroastrians.

This marble slab from a third century Roman tomb depicts the Magi in adoration of the Messiah–their clothing is distinctly Persian.

Note the star, a ubiquitous sign of the expected Jewish savior, which we also saw on King Herod's coin.

Messiahs were plentiful in the first century.

From my collection: a coin from the Great Jewish Revolt.

Inspired by a Galilee-based messianic contender, the uprising against Rome ended with the Temple's destruction.

Nonetheless, there were glimpses of success.

This coin minted by the Zealots bears the inscription, "freedom of Zion" and "year three" in Hebrew script, indicating the messianic warriors' autonomy and belief that redemption was at hand.

THE ANTICHRISTS

Paradise Now

Of all his teachings, one of the most relevant to our age is Jesus' treatment of the Kingdom of Heaven as an accessible event. But it is not a political aspiration or an after-death expectation. This is the point upon which I and my Muslim Brother were confused. There is no revision of policy that can make this happen; it can only occur in the realm of consciousness, which indeed will change our lived experience. But it cannot be imposed, which is ever the mistake of Babylonians and millenarian zealots alike. Paradise right now is for any sheep whose left hoof is unaware of the good his right hoof has done.

"And when he was demanded of the Pharisees, when the kingdom of God should come, he answered them and said, The kingdom of God cometh not with observation: Neither shall they say, Lo here! or, lo there! for, behold, the kingdom of God is within you."[1]

Not observed. Not here and not there. Within you.

It was like the universe, eternally now and not bound to our material state. It can't be observed, it can't be reified—it can't really be explained. So, for Jesus, eternal reality lies in physics beyond gross measurement or brusque knowledge. Specifying a fixed "when" and "where" is simply not applicable, any more than it would be in quantum physics. Instead, Paradise is experienced within, between, among, behind, and beneath the observable. Its effects upon material, time-bound life may be felt, but those are effects, not the "the kingdom of heaven" itself.

When the masses complained about his parables being obscure (as perhaps the reader does of my explanation!), Jesus told them that this reflected Reality better, and was, in fact, a way of testing their intentions. "To you it has been given to know the secrets of the kingdom of heaven... the reason I speak to them in parables is that 'seeing they do not perceive, and hearing they do not listen, nor do they understand'... but blessed are your eyes, for they see, and your ears, for they hear."[2]

All this comes into focus in connection with the question Jesus faced in his temptation by Satan-inspired Peter—the ethos of violence to end all violence. When the Kingdom of God came, the people around Jesus assumed it would come as their God-empowered victory over their enemies. There would be bloodshed, but it would not matter, because their final act of violence would bring the age of everlasting peace. You know the rationale— it's the same redemptive violence espoused by Crusaders, jihadists, and Bolsheviks.

Where does that come from? Popular opinion in this first wave and prototype of millenarian violence relied heavily on two prophecies, one from Daniel and the other from Ezekiel. Both promised a warrior savior to give victory to the righteous oppressed who would use this deliverance to make the world new and better. Let's have a look at those prophecies—what did their writers really want to tell us?

First, we know that Jesus accepted them. He said he was the Son of Man promised by Daniel. Daniel writes that the Son of Man will arrive with the angelic host to usher in the new day, and hand dominion over to the saints. It is a stirring Zoroastrian image of time's end, which on its face, is a scene of conquest. So what did Jesus read in this prophet that so many people missed?

I think it is clear. Daniel places an emphatic asterisk in this dramatic story. He says straight up that this is a mystery, which occurs in this text as the word *rāz*, the special Zoroastrian word that he borrowed for the occasion (and that still means "secret" in modern Persian). It means extraordinary, esoteric, hidden—anything but mundane. Daniel's story is like the teaching method of Jesus, a parable requiring spiritual eyes and ears to comprehend its "secrets of the kingdom of heaven." It should be obvious, shouldn't it? Angels riding on the clouds? Are we really to read that literally? If the angels have not appeared, what possible cause is there for the violence?

As for Ezekiel, he creates a metaphor for the fallen world order, calling it

Magog. His thorny tale is the origin of the literary concept of Armageddon, a perennial bestseller in print and film. I can guarantee you that right now any number of Jewish, Muslim, and Christian leaders claim to know the true identity of Magog. (All three religions embrace the idea.)

But Ezekiel's stories are even more wildly ecstatic than Daniel's. They bear no resemblance to nature! His entire oeuvre reads as hallucination. Bones reassemble themselves and flesh grows on them. (Time in reverse!) Fish of the sea and the creeping things quake in terror. (Disney animation!) The mountains throw themselves to the ground. (Hollywood special effects!) Not exactly ordinary politics or everyday events, and yet even as I write, people die and kill over these phantasmagoric words. Islamic State, Taliban, Israeli settlers, Christian warmongers—they all talk about Magog and envision a literal future that looks like that.

Hebrew University professor of psychology Benny Shanon makes a strong argument for why the scenes are so far out: Ezekiel and others were on drugs.[3] Corroboration comes from the Zoroastrians who invented End Time allegories centuries before Ezekiel used them. They and their Vedic cousins frankly admitted to using hallucinogens. It is a strong hypothesis and nothing to be scandalized about, as these were not laboratory-refined party drugs. To the contrary, they were natural mind expanders like ayahuasca, painfully difficult-to-consume plants, used by our answer-seeking forbears to break the mold of constructed reality. God bless them for it.[4]

How about Moses? It would explain that burning bush which is not consumed, just as here in Ezekiel it explains the fall-down-drunk mountains and backward-running clocks. If not hallucinogens, then we must consider mind-altering forms of trance.

Whatever the inspiration, these prophets are not writing tactical manuals. Upon what do the holy warriors rely, then, when the sources are so fantastically not of this world? If you focus with narrow enough vision, some phrases might just suggest a practical instruction. A single line from Ezekiel says of Magog that the LORD will "call for a sword against him throughout all my mountains" and "every man's sword shall be against his brother."[5]

Upon this slender stanza of possibly drug-fueled poetry, many people hang an entire ideology of religious violence—they imagine that eternity requires them to be God's sword. Clearly, Jesus was not one of them.

It's not because he was unaware of these prophecies—his ministry relies heavily upon them and, as we've noted, he presents himself as a fulfillment of Daniel's delivering hero, the Son of Man. Rabbi Dr. Kaufmann Kohler, a pillar of American Judaism and president emeritus of the Hebrew Union

College, is very helpful in summarizing Jesus' connection to this prophetic tradition:

> The greater the oppression of the Worldly Kingdom (Rome), the more eager the Jewish people, particularly the pious ones, were for "the Kingdom of Heaven," as they called it, to come speedily. This is the ever-reiterated object of the prayers... Jesus preached the same Kingdom of God (Matthew has preserved in "Kingdom of Heaven" the rabbinical expression "Malkut Shamayim.")[6]

The difference is that Jesus said the kingdom was not an object, not observable and therefore not achievable by political means. As for possession by the sword, the Gospel of John remembers Jesus stating unequivocally that this Son of Man would countenance no swordplay: "My kingdom is not of this world. If my kingdom were of this world, my servants would have been fighting... but my kingdom is not from the world."[7]

And this, after all, was what differentiated the meaning of Jesus from other messianic contenders. Some might contest the historical validity of the man, but the revelation is valid nonetheless. Here is a Messiah in the vein of Jeremiah, who saw nothing but foolish idolatry in the material trappings of the Temple, and here is a Messiah who, in line with Zoroaster, urged his followers to enter the Kingdom now and for eternity through an exercise of truthful consciousness. If the world was to change, consciousness must change first, not the other way around.

Terrorism

When the Gospel of Matthew was written, Herod was no longer on the throne. No one was. The Temple was gone, the Jewish kingdom abolished. Jesus talked about this when he pointed to the Temple's buildings and said to his students, "You see all these, do you not? Truly, I say to you, there will not be left here one stone upon another that will not be thrown down."[8] This was no prophecy; it was Matthew reflecting upon the meaning of recent events—namely, the destruction of Jerusalem and the Temple after Judas of Galilee and his progeny's Great Revolt.

This was a familiar situation for Jews. When Babylon destroyed the Temple, prophets wrote ex post facto predictions about the calamity. Now, when the Temple was again destroyed, new voices spoke prophetically into this situation, too. Herod was a wicked, corrupt, and illegitimate king; some thought that the demolition of his architectural masterpiece might be a sign that the true King Messiah was at the doorstep. Surely YHWH would not leave them without a Temple for long, and so they prepared to join him in one last battle.

Or did it mean something else? The Pharisees, at least those who lived in remote places like Galilee, were already accustomed to thinking of worship outside the Temple. The Messiah would come at the right time, but only when the people's hearts were pure and their lives sufficiently governed by the Law. It was to be an age of humility and instruction, and they had the tools to go on indefinitely. Rabbinic Judaism, centered on the Torah and the local synagogue, is their legacy.

The diaspora Jesus movement can be considered part of both options; it put forward a way to live without the Temple and yet still argued that the Messiah had come. Spearheaded by the Apostle Paul, who described himself as a "Pharisee, the son of Pharisees," this Jesus community developed a unique interpretation of the Temple's destruction. Unlike other Pharisees, Paul said that the Messiah had already come, and that he fulfilled Temple obligations. The Temple was no longer needed; Jesus died as the last sacrifice, slain on the authority of the priests who wielded a Roman knife. In this way, Jesus fulfills Jeremiah, who said that the Temple was an idol and that one day the Law would be written on our hearts. When the Temple was finally lost, it was a gift—the first stage toward fulfillment of universal salvation.

The message was even more compelling because Jesus' rivals had colossally failed. Israeli journalist and scholar Gershom Gorenberg reflected upon these events in the light of the contemporary Middle East: "The choice of terror is even more likely when the End is overdue. Those unwilling to accept failure may conclude that God is waiting for them to act, or that the type of action they have already tried—be it proselytizing or building settlements—wasn't enough."[9]

That impatience was readily apparent in the first-century Jewish survivors of the Great Revolt, who placed their faith in yet another would-be King Messiah just a few decades after Jerusalem's destruction. The new hope was Simon Bar Kosevah, a true descendant of David and leader of a widespread and deadly guerrilla campaign that ended with the permanent banishment of Jews from Jerusalem and the demise of Judea as the practical center of Judaism; in short, a disaster bigger than the one Jesus seemed to predict.

A near contemporary estimated the death toll: "Five hundred and eighty thousand men were slain... and the number of those that perished by famine, disease and fire was past finding out. Thus, nearly the whole of Judaea was made desolate."[10]

After the disaster, the rabbis dubbed him "Bar Koziba" or "son of the lie," a remarkably Zoroastrian-tinged denouncement and a play on his self-chosen title, "Bar Kokhba," which means "son of a star."

This chosen moniker has messianic significance. The reference is to a prophecy by Balaam: "A star shall come out of Jacob, and a scepter shall rise out of Israel." Although there is some scholarly debate as to whether Simon explicitly claimed messiahship, few in his day would doubt what he was up to —the star is on his coins and he did everything he could to fulfill messianic prophecies. After he produced such horrible results, the rabbinical disavowals of his messianic claim suggest he most certainly must have made them—they protest too much otherwise.[11]

Since the followers of Jesus had their own Messiah, and one who repudiated militancy, they naturally did not participate in Bar Kokhba's rebellion. As you can imagine, he did not take this rejection casually. Writing not long after the fact, Justin Martyr reports that the Jewish prince severely persecuted Jesus' followers. He would not likely have mentioned it, within the living memory of many eyewitnesses, if there were no truth in this claim. Jerome mentions it, too: "Because the Christians are not willing to help him against the Roman army, Barcocheba, leader of a party of the Jews, murders them with every sort of torture."[12]

Whatever their relationship in the harsh circumstances of the uprising, Jewish followers of Bar Kokhba and the Jewish Christians of Judea shared the same fate after the rebellion was put down: permanent banishment from Jerusalem and its holy sites. Jewish life was forced to carry on elsewhere.

Many of the Jewish refugees headed north into Galilee and west to the new rabbinic center at Yavneh, while still more landed in diaspora cities like Antioch, where post-Temple Judaism was already struggling to reshape itself. In those non-Semitic regions, the Jewish and Judeo-Christians mixed with Zoroastrian-influenced Gentiles and Greco-Romans. One result was Paul and Matthew's form of Christianity. Another was diaspora rabbinic Judaism, both of which learned to cope just fine without a Temple.

Some of the refugees, however, decamped to Arabia, where they became rich as middlemen on the trade routes that once entranced the Babylonians.

This may seem an odd destination to us now, but it was only natural since Jews shared important traditions with the Arabs of this region, including a common reverence for Abraham and Moses. That camaraderie was felt both ways—several Arab tribes around Mecca and Medina converted to Judaism.[13]

The last Jews to leave Jerusalem after Bar Kokhba's defeat certainly contributed to the numbers of those heading east and into Arabia. Some of them, I believe, included Jerusalem's early Christians. That's important, because as the New Testament's Book of Acts suggests, they were a more traditionally Jewish group led by Jesus' brother James, who was portrayed as being at odds with the Apostle Paul. Carrying with them not just the Jewish traditions, including the importance of the Temple Mount, they would also bring the news that Jesus was the Messiah, only without the trinitarian beliefs that would later characterize Roman Christian orthodoxy. And since James' legacy would not be touched by the later ecumenical councils of the Church, this isolated view of Jesus, coupled with a strongly traditional Jewish practice, would in turn help shape the basic tenets of Islam, which emerges from this same part of Arabia in a predominantly Jewish town. There is a logic behind why Islam recognizes both Moses and Jesus.

That is a lot of history to keep track of, but I trust it will stick with you as you see how it unfolds into what happens next: the births of Christianity and Islam, the twin offspring of the Jewish-Zoroastrian marriage.

Peaceniks

While it is tempting to look at Bar Kokhba as the parting of the ways between Christians and Jews, the evidence shows that for several centuries the lines were blurry. Even 200 years after Matthew, St. John Chrysostom writes that Christians in Antioch frequented the city synagogues on the Sabbath and during the Jewish feasts. Clearly, Christians remained attached to their roots, including the taproot of forbidden Jerusalem.

Arguably, it was the next generations of Romans who drove the deepest wedge between Christian and Jewish culture by stigmatizing Christianity as a cult. Although widespread persecution was rare until the middle of the third century—usually the Roman hierarchy practiced a policy of don't ask, don't tell—the Christians had a bad reputation nonetheless. The Eucharist led to charges of cannibalism, while rumors of sexual impropriety dogged the community for centuries. (This slander, already hinted at in the story of Jesus and the sinful woman, was due to the Christians' liberal mixing of sexes, unprecedented sexual equality, and reputation for "love feasts," a term easily misunderstood.)

When there were occasional persecutions, they were severe. As early as 64 CE, Christians were singled out for abuse when Emperor Nero blamed them for Rome's great fire. Finally, in 250 CE, Christianity was completely outlawed. Why weren't the Jews banned? Firstly, Judaism was respected as an ethnic religion with a deep history, while Christianity seemed to be a bizarre new cult that infiltrated all ethnicities, gaining Roman converts throughout the empire and demanding that every one of them renounce their family's pagan traditions. Furthermore, it attracted the poorest of the poor and slaves, a real concern for authorities that had not too long ago put down a slave rebellion.

Through it all, Christians waited patiently. There was no thought of rebellion or resistance. There was nothing to be done: they belonged to a heavenly kingdom but were consigned to live corporeal lives as subjects of Rome. Christians compared their situation with the Jews in the first Babylonian exile. As Tertullian articulates, they believed that Rome was a revived Babylon and that the prophecies relating to the old empire now applied to its successor. ("Babylon... is a metaphor of the Roman city, which, like Babylon, is great, and proud of empire, and at war against the saints of God," wrote Tertullian.[14])

Christians were obedient, unless obedience required denying Christ, in which case they would submit to death rather than rebel. Such stalwart obedience raised practical questions, however: What was Caesar's and what was Christ's? It was up to the Church Fathers to provide guidance. Of them, Origen's teaching is exemplary, as he affirmed the separation of spheres and the apolitical nature of the Kingdom of God. Renowned scholar of apocalypticism Norman Cohn highlights him as an important voice against millenarian literalism: "Origen, perhaps the most influential of all the theologians of the ancient church, began to present the Kingdom as an event which would take place not in space or time but only in the souls of believers."[15]

Amen to that. In fact, Origen's eschatology is quite representative of the early Church. Relying on the apocalyptic idea of history as a succession of stages ending with eternal perfection (so vividly described by Daniel), the early Christians were able to cope with Roman subjugation as a necessary if uncomfortable phase. Like Karl Marx, another great mind in this dispensational apocalyptic tradition, Origen believed that the penultimate phase required coercion. For Marxists, it is the dictatorship of the proletariat that wields the necessary sword; for Origen, it was the Roman state. He wrote that Emperor Augustus acted at God's behest and "fused together into one monarchy the many populations of the earth." This because "the existence of many kingdoms would have been a hindrance to the spread of the doctrine of Jesus throughout the entire world." Of course, there is an important difference between Soviet theories and these Christians: the early Church never saw itself as the coercive agent—rather, the fallen world itself was coercive by nature and God used this against it to drive people to salvation. This was emphatically never a call to revolution.

Moreover, Origen argued, if Rome did not impose order, these many smaller kingdoms would remain in constant warfare, leading to more bloodshed and violence than would occur under Rome's disciplining hand. Concludes Origen, "How, then, was it possible for the Gospel doctrine of peace, which does not permit men to take vengeance even upon enemies, to prevail throughout the world, unless at the advent of Jesus a milder spirit had been everywhere introduced into the conduct of things?"[16]

In other words, Christians who must love their enemies surely cannot spread the Gospel by force. There can be no holy war. And as difficult as Roman domination might be, it was temporary and served a purpose and was the lesser of evils. That's not to minimize the Christians' resolve and commitment, however. They did not live passively. So many Christians gave themselves up to death in lieu of disobedience that one Roman emperor accused them of practicing a death cult.

In my view, Origen's personal circumstances add tremendous authority to his argument. Non-violence was a tenet tested in his own life as a martyr's son who had to personally make the decision not to fight for his family. His appreciation of the very sword that slew them is not academic—to say that it had a divine purpose must have been extremely difficult for him.

Tertullian, another Church Father (he gave us the Trinity), likewise wrote that the sword had no place in a Christian's life. ("Only without the sword can the Christian wage war: for the Lord has abolished the Sword."[17]) He also viewed the Roman weapon as the means of temporal peace and counselled obedience to the authorities as far as possible, and beyond that, submission to the required penalties. As you can imagine, this established a paradox and a dilemma with regard to Christian membership in the Roman army. The sword had no place in Christian life, but could a Christian wield a sword not as a Christian, but as a Roman? Not in rebellion, but in obedience? The Roman army brought Gospel peace to the world; if God used it, why couldn't a Christian be a soldier, given his dual status as a citizen of heaven and a subject of empire?

The answer was not easy. Soldiering was discouraged but it was noticeably practiced as a Christian profession nonetheless. At one point, the prayers of Christian soldiers were even cited as the reason for a Roman victory. A logical rationalization was seeping in: it was unthinkable to bear

Christ's sword—but yes, it might be possible for a Christian to have a day job as a soldier because God supported the Peace of Rome.

There were rules, however. Hippolytus, writing guidelines for new converts, stipulated that "a soldier who is in authority must be told not to execute men; if he should be ordered to do it, he shall not do it... if he will not agree, let him be rejected" (meaning rejected from Church membership).[18] In a similar vein, a gladiator or gladiatorial showrunner or "one concerned with wild beast shows" had to quit his profession or be barred from the Christian table. Otherwise, a Christian could serve. I should note that the ban on execution was because Jesus said we cannot be judges—this is a role only God fulfills and, as we know, it has a lot to do with the Tree of Knowledge.

In summary, Roman politics was understood to be ordained to foster the Gospel's advance; just how far the Christian might be involved in it was open to interpretation. Logically, if the Roman state was the pacifying sword that allowed the Gospel to spread, it might be further employed on Christianity's behalf. This line of reasoning approached an endorsement of violence by proxy. For now, as an often-persecuted minority, it wasn't a serious problem, but if the Christians ever gained imperial favor, this question would have to be answered definitively. Did it mean the Kingdom of Heaven had arrived or was it a plot to corrupt the faithful? This very real test, unthinkable to Origen and Tertullian, will appear less than a century after their deaths.

Caesar of Christ

Origen was a scholar of Greek philosophy, Tertullian was not. Whereas the former was adamantly transcendent, the latter was a man of substance who gives us an inkling of how the balance between church and state might tip in the wrong direction.

Tertullian was influenced by Irenaeus, another important Church Father, whose own *Against Heresies* has a certain affinity with the book you are reading now—Irenaeus takes a long view of human development and sees an unfolding story.

Unfortunately, he misses the point of the Axial Age. Writing in 180 CE, he concludes his laudable work with several chapters pertaining to interpretations of Daniel, Ezekiel, and the Apostle John's Revelation, warning us that we are woefully mistaken if we "shall endeavor to allegorize prophecies of this kind."[19]

Irenaeus was a hardcore literalist. Everything was concrete. The

Kingdom of God was an "inheritance in the kingdom of the earth." He explains that the "renovation" of the earth (a term obviously derived from Zoroastrianism) would begin "in that very creation in which they [the righteous] toiled or were afflicted." They would "receive the reward... in the creation in which they were slain... in the creation in which they endured servitude, in that they should reign."

And that place was none other than the glorious concrete of the Roman Empire. For Irenaeus, heaven is on Earth, material and political. "It is fitting that the creation itself, being restored to its primeval condition, should without restraint be under the dominion of the righteous."[20]

As his ideological successor, Tertullian was more complicated, and an eloquent pacifist. "The Lord, by taking away Peter's sword," he wrote, "disarmed every soldier thereafter." Beautiful. And yet he believed there will be an earthly kingdom for Christians, and like his Jewish predecessors, his eschatological focus was on Jerusalem, or more to the point, the "New Jerusalem," which was now the hope and sign of redemption.

Falling in line with the likes of Menahem and Bar Kokhba, Tertullian encouraged the idea that "a kingdom is promised to us upon the earth... before heaven... in the divinely-built city of Jerusalem."[21] By this he means that God has literally built a new Jerusalem that will be, in his words, "let down from heaven." Take note that he believes there must be an earthly Christian kingdom before the final redemption can happen.

In assaying the Apostle John on this matter, Tertullian leaves no doubt; while conceding that the beloved apostle was "declaring that our citizenship is in heaven," he argues that the author "predicates of it that it is really a city in heaven." A city that must first be manifest on the earthly plane.

To back up this hypostatization, Tertullian turns to Ezekiel, whose descriptions of the New Jerusalem he read as coming from an actual extraterrestrial visit to this God-built metropolis. All this was bolstered by recent headlines: "This prophecy, indeed, has been very lately fulfilled in an expedition to the East," effuses Tertullian, "for it is evident from the testimony of even heathen witnesses, that in Judaea there was suspended in the sky a city early every morning for forty days. As the day advanced, the entire figure of its walls would wane gradually, and sometimes it would vanish instantly."

That's right. He and many others believed that the New Jerusalem had been sighted hovering above the old Jerusalem, a sure sign of the nearness of the kingdom, which was to be lived out for 1,000 years "as a kingdom upon this earth."

Christians kept their eyes peeled for more signs of the times. They got a big one in 166 CE, when Emperor Lucius Verus went to battle against the Zoroastrian Parthians, emerging victorious. As he returned with his triumphant legions, they began to drop like flies. This was the Antonine Plague; it decimated the army and then moved through every corner of the empire, killing off roughly 15 percent of the population, eventually taking the emperor, too. The situation was so dire that his co-emperor (and survivor) Marcus Aurelius lowered the bar for membership in city councils (notably in Athens) because there simply weren't enough qualified people left alive to fill the positions.

Worse, as the core population was decimated by the plague, the barbarians were pounding at Rome's gates. As is wont to happen in a crisis, more and more power shifted to the military. This in turn triggered political instability and a shift of wealth away from broader public benefit to support the army. Scholarly and cultural pursuits collapsed. From this point forward, Rome's vaunted building projects and inscriptions came to a sudden halt.

With the empire fractured and under threat, events finally came down to the pivotal moment when rival emperors Maxentius and Constantine battled to re-establish the unified glory of old Rome. It seemed unlikely that Constantine would prevail. His troops had fought every inch of the way from their northern strongholds and were exhausted by the time they neared the capital, where the outcome hinged on whether Constantine's forces could manage to cross the choke point at the Milvian Bridge, gateway to Rome.

For Maxentius, this was the home field, and his army was twice the size of Constantine's. Omens read by soothsayers and priests in both camps predicted that Maxentius would prevail, causing bewilderment among Constantine's officers when he nonetheless decided to march on. The omens also led Maxentius to confidently position his troops with their backs to the river on its far side, certain that he could conclude the civil war there and spare Rome from becoming a battleground.

Clearly a greater omen was necessitated, so on the eve of battle, Constantine reported a vision: he saw a cross in the sky, and below it the words, *hoc signo vinces*, "in this sign conquer." He instructed his men to mark their shields with the sign of Christ in place of the Roman eagle.

We might ask why the sign of this dubious "death cult" would be a source of encouragement to the troops. Christians were likely no more than 5 million among a population of 60 million. They'd also just endured eight years of severe persecution—only recently relieved through the edict of toleration. What's notable for us is that Christians had somehow become enough of a force to warrant this widespread persecution and merit the unprecedented amnesty. A clue lies in the list of notables singled out during the persecution—anti-Christian measures specifically targeted people of rank, such as soldiers, bureaucrats, and even senators. Whereas Nero might have used Christians as a scapegoat, the emperor behind this purge, Diocletian, took aim at them because they had become powerfully influential people who refused to worship him.

Their growing influence in the empire can be understood by considering the effects of the plague. Christians were unusually clean. They wrote pamphlets on personal hygiene to train their converts and children in "temple maintenance"—"temple" here meaning the body, the temple of the Holy Spirit. Those same habits made them more likely to survive epidemics and made them particularly good at caring for the sick. "At the same time that they were undergoing persecution," writes Gary Ferngren, a specialist in the social history of ancient medicine,

> Christians carried out an active program of philanthropy, which included the widespread care of the sick both within their own community and, especially during the times of plague, outside of it. Their long experience in medical charity prepared the way for the eventual establishment of the first hospitals as specifically Christian institutions.[22]

Another social factor was the growing wealth gap that marked the decline of Roman culture due to the plague. Harvard Divinity School theologian Helmut Koester writes, "In spite of all the glories of the Roman Empire... there was great poverty on the one hand and immense wealth in the hands of a very few people. There were sickness and disease and there were no public health services, and doctors were expensive." Koester notes that such inequalities were entrenched in the Augustan hierarchical system, modeled as it was on Sumeria. "If you're at the bottom of that social pyramid, not a whole lot of things are coming down to you anymore."[23]

By contrast, says Koester, Christians in the century preceding Constantine oversaw

> the establishment of hospitals... a clear establishment of social service— everything from soup kitchens to money for the poor if they need it... Christianity really established a realm of mutual social support... And I think that this was probably in the long run an enormously important

factor for the success of the Christian mission. And it was for that very reason that Constantine saw that the only thing that would rescue the empire is to take over the institutions that the Christians had already built up.

Also pertinent: it was the Christians, of all people, who kept intellectual life alive. The fathers of the church were devoted scholars, vibrant in comparison to the tired pagans whose social model had evolved little in thousands of years. The Greek philosophical tradition was largely picked up by the Christians exactly when the emperors were pushing it away in favor of more primitive Mesopotamia-style paganism. This was the key point of contention when Diocletian instigated the great persecution. As James Carroll notes in his history of Christian-Jewish relations, "The great exception to the third-century decline of intellect and culture in the Roman Empire had been the flourishing of Christian theology."[24] Origen, Tertullian, and Cyprian all worked into the third century.

Christians sponsored literacy schools because they wanted their members to be able to read the scriptures. As Koester states, "We find that... a large number of the people in the imperial administration are Christians, because they could read and write. Which constituted a big problem with the persecution of the Christians, because they were thrown out of their office first when the persecution began, and suddenly the government didn't work anymore."

In short, by the time Constantine prepared to "cross the bridge" (in so many ways!), the Christian religion, famed for its healing and erudition, had become indispensable. All this must have factored in the reported encouragement that the troops demonstrably took from the news that the Christian god was on their side. They rallied impressively and took the battle decisively.

Thus, the Roman Empire became Christian. Carroll put it well:

In a way, this is the second-greatest story ever told, at least concerning what we think of as Western civilization. After the death and Resurrection of Jesus, the conversion of Constantine may have been the most implication-laden event in Western history. If we rarely think so, that is because we take utterly for granted the structures of culture, mind, politics, spirituality, and even calendar (Sunday as a holiday) to which it led. None of those structures was foreordained, and indeed, to grasp the epoch-shaping significance of Constantine's embrace of Jesus, his sponsorship of Jesus' cause, imagine how the history we trace in this book would have unfolded had the young emperor been converted to Judaism instead.[25]

Indeed.

Christendom

Constantine didn't stay long in Rome, but he did have the first Vatican basilica constructed there. This was the Archbasilica of St. John Lateran, the preeminent papal basilica, outranking St. Peter's. Constantine pointedly erected it over the ruined headquarters of enemy Maxentius' imperial cavalry bodyguards. Leaving Rome for good, the *pontifex maximus* built a new imperial palace in Byzantium, renaming the city Constantinople.

"It must never be forgotten that Constantine's revolution was perhaps the most audacious act ever committed by an autocrat in disregard and defiance of the vast majority of his subjects," writes John B. Bury in his *History of the Later Roman Empire*.[26] Imagine the thrill if you were a Christian! They still numbered just under 10 percent of the empire's population.[27] With the common belief that the saints would acquire an earthly kingdom, Christians could not but meet Constantine's embrace as anything but an eschatological event—possibly the beginning of the end of history. Christian literature of the day bears this out; they greeted "the Emperor Constantine as the messianic king." It also served to validate Tertullian's teaching on the subject —he'd been proved right.

Christians also testify that Constantine saw himself as an eschatological figure, too. "His conversion made it possible for him to take part in what he regarded as a supernatural epic," historian Paul Veyne reminds us, "to direct it himself and thus ensure the salvation of humanity." Although it was once in vogue for historians to doubt that Constantine saw himself this way, the preponderance of evidence suggests that Veyne, one of his most credible biographers, is correct: Constantine believed his salvation to be history's turning point. In 314, "he declared in a letter to his "very dear brothers," the Christian bishops, that "the eternal and inconceivable holiness of our God will absolutely not allow the human condition to wander in darkness any longer."

Even so, sober-minded Christian leaders did not yet consider this to be a theocracy; the Roman Empire was still an earthly kingdom awaiting judgment, but the paradox became more fraught. With Caesar himself supporting the Church, eventually to be baptized and included into Christ's body, how could one tell exactly what belonged to Caesar and what belonged to God? Certainly early Christians would not have taken up the sword to hasten the day of the Lord—even the literal-minded Tertullian was resolutely pacifist—but what does one do when the Lord seems to thrust the sword into your hand?

A sign of the changing times glares at us through the robes of the clergy. When Christians were a despised minority, Hippolytus warned that a "military governor or magistrate of a city who wears the purple robe" would have to resign from office if he wanted to be baptized and enter the communion of the saints.[28] Now those very robes would adorn the princes of the Church as they paraded to the altar of Christ under Roman-style insignia and standards.

Constantine reified Christ. "Theologians, as if by imperial fiat—or rather, precisely by such fiat—now found ways to put the heretofore ineffable mystery into words, while liturgists gave it expression... The identity of Jesus became sharply defined from now on."[29]

The Council of Nicaea, held at the emperor's behest, was called to codify a uniform doctrine and establish a single hierarchy across the body of believers. That it was the emperor's program imbued the council's members and its decisions with the coercive power of the imperial state. The change is immediately visible. Christian art, which previously had depicted living scenes of Christ performing miracles or Jesus as the Good Shepherd or the visitation of the Magi, was subsequently composed of images transcribed directly from imperial art and paganism. Jesus now appears as Jupiter on a throne.

Before Constantine, the cross was not a totemic object; it was a powerful statement about self-denial. Signing the cross was an action reminding the believer that they were executed along with Jesus, dead to the Cosmic Order and the Big Other. The cross as an object was a hangman's rope, the means by which Jesus and tens of thousands more were executed by the worldly order. The cross was remembered from the victim's point of view.

Constantine's cross reversed this, making it a sign of power. Remember, the cross was not new to the empire; it had always been a gruesome tool of torture and subjugation. Constantine's first symbolic cross was made by lashing two spears together at the Milvian bridge. It is astonishingly perverse —Constantine took spears, not to beat them into pruning hooks as Isaiah dreamed, but to transform the emblem of Christian sacrifice into one of Christian domination. Thereafter, he placed the symbol of Roman cruelty as a sign of authority in the churches, front and center of worship, above the community and opposed to it.

For Jews and non-believers, the cross would therefore remain what it always had been, a sign of state terror, a fear-inducing symbol of domination, but now carried by the state-sponsored Church. By the end of Constantine's century, to contravene the new Christian orthodoxy was to commit a crime against the empire, and heresy could end with execution.

An immediate effect was to criminalize and scapegoat Jews. Since Christianity was originally a Jewish religion, officially sanctioned Christian doctrine automatically impeached Jews who rejected Christian interpretations of the Hebrew Bible—specifically, Jesus' claim to be the Messiah. By not believing in Jesus, they now effectively contradicted the foundations of the state religion, something that was never a problem under pagan Rome.

St. John Chrysostom demonstrates the virulence with which the tide was turning. His ranting homilies show us something surprising. Up until Constantine, Christians in Antioch still visited synagogues and celebrated the Jewish feasts. That's amazing since this was the city where faith in Jesus first spread widely among Gentiles, and according to the Book of Acts, the place where the disciples were "first called Christians." Here, Paul quarreled with Peter, who under James' influence insisted that Gentile Christians follow Jewish law. Now, more than 200 years later, it is clear from Chyrsostom's ire that there were many followers of Jesus still comfortable in both worlds. That had to change.

As Archbishop of Constantinople, Chrysostom laid down the law:

> I invoke heaven and earth as witnesses against you if any of you shall go to the Feast of the Blowing of the Trumpets, or participate in the fasts, or rush off to the synagogue for the observance of the Sabbath, or observe any other rite of the Jews great or small, I call heaven and earth as my witnesses that I am guiltless of the blood of all of you.[30]

Respected scholar and professor of rabbinic literature H. L. Ginsberg recognized this as the beginning of European antisemitism. "With Chrysostom there began the endeavor, which eventually brought so much suffering upon the Jews, to prejudice the whole of Christendom against the latter, and to erect hitherto unknown barriers between Jews and Christians."[31]

Indeed, the "golden-mouthed" archbishop even put a barrier between Christians and their Jewish doctors. He said they should choose death over treatment by a Jew, "for what is a man profited, if he shall gain the whole world, and lose his own soul?"[32] In conclusion, he determined that it was a Christian duty to hate Jews. "And so it is that we must hate both them and their synagogue."[33]

As for Christianity's old Zoroastrian friends, there was an especially thorny problem. Jewish friendship with Persians had been fostered by their mutual status as oppressed peoples under Greek rule. This continued among Christians, too, while under Rome's pagan heel. But now the Christians had won the lottery—they *were* Rome—while the empire's greatest enemy was still the Zoroastrians in Persia; they'd been at war with them for centuries. So regardless of the role that Zoroastrianism had played, or the significance of the Magi to Christianity, as soon as "Roman" and "Christian" became synonymous, the Zoroastrians had to be considered enemies of Christ.

Zoroastrians and Jews faced the same charge: they had a chance to embrace Christ and they didn't. Of course, that is not quite true. In the first century, many Jews and Zoroastrians had followed Jesus. Over time, these believers generally began to identify only as Christians. But as Chrysostom's harsh words make very clear, many felt comfortable as hyphenated Christian-Jews, at home in both church and synagogue. (*Opus imperfectum* also mentions Gospel-preaching Magi.) Unfortunately, this fuzziness threatened the unity of the state, which above all sought uniform doctrine from top to bottom, as all such Babylonian hierarchies did. The church councils that Constantine convened established the canon of scripture and the exact wording to fully reify the faith. Hypersensitive to divergents, it was in or out, right or wrong, with us or against us.

Meanwhile, outside of Roman Christianity's domain, the same dynamic occurred in reverse: Zoroastrians and Jews living in Persia had to declare their allegiance—was it to Persia or enemy Rome?

The advent of official Christian dogma was thus inherently alienating, a brand-new branch of the Tree of Knowledge of Good and Evil. As the enemy of Rome automatically became the enemy of the Church, and as non-Orthodox beliefs meant disloyalty to the state, the never-ending Persian-Roman conflict took on the attributes of a holy war. When the conflict heated up under Emperor Heraclius in the early 600s, it became an occasion for out-and-out eschatological ecstasy—a genuine apocalyptic battle between Zoroastrians, Christians, and Jews, and the furnace in which Islam was forged.

The Last Emperor

As avid readers of prophecies, Christians, Jews, and Zoroastrians alike were especially drawn in this period to works exemplified by the Sibylline Oracles, a body of literature inspired and sourced from the old Greek-era apocalyptic texts.[34] All three faiths puzzled over the End Time, looked for signs of its advent, and in this war, regarded the other as the agents of darkness. If Ezekiel, Daniel, and Zoroaster were too imprecise for literal-minded holy warriors, the ever-accommodating Oracles were clear, specific, and overtly political.

The genre is still with us through modern-day television evangelists and authors. Simply look up the Christian Broadcasting Network's Pat Robertson on YouTube talking about Gog and Magog, or pick up a copy of Tim LaHaye and Jerry B. Jenkins' book *Left Behind: A Novel of the Earth's Last Days* (with series sales in excess of 80 million copies[35]). Or Hal Lindsay's immeasurably successful *The Late Great Planet Earth*, which so affected me as a teenager, and which is even more like the Oracles, as it purports to be non-fiction. The ingenious conceit shared by all this literature is to interpret the old prophecies through current events: lately, the Cold War, the regathering of Israel, contemporary moral decline, Islamic extremists, and so on; back then, the Persian wars and the Jewish reclamation of Jerusalem.

In every age, this literature rivals or surpasses official religion in popularity and influence. *The Late Great Planet Earth* was so successful in its original 1970 edition, published by evangelical publisher Zondervan, that juggernaut Bantam House acquired rights for a re-release with a cover patterned explicitly on Erich von Däniken's hyper-successful alien-origins book, *Chariots of the Gods*. It was a prescient move. To date, *The Late Great Planet Earth* has sold in excess of 35 million copies, making it one of the top forty best-selling books of all time.[36] By 1978, the *New York Times* was calling Lindsay "one of this decade's biggest-selling authors."[37] This is exactly what the Sibylline literature was: enormously popular and transformative of culture to the point of guiding global politics. (When we get to the twentieth century, we will see how *The Late Great Planet Earth* and its ilk influenced world leaders.)

In their day, the Oracles instructed Byzantine Christians—who were by then the vast majority of the population—to be on the lookout for events and personalities that corresponded to scenarios, imagery, and sequences of biblical End Time predictions. Of special concern was the return of Christ as pictured in John's Revelation, where he appears as a victorious warrior. Wiser theologians like Origen and Augustine understood John's vision as allegorical, whereas the Christian readers of the Oracles took it literally.

Despite efforts to suppress it, the legacy of Irenaeus remained strong and all the more so as huge numbers of less-educated converts filled the churches. With Christendom's reign palpable all around them, and Church dogma indistinguishable from the state's, it was easy to picture the warrior-Jesus appearing if the right circumstances arose. Christ's kingdom already possessed a worldly estate and an army that fought in its name. Why, then, would anyone read the prophets as anything but that?

For the masses, these non-canonical updates to prophecy were as authoritative as the biblical ones, and the flexible Oracles kept up with current events, keeping it all fresh. Christendom's very structure fostered one of these amendments, one that proved to be particularly useful in times of war. "Thanks to them," writes Norman Cohn, "in the imagination of Christians for more than a thousand years the figure of the warrior-Christ was doubled by another, that of the Emperor of the Last Days."[38]

Through the innovation of the Last Emperor, prognosticators predicted that there would be a geopolitical challenge to Christendom and a period of tribulation when the "Golden Age" of Constantine's realm would almost be snuffed out. Then, the Last Emperor would rally for battle in Jerusalem. Once the saints miraculously delivered the city, he was expected to lay his crown and royal vestiture at the place of Christ's crucifixion, thereby handing the empire over to God's direct rule.

That's still not quite the end, however. There would be one last battle for Jerusalem when Ezekiel's Gog came from the land of Magog to confront the saints one last time in Jerusalem. This would be the final, last, and definite end, concluding with Christ triumphant. It is yet another "last battle" focused on Jerusalem, part of a repeating pattern, with the Christian versions of the Oracles based on earlier Jewish ones, to be passed along in due course to Muslims before returning to Jews and Christians in the twentieth century.

And so it was that in the early seventh century, the prophecies appeared to find fulfillment as the Sassanid Persians inflicted defeat after defeat upon the Christians. For some years it looked as though Christendom would be lost entirely—it really was as bad as that.

To Jews—who were reading their own apocalyptic literature, supplemented by Sibylline updates—Constantinople's troubles looked like a prophesied sign of redemption. As ever, the Persians represented the hope of Cyrus. He had reinstated Jerusalem as the Jewish capital after Babylon destroyed it and exiled the Jews. Apocalyptic literature suggested that this was just a precursor. Now in the days of the new Roman Babylon, it appeared as though the Persian Zoroastrians would again be chosen as the sword of YHWH.

When the Persians appointed a charismatic Jewish leader to spearhead the battle to wrest Jerusalem from the Romans, full redemption appeared to be within reach. The leader was Nehemiah ben Hushiel ben Ephraim ben Joseph—a name that laid claim to the messianic throne of David if ever there was one. He was no figurehead. He brought with him an armed force of 20,000 Jewish troops and successfully secured Jerusalem in 614 CE.

Victorious, Nehemiah donned royal robes and took his place as the successor of David, from whom he was genuinely descended (something the Maccabees and Herod could not claim). At last, the Jews had a legitimate candidate for King Messiah. Nehemiah immediately began work to rebuild the Temple and took steps to restore the priesthood and regular sacrifice for the first time in half a millennium. Elsewhere, as Roman fortunes collapsed across the empire, the Jewish population of Antioch rose up and assassinated the Christian patriarch.

If there was any doubt on the Christian side about the End Time, it was removed. Under Constantine, Syria Palaestina had become Terra Sancta, the Holy Land. Christendom revolved around Jerusalem, which Constantine and his mother consecrated with great devotion. He tore down the abominable temple of Jupiter and built the Church of the Holy Sepulchre over the place of Christ's burial and resurrection, to which thousands of pilgrims flocked every year. All awaited the descent of New Jerusalem to complete the last step in finalizing Christ's rule on Earth, but they knew that before that, the Antichrist would appear to test the faithful. That these two rejectors of Christ, the Persians and Jews, could conquer Terra Sancta, burning and looting the churches, was nothing less than a fulfillment of the prophesied last tribulation.

I should mention that one church was spared: in 614, when the Persian forces desecrated and mutilated the churches of Jerusalem, they did not have the heart to touch the Church of the Nativity in nearby Bethlehem. You know why, of course: this was the Magi's church, set apart by a mosaic showing the Zoroastrian priests in their traditional dress.

By 622, with the Persians at his doorstep, the current emperor considered abandoning Constantinople; he planned to reboot Christendom in Carthage and would have done so if not for the intervention of Sergius, the ecumenical patriarch. Understanding very well the eschatological significance of this war, at least in the minds of the people, he urged emperor Heraclius to stay and fight. If this was the great tribulation, it was up to the emperor, with God's help, to retake Jerusalem so that Christ could return.

And so, with the Persians now literally at the city gates, it would surely take a miracle to turn the tide. That was OK. True believers had read the Oracles. To do his part, Sergius provided the wealth of the Church to support the state and its army, stripping precious metals from Hagia Sophia and emptying the church coffers. This provided the emperor enough material to strike new coins for circulation, bearing an inscription that was at once nakedly sincere and electrifying: GOD HELP THE ROMANS!

I'm looking at one of those coins right now on my desk, and I have to say, it gives me a thrill! The effect was instantaneous then, too. Apocalyptic heat galvanized the troops and inspired waves of volunteers. Their inspiration was the patriarch's passionate support of the emperor and their own familiarity with the likes of apocalyptic commentator Commadanius, who, as Cohn reports, retooled "the usual phantasies of vengeance and triumph" into a practical "urge to take up arms and fight."[39]

Now with the End Time scenario unfolding before their eyes, thousands of ordinary Christians rose up to be in Christ's army. This was to be a full-blooded holy war, the first Christian Crusade, with Jerusalem and Christ's return its goal. By the fall of that year the Persians had a major defeat (it still isn't exactly clear how that happened) and by 628 the emperor had reached the Persian capital and forced the surrender of the entire Near East on his terms. Salvation was at hand.

At the broken Persian court, Heraclius secured the holy artifacts they'd taken from Jerusalem and marched with them back to Terra Sancta, finally re-entering the holy city triumphantly in 629 on Newroz Day.

Naturally, this seemed a fulfillment of the Emperor of the Last days, who was to lay his royal vestiture at Golgotha after delivering Jerusalem from the Antichrist (now known to be the false messiah Nehemiah). Newroz Day was chosen because Zoroastrians celebrated eternal redemption on this day through ceremonial gifts to the King of Kings—a title that Heraclius now chose for himself as the deputy of the eternal King of Kings, Jesus Christ. He was the first Roman emperor to ever assume this title, and he did so on this day for purely eschatological reasons.

Muhammad

IF WE HAVE ANY DOUBT ABOUT HOW HERACLIUS' PEOPLE VIEWED HIM, we've only to read the histories written by his contemporaries. "Heraclius' victory and his actions thereafter convinced many that the end of time had truly come upon them," writes Stephen J. Shoemaker in *Arabica*.[40] The author cites Heraclius' court poet, George of Pisidia, who couched the emperor's reign in "boldly eschatological terms" while contemporary historians "saw the events of their day as presaging the impending final judgment and the end of time."

Shoemaker continues, "They also disclose the extent to which Byzantine eschatology viewed the Empire itself as a positive eschatological agent... that the Kingdom of God was somehow beginning to be realized." It isn't just about Christendom, however. For this is the century that Islam first appears. Again quoting Shoemaker, understanding Heraclius-era Christian eschatology "is crucial for understanding the mixture of eschatology and empire in primitive Islam."

And it is to this that we now turn. As you may have noticed, Islam first appears just after the events surrounding the Jewish revival in Jerusalem and Heraclius' miraculous reconquest. It is this eschatologically fevered environment that shapes Islamic beliefs and practices. No one can understand the Middle East without grasping this fact.

There is some uncanny occurrence of coincidence in the 600s, as there will be again and again in the remainder of our story. It wasn't just the near demise of Christendom, or the fortuitous convergence of Zoroastrian and Jewish interests. Another viral idea infected Jews and Christians, causing this otherwise predictable clash of empires to burn with the fever of apocalyptic fury. It is simply math: the ever-recurring 70×7 years, Daniel's promised 490 years until "eternal righteousness [is] ushered in and prophetic vision ratified."

The first 490 years counted from the Babylonian exile and came due when Jesus was born, keeping the fever high until Bar Kokhba's devastating defeat in 135 CE. His humiliation resulted in the second exile of the Jews from Jerusalem, this time imposed by Rome, "the new Babylon." It was a reset. Counting 490 years from the date of this second exile, it came due again in 625. Or, if you like, counting from the start of the rabbinically cursed Bar Kokhba's uprising, it comes in 622.

Don't underestimate the propensity of people to make a big deal out of these calculations. It is still being done today. *Left Behind* and *The Late Great*

Planet Earth built their popularity around the same 7×70 formula, and entire Christian denominations sprang from it. If you want a flavor of this, search YouTube for "7×70 prophecy." Preachers and prognosticators remain obsessed with this math.

In short, the 600s appear on the calendar with as much significance as the year 1 AD. Just look what happened:

- 610 – Heraclius was crowned emperor.
- 610 – Muhammad was called to prophethood.
- 614 – Jewish army retakes Jerusalem; Temple services restored.
- 619 – 20,000 Jews slaughtered by Christians outside Jerusalem's Golden Gate; the year remembered by Islam as the "Year of Disaster" or "Year of Sorrow."
- 620 – Traditional date of Muhammad's miraculous "night journey" to Jerusalem; Muhammad meets Jesus there and is instructed how Muslims should pray.
- 622 – Heraclius mints "God Help" coins.
- 622 – The Hegira from Mecca to Medina—start of Islamic calendar.
- 629 – Heraclius restores True Cross to Jerusalem, is ordained as "King of Kings."
- 637 – Muslim armies conquer Jerusalem and begin worship on the Temple Mount with Jewish priests in attendance.

We would be utterly obtuse not to recognize the correlation between the founding of Islam with this intense Christian, Jewish, and Zoroastrian eschatological period. I'll just say it: Islam is a function of Jewish and Christian apocalypticism.

Islam never claimed to be a new religion; it evolved from others, and Muhammad avows as much. The Holy Quran presents Abraham as the starting point, Jesus the middle, and Muhammad the final seal of Judeo-Christian religion. It's a full circle. The whole tradition of Moses, the burning bush, and the giving of the Law takes place in Muhammad's back-yard, the desert territory inland of the Red Sea, including the Ḥijāz region of modern Saudi Arabia, the southern deserts of Jordan, Egyptian Sinai, and Israel's Negev. As we've read, YHWH, the idea that became Abrahamic monotheism, was first contemplated in these deserts by civilization's discontents, the tent-dwelling traders like Abraham, despised by their urbanized Egyptian neighbors as uncivilized. In other words, they were the Bedouin of northwestern Arabia, Muhammad's kin and actual ancestors.

Muhammad claims to be a direct descendant of Ishmael, Abraham's first-born son, who came to live in these deserts. But Ishmael the son of Abraham appears exclusively in the Hebrew Bible, and no other ancient source. This continuity between the origins of Israel's religion and Muhammad's is beyond logical dispute. Not only do Muslims believe that Muhammad is descended from Abraham, but as often as not, Islam is called "the religion of Abraham" in the Quran. In sum, Jews and Muslims share a starting point and a trajectory. Monotheism did not suddenly sprout from the sandy soil here in the seventh century.

Moreover, by that time, Jerusalem's exiles had been living among their Arab cousins for at least 500 years, plenty of time to share how their common Midianite roots had grown and blossomed in Judah. In fact, Muslim tradition does not remember the Ḥijāz ever belonging to any people but the Jews, to whom the Arabs happily credit digging the wells, planting the date palms, and organizing trade.[41] The Jews here spoke Arabic and were known by tribal and clan affiliations, just as everyone else was, going by the title *banū*, meaning "sons of." Muhammad was of Banū Hāshim, and famed Jewish tribes included the Banū Ḳuraiẓa and Banū Naḍīr.

Medina, Islam's founding city, was originally Yathrib, a city dominated by Jews. But even outside of Medina, Jewish beliefs were well-known. A passage in the Quran reveals to what extent. The story shows the Prophet rebuking a challenger, sounding very much like Jesus scolding a Pharisee: "Is he not acquainted with what is in the Books of Moses? And of Abraham?" asks Muhammad.[42] The scene is set in the earliest phase of Muhammad's career in Mecca, meaning that the encounter reflects the default culture. The Prophet's incredulousness assumes that everyone around there knew Abraham and the books of Moses quite well. Indeed, out of context, we would most certainly assume he was a Jew speaking to a Jew. (He actually addresses a fellow tribesman, Al-Walid ibn al-Mughira.)

Persian and Christian influences were strong, too. The two regional empires had forged alliances with different Arab tribes across the ill-defined desert borders. Some of the Byzantine-influenced Arabs became Christian, especially in the north toward Damascus, and there were probably all sorts of exiles, such as unorthodox Christians and heretics who had taken refuge beyond the reach of official Christendom—particularly those who did not believe in the divinity of Jesus.

It is even possible that some were those James-affiliated Christian-Jews from Jerusalem, banned from the holy city after Bar Kokhba's revolt. If so, they would have a very different take on Jesus than Orthodox Christians, accounting for some of the Quran's claims about him—specifically, that he could not be God's son, even though he was the Messiah.

As for the Persians, textual evidence in the Quran shows more than a passing familiarity with the Zoroastrianism of their Persian trading partners. Arabian Jews also had very strong connections with Persian Mesopotamia, where large numbers of Jews lived, and there were refugees from the Persian-affiliated Jews of that short-lived messianic kingdom in Jerusalem.

All these communities mixed in northwestern Arabia, influencing each other in matters of eschatology, combining to shape Muhammad's message as a sort of medley with its own set of variations.

The exact process, however, is obscured by layers of redacted tradition. We don't need to worry about that or bother ourselves too much with what is myth and history. (If you wish to pursue it, see the citations for this chapter.) No matter when it was codified, the results are the same, and manifest in the text of the Holy Quran.

For example, Islam is not embarrassed to say that Muslims first prayed in the direction of Jerusalem, not Mecca. Nor is it hesitant to claim Muhammad as an eschatological end point, the culmination of a long line of Jewish patriarchs, kings, and prophets—all named in the Quran. There is not a single prophet in the Quran who is not a Jew, and Muhammad is the Seal of the Prophets. You may ponder for yourself what it might mean that Muhammad alone is not a Jew.

In any case, his task is to restore the pure worship of Abraham's, Moses', and David's One God, and to prepare the world for the End Time, the Day of Judgment.[43] Whatever the eschatological purpose of the Jews had been, Muhammad proposed to fulfill it.

In pursuit of this, he moved to create a theocracy, fusing religious and political authority. It was the Jewish apocalyptic ideal of God's direct rule, more lately seen in Byzantine Christendom. That Medina was autonomous and largely ungoverned helped his project immensely; he could call for submission to God alone without causing alarm to an imperial authority (the problem the Jews had always had). And given the anarchic situation in Medina, his efforts were met with applause by all parties, Jews included.

Thus, in 622, a new state enterprise became official through Muhammad's Dastūr al-Madīnah, or Constitution of Medina—it was a theocracy based on the Jewish prophetic tradition. This is the same year that Heraclius minted his "God Help" coins and 490 (7×70) years after Bar Kokhba declared his disastrous messianic revolt against Rome. Daniel's prophecy was fulfilled!

If Muhammad wholeheartedly embraced the sword in this endeavor, he can hardly be blamed. His role model was Byzantine Christianity which, although it did not admit to theocracy, professed what they called *symphonia* between church and state, whereby "the temporal power and the priesthood relate to each other as body and soul."[44] Although these Christians hadn't forgotten that Jesus said no to the sword, they found an eschatological loophole: since Christ promised to fight alongside the saints upon his return—a picture John's Revelation painted in unforgettable detail—Christians could cast themselves as soldiers in that battle if they were absolutely sure the end had come. This was to become an often-cited precedent by all concerned.

Muhammad was right with them. His whole enterprise was conceived of as this Last Battle. The Quran references the Day of Judgment literally hundreds of times using the same metaphors and signs (blowing of heavenly trumpets, for example) that we find in Jewish and Christian apocalyptic literature. Often the words are identical. For example, "in the twinkling of an eye," the dead will rise as the angels descend from heaven with judgment. Echoing Jesus, the Quran instructs us on the proximity of the hour: "Do they then only wait for the Hour, that it should come on them of a sudden? But already have come some tokens thereof."[45] Comments the *Oxford Handbook of Eschatology*, "The Koran speaks of death, the end of the world, and resurrection more than any other major scripture. The hadith, or corpus of prophetic sayings, follows suit, as does the tradition in general."[46]

At the end of the struggle waited *firdaws*, "Paradise," borrowing the word directly from Zoroaster just as Jesus did. This is the highest expression of heaven. More generally, the eternal reward "for those who believe and do righteous deeds" will be *jannāh*, literally "a garden," which correlates with *Jannāt ' Adni*, the Garden of Eden, where Islam affirms Adam and Eve lived until the Fall and exile. As Paradise was lost in Adam, so it will be restored through the second Adam, Jesus—the only other human not born by man's seed. "Jesus to Allah is like that of Adam," Muhammad prophesies; "He created Him from dust; then He said to him, 'Be,' and he was."[47]

This is Pauline theology, and important to our understanding because it makes Jesus the key to Paradise in early Islam. Jewish and Zoroastrian apocalyptic literature expected the Son of Man and the Saoshyant at the final hour. The Muslims imported this idea, too, accepting with the Christians that Jesus was the principal figure on the Day of Judgment. He is also the Messiah, which in the Quran is a Hebrew loan word, *Masîḥ*. Jesus' other titles call attention to unique messianic attributes: Jesus is the *kalimatin min Allah* ("Word from God"), and *kalimatu* ("His Word"); both are characterizations reserved exclusively for Jesus in Islam, as is *ruhullah* ("the Spirit of God").

With the centrality of Islam's virgin-born Jesus, it is only natural that the Muslims adopted Christian expectations of the Antichrist, too. *Al- Masīḥ ad-Dajjāl* ("the False Messiah") will appear in the final, darkest hour. They called this tribulation the *fitna*, a period of godlessness that sets the stage à la John's Revelation and Ezekiel for a final showdown between returning Jesus and Gog and Magog (rendered *Yajuj amd Majuj* in the Quran).[48]

History is clear that within decades of Muhammad's birth, the Muslims marched out of Arabia to enlarge the domain of submission to the One God. The details, however, are unexpectedly fuzzy. For help, we turn to an Armenian churchman Sebeos, who wrote a history of what he saw. His close witness of Islam's rise makes him indispensable to the otherwise impossible task of understanding exactly what happened during Islam's swift and unexpected conquest of Syria and Palestine.

His testimony is so convincing because Sebeos tells it as an aside: his real interest is in the Christian/Persian conflict. Reporting on the Christian liberation of Edessa from the Persians, he notes that a Jewish delegation (allies of the defeated Persians) was dispatched to Medina. Their mission was to win over their Arab Abrahamic cousins in support of a fresh bid to reconquer Jerusalem from Heraclius' Christendom. Is this what the Arabs thought they were doing when they conquered Jerusalem?

I'll let Sebeos tell the story:

> The Jews called the Arabs to their aid and familiarized them with the relationship they had through the books of the Old Testament. Although the Arabs were convinced of their close relationship, they were unable to get a consensus... In that period a certain one of them, a man of the sons of Ishmael named Muhammad, a merchant, became prominent. A sermon about the Way of Truth, supposedly at God's command, was revealed to them... he ordered them all to assemble together and to unite in faith.[49]

Sebeos then paraphrases Muhammad's message to the Arabs, capturing a snapshot of the Prophet's view of their position regarding the Jews and the Promised Land:

God promised that country to Abraham and to his son after him, for eternity. And what had been promised was fulfilled during that time when God loved Israel. Now, however, you are the sons of Abraham, and God shall fulfill the promise made to Abraham and his son on you. Only love the God of Abraham, and go and take the country which God gave to your father, Abraham. No one can successfully resist you in war, since God is with you.

And go they did—Arabs as the new Israel. The question is whether they went together with those Jews, and if Muhammad went with them, if not as their Messiah, then as the Messiah's champion.

The Mi'raj and the Dome of the Rock

It had been a chaotic century; Jerusalem changed hands twice, the Byzantine Empire nearly collapsed, a Jewish ruler ascended in Judea, and then, miraculously, it was all back in Christian hands. At the end of the day, the Zoroastrians were finished, never to recover. What happened next is obscured by a cloud of dust rising from the thundering hooves of Islam.

As they stormed from Arabia into western Syria and the Holy Land, the Byzantine Christians, weakened by decades of war, could not at first comprehend what was happening. The emperor, if he had a chance to think at all, might have thought he was being attacked by a revived Jewish messianic movement. Considering the commentaries of other Christians near the scene, that is exactly what it appeared to be.

After all, there was no precedent for an Arab conquest of this kind, and in Christian minds, nothing called Islam would exist yet for decades. Sebeos' account sees the Jews and Ḥijāz Arabs united in a common-faith initiative. He is corroborated by Jewish sources from this time that speak of Jews hailing Muhammad as the Messiah.[50] Was Islam's conquest of Jerusalem a messianic campaign led by Muhammad and filled with the ranks of both Jews and Judaized Arabs?

The details are hard to come by. It was much easier to piece together an objective history about Jewish and Christian development simply because it was a much busier scene, with numerous antagonistic voices on the record for comparison, and mountains of material evidence. The Ḥijāz was not Babylon or Rome, where archives recorded transactions and legal rulings, and officially decreed persecutions and amnesties. The archeological and documentary record is extremely sparse—practically non-existent. When the official account was written 100 years later, Muslims were not concerned with journalistic accounts. Insulated to an unprecedented degree, they could write their own story without contradiction. Until we find an Arabic equivalent of the Dead Sea Scrolls, we have only one carefully crafted version of events.

Still, considering the surviving external accounts, there is at least the intriguing possibility that Muhammad himself led the conquest of Palestine as a Messiah heading for the last battle.[51] It's not a far-fetched idea at all. At least eleven diverse sources, all concurring on important details, report it just that way. There is also the smoking gun of a Jewish apocalyptic, *The Secrets of Rabbi Shim'ōn b Yoḥai.* A scholarly consensus puts the source as a near contemporary of the events. The text views the Islamic conquest of Jerusalem as YHWH's work, part of the promise to restore the Jews and the Temple.

As the story goes, the titular Rabbi Shim'ōn gets a Joseph-and-Mary-like visit from an angel to tell him that Muhammad is the chosen Savior. "Do not be afraid, mortal, for the Holy One, blessed be He, is bringing about the kingdom of Ishmael only for the purpose of delivering you from that wicked one that is, Edom."[52] ("Edom," in these days, was Jewish code for the Byzantine Christians.)

That this reflects a contemporary Jewish voice is plain: there is no way that a Jewish writer would write such an endorsement after Islam was established in its final form, when relations had demonstrably soured. The source has to be a Jewish participant in early Islamic life.

Some chroniclers are so specific as to say they met Muhammad personally near Jerusalem. If they had said the "armies of Muhammad," there would be some ambiguity, but these claims, told in a casual off-hand way as part of a longer story, describe meeting and speaking with him. And this was well before Muhammad was generally known. In my mind, this defies explanation —why make such a thing up at a time when no one cared?

Although I do believe there is something to the theory outlined above, accepting the traditional story does not change the picture much. Islam is still concerned with the End Time and Jerusalem's role in it. Given the overwhelmingly eschatological character of the Quran, Muhammad's surviving to lead the battle is not essential. The fact is the armies of Islam very quickly captured Jerusalem—it was the top priority—and their motivation was undeniably eschatological. That is not controversial: Jerusalem to this day remains a prophetic lightning rod for Muslims.

To this point, the traditional Muslim version of Muhammad and Jerusalem speaks volumes. As it turns out, Muhammad's approved biography admits that he did go to Jerusalem after all. But there is a twist designed to solve the inevitable problem that God never shows up for the fight in any End Time battle. If Muhammad indeed took Jerusalem with an army expecting the Apocalypse and it didn't happen, this requires an explanation. Islamic tradition handles this deftly by having the Prophet enter Jerusalem and experience the expected Apocalypse—the unveiling of heaven—by miraculous means. It is called the Isra and Mi'raj—an entirely metaphysical apocalypse that allows the events of the Last Day to be with Muslims always and every day as they await its political fulfillment.

In Muhammad's Isra, the prophet visited Jerusalem's Temple Mount over the course of a single night, whence he was translated into heaven (the Mi'raj), received instructions on *ṣalāt* (the form and number of daily prayers), and spoke with Abraham, Moses, and Jesus (needless to say, three Jews). The angel Gabriel took Muhammad from the Foundation Stone, the heart of Solomon's Temple, to the true foundation in heaven. This account transforms Muhammad's (or his successor's) actual military campaign against Byzantine Jerusalem into exactly what he believed it would be: the moment when heaven comes to Earth.[53]

As per Islamic tradition, it was just a year or so after the Mi'raj that Muhammad established the constitution in Medina; then a year later, he changed the direction of prayer to Mecca. The sequence is significant. Mecca and Medina are famously Islam's holiest cities, but Muhammad first had to connect with heaven and get the blessing of the prophets at Jerusalem. In Islamic eschatology, Jerusalem is the primary address and the one that validates the others.

Understanding this is indispensable because today Jerusalem is the locus of great tension. And it is not just Jerusalem—it is the Temple Mount in Jerusalem that is the bone of contention. From that specific spot, the Foundation Stone on the Temple Mount, Muhammad bridged heaven and Earth. It is the stone upon which Abraham laid his son in symbolic offering and over which the Israelites built their temple.

No wonder, then, that Jerusalem's most recognizable feature—the Dome of the Rock—was built over this same stone. The builder was Abd al-Malik ibn Marwan, arguably the caliph who established Islam's first true empire. He certainly was the first Muslim ruler to mint coins and raise taxes uniformly across the Islamic realm. Because of a lack of evidence prior to his rule, we may never know to what extent he shaped Islam as we know it today —some think it's practically his invention—but we can get a good idea of his importance from the simple fact that the first written examples of the Quran and references to Muhammad are his, elaborately adorning the walls of the Dome of the Rock. To reiterate: far and away the earliest versions of the Quran's text appear on Abd al-Malik's Dome of the Rock.

The Dome is also the earliest Islamic monumental structure, the oldest surviving building associated with Islam of any kind, pre-dating any mosque. We have to ask: why did they give the Temple Mount such priority and the honor of first preserving the Muslim creed in writing?

It's not just Muhammad's Night Journey, because that story most certainly post-dates the building, as if the building required the story. The answer is in what the story does: it connects the Arabs to the Jewish temple, which is the reason for the site's importance to Islam in the first place. It's all about the Jewish foundation of Islam.

Until modern politics made Muslims uneasy with this topic, Islamic tradition and high-ranking Muslim scholars never hesitated to give that very answer. Fortunately, we can look at what they wrote.

Here is an example from as late as 1929. In *A Brief Guide to al-Haram al-Sharif*, a pamphlet printed by the Supreme Islamic Council overseeing the holy sites on the Temple Mount, we read, "The site is one of the oldest in the world. Its sanctity dates from the earliest (perhaps from pre-historic) times. Its identity with the site of Solomon's Temple is beyond dispute. This, too, is the spot, according to universal belief, on which 'David built there an altar unto the Lord, and offered burnt offerings and peace offerings.'"[54]

Older sources continue to astonish us. The earliest Muslim traditions, dating from the late 600s and preserved in later anthologies, describe how after acquiring the Mount, the Arabs called Jewish experts in to purify the site and teach the Muslim community how to conduct services after the Dome of the Rock was built.

Indeed, the rituals described there relate to Jewish practices, including the type of clothing required for those conducting services, the days assigned for special requirements, the manner in which they used incense, and more. Thus, the Islamic record unabashedly shows the way these traditions were passed from Jews to Muslims. The intention was to revive worship as per the Temple of Solomon. There is no reason for this to be controversial: why wouldn't Muslims want to do that, given the Quran's premise that Islam is the purified continuation and indeed restoration of the religion of Abraham, Moses, David, and Solomon? Jewish messianists were trying to do the same thing just a few decades earlier. Why would these Arab followers of Moses, Abraham, David, and Solomon want anything less?

We can see it in the names by which Muslims called this place, too. In

Hebrew the Temple is *Bayt ha-Mikdash*, meaning "the Holy House." Likewise, esteemed ninth-century Muslim chronicler al-Tabari calls Jerusalem *madīnat Bayt al-Maqdis*, meaning "city of the Temple," an Arabicized use of the Hebrew name. The *Encyclopaedia of Islam* concurs that in the first centuries of the faith, Muslims mostly used the Hebrew name: "the older writers call it commonly Bait al-Makdis which really meant the Temple (of Solomon)."[55]

Its real importance isn't just to do with the past, however. The Dome of the Rock is about Paradise and especially the Paradise to come. "Muslim eschatologists often asserted that Jerusalem was the site of the future earthly paradise, a Jewish notion that was taken up in Islam," writes Utrecht University's Christian Robert Lange in his survey of Islamic eschatology.

Early Muslim writers wrote effusively about Jerusalem's heavenly connections. Here is a sampling: It is the closest place on Earth to heaven, the closest to Allah's throne, the place where heaven and Earth meet. A tree of the Garden of Eden (the Tree of Life) is said to support the foundation itself and the rock is the entrance gate—there is nowhere closer to Paradise than this. Praying in Jerusalem is like praying in heaven, we are told.[56] The rock is a Rock of Paradise, the center of global geography. On Judgment Day, the angel Israfil will blow his trumpet standing on this rock to call humankind to its fate.

Then there is the building itself. Everything about the Dome of the Rock's architecture references Paradise, from the ubiquitous Tree of Life in the ceramics, to the Dome's inscriptions, which preach the coming Day of Judgment and resurrection. Writing in the *Islamic Quarterly*, Carolanne Mekeel-Matteson observes that while Christian architecture in Jerusalem commemorates eschatological events that have been fulfilled—that is, the birth, death, and resurrection of Christ—in the Dome of the Rock, Muslims refer to events awaiting fulfillment in the End Time. "In the first great structure of Islam, the commemoration is eschatological and thus points to the future..." It is about "the Resurrection, Judgment, and final rule of God upon earth."[57]

But what about Mecca and Medina? We can't really separate the three holy places of Islam. The three sacred mosques of Mecca, Medina, and Jerusalem stand together. The Quran says that in bridging Earth and heaven, the Mi'raj connects Mecca with Jerusalem. "Exalted is He who took His Servant by night from al-Masjid al-Haram to al-Masjid al-Aqsa, whose surroundings We have blessed."[58]

Whereas the first of these, Mecca's Masjid al-Haram, looks back to

Abraham ("We showed Abraham the site of the House, saying... Purify My House for those who circle around it"), Medina is about Muhammad's political life; Islam's Jerusalem looks forward to the living Jesus who will return to that exact spot where heaven and Earth were bridged.[59]

Indeed, in the age to come, the differences do not matter. On the Day of Judgment, Mecca's Kaaba will be transported here. It is here and nowhere else that the archangel will blow the trumpet of final judgment. Jerusalem alone is the connecting point between Earth and heaven, this age and the next.

The seventh century was rich with messiahs and portents of the End Time.

A Jewish messiah in Jerusalem was complicit in the near-obliteration of Christendom, prompting the emperor to melt down the precious metals of the churches and mint these coins bearing the plea "God Help the Romans!"

Emperor Heraclius then miraculously prevailed, reclaimed Jerusalem, and re-christened himself "King of Kings."

His biographers saw all this as part of the pageant of the End Time.

From my collection: One of Heraclius' supplicant coins, showing the emperor and his son (*L*) and bearing the inscription *Deus Adiuta Romanis* (*R*). Note the *staurogram* (*tau-rho*) in the right field, which Herod also used on his coins. A symbol of Christ, it may well have been an older messianic sign of salvation.

Next to my Heraclius coins, I display coins of Abd al-Malik, builder of Jerusalem's iconic Dome of the Rock. He was the ultimate winner in the seventh-century fight for Jerusalem.

In one coin, we see the caliph standing with hand on sword.

In another, there is a menorah. In the early days of Islam, Muslims even employed Jewish priests to serve at the Dome of Rock. At the same time, some Jews embraced Muhammad as a forerunner of the Messiah.

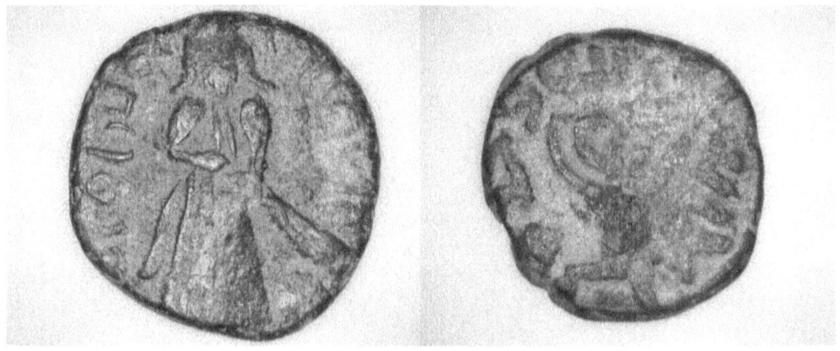

The Jewish Temple stood here where I am standing.

I think early Muslims believed they were restoring the Temple when they built the Dome of the Rock.

Around the time Muhammad was born, a Jewish messianic claimant took Jerusalem and also attempted to rebuild the Temple here. He was followed by the Christian emperor Heraclius, who was crowned "King of Kings" on this spot.

It's all a part of the competition for Paradise which continues to manifest itself here.

❧ 13 ☙

THE MILLENNIUM

Abyss and Ascent

As much as living in Galilee opened my eyes to the real experience of Jesus and the disciples, I would live in Israel for many months before seeing the wonders of Jerusalem. It was still a fantasy. And since Tel Aviv, the kibbutz, and the Gentile unholiness of Galilee already fogged my view of the Holy Land, I began to wonder what disillusionments awaited me on Mount Zion.

I'd already met a foreign traveler, a short-term volunteer, who was driven mad by his pilgrimage to the holiest of holies. By the time he came to the kibbutz, he was near the end of a forty-day fast and looked at us through eyes the likes of which I had never seen before. I viewed this pilgrim with alarm; his high was hyper-awake, as if he were seeing too much, things no one would want to see and live.

"I am the prophet," he said. It was a statement as convincing as it was absurd. His mission was to pave the way for the Lord. We should listen to him. We should repent. He was one of the "two witnesses of Revelations chapter 9." We ought to take heed.

"Jerusalem syndrome," one of the kibbutzniks sneered; "it happens all the time." I found this disconcerting, not only because of the apprehension of its possibly infecting me, but also because of the awareness that, to some extent, it already had. What should I expect when I got there?

It was time to find out. At last, the kibbutz announced it would foot the bill for a visit. Yes, I would see Jerusalem! But would I come back sane? There was little opportunity to think about it. The decision was made and off we went.

Our guide took a route similar to the one Jesus most likely used—a longer and more circuitous path, but in his day, the safer option. First, we went down from our Galilean heights to Tiberius, brushing by Capernaum, where Jesus preached and lived. We saw the excavations of Peter's house and the second-century Roman-style synagogue, built over the one where Jesus preached and refurbished to its present glory, most probably by his Jewish followers. I could visualize him there, standing on the shore of the Sea of Galilee, calling to his disciples to become "fishermen of men."

Jesus, too, was just a Jerusalem Syndrome fool, my kibbutz buddy suggested. I frowned. He laughed. Then we headed straight down the river valley, shadowed from the east by Jordan's ruddy highlands, and after some hours, when the soil transitioned to a chemical white, we stopped by Jericho. There, we talked about Moses, who could only look across the river from those heights, barred from entering the Holy Land; we spoke about Joshua, who fought the battle here at Jericho (by one biblical account) or who did not have to fight much at all (according to another). My Jewish friends assured me it was a collection of fantasies, penned by ancients themselves stricken with Jerusalem Syndrome.

I couldn't yet understand what these scriptural contradictions might mean—I was still very much a literalist. But they weren't being cruel. Their intention, I think, was to inoculate me as we made our ascent to Zion. They looked to spare me from the ravishments of the disease and the treatments were administered by pointing out contradictions in the Bible's account—for instance, how the Canaanites were all wiped out at the end of one book and in the next are miraculously alive again, their cities whole and their religions a temptation to the fragile and tenuous alliance of tribes that will one day be Israel.

What? The Bible is perfect and without ambiguity! I looked it up. To my dismay, all they said was true. For now, all I could do was take my inoculations with a wince of denial and move on.

From Jericho, we drove down to have a look at the Dead Sea and the caves where David hid from Saul. Was this part true, I asked? They said only that there was "some truth in it." What was sure, I learned, was that this was the lowest spot on the face of the earth, and by God, it felt like it.

As we started the climb from the valley toward Jerusalem, a short and steep ear-popping drive, a powerful vision flooded my awareness. The dream, the ambition of all humankind, had something to do with this half-hour car ride, for all those dreams stem from the Abrahamic quest for the "city whose foundations and builder is God." That's what everyone was looking for in Jerusalem—the idea of a better world, of Paradise restored—and, at the very least, it was ritually enacted in this ancient route from the depths of hell to the holy city on the hill.

Abraham, if I was to believe there was such a man, would have come this way from Sodom and Gomorrah, which lie buried just south of Jericho. Later, the evidently mythical Israelites came out of Egypt along the same path, forced by the mythologists to go this way, although there were much easier, far more straightforward routes to take. A shout from my guide interrupted and confirmed my reverie.

"We make Aliyah, *motek!*"

Jews "make Aliyah" when they return to Israel from the diaspora. In Hebrew it means "ascent." In the deepest sense, it is the ascent from this symbolic hell and its pillars of salt, the journey of God's people out of bondage in Egypt through this underworld to Jerusalem's heavenly heights. It felt inescapably visceral, hell and heaven from the viewpoint of an ancient traveler. I searched for analogies; it was as though one walks through a door in Death Valley to appear suddenly in the cool hills above San Diego. Except the Dead Sea is more dead, literally packed in salt, and somehow more ominously judgmental, as it is hemmed in by yet more desert and those soaring heights, which always remind the salt-encrusted lowlanders of the heaven they do not possess.

It isn't that it is so high, exactly—Jerusalem stands at only 2,700 feet above sea level. It is rather that the Dead Sea is such an abyss. The ground at the shore is 1,400 feet below sea level, and as such, is a genuine matter-of-fact hell; escaping from it is the story of salvation.

Aliyah, this modern term for Jewish immigration to Israel, is therefore straight from the Bible; in fact, *aliyah* is the very last word of the Hebrew Bible.

I never knew this growing up—no preacher I was familiar with ever mentioned it—but Hebrew scriptures end with the Book of Chronicles, preceded by the great Last Days prophet Daniel and the books of Nehemiah and Ezra. The significance was obvious: these books were about the end of exile in Babylon and the promise of redemption. The last books tell of the Jewish people's liberation by Cyrus and end with an appeal in the final line for able-bodied Hebrews to return to their Promised Land and rebuild their

Temple on Cyrus' dime—to make Aliyah, to come up from Babylon's fallen realm to the higher plane of enlightenment.

In fact, the very last words of the Hebrew Bible are spoken by none other than the Zoroastrian King of Kings: "Thus said King Cyrus of Persia: The Lord God of Heaven has given me all the kingdoms of the earth, and has charged me with building Him a House in Jerusalem, which is in Judah. Any one of you of all His people, the Lord his God be with him and let him go up." (The translation of "go up" is, of course, *aliyah*.)

So here I was, obeying Cyrus the Persian. And we were definitely going up, and my ears were popping. The steady incline did make Jerusalem feel remote like heaven—aloof and, for that reason, alluring. I could feel for the first time what the journey from the lowest of lows to the golden city meant to the ancients.

Finally, we arrived. There it was. Jerusalem's Old City sat high as expected, and its peculiar stone reflected the famous golden hue as it always has, walls now layered according to epoch, with mostly Ottoman stones on top and Roman ones at the bottom. Transversing this relatively modern configuration, jagged gashes appeared in the fabric of time, ripped open by archeologists to expose the walls going back to the 700s BCE.

It was too easy to walk over such things without comprehending them and it was too difficult to sort out the modern from the old, the old from the classical, and the classical from the truly ancient.

Most of what I heard just muddled the brain of a simple believer. Television and Sunday school had accustomed me to seeing those familiar walls complete, unbroken, and unburied, and to imagine David walking on them or Jesus arguing with the money changers in front of them. Jerusalem is Jerusalem, then and now, I'd thought.

Told that these assumed-to-be-biblical walls were built by a Turk named Solomon—"only 450 years ago, *motek*"—I was confused. What? Solomon is a Turk? "*Nu*, the Ottoman one, Süleyman the Magnificent, named after King Solomon. He ordered to rebuild the walls. Who you think makes it? What you think you see?"

I did not see at all. It was a Muslim Solomon who built Jerusalem? But why would he do that? Why was this important to any Muslim except to take something away from the Jews? And if they hate Jews so much, why did they name him Solomon, after a King of Judah?

As we explored further, I found comfort on the opposite side of the Old City. Here, things were refreshingly biblical and simple. We walked through Hezekiah's tunnel, which was built long before the Romans or the Turks were anything at all. At face value, it was a utility, a way to provide the city with water while under siege. But the tunnel was dug by dreamers, so happy to no longer live in the abyss that they would do anything to protect the heavenly city, even defy the world's greatest empire.

Thankfully, Hezekiah's tunnel meant the Bible was true and testified to its message—the whole story of how it was built is in the Bible. Walking through it, long before the days when tourists were allowed here, we saw the chisel strikes turn the other way at the point where one team of biblical engineers met its opposite. The sloshing trek once again gave me something akin to time travel; I felt very much like I was one of those workmen.

They had left an inscription where they met. "And this is the story of the tunnel," they wrote; "the axes were against each other and while three cubits were left... the voice of a man called to his counterpart... and on the day of the tunnel being finished the stonecutters struck each man towards his counterpart, ax against ax and flowed water from the source to the pool..."

On this point, the atheists were happy to indulge me. "It's history—we have records of this war from other kingdoms. We have the evidence. It is stone. This is a political reality, *motek*—this is the sovereign Jews fighting for our land and our city. This is not religion, it's facts on the ground!" Pausing to let that sink in, the point was driven home with the palm of his hand striking the stone: "This is what's important." Stone, ground, land, hard facts.

My Mi'raj

Exiting the tunnel and going north brought us again to the current walls (Turkish Solomon's walls, meaning that "current" in Jerusalem equals 450 years old). Obscured below them were the actual steps that led to the gates Jesus used to enter the Temple courtyard, sealed up since the time of Heraclius. Beyond that were structures from the first Islamic caliphate. The Romans had destroyed the city, but the first Muslims had restored a passageway through these southern gates. It was an attempt to facilitate pilgrimage to what had been the center of Jewish worship. I began to understand what we have just explored in this book—that Jerusalem was central to Islamic expectations.

I knew that, of course, but it had always seemed to be against something, not for something. The possibility that theirs was a vocation like mine did not enter into it. For the first time, I began to see that Muslims thought they were part of the Bible story—as misdirected as I thought they were, their intentions and mine agreed.

Alright, then. Time to ascend the last few hundred feet to approach the Foundation Stone, and the Holy of Holies over which Muslims built the Dome of the Rock. I had to see this abomination, this counterfeit Temple and counterfeit pilgrimage that mocked Jesus' steps. In all honesty, it spooked me: what demons lurked therein? I read Jesus' words, "So when you see the desolating sacrilege spoken of by the prophet Daniel, standing in the holy place, then let those who are in Judea flee to the mountains." What was I thinking walking right up to the thing? I was supposed to run away!

The excursion itself didn't provide any relief. Already nervous, the short walk up to the mount presented unexpected obstacles that read—at one point literally—as further warnings.

First, the venerable southern route was inaccessible in modern times, so we had to go up the ramp that climbs from the Western Wall courtyard. It presented a dramatic scene, the Wall sprouting history, faced by the prayer-fully bobbing Jewish faithful, and directly above them the golden Dome of the Rock peaking over the ledge, taunting the righteous to tear it down and rebuild the Temple.

Going up the ramp, I was challenged: "Jews are not allowed!" The objection was from a Jewish Israeli who mistook me for one of their own. He pointed to a sign: "Announcement and Warning. According to the Torah it is forbidden for any person to enter the area of the Temple Mount due to its sacredness. The Chief Rabbinate of Israel."

Insisting upon my Gentile ancestry, I pushed on to the top in the wake of shouted Hebrew skepticisms about my grandparents' religion, earning therefore the suspicion of the Arabs up top as well. Scrutiny trailed closely behind.

Once aloft, I pondered the vicissitudes of taboo. My guidebook said that from Jesus' time a similar sign has been discovered, then written in Greek. But that one was aimed at a different brand of human, this time advising non-Jews that visiting the mount was a no-no. "No foreigner shall enter within the balustrade of the Temple, or within the precinct," it reads, "and whosoever shall be caught shall be responsible for (his) death that will follow in consequence." I was judged on all accounts.

I was surprised by the size and flatness of the place. Yes, the Temple certainly did sit here; you could feel it, and it was clear to me that whatever the current name, everyone who had visited here in the past 2,000 years had felt it, too. No wonder the first Muslims built the Dome of the Rock—a building that is not a mosque and not a tomb but rather an evocation of what was and will be. The way the space was used going back at least 3,000 years has dictated to all newcomers its sanctity.

Wandering around trying to look inoffensive, I circled the structure, praying in tongues and taking deep breaths in preparation for entry into what must be, I thought, a house haunted by Satan himself. It was unseemly to feel awe in the face of such evil, but because of the unexpected breadth of the plaza, perspective played an unexpected trick, one that the Muslim architects surely counted on: the building was farther away than it appeared and therefore grew ominously in stature as it was approached. By the time I reached the entrance, it had become a formidable piece of sacred architecture, calling the eye upward in submission to Allah. I did not like that.

Entering, I could feel the awful accumulation of history that weighs on this stone—the "Rock" of the Dome. It has powers, massive and dense and capable of drawing the entire planet into its interior to be crushed and consumed back to the dust from which it came. Tradition holds that the Garden of Eden was here. The Foundation Stone is the beginning of everything and is predicted to be the end—if not of everything, at least of the phase we know as history or ordinary time. This rock presumes to destroy us and translate us to another dimension, that of eternity. Too esoteric a reading? I didn't think so then, and I don't think so now.

But the decorations that plaster the building do not depict or refer to Muhammad's visit, his famous Mi'raj. Portraiture being frowned upon in Islam, all the art here is in the form of mosaic calligraphy; hence the decor is explicit and rather preachy, and it is all about the Judgment Day, the Day of Resurrection, and the establishment of God's rule on the earth. All in all, the theme is Allah's supremacy. The inscriptions summarize the finished story, not the past; it is about the victory, not the struggle; the Dome of the Rock directs our attention to prophecies remaining to be fulfilled, not those that have already come to pass.

The closest to realistic art I could find here were the ubiquitous representations of the Tree of Life, reflecting the belief shared by all of Abraham's estranged children that this place was the location of the Garden of Eden and the beginning of Paradise restored. A nice thought betrayed by the enmity of those who believed it.

No matter, for the eye is directed upward, and hovering like a halo over the Holy of Holies, the interior calligraphy of the Dome of the Rock spits out this insult: "In the words of truth, Jesus the son of Mary... it is not conceivable that God should have taken unto Himself a son... !"[1] Told of its meaning, I could only think that no rabbi would dissent from this declaration which quotes from the Quran—or rather I should say that the Quran quotes from it, for the Dome is the first place it was written, as far as we know.

Despite those similarities, however, there can be only one carrier of Abraham's torch, and excepting for a few misguided Jews of antiquity, none believed Muhammad to be the one. This Dome is therefore to be blown up or moved, and the Third Temple built—or so I thought, and so said many Israelis, in those days.

Agog for Gog

My first encounter with Zion was an important few days that left me not so much stricken with Jerusalem Syndrome as introduced to its antidote, something real that would incubate for a number of years. I have to thank my clear-eyed kibbutz friends for jostling me from slumber. Sometimes there is nothing so truly prophetic as a Jew who has lost his faith.

I'll come back to them, as they will introduce me to Arabs for the first time and to the complexities of Israeli politics. For now, we will continue where we left off in our history and where I just arrived in mine, the Dome of the Rock and rise of Islamic civilization. We must find out how it was that a Muslim named Solomon built Jerusalem's walls.

For the most part, the 700s through the 900s was a period of gestation for the Islamic world and diminishing fortunes for the Byzantine Christians, while the European side of the Roman Empire continued its long decline. Rome remained a cultural backwater after Constantine moved the capital, and overwhelmed by the ruffian heirs to the barbarians, Europe was deep into the night of the Dark Ages.

Ever so slowly, however, Europe began to find illumination. The pivotal figure was Charlemagne, the brilliant ninth-century emperor of Rome and the Franks and "ruler of all their dominions." A fervent Christian, he converted the Saxons and held in check the Córdoba Muslims, stopping the further spread of Islam into Europe.

Charlemagne also championed classical scholarship. He especially favored the establishment of monasteries, particularly in the newly Christianized hinterlands. Hereafter, monastic centers would proliferate under the patronage of those local nobles, and their monks would become the repository of classical scholarship. For this, we must thank the Muslims. If Caliph Umar II had not rescued Greek works of science and philosophy, translating them into Arabic and preserving them in his university at Harran, they would all be lost to us. By a twist of fate, Charlemagne brought them to Europe's monasteries via Islamic Spain—a side effect of his military ventures there.

Over this time, as Europe's pagan tribes became more and more Christian, Rome gained more and more autonomy, and the eastern capital at Constantinople became more and more feeble. Finally in 1054, the Great Schism firmly divided East from West, Catholic from Orthodox. All very important, but perhaps it is not the biggest news. The headline should be that we've just passed the Millennium, a magic number that appears in John's Apocalypse.

The Millennium deserves comment: it was not like Y2K, which was awaited the world over with a calendar in one hand and a stopwatch in the other. Y1K occurred in an era of looser timekeeping, the idea of it more important than the precise agenda. Christians more or less knew that the first thousand years had passed and that it marked the end of time. This lent the concept plenty of latitude. From when is the thousand years counted? Was it the birth of Jesus or his death and resurrection? Or was it from the time the Temple was destroyed, since this was the sign that Jesus gave? The math was just smudged enough to heat up expectations and keep them simmering for a long while.

Occasionally, something would bring it to a boil, and no Millennium event generated more historical heat than the first appearance of the Turks, recent converts to Islam from the mysterious and dreaded northeastern lands thought to conceal Gog and Magog. At last, the gates of Armageddon were opened!

Armenian historian Matthew of Edessa described the scene:

When the year 467 of the Armenian era began [1018 CE] a fatal dragon with deadly fire rose up and struck those faithful to the Holy Trinity... the very foundations of the apostles and prophets were shaken. This was the first appearance of the bloodthirsty beasts. The savage nation of infidels called Turks gathered together their forces... and mercilessly slaughtered the Christian faithful with the edge of the sword.[2]

Until then, Christendom had never encountered a Turk; and as far as the Armenian defenders of Asia Minor were concerned, they may as well have come straight from the pit of hell.

For starters, Turkish military tactics were outlandish, employing a short, recurved composite bow and units of flexible mounted horsemen. The Turkish bow was state-of-the-art technology, beyond anything that Europeans had seen or could produce. It took a year to make, and by all accounts, it was extraordinarily accurate and powerful.

Turkish horsemanship baffled the Christians, too. Their ponies were small and fast, bred for the harsh terrain of the Central Asian steppes and famously hardy: they barely ate anything. Disconcertingly, Gog's warriors appeared to be one with the animal. Riding up front with their signature short stirrup and leaning forward, their long "flowing hair like women" was indistinguishable at a distance from the horse's mane; it appeared as though the barrage of stinging arrows emanated from a single hellish beast.

As if a pestilence of supernatural origin, the Turks swarmed in and fell back, vanishing, only to reappear again and again. The overall effect was mystifying. "They were like flies that could be beaten off, but not driven away," wrote one Christian warrior. Another marveled that the Turks "were to be feared while they fled, as well as when they pursued," because they were the reigning masters of the "Parthian shot," turning on their state-of-the-art stirrups and firing as they rode away.[3]

At first the Byzantines pursued—sometimes for days—too late realizing that it was a plan to exhaust them while the devilish Turks methodically cut off the rear, encircling them.

Matthew reports that after the first unhappy encounters, defeated Armenian King Senek'erim sat devastated, poring over the works of a leading interpreter of biblical prophecy. "He examined the chronicles and utterances of the divinely-inspired prophets, the holy vardapet, and found written in these books the time specified for the coming of the forces and soldiers of the Turks." Our historian dryly appends a footnote: "He also learned of the impending destruction of the whole world."

As fourth-century converts from Zoroastrianism, the Armenians may have had a particular knack for apocalyptic analysis. They certainly had a way with words. Soon their findings were tickling the ears of the pope in Rome and were being picked up by populist preachers along the way. Matthew assembled a litany of omens to prove the case for imminent Armageddon:

- 952 CE – A severe famine and plague of locusts ("numerous as the sands of the sea") devastated upper Mesopotamia. "Many went mad, and attacking one another mercilessly and savagely, devoured each other. The princes and the nobles fed upon seeds and berries."

- 997 CE – A comet appeared, "dreadful in appearance, bright and marvelous." It was reported as a "horrible and dreadful" omen.
- 1003 CE – "A certain star, appearing in the form of fire, arose in the heavens as an omen... and also a sign of the end of the world. There was a violent earthquake throughout the whole land—many thought that the day of the end of the world had arrived."
- 1003 CE – (It was a bad year.) "A plague of bulbous sores came upon the area... because of its harshness, many had no time to make their confession or take communion."
- 1022 CE – "The upper firmament of the heavens was torn apart from east to west; and thus the blue sky was cleft in two. A dazzling light fell upon the earth... and the whole land shook with a tremendous movement. Before the light abated, a horrible roaring and reverberating sound fell upon all living creatures."
- 1036 CE – "The sun darkened with a frightful and horrible appearance... The luminaries of the heavens turned gloomy and black, and the whole sky was stretched out like a vault in darkness. The mountains and all the rocks, shaken to their foundations, trembled; the vast large Mediterranean Sea, moving back and forth, billowed..."
- 1045 CE – A series of earthquakes devastated large areas. The Moon appeared red "as blood."
- 1058 CE – A toxic "red snow" fell for sixty days across northern Syria.
- 1071 CE – Last of all, and most importantly, the Turks definitively defeated Constantinople's armies.

Many of these descriptions recall natural disasters and astronomical occurrences such as earthquakes and comets, some of which are reported elsewhere. Others may not be documented but are plausible.

Does he exaggerate when he says things like the heavens "torn apart from east to west" and "the blue sky was cleft in two?" I used to think so, but then I saw cell phone footage of the relatively benign 2013 Chelyabinsk meteor strike. It perfectly fits Matthew's portrait of a tear opening in the heavens from east to west. (Go on Youtube and see for yourself.) Eyewitnesses of this meteor strike sound as spooked as Matthew. They talk about the terrifying sonic boom, imploding windows, glass flying. It damaged over

7,000 buildings, injuring over 1,000 people. Some witnesses reported feeling heat as the heaven-rending object streaked 30 kilometers above them.

A moderately larger object would produce an exponentially more dazzling effect, a blazing fire against the blue sky, and a trail of smoke leaving an open seam like a knife cutting through blue velvet. Red snow? It happens, too. The 1815 eruption of Mount Tambora in Indonesia caused red snow to fall in faraway Italy over the course of a whole year; this caused 1816 to be known as "the year without a summer."

So, these were not unprecedented events, but neither were they common. Imagine if there was a chain of astronomical or geophysical disasters near you. In spite of having scientific explanations at hand, we would still intuitively wonder, as people do: Why now? Why us? What does it mean?

To make sense of it, the Armenians turned to their leading expositor of prophecy, John Kozern. His verdict was straightforward: "Misfortune and disaster have come to all mankind, for today is the thousandth year of the imprisonment of Satan."

To make sure we understand, Kozern tutors us in the math, explaining that it is the year 1030 (not something everyone would know), and then instructing us that if we "subtract thirty years for the period before the baptism of Christ you have 1,000 years at the present."

Those natural signs, along with the Turks' bewildering appearance and prowess, matched the prose of St. John's Apocalypse, the very book that tells us about the significance of the Millennium: "I saw a star that had fallen from heaven to earth," John wrote, "from the shaft rose smoke... and the sun and the air were darkened..."

He seemed to describe the Turks, too: "locusts on the earth... like the authority of scorpions... like horses equipped for battle... their faces were like human faces, their hair like women's hair... they have tails like scorpions, with stingers..."[4]

To Christians of the tenth century, that picture was the spitting image of the long-haired Turks, who appeared to be a single piece with their indomitable horses, stinging the Christians to death like a swarm of locusts with tail-fired arrows. And the swarm just happened to pour out of the land of Magog after years of celestial and territorial fire and smoke. The Apocalypse had begun.

It was not just the Armenians who thought so. Far away in England, Wulfstan ("the Wolf"), Archbishop of York, wrote his *Sermon of the Wolf to the English*, just after the turn of the Millennium.

Beloved men, know that which is true: this world is in haste and it nears the end. And therefore, things in this world go ever the longer the worse, and so it must needs be that things quickly worsen, on account of people's sinning from day to day, before the coming of Antichrist. And indeed it will then be awful and grim widely throughout the world.[5]

Having just been warned so sternly about the coming Antichrist by the Wolf, just imagine the effect it had on his parishioners when news of the Turks reached England, just a few short years later.

Navel of the Earth

By now Charlemagne's united Europe had broken into ever smaller provincial lordships. Born and bred to battle, and despite their deepening Christian piety, they took to fighting one another. St. Augustine's carefully delineated separation of church and state was beyond the grasp of Europeans. Here, devout princes had to mete out justice ad hoc, according to tribal traditions that included honor-based blood feuds and vendettas. It was a known problem, and one that important Christian leaders wanted to solve.

This is where the specter of Magog came in handy. In 1071, the Turks had crushed the Byzantine Empire at the Battle of Manzikert, an eschatological tragedy that disposed Emperor Alexis I to call upon his European brothers for help, despite the recent schism. Pope Urban II responded spectacularly. On November 27, 1095, he called the warrior class of Europe to a holy war. It was to be pilgrimage as battle. The pope thus found a way to bring peace to Europe through a common enemy: Islam.

This was the political rationale that launched the Crusades at the Council of Clermont, but it was not divorced from an overarching vision of the End Time. Pope Urban was a sincerely God-fearing man who grew up in a troubling environment of inter-Christian violence. That the Antichrist invasion coincided with healing Christian divisions made sense to him. There was a logic to it: the days of tribulation were coming to an end, and the last battle would bring peace, first to Europe and then to the world.

He found a willing audience. The Europeans were well aware of Islam by this point, and they were acutely conscious of the Millennium. The calendar was becoming a sort of scale upon which history was weighed; each century felt heavier than the last, a phenomenon that is still with us.

Norman Cohn adroitly summarized their anxiety: "The coming of Antichrist was even more tensely awaited. Generation after generation lived in constant expectation of the all-destroying demon whose reign was indeed to be lawless chaos... but was also to be the prelude to the longed-for consummation, the Second Coming and the Kingdom of the Saints."[6]

All this is reflected in Urban's speech. Leading Crusaders remembered it as a summons to fight the last battle and, of course, Jerusalem was the heart of it: "Jerusalem is the navel of the world," Urban declared to the assembly. "This royal city... is now held captive by His enemies, and is in subjection to those who do not know God... Therefore, she seeks and desires to be liberated and does not cease to implore you to come to her aid."[7]

There is a common misconception that participants in the First Crusade were motivated by greed, but this is untrue. They were motivated by spiritual angst, the same deep desire to escape history that motivated the first villages. It was the burden of guilt and anxiety over mortality; again, a fear not so much of dying as of being dead and the fate of consciousness thereafter. Pope Urban underscores this heavily in the tagline of his speech: "Accordingly, undertake this journey for the remission of your sins, with the assurance of the imperishable glory of the kingdom of heaven."

His audience was ecstatic: they cried out, "God wills it! God wills it!" The pope, "with eyes uplifted to heaven," gave thanks to God and, lowering his hand to silence the ecstatic crowd, said, "Whoever, therefore, shall determine upon this holy pilgrimage... shall wear the sign of the cross of the Lord on his forehead, or on his breast." The reason, Urban said, was that they were by this act fulfilling "the precept of the Lord, as He commands in the Gospel, 'He that doth not take his cross and follow after me, is not worthy of me.'"

This requires a little more context. Venerable historian of the Crusades Steven Runciman summed the culture up thus:

> Medieval man was convinced that the Second Coming was at hand. He must repent while yet there was time and must go out to do good. The Church taught that sin could be expiated by pilgrimage and prophecies declared that the Holy Land must be recovered for the faith before Christ could come again... The distinction between Jerusalem and the New Jerusalem was not very clearly defined.[8]

Of Pope Urban's commission, he writes that many "believed that he was promising to lead them out of their present miseries to the land flowing with milk and honey of which the scriptures spoke. It would be hard; there were the legions of Antichrist to be overcome. But the goal was Jerusalem the golden."

This literal-mindedness may be compared to Tertullian's impassioned belief that the New Jerusalem was spotted above the earthly one. The would-be Crusaders saw signs and miracles all around them, and they were therefore vulnerable to demagogues and outlandish reports. Bear in mind, however, the serious intent with which these people led their Christian lives. These were not Sunday Christians. For them, there was no divide between secular and sacred time.

Thomas Asbridge, a fresh voice among historians of the period, stresses how important that context is to our understanding of the Crusades and Pope Urban, who grew up in a society where "the full pantheon of human experience—birth, love, anger and death—was governed by Christian dogma, and the cornerstone of this system of belief was fear." Asbridge notices our thesis of historical angst here, too. "Medieval minds were plagued by an overwhelming anxiety: the danger of sin."[9]

It was nearly inescapable. Common people were continually reminded of the consequences by blistering sermons and vividly terrifying religious art. For people who had no other visual representations—no photographs, moving pictures, or even accurate mirrors—paintings had a power that we cannot now easily conceive. The specter of eternal anxiety completely filled their imaginations.

Local rulers and knights were no exception: "Bombarded by a stream of warnings about the dreadful danger of sin, but forced to resort to soul-conta-minating violence in order to fulfill their duty and defend their rights in this lawless age, most knights were trapped in a circle of guilt, obligation and necessity."[10] There is something astonishingly modern about that assessment —the very reason for Prozac.

Pope Urban genuinely grieved for his flock, knowing they longed for absolution. This may be hard for us to grasp, but this was not the self-help religion of the modern age—sin was hard to get rid of in those days. Urban was raised in this climate, too, becoming a clergyman with the best of motives. When he promised Jerusalem and forgiveness to anyone who would take up the cross, he meant it.

No wonder, then, that warriors and knights jumped at the offer to be freed of a lifetime's accumulation of guilt. They set their houses in order and made plans for a campaign to Jerusalem. But the more flexible peasants were faster off the starting block. They beat their plowshares into swords and headed out immediately. Inspired by prophets and visionaries—most notably,

Peter the Hermit—it was these poor who filled the ranks of the First Crusade.

Some historians wonder if Peter came up with the idea in the first place. It is possible that Pope Urban simply endorsed what was already a popular movement fueled by apocalyptic literature. We may never know for sure, but the masses—numbering as many as 100,000—did get a good head start on the knights, practicing their dragon-slaying tactics on Europe's innocent Jews before making their way to the Muslims. (Both were the Antichrist as far as the Crusaders were concerned.)

When the holy warriors captured an area, they sometimes gave the residents a choice between conversion and death. One of the Crusader diarists writes, "To this camp went the pilgrim knights... and it was straight away captured by them with the aid of Christ. They took all the inhabitants of this place and killed those who were unwilling to receive Christianity. And when this had been accomplished, our Franks returned with great joy to their former camp."[11]

Cohn described these acts as devotional: "In the eyes of the crusading *pauperes* the smiting of the Moslems and the Jews was to be the first act in that final battle which... was to culminate in the smiting of the Prince of Evil himself."[12]

I'll spare you the gory details of the three-year campaign and jump ahead to the final battle. On July 15, 1099, the Crusaders breached the walls of Jerusalem. Mad with millenarian zeal, they hacked down every Muslim they encountered—man, woman, and child—and then, driving all the Jews into the synagogue, they burned it. Hardly a single Jew or Muslim was left alive in the city.

I will now quote at length the eyewitness report of Raymond of Aguilers. It is, I think, important to hear these words because of their modern resonance, speaking as they do of Jerusalem's capture by the army of God and the wonders of beheading and burning alive infidels. The actions of holy warriors 1,000 years ago appear identical to those of today's holy warriors:

> But now that our men had possession of the walls and towers, wonderful sights were to be seen. Some of our men (and this was more merciful) cut off the heads of their enemies; others shot them with arrows, so that they fell from the towers; others tortured them longer by casting them into the flames. Piles of heads, hands, and feet were to be seen in the streets of the city.

But these were small matters compared to what happened at the Temple of Solomon, a place where religious services are ordinarily chanted. What happened there? If I tell the truth, it will exceed your powers of belief. So let it suffice to say this much, at least, that in the Temple and porch of Solomon, men rode in blood up to their knees and bridle reins. Indeed, it was a just and splendid judgment of God that this place should be filled with the blood of the unbelievers, since it had suffered so long from their blasphemies.

One Little Word

Despite filling the Temple Mount with apocalyptic blood, the conquest was not met with Christ's appearance. And of the numerous other millenarian outbreaks to follow this first Crusade, few would be of lasting significance. Norman Cohn is recommended to the reader who would like to know more; for us it will be enough to focus on a few links in the historical chain, and the first substantial one is to be forged by Martin Luther.

Like most in his time, Luther believed he lived in the End Time, and had plenty of evidence to support his views. Waves of plague swept through European cities; the Catholic Church, the only source of eternal security, was ethically calloused; and the Turks, regarded still as the vanguard of the Antichrist, were pounding at the gates of European Christendom.

By Luther's time, the long-haired nomads had seized the authority of the caliphate and settled into civilized splendor. The definitive moment came in 1453, when the Turkish Ottomans conquered Constantine's city, converting the first and greatest church, Hagia Sophia, into a mosque. Soon, the Ottomans had Mecca and Jerusalem, too. They placed Muhammad's sword, mantle, and banner in the nearby Topkapi Palace to signify that this was now unequivocally Islam's capital.

Until modern times, Constantinople (Turkish Istanbul) remained the seat of the caliphate, which in Luther's day extended across half of Europe. The future hinged upon Vienna, which the Muslims besieged in 1529 in a heated war that lasted some 150 years. With plague, apostasy, and the Antichrist part of everyday experience, life was lived with spiritual urgency. Luther's was no exception. We can feel the portent in the words of his most renowned hymn, "A Mighty Fortress is Our God," a clarion poem forged in the fires of spiritual warfare:

A mighty fortress is our God, a bulwark never failing;
    Our helper He, amid the flood of mortal ills prevailing.

> For still our ancient foe doth seek to work us woe;
> his craft and pow'r are great, and armed with cruel hate, on earth is not
> his equal.

In the face of the craft, power, and cruel hatred of the enemy, we might expect Luther to follow Peter the Hermit and Simon Bar Kokhba down the militant path against "our ancient foe." But even "amid the flood of mortal ills," Luther went another way. To the perennial question of whether Paradise is restored through one final apocalyptic act of redemptive violence, Luther said no; salvation is by grace.

Anyone who has heard of Martin Luther knows him for this message if they know anything at all. We can appreciate it even more because this was not an obvious time to preach grace. To the contrary, it was a time when wars of religion dominated world events—and for that reason, too, his teaching is particularly relevant to our time. Whatever we face today, Luther faced it at closer quarters, including having what he believed to be the armies of the Antichrist just over the horizon. Others took that as a justification to become God's warriors. Luther saw God's mercy as the only solution.

We usually think of grace as a matter of personal salvation, but what this means in a sociopolitical setting is apparent in Luther's approach to the Turks. His teaching warns against self-assumed righteousness and the hubris of self-deliverance, a message addressed to personal faith, but also fundamental to political behavior. Self-deliverance is the creed of holy warriors. They choose violence to make the day of salvation happen at their behest. When the principle that one cannot save oneself is spread to the political realm, it transforms the way any conflict is handled.

Grace, however, is not soft—it is tough. It does not mean coddling delusions of redemptive violence in others. Often, modern concerns for human rights turn into a perverse self-righteousness, where we condemn regressive behavior in our own group but defend it in another. For example, excusing militancy in an oppressed group, or allowing for religious violence because a group is a minority and perhaps therefore exempt from our own standard of not resorting to violence. I've seen this many times among colleagues who promote the highest criticism of Judea-Christian beliefs and practices but who would not dare to question Muslims who hold fundamentalist views.

Luther did not have this problem. God's grace did not mean that Luther had to endorse Islam. He might have celebrated the fellowship of humanity, but he remained convinced of Islam's intentions to subdue Christians and wrote extensively about Gog and Magog, persuaded that the Turks fulfilled those prophecies: "I believe that the Turk's Allah does more in war than they themselves. He gives them courage and wiles; he guides sword and fist, horse and man."[13]

That Luther felt this way makes his studied disavowal of violence and self-deliverance all the more convincing. It shows the possibility of holding strongly opposing beliefs without resorting to coercion or hateful behavior. "The Turks are certainly the last and most furious raging of the devil against Christ... After the Turk comes the judgment," Luther wrote. Yet he did not see this as a justification for acts of Christian political domination.

"A Mighty Fortress" reveals the key—the battle and the deliverance were not in human hands:

> Did we in our own strength confide, our striving would be losing;
>> Were not the right Man on our side,
>> The man of God's own choosing.
>> Dost ask who that may be?
>> Christ Jesus, it is He! Lord Sabaoth is His Name,
>> From age to age the same; And he must win the battle...

A spiritual battle, in Luther's conception, assumes that all parties are utterly dependent on the gift of grace. If Christians were saved from the demonic possession that drove the Muslims in battle, it was only by the grace of the "Man on our side." And by virtue of the universality of Christian beliefs, that "Man" was also on the side of the Turks. All were dependent on grace in the end, and the eschatological war was only to be won through the Word of God with salvation for all:

> And tho' this world, with devils filled, should threaten to undo us;
>> We will not fear, for God hath willed His truth to triumph thro' us.
>> The Prince of Darkness grim—We tremble not for him;
>> His rage we can endure, For lo, his doom is sure,
>> One little word shall fell him.

It's not just in the hymn, of course. Luther was methodically critical of the Crusader mentality, preaching specifically that the Crusaders confused fleshly and spiritual realms. Because it was such a hot topic in those days (Pope Leo X was vigorously advocating for a huge crusade), Luther put it on paper for wide dissemination, writing two tracts, *On War Against the Turk* and

Military Sermon Against the Turk, in 1529–30, at the beginning of the Turkish siege of Vienna.

His explicit purpose was to lay out the errors of Crusading to establish for his followers a dividing wall between the Christian as a person of faith and the Christian as a subject of state power. As a citizen, one might be obliged to fight the Turks because the principality was justifiably at war in defense of the realm, said Luther; but a Christian could not fight as a Christian against a Muslim. It could not by any means be a holy war.

Fudging of this issue was not tolerated: Luther said that there could be absolutely no Christian justification for civilian military enterprises, not even against the devil-inspired Turks. Sovereign state or monarchal power was not permitted to pose as the Kingdom of Heaven or even claim its endorsement in war. Luther believed that for the Church or its leaders to foment military action was to invite the wrath of God, going so far as to argue that soldiers had the moral obligation to disobey orders if called to fight in a holy war or told that their action was demanded by God.

He took this stance not because he felt a lack of urgency. Luther, one of the pivotal historical figures of the past 500 years, saw his reformation as an eschatological event, and was not shy about describing it as such, believing that his generation was at war with the Antichrist. It's just that he saw it more like Zoroaster did: a war between Truth and Lie in the human mind and heart.

"One little word shall fell him" was essentially the Reformation's Armageddon thesis. Along with the explosion of Protestantism, it would grow into the next big Christian thing, a global missionary movement through which the earth was to be subdued—not by the sword, but by preaching. Over the next 400 years, the eschatological framework primarily hung on the proclamation of the Word.

Historians often call this idea "amillennialism" or "postmillennialism," meaning that the 1,000-year reign of Christ described in John's Revelation is already underway through the proclamation of the Gospel. Postmillennialist evangelism is an impassioned effort to preach the Gospel to every tribe, tongue, people, and nation to fulfill the conditions for Christ's return. It is as vividly millenarian as the Crusades or Bar Kokhba's rebellion, but it is purely a battle for hearts and minds.

In brief, Christians believed that as the saints preached the Gospel, more and more of the world would be included in the Kingdom of God. The *Evangelical Dictionary of Biblical Theology* provides a handy consensus:

Such activity will result in a more godly, peaceful, and prosperous world... Evil will not be eliminated during the millennium, but it will be reduced to a minimum as the moral and spiritual influence of Christians is increased... This period is not necessarily limited to a thousand years, because the number can be used symbolically. The millennium closes with the second coming of Christ, the resurrection of the dead, and the last judgment.[14]

At times the push to evangelize the world expressed itself counter to Lutheran wisdom; the expansion of the Gospel was enhanced by the sword and by authoritarianism. In America and Africa, the Gospel went hand-in-hand with colonial violence and exploitation—the divide between church and sovereign power was paper-thin. There is an echo of this when even the best-intentioned missionaries intuitively call their efforts a "crusade," as did the great Hudson Taylor, founder of the China Inland Mission, and John Mott, the founder of the influential Christian Student Movement. But despite this cozy relationship between empire and church, none of this was really a crusade. Luther's dividing wall held.

It helped that Jerusalem was not a factor. From the mid-1500s to the mid-1800s, missionary efforts were directed away from the center, away from Jerusalem, to the unevangelized and bedeviled ends of the earth—the heathens of the Americas and Africa and the exotically deceived peoples of Asia. But as Christian efforts pushed ever closer to accomplishing the Great Commission, thoughts inevitably turned again to Jerusalem, the place where it all began, and the place where it was expected to end.

Muslim Solomon

Luther's century was pivotal. He was born in 1483. Süleyman the Magnificent, the presiding Islamic caliph and leader of what Luther called "the devil's raging," was born in 1494. As I learned on my first visit to Jerusalem, Süleyman was named after biblical King Solomon, and it was he who built the city's famed walls. That was made possible by Süleyman's father, the terrifically named Selim the Grim, who unified Mecca, Jerusalem, and Constantinople, giving him possession of the caliphal artifacts and control of all that was holy. This made Selim the undisputed caliph and successor to Muhammad, a right passed down to his successors until 1924.

No wonder Luther thought it was the End Time—it was Süleyman's great-grandfather, Mehmed the Conqueror, who took Constantinople from Christian hands, turning the great Hagia Sophia church into a mosque. It became nothing but a sign of submission to Islam, the religion of the Antichrist, for "He is antichrist who denies the Father and the Son," wrote John the Apostle. As we saw, those very words are xeroxed in the Dome of the Rock as the first example of Quranic writing. Half of Europe fell, too. The end was undoubtedly at hand.

These developments had no less impact in the Islamic world, where Muslims viewed the same events as their completion of Muhammad's task of preparing the world for Jesus' return. Especially important was the reunification, which brought the three Muslim holy cities under the restored caliphate. As Muslims believed the Dome of the Rock to be a restoration of Solomon's Temple, the new, young, "Magnificent" Solomon knew full well what his duty was. To fulfill prophecy and prepare for the Judgment Day, he'd have to live up to his name by restoring Jerusalem to its full former glory.

Gülru Necipoğlu, a highly awarded Turkish scholar and expert on Islamic architecture, addresses this subject with aplomb. Her study of the Dome of the Rock shows how Süleyman's work in Jerusalem was indeed motivated by the fast-approaching Day of Judgment, pointing out in detail the way millennial dates cast their magic spell over the caliph and his subjects.[15]

What millennium, you ask? Isn't this the 1500s approaching? Not for Muslims; their calendar dates from Anno Hegirae (AH), the year of Muhammad's migration from Mecca to Medina. So this really was the tenth and final century of the Muslim era, the time when a messianic final caliph was supposed to conquer the world and prepare it for Judgment Day. Süleyman ascended the throne in 926 AH and ruled until 973 AH. Furthermore, Muslims had a plethora of signs to go along with the magical date—the same signs that worried Martin Luther and the Christians.

Make no mistake, Süleyman's name is not coincidental. The associations I've made between Süleyman and King David's son appeared obvious to his contemporaries, too. Prominent inscriptions explicitly call him "the second Solomon," linking his work on the Temple Mount with the Temple's original Jewish builder. Süleyman dedicated his life to this task, pouring his energy, wealth, and time into the city, sprucing it up for Jesus and Israfil's imminent arrival.

An inscription left to honor Süleyman at Jerusalem's Tower of David illuminates the picture nicely:

The order to restore this noble fortress was given by the great Sultan... the possessor of the necks of the nations, the patron of the people of the sword and the pen, the servitor of the Two Harams [Mecca and Medina] and the Most Holy Precinct [Jerusalem's Temple Mount], may God sanctify... the source of security, and faith, and safety, the Sultan, son of the House of Osman, the second Solomon, may god prolong his existence as long as the duration of the dome over the Rock!

He was also "the caliph resplendent with divine glory who performs the command of the hidden book and executes its decrees" and "possessor of the kingdoms of the world, shadow of God over all peoples..." That's quite something.

As Necipoğlu notes, "The tenth and foremost ruler of the House of Osman thus claims to be the divinely appointed messianic renewal of religion and justice in the tenth and last century of the Muslim era, Süleyman continued until the end of his life to refurbish the Dome of the Rock, which marked the future site of the Last Judgment."

As I've said, European Christians were as vexed by all this as the Muslims were hopeful, and it rang a clarion bell for Jews, too, as we shall understand presently, for Süleyman protected them in his empire, saving them from the ravages of antisemitic Europe.

It was 1492—that date of primary-school import—when Spain and Portugal expelled the Jews in a frenzy. No one else in Europe wanted them either. To European Christians, the Jews were part of the Antichrist spirit, along with Muslims; even Martin Luther turned on them when they failed to convert to his reformed Christianity.

Friendless among Christians, Süleyman's grandfather took them all in without reservation. As the *Jewish Encyclopedia* says, the Sultan "ridiculed the foolish conduct of Ferdinand and Isabella of Spain" who "impoverished his own country and enriched mine!" He ordered his governors "not only to refrain from repelling the Spanish [Jewish] refugees, but to give them a friendly and welcome reception. He threatened with death all those who treated the Jews harshly or refused them admission into the empire."[16]

Well then! It makes sense that Jews thought of him and his progeny as a new Cyrus. Writing in Hebrew in 1523, noted historian and scholar Rabbi Eliyahu Capsali expresses the sentiments common among Jews of this time: he wrote that the caliph fulfilled prophecy as the ruler of the final world empire, that God was regathering the Jews to Jerusalem where they would await the Messiah, and that he would restore them to the Holy Land by way of Istanbul. He wrote of Süleyman, "He is the tenth king of the Turks, and the tenth one shall be holy to the Lord; in his days Judah shall be delivered and a redeemer shall come to Zion."[17]

Not that I knew any of this when I first learned about Süleyman's walls. Curiosity piqued, I started asking kibbutzniks questions about history and faith. What did it mean that my irreligious kibbutzniks connected with Jerusalem as a nakedly and harshly political piece of geography—an exercise of ethnic will? Or that Süleyman, a Muslim, dedicated his life to it as a man of faith? He devoted everything to readying the city for the return of Jesus, whom he regarded as the Messiah. How could I fault him for that?

Bringing up the Turks, I got an odd answer one day as I chatted with a person whose parents came to Israel from Turkey. My friend told me that he and his family were Sephardic "Spanish" Jews. Their family went to Istanbul in 1492 after being driven from their homeland by Christians. Because of the date, I asked jokingly if it had anything to do with Columbus. To my shock, they said yes, of course it did.

1492

1492. Columbus. "Don'joo know this, *motek*?"

This is what I did not know: In 1492, Columbus sailed the ocean blue... and Queen Isabella sent packing all the Jews.

This was my new nursery rhyme. Actually, it was March 31, 1492, when King Ferdinand and Queen Isabella issued their edict against them. It was a choice: convert or be gone within four months. Many converted; they were known then as "conversos." Others converted as a sham and practiced Judaism in secret—the "marranos."

There is some evidence that Columbus was one of the latter. His private correspondence bears Hebrew letters, invocations that only pious Jews would use or know about. In his will, he instructed his descendants henceforth to use a Jewish symbol as their family sign. His legacy included a tithe of all his assets to support the poor (a Jewish custom). Also, Columbus sailed on August 3, 1492, having delayed a day from the originally scheduled departure, which was Tisha B'Av on the Jewish calendar, the date of the Temple's destruction and a day of mourning. It was also the week that any non-converting Jews had to leave Spain.

Coincidence? Not when we consider that the venture was provided for by three wealthy Jews. Columbus' first report of finding land was to these men, not to the Crown. Two were conversos, Louis de Santangel and Gabriel Sanchez; the third was Rabbi Isaac ben Judah Abravanel, who made himself extraordinarily wealthy as a royal financier. He has been called "the greatest codifier of messianism in his day."[18] As such, he was one of the begetters of what is now Religious Zionism or political messianism among Israelis. Abravanel therefore had a huge impact on the modern world through Columbus in America and Jewish settlers in Palestine, both exercises in repossessing land for God's kingdom, and two historical phenomena that resemble one another because of their shared paternity.

Interesting stuff, but it doesn't mean Columbus himself was a Jew. What it does mean without a doubt is that the explorer sympathized with a Jewish ambition. Actually, his motivation is not in question—he fully believed that his generation lived in the Last Days, and he publicly committed his life to fulfilling prophecies concerning Jerusalem. I wonder if he was like many Christians I've known, so steeped in the End Time as to adopt Jewish symbols and customs as their own. Columbus' Jewish signage could be something like that—an End Time–obsessed Christian's homage to the Chosen People.

How obsessed was he? Columbus pitched his voyage to Queen Isabella as an attempt to reach the Far East, where he hoped to find the legendary Great Khan. The widespread belief was that this mythical figure had repeatedly sent messages to the West for instruction in the Christian faith. He ruled a great empire as the head of a huge army. Columbus, along with most of Europe, believed that once converted, the Great Khan would join Christians at Jerusalem, defeat the Muslims, and destroy the Dome of the Rock. It was exactly this plan that Columbus presented to the queen.[19]

Bear in mind that Columbus spent his life up to this point fighting Muslims. Although the Turks would be good to the Jews, Columbus and his patrons could not know this when he sailed to the West hoping to find the East. He died decades before Rabbi Capsali wrote his tribute to the Ottomans. The Jews' immediate fate was unknown as Columbus left home, departing in the same fateful week—in many ways, just one of them.

There should be no surprise that Columbus was essentially an anti-Muslim Crusader. Our shock comes from a failure of educators to cover what's important in history. The fact is, Columbus' long career as a holy warrior against Islam was not unusual in the fifteenth and sixteenth centuries when this was the most important political struggle in Europe. Everyone— yes, everyone—saw it as an End Time war. As Yale historian Alan Mikhail writes, "The Ottoman Empire, contrary to nearly all conventional accounts of world history, was the very reason Europe went to America."[20] Mikhail further summarizes the history, writing that "Christopher Columbus crossed the seas in hopes of funding a new Crusade to retake Jerusalem. His project was the culmination of a long career battling Muslims as a man who firmly believed he lived in the last days."

Lest there is any remaining doubt, Columbus reiterates this purpose on the first page of his ship's logbook—he explicitly dedicates the voyage to the purpose described above. His crew included Arabic and Hebrew speakers, which would be needed to accomplish the venture—remembering, of course, that he thought he was heading to Asia, and that he would march with this army onward to Jerusalem.[21]

As we know, that didn't work out so well. There was that whole new continent in the middle of it all, a fact that actually took some time for him to digest. After much strife and turmoil, Columbus returned to Europe where he lived to complete his life-long project: not a voyage, but a compendium of End Time literature, *The Book of Prophecies*. He began it in earnest as a young man, scouring the prophetic scriptures and biblical genealogies to determine exactly when the end would come. Naturally, he calculated it would be very soon.[22]

I said it should be no surprise, but I confess that I am still astonished by all this. Columbus was not only a holy warrior, but the author of an apocalyptic book that would not be equaled until the evangelicals put their pens to the task in the twentieth century. Moreover, his legacy in America bore his philosophical mark for centuries and those evangelicals are part of it. Columbus' ideas of holy war affected the length and breadth of the settlement of the Americas.

I heartily recommend your reading Professor Mikhail's fine book on Ottoman-European relations if you want details and examples. In the meantime, I can summarize it like this: The dream of America as a relay point on the road to Paradise did not die with Columbus. It lingered on in the ideas of the Spanish conquistadors and then again in the Puritan colonists.

Going forward, Americans couldn't help but to see themselves as a vector of God's redemptive purposes. They were Joshua in Canaan. One such early advocate of America's place in the holy scheme articulated a point of view that remains current and politically potent in our time. He was none other than Harvard's sixth president, the Reverend Dr. Increase Mather, author of *The Mystery of Israel's Salvation*.

The First Shall Be Last

FROM THE DESK OF THE PRESIDENT OF HARVARD UNIVERSITY: "ONE OF those great and glorious things which the world, especially, the people of God in the world, are in expectation of at this day, is, The general conversion of the Israelitish Nation."[23]

The Rev. Dr. Mather wrote *The Mystery* in 1669. In those days, America's pioneers thought of New England as a second Promised Land, and they did not mean it poetically. This was a serious business. Puritan America was to be the New Jerusalem, a "city upon a hill" in the words of founding pilgrim John Winthrop.[24]

It's an idea that stuck: American history is saturated with it. To this day, Winthrop's words are quoted by American politicians and preachers. Presidents Kennedy, Reagan, and Obama invoked Winthrop's "city on a hill" at pivotal moments. The purpose is to remind Americans of their special calling and responsibility. The Puritans likened their experience to Israel's deliverance from Egypt. Europe was Egypt's godless land of false religion, and the New World was the Promised Land where God's kingdom would be fully realized. From here, the Gospel would be preached in purity and all the nations would learn the ways of the Lord. In other words, America was an exact parallel and partner to eschatological Israel.

This vision might have fit postmillennialism's progressive salvation well. But Mather did not focus on the gradual effect of Gospel yeast in the dough. Instead, he saw increasing evil. The millennium of Christ, he thought, is not an incremental process of enlightenment through preaching, but an emerging crisis between light and darkness to which history is leading.

The decisive marker was the Jews. According to Mather's reading of the Bible, they would first be regathered to the Promised Land and then be saved, accepting Jesus as the Messiah. After that, the Antichrist would be defeated and only then would Christ descend to commence his 1,000-year reign in person in a physical, temporal Jerusalem. This scenario is therefore called premillennialism, because Christ's earthly millennium will begin only after the crisis. Emphatically, then, it is not a progressive redemption through Christ's teaching; it is a victory after a decisive battle. That distinction is all-important.

While Mather and his ilk still believed in preaching the Gospel to the nations, the task would be completed only after the Jews returned to Jerusalem. "There is indeed a fulness of the Gentiles, which shall be after the conversion of the Jews," he assures us. "In bringing in which fullness, the saved Tribes of Israel, shall be very instrumental..." Here he means that the completion of the Great Commission ("the fulness of the Gentiles") will require the help of these newly enlightened Jews living in Zion. This is no reason to stop preaching to the nations, however: "But there is also a fullness of the Gentiles, which shall precede the Jews' conversion." In other words, keep preaching the Gospel to the nations, but understand that it won't be complete until the Jews are back in Israel and saved—keep your eye on the Jews as you go about your missionary work.

In his arguments, Mather culls verses from Ezekiel, Daniel, Revelations, and Luke's Gospel. The simplest and most graphic of these is Ezekiel's vision of the dry bones, which envisions redemption as an anti-entropic process, reversing the subjective experience of time like a film playing backwards. It's a psychedelic trip—scattered bones come together into skeletons, then lifeless flesh appears on the bones; finally, it all comes to life through the breath of God. Mather, unaware of the possibility that Ezekiel used hallucinogens, asks us to read this as literally as possible, which is to accept that the prophet is talking about the politically sovereign nation of Israel, just as Ezekiel says: "Mortal, these bones are the whole house of Israel."

The literal specifics of Ezekiel's words are there for all to read: "I will bring you back to the land of Israel. And you shall know that I am the LORD... I will put my spirit within you, and you shall live, and I will place you on your own soil..."[25]

Mather's literalism found encouragement in rumors that Jews were already returning to Palestine. (These began when followers of Ottoman Messiah candidate Sabbatai Zevi prepared to return to Zion in the 1650s–60s. Plans were thwarted when the "Messiah" converted to Islam.) Mather cites "constant reports from sundry places" saying "the Israelites were upon their journey towards Jerusalem." This must be, he argued, a current fulfillment "of that Prophesy concern ing the noise and shaking, and coming together of those dry bones... which was preparatory to that which followeth..." That which followeth was in the next verses, in Ezekiel's detailed description of the new heaven and Earth—Paradise.

From the Gospel of Luke, Mather quotes Jesus regarding the prophetic destiny of the Jews:

> And they shall fall by the edge of the sword, and shall be led away captive into all nations: and Jerusalem shall be trodden down of the Gentiles, until the times of the Gentiles be fulfilled... When ye see these things... know ye

that the kingdom of God is nigh at hand... This generation shall not pass away, till all be fulfilled.[26]

Thus the definitive sign of the end is to see Jerusalem no longer trodden down by Gentile occupiers. To Mather, that meant booting the Gentiles out. His pamphlets predict a joint Christian-Jewish war against the Turkish Muslims who were the Gentiles du jour.

The hard foundation for all this is Mather's literalism. He did not believe in allegory. "If Men allow themselves this Liberty of Allegorizing, we may at last Allegorize Religion into nothing but Fancy, and say that the Resurrection is past already." His is the slippery-slope thesis of religious fundamentalism —confusing nervous priggishness with faith. He is adamant that "in the Interpretation of Scripture we may not depart from the Literal Sense" lest we "make Allegories where there are none" and impose "our own Imaginations instead of Scripture."

That means any promise about Israel's restoration anywhere in the Bible has to be a political one. In case we miss his meaning, professor Mather repeats his conclusion: "The time will surely come, when the body of the twelve Tribes of Israel shall be brought out of their present condition of bondage and misery, into a glorious and wonderful state of salvation, not only spiritual but temporal."[27]

Mather's temporal literalism might not have caught on—he was in the minority when he wrote this. But over the next two centuries, scientific materialism spooked preachers to such an extent that Mather's extreme biblical literalism appeared as a bulwark, a kind of alternative science. It was a false choice, but lazy minds took the easy way out—Mather's approach was dead simple.

Ironically, the scientific revolution was spurred on principally by other Puritans and their close associates. Modern science was incubated in Britain's Royal Society by Bible-believing Protestants who had cast off the fetters and meddling of church and king. It was their Protestantism that allowed them to think freely, unencumbered by the ecclesiastical interference that stifled early pioneers like Copernicus and Galileo.

The most important of these was Sir Isaac Newton. What is astonishing, however, is that this cornerstone of the scientific method was a dedicated millenarian: "the Gospel must first be preached in all nations before the great tribulation and end of the world," wrote the father of modern physics.[28] This is the man who gave us calculus, upon whom NASA relied to go to the moon, upon whose shoulders every physicist and engineer stands today.

Moreover, it is worth noting that Newton was not merely a millenarian, but a passionate aficionado of the apocalyptic. In the prime of his life, while tending to his scientific research, he nonetheless penned thousands of pages breaking down history in terms of biblical prophecy and diagraming mathematically precise graphs to describe his conclusions. My favorite illustrates the progression of the Seven Trumpets of Revelation as historical phases superimposed over Jerusalem trod underfoot by the Gentiles and other complex factors, like some kind of occult polynomial equation.[29]

Despite Newton's example, poorly schooled theologians felt under attack by science. Most frightening of all was Darwinism. The response was to defend the Bible as Mather did by trying to make it an encyclopedia. The Bible was no longer allowed to be a spiritual revelation; it was made to be a collection of facts. This was an unnecessary envy of scientific studies. Over time, science turned more and more mysterious with the discovery of the quantum realm while Bible scholars became more and more concrete.

Biblical literalism thus grew in opposition to science because of a lack of faith in its own metaphysical premise. Newton, of course, knew better. He understood that such an antithesis was false and unnecessary, that science and allegory were both interpretations of reality. His intellectual great-grandchildren concur: as science has moved beyond mechanics, physicists confirm that reality can only be approximated by human language via allegory and metaphor—admitting that, on this level, mathematics is itself a language at best. An allegorical Bible, it turns out, suits the purpose of describing truth quite well.

Perhaps this happy relationship between fact and truth, science and transcendent perception, will be more widely restored someday. Until then, we live with the legacy of Increase Mather, whose ideas grew over the next three centuries, coming to dominate, oppress, and threaten the entire human race.

Matt. 24.15.

Isaac Newton is the archetypal scientist. Engineering, flight, space travel, electronics, and more, all depend on his discoveries.

But just as important to him: studying eschatology. Pages from his notebooks show a an abiding concern for solving the puzzles of Daniel's prophecies. We read references to the "seventy weeks of years" and the "prophecy of the seventy weeks."

On other pages he refers to King Herod's messianic claims, "the Jews who took Herod for the Messiah..."

His goal in this work was to determine our place in prophetic history so that we might be better prepared for the Second Coming of Jesus.

For Isaac Newton this too was the stuff of mathematics and physics.

The Land — The People.

Hon. Woodrow Wilson,
     President of the United States,
          Washington, D. C.

Dear Mr. Wilson:

          Congratulations and best wishes for the __________ ____ __
Presidency of th   W. W. #3.

          It was
in the presentat
for the Jews".
mit of a trip En
present the Memo
October, but was

          It wou
signatures of th
this was so evid
of the Presbyter
Methodists and B
ficials, evidenc
our entire popul

          Pardon
I sought the sig
his Campaign Hea
Mr. Willcox, as

          The ne
the Memorial and
think I ought to
want to sign a p

          I was
the President of
And I was grieve
people in Europe
Immediately I th
bless Abraham (a

          During the whole of this campaign, since that time, there has
been no question in my mind as to who would be our next President.

          And now I would emphasize that there is no surer way of your
being unerringly led in the difficult task, which is still upon you,
at the helm of our Nation, in the maelstrom of difficulties which are
arising, than to evidence determinedly your sympathy for suffering
Israel, by such proper use of your official position and influence, as
may show your own and the combined kind interest of our Nation in God's
ancient people, and the recovery of their predestined Palestinian Home.

          Dear Mr. Wilson, may I add, that it seems convincingly clear
from the prophetic Scriptures, that the world is on the verge of unprecedented horrors; that either this winter or the coming spring, the
warring nations of Europe, with the exception of Russia, will be
plunged into a synchronous governmental destruction, and that all next
summer and the following winter a perfect pandemonium and chaos will
prevail, and that this will result in an entirely new form of government
for all of the large territory, embracing Persia, Turkey, all the North
of Africa, and everything in Europe South of the Rhine and the Danube,
to be governed by ten co-existant kings.

          A marvelous sphere of usefulness seems clearly predicted for
our Nation as God's chosen instrument in these last days. Just as surely as God raised up Cyrus to befriend His ancient people, in the days of
Persia's supremacy, so I believe, has he raised up you, for leadership
of our Nation in this crux of opportunity. And just so sure as you
are true to God's Word and His purposes revealed therein, will you be
supernaturally upheld and guided to bring blessing, not only to Israel,
but to the whole world.

          Assuring you of my constant prayers, I am very respectfully,

               Your obedient servant,

                    Wm. E. Blackstone

William Blackstone published *Jesus is Coming* in 1878.

Selling in the millions, and translated into dozens of languages, his book convinced many that the End Time was at hand.

Blackstone was well-connected. Supported by bankers like J.P. Morgan and allied with liberal Jewish Supreme Court Justice, Louis D. Brandeis, Blackstone encouraged progressive icon President Woodrow Wilson's support of Zionism.

It was not a hard sell: Wilson already saw himself as a God-ordained leader set to bring the Kingdom of God to earth through social reform and a transformation of the international order.

Thus, the founders of modern American progressive politics felt right at home with End Time Zionism.

❧ 14 ❧

TWENTIETH-CENTURY
CRUSADE

Donkeys and Chickens

As a teenager at Caesarea Philippi, picturing the likes of Herod and the Roman-influenced Jews there, I'd begun to make sense of my experience. The more I reflected on Jews in Roman times, the more clearly I understood what living in modern Israel entailed. This was not the Holy Land, not yet. But it hadn't been for Jesus, either.

The kibbutzniks I lived with were like those panolepsy-stricken Jews reveling at Herod's northern palace. My colleagues, even my Hebrew teacher who knew everything about the Bible, were atheists down to the last man. Apart from a few exceptions, they were materialistic, crass, and inclined toward debauchery. No problem. Jesus dealt with similar relationships all the time. I was happy with the situation.

I could think about Jesus and his dealings with sinners and tax collectors. They were still Jews, weren't they? It wasn't just the Pharisees who were Jews. What does it mean, after all, to be a Jew? Is it a religion or an ethnicity? It is both, I figured, but not always simultaneously. Certainly, not all Jews believe in God or the Bible. Neither were they all like Mel Brooks and Oscar Levant, the Jews of my childhood, bon vivant wits and icons of urban sophistication. The kibbutzniks were, by and large, none of these things—neither pious nor urbane—but they were Jews fulfilling God's promises despite themselves.

My kibbutz Jews did have faith, however; it just wasn't in God. Instead, they believed in redemptive labor, the hammer and the sickle. The first lesson during my kibbutz orientation was pure Marxism: "From each according to his ability, to each according to his need." That's all right, I thought. The prophets promised that the returning Jews would make "the desert blossom as the rose," so surely the socialist labor ideal was part of the plan.

Apparently my social "ability" was to clean giant pots and pans. I pulled this assignment for a straight month before moving on to the biblically inspired roses. (I learned later that it was not a hazing: I really was the best pot-scrubber they'd seen—only their Marxian sense of equality saved me from permanent confinement to the kitchen.)

When told about Columbus perhaps being a Jew, I thought, well, at least he seems to have understood the plan. My kibbutz friends certainly did not. End Time? Nonsense! Jesus? A despicable fraud! No, young man, we are here to create an existential statement; it has nothing to do with God.

Or did it? In the next breath I was likely to hear that God was out to get them. He allowed the Holocaust! God turned his back on us! It was the kind of atheism that says, "I hate you! You're not my daddy anymore!"

Feeling defensive of Israel, they tried to reassure me. They told me there were Israelis who thought like I did. Settlers and Religious Zionists were more like me, they said, but they won't like me because they despise Jesus.

"By the way, they don't really like us, either. The Religious Zionists came to the land believing that people like us are donkeys," a coworker explained.

This thought was delivered with unintended poignancy during a break from our laborious task of the day: chicken harvesting. If you've never done it, imagine yourself in a building the size of a football field. It has been sealed shut for months while baby chicks ate and shat their way into plump adulthood—until today, when the lights were turned on in full so as to disorient the creatures. As the doors were flung open, our team stepped in (assigned on rotation to a job no one wanted). The task was to get six chickens at a time by grabbing one leg, slotting it between two fingers, and then grabbing another leg of another chicken, slotting it between the next fingers, and so on. With the birds thus seized, they were to be stuffed together in a cage (don't break the legs or the wings!) and hauled off for processing.

OK, the donkey thing makes sense. This was donkey work. Something about packing live chickens to feed the children of Israel was as much a fulfilled prophecy as any assent to correct dogma. Still, I needed some details. How exactly are you a donkey?

"The Messiah's donkey," a workmate chimed in. "The Messiah will come on a donkey. We are it. That's what religious people think of us. They think you are, too. You Christians support Israel in politics and with dollars. This is why they tolerate you here."

It had to do with those dry bones of Ezekiel. Rather than a single messianic event, redemption would come in stages and through uncomprehending hands, like these non-observant Jews or Christians in America, or even me. OK, I was delighted to be the Messiah's donkey.

I later learned that it was Rabbi Avraham Isaac Kook, the Ashkenazi Chief Rabbi in Palestine, who anointed secular Zionism as an act of God, in effect recognizing the godless labors of the kibbutznik as part of the Lord's plan to restore and redeem Israel. He taught that all Zionists are part of redemption, whether they recognize God or not. It was Kook who made the connection between them and the Messiah's donkey.

But Kook—a man of immeasurable influence over the course of modern Israeli religion—relied on the teaching of another man, a great rabbi whose thesis was met with skepticism by European Jews of his time. He found a ready audience, however, among Christians, the very people who in the nineteenth century laid the foundation for the return of the Jews to the Holy Land. It simply wouldn't have happened without the evangelical Christian donkey.

Back to Zion

There had not been a serious bid to restore Jewish sovereignty since Muhammad, and it would not be championed again by Jews until 1897, when Theodore Herzl would write his influential book, *The Jewish State*.

But we should really look at 1862, when Rabbi Zvi Hirsch Kalischer penned one of the first Jewish discussions of Zionism as a hands-on project. His work deals with religious questions; for example, could priestly sacrifice be reinstated after Jews return to Jerusalem?

This book, *Zion Quest*, leads directly to Herzl and twentieth-century Zionism. It also forms a direct link between modern Israel and the American Puritans, for Kalischer was a serious scholar of Christian ideas—he spends half the book appealing directly to Bible-believing Christians raised in the school of thought so well-articulated by Increase Mather. Kalischer knew that they would be the most likely people to champions his ideas.

His argument was that Zion's redemption could not be expected to come supernaturally. It would have to come through natural means. He therefore called for Jews to stop waiting on the Messiah and to act now. They must begin to settle Palestine now and make the land a fruitful and safe home. This was to be the first part of redemption; the Messiah would follow after believers did their part. Again, it's the idea of dry bones first, spirit second that comes from Ezekiel's ever-popular vision of Israel's redemption.[1]

Most of his rabbinic colleagues disagreed—they believed the Messiah would have to act first and that Kalischer's proposal was dangerously presumptuous.

This is where the donkey business came to the fore. Non-believing Jews, Christians, or the gracious authority of the Ottoman caliph (who still controlled the Holy Land) could be the vehicle for assembling those dry bones. Moreover, this was the plan: the physical, skeletal aspect of Israel's redemption must take place before the Messiah can come. The emphasis was on human action—if not self-deliverance, then putting oneself into a mandatory position to be delivered. Just waiting wouldn't cut it.

Although his idea would catch on among Israel's rabbis in the twentieth century, he had more immediate success convincing secular Jews and evangelical Christians.

Kalischer was a big influence, for example, on Sir Moses Montefiore, the British Jewish politician who built the first modern Jewish settlement at Jerusalem and who famously corresponded with Charles Henry Churchill, the British consul in Ottoman Syria, which included Palestine. Churchill, in turn, was the first British official to seriously propose support for resettling Jews in Palestine.

Writing to Montefiore, Churchill can't hide his religious bearing: "The blessing of the Most High must be invoked on the endeavour. Political events seem to warrant the conclusion that the hour is nigh at hand when the Jewish people may justly and with every reasonable prospect of success put their hands to the glorious work of National Regeneration." He stresses his eschatological motive, "which is simply an ardent desire for the welfare and prosperity of a people to whom we all owe our possession of those blessed truths which direct our minds with unerring faith to the enjoyment of another and better world."[2]

Kalischer, Montefiore, and Churchill represent elements of an evolving movement in the nineteenth century that gained momentum as biblical literalism became more popular. Mather's insistence on a non-allegorical reading of prophecy fit nicely with Kalischer's idea of acting first to prepare for the Messiah's coming. Completing the cast are a handful of similarly minded British and American Christians.

None are more important than John Nelson Darby. Darby was an

Anglican priest who broke away from the Church as a founding member of the anti-denominational Plymouth Brethren. The Brethren, like their Puritan antecedents, believed the Church to be hopelessly corrupt. Darby, convinced that the end was near, turned his attention to a literal reading of the prophets. The result was a precisely defined system of premillennialism —apocalyptic literature as science.

He was tireless. For decades, Darby travelled the world promoting a system in which history could be divided into seven great epochs or "dispensations." What Zoroaster meant as metaphor Darby turned into a Christian version of Darwinism: the dispensations progressed from Creation to Fall, to Flood, to Abraham, to Israel, to Christ. He said Christians were now at the tail end of evolution, in the Christian sixth period, the age of Grace.

What happens next is all to do with the Antichrist, Armageddon, Gog and Magog, and the return of Jesus to Jerusalem. True Christians will get to leave early; they will be "raptured" and escape the seven years of global torment perpetrated by the Antichrist. The greatest signpost before the rapture: the regathering of Israel to the Promised Land.

This idea would have a big impact on America in the twentieth century, but before then, it was influential mostly among a subset of critically positioned Englishmen. This group was a crowded field of Christian Zionists, including such unlikely characters as Lawrence of Arabia, the man who would gain the support of the Sharif of Mecca in Britain's campaign against the Ottoman Empire in the First World War. Lawrence, a Sunday school–inspired archeologist, philologist, poet, and lover of biblical antiquity, was the consummate Arabist; however, he nonetheless dreamed of "Arab and Zionist policy converging" in a process by which the Arabs would be redeemed by Jewish influence.[3]

Lesser-known figures in the dispensationalist orbit would be key to the development of Western support for Zionism. Chief among them was Anthony Ashley Cooper, better known to us now as Lord Shaftesbury. His Christian influence was felt foremost in social reforms: famously, in legislation to institute child labor laws, to improve conditions of factory workers, to establish schools for the poor, and to create laws providing better treatment of the mentally ill.

All history-making and impressive achievements, but his avowed passion was the restoration of the Jewish people to their land. As a Darby-influenced premillennialist (by way of firebrand Scottish preacher Edward Irving), Shaftesbury ultimately used his influence to develop an official Anglican mission society devoted entirely to the restoration of the Jews.[4] He is responsible for the creation of an Anglican bishopric in Jerusalem; the first bishop was a Jewish believer in Jesus. His influence likewise ensured the establishment of a British proconsul in Ottoman Jerusalem with authority to protect all Jewish settlers as though they were British citizens.

Shaftesbury's power to shape opinion should not be underestimated: I agree with popular historian Barbara Tuchman when she describes Shaftesbury as "the most influential nonpolitical figure, excepting Darwin, of the Victorian age."[5]

In particular, he influenced the foreign secretary, Lord Palmerston, who was moved by Shaftesbury's argument to favor a homeland for Jews in Palestine. It was under Palmerston that the matter was first discussed at the governmental level as a serious, actionable proposal, a discussion that was revolutionary enough to warrant considerable attention from the press.

What Shaftesbury and company represent is an evangelical culture on both sides of the Atlantic that colored the opinions of countless up-and-coming leaders, government officials, and military commanders. It grew naturally out of Protestant reforms dating from the 1600s and spread organically through the culture as open access to the vernacular Bible allowed people to study the prophets for themselves.

Now the dominant world power, Britain's interest was piqued by the Bible's promises to the Jews. Their restoration was inextricable from the Christian promise of Christ's return. Helping the Jews return to Zion was therefore something Bible-believing politicians and men of wealth and influence could practically do to further the Kingdom of God. But what could they do about that other great world power? The Ottoman Empire still possessed the Holy Land. Little could be done unless God acted to change that.

Khaki Crusaders

Uncanny as it seems, just as Herzl and Jewish Zionism began to see serious numbers of Jews ready to return to Palestine, and just when Britain's leading lights reached a peak level of Christian sympathy for the idea, history produced the most terrifying and widespread war of all time, a version of apocalypse that made the Zionist dream come true.

This was of course the First World War, by the end of which Britain had possession of the Holy Land and largely controlled the fate of the Arabs. Mather would not have been surprised. He had linked the restoration of Israel with a catastrophic war to end the Muslim Ottoman Empire. It turns out he was a real prophet: the war indeed ended with the dissolution of the 400-year-old empire and, soon after, the abolition of the caliphate. For the first time since Muhammad, the prophet would have no successor.

Jerusalem was not strategically important. There was no militarily compelling reason to take it. The only reason it mattered was its religious significance, which British prime minister David Lloyd George recognized when he ordered General Edmund Allenby to take it "as a Christmas present" for the British people in 1917.[6] After King David, Nebuchadnezzar, Alexander the Great, Pompey, Herod, Titus, Omar Ibn Al-khaṭṭāb, Godfrey, and Saladin, to name a few, Allenby became the thirty-fourth conqueror of Jerusalem on December 11 of that year, dismounting his horse and walking into the city in homage to the humility of Jesus. Muslims lost control of Jerusalem after 500 years of rule.

It's no wonder, then, that both the newspapers and government propaganda described the victory as the final chapter of the Crusades—an interpretation, also widely accepted among Muslims, which would be the fount of every war in the Middle East since then, as we will soon see.

Looking at official British propaganda, popular journalism, statements of senior clergy, and correspondence from the field, the First World War's entire campaign against the Ottoman Empire did indeed frequently take on a Crusader identity. This is not surprising, given the longstanding British view of its empire as the vessel of blessed Christian rule.

Despite a warning from the Ministry of Information about the danger of upsetting British Muslims, the government and popular press continued to present the Palestine campaign in this light. Books like the *Khaki Crusaders*, *The Modern Crusaders*, *The Last Crusade*, *With Allenby's Crusaders*, and *The Romance of the Last Crusade* all chose to tell the story of Jerusalem's recapture in those terms. The Ministry of Information itself released an early documentary during the war, titled *The New Crusaders: With the British Forces on the Palestine Front*.

Why isn't this considered more seriously in addressing Middle East conflict today? It is partly because Western historians and journalists generally avoid religion as a causative factor in their own stories. We live in a materialist society that looks for problems and solutions rooted in material wants. That's a mistake. The underlying religious bias that determined important Western policies should not be ignored. Certainly in the Middle East, most people look at the First World War as the West's continuation of the Crusades, not infrequently talking about contemporary Western policies as part of the "Crusader-Zionist Alliance" that began with the Great War.

They are wont to cite examples. A striking one comes from *Punch* magazine: in covering the news of Allenby's occupation of Jerusalem, Richard the Lionheart appears in a sketch looking across the subjugated holy city. The caption reads: "The Last Crusade... My dream come true!"

Across the Atlantic, the *New York Herald* headlined Allenby's victory on the front page as "Jerusalem is Rescued By British After 673 Years of Moslem Rule—GREAT REJOICING IN THE CHRISTIAN WORLD."

And, of course, there is the greatest concrete example of all. As Allenby's troops swept through Palestine, Lord Arthur Balfour, the British foreign minister, swung into action. He issued a declaration that read, "His Majesty's Government views with favour the establishment in Palestine of a National Home for the Jewish people, and will use their best endeavours to facilitate the achievement of that object..."[7]

This official endorsement of Zionism, by the world's leading power, was the first step toward statehood and, as such, was celebrated by Jews with dancing in the streets. Ultimately, it would lead to the formal establishment of the State of Israel. Why did Lloyd George and Balfour do this? None of the presumed geopolitical benefits fully account for it. It simply would not have happened if Lloyd George and Balfour had not possessed an innate sympathy for Jewish restoration.

They didn't need to be aficionados of premillennial dispensationalism. They were already products of the same Puritan culture that birthed premillennialism. What swayed them was their feeling for the place of the Jewish people in the Promised Land, carried with them from childhood. As Lloyd George noted some years later about his Baptist upbringing, "We had been trained even more in Hebrew history than in the history of our own country." In fact, he confessed, "I could tell you all the kings of Israel. But I doubt whether I could have named half a dozen of the kings of England, and not more of the kings of Wales."[8]

Progressive Zionism

In 1909, just a few years before the First World War, Oxford University Press published the Scofield Reference Bible. Very much a product of the English evangelical culture that shaped Lloyd George, it is the most influential book you've never heard of, especially consequential in shaping American political life. For millions of people, including some of the most powerful actors in the mid- to late twentieth century, this ground-breaking text provided a clearly articulated libretto with which to interpret the times.[9]

Scofield's genius was his relentless incorporation of commentary and cross-references within the body of the scriptural text. Without knowledge of ancient languages and history, most Christians found the Bible inscrutable. This state-of-the-art publication deciphered it for them—no scholarship required—and it did so with unblushing confidence. It really shines in the most puzzling parts—the apocalyptic literature and the prophets—and since editor C.I. Scofield was a premillennial dispensationalist, his work explained these allegorical texts in rigidly Mather-like concreteness.

His Bible made average churchgoers into armchair experts on the End Time. But their education was one-sided, based fully on Darby and his ally, the father of modern evangelicalism, America's Dwight L. Moody. By empowering the pew, Scofield forced preachers to change the way they delivered sermons. Even if they were uncomfortable with Darby's ideas, they still had to convince parishioners who had read Scofield's Bible at home, forcing preachers to adopt the same relentless "chain references" technique pioneered by Scofield. If you've ever heard a sermon where the preacher jumps hither and thither from verse to verse, building circular arguments, it is due entirely to Scofield.

All the big names of twentieth-century evangelicalism were affected: Billy Graham, Pat Robertson, and Jerry Falwell were perhaps the most influential Scofield disciples. In turn, presidents Jimmy Carter, Ronald Reagan, and George W. Bush had their basic religious worldviews shaped to lesser and greater degrees by Scofield-influenced institutions such as Moody Bible Institute or Dallas Theological Seminary. Even if one's church didn't endorse it, the ideas easily seeped into the Christian psyche through the ubiquity of radio and television preachers. Any movement labelled "evangelical" was affected.

Most people who consider themselves to be well-educated, modern, and open-minded can happily sneer at the comical beliefs of Scofield's followers. But to do so belies an ignorance of a parallel development that is as steeped in millennialism as it is liberal and progressive. This, too, gained momentum with the start of the First World War and is best exemplified for us in the life of Lloyd George's American counterpart, President Woodrow Wilson.

Wilson was a Bible-believing pastor's son. Sunday school was in his blood, and his Christian faith was deep, attested throughout his life in literature, correspondence, and on-the-record conversations. But Wilson was not a grassroots evangelical and was too well-educated to need a Bible like Scofield's. This makes him, therefore, an excellent study of the other kind of millennialism—the more mainstream, liberal kind that we tend to think of as less maniacal. In my view, it's just as troubling and possibly more dangerous since it is readily accepted by secularists.

As a young man, Wilson articulated beliefs that he would apply as the architect of the twentieth century's international system: "We should perform every act as an act of which we shall some day be made to render a strict account, as an act done either in the service of God or in that of the Devil." Lest we think this didn't apply to his presidency, he also said that no aspect of life could be separated from faith: "The Christian character is not one to be assumed only upon the Sabbath... but is a character which is perfected only by... a religion pervading every act—which is carried with us into every walk of life and made our one stay and hope."

An avowed pacifist, President Wilson entered the First World War with pained reluctance, having convinced himself that he could achieve the noble ambition to end not just this war, but all war for all time, by undertaking this one last act of violence. For Wilson, America was fighting as God's agent for eternal peace. "The world must be made safe for democracy," was his declaration to Congress, insisting that America's place in the war was elementally different from other combatants; "We desire no conquest, no dominion," and America fought with "no selfish ends to serve."

This wasn't rhetoric; Wilson truly believed America's involvement would allow the war to end without either side's defeat and, in so doing, achieve lasting peace in the world—an extraordinary idea that pointed to a vision of Paradise-sized proportions. When all was said and done, he looked to establish the League of Nations to shape international relations in line with his millenarian ideal.

In 1918, he laid out the Fourteen Points to guide the world after the war:

> The day of conquest and aggrandizement is gone by... All the peoples of the world are in effect partners in this interest, and for our own part we see very clearly that unless justice be done to others it will not be done to us. The programme of the world's peace, therefore, is our programme; and that programme, the only possible programme.

Fundamental were points two and three, which became cornerstones of globalization: "Absolute freedom of navigation upon the seas," and the "removal, so far as possible, of all economic barriers and the establishment of an equality of trade conditions among all the nations." Point four was to begin the process of beating swords into plowshares—global disarmament: "Adequate guarantees given and taken that national armaments will be reduced to the lowest point consistent with domestic safety."

In his summary, he preached a universalist vision: "We cannot be separated in interest or divided in purpose. We stand together until the end... in the new world in which we now live." It is easy to forget that the United Nations, that most liberal of institutions, came out of Wilson's theistic vision.

Like his Puritan forebears, Wilson saw America's opportunity as a mandate to institute God's reign of peace. But it was postmillennial, the incremental establishment of the Gospel kingdom through education and social action. We must ask, then: what's the practical difference between a Darby and a Wilson? If anything, Wilson demonstrates how much the premillennial and postmillennial Christian dreams have in common. As much as it talks of peace, progressivism has historically been just as apt to impose its will on the world through political and military power as any other kind of millenarianism. Indeed, of all people, it was Wilson who succumbed to the temptation to solve violence with violence through world war.

The Wilsonian spiritual battle is not the hot-headedness of the Crusades. But it is a steady march in the betterment of the world under Gospel influence. It is Progressivism. (Wilson was the first Democratic president to espouse that term.) By virtue of its optimism, however, the progressive cause he promoted was as proactive and interventionist as the Crusaders ever were. The difference between pre- and post-millenarian camps, liberal and conservative dreams, or blue and red politics, is academic—both poles are fighting a spiritual war for Paradise on Earth.

Critically, both Christian millenarian visions have a place for Israel's restoration in their New World Order. It is in each scenario the last great sign of the end of history; for both, the regathering of the Jews to the Holy Land became irresistibly compelling.

Woodrow Wilson was no exception. When the British afforded him the opportunity to review and approve the Balfour Declaration before it was issued, the president did not conceal his enthusiasm; he had voiced deep sympathies for the Jewish people throughout his life.

> I have before this expressed my personal approval of the declaration of the
> British Government regarding the aspirations and historic claims of the

Jewish people in regard to Palestine. I am, moreover, persuaded that the allied nations, with the fullest concurrence of our own Government and people, are agreed that in Palestine shall be laid the foundations of a Jewish Commonwealth.[10]

He didn't need any help from Darby's dispensationalism, but he got it nonetheless—not by way of his church but through a prominent Jewish friend. That's the feature of Darby's influence that is so intriguing: its fibers are woven deeply into the fabric of Western culture, yet even those it most profoundly affects are unaware of it. This is a virus in every sense.

To see how Darby got under President Wilson's skin, we have to look back a few decades to William Blackstone, author of the runaway bestseller, *Jesus is Coming*, published in 1878. Through *Jesus is Coming*, Blackstone introduced Darby's science of the End Time in dozens of languages, selling millions of copies. Blackstone was a volcanic and passionate Zionist, as we'd expect from a disciple of Darby, and he was wealthy, politically well-connected, and exceptionally persuasive. Having secured the backing of banking magnates J.P. Morgan and John D. Rockefeller, he set his energies to lobbying then president Benjamin Harrison in support of a Jewish state. This was history's first pro-Israel lobby, started in 1891. Let that sink in: this is six years before Herzl, the father of modern Jewish Zionism, published his work, *The Jewish State*. That's how deeply the idea is embedded in the American identity.

Wilson's Blackstone connection came through the president's Kentucky-born Jewish appointee to the Supreme Court, Louis D. Brandeis. A pillar of progressive social reform, opponent of large corporations, buster of monopolies, and godfather to modern privacy and free-speech laws, "the people's lawyer" was also a leading Zionist and a big fan of Blackstone's efforts on behalf of the Jewish people. Again, we must pay close attention: Zionism was a progressive project.

In 1916, Brandeis asked Macy's department store owner Nathan Straus—Jewish, and one of America's most generous philanthropists—to contact Blackstone on his behalf. In a letter dated May 16, Straus relayed his friend's message. It reads like fan mail: "Mr. Brandeis is perfectly infatuated with the work that you have done along the lines of Zionism. It would have done your heart good to have heard him assert what a valuable contribution to the cause your document is. In fact he agrees with me that you are the Father of Zionism, as your work antedates Herzl."[11]

Just think about that: America's most prominent Jewish leader called

America's most successful Christian apocalyptic writer the "Father of Zionism."

It was with Blackstone's example in mind that Justice Brandeis lobbied President Wilson to support the establishment of a Jewish state after the war. Brandeis believed that the key was appealing to the president's biblical faith.[12] We aren't privy to the details of his appeal to Wilson, but we know that Justice Brandeis felt it was necessary to encourage the president to stand up for the Jewish homeland, and that he thought that Wilson's famously active faith predisposed him to it.

Once convinced, Wilson wasn't at all shy about declaring the importance of regathering the Jews. In 1916, he named it one of his greatest accomplishments: "The Jewish Homeland was one of the two primary achievements that would come out of the war." And toward the end of his life, he reflected with awe on providence: "To think that I, the son of the manse, should be able to help restore the Holy Land to its people."[13]

It fell to Wilson's successor, Warren G. Harding, to make all this official.[14] Like Isaiah before successive kings of Judah, Blackstone appeared yet again, now standing before the Baptist Harding with the Word of the Lord. It was delivered in 1920, only weeks before Harding took office. "God has reserved our nation for special service in the impending crux of human history... the restoration of Israel to their homeland in Palestine," Blackstone prophesied to the president-elect.[15]

Then, to make certain Harding understood the gravity of his responsibility, the author informed him that this "is very significant for it betokens the approaching end of the times of the Gentiles."

This refers to Increase Mather's interpretation of Luke 21 as the final sign of the End Time—Blackstone is effectively calling on the president of the United States to end history by fulfilling a prophecy that originated in ancient Zoroastrianism.

Six months later, Blackstone got his wish. Harding wrote regarding a visit to the United States by Dr. Chaim Weizmann, head of the Zionist Commission:

I want to add an expression of my most friendly interest in and for the Zionist movement. It is impossible for one who has studied all the services of the Hebrew people to avoid the faith that they will one day be restored to their historic national home and there enter on a new and yet greater phase of their contribution to the advance of humanity.

The remarks were read into the record of the *Congressional Hearings on the Establishment of a National Home in Palestine*. The result was a joint resolution endorsing the establishment of a Jewish state in Palestine between the Mediterranean Sea and the Jordan River. Harding signed it on September 21, 1922.

Fait Accompli

In the end, Wilson's hope that his would be the war to end all wars was gravely dashed. As the reality of the First World War's unprecedented carnage became clear, the West slid into the Great Depression and took a headlong dive into yet another, even greater, cataclysm. The gloom tipped the millenarian scales in favor of the more pessimistic premillennialists— Wilsonian optimism was in popular decline.

As Matthew Avery Sutton ably demonstrates in his book *American Apocalypse: A History of Modern Evangelicalism*, it was in this state of shock that many traditional postmillennialists like Wilson were finally converted to the alternative view, convinced in the end that the world was not getting better after all. Mather may have been right all along—the end would come with a bang, not a gentle Gospel breeze.

What happens repeatedly is that the world finds itself involved in self-fulfilling prophecies. This is certainly true for the European side of the Second World War and the Cold War that lay beyond it. Not all the actors were self-aware; they acted out of a cultural predisposition, carried away by an intoxicating sense of destiny. Be it Hitler and Stalin or Wilson and Lloyd George or Bush and Obama, they act on programming that has been running for thousands of years. Of course, this hidden hand of history can feel very much like the hand of God: fated, inevitable, and irresistible.

That's why reflecting on history is so important. We become more aware of its power, able to understand that history's plotlines have momentum, that history literally writes our story and shapes our characters. Unfortunately, most world leaders have not and do not understand this at all—they fail to see that they are acting in line with a script, they are too shallow to grasp the power of a collective narrative, and they attribute to themselves too much efficacy.

In this story of human history, the next line of the plot really is the Apocalypse, because only in the past century has our technology reached the point that it can match the awful visions seen by the prophets. Are we capable of re-writing it? Do we have the energy and the motivation to do so?

Can we be that mindful? Or will we remain so entranced with the minutiae of material existence and so distracted by infotainment that we simply don't notice as we are swept away?

We've discussed Christians, Jews, and Muslims, but lest we think other ideologies are immune, we should remember their non-theistic offspring. We cannot address either in detail, but that will not be necessary. Before moving on, keep in mind that communism and Nazism are left and right expressions of exactly the kind of errors we see in all religion, for utopian ideologies are always religious, no matter how much love of humanity they claim to possess. Mao's cultural revolution was for love of the greater human good. Hitler's dream was a literal millennium. What we might call Trumpism and Wokeism are no more benign. All these are currents of history carrying nations away before anyone is self-possessed enough to build a dam against it. Afterwards, we always say, "How could that have happened?" Next time, there may be no afterwards.

What will be the catalyst? A very likely candidate is the State of Israel. It is a lightning rod for every ideology. Is it because God destined it to be that way? That is, of course, solely a matter of nomenclature. Inevitability comes from the flowing narrative of history. It is a kind of improvisatory theater. The elements of the plot, set in motion long ago, place Israel and the Middle East at center stage. Most actors in this drama are carried away by sheer momentum and adrenalin. You can feel the heady exhilaration when world leaders and journalists discuss the Middle East. They are excited. They've been swept away by the current of history.

Believers and unbelievers alike are equally ignorant of the power of the narrative. Some are in denial. They bristle at the suggestion, for example, that Israel's rebirth is a fulfillment of prophecy. But by whatever mechanism, the prophecy in actual fact was fulfilled and its consequences are real. It should be understood, then, that the centuries-long ripening of even self-fulfilling prophecies is indeed God-like: it is bigger than a single life or a lifetime and is awe-inspiring in its own right. There is no practical difference between fate and fait accompli.

The flow of history's river is swift and powerful and not to be disrespected. If we are ever to grow up and manage to take responsibility for this story, we have to come to grips with that and act with wisdom. For that reason alone, Israel's restoration should be taken very seriously, and despite a rational insistence that it is just another country in the world like any other, objectively speaking, it plays a special part. It remains the focus of mimetic rivalry for billions of people. Israel's uniqueness cannot be wished away.

The Call

I was unaware of all of this when that bigger story swept me to Zion's gates. I wasn't aware of much at all. Like everyone else, I just went along with the current.

While in Jerusalem on that first visit, I was in love. I was not traveling alone, but with a small group from the kibbutz that included an English girl, a miniature ballerina who held beliefs like my own. She did not know how I felt, as I assumed she could not feel the same about me. I never knew what to do.

Stricken unsociable because of this and everything else, I went to sit in the cool air on the hostel's rooftop in companionable rejection with Jesus. He lived alone, the loneliest man, and was painfully alienated by this city. That's what I was thinking, perched on the edge of Jerusalem Syndrome and at risk of being pushed over by the right combination of religious fantasies and heartbreak. A Mi'raj of my own was imminent.

Then, entranced perhaps by the city's powers, or brought there by more legitimate urges, or by both (for why should these be in opposition?), she appeared and sat down. She sat close. I was thrilled, terrified, intoxicated, and lovesick. Paralyzed and certainly doomed to say the wrong thing if I dared say anything at all, I just stared, looking over the lights of the city and feeling the cool stones of which everything in Jerusalem is built.

But I was acutely aware of her, this potential Eve. A light breeze caressed her face, as I wished to do, playing with an exquisite lock of raven hair that had strayed across her temple, as pale as her hair was dark—judged by me to be angelic and, in that moment, the most beautiful thing I could ever hope to see. For a moment, I conceived of Paradise found. But then, for no reason I can account for other than habit, I despaired. Maybe deep down I knew that idolizing a girl was a dead end on the Paradise road.

"You're pensive," she said. "What's wrong?"

"I love you..."

She was silent, then took my hand and leaned into me. "I love you, too."

That was that. It was surely more important than the Dome of the Rock and the Last Days. Surely it was. I'd waited my whole life for that: Eve in my Eden. And for a while, her aura displaced the incense that men had burned since first exiled from that place, the incense and burnt offerings set ablaze in Jerusalem in empty hopes of constructing a new Paradise. Ours was the real thing.

Not to dwell on the details, the minutiae of which appear to me now absurd, but here is the proof that I was already mad with Jerusalem Syndrome, a true brother of those who would destroy the world to see a better one revealed: within a year, pressured by religious peers to fulfill our destiny, and addled by the calling to save the world, we let each other go. We were driven apart by the dream. It was insidious, a contagion that fevered the mind and made us doubt the simplicity of Paradise-in-hand.

It is clear to me now that these halcyon days could not have lasted in any case; but they could have lasted as long as any earthly stability does, balanced in equanimity and enlightenment of the true nature of things. In other words, we might have made it work, lived quietly and constructively, but in the confusion of wanting to be holy and do the right thing and live for the coming kingdom, we separated. Our spiritual guides insinuated that we had not handled ourselves in a spiritually skillful manner; if we cut ourselves off, severed proximity and communication, then if it was right, God would resurrect it—a test that smacked of Puritan witch trials, although I did not understand that then. Predictably, it died on the vine instead, unwatered and deprived of the light of day. We never saw each other again.

To sum this up, I was simply too sick with the fantasy of Paradise to experience Paradise in any truth. I either idolized Eve or renounced her for greater things. I couldn't just relax and live in Paradise. Having failed, all I knew to do was to double down. As had happened with similar debacles, I emerged from this one hyper-zealous.

Over the next year, I made plans to leave the Holy Land and preach the Kingdom of God in the House of Islam. I'd go out in glory. It was a total and eclipsing obsession: go deep into the heart of darkness and there be consumed by the eternal flame, freed of this world and delivering a good chunk of oppressed humanity along the way.

My understanding was that the Muslims had been led astray from the true Messiah by the Antichrist. They had good intentions, but they were misled. They would surely embrace the Gospel when they heard it in its purity. I'd strip off the obscuring affectations of traditional Christianity and show them the true Gospel as preached by Jesus! Just look at Jerusalem— what a terrible witness it was. No wonder they could not see clearly. Jerusalem's churches looked like they were stricken with leprosy, encrusted in dead flesh, bandaged and adorned in rococo garb, all to divert the eye from the rot within. The Gospel had no place there, I thought, and if anything, these churches practiced some kind of anti-propaganda, ensuring that none would seek the message of Jesus therein. All Muslims needed was a clear hearing of the Gospel.

Preach the Gospel until it filled the earth: that's what Keith Green told us to do. We were so close! So much of the world had already been reached! Evangelize the rest of the nations in preparation for Christ's return and salt the world's institutions with leaders prepared to administer God's rule. We had a good start already in America, where Christians systematically took over school boards, engineered Republican politics, and placed God's people in key positions—the preservative that would sustain us through the Last Days. That this political, rule-based Kingdom of God was more or less identical to Islam was beyond my comprehension.

What of Armageddon and Antichrist? Sure, that was expected, but it was a last-gasp strike by a defeated enemy, a short cleansing procedure. Bring it on! The sooner the better! All would be well in the End!

My choice of field was intuitive. I would go to Istanbul where Muhammad's relics rested. Once there, I would seek out one of the "most unreached peoples of the earth" in terms of Gospel influence. Turkey, with its 99.9 percent Muslim population, fierce opposition to Christian proselytism, and inheritance as the last great Islamic empire was appealing: it had fascinated millennialist Christians for centuries, and indeed was, to the mind of Mather, Newton, Luther, Columbus, and number of others, the epitome and sum of Islam. My ambition was therefore to tackle this last giant of resistance to the Gospel—to strike at the root.

I started out with just over US$100. I had no credit card. The only other asset available was an airline credit. That's what got me a one-way ticket to Turkey. Of my cash reserve, I'd spend a lot of it staying at a flop house on the Arab side of Jerusalem during my final days in the Holy Land.

It would be a transition from my Jewish homeland into an entirely Muslim world, but I hadn't really planned it that way. I stumbled into it having left the kibbutz, and with a few days to kill, I wanted to see Jerusalem again. How I came to the hostel where I lodged, I don't know. It must have been very cheap, a dormitory where I dozed with my hand on my wallet, fully clothed. But that is irrelevant. What stuck with me was the feeling of being in a Muslim world now. It felt right; I felt called.

This was an experience of East Jerusalem, for the first time untended by Jews, and it revealed a side of Araby I'd not encountered in the Galilee where I'd made Bedouin friends. No, this was less *Lawrence of Arabia*'s desert and more that urban scene where José Ferrer licks his lips before whipping the bound and subjected Lawrence. It was seedy and strangely musky and menacing in a sensual way; it smelled seductive and off-putting at the same time.

I noticed new things now because we no longer stayed in the modern Jewish part of town. I was sleeping, eating, and walking exclusively in the Arab part. When tasseled and hatted Jews made their way through the street, they looked like intruders.

I was less naive at this point, having read a book called *The Arab Mind* by Rafael Patai, which magnified my sense of this place. It's a sociological work in which Patai details the modern Arab urban mentality by means of Arab scholarship on the subject. "The pink elephant in the alchemy of Arab life is the sex taboos," Patai notes. "Parents and other authority figures imbue the Arab child with the notion of the sinfulness of sex, and the culture as a whole surrounds the individual with an atmosphere which constantly reminds him of the same subject." Hmmm. I'd read that and now I felt it. It stuck to your shoes in the streets, icky and hard to clean off.

> Segregation of the sexes, the veiling of the women where it is practiced and all the other minute rules that govern and restrict contact between men and women, have the effect of making sex a prime mental preoccupation in the Arab world. The very taboo of sex creates a kind of fixation on the subject.

Indeed.

There was a familiarity, of course. Conservative Evangelicals should recognize the dynamics of sexual repression immediately. If the Arab Muslim version felt far more intense here in the city, the separations sharper, the taboos more pronounced, I still felt a shared experience, which provoked sympathy in me for so many young Muslim Arabs who were molded by powerlessness and shame. Yet, for some reason—a blind spot—I did not connect any of this with their zeal for the End Time, nor my own. I still couldn't see the most obvious thing of all: that I was exactly like them.

I ought to have known better, since Jesus taught sternly about judging others with a measure different from the one used to weigh one's own failings. As I say, it was a blind spot: a log in the eye! Ignoring it, I resolved to work all the more diligently on the splinters in theirs. These Muslims needed forgiveness. They must be set free from their guilt and shame. And so, to this end, I headed to Tel Aviv and boarded a flight. Two hours later I was in Istanbul.

Me and Muhammad's Cloak

The next day, I woke up in the early hours to the mercilessly amplified muezzin. As the ego fought to rise above the waters of sleep, I was disoriented and disembodied. I often wake up that way: Who is this lying there? What bed is this? Where is it? As I came to myself, it was not much better. Now my consciousness was time traveling: I am a little boy again, at school. It is the end of first grade, and I am waiting for my mother to pick me up. I'm sure she won't—absolutely positively certain of it. Finally, as the call to prayer came to a close, the desire to be one with the dead began to pass and I settled into a time, a place, and the familiar iteration of being myself in the world.

My self was cold. It had been icy when the flight from Tel Aviv landed the previous afternoon, the sun rapidly setting. There wasn't much time to notice anything more than the hovering Lenin-like busts of Turkey's founding father Mustafa Kemal Atatürk and the omnipresent hungry apparitions of very tense young men with guns. Atatürk's constancy was armed and dangerous, it seemed.

There had been guns in Israel, of course. But over there they felt like my guns, the Lord's sword wielded in common cause and ready for use against the Antichrist's armies. These Turkish guns seemed to be not only against me but against everyone. I wasn't yet sure why.

I had arrived with $30 in my pocket, a phone number, and an address in Kurtuluş, an old Jewish and Armenian neighborhood of apartment blocks and cobblestone streets; it was not far from Taksim Square in the city center, but still had many wooden structures. I was to stay with some Americans who ran an illegal Bible correspondence course from their tiny flat. That suited me fine.

Our lodging was frigid—it seemed colder than outside—and there was a dense stink in the air of something impure having been set alight. I got up to look out the window. It was snowing. Istanbul in the snow is a thing to behold: it is such a big, dense place that the proverbial blanket of snow appears to be the work of a gigantic benefactor, the bestowal of a sanctifying robe over the soot-stained marble, concrete, and brick. There was music. My hosts were blaring Kansas' philosophical hit, *Dust in the Wind*. (Kansas composer-in-chief Kerry Livgren had come to Jesus not long after composing this.)

Awake now, I made my daily gamble, chose life, and roused myself from my corner of the apartment. After dressing, I refused tea and walked down three flights of stairs hoping for fresh air. Each step was disorienting because the marble edges had eroded, giving one the feeling of falling, a common attribute of Istanbul stairwells. How many comings and goings of unremembered lives were marked by those eroded steps, I wondered.

Safely on the landing, I was foiled again by the old building; I couldn't get out. It took a good ten minutes before I was free, mostly spent puzzling over the unfamiliar latch on the iron-gated door with its sliding bolt—a modern Gordian Knot. At last, it was understood that I was to pull a brass thumb tab, making the door click open heavily toward me with a gust of icy wind and the sulfuric stink of 10 million people burning low-grade coal. The air was worse outside than inside.

But something about the snow and that stink of coal brought me back to Appalachia. I breathed in and each breath pinched my heart and I liked it. Maybe this is why I'm here, I thought; I've come to face my demons. It was a mix of sadness and joy, an embrace of pain that only genuine flagellants can appreciate. For us, such pangs represent being alive—they are a semblance (at least) of meaning, even if our daily marble-grinding footsteps might be pointless.

Invigorated by the strangeness and how much I took to it, I walked down the hill, finding a cafe. I ordered what looked like thick milk from a mustached gentleman who seemed to leap from the 1950s. It was the white uniform and tent-like paper hat he wore, and it was also something about his tight haircut and the pride with which he executed his service, offering me my drink, something called *sahlep*, as if I were royalty.

Sahlep, I soon learned, was made from orchid roots. It is the most warming drink ever invented. Sitting with it then, I took out an aerogramme, writing my lost sweetheart a letter and, in the writing of it, for the time being, purging myself of the need of her. I never sent it.

As I say, I'd arrived with $30. Paying for the *sahlep*, it finally occurred to me that this was not going to be enough to sustain me for long. Like the morning's encounter with the metal door, the need for money showed that my formative years in Israel had left me unprepared for the outside world. We'd had no locks and no use for money. I no longer understood money. The kibbutz had taken care of everything. What little pocket money they provided was only negotiable in the community shop, the *kolbo*, which took only the kibbutz scrip that we were paid in. This was much like my great-grandparents, who lived in the mining company's housing and who were likewise paid in company scrip, good only at the company store. Suddenly, considering what portion of my entire fortune a cup of orchid milk had cost me, I wondered at the cult-like insulation—so warm and secure—that was our communal life. I also wondered why it should be any other way.

But I had no choice now: I would live by faith while trying not to be a burden. Over the next months and years, word got out that I was serving the Lord in a Muslim land. Without intentional effort to raise funds, funds were anonymously provided. I had no idea how it worked. Money just appeared in my account and I thanked the Lord. This gave me time to work on the local language and learn more about the world I was called to serve, beginning with the vast city of Istanbul. It was a university and I majored in history and religion, all to prepare and equip myself for the great final task of preaching the Gospel to Islam.

The geographical heart of all this was Istanbul's Topkapı Palace, a place haunted by the ghosts of caliphs past. Over and over again, my friends and I visited it and marveled at what we saw. There was Muhammad's sword! There was his cloak and his banner! And the swords of the first caliphs, the fathers of Islamic civilization! These were physical reminders and a present witness that Islam was in its first centuries undeniably a religion of conquest.

What were they now? They were artifacts in a museum. Why and how? I didn't know anything about the First World War, the Last Crusade, and what that meant to the Middle East. Sure, I knew this was the last caliph's palace. I knew that his ancestor Süleyman rebuilt the walls of Jerusalem. But like most people, I never really thought about what changed to make all this a secular museum today, what that might mean for Muslims in the Middle East.

Honestly, I didn't think to ask these questions because I could see these objects remained touchstones of prophetic significance. This part of the palace did not feel like a museum at all. Those artifacts were venerated, continuously bathed in recitations of the Quran. They lay there, seemingly rendered impotent by the modern Crusaders' conquest of the Ottomans, and yet they held their power as visitors from across the old realm looked upon them in silence and awe, reminded that something was amiss and that something should be done to restore the primary Islamic mission. I felt the drum call of war in the footsteps of those pious visitors, even if I didn't understand why.

The Quran makes clear why that is: "He it is Who sent His Messenger with... the religion of truth, that He might cause it to prevail over all religions." These forlorn swords testified to what every passerby was called to do: make Islam prevail over all other religions again.

This much was clear. I was uneasy. Just across the way from the palace was Hagia Sophia. I had never doubted that Islam was triumphalist and often militant; I just had not understood the root of it. Now living in the city that was Christendom's capital for 1,000 years and then the capital of Islam for over four centuries, I was forced to consider the connection between the two more deeply, the possibility that Islam came by its impulse to conquest honestly. For if Islam was a follow-on to Christianity, which it surely was, the example of Christianity it reflected was an imperial one, one that had nothing to do with the teaching of Christ. Yes, Islam inherited the idea of domination from Christians and Jews. It was another seed of truth waiting to explode in my soul.

House of War

I thought hard about all this, looking at those swords, and remembering that Jesus did not carry one. No matter how far astray Christians had wandered, I thought, to be a fundamentalist as a Christian must mean to become a pacifist like Jesus. To be a fundamentalist in Islam, however, to see faith restored, must mean to take up arms, for that was its primal condition and the teaching of the Prophet.

Muhammad's message was God's rule and an imminent exit from history. When he died without the Day of Judgment coming to pass, the mantle was passed on to a succession of caliphs charged with continuing the march to domination.

The word "caliph"—*khalīfah*—means "deputy" or "envoy," and came to mean the representative of Allah and the successor to Muhammad. The Islamic caliphate conveyed the authority of God's rule on Earth, a concept that respects no separation of secular and sacred within society. Instead, the separation of spheres in Islam was totalitarian, divided between those under God's rule and the unruly infidels who were not. These are the realms of *islam* ("surrender") and *ḥarb* ("war").

Islam is said to mean many things. Most commonly we hear that it means either "submission" or "peace." Those terms might not appear to have much in common, but both are accurate, and you can add more to the list: "capitulation," "surrender," and "reconciliation." The idea is something along the lines of "pacification"; it is peace through conquest and surrender.

Those who chose not to live in the *Dar al-Islam*, "the realm of Islam," assigned themselves to the alternative *Dar al-Harb*, "the realm of war." Incidentally, the word *ḥarb* is related to Hebrew *kherev*, a word for "sword" and "destruction."

There is a name for the process of achieving peace; it is *Jihad*, the exertion of the believer to convert more and more of the realm of war into the domain of peaceful submission. It is akin to the evangelism of the Crusades, and there should be no doubt about the original concept: jihad can be a private battle, the struggle to bring one's own thoughts and actions under heaven's peaceful aegis. Or it can mean a social or material struggle. In Islam, Muhammad's example supersedes all interpretation, and he exemplified jihad by military conquest.

Over the course of history, within the ebb and flow of the first Islamic conquests of the Middle East, the Crusades, and then Islam's deep infiltration into Christendom, the ideal of Islam's steady progress remained intact. As we might expect, then, the events of the twentieth century that so excited Christian and Jewish passions also appeared to Muslims as laden with eschatological significance. In Muslim eyes, the huge setback to the caliphate in the First World War was a fulfilled prophecy of the End Time.

The signs were all there. Islamic tradition delineates a number of indications that the Day of Judgment is near: open sexual immorality and proliferation of sexual diseases; corrupt and exploited Muslim rulers; prolific consumption of alcohol; a vast increase in trade and illicit wealth; a growing disparity between rich and poor; Christian nations attacking Muslims; and war with the Jews.

Islam predicts hard times of tribulation and apostasy in the Last Days. For example, an often cited and authenticated hadith of Ahmad b. Hanbal preserves a prophecy of Muhammad's about the course of history. Muhammad says that prophethood (his own life) would last as long as God wills, then would be replaced by the age of the caliphs, modeled on his own example. After that will come a period of harsh rule by tyrannical rulers until God once again raises up a righteous caliphate like his own.[16]

This and other signs, it has been argued, came to pass during the First World War when the Crusading powers divided the caliphate and corrupted the Muslim world through its defeat of the Ottoman Empire. This was Lawrence of Arabia's project, which was to make allies of the rulers of northwestern Arabia and turn them against the caliph. Adding enormous gravity to the situation, these Arab allies were none other than princes of the family responsible for protecting the House of Allah, the Kaaba in Mecca. It was they who fought alongside the English to overthrow the Ottomans.

Those relics that fascinated me in the palace—Muhammad's cloak, battle standard, personal seal, and swords, along with the swords of his first four successors—had been protected and passed along by the Umayyad, Abbasid, and Ottoman caliphs as emblems of caliphal authority. After the war, they came into the possession of Mustafa Kemal Atatürk, an unbelieving lover of alcohol and European-style suits who disavowed the Islamic past and turned these symbols of sacred authority into museum curiosities.

When he made Turkey into a secular state, he made it in his image, banning Islamic dress, forbidding the call to prayer in Arabic, and adopting the Roman alphabet to replace the Arabic-based script. The new government brought Islam firmly under its control through a directorate of religious affairs charged with controlling Islam's teachings and practices. It was he who finally abolished the caliphate.

Atatürk dealt so harshly with Islam because he understood its vitality, even its militancy. It couldn't be educated or rehabilitated or treated gently. Islam may mean peace, but not passively so. Atatürk understood that Islam means to bring all ideas under its dominion—either he was the boss or Islam was. It was a zero-sum game.

He wasn't the only one. The outcome of the war meant a slew of new countries. Jordan, Syria, Iraq, and Saudi Arabia never existed before. The Arab world was summarily divided between French and English spheres of influence, with the newly appointed Arab leaders entirely beholden to them. (Under Lawrence's guidance, Meccan Prince Faisal even made a deal with the head of the World Zionist Organization, Chaim Weizmann.)[17] Just twenty years later, the Jews declared a state, making war on Muslims with the support of Western Christian powers.

For Hassan al-Banna, an Egyptian school teacher, these developments were a call to action that rapidly grew into the largest Islamic revival movement of the twentieth century: the Muslim Brotherhood. The Brothers advocated pan-Islamic unity and a government based firmly on Islamic law. Still today, the Brothers explain their religious duty in terms of the war that ended the caliphate:

"A century has passed since the secret agreement signed on May 17, 1916 by the French diplomat François Georges-Picot with Britain's representative Mark Sykes," wrote the Muslim Brotherhood's spokesman in an official statement released in 2016. The Brotherhood described the treaty as an agreement "to partition and share Ottoman Empire areas, the last Islamic caliphate, with the help of local allies who lusted after power, traitors who betrayed their Arab identity and Islam—their faith." The French and British "cut and occupied our homeland, and set Arab against Arab, Muslim against Muslim;" furthermore, he adds, Arab rulers today continue to be "slaves to foreign influence."[18]

The same anniversary statement focuses on how the occupiers "broke the Islamic caliphate" and then describes their revival movement as a quest to "restore the soul of the Islamic homelands" and free them from "a secular Westernizing plot that still works its way among us."

Obviously, the ruling Arab elite—villains in the Brotherhood's story—regarded the group's explosive growth as an imminent threat. The Brotherhood was banned in Egypt in 1948 and al-Banna was assassinated in 1949. This was regarded by the Brothers as proof of their case, and fortunately for them, al-Banna's successor was a prolific writer, a brilliant, innovative intellect and man of truly extraordinary conviction and integrity.

Sayyid Qutb's diagnoses of the world's ills and his prescribed cure impacted the lives of hundreds of millions. World history from 1970 would be unrecognizable to us if this man had not written what he did; his influence has only grown with each successive decade since Egypt executed him 1966.

Qutb lived for a time in the United States, leading him to judge the condition of global humanity to be at a breaking point: humans lived in abject alienation from their natural, God-given state, and all lived in bestial degeneracy, as evidenced by unbounded sexual licentiousness, alcoholism, and drug addiction. All were symptomatic of existential bankruptcy, and in his view, it was this rot that the Western powers sought to impose on the Islamic heartland. As it blazed the trail on this headlong drive into depraved ignorance, the Christian West's "treacherous orientalists" utilized the "evil designs" of "world Jewry" to suck the Muslim world into its folly.[19] Two aspects of this "trickery" are worth our notice, as they shed light on the logic of militant Islam.

First, Qutb deplored the West's idea that religion is a set of optional personal convictions, "merely a name for 'belief' in the heart," he scoffed. Muslim scholars living in the West, the cherished moderates, "with their defeated mentality," bore Qutb's judgment for having adopted this shopping-cart style "Western concept of 'religion.'"

No, he said. The truth is not a matter of opinion or personal conviction. "Islam is not merely a belief... Islam is the way of life ordained by Allah Almighty for all mankind, and this way establishes the Lordship of Allah alone."[20] For Qutb and his millions of followers, religion is not a choice but a detailed system for living, handed to us from God as a finished corpus *in toto*, which applies to everyone whether they believe in God or not. This is particularly prickly with Islam, because this true religion, as Qutb writes, is the

"Haakimiyah (sovereignty or kingdom) of Allah—and orders practical life in all its daily details."

Moreover, argues Qutb, this head-to-toe monopoly on belief "throws a completely new light on the Islamic Jihad." Westernized Muslim scholars wrongly "conceive of religious war as a war to impose belief on peoples' hearts." Not so, says Qutb. It has nothing to do with beliefs; therefore, "Jihad in Islam is simply a name for striving to make this system of life dominant in the world."

Note that the key words are "system" and "dominant." Jihad is not a moral argument—it is law enforcement. In the early days of Islam, writes Qutb, "Jihad bis-Saif (striving through fighting with the sword)... was a movement to wipe out tyranny and to introduce true freedom to mankind." Qutb thus taught that jihad's aim to make Islam the "dominant system in the world" was an act of liberation. "Only in this manner can the way of life be wholly dedicated to Allah, so that neither any human authority nor the question of servitude remains." In other words, true freedom only occurs in total submission to Islam; everything else is subjection to mere human ideas.

For Qutb and the Muslim Brothers, the first order of business was to rid themselves of the Westernized Arab elites. They would replace them with genuine Islamic states based on Islamic law. Then the overarching universality of God's sovereignty would supersede local secular nationalism. Because it is transnational, this superseding authority also applies to all Muslims wherever they live, even if they are citizens of the Western nations: "Other societies do not give it [Islam] any opportunity to organize its followers according to its own method, and hence it is the duty of Islam to annihilate all such systems, as they are obstacles in the way of universal freedom." Please pay attention to what he says—namely, that the duty of Islam is to annihilate other systems.

Qutb and the Brotherhood's founders inspired generation after generation. We've seen it in their powerful presence in the Arab Spring and their ascendency to power in Egypt. We see them also in the outlook of Hamas, in Egypt's Islamic Jihad, in Turkey's longest ruling party, and in Islamists in Syria and North Africa. We see the same ideas in extreme offshoots like al-Qaeda and the Islamic State—all these various Islamist movements are founded upon precepts cultivated by the Brotherhood. Even Iran's Ayatollah Khomeini, although a Shiite, admitted to the influence of Muslim Brotherhood ideas. Iran openly honors Qutb in particular.

In these terms, we can see an illustration of Islam's peace as it evolved in modern Egypt. In 1981, President Anwar Sadat was gunned down by members of Egyptian Islamic Jihad. His crime was making peace with Israel's prime minister, Menachem Begin. The deal, signed under the watchful eye of US president Jimmy Carter, was the last straw for the Islamists. In their eyes, Sadat's agreement with a born-again Christian and Israeli Jew showed him to be the steward of Crusader ambitions. But it was not anything like that: it was an honest agreement to live in peace agreed to by rival siblings prepared to live equitably as part of the human family. It wasn't good enough because it wasn't a peace achieved through domination—it wasn't pacification.

Over the years, I've known many Muslim Brotherhood members and others inspired by their founders. I know them well enough that they speak honestly with me, without obfuscations and ambiguous terms. They present their support of violence in Quṭbian terms: it is a benevolent act of liberation—done in my best interests, they assure me.

From my first cloak-and-dagger meetings with exiled Muslim Brothers in Athens in the 1980s, to ISIS supporters I've encountered in the 2010s, all have described to me their militancy as an act of grace that promises to free me from idolatry and subjugation to limited human ideas. They want me to know the peace of the House of Islam, to surrender to Allah and thus remove myself from the House of War that I've imprisoned myself in.

And if I remain captive in the *Dar al-Harb*? As long as I'm in it, I am subject to jihad, but it is my fault. Their deepest wish for me is that I might know the true liberty of obedience to God as presented untainted in Islam. I have no reason to doubt their sincerity.

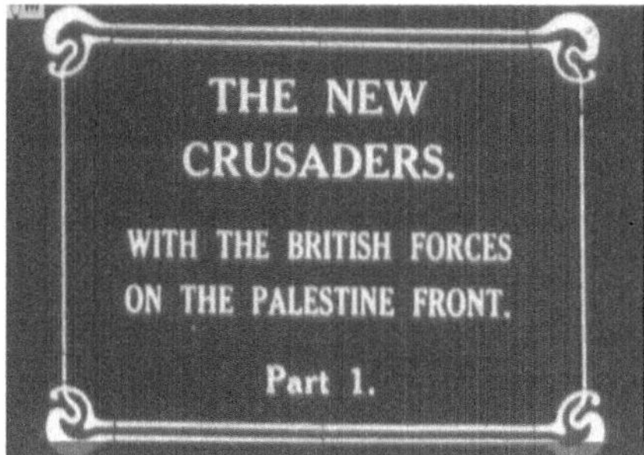

British government film from WW1

Christians invoked the Crusades during the First World War when Britain fought against the Muslim Ottoman Empire.

War's end led to the dissolution of the caliphate.

To this day, the Muslim Brotherhood and Hamas cite the war and its aftermath in terms of the Crusades and the End Time.

The Muslim Brotherhood's ideas spread beyond the Arab world to deeply influence non-Arab and non-Sunni Muslims.

The Iranian Shiite leader, Imam Ayatollah Ruhollah Khomeini, relied heavily on the scholarship and inspiration of the Egyptian Muslim Brotherhood's Sayyid Quṭb.

He is honored here on an Islamic Republic of Iran postage stamp from my collection.

Recep Tayyip Erdoğan, Turkey's president, also espouses the Brotherhood's ideals. In this photograph, from the centennial of the Battle of Gallipoli, Erdoğan prays with Prince Charles.

Erdoğan has been quick to remind his nation that this World War One battle was a continuation of the Crusades.

A powerful political lobby developed as many American Christians and Jews came to see Israel as the definitive sign of the End Time.
Menachem Begin's Likud Party supported evangelicals who campaigned for Ronald Reagan, a true believer in End Time prophecy.

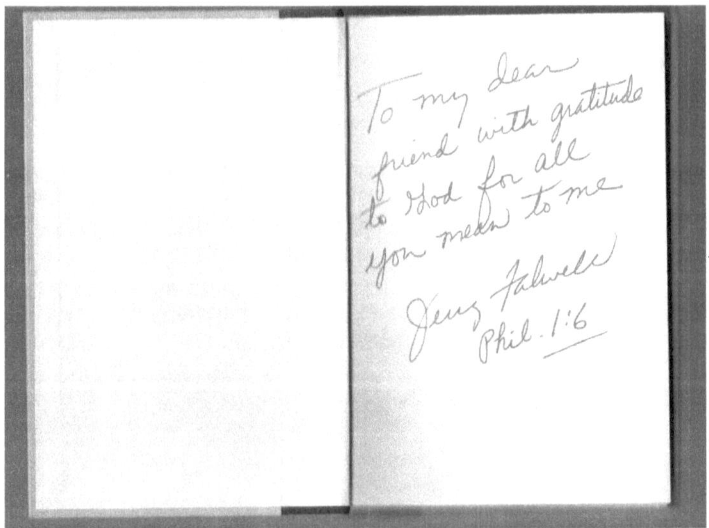

Moral Majority founder Jerry Falwell was among the Christian leaders that Israel supported.
His 1979 biography, *Aflame for God*, was written by a conservative Jewish activist with strong links to Likud Party stalwarts in Israel.
Pictured: my copy of *Aflame for God*.

15

APOCALYPSE NOW

Islam's Armageddon

It is not only the assassins who are enraptured by this false Paradise—their acts of violence are buoyed by a larger society. What does millenarian populism look like in the modern Muslim world? Unfortunately, it looks a lot like Syria and Iraq.

In 2012, the Pew Research Center sampled opinions across the Middle East, North Africa, and Muslim South Asia; it was not biased toward particularly pious Muslims or activists, but rather included a cross section of the population in Muslim-majority nations. They found that more than half believe they will live to see the appearance of the Mahdi, the prophesied leader who will appear with Jesus in the Last Days to combat *Al-Masīḥ ad-Dajjāl*, the "False Messiah" or Antichrist. The figures for those expecting to see this glorious day were especially high in Afghanistan at 83 percent, Iraq at 72 percent, and Turkey at 68 percent.[1] (The poll was not conducted in Iran, Saudi Arabia, Syria, or Yemen—all of which presumably exceed the higher percentages.)

As in the West, modernity has not mitigated these beliefs—if anything, it's made them more urgent. Owing to the ubiquity of mass media in the Information Age, specific End Time theories have taken on the authority of religious canon. Television imams mimic the phenomenon of Christian television evangelists, and high literacy rates (like those in Enlightenment Europe) have enabled ordinary Muslims to choose from a broad spectrum of eschatological interpretations. For every narrow ideology, higher literacy has meant the rise of a majority that is just educated enough to get into serious trouble. There is little real intellectual rigor or discipline.

The template was cut by Egyptian author Said Ayyub, who wrote his book *Al-Dajjal* (The Antichrist) in 1987. Echoed by countless copy-cat books and TV imams, it was to the Islamic world what the *The Late Great Planet Earth* was for Christians—a runaway bestseller that rabidly interpreted traditional prophecies through modern geopolitical realities.

Barbara Stowasser summarized the genre for the Yale Center for International and Area Studies: "This contemporary apocalyptic literature, then, is anti-Western in that it sees the West (often equated with Christianity) as the main breeding ground of immorality."

She adds that in the Islamic apocalyptic context, the Arab-Israeli conflict was drawn into "popular sermons, pulp-fiction narratives, on Websites" to "set the tone for an apocalyptic millenarian mind-frame in their mass audiences and readers." Invariably, "Israel is seen either as an embodiment of the [Antichrist] Dajjal's power, or as his agent and instrument in accomplishing his goals."[2]

Stowasser noticed that the information was passed along in "an Islamist-fundamentalist information loop of oral communication, video and audio cassettes of sermons delivered by Islamist preachers, popular pulp fiction narratives, and the new electronic media including Web sites and Home pages." Writing in 2002, she could not have known how awfully effective this would be in the hands of global jihadists a decade later. The way the Internet would circumvent state censorship to create large bodies of virtually connected brothers in arms was entirely unforeseen by scholars and a total surprise to our spy masters.

The most glaring example was ISIS, whose propaganda relied heavily on Last Days interpretations popularized by Ayyub—something obvious right from their first publication. I'll leave it to you for further reading, beginning with a highly regarded article by Graeme Wood in the *Atlantic Monthly*. The subheading tells us enough for now: "The Islamic State is no mere collection of psychopaths. It is a religious group with carefully considered beliefs, among them that it is a key agent of the coming apocalypse."[3]

ISIS is just one example. All the Sunni Muslim fighters in Syria and Iraq —some affiliated with al-Qaeda and some bizarrely supported directly by the United States—also believe that they are waging the last war. As a Syrian Islamist rebel told Reuters, "If you think all these mujahideen came from across the world to fight Assad, you're mistaken. They are all here as promised by the Prophet. This is the war he promised—it is the Grand Battle."[4]

This young warrior reflects the thinking of Abu Musab al-Suri, a Syrian Muslim Brotherhood member who joined Osama bin Laden in Afghanistan as part of al-Qaeda's inner circle; he gets credit from numerous sources for "radicalizing" a hitherto moderate bin Laden (who was, of course, originally fighting America's war against the Soviets, with American-supplied weapons).

After 9/11, al-Suri took the opportunity afforded by a lengthy period in hiding to write his 1,600-page book, *A Call to Global Islamic Resistance*. Published on the Internet in 2004, it had an enormous impact on the development of the Syrian Civil War and the global recruitment of jihadists. It is at once a rationale for jihad, an explicit justification for terrorism ("terrorizing the enemies is a religious duty"), and a practical training manual for how to do it.[5] To that end, al-Suri relies on the Quran: "And prepare against them whatever you are able of power and of steeds of war by which you may terrify the enemy of Allah and your enemy and others besides them whom you do not know [but] whom Allah knows. And whatever you spend in the cause of Allah will be fully repaid to you, and you will not be wronged."[6]

French scholar Jean-Pierre Filiu analyzed this material for his award-winning research on Islamic apocalypticism, concluding that al-Suri's work should not be misunderstood: "There is nothing in the least theoretical about this exercise in apocalyptic exegesis... It is meant as a guide for action."[7] That's exactly what we've seen in the Middle East from 1990 until now—it is End Time action, not a conventional war over resources or power.

So why are Sunni fighters fighting Shiite Muslims? It's a house of apocalyptic mirrors. Listen to the young Shiite fighters, and you'll hear the same motivations recited by the Sunnis for killing Shiites. They see one another as prophesied apostates—one of the signs of the end. Each sees that role fulfilled by their brothers, based on differences in offerings made to the same God—not unlike Cain and Abel.

Abbas, an Iraqi Shiite fighter in his mid-twenties, is representative of the young Shiites who joined the war by the tens of thousands. He told Reuters that he knew he was living in the era of the Mahdi's return when the United States invaded Iraq in 2003. "That was the first sign and then everything else followed." It didn't matter that the United States was there to oust Saddam Hussein, a vicious enemy of Shiites, or that the result was a Shiite-dominated government. All that matters is the millenarian significance of it. As of this writing, he is on his fourth tour of duty in Syria—assuming he's still alive.

Messianism among Shiites is not new. *Encyclopaedia Iranica* introduces the topic by stating that "Messianism is one of the most powerful, diverse and enduring expressions of Islam in Iran throughout its long history. Messianic speculations are evident especially in Shi'ite literature ranging from Hadith, theology, and philosophy to occult sciences, and folklore."[8] These speculations have real consequences. "Messianic yearnings also motivated a number of epoch-making popular movements with political ambitions and lasting influence on Iranian cultural identity."

The 1979 Iranian Revolution is the leading example. It is, in essence, a Shiite version of Quṭb's rejection of Western contamination, but a more successful application of what the Muslim Brotherhood aspired to do—in Iran, it resulted in a true Islamic state.

We could illustrate Shiite views further by quoting from dozens of established clerics and mainstream politicians in Iran, Iraq, and Lebanon, but one example is sufficient: former Iranian president Ahmed Ahmadinejad. He speaks as a genuine populist voice of the End Time–enraptured masses. All we have to do is read his Paradise-themed speeches to the United Nations General Assembly to understand what at least 17 million Iranian voters believe.

On one occasion, he calls on humanity to tread "the path of the divine prophets and the righteous under the leadership of Imam al-Mahdi, the Ultimate Savior of mankind."[9] At another session, he announced, "I am here to voice the divine and humanitarian message of learned men and women of my country to you and to the whole world; God Almighty has promised us... a man who is a perfect human being and is named Imam Al-Mahdi, a man who will come in the company of Jesus Christ (PBUH) and the righteous... He will lead humanity into achieving its glorious and eternal ideals."[10]

All this by way of explaining Iran's foreign policy, which rests largely upon supplying militias to fight in Lebanon, Iraq, Syria, and ultimately against Israel's existence. Israel's annihilation is the objective celebrated every year on Iran's holiday, Jerusalem Day. According to Mr. Ahmadinejad, the goal of Iranian policy is "the arrival of the Ultimate Savior" who will "mark a new beginning, a rebirth and a resurrection. It will be the beginning of peace, lasting security and genuine life... He will establish a world brimful of prudence and he will prepare the ground for the collective, active and constructive participation of all in the global management."

We can almost see Paradise's verdant gardens when the Iranian president concludes with this evocative image of the Mahdi's nearness—it is so close we can smell it:

Now we can sense the sweet scent and the soulful breeze of the spring, a spring that has just begun and doesn't belong to a specific race, ethnicity, nation or a region... He will be the spring of all the justice-seekers, freedom-lovers and the followers of heavenly prophets. He will be the spring of humanity and the greenery of all ages.

Spring, we should recall, begins with Newroz Day, the Zoroastrian idea that started it all, and which is still celebrated in Iran.

With the collapse of ISIS, Iranian militias now dominate Iraq and Syria, building missile bases that target Israel. ISIS fighters have not vanished, however; they've regrouped, many joining other Sunni militias including al-Qaeda, and others going home to plot another insurrection. They will work to infiltrate and undermine Arab governments and regimes across the region. Could it be that this awful civil war was only the prelude?

If so, it may be because the Muslim warriors are not alone in confusing peace and pacification. If we removed their specific identifying characteristics and listened only to expected outcomes, Israeli and Christian millenarians can be heard espousing ideas remarkably similar to the Muslim warriors.

Times of the Gentiles

In Israel today, 22 percent of the Jewish population believes that the Israeli state is a fulfillment of prophecy and portends the End of Days.[11] This group is what Israelis call the National-Religious block, but outside of Israel, they are more commonly known simply as Religious Zionists. What sets them apart is their contention that it is a religious duty to possess all the biblical lands of Israel and Judea.

Affiliation with this ideology does not exactly equate to religious practice or beliefs, however. Although about 50 percent of the Israeli Jewish population identifies as secular, a sizable sampling of this demographic nonetheless supports the Religious Zionist ideal. The term "Religious Zionist" can therefore be misleading; you can be a Religious Zionist without keeping up strict religious practices.

Confusingly, this statistic mirrors the well-known fact that many devoutly religious Jews do not endorse the political ideology of Religious Zionism at all. The ultra-Orthodox (about 10 percent of Israeli Jews) believe that the restoration of Israel can only be the work of the Messiah, not of ordinary human political efforts. They are extremely religious, but pointedly not Religious Zionists.

Affinity for Israel's biblical identity therefore comes in various shades of intensity across a wide range of more and less religious and secular beliefs and practices.

This ought to be expected given the origins of Zionism with Zvi Hirsch Kalischer and his practicalities-first, let-the-donkey-do-the-work strategy for redeeming the Holy Land. Most early Zionists were not religious at all. Those who actually ascended to Zion in the 1800s and early 1900s tended to be agnostic socialists, like my kibbutzniks.

Religious Zionism took some time to catch on. It was Rabbi Avraham Isaac Kook, who became the Ashkenazi Chief Rabbi in Palestine in 1924, who legitimized Zionism as a religious act, recognizing it as part of God's plan to restore and redeem Israel, making the connection between secular Zionism and the Messiah's donkey.[12]

But all Zionism is built on biblical promises of restoration, which even agnostic Zionists were wont to quote for nationalistic purposes; and because the state was brought into being on the basis of Jewish identity, the whole thing is inescapably connected to religion, no matter how nominally it is practiced. Over time, nationalist feelings naturally became conflated with religions ones—hence the large number of secular Israelis who identify with Religious Zionism.

Not even an atheist can escape it completely. Israel is a Jewish state; the religious hierarchy determines who is allowed to live in it and significant matters relating to how one lives, whom one can marry, and where one is buried. The secular half of the country can't easily write themselves out of the religious story. They live within the narrative of redemption just by being Israeli.

They are not alone; they have a considerable number of Gentiles to keep them company. The Christians who helped inspire the Zionist movement naturally met Israel's statehood in 1948 with ecstatic joy—they'd been predicting it for years. The *Moody Monthly*, a representative mouthpiece of evangelicalism, evaluated Israel's statehood in terms of Ezekiel's prophecy of the dry bones, just as Kalischer and Mather predicted: "The valley of dry bones, the arid land, the stony hills, and the swampy marshes are coming to life." *Moody Monthly* summed up Christian sentiments with this headline: "God's clock has struck."[13] Thus, Religious Zionists and Christian dispensationalists regarded Israel's restoration as a sovereign state to be the beginning of a final countdown. They were excited and hopeful, even if the next stage—control of the Temple Mount—was utterly inconceivable.

Among the nations, a similar Messiah's-donkey pattern emerged. Christians believed that prophecy was being fulfilled by unwitting secular Gentiles, namely the leaders of America and Britain. For the most part, as in Israel, the unwitting played along just fine.

When the biggest donkey of all, the United Nations, voted to establish Israel, much of America found itself caught up in the chronicle of prophetic zeal. Mainstream news media depicted Israel as a David against the Arab Goliath. During the war in 1948, for example, typical headlines included this, from the front page of the *Los Angeles Times*: "Holy Land Will Be Under Attack Tomorrow."[14] It sounds like a passage heading in the Bible—Joshua and the battle of Jericho.

"The armies of four Arab nations were reported closing in tonight... before the British surrender their Holy Land mandate... Jewish defenders... on the Jerusalem–Hebron Road withstood the Arab assault for more than 48 hours..." There is no hint of the complex reality that Arabs lived there already. American news generally portrayed Arabs as aggressors against the Promised Land, as if it had sat unchanged since the days of King David.

The secular media's romantic crush on Israel did not quickly fade, either. A survey of leading newspapers and magazines for the period bears this out. Nearly two decades later, under the heading "The Promised Land," *Time* magazine explains the background of Israel's tense position in the Middle East by telling its well-educated readers the story of Jacob's wrestling with the angel.

Israel "is the fulfillment of a struggle that has pitted the Jews against the world for 2,000 years," says *Time*'s writer, noting matter-of-factly that "it was the land of Canaan to which Abraham was given the divine deed."[15] This was the Old Testament as political science. Seeing Jewish Israel through biblical glasses was in America's blood.

The Arabs were not helped in this regard by the bellicose nationalism that came to dominate Egypt, Syria, and Iraq in the 1950s. Nor were they endeared to the American public by receiving arms and support from the Soviet Union, mixing rampant nuclear fears into an existential conflict that already seemed to come from the pages of the Apocalypse. These threats merged in America's popular imagination: godless Soviets allied with Arabs against the Puritans' New Jerusalem and the restored Jewish nation.

There had to be more, however. In 1948, the new State of Israel was missing the key pieces of Judea and Samaria, the core of the two biblical kingdoms of Judah and Israel. Presently they belonged to the Arabs, as did sacred Jerusalem, including the site of the Temple and the City of David. That had to change, and Christians knew exactly what to look for.

At least since the days of Increase Mather, Christian End Time interpreters focused on Luke's Gospel. There, the clearest sign was given when Jesus described the destruction of the Temple and the exile of the Jews from the city: "They shall fall by the edge of the sword, and shall be led away captive into all nations." That much had happened just as Jesus described it —this was the experience of the Jews over the past 2,000 years, and now with the Holocaust, it appeared to have reached its zenith.

Luke's story continues in the Book of Acts, where the disciples gathered around Jesus, just moments before he ascended to heaven, to ask, "Lord, is this the time when you will restore the kingdom to Israel?" He said no, they must wait and watch. For what? He had already told them the sign: "Jerusalem shall be trodden down of the Gentiles, until the times of the Gentiles be fulfilled."

This did not quite happen in 1948. While many prophecies from the Hebrew Bible were arguably fulfilled by the ingathering of the exiled Jewish people, this precise scenario given by Jesus required an end to Gentile hegemony over old Jerusalem and, specifically, the Temple Mount. In 1948, what they got was the land to the west of the city walls, while Muslims held the Temple precinct and the entire Old City under Jordanian rule.

It was a setup for an implausible miracle. The likelihood of the Arabs ever surrendering this sacred ground was non-existent. Jerusalem's Arab rulers had already fought a bitter war to contest Israel's statehood, had the backing of the Soviet Union, and were going from strength to strength.

By 1967, a series of escalations, misleading Soviet intelligence, and a web of mutual defense agreements brought Egypt, Jordan, and Syria to the brink of all-out war with Israel. Egypt's Abdel Gamal Nasser was the main instigator, and his rhetoric played straight into the biblical scenario of Armageddon. Typical is this Nasser gem from 1965: "We aim at the destruction of the State of Israel. The immediate aim: perfection of Arab military might. The national aim: the eradication of Israel."[16]

Radio Baghdad concurred: "Kill the Jews!" Syrian radio's forecast predicted glory: "We will destroy Israel in four days." Egyptian radio joined the chorus: "Our people have been waiting twenty years for this battle... Now they will teach Israel the lesson of death!"[17]

Although Israel was judged to have a qualitative military advantage, this was by no means a guarantee of survival. If war broke out, most experts believed the Israelis could defend themselves, but only at great cost in human life and property. Two and half million Jews were packed into narrow, feebly connected strips of land.

This is a talking point that Israel still deploys as propaganda, but it also happens to be true. On the brink of war, Egypt's state-controlled media emphasized exactly this vulnerability: "Jordanian artillery, coordinated with the forces of Egypt and Syria, is in a position to cut Israel in two... where Israeli territory between the Jordan armistice line and the Mediterranean Sea is only 12 kilometers wide."[18]

With such rhetoric encouraging all the Arab states to join together to push the Jews into the sea, the Israelis understandably felt that another Holocaust was in the making.

Jerusalem Syndrome

Israeli historian Tom Segev considers the domestic background of the 1967 war to be as important as Nasser's threats. Segev is regarded as a revisionist, meaning that his research has led him to conclusions that do not support the traditional—some would say, mythological—way that Israel has told this story. I think both versions are important, valid, and real—in fact, the mythological one has a reality and effect of its own, matching or exceeding the more earthly dynamics that historians like Segev uncover. One is the key to understanding the other.

As for the political background, the true intentions of Nasser, the genuineness of the threat, and any possible ulterior motives the Israelis had are all worthy subjects about which a slew of books may be read. My conclusion is that forces greater than any of the players—not necessarily *the* higher power, but *a* higher power, nonetheless—caused the crisis. Once again, the non-human archetypes, the overarching structures, the narrative force of collective story and corporate behavior, the ideological frameworks and virtual identities: it is those things that combined here to cause a war, which, according to the clear accounts of every actor involved, no one actually wanted.

How did it happen, then? How does a war involving multiple states and two global superpowers get started when no one wants it? The answer lies in the accumulation of details, the specific stories of individuals, and that's where Segev's research sheds light; it shines most brightly through the lenses of ordinary people.

The cumulative testimony of private diaries and correspondence shows to what extent the epoch-making events of 1967 were beyond the control of decision makers. As in a hurricane, the storm will probably form if certain conditions are present: deep, warm water for energy, a lack of interfering wind shear, and, critically, an atmospheric depression. In 1960s Israel, the heat and depression were unrelenting.

As we read newspaper editorials and private correspondence, national malaise strikes us at every turn. Israel's economy was in terrible shape and disillusioned young people were leaving by the thousands. Segev recounts evidence reflecting "an extremely solemn mood, almost one of bereavement." In a typical example from 1966, the Israeli daily *Haaretz* laments, "There is bitter desperation everywhere." Another editorial in the same paper wondered, "When all hope is lost, what else can one hope for if not a miracle?"[19]

Many readers will be surprised to know that before the early 1960s, discussing the Holocaust was nearly taboo in Israeli society. It was too fresh, the pain too close. Also, many Israelis were embarrassed by their European kin, by the weakness they perceived in them. Sabras, native-born Israelis from the first waves of Zionism, had never lived in Europe and knew nothing but self-sufficient strength. They spoke Hebrew as their mother tongue and grew up as victors in every war they had fought. They had little in common with the wave of European-born Jews that arrived after the Holocaust. It was incomprehensible to them that Jews would have allowed themselves to be led as lambs to the slaughter.

That changed with the capture and public trial of Nazi fugitive Adolph Eichmann in 1961. It was a catharsis and a catalyst for bringing Israelis together. The Holocaust was transformed in the Israeli psyche; it become a symbol not of weakness but of survival, and a bitterly rooted motivation to never, ever allow anything like it to happen again, at all costs.

Young Ofer Feniger felt compelled to write to his girlfriend after witnessing the Eichmann trial: "I feel that from all the horror and the helplessness, a hugely powerful strength is growing in me." A typical native-born Israeli, Ofer speaks as the voice of a generation reconstructed by its vicarious experience of the Holocaust, which is what the very public Eichmann trial afforded to many. It was a communal rite that united all Jews.

Ofer reveals a widespread response when he writes that the trial made him "strong to the point of tears; sharp as a knife; quiet and terrible; that's how I want to be! I want to know that never again will hollow eyes look out from behind electric fences! Not if I am strong! If we are all strong! Strong, proud Jews! Never again to be led to the slaughter."[20]

Now we have to juxtapose that with Arab political hyperbole. After Eichmann, rhetoric like Nasser's vow to complete the "eradication of Israel" could not be heard only as the words of a blowhard. "Nasser speaks clearly, as

Hitler did on the eve of the Second World War," wrote columnist Ze'ev Schiff for *Haaretz*, expressing an opinion that was growing at precisely the rate of Nasser's increasingly malignant threats. When Hitler talked like this, no one took him seriously.[21] The post-Eichmann thinking said, "Let's not make that mistake again."

It was impossible to shut out. The Eastern Mediterranean is a crowded house and Israelis could easily receive broadcasts from Cairo and judge Nasser's Hitler impersonation for themselves. No Arabic? Not a problem. As a courtesy to its audience, Egypt broadcast the threats in Hebrew, too. "Your leaders will not help you," the Cairo propagandists raged, "they will bring a Holocaust upon you!" A letter from a Tel Aviv woman to her family back in Boston captured the ambience: "Anyone who can pick up Cairo television must have been wetting themselves with fear over the past few weeks."[22]

Israel's leaders were frightened, too. They were confident they could win a war, but not if they waited to be attacked first. Generally, the civilian and military leadership thought the situation was far more dangerous than anything Israel had experienced, far more serious than the 1948 War of Independence. If convinced that Nasser really was going to attack, they would have to preempt or be annihilated.

Yitzhak Rabin was military chief of staff. As war became imminent, he instructed schools and public buildings to prepare to serve as hospitals, stating that he anticipated casualties in the tens of thousands. Rabbis were dispatched to go through public parks to sanctify them as burial grounds. As Segev notes, "Only a society drenched in the memory of the Holocaust could have prepared so meticulously for the next one."[23]

American Christian leaders expressed the same fears. They joined together in signing a petition in the name of "Americans of all persuasions and groupings" to "urge the Administration to support the independence, integrity and freedom of Israel." The Johnson White House had to listen: the petition was signed by a host of Roman Catholic, Protestant, and Russian Orthodox leaders. This is already an unusual coming together of minds, but the breadth of support is illustrated best by considering two prominent signatories, hardly figures associated with conservative politics: Rev. Dr. Martin Luther King and Dr. Reinhold Niebuhr.[24]

To reiterate: no one wanted this war. Nasser did not want it and Israel did not want it. This is absolutely clear from the archival record. As often happens, a series of unintended consequences, energized by foolish, difficult-to-retract verbal bombast, escalated and spun out of control. Key factors: Nasser had painted himself into a corner with his big mouth and was forced to position armor and troops into a threatening stance, poised apparently for an invasion; Israel mobilized its reserves in response, thinking he would not invade, but not quite sure. The tipping point: Soviet disinformation led Tel Aviv to judge that the invasion was imminent and that a preemptive strike on Egypt's air forces was their only chance. Once it started, treaty obligations drew in the remaining unwilling parties of Jordan and Syria.

This is, of course, the Six-Day War, so-named by Minister of Defense Moshe Dayan, who was given the honor when it was all over. The name is not so much about the war's length as it is about Israel's inexplicable success. God did the work of Creation in six days and rested on the seventh; Israel's deliverance from Nasser's Egypt appeared to be every bit as miraculous.

At war's end, Israel was left in control of Gaza, the Golan Heights, Moses' Sinai, and all of the West Bank's biblical Judea and Samaria. It was a wholly unexpected and exhilarating outcome. The lands they acquired were the lands of the Bible, the missing pieces of prophetic fulfillment. The acquisition of Jerusalem and the Temple Mount was the most surprisingly miraculous thing of all. Jewish people now had access to the Western "Wailing" Wall, the only surviving part of Herod's Temple, and furthermore, they had absolute control of the Muslim holy sites.

For the Arabs, it was equally stunning. Jordan and Egypt's armed forces were totally decimated; Syria was humiliated. Ten Arab soldiers were dead for every Israeli killed in combat, despite the Jews being on the defensive in a confined space.

At first, it wasn't clear even if Muslims would be allowed to worship again at the place of Muhammad's ascent into heaven. It was for Arabs a disaster of biblical proportions every bit as much as it was a Bible-sized epic of salvation for Israelis.

Dispensationalist Christians were elated. The second portion of Jesus' prediction about the End Time was fulfilled! The long dispensation of Gentile rule over Jerusalem was finished! The City of David was now firmly under Jewish feet for the first time in 2,000 years! Evangelical leaders in America at once recognized the implications: this was something that was supposed to happen, something predicted and expected—but wow, it really happened! And against overwhelming odds! Angels must have fought on Israel's behalf to secure such a lopsided victory! The Bible had come to life!

John Walvoord, president of Dallas Theological Seminary, characterized the war's outcome as having "climaxed one of the most remarkable fulfillments of biblical prophecy since the destruction of Jerusalem in A.D. 70."[25]

In short order, Carl Henry, the editor of the highly regarded *Christianity*

Today magazine, called for Christian leaders to assemble in newly restored Jerusalem. This "Jerusalem Conference on Biblical Prophecy" hosted over 1,500 delegates gathered from thirty-two nations.

Israel's founding prime minister, David Ben-Gurion, addressed the delegates quoting from Isaiah.[26] Although Ben-Gurion was a socialist pioneer, and not a religious man, he disclosed here, as he'd done many times in his life, the underlying inspiration of the Bible in his secular nationalism and humanistic ideals. Standing before the applauding Christians, he appeared every inch the Messiah's donkey.

The conference was not for dilettantes: these were serious leaders, including the pillar of the Southern Baptists, W.A. Criswell; representatives of the National Association of Evangelicals; the venerable Dr. John R.W. Stott from London; leaders of powerful youth organizations, including Inter-Varsity Christian Fellowship and Youth for Christ; and prominent theologians from the Dallas and Talbot theological seminaries, plus the Gordon-Conwell Divinity School, among others.

Talbot's dean, Charles Feinberg, spoke in reference to Ezekiel 40–48 to show that, with Jerusalem now freed from the feet of the Gentiles, the next prophetic event had to be a rebuilt Temple. His closing remarks: "With charity toward all and not one whit of malice toward any, we hold unswervingly to the literal interpretation of Ezekiel 40–48: THE TEMPLE WILL BE REBUILT!"[27]

A reporter commented that the majority of delegates showed their agreement with Feinberg through their enthusiastic applause. Dr. C. Everett Koop, a prominent Presbyterian and legendary pioneer of pediatric surgery, was one of them. The future United States surgeon general remarked that all agreed on "the soon return of the Lord."[28]

Meanwhile, Pat Robertson was literally breaking ground on what would become the Christian Broadcasting Network (CBN) when news of the Israeli miracle broke. He saw the two events as divinely connected. Pat would go on to become immensely influential—not just on yours truly, but at the highest levels of American politics, as founder of the Christian Coalition, the American Center for Law & Justice (ACLJ), and Regent University, to name a few of his achievements. CBN was the foundation of it all, a foundation laid exactly as Jerusalem was being reclaimed by the feet of Jewish warriors.

Fittingly, in honor of the 50th anniversary of the Six-Day War, CBN produced *In Our Hands*, a film about Israel's 55th Paratrooper Brigade, which had led the battle for Jerusalem. It was their soldiers who telegraphed the news to the world: "The Temple Mount is in our hands!"

Commenting to the *Jerusalem Post* on the film, CBN spokesman Michael Conrad effectively summarized the feelings of a great many evangelical Christians, including, no doubt, a few who managed to be elected president of the United States:

> The Six Day War is of tremendous importance to Christians... It is seen as the fulfillment of a prophecy given by Jesus in Luke 21:24: "And they will fall by the edge of the sword, and be led away captive into all nations. And Jerusalem will be trampled by Gentiles until the times of the Gentiles are fulfilled."

"We believe the times of the Gentiles have been fulfilled—the Jews are back, and Israel has been reborn," he said. "The Jews have been set apart, unable to assimilate into the cultures of the dispersion and are being gathered once more to the land of Israel."[29]

Mather's prophecies continue to be fulfilled.

Fulfilling Prophecy

We might expect that CBN would mythologize the Six-Day War, but most mainstream reporting in 1967 did the same thing. *Time* set the tone with its star-struck description of Moshe Dayan, Israel's "dashing, one-eyed Hero of Sinai," who led his troops through "astonishing hours of incredibly accurate bombing and strafing."[30] Israel's white-hat heroism glows bright against the darkness of communism. "Israel erased an expensive decade of Russian military aid to the Arab world."

Nasser and company lay on the page in vivid contrast to Dayan's suavité and cowboy derring-do. *Time* magazine paints the Arabs as inept, insanely violent, and cowardly, calling Nasser "venomous." (Only King Hussein's troops received praise, although the editors cast the king himself as Nasser's dupe.) *Time* further describes Arabs as "hostile" and "menacing"; their desire for Israel's destruction isn't geopolitical, it is "lustful."

This opinion-setting report, the first and most widely read, evokes a pistol-packing Jewish maiden under the threat of Arab rape. "Ever since Israel was created 19 years ago, the Arabs have been lusting for the day when they could destroy it... With a hostile Arab population of 110,000,000 menacing their own 2,700,000, the Israelis could be forgiven for feeling a fearful itch in the trigger finger." An innocent teenager, Israel will be excused for blowing the head off of this Arab predator.

A photograph shows Dayan and Yitzhak Rabin at the Western Wall just after its capture; both are dressed in battle fatigues and helmets, the subliminal message being that the cowardly, loud-mouthed Nasser never got close to the fight he started, while these biblical heroes led their troops from the front. The image caption speaks volumes: "RABIN & DAYAN AT THE WAILING WALL—THE SYMBOL OF THE NATION BECAME THE SYMBOL OF GREATNESS."

The chances for future peace were judged to be slim because, "envenomed by their latest defeat," the Arabs were likely to "embark on a new orgy of irredentist fervor."[31] If they were defeated again it was their own fault, owing to their "ruinous enmity toward Israel." Envenomed, Lustful, and Menacing versus Dashing, Astonishing, and endowed with Greatness: who would you root for?

Seth King chimed in for the *New York Times* to assess the Israeli capture of Jerusalem as the return of "the site of King Solomon's temple to the control of a Jewish state after nearly 2,000 years."[32] On June 28, an editorial in the same publication, while cautioning that Israel's plans to annex the Old City of Jerusalem did not bode well for peace, nonetheless states that "no one can seriously dispute the legitimacy of Israel's interest in the Old City nor the reasonableness of its demands."[33]

I've cited these reports to show how quickly non-religious people raised in a Judeo-Christian culture can fall in line with serious millenarians regarding sacred Jerusalem. If space allowed, we could do the same thing with reference to media reports from the Islamic world, colored instead by their own mythologies of Jerusalem. To this day, Arab and Turkish press paints geopolitical developments in terms of victimization by the rapacious Crusader-Zionist alliance. It is very difficult to filter out the lexicon of millenarianism from political developments in Jerusalem—perhaps impossible—and the more intense the struggle, the more likely we are to see the world polarized into camps supporting one side or the other.

In Israel, secular autonomy was the war's biggest casualty, transformed forever by a transfusion of religious Zionism into the modern Israeli bloodstream. Fear was transformed into messianic fervor. "The people are drunk with joy," was how Israeli poet Natan Alterman put it. Segev summarized the euphoria as a quest "for the most elaborate superlatives; no flowery phrase or cliché was left unused."

Their euphoric speechlessness drove secular-minded Israelis to the Bible for the right words: "The Messiah came to Jerusalem yesterday... and he rode in on a tank," was the assessment of the centrist daily newspaper *Maariv*. Other papers carried headlines straight from the biblical conquests of Jericho and the cities of Canaan—often word-for-word quotes from the Hebrew Bible. The media repeatedly characterized the six days as "days of miracles."[34]

Hard-nosed Moshe Dayan was no exception: "We have returned to all that is holy in our land. We have returned never to be parted from it again."[35] Among the first to reach the Western Wall, which no Jew had been able to visit since 1948, it was Dayan who placed a written prayer within its cracks before anyone else could—it was for everlasting peace. It is a lovely prayer and the cornerstone of Isaiah's vision, but General Dayan's placing it there reminds us that since the day the prophet uttered it, his transcendent words have mostly been a cause for war.

For Religious Zionists, the days of miracles were proof again that God worked through their secular kin. Rabbi Avraham Isaac Kook's son, Zvi Yehudah, rose to the occasion, interpreting the Six-Day War as evidence that his father's teaching was correct: the Jewish people were in the middle years of an unfolding messianic redemption that had already begun, and all Israelis, even unbelievers like Dayan, were active participants in fulfilling it.

With the promised lands of Judea and Samaria—the West Bank—under Israeli control, logic dictated that redemption would be advanced by settling on those lands, just as Joshua did after the first deliverance from Egypt. Micah Goodman summarized the logic for *Haaretz*: "Settling the land is, then, both mitzvah and prophecy. It fulfills the initial parts of the vision of redemption and causes the fulfillment of the subsequent parts of the visions."[36] (A mitzvah is an act of religious obligation and a righteous deed.)

Ezekiel's prophecy of the dry bones was in the midst of fulfillment: in 1948, the dry bones were knit together, the skeleton of redemption was assembled. The Six-Day War put flesh on the bones. *Time* noticed the sequence. Less than a month after the war, the magazine's editors reminded readers of the rabbinical claim: "Israel has already entered its Messianic era." In 1948, recalls *Time*, "Israel's chief rabbis ruled that with the establishment of the Jewish state and the 'ingathering of the exiles,' the age of redemption had begun." And now, after the Six-Day War, "many of Israel's religious leaders are convinced that the Jews' victory over the Arabs has taken Judaism well beyond that point."

If 1948 put the bones together, and the Six-Day War put flesh on them, this, says *Time*, "raised an interesting theological conundrum." YHWH's life-giving spirit could enter the assembled flesh and bones only once the LORD's *shekhinah* glory returned to a rebuilt Temple. Indeed, in the chapters immediately following the dry bones, Ezekiel's next step is to describe the gloriously rebuilt Temple in detail. *Time* poses the obvious question: "Has the time now come for the erection of the Third Temple?"[37]

They got an answer from historian Israel Eldad: "We are at the stage where David was when he liberated Jerusalem. From that time until the construction of the Temple by Solomon, only one generation passed. So will it be with us." When *Time* asked, "And what about that Moslem shrine?" Eldad replied, "It is of course an open question. Who knows? Perhaps there will be an earthquake."

What would clear-minded Israeli secularists say? *Time*'s editors note that "although Zionism was largely a secular movement... one of its sources was the prayers of Jews for a return to Palestine so that they could build a new Temple." It's a sound observation, acknowledging the inseparability of Israeli nationalism from religion.

If any anecdote can illustrate Jerusalem's power to intoxicate the non-religious mind, it is Dayan's statement shortly after taking the Temple Mount. When asked his motivation in the battle, this icon of native-born profanity was suddenly smitten by the Holy Spirit: "Everybody fought for something that is a combination of love, belief and country. If I may say so, we felt we were fighting to prevent the fall of the Third Temple."[38]

The "Third Temple" means Ezekiel's prophesied Temple. If a secular icon like Moshe Dayan could become a warrior-prophet, the whole nation could. Why wait for an earthquake? If the actions of the Israeli people cause prophecy to be fulfilled, if settling the land is a mitzvah, wouldn't removing the Dome of the Rock also logically have to be a mitzvah—an act that would lead to the next stage of redemption? A significant number of well-placed and well-financed Israelis and their Christian supporters thought so.

If they had to, they'd make a geopolitical earthquake of their own.

Driving the Messiah's Donkey to World War III

In the early 1980s, a conspiracy of twenty-seven such believers tried to fulfill the mitzvah. The plan was not just to destroy buildings sacred to Islam, like the Dome of the Rock, but also to assassinate Palestinian leaders, blow up Palestinian passenger busses, and kill as many Muslim worshipers as possible. The plotters were not on the fringe; they were ordinary citizens, scholars of religion and veterans of the Israel Defense Forces.

In 2004, when a similar conspiracy surfaced, Likud Party parliamentarian Ehud Yatom sounded the alarm. As a commander of the Shin Bet unit that broke up the original plot in the nick of time, Yatom wanted everyone to understand how "very close" it had come to succeeding. His concerns are all the more compelling in light of his proximity to the case and his ideological position: Yatom was a hawkish member of the conservative Likud Party. The Likud is entirely sympathetic to Religious Zionist plans and a champion of settlement on the West Bank.

Also, it must be said, Ehud Yatom does not possess a squeamish disposition. He once obeyed unlawful orders to execute two Palestinian hijackers after their capture ("I smashed their skulls"); this led left-wing Meretz party boss Yossi Sarid to describe him as "the vermin of Israeli society, the rotten fruit of a military mentality devoid of values."[39] And yet, with all that, the possibility of blowing up the Dome of the Rock gave Yatom chills.

If the plot had succeeded, he said, "it would have meant the entire Muslim world against the State of Israel and against the Western world, a war of religions... Today's terrorist attacks would be nothing compared to what could happen—even World War III."[40]

This would have been fine with the 1984 plotters. That was their goal: to cause an apocalyptic war, one which they truly believed would conclude as miraculously as the Six-Day War had, only this time with the rebuilding of the Temple and Israel's refounding as a kingdom under the Messiah.

What would the plotters say today? Just ask them. Yehuda Etzion has prominently dedicated himself to provocative action on the Temple Mount, incessantly challenging Israeli government prohibitions against Jewish activities there. Etzion was not only a member of the 1984 conspiracy—he was the man who planned the bombing. (Though convicted of terrorism, all the plotters were pardoned by 1990.)

Other Temple Mount activists hope to negotiate a Muslim surrender. The terms of capitulation would see the relocation of al-Aqsa and the Dome of the Rock to another site. "This is the place that symbolizes Zionist redemption, without it there is no meaning to Jewish life in this land," says Gershon Salmon, the founder of the Temple Mount and Land of Israel Faithful Movement.

Like many, Salmon's passion for the Temple Mount was aroused by the Six-Day War. He typifies those messianic enthusiasts who do not come from a religious background. Since the Six-Day War, his secular views have evolved into a kind of nationalist messianic vision—religion formed in an improvised rather than orthodox mold, the Messiah's donkey suddenly aware of its reason for existence. Salmon's biography illuminates the many "non-religious" Israelis who identify with Religious Zionism in the polls.

His more traditional counterparts are found in the Temple Institute, a religious body promoting a scholarly view in which the rabbinical sages have sanctioned rebuilding the Temple. Their work includes manufacturing the requisite clothing and tools for the priests, including the identification of the "Red Heifer," a flawless cow that must be used to consecrate the new sanctuary.

Have a look at their web site; maybe they've found the heifer by now.[41] And by all means take a break from reading and look at their slick videos on YouTube. One in particular is especially powerful: a young boy awakes on the morning of Tish'a b'Av, the anniversary of the destruction of the Temple. With keenly Paradise-laden phraseology, the synopsis explains that the boy "discovers the possibility of a better world, one in which the Holy Temple has been reestablished, and peace and happiness fills our lives."[42]

The special effects are startling. We walk in live action from the boy's point of view through the streets of Jerusalem's Old City until we reach the Western Wall Plaza. There, over the top ledge, we see the looming, unmistakable facade of the Holy Temple, sitting where we are accustomed to seeing the Dome of the Rock. As a former Jerusalemite, I can vouch for the realism and emotional effectiveness of this piece. It will without doubt serve to convince more than a few young Israelis that this dream is within reach.

The truth is that it would not take anything so extreme as demolishing the Dome of the Rock to set off an apocalyptic chain reaction. Every little thing is like a finger on the trigger. For example, when Salmon's group announced a plan to lay a cornerstone for the new Temple in 1990—just one symbolic stone—it provoked a protective response from Muslim Arabs that overwhelmed the Israeli police and ended in 21 deaths and 125 wounded. In 2000, soon-to-be prime minister Ariel Sharon sparked the Second Intifada simply by making a walking tour on the Mount.

The tensions run both ways. What would happen if an Israeli leader were to decide that Judea and Samaria were negotiable, that things might be returned in some measure to the pre-1967 status quo? That was put to the test when Prime Minister Yitzhak Rabin signed an agreement with King Hussein of Jordan and Yasser Arafat in 1993. The world applauded, but the mayor of Jerusalem described the agreement as "a dark cloud over the city."

If anyone had the right to reset the West Bank to pre–1967 lines, it was Rabin. He had been the armed forces chief of staff in 1967, the secular vehicle by which the Temple Mount and all the West Bank were secured.

With Dayan, he was one of the first to reach the Western Wall, making him a biblical hero. Now, as prime minister, he appeared ready to give it all away to Arafat, a bona fide terrorist.

Nothing could protect Rabin. Despite his historical credentials, he was summarily condemned by Israel's right wing and denounced as worthy of death by numerous influential rabbis. Settlers portrayed him as a traitor who stood in the way of fulfilling prophecy. Yigal Amir, a life-long scholar of the Talmud, determined it was a mitzvah to shoot and kill Rabin in 1995 at a peace rally; his stated reason was that any withdrawal from the territory captured in 1967 would deprive God's people of their "biblical heritage."[43]

For a sober and complete study of the link between Rabin's assassination and its religious cultural foundations, see *Murder in the Name of God: The Plot to Kill Yitzhak Rabin*.[44] Or, for a more hot-blooded account, Israeli author Seffi Rachlevsky writes compellingly to connect the dots between religious teaching about the End Time and acts of violence like this. "The Jewish underground of the early 1980s... and Amir should not be viewed as the acts of a few deranged individuals," writes Rachlevsky, "but as something much more."[45] The something more is broad popular belief in redemptive violence. Violent extremists do not exist in a vacuum; they take action on what thousands believe and say should be done.

What does the average Israeli think about the Temple Mount? In a 2010 poll by Israel's parliamentary television service, 49 percent of Israelis said they favored rebuilding the Holy Temple. Only 23 percent said they did not want it to be rebuilt; the remainder were undecided. The poll also showed that 42 percent believed that, in fact, it would be rebuilt at some point.[46]

"Messianists have hijacked Judaism," writes Rachlevsky, "leading us all down the garden path to Armageddon." He fears for his nation, arguing that if this trend is not contained, the "black hole" of those utopian ideologies will "swallow up religious Judaism, and after that perhaps Israel as a whole."

The Black Hole

All sides frame the Jerusalem question in irreducible terms; every aspect is non-negotiable, every decision an escalating provocation, every death a martyr's. Figures as fundamentally different as Donald Trump and Ayatollah Khomeini have been irresistibly sucked into the Black Hole.

Iran is so drawn to it that the last Friday of Ramadan is "Jerusalem Day," dedicated to the liberation of Jerusalem and the destruction of the "cancerous tumor" that is the State of Israel.[47] Why would Iran be so interested in a city that possesses no resources or practical strategic assets and that does not have access to shipping lanes nor even a decent airport? It has nothing to do with the plight of the Palestinian people—the answer lies entirely with eschatology, Muhammad's transit between heaven and Earth from Jerusalem's Foundation Stone.

Iranian moderates are as vigorous on this issue as the most rabid fundamentalists. Former Iranian president and champion of interfaith dialogue Mohammad Khatami instructed his people on their responsibilities: "In the Koran, God commanded to kill the wicked... If we abide by human laws, we should mobilize the whole Islamic World for a sharp confrontation with the Zionist regime. If we abide by the Koran, all of us should mobilize to kill."

Consider also Israel's trade partner, Turkey. President Erdoğan is known for his revival of Ottoman principles and his unprecedented defense of Palestinians, notable mainly because Turks and Arabs have not historically gotten along very well. The Ottomans were much kinder to Jews than to Arabs. Erdoğan, however, has been heavily influenced by modern Arab Islamic revivalism. As it turns out, a great many Turks felt as offended and oppressed by post–World War modernism as the Arabs did. Longing for the proud days of the caliphate brings devout Arabs, Turks, and Kurds together as never before.

Erdoğan made this clear when he reconsecrated Hagia Sophia as a mosque in 2020. You will recall that this was the Byzantine mother church and then the caliphal mosque under the Ottomans. Turkey's anti-Muslim post-war ruler, Mustafa Kemal Atatürk, turned it into a museum along with the sultan's palace. When President Erdoğan reconsecrated it as a mosque, he linked this decision explicitly to Jerusalem. "The resurrection of Hagia Sophia is a harbinger of the Masjid al-Aqsa's attainment of freedom. The resurrection of Hagia Sophia is the footsteps of the will of Muslims all over the world to exit the interregnum." ("Interregnum," Turkish *fetret devri*, is a period without revelation, often used in the Middle East to refer to the period following the First World War.)[48]

The soon-to-be freed Masjid al-Aqsa is of course the Muslim mosque adjacent to the Dome of the Rock in Jerusalem. It is the way Muslims refer to the entire Temple Mount upon which both sit. This is one of the three holy places of Islam—not the third in importance, but one of three together. The Quran says that in bridging Earth and heaven, the Mi'raj connects Mecca with Jerusalem. "Exalted is He who took His Servant by night from al-Masjid al-Haram to al-Masjid al-Aqsa, whose surroundings We have blessed."

By making this connection, Erdoğan says that restoring Hagia Sophia as a mosque is the first step to Muslims taking Jerusalem back. According to President Erdoğan, we hear it in "the footsteps of the will of Muslims all over the world." Jerusalem remains the focus, again not for geopolitical interests but eternal ones.

Erdoğan clearly made that point again while opening the October 2020 session of Turkey's parliament: "Knowing that this struggle will continue until the Judgment Day, we will always be prepared, always strong and always vigilant." He uses the Turkish word *mücadele* (mujah-deh-leh) for struggle, formed from the Arabic word *jihad*. The struggle, or jihad, toward Judgment Day, is over Jerusalem: "Here I underline the following point. The Jerusalem matter is not an ordinary geopolitical problem for us... Jerusalem is our city, it is a city belonging to us."

This wasn't the first time Turkey's president expanded on Jerusalem's meaning. In another official statement in 2017, he summed up the city's importance to Islamic eschatology, which emphasizes Jerusalem as the place connecting Earth and heaven:

> Time flows in Jerusalem, not according to the cycles we know, but in its own course. Jerusalem is passion, longing. The illumination of humanity's eye, the bliss of its heart. Jerusalem is the closest place on earth to Allah's heavenly throne. Because Jerusalem is the second stop of the Isra and the first step of Miraj; The first qibla of the ummah, Jerusalem, the city of the Prophets, is the holy glory and honor of all Muslims. The messages of the Prophet about Jerusalem are that transparent and clear. For this reason, every day Jerusalem is under occupation and captive under the Crusaders' dirty feet, shame is brought upon Muslims. Until he freed again Jerusalem Salahadin Eyyubi's eyes knew no comfort of sleep.

So much is there. The different flow of time, Jerusalem as the closest place on Earth to Allah's throne: President Erdoğan says it all.

On another occasion, when three Molotov cocktail–throwing Muslim youth were killed by Israeli police in a riot, Erdoğan made a heart-tugging appeal to Muslim listeners the world over: "Today it is *cuma* [Friday], for Muslims it is a holy day, and today in Jerusalem the police, military and all the security forces there have attacked Muslims." Erdoğan made his motives clear: "If Israeli soldiers are dirtying al-Aqsa with their boots, the reason is we fail to defend it decently. Let's defend Palestine just as we defend Mecca and Medina."[49] For Erdoğan, Palestine is Jerusalem—it is al-

Aqsa. "Jerusalem is the red line for all Muslims," he declared a few months later.[50]

Jerusalem even overcomes the division between Shiite and Sunni End Time warriors. The liberation of Jerusalem from Crusaders and Jews eclipses the antipathy that elsewhere drives Sunni and Shiite to slaughter each other by the thousands. It explains why Iran sponsors anti-Sunni militias everywhere, but supports Hamas, a Palestinian Sunni movement originally part of the Muslim Brotherhood. It's because Hamas is dedicated to liberating Jerusalem and killing Jews.

The founding covenant of Hamas describes Palestine as "the navel of the globe" and refers to a prophecy saying that "the Holy Land... will be in constant struggle till the Day of Judgement." This effectively puts the Palestinian question beyond normal politics; it isn't as simple as a question of national sovereignty or statehood. Article 11 of the Hamas charter declares all of Palestine to be consecrated ground and says that no politician has the right to give any of it up. It says, in other words, exactly what Jewish settlers and Christian Zionists are saying.

Article 7 quotes Muslim scripture in a way that contradicts any effort by moderates to resist the terrorist-jihadist call. "The last hour would not come unless the Muslims will fight against the Jews and the Muslims would kill them until the Jews would hide themselves behind a stone or a tree and a stone or a tree would say: Muslim, or the servant of Allah, there is a Jew behind me; come and kill him..."[51]

This is a favorite prophecy of militant jihadists, the sentiment of which —death to the Jews—finds its way into a great many Muslim sermons and prayers, and not just in the Middle East.

Following the July 2017 incident that enflamed Turkey's Erdoğan, two prominent California imams called for the destruction of the Jewish people citing this hadith. At the Islamic Center of Riverside, Mahmoud Harmoush preached that Israel was plotting against the holy sites of Mecca and Medina and told the faithful that to thwart Israel's plots, they must "wake up" for "prayer is not the only thing." What else could there be? He left it to their imaginations, then prayed, "Oh Allah... destroy them... and rend them asunder... turn them into booty in the lands of the Muslims." Harmoush prayed further for God to "destroy them... disperse them and rend them asunder."[52]

Meanwhile, in the university town of Davis (noted for its liberal concerns —e.g., a toad tunnel to protect amphibious passage across the I-80 freeway, and municipal fruit trees to allow foraging for the homeless), local imam Ammar Shahin prayed that God would "liberate the Al-Aqsa Mosque from the filth of the Jews" and "annihilate them down to the very last one. Do not spare any of them."[53] This is hardly in the spirit of Davis, a sanctuary city whose "Principles of One Community" hails diversity and affirms "our shared responsibility to promote and sustain a united community that acknowledges and celebrates differences..."[54] The Islamic Center presumably thrived happily in this embracing culture.

There is no doubt about the language used. It is awful, because the language of the source, the original hadith, is awful. What can we make of this ubiquitous, poisonous text? It is certainly not unorthodox—it is *sahih*, meaning it is of the highest order of reliability and authority. Put in the most flattering light, it might be interpreted as a prediction of something evil: "In the End Time Muslims will kill Jews and the rocks will not hide them." But most read it as prescriptive: "Before the end can come, you must kill the Jews."

By coincidence, I saw an article just today from a Turkish Islamist news site close to the ruling party: "The Final War Between Jews and Muslims." It quotes the same hadith, stating that Jesus will come only when this last battle-to-end-all-battles over Jerusalem takes place. It is the war "that will finish off the Jews."[55]

A number of verses in the Quran also urge their slaughter. Moderates argue that these must be considered in context, and that under Islamic dominion Jews were historically protected. They can point to Hebrew passages that have similar calls to kill worshipers of Baal, and they may say correctly that regards the Jewish Temple Mount, Jewish terrorists and settlers use a similar logic.

All true. Christians and Jews, however, are more easily rid of the problem, since there are no Baal worshipers today, whereas there are a great many Jews. Sure, we can find Christian and Jewish preachers sputtering hate, likening Muslims to the Moabites, for example. But those preachers are quickly recognized and condemned. To read a scripture about Baal and equate it with a living community is simply not possible; for Muslims, however, there is an easy and direct identification between Jews then and now.

Muslims should not be exempt from the criticism that their Abrahamic brethren apply to themselves—and especially not in a place like Davis, California, where no measure of hate speech is normally allowed. Not even toward toads.

Considering now the Black Hole as a total phenomenon, a picture of jarring paradoxes materializes. As it stands, pragmatic moderates like the late

Prime Minister Rabin or Jordan's King Hussein have more in common with one another than they do with their own millenarian constituents. Meanwhile, Hizbullah, Hamas, or Islamic Jihad agree entirely with Israel's settlers and Christian millenarians in denouncing any compromise over Jerusalem. As James Walsh noted for *Time* shortly after Rabin's assassination, "the crowning irony now is that Palestinian bus bombers and Jewish extremists have unwittingly found common cause in trying to destroy any workable peace."[56]

16

NEW WORLD ORDER

Born Again

Columbus brought the Americas to Europe's attention while on a holy war to liberate Jerusalem. His vision never waned. Puritans, Great Awakening revivalists, Darbyite premillennialists, Wilsonite postmillennialists: they all kept the vision fresh, if somewhat veiled by the strictures of politeness. Then, at last, in the 1970s, a more explicit millenarian narrative found its way into American politics. This was when presidential candidate Jimmy Carter proclaimed himself a born-again Christian.

This was my decade. Just before Carter made his announcement, God appeared to my mother in the form of Brother Whipple, a Baptist preacher. His opening words were masterfully put: "You can't make anyone love you, can you, Rita?" Like all great spiritual guides, Brother Whipple was an empath who could read a soul and cut it to the quick. Being a Baptist minister, he used this gift in the service of Jesus. My Mom got saved, born-again, like Jimmy Carter.

That week a book appeared in my room: it was titled *The Way*. The cover had groovy lettering and a cute hippy girl; the language was simple, a paraphrase edition of the Bible. I became obsessed with it. It was so honest! Absolutely filled with debauchery, homosexuality, incest, polygamy, child sacrifice, slave girls, murder, and such base-level dysfunction as to put our clan's troubles into needed perspective. The Bible's horrors gave me the universal context that had been missing. Moreover, if there was a big picture —a real reason and meaning to be found—this had to be the best resource. It was God's story, after all, and I found comfort in seeing how messed up the deity's family was.

I started going to church with Mom and began to hear an important message: God was gracious. Brother Whipple taught about Jesus being the second Adam. He said this second Adam could reverse the horrible state induced by the first Adam's fall. The key was forgiveness. You forgive, you will be forgiven. I wanted in on that.

Billy Graham sealed the deal. His "crusades" were on television a lot in those days. His message was simple and direct and convincing—quite literally moving—and he had a knack for making people get out of their seats to repent. When he called for action this night, it was impossible for me not to kneel in front of the TV. I confessed and "asked Jesus into my heart." Brother Whipple baptized me shortly after that. I was born-again, too.

Carter was therefore our man. What was new with his candidacy was the idea that we believers might write our story large—see the world reborn instead of merely shunning it. This was a meshing of premillennial dispensationalism (hunker down until the rapture!) and postmillennialist transformation (preach the Gospel, reform the system!).

Carter's declaration, made during the March 1976 North Carolina primaries, marked the beginning of this new epoch. For decades, premillennialists had kept their heads down, slightly embarrassed among their tweedy Protestant brethren who dominated the eastern elites. With Carter's proud identification as a born-again Southern Baptist, the possibility arose that they could be kingmakers in the End Time, and just ten years after the Six-Day War. Although Carter did not embrace all of his supporters' dreams, he made no apologies for them, either, and most importantly, he was not embarrassed by their company.

The magnitude of this moment was not lost on the establishment. The bellwether *Washington Post* began reporting frantically on Carter's born-again status and what it might portend. Premier political analyst Joseph Kraft best framed the question on everyone's mind: "Is America ready for a Christian President from the South?"[1] His analysis bore a note of surprise that Carter's "fundamentalism has carried him far already and... is still working for him." But Kraft also figured that there could be trouble for the candidate as he "moves into more hotly contested [northern] industrial states." The prediction? Carter just might be able to wrangle the vice-presidential nomination, if he's lucky.

Of course, that's not what happened. Carter won Ohio, Pennsylvania, and New Jersey and dominated the convention—not in spite of, but because of, his "unblushing and repeatedly articulated belief in God and family," which Kraft described as "that religious quality... that sets Carter apart from all other Democratic candidates."

In April, the *Post* devoted two full pages to an essay by philosopher Michael Novak to help explain the Carter phenomenon to the ruling classes. Today it reads like a first-grade primer, but then it was the very frontier of esoterica. "There is a hidden religious power base in American culture," he writes, "which our secular biases prevent many of us from noticing. Jimmy Carter has found it... When commentators marvel at Carter's broad appeal, it is because highly educated people hardly ever study the lives of the vast majority of American Protestants."

Novak observed that while the Protestant intelligentsia went through their "god is dead craze," Billy Graham's and Hal Lindsay's books "were selling at hundreds of thousands of copies per title." The writer identified the support that Carter was finding in unexpectedly northern climates as due to the "overwhelming numbers of Protestants in the United States [who] are evangelicals fresh from an experience of conversion." He described them as "the most underrated demographic reality in the United States."[2] To be clear, by "experience of conversion," he means traditional mainline post-millenarian Protestants—Presbyterians, Methodists, Lutherans, and so on—who "got born again" at Billy Graham crusades or by similar means.

"Born Again!" screamed *Newsweek* magazine in its pre-election cover story, and pollster George Gallup proclaimed 1976 the "Year of the Evangelical."[3] Gallup's research showed that 34 percent of the population claimed to be born-again, which amounted at the time to about 50 million voting-age adults.

Increase Mather was proving yet again to be a visionary. He'd argued centuries ago for a literal reading of the Bible, and now Gallup's research showed that four out of ten Americans had come to believe that the Bible "is to be taken literally, word for word." Gallup, an Episcopalian who would not normally be counted in Mather's camp, told *Time* that while many members of mainline denominations may think that "religious enthusiasm does not go hand in hand with intellectual seriousness and emotional balance," he now questioned his own Christian quiescence: "Isn't it time for us to bring our religious feelings out of the closet?"[4]

It was a watershed year. Every presidential candidate since Carter has had to find a way to apply the born-again brand to themselves. Like being native-born, being born-again is a prerequisite for the presidency.

Today candidates might fake it. For Carter, it was not a calculation; he was absolutely sincere. This same integrity—some might say stubbornness—is also what got him into trouble with his support base.

At heart, Carter was a Woodrow Wilson, a passionate Christian activist, but of the liberal kind. And like Wilson, he was some kind of hybrid millenarian who was at times hard to gauge. Sailing by his own star, he confused his followers and was soon perceived to be adulterating his Christianity with a humanist agenda. This put his followers' new-found political might to the test: How powerful were they? Could they make Carter live up to their vision?

Enter Jerry Falwell, a fellow Southern Baptist who had positioned himself as defender of the status quo during desegregation. Now recognizing the opportunity to galvanize the energy of 50 million conservative Christian voters, Falwell developed a strategy that focused on moral decay in the End Time. "It was important to speak of ERA [the Equal Rights Amendment, which fundamentalists believed to be a libertine rubber stamp], the Roe decision [legalizing abortion], and protections for homosexuals as examples of laws contrary to the traditional American family," he said. "It helped marshal the troops."[5]

Until then, abortion had been a concern mainly to Catholics. In 1978, it became the evangelical rallying cry and the means test for Carter's biblical-literalist bona fides. The cultural tipping point was Francis A. Schaeffer's pro-life film, *Whatever Happened to the Human Race?*[6] It swept through churches and campuses across America, awakening millions to their responsibility as God's agents in society.

Schaeffer, who went on to author the political call-to-arms *A Christian Manifesto*, gave the new Christian voting block a strong intellectual foundation. He was something of a Quṭb or Rabbi Kook for revivalist Christianity. (He made the film with C. Everett Koop, whom we met at the Jerusalem prophecy conference. Koop was the most important pediatric surgeon of the twentieth century, and fiercely anti-abortion.)

In this climate, Carter convened the White House Conference on Families. The name sounded good to born-again ears, but it turned into exactly the kind of licentious ruckus they'd feared. With content emphasizing single-parent homes and gay rights, it made Carter appear to be a traitor—a perverter of the word "family." Falwell and Pat Robertson seized on it, bringing to bear the full weight of the now mighty Christian Broadcasting

Network. Falwell described the conference agenda as an attempt to "to sanction homosexuality, expand day care, create new government programs to regulate families, and ensure federal funding for abortion." These "anti-family forces" had to be stopped.[7]

Carter's poll numbers shriveled while Christian church attendance continued to shift away from mainstream Protestantism to fundamentalist and independent Charismatic churches. The "Born Again!" were only getting stronger.

Back home, the news was that the big Presbyterian church in town broke away from the mother church when the pastor was "baptized in the Holy Spirit" and spoke in tongues. He and his flock formed an independent fellowship. As I've said, a few years later I too experienced baptism in the spirit and glossolalia after being prayed for by, of all things, a born-again Lutheran.

That's just the tip of the iceberg. Many loyal Presbyterians, Lutherans, Catholics, and Episcopalians became de facto born-again evangelicals, adopting literal readings of the Bible and experiencing the charismata without ever leaving their churches. Outside of Sunday services, they attended mixed meetings—for example, a screening of a Schaeffer film or a Christian rock festival, where they'd get heavy doses of the new political agenda along with empowering Pentecostal experiences and updates on the signs of the times. Enrollments in Christian colleges and universities soared. (In 1978, Falwell's own Lynchburg Baptist College was able to raise $7 million in a single day to expand the campus that is today Liberty University, sporting an endowment of $1.2 billion.)

It is significant that Schaeffer and Koop of *Whatever Happened to the Human Race?* and *A Christian Manifesto* were Presbyterians, not Baptists or Pentecostals; it shows how End Time concerns and Mather's literalism were becoming part of well-established and staid Christian institutions, illustrating very well the merging of post- and premillennialism.

Keep in mind that these evangelicals, the old and the new, were all irradiated with dispensationalism's ideas about Israel as God's timepiece, and they were still glowing after the Six-Day War. They watched Carter very carefully, therefore, as a seismic shift in Israel's internal politics became the ordeal by which the American president's born-again claim would be tried. It would produce an astounding residual: that same trial by fire would forge the metal to build the New World Order and spark the flame that would reignite the Crusades.

The Ordeal

Not long after Carter's inauguration in 1977, Israel elected the right-wing Likud Party to office for the first time. The new prime minister was Menachem Begin, former leader of the Irgun, the pre-state Jewish underground organization. Under the British Mandate, they had demanded unhindered immigration and rapid settlement of Jews, but their most striking distinction was a maximalist ideology—the establishment of a Jewish state on both sides of the Jordan River.

In other words, they believed that Israel should include the west and east banks of the river, encompassing the entire Kingdom of Jordan and a chunk of Syria. (At the time, this was not as unreasonable as it sounds: both Arab countries were brand new creations, cobbled together to fulfill pledges of sovereignty made by Lawrence of Arabia to the Meccan Hashemites; neither had ever before existed in history, and their new British-appointed kings were not native to those lands.)

Young Begin's tactics were harsh; the Irgun hanged captured British soldiers and bombed the King David Hotel in Jerusalem, killing ninety-four people. His installation as prime minister took President Carter by surprise: "I had not dreamed that Menachem Begin, once declared by Great Britain to be a foremost terrorist leader in the region, would win the election that May and become Israel's leader."[8]

As prime minister, Begin kept with his ideological roots, favoring accelerated Jewish settlements in the West Bank, which he always referred to as Judea and Samaria, biblical terminology that played very well with Americans who believed prophecy was being fulfilled before their eyes. It seems the Likud understood the power of Scofield-inspired American politics better than born-again Carter did, and Begin spoke their prophetic language with far greater conviction.

This became clear as Carter moved to press the Israelis into concessions toward the Palestinians through a joint US-USSR statement calling for a "comprehensive settlement" to the Arab-Israel conflict "as soon as possible." Alarmingly, the statement specified "withdrawal of Israeli Armed Forces from territories occupied in the 1967 conflict" and "the resolution of the Palestinian question, including insuring the legitimate rights of the Palestinian people based on mutual recognition of the principles of sovereignty, territorial integrity, and political independence."[9] Did Carter mean Israel must vacate old Jerusalem, too?

It wasn't going to happen. Begin was busy doing just the opposite, annexing Palestinian and Syrian lands—he was not elected to withdraw from them—and politically active millenarian Christians understood this to be the correct procedure to hasten the day of the Lord. Carter's bold call for a withdrawal seemed to be against God's plans. Had he been brought under the sway of Gog, whose traditional land of Magog was now part of the USSR?

Israelis and evangelicals were not the only ones panicked by the urgent superpower memorandum, however. Since it specified "incorporating all parties concerned," the Syrians and Egyptians were also worried that they would be forced to act against their interests. The Palestinian problem was a propaganda asset and although solving it was a nice thought, actually doing so provoked nothing but anxiety in Damascus and Cairo. Egypt's Sadat wanted no part of it. He wanted the Sinai back and thought he could achieve a separate cold peace with Israel that he could defend to his people as a tactical, not an ideological, move, the Palestinians be damned. He did not want a "comprehensive solution."

Neither did Sadat trust the Soviet Union's intentions. Fearing he would be trapped in a net woven by the self-interests of the superpowers, Sadat brilliantly seized the agenda by making a dramatic and unprecedented visit to Jerusalem.

It took the world by surprise. His voice convincingly genuine, Sadat addressed the Israeli Knesset: "If you want to live with us in this part of the world, in sincerity I tell you that we welcome you among us with all security and safety." This was the first and so far the only time an Arab state leader has addressed the Knesset. Sadat summed up his intentions with gravity: "I sincerely tell you that before us today lies the appropriate chance for peace, if we are really serious in our endeavors for peace. It is a chance that time cannot afford once again. It is a chance that, if lost or wasted, the plotter against it will bear the curse of humanity and the curse of history."

Israel's prime minister and parliament were left with no choice but to rapidly negotiate peace terms. What else could they do? The Israelis wanted official recognition of their right to exist. Here at last they had it. But the concessions and compromises that accompanied the peace treaty were unnerving; they could not quickly cede more ground to the Palestinians, and as Carter pressed harder, most Israelis felt they were being pushed without due consideration.

Their evangelical allies rallied in support. Full-page advertisements began to appear in major American newspapers soon after the joint memorandum was announced. Well-educated readers of the *New York Times* got a jolt as they thumbed through the world news section. There, among other Middle

East stories, was a full-page statement. It was signed by three recent leaders of the National Association of Evangelicals and numerous luminaries, all comfortable with Begin's prophetic dialect. "The time has come for Evangelical Christians to affirm their belief in biblical prophecy and Israel's Divine Right to the Land," scolded the text.

Signed by a host of leading figures, the admonishment targeted the Carter administration directly. "We voice our grave apprehension concerning the recent direction of American foreign policy vis-a-vis the Middle East... We are particularly troubled by the erosion of American governmental support for Israel evident in the joint US-USSR statement."

As to the specifics,

> While the exact boundaries of the land of promise are open to discussion, we, along with most evangelicals, understand the Jewish homeland generally to include the territory west of the Jordan River. We would view with grave concern any effort to carve out of the historic Jewish homeland another nation or political entity, particularly one which would be governed by terrorists whose stated goal is the destruction of the Jewish state.

The *Times* placed the appeal on page 12 of the November 1, 1977, edition. Before flipping to this page, however, most readers first saw a genuine news piece on page 9—it was a perfect set up: "Study Finds Dispute With Israel Would Hurt the Carter Race in 1980." The story cites *Commentary* magazine research and reads like a warning to President Carter that if he doesn't get the Israelis on his side, he will not be re-elected.

The ad caused many to wonder who was behind it, and if indeed "most evangelicals" were really this upset. Carter was Christian America's own born-again candidate. Had that changed?

The numbers didn't lie. Going by the organizations represented by the letter's signatories, the statistics were staggering. The National Association of Evangelicals was huge (currently representing 45,000 churches). The remainder were a "who's who" of American conservative theological scholarship.

But this didn't entirely answer who was behind the campaign. A peek behind the curtain revealed another figure, a media strategist. He was none other than New York–based Jewish activist and writer Gerald Strober.

If this causes you to scratch your head, allow me to set the scene. Strober helped found the Committee of American Jews in Support of Prime Minister Begin. A true believer in Begin's biblical narrative, Strober recognized at a critical moment who Israel's natural allies should be. The result was a new political block. It forged together Jerry Falwell's Moral Majority, the Evangelical Alliance, Pat Robertson's millions of TV followers, and conservative American Jews. Their overseas and not-so-silent partner was of course Begin's Likud Party. The common denominator: a literal belief in biblical prophecy.

Their alliance proved to be wildly successful. Neither the White House nor Congress has since successfully defied what came to be called "The Israel Lobby." Let's think about that: one of the most successful American political organizations of the past half-century, arguably more consistently successful than either of the major parties, is based mainly on a belief in the inviolability of the Promised Land in the End Time.

By the time Jimmy Carter commenced his re-election campaign, he was no longer seen as the Christian candidate. Evangelicals distrusted his social agenda and his faith in biblical prophecy. Jerry Falwell was positioned to swing the election. According to Carter, "Jerry Falwell purchased $10 million in commercials... to brand me as a traitor to the South and no longer a Christian."

Begin's party is apparent at every turn. Israel's cozy relationship with the evangelicals was such that when the time came to boost Falwell's national profile, it was Strober who authored Falwell's biography for Christian publishing house Thomas Nelson. Penned in 1979, the wholly uncritical *Jerry Falwell: Aflame for God* came out just in time for the presidential campaign. How many people noticed it was written by a conservative New York Jew working hand-in-hand with the Israelis?

It is not as though Israel's government concealed its presence. Begin gave Falwell a Learjet for his personal use and then awarded the evangelist the Jabotinsky Centennial Medal at a gala celebration in New York City. The prize was a special one that marked the 100th anniversary of the father of Revisionist Zionism, the ideology that the Irgun and the Likud was founded upon; the award celebrated the triumph of Jabotinsky's maximal Zionist position over Israeli politics. This hugely symbolic medal was created to honor the Likud's most influential partners. Billy Graham got one, too.

As the 1980 presidential campaign got underway, the messianic End Time power block had given up on Carter. They anointed Ronald Reagan as their shadow messiah. Early on, Reagan identified Carter's problem: "The Carter record is a litany of despair, of broken promises, of sacred trusts abandoned and forgotten."[10]

President of Armageddon

Reporting from the Republican Party convention, the *Washington Post* noted an evangelical stampede. "The white, right, born-again faithful, once safe in the fold of Jimmy Carter... are flocking to the Republican mother church this year where they feel they have a friend in Ronald Reagan."[11] Approaching an old-guard party member for a comment, they naively asked if the severely conservative planks of the new Republican Party platform were "chiseled in stone." The delegate's reply said it all: "They ought to be. It's down the line an evangelical platform." The new Republican canon was a veritable Ten Commandments.

Falwell bragged that his Moral Majority was giving Reagan at a minimum 4 million votes that otherwise would not have been available to any candidate at all—brand new voters, awakened to political action by the need to support Israel and protect America from moral decline. With an estimated 25 million television viewers and 72,000 clergy within its ranks—including Catholics, Mormons, and Jews—it was a plausible claim. The Moral Majority had discovered that only 55 percent of evangelicals were registered to vote, compared to a national average of 72 percent. Their motto famously became "Get them saved, baptized and registered."[12]

"Carter last time got the [church] vote because he campaigned as a born-again Christian," the *Post* quoted Falwell. "But this time people will be more concerned about issues than general characterizations. Carter has proceeded to undermine the American family."

One of the newly registered Republican delegates explained their position in terms just as well suited to the Muslim Brotherhood: "I look to God as my government, not man..."[13]

There was considerable grumbling among traditional Republican delegates. One told the *Post*, "They're a one-issue people; they won't last long." Ronald Reagan knew better. As early as the Iowa caucuses, Reagan derided the gentrified old-school Republicans as "charity ball types who love to go to committee meetings."[14] More than any other candidate, Reagan understood which way the winds of history blew and that it was decisively at his back.

He was also completely sincere. Ronald Reagan's affinity for what the *New York Times* was calling the "New Right" was not in the least bit cynical—he was one of them. Reagan was raised and baptized in the Disciples of Christ Church and remained a simple but serious Bible-believing Christian all his life.[15] His personal correspondence, handwritten notes, speech annotations, and casual conversations reveal a man comfortable with the Bible and prone to evangelism. Very much in keeping with his Campbellite church roots, he read the Bible as simple fact, more like Falwell's literalism than Carter's tortured intellectualism. Reagan prayed regularly and earnestly.

A letter to his friend Greg Brezina reveals how at ease President Reagan was with the Bible and with the Lord. Writing to the professional Atlanta Falcons footballer early in his presidency, Reagan described his historic position in terms of Christian morality and biblical literalism.

> I have long believed that the American people are hungry for a spiritual revival. I also believe there are evidences that such a revival is taking place. It is true that we can still see pornography, drug use, profane and obscene language commonly used etc. But there are other signs, increased membership in the more fundamental religions where social gospel has not replaced the Bible. Let me assure you that II Chronicles 7:14 is ever present in my mind. My daily prayer is that God will help me to use this position so as to serve Him. Teddy Roosevelt once called the presidency a bully pulpit. I intend to use it to the best of my ability to serve the Lord.[16]

His approach to Israel and the End Time was just as matter-of-fact. Speaking to the executive director of the American Israel Public Affairs Committee (AIPAC), Reagan went straight to the signs of the times. "I turn back to your ancient prophets in the Old Testament and the signs foretelling Armageddon, and I find myself wondering if we are the generation that is going to see that come about."[17]

Quoted by the wire services and reported prominently in the *Jerusalem Post*, no one could miss what his comments signified: the president of the United States viewed the Middle East problem as an End Time problem. When Reagan confessed to receiving counsel about Middle East policy from the Hebrew prophets, no one doubted that he meant it. Anyone reading this news had to adjust their political calculations accordingly.[18]

Reagan is on the record as having read Lindsey's *The Late Great Planet Earth*. Did he believe it? Reviewing his collected papers and recollections, the only conclusion we may draw is that he viewed world events through the lens of popular Scofield-dispensationalism, and that he was uncritical of it—so yes, he believed it. That's important because Lindsey identified so many international players, including the Soviet Union, Iran, and Israel, with End Time events linked to specific Bible prophecies. It could not but influence Reagan's decisions.

"We got into a conversation about how many of the prophecies concerning the Second Coming seemed to be having their fulfillment at this particular time," Reagan said, recalling a conversation with Billy Graham.

[He] told me how world leaders who are students of the Bible and others who have studied it have come to this same conclusion—that apparently never in history have so many prophecies come true in such a relatively short time. After the conversation I asked Donn to send me more material on prophecy so I could check them out in the Bible for myself. You know I was raised on the Bible. I also taught it for a long time in Sunday school.[19]

(Donn is Rev. Donn Moomaw, College Football Hall of Famer, evangelical minister, and friend of the Reagans.)

When Antiochian Orthodox Metropolitan Philip visited Reagan in the White House on April 7, 1982, "the President alluded to the Bible and the prophecies of Armageddon. He mentioned the natural disasters that the entire world was suffering and has suffered of late, and felt all these happenings were warnings that should be heeded for the avoidance of that doom."[20]

Alabama senator Howell Heflin visited the Oval Office in October 1981:

We got off into the Bible a little bit. We were talking about the fact that the Middle East, according to the Bible, would be the place where Armageddon would start. The President was talking to me about the scriptures and I was talking a little to him about the scriptures. He interprets the Bible and Armageddon to mean that Russia is going to get involved in it.[21]

(The "it" Senator Heflin refers to is the Middle East.)

Reagan loved to talk about Armageddon. This is from his official White House documents:

Some theologians quite some time ago were telling me, calling attention to the fact that theologians have been studying the ancient prophecies—What would portend the coming of Armageddon?—and have said that never, in the time between the prophecies up until now has there ever been a time in which so many of the prophecies are coming together. There have been times in the past when people thought the end of the world was coming, and so forth, but never anything like this.[22]

California State senator James Mills vividly recalled a conversation he had with Reagan after an official dinner where Mills was the honoree:

It can't be too long now. Ezekiel says that fire and brimstone will be rained upon the enemies of God's people. That must mean that they'll be destroyed by nuclear weapons. They exist now, and they never did in the past. Ezekiel tells us that Gog, the nation that will lead all the other powers of darkness against Israel, will come out of the north. Biblical scholars have been saying for generations that Gog must be Russia. What other powerful nation is to the north of Israel? None.[23]

"Oh, no!" The microphones picked up Nancy Reagan's gasp when Marvin Kalb asked her husband to explain his take on Armageddon in the final presidential debate of the 1984 campaign. She knew her husband's beliefs and how candid he was with them. Kalb went straight to it: "You've been quoted as saying that you believe deep down that we are heading for some kind of biblical Armageddon... Do you feel that we are heading, perhaps, for some kind of nuclear Armageddon? And do you feel that this country and the world could survive that kind of calamity?"

Reagan's answer, guileless as ever, reckoned that a majority of Americans agreed with him. He assured Mr. Kalb that he "never said we must plan according to Armageddon." But he affirmed his interest in the subject as a "philosophy" and his wide-ranging discussions of "prophecies down through the years, the biblical prophecies of what would portend the coming of Armageddon and so forth... and the fact that a number of theologians for the last decade or more have believed that this was true, that the prophecies are coming together that portend that."

After the debate, he was easily re-elected.

The New World Order

The complexities of religious political movements can be confounding. Are they premillennial or postmillennial? Does the Muslim Brotherhood have the same philosophy as al-Qaeda? Why do secular Israelis support messianic policies while ultra-Orthodox Jews reject the Israeli state—shouldn't it be the other way round?

As for recent America, its millenarian impulse vacillates between apocalyptic pessimism and triumphalist optimism, between pre- and post-millennialism. Presidents Wilson and Carter were progressives, while Ronald Reagan and George W. Bush were conservatives. Yet all four preserved the Puritan dream of America as a place uniquely blessed with the power and responsibility to restore Paradise to the earth. None escaped the End Time virus that caused utopian hallucinations. The only thing that really divides them is how America will deliver the Paradise of the world to come.

Carter's post-millenarian liberalism, like Wilson's, led him to a social agenda that troubled literalists. But it also brought him a peculiarly biblical success in negotiating the Camp David Accords between Egypt and Israel.

It was his life's greatest achievement. Over a twelve-day marathon, Carter personally played the role of Christ, reconciling Sadat and Begin and "staying up deep into the night... singing Israeli folk songs with Begin's delegation."[24] This anecdote is telling: Carter's familiarity with Israeli folk music illuminates how deeply his Baptist-bred feeling for Zion ran. I doubt he could have pulled it off without his genuine affinity for Israel and for Egypt, too—both nations being great kingdoms of the Bible whose End Time peace is literally prophesied by Isaiah.[25] It is notable that the three leaders jointly issued a call for prayer at the beginning of the summit. All three were true believers and practitioners of their faiths.[26]

Ronald Reagan began on the other side of the coin, a premillennialist prepared to ride out Armageddon. But he ended his second term committed to reshaping the world for peace like a new Woodrow Wilson.

Veteran news analyst Daniel Schorr—easily one of America's most respected and experienced journalists—took note of this in his nationally syndicated column in an editorial entitled, "Reagan Recants: His Path From Armageddon to Detente." What strikes me is how Schorr, a no-nonsense veteran who'd covered the Second World War with Edward R. Murrow and the entire epoch of the Cold War, resorts to describing Reagan's transformation as a metaphysical mystery:

> When President Reagan, on the eve of his summit with Mikhail S. Gorbachev, rejected the inevitability of war between the superpowers, he was bearing witness to a remarkable transformation in his longstanding view of the world. Reagan, by some process not yet fully understood, put behind him the belief that his mission was to prepare for the ultimate conflict that would usher in the Millennium.[27]

Schorr didn't understand the flip that nearly always occurs when oppressed millenarians become political victors. Just as Constantine's success on the Milvian Bridge transformed Christians, Reagan's defeat of Communism marked a shift in the End Time outlook of his Christian supporters. Make no mistake: they saw victory over the Soviets as a win for Jesus. Reagan's mission had not essentially changed. The millennium was still on his agenda, only now he thought of it as a mandate to build the rule of Christ piece by piece, beginning with disarmament. On April 30, 1985, he wrote to Soviet leader Mikhail Gorbachev that their goal had to be "total abolition of nuclear weapons." Peace on Earth, here we come.

In Schorr's terms, the president's earlier "longstanding view" had led Reagan to stand up unflinchingly to what he called the Evil Empire, pushing right up to the line of a civilization-ending nuclear conflict and the militarization of space. No one doubted he would cross the line if necessary, nor did they doubt that he believed God was on his side. Critically, the Soviet leadership didn't doubt it, either. When they realized Reagan was seriously open to the end of the world, he in effect called their bluff. At first, they responded with an even bigger gambit—intensifying their invasion of Afghanistan—but the Soviet leadership was composed of tired materialists bereft of ideology. They were not about to set the atmosphere on fire for that.

In contrast, Reagan's faith was rock-solid. He upped the ante with unprecedented increases in military spending, such as the Strategic Defense Initiative (Star Wars), and laid a yet heavier bet on the efficacy of his fellow End Time warriors, the mujahideen Islamic fighters of Afghanistan, whom he saw as fellow monotheists fighting against the godless Soviet ideology.

In broad terms, I believe Reagan saw all this within the framework of the battle of Armageddon. His obsession with Armageddon wasn't because he wanted the world to go up in nuclear flames; he believed in salvation through whatever means God chose. Everything he'd done was for this. If it was to be through apocalypse, he was willing to go there, but this was not the objective, only the means—the Gipper's goal post was Isaiah's dream of total peace.

To get there required this cold-eyed showdown on Afghanistan's dusty roads. There, the desperate Soviets laid their last bet, but it was too late— they had already spent themselves into a disastrous position trying to keep up with America. If Marxism's god is historical development, it had turned against them. By the middle of Reagan's era, every bid had failed and the state was teetering on the edge. Meanwhile, Reagan's God had deep pockets and millions of unfaltering true believers, including those Islamic warriors.

The modern reader must understand that 1980s Afghanistan was the template for Syria of the 2000s. Local and foreign jihadists were backed by myriad wealthy foreign states to fight a war of ideology and religion. Although the number of foreign fighters was comparatively small, this is where Qutb's tenets were tested and made practical. Reagan did not understand the Quṭbian anti-Western foundations of the movement, nor did he grasp the meaning of mujahideen—"those who make jihad."

Israel did not really get it, either. The god-neutral PLO and the socialist-nationalist Baath regime in Syria were Soviet clients. In those days, Israel happily backed Islamist movements to undermine these powerful enemies. Afghanistan was more of the same. The coalition was astonishingly diverse. With Israel's connivance, America supplied powerful arms and training to the anti-Soviet Muslim warriors, helped by Saudi Arabia and Egypt. For the time being, the strategy was a glorious success. The known common enemy, the Soviet Union, was waving the white flag. America had won the Cold War and Israel's Soviet-backed enemies would presumably collapse without Russian support and all would be well. Peace at last.

Victory secured, Reagan turned to constructing a benevolent Christian dominion to rule the world he had just conquered. This is how Constantine saw himself, too; both thought that after their God-ordained victories they could prepare the world for Christ. That's the shift that befuddled Daniel Schorr and explains how a fundamentalist-conservative became the father of a liberal-progressive system that Woodrow Wilson only dreamed of, and what Vice President George H.W. Bush called the "New World Order."

As the founder of the New World Order, Reagan was Wilson's true successor, not Jimmy Carter. The latter had tried to achieve a liberal global order through the niceties of detente. Reagan rejected detente, choosing hard, honest confrontation. History favored Reagan with its blessing, allowing him to leave the legacy that Carter hoped to bestow upon the world. Now, just as Constantine-era Christians had changed tack when history thrust them into power, President Reagan's born-again supporters readily took to their new task of filling government positions with believers who could straighten the moral backbone of America and then transform America's allies and supplicants across the globe.

And like the Byzantine Christians, they adopted new versions of the End Time story. Yes, one day there would be an evil revolt against the New World Order. Armageddon would take place. Gog and Magog would attack Israel (although with the Soviets gone, a new candidate would have to be found). The critical new assumption was that God's people would occupy positions of power and influence, ready to administer the divine rule of Christ after the Last Battle.

Enter Reagan ally Pat Robertson, architect of the Christian Coalition, a more structured and long-lasting version of Falwell's Moral Majority. American readers are familiar with it; the political networks Robertson built still determine elections. Trump would not have been elected without it, and the Coalition's influence explains the Tea Party and the presence of Sarah Palin on the Republican ticket with John McCain.

Pat wasn't always a champion of changing things from the inside, however. He had spent twenty-five years of his career in full premillennial-dispensationalist mode. Day after day, he brandished battle maps on his flag-ship *700 Club* Christian talk show. They decoded for his viewers a Soviet-Iranian attack on Israel, indexed to the identities of mysterious figures in Hebrew prophecy—Gog, Meschech, Tubal, Put, Persia, and Cush. (Names, incidentally, that President Reagan sprinkled liberally over his conversations.)

Millions watched the *700 Club* (myself included) and wondered what to do. The answer was simple: vote Republican and prepare for the rapture. I know this part of the story well and watched keenly as Pat's message evolved along with Reagan's.

It started midway through Reagan's first term. Pat's 1982 book, *The Secret Kingdom*, explains that Christians and Jews are the leaven in the dough of human culture; it would expand and rise to fill the earth.[28] Little by little, the Kingdom of God would emerge as Christians took positions of power in government, business, and the arts. The Great Commission would be completed through their influence, reaping a final great harvest of souls before the Antichrist appears to take his last stand by attacking Israel. That's when Jesus will appear to strike down the rebellious and take his seat on the throne as "King of Kings, and Lord of Lords" at the head of an already-in-place government of God.

This is essentially postmillennialism, but in an extremely acute phase. It is also exactly the way Byzantine literature adapted to its victory between the reigns of Constantine and Heraclius. America's evangelicals had turned from a pessimistic focus on an imminent rapture rescuing a put-upon Chris-tian minority, to a single-minded endeavor to build a precursor to the global millennial Kingdom of God. The end could still come like a thief in the night, but in the meantime, the task was to build God's bureaucracy.

This Crusade, This Holy War

Christianity's sibling religions adopted a similar pose. All had undergone this millenarian hybridization. Much like premillennialist Christians who had opted out of politics to await the rapture until their political awakening in the 1970s, traditional Jews had eschewed politics to wait for the Messiah.

Now, Religious Zionists believed that Israel's political establishment heralded the coming kingdom, which had to be constructed in advance to prepare the way for the Messiah.

Islam's premise was already a unified concept of religion and governance —it had always been a total head-to-toe theocracy established in preparation for the imminent return of Jesus. With the Iranian Revolution and the war in Afghanistan, however, the template for how to do that in post-caliphate times was molded and tested. Islamic revival movements, either militant or winner-takes-all political action, were the new normal.

Taken together, all this meant that by the end of the twentieth century, the problem was the same as when the First Crusade was fought: an intense mimetic rivalry between Abrahamic millenarians focused on Jerusalem, where Abraham's children were getting in each other's way. But now the stakes are much higher: when we next collide at the Temple Mount, it will not be with swords—it will be with powerful Armageddon-capable weapons.

This reality burst through the doors of public perception on September 11, 2001, when one faction of the millenarian army attacked the other in a bid to hasten the day of the Lord. Very few really understood what was happening. Every attempt to face it honestly as the act it was—a provocation designed to spark the Apocalypse—was met with incomprehension and knotty punditry. Public analysis desperately tried to root the affair in conventional politics; surely this was about land, or oil, or national identity—it couldn't possibly really be about heaven, could it?

Let's consider Turkey's president, Recep Tayyip Erdoğan, a modern champion of the Palestinians and the first leader of Turkey to successfully challenge Atatürk's secular, Islam-hating revolution. As thousands made plans to visit Turkey in remembrance of those lost in the Battle of Gallipoli (death toll: 100,000), Mr. Erdoğan urged vigilance. "The Crusades were not finished nine centuries ago in the past! Do not forget, the Gallipoli campaign was a Crusade!"[29]

Gallipoli was fought just over 100 years ago in the course of the First World War. Western historians most often see it as a deadly episode in a tragic war. But millions of Middle Easterners see it as Erdoğan does: they view the Great War's Middle East theater as a late phase of the Crusades, ending with the 1,000-year-old Christian dream of destroying the caliphate.

We know already that the Muslim Brotherhood exists as a response to that prophesied End Time setback for Islam. Erdoğan's interpretation of the war shouldn't come as a surprise—it is typical, no more unusual than the daily weather report. Major newspapers across the Middle East use the same language as a matter of course. It is so common that veteran Turkish columnist Taha Akyol felt compelled to comment on it in the *Hürriyet*, Turkey's highest-circulation daily. Under the headline "Crusader-Zionist Alliance Saga," he noted that references to the Crusades are commonplace in leading Turkish circles. This was taken for granted. What bothered him was the way this obsession was allowed to drive foreign policy. He urged the government "to prioritize diplomacy over ideology."[30]

Listen to any number of Muslim leaders regularly—even secular ones—and you will hear a reference to the Crusades. It is there in its most benign form as a catch-all for anything the West does that smacks of colonialism, but it is also the paradigm for millenarian jihadism. Holy war is the lens through which international relations is viewed.

There are layers of one-upmanship in the Crusader blame game. Several months before Erdoğan's 2017 remarks, an ISIS member attacked an Istanbul night club on New Year's Eve, killing thirty-nine trapped partygoers. The Islamic State released a statement justifying the massacre as "revenge on the servant of the Crusaders." By celebrating New Year's Eve, the partygoers joined what ISIS deemed a "Christian polytheist feast."

Osama bin Laden used the same language as the Turks: "We are assured that we can wage a jihad against the enemies of Islam, in particular against the greater external enemy—the Crusader-Jewish alliance."[31]

Loving the region and the people as I do, I've not wanted it to be such a popular idea, but after many hours of sitting in tea houses, looking at local newspapers, and listening to sermons, it is inescapable. In Beirut or Istanbul, all it takes is a mention of Israel (if you dare) to find your conversation turned suddenly into an impassioned discussion about the End Time, the Crusaders, and their Jewish allies.

I've had the same discussions in Sydney, London, and in America's Midwest. It may not be something raised ordinarily with non-Muslim friends, but if you know how to approach it, if you speak in a way that gives the impression that you are experienced and sympathetic, you would be amazed at how a casual conversation—for example, one I had not long ago while shopping for a cigar in the United States—can turn into an excited discussion of the glorious day, soon to come, when the Mahdi and Jesus will appear to judge the Jews and revert the likes of me to the true religion of Islam. All the signs are there, after all.

What about Western views? Surely such biases have long been purged from secular Western culture. Not quite. We rarely consider why our sports teams are called the "Crusaders," or why there is a Crusader-style flag in many churches. Private Christian schools overtly celebrate crusader imagery and narratives, bolstered with Bible verses about the "full armor of God." Crusader costumes are sold as alternatives to evil Halloween garb, as if an armor-clad, sword-carrying soldier emblazoned with a cross is not an expression of evil.

These may seem trifling examples, but Westerners adopt such symbols without reflection or consideration of what they mean. We don't understand how this tills the soil of violence and perpetuates a paradigm of holy war. How do these emblems read to Muslims? Imagine if the high school next door to you named their football team the "Jihadists."

If the West was truly free of the crusades paradigm, we would expect George W. Bush to counter bin Laden's thesis on 9/11. He didn't. His immediate response was to launch the Global War on Terror with the words, "This crusade, this war on terrorism is going to take a while."[32] Not as eloquent as bin Laden, but strangely, they seem to agree on what this is.

When I first heard these words, still trying to get home after 9/11 (I was in a major Middle Eastern city when it happened), I could feel a shudder radiate through the lounge where I was sipping whisky. My alcohol-drinking, non-observant Muslim associates heard what I did—namely, the president of the United States endorsing Osama bin Laden's worldview by declaring America's response a holy war, that is to say, a crusade. My friends and I ordered a fresh round of drinks and wondered if Bush had had a few, too.

He misspoke, his staff said later.

Did he? Although President Bush was told to watch his mouth and spoke carefully crafted lines to assure the world that this was not a religious war, in less controlled settings, he continued to reveal his personal religious motivations. It came out most frequently in his chronic description of the enemy as "evil." (For example, "This is a new kind of—a new kind of evil."[33])

Former Palestinian foreign minister Nabil Shaath told the BBC that when President Bush met with an Israeli-Palestinian delegation during the Sharm el-Sheikh summit in 2003,

> President Bush said to all of us: "I am driven with a mission from God. God would tell me, George go and fight these terrorists in Afghanistan. And I did. And then God would tell me, George, go and end the tyranny in Iraq. And I did. And now, again, I feel God's words coming to me, Go get the Palestinians their state and get the Israelis their security, and get peace in the Middle East. And, by God, I'm gonna do it."

He also mentioned the Crusades as one of the motivations "Islamic radicals" used to justify their attacks.

These quotes were denied by a White House public relations official (who was not in attendance), but the comments had appeared independently in a set of memoranda from the meeting acquired by the Israeli newspaper *Haaretz*.[34] If Bush didn't say this, it raises another question: Why would Shaath fabricate such a thing? And if he did make it up, he should get an award: this sounds just like George W. Bush. He got his syntax correct right down to the last jot and tittle.

Moreover, this picture fits a larger frame. During the 2003 Iraq War—the same year as the Sharm el-Sheikh summit—the daily intelligence briefing prepared for President Bush featured a cover page with a fresh image from the battlefield, below it a verse of scripture. Some of these were leaked. On April 3, it featured a US Army tank racing through the double-sword gates of Baghdad bearing this prophetic biblical caption: "Open the gates that the righteous nation may enter, the nation that keeps faith."[35] The Pentagon later confirmed the practice by way of disavowing it, stating that "it no longer includes a Bible quote on the cover page of daily intelligence briefings it sends to the White House as was practiced during the Bush administration."[36]

Clash of Civilizations

President Bush made his Crusades reference on live television with the whole world watching. Was it shocking because it was wrong or because it was true? Efforts to sweep the statement under the rug painted the Global War on Terror (GWT) as a confrontation not with Islam but with "extremists," somehow religiously neutered and without connection to Muhammad's faith.

Does anyone really believe that? Ordinary Muslims celebrated 9/11 on Middle Eastern streets as a victory against those they called Crusaders. The bombers killed themselves and thousands of people for Islam. Who are we to tell them they are not real Muslims?

Bush labelled the GWT a crusade because of an honest impulse. Moreover, the White House's denials rang hollow because the Bush administration was populated with conservative evangelicals, many of them connected to the Christian Coalition one way or the other. These were Reagan-era Christians who methodically worked their way from Christian private schools and universities into government. They weren't the kind of people to shy away from crusades.

Outside the White House, two of Bush's most prominent veteran evangelical supporters loudly agreed with their Muslim counterparts, choosing to take them at their word—this was a holy war. First was Franklin Graham, Billy Graham's eldest son and successor. He responded to 9/11 by urging the president not to equivocate. Graham called Islam "a very evil and wicked religion," emphasizing his unshakable knowledge that Muslims worship a demon.[37]

The second was Charles Colson. Regarded as a thinking-man's Christian, Colson was politically savvy and influential. This was the man who was appointed as special counsel in Nixon's White House, becoming the "political point man." Nixon wrote in his memoirs, "When I complained to Colson, I felt confident that something would be done," adding, "I was rarely disappointed."[38] Colson is best known as a key Watergate conspirator, for which he was convicted and served time in prison. It was there that he was born-again, going on to become a highly respected conservative Christian leader and founder of Prison Fellowship, a truly laudable ministry for convicts. I have greatly appreciated Colson's work.

In 2001, shortly after the al-Qaeda attack, he wrote to his large, prominent, and generally well-educated audience that 9/11 showed Islam for what it really is. Colson cited a scholarly book, *The Clash of Civilizations and the Remaking of World Order*, reminding his readers of Harvard historian Samuel Huntington's thesis that the world is locked in a monolithic conflict between irreconcilable civilizations. Colson quoted Huntington's description of the civilizational boundary line: "Islam has 'bloody borders.'"[39]

Colson illustrated his contention with examples of Muslim atrocities against Christians—murder and rape—and said that "Muslims are involved in a disproportionate percentage of violent conflicts between religious and ethnic groups."

He also directly addressed President Bush's remarks:

Since September 11, Americans have been told repeatedly that what happened that day should not be held against the Islamic world. The president told us that the terrorist acts were a kind of "blasphemy" and that the terrorists had "hijacked a great and peaceful religion." Now, I understand why the president and his administration say this... But Christians ought to be aware it just isn't so... Bin Laden and his followers did not hijack Islam, they simply took it seriously.

Colson concluded his letter by encouraging Christians not to be fooled by political correctness. "All of this runs contrary to the obligatory political rhetoric of the day. Anybody who denies Islam's peaceful nature runs the risk of being called a hatemonger... And meanwhile, Christians all over the world are dying in conflicts that, according to this rhetoric, couldn't be taking place."[40]

To be clear, in Huntington's thesis, the clash is not about religion—it is about "civilizations." But Colson is right. To say, "it is not religious, it is civilizational" ignores the obvious. One of the clashing civilizations is based on the foundation of Christendom, the other the Islamic caliphate.

Old hands in the Middle East scratched their heads when Huntington's book hit the newsstands; where had we heard this before? In fact, the idea and even the title of the book goes back to Bernard Lewis, esteemed scholar of Islam, who coined Huntington's titular phrase way back in 1990. For Lewis, the expression was used to elucidate what in his considered view was the historical state of conflict between Judeo-Christian civilization and Islamic civilization.[41] Lewis looked at it as a simple evaluation of how things are, without being overly concerned with the politics. Colson would have done better to quote him.

Meanwhile, compared to their political bosses, those actually prosecuting the Global War on Terror seemed impervious to political correctness. Major General William G. Boykin was the most vocal, openly revealing what most of us in the arena knew—namely, that many top US leaders in the GWT mirrored bin Laden's belief that this was a holy war.

North Carolina–born Boykin is a man of faith and a brave hero. His personal integrity is unimpeachable. He also regularly spoke at churches in uniform, pledging allegiance to two flags: the Stars and Stripes and the "Christian flag," a banner modeled on Crusader signage that sits to the side of the altar in hundreds of thousands of American churches. ("I pledge allegiance to my flag and the Savior for whose kingdom it stands; one brotherhood uniting all mankind in service and love.")

General Boykin made clear on many occasions that he viewed Islam as demonic, a religion inspired by Satan. "There is no greater threat to America than Islam," he said.[42] Moreover, the United States was a "Christian nation" waging a "spiritual battle." As for his confrontation with a Muslim Somali militia leader while fighting there with the Delta Force, Boykin stated, "I knew that my God was bigger than his."[43]

General Boykin was an original member of the Delta Force and later part of the Joint Special Operations Command. He is unquestionably one of the most experienced ground operatives alive, having served in Afghanistan, Iran, and Somalia. He was also just the kind of Christian I was raised to be: a believer in the End Time, committed to the transformation of the world through evangelism, and sure of America's special place in that regard.

During the Bush years, Boykin was appointed to the critical position of under secretary of defense for intelligence. Along with General Stanley A. McChrystal, he was tasked with nothing less than hunting down Osama bin Laden and finding and eliminating al-Qaeda's leadership. One officer close to the scene described the generals in charge of the Joint Special Operations Command as "fellow travelers in the great crusade against Islam" who "presided over this black world where any actions were justified against Muslims because you were fighting against the Caliphate."[44]

On the frontline, we might consider the example of "American Sniper" Chris Kyle, known best as one of America's most lethal soldiers, with 160 confirmed kills. When jihadist insurgents put out a bounty on Kyle, whom they dubbed "the Satan of Ramadi," he rejoiced, saying that he "hated the damn savages." Award-winning journalist of the GWT, Nicholas Schmidle, whose work is notably steeped in long experience on the battlefield, wrote sympathetically of Kyle for the *New Yorker* in 2013: "Like many soldiers," Schmidle reported, "Kyle was deeply religious and saw the Iraq War through that prism. He tattooed one of his arms with a red crusader's cross, wanting 'everyone to know I was a Christian.'"[45]

The new-wave jihadists must have approved of Kyle's honesty. We can deduce this because the Islamic State reported favorably on President Bush's gut response to 9/11 in a 2015 article that appeared in *Dabiq*, the organization's flagship magazine. "As Shaykh Usāmah Ibn Lādin (rahimahullāh) said, 'The world today is divided into two camps. Bush spoke the truth when he said, "Either you are with us or you are with the terrorists." Meaning, either you are with the Crusade or you are with Islam.'"[46]

The same edition assailed the spin the White House tried to put on the GWT and denounced Muslims who painted Islam as "a religion of peace." In other words, ISIS agreed wholeheartedly with Colson and Graham:

So how can the heretics or even those who blindly follow them—Bush, Obama, and Kerry—obstinately claim that "Islam is a religion of peace," meaning pacifism? One of the biggest false arguments propagated by the heretics is the linguistic root for the word Islam. They claim it comes from the word salām (peace), when in actuality it comes from words meaning submission and sincerity sharing the same consonant root.[47]

I must emphasize, because it can be confusing, that these are Muslims saying this, and this Muslim resistance to political correctness is not limited to the fringes of the Islamic State. Islamic revivalists of all kinds believe that the West's insistence upon "peaceful" Islam is an attempt to trick Muslims into passivity. Why should they be the "peaceful religion" while Christians and Jews bomb the Middle East, killing millions?

In my experience, obfuscation is not helpful. When Muslims say they are fighting Crusaders, they mean it, and we should respect them enough to believe it. There is nothing more colonial-minded and disrespectful than saying to Muslims that we know their beliefs better than they do.

Black Jesus

> I came to see faith as more than just a comfort to the weary... but rather as an active, palpable agent in the world and in my own life. I was finally able to walk down the aisle of Trinity one day and affirm my Christian faith. Kneeling beneath that cross on the South Side, I felt I heard God's spirit beckoning me. I submitted myself to His will, and dedicated myself to discovering His truth and carrying out His works.[48]

That's how candidate Barack Obama came out as a born-again Christian. His faith in Jesus would make him "an active, palpable agent in the world." Welcome to the club.

I liked Obama just fine. For the record, I'd had my political coming of age as a middle schooler when Carter ran for office in 1976. (We had a mock election—I campaigned for Jimmy.) Later, in the Reagan years, I worked in the Middle East as a stalwart supporter of the Gipper and his friends and allies. When they asked me to help investigate claims that Saddam Hussein had just used chemical weapons against the Kurds, I hastened to the arena to interview the victims and understood immediately that the Reagan administration had a hand in it—I was vociferously appalled.

A few years after that, as George H.W. Bush cited those same atrocities to stir up support against Saddam Hussein, I was one of those who knew first-hand that Republican administrations had befriended the dictator, helped him commit those atrocities, and then denied that they happened until it suited their purposes. It was time for a change of tack, so back in America, I supported the Democrats and wrote a foreign policy piece on the Middle East for Ralph Nader's campaign newspaper as a supporter of the Greens.

I also voted for Obama and supported his campaign. My vote was prag-matic and conditional. Knowing that government at this level is an enor-mous, powerful ship whose inertia and orientation leads the leaders more often than the other way around, my expectations were low. I voted more against a continuation of the party in power than for the new one.

My skepticism, however, was rare among Obama's supporters, where a messianic halo was forming. I prayed it would not blind Mr. Obama, who assured us that he loved Reinhold Niebuhr, describing him as one of his favorite philosophers. He would presumably hold the theologian's call to humility close to his heart, especially Niebuhr's dictum, "Democracy is a method of finding proximate solutions for insoluble problems."[49] Indeed, Obama echoed Niebuhr, saying that when it comes to solving the world's evil and pain, "we should be humble and modest in our belief we can eliminate those things."[50]

In the end, I am afraid that there was little humility to be found. It's not that I doubt Obama's sincerity; I believe he really meant it. Perhaps humility went against his nature. Or maybe his head was turned by adulation. What-ever the case, his solutions at home and on the international scene became as maximalist as Reagan's. Maybe it was that three-tone poster's fault, with his tilted head looking beatifically toward the sublime space to which he would take us, the place of HOPE.

The liberal British newspaper the *Guardian* noticed it early in the campaign. The image, they wrote, "acquired the kind of instant recogni-tion of Jim Fitzpatrick's Che Guevara."[51] Actually, Che and Lenin both adopted this quasi-religious pose on purpose, modeled on Christian iconography, because it was the hope of messianic Paradise that commu-nism offered to fulfill. This shouldn't be understood as an accusation of cynical manipulation on Obama's part. My point is that the iconography eclipsed the man.

Looking at the timeline, we can understand to what extent the poster made the man. This was not a commissioned work of art. Unbidden by the campaign, Shepard Fairey did what artists do: he expressed the zeitgeist, taking campaign planners by surprise and forcing them to scramble in pursuit of HOPE's extraordinary and un-Niebuhrly conceit. Having made Obama an instant object of devotion, the challenge was to hammer out poli-cies that could live up to it. HOPE was the new candidate.

How could that happen among such a sophisticated body of supporters? Most considered themselves evolved past the stage of primitive religion and iconography—like their candidate, they were more intelligent, wiser, and therefore better equipped to lead not just America but the world into the twenty-first century.

The problem is that most were unaware of how religious that aspiration is. Obama's supporters were in denial. They were spiritually hungry, and their Paradise-starved hearts betrayed them as they became as unbalanced as the Religious Right of the late 1970s.

Consider again what the HOPE campaign promised. As the face of HOPE and CHANGE, Barack Obama could not just be about jobs, taxes, or foreign policy. If that's all it meant, a simple change of fiscal policy and refocus of diplomatic priorities, any of which might be overturned in the mid-terms, no harm done. But this campaign didn't mean ordinary change; this had to be eschatological change, like St. Paul's definition of resurrection: "In a moment, in the twinkling of an eye... we shall be changed."[52]

Before HOPE, there were already signs that candidate Obama might be quite comfortable with messianic acclaim. Echoing Ronald Reagan, Obama told his audience of 2,400 churchgoers in Greenville, South Carolina, that he aspired to be "an instrument of God." Then he promised with Christ-like assurance, "I am confident that we can create a Kingdom right here on Earth."[53]

That's a mighty big promise. Even Jesus did not make that claim. But Obama's followers put their faith in him without reservation. The *Economist* observed that Obama alone among modern public figures effected ecstatic, nearly medieval reactions. "Mr Obama has inspired more passionate devotion than any modern American politician. People scream and faint at his rallies. Some wear T-shirts proclaiming him 'The One.'"

Written early in his presidency, the piece correctly notes that it was not just campaign hyperbole. He had promised to "change the world" and "transform this country," and now as president, "he keeps adding details to this ambitious wish-list. He vows to create millions of jobs, to cure cancer and to seek a world without nuclear weapons."[54]

In Italy, Sandro Magister, a journalist known for his coverage of the Vatican, looked at this phenomenon and recalled a fascinating historical precedent. The Italian marveled at Obama's "messianic vision" and the president's startling resemblance to Joachim of Fiore, a twelfth-century millenarian monk who declared the dawn of a new age in which there were to be no divisions among humanity, and specifically no religious divisions. Magister found the "messianic rhetoric that pervades Obama's speeches," including his repeated proclamations of a "new era," of a "new beginning," and an "age of peace," to be vintage Fiore.[55] (Rumors had already circulated that Obama based his philosophy on Fiore; Magister refuted this but wanted to point out the uncanny similarities between the two nonetheless, and to warn of dangers attested to through his extensive experience of such things at the Vatican.)

Historians will have to assess Obama's presidency in terms of success or failure as he defined it. And he defined it big. Esteemed historian Morton Keller has already chosen to begin his early Obama retrospective with the only stick by which this presidency can be measured: "The media and the educated classes in particular had a strong belief in his unique talents and the prospect of an epochal presidency. (So, apparently, did Obama. Early on he asked a group of historians what it took to be a transformative president.) His staff had even higher expectations. With minimal irony, they referred to him as Black Jesus."[56]

Jesus he was not. There is no doubt that he brought some change, but it was not capitalized, messianic Change. Transformative? On some levels yes, of course. Most presidents are, for better or worse, transformative of something, and Obama can point to some historic ground-breaking.

In the greater scheme, however, nothing much changed at all. His path to the White House was well trodden and clearly illuminated by the correct education, the right friends, and the obligatory money connections. Obama's "Kingdom right here on Earth" was Reagan's bequest. He may have taken a different approach to it, but it was still the Gipper's New World Order that Obama championed—he was at best a novel dynastic successor. Obama's ambition was to hone and perfect the New World Order at home through his social agenda and to extend it to those last resistant corners of the globe. The idea that Obama would be truly, fundamentally different from Reagan, Bush, or Clinton was only a religious delusion.

Neochange

But wasn't President Obama liberal and Reagan conservative? Sure, why not? But do their differences matter as much as what they agreed upon? What they shared was an overarching dream of a global society, characterized by a free-market economy, free trade, democracy, and human rights. The differences are in the details of social balance and the means by which recalcitrant international players can be compelled to comply with the New World Order.

Obama often sounded like Reagan—the same grand narrative that promised God's kingdom on Earth—because he was indeed exactly like

Reagan on that point. Both promised the same End of Days liberation and were all about, in a word, Hope. (Reagan's appeal was the absolutely believable optimism he projected; his breakthrough message, "It's morning again in America," was pure hope and it brought tears to people's eyes.)

Many of Obama's supporters soon began to realize this, understanding finally that, just as before, there would be no Change. His iconographer noted the similarity to Reagan-Bush with a disenchanted shrug.

"Do you think Obama has lived up to your 'Hope' poster?" *Esquire* asked the image's creator in 2015.[57]

"Not even close." How come? "There have been a lot of things that he's compromised on that I never would have expected. I mean, drones and domestic spying are the last things I would have thought [he'd support]."

Sad to say, these are not compromises; they are the standard policing tools of the New World Order, the same type of weapons and invasive hand that appeared originally with the Old World Order—the Cosmic Order of Sumeria. Sovereignty has always been coercive, and Obama's reign was, too. Wars to end history are brutal, and Obama's was no exception. Yes, he fought wars; a vicious one in the Middle East against two different factions, with religious fundamentalists on the one side and supporters of Syria's dictator on the other. At the same time, he conducted an aggressive culture war at home against those whom he considered to be regressive. We are not accustomed to thinking of liberalism as waging a millenarian holy war but it surely does, just any other -ism would.

Here is where we see the link between Reagan and Obama most clearly. As early as 1989, Francis Fukuyama identified democratic liberalism as history's exit point. Fukuyama's best-selling and highly influential *The End of History and the Last Man* evangelized the end of conflict between ideologies and the dawn of an age of universal humanity. After the Soviet giant's fall, all would embrace the triumph of freedom, democracy, equality, and human rights—the lion will have lain with the lamb.

This picture fits Barack Obama very well indeed. But that New World Order gospel came from an influential neoconservative planner in the Reagan White House. Fukuyama was one of the first young disciples of the administration, brought in by neocon intellect Paul A. Wolfowitz in 1981, soon after Reagan was sworn in. Fukuyama and team were tasked with devising the president's strategy for global domination. The result was the Reagan Doctrine, the hardline principles for taking down the USSR and establishing worldwide liberal democracy.[58]

It wasn't just for Republicans, however; the Clintons were true believers in Reagan's New World Order (NWO), too. Bill's job was to rebalance the economy after half a century of Cold War and, if possible, to talk government-skeptical Americans into accepting social services that were becoming the norm in the rest of the NWO. All that was left for the Clintons was to tidy up and cash in. There was no grand vision here: their entire agenda was to reinforce Reagan-Bush gains and utilize them to begin to marginally spread the booty around.

Bill Clinton's international energies were spent sweeping up after the Soviets and trying to figure out how far to go in employing American military power to further the NWO. He also brokered the peace deal between Israel and the PLO, an organization that had lost its international sponsor with the collapse of the Soviets.

When force was needed, Clinton used it, most prominently in Yugoslavia, Somalia, and Haiti. And when it became clear that Islamic revivalists were going to be among the last resistors to Western hegemony, he acted militarily against al-Qaeda's network wherever and whenever he chose. Lest we forget, it was Bill Clinton who signed the Iraq Liberation Act in 1998, officially sanctioning the neoconservative theory of unilateral regime change in the Middle East. Operation Desert Fox was launched by Clinton to show he meant business. (If you've forgotten, this was a seventy-hour air campaign involving 300 sorties, 600 air-dropped munitions, and 250 or so cruise missiles. Targets included six of Saddam Hussein's palaces.)

After Clinton, George W. Bush took the helm. Paul Wolfowitz returned as deputy secretary of defense. The world was quiet except for a few segments of resistance: jihadists and the dictatorial poles of the North Korea/Iraq "axis of evil." Now finding his ideological seat still warm after the Clinton years, Wolfowitz found his chance to test the limits.

The Bush team developed the Reagan Doctrine into a determination that the United States has an obligation to depose unsympathetic regimes and install NWO-style democracies. This became the Bush Doctrine. It is quintessentially millenarian because of its unreserved faith that America can successfully bring holy judgment upon the rulers of darkness and miraculously transform their nations into exemplary members of history's final society.

The test case was an obvious one. As soon as the Bush team settled into the White House, plans to invade Iraq went front and center—not in response to 9/11, which had yet to take place, but to prove America's ability to deconstruct a dictatorship and build a liberal democracy in its place. This was important—Fukuyama's End of History was depending on it.

Al-Qaeda's attack helped make the plan palatable, but of course there was never any connection between the two, except that both groups did not submit to the post-Soviet order. I have no doubt that without 9/11, the war would still have been pursued solely for the reasons that Colin Powell presented to the United Nations: Iraq's support of global terror and the development of weapons of mass destruction. The same pack of lies would still have been effective without al-Qaeda's help.

Bush's war was therefore an evolution from Reagan, George H.W. Bush, and Clinton; when Congress authorized the invasion in 2002, it cited nothing less than Bill Clinton's own Iraq Liberation Act as its precedent.[59] Senator Hillary Clinton cited it, too, when she voted for the authorization. Her proviso was that her vote did not mean adopting a doctrine of unilateralism or preemption. What did she think of regime change per se? A-OK. Before casting a "yes" vote, Senator Clinton noted this in her floor speech: "In 1998, the United States also changed its underlying policy toward Iraq from containment to regime change."[60] That is to say, her husband's Iraq Liberation Act did that.

The big difference between Bill and Hillary's precedent-setting regime-change doctrine and Bush's was the Clintons' insistence that such actions be done in a coalition and only after being provoked. In practice, there has been very little to distinguish the two—just nuances over what constitutes a provocation, and how much of the army to field. If you listen closely, however, you will hear the real question: "How much will this cost?"

The Bush people imagined the invasion would be a relatively easy task and that it would recoup the costs by way of Iraq's booming economy once free. They were confident that the military phase would be quick and painless. The nation building should go well, too, because everyone in the world wanted our Western liberal system and values, they thought. The only thing holding those poor people back were leftover dictatorships from a bygone age—pathetic vestiges of the time before history ended, caricatured perfectly in Saddam Hussein, Muammar al-Qaddafi, and Kim Jong-il.

Obviously, the experiment did not go well. As the failure in Iraq became clear, Fukuyama stopped preaching the End Time Gospel. He wrote a critique of the invasion for the *New York Times Magazine*, now arguing that history cannot be pushed along to its final point. Not only was history not over, there was nothing to be done to hasten its end. Such activism was founded upon Bolshevik Leninism, Fukuyama said.[61]

It is a spot-on insight: we can't make Paradise happen by force. But as we know, this belief that history can be compelled did not begin with the

Bolsheviks. We have seen it in every attempt to secure Paradise: Jewish rebels, Muslim jihadists, Crusader armies, global Christian imperialists, New World Puritans, Nazis, and, yes, communists.

As a lowly state senator, Barack Obama vehemently opposed the invasion, calling it a "dumb war"—not hard to say as a local official whose position rendered the opinion without consequence.[62] As he was not specific, I'm not sure what part of the invasion he thought was "dumb." It couldn't have been the military part of the experiment, which was actually a rip-roaring success: getting rid of Saddam was not hard to do. Setting up a democracy was easy, too—free and fair elections took place within eighteen months.

Judging by Obama's later actions, he did not really understand the "dumb" part. Here it is: Bush defeated Saddam and installed democracy without accounting for the possibility that Western democracy and morals might be rejected by a majority of the people there. Newly democratic Iraq elected a majoritarian tyranny of Shiites who were increasingly beholden to Iran. Very large parts of the population, in and out of power, did not want this New World Order. Democracy (of a less-than-liberal kind) allowed them to make that clear. Now all that was left was to begin killing one another to impose their own flavors of absolutist oppression. Were there NWO-style liberal democrats there? Sure. They just couldn't win an election.

So it was the ideal of world-saving liberal democracy that was the "dumb" part. Unfortunately, this is the very part that Obama held on to as president. The supposed stupidity of the exercise, the only part that failed, was the aspect that Obama went on to embrace most fully and most foolishly in the Middle East. President Obama did not wait for history to meander its way to its own conclusion, as penitent Fukuyama suggested he should. Instead, he pushed and coerced with every bit as much ambition as Bush. Both were out to save the world for global free-market democracy, human rights, and freedom. Both cited God's authority. And both failed.

First Do No Harm

What divided Bush and Obama was not fundamental to the globalist faith; it was instead cultural and technical differences highlighted in domestic social programs (such as those relating to transgender rights) and military tactics (such as the role of expensive ground forces versus remote-controlled bombing and proxy armies in deposing dictators). Bush and Obama would apportion public wealth differently, slicing the negotiable public monetary pie—a beggar's portion to begin with—in favor of different biases.

But just like Bush, President Obama found much of the world unreceptive to his plan of salvation. There is more to the New World Order and liberal democracy than simply voting. Hitler won votes. Putin wins votes. The fault was the NWO's assumption that it knows what is best for everyone and that the majority always wants what Western globalists want. When given the option to choose, people often choose to reject liberal modernity and embrace their own "religion," which from Russia to Egypt to China has lately been some form of structured intolerance.

Why didn't Obama see this? Because his is as much a religion as any other; any comprehensive utopian ideology is a millenarian religion, and it suffers from the overreach that characterizes all such fantasies.

At home, President Obama made this miscalculation as he tried to perfect the ideal of equality—a nice idea that is impossible to achieve peacefully by the force of law. The aspiration for a truly equitable and peaceful world is wonderful, but it requires an innate sense of the universal human family, accepting of its natural differences in strengths and abilities, roles and preferences. Trying to impose that equality through abstract power and coercive legislation only brings more division, deeper alienation.

Let's consider the word "inclusive." It seems a wholly unobjectionable word. But who really means it? Do progressives want to include conservatives? I find it hard to grasp, for example, the youthful impulse to "cancel" people who think differently, very often in the name of "inclusion." How is that possible?

The answer is exceptionalism, which has always been a hallmark of millenarian religious exercises. "We know best; what we are doing to you is for your own good." Global liberalism makes itself the one exception that rises above the level field of other ideas. If it is anything at all, it is a universal religion. It conditionally tolerates other religions: one can be a Christian, Muslim, Satanist, or whatever, as long as democratic liberalism overarches the whole thing. You can be a Christian as long as you include non-Christian beliefs in your church.

I'm reminded of George W. Bush's response to a question from a Muslim student: "People view America imposing its beliefs. If you believe that freedom is not universal then it could be viewed as an imposition of beliefs."[63] It's a frank admission and reveals so much about the whole enterprise. Obama would agree with him, of course: somehow the imposition of

Western-style freedom is exempt from the charge of imperialism. Why should that be?

The Arab Spring was President Obama and Secretary of State Clinton's test case on this matter. How should diversity-minded, inclusive neoliberal leaders respond to a mass movement dominated by anti-globalist Islamic revivalists? The answer, it seems: with studied incomprehension.

"Obama upended three decades of American relations with its most stalwart ally in the Arab world, putting the weight of the United States squarely on the side of the Arab street," judged the otherwise Obama-friendly *New York Times*.[64]

That upending took place in February 2011, when the president rebuked Egypt's Hosni Mubarak in a telephone call and then immediately appeared on television in a hastily called news conference to say that Mubarak must go. It looked and felt like a superior dressing down a subordinate and that's what it was. Such a display of dominant coercion is unusual from American presidents, perhaps an expression of President Obama's messianic confidence.

Mubarak, now without a superpower ally, duly resigned and democracy had its day in Egypt. Yay! For Bush, it took a military invasion to overthrow Saddam and give democracy to the Iraqis! Obama did it with a phone call!

Although Obama's circumstances were different, in both cases democracy proved to be anything but liberal. The people of Egypt predictably chose the Muslim Brotherhood to rule over them. The outcome was as far from Western ideals as what transpired in Iraq.

Did the president understand the situation better when, just eighteen months later, the streets again filled to attack US diplomatic missions in Egypt and Libya? The latter resulted in the death of Ambassador J. Christopher Stevens and led to Hillary Clinton's Libya debacle. Meanwhile in Cairo, the protesters burned effigies of their liberator, President Obama, in the streets. "Democracy" soon erupted in Yemen, Bahrain, and Syria, and the president's responses indicate that he remained as blind to the reality as Bush had been.

Meanwhile, in the Garden of Eden, things were about to get very ugly. As Syria began to disintegrate in 2011, my associates and I rushed aid to Christian victims of the anti-Assad forces favored by America. There, the "democratized street" meant locally imposed Islamic law and curtailment of Christian rights (and, in some areas, outright atrocities). How did it come to this? It seemed almost too perfectly symbolic: the upper Euphrates, where the worst of catastrophes unfolded, was the biblical setting of the Garden of Eden and the actual location of humanity's conscious birth. How is it that things were worse here now than they were 12,000 years ago? Where is the progress?

We shook our heads and recalled President Obama's unprecedented speech at Cairo's Al-Azhar University in 2009, where he spelled out his vision calling for "governments that reflect the will of the people" across the Middle East. The latter part of his remarks referred to America's unique calling: "The United States has been one of the greatest sources of progress that the world has ever known... shaped by every culture, drawn from every end of the Earth, and dedicated to a simple concept: E pluribus unum: 'Out of many, one.'"

Was there some suggestion that this was a motto applicable to the world—come under the unity of the New World Order? Or was it a subliminal appeal (or possibly affront) to Islam's cardinal doctrine of *tawhid*, the indivisible unity of God? It's unlikely anyone in the administration understood that these words could be read as a rival creed. I can only assume the line was written without guile. Nonetheless, it again failed to recognize that many people do not want to be "one" with Western liberalism at all.

It did have an effect, however. The Arab Spring erupted in the wake of his speech with unintended consequences, the Syrian Civil War being one of them. Clearly, universal tolerance under the aegis of liberal democracy was not the will of the people who took to the streets and picked up weapons to depose Assad. Nor was it that of the people in Cairo's streets who happily burned Obama in effigy. As for the rest of "the people," most would have been better off with their tyrannical leaders who generally operated under the maxim of "don't bother me, I won't bother you."

In his fateful telephone conversation, Mubarak had correctly predicted chaos, warning President Obama that he didn't have a good grasp of how the Middle East works. Questioning the American president's acumen was a bad tactic, however. It most certainly backfired on Mubarak. The president was used to giving lectures, not receiving them. (In the words of Congressman Dennis Cardoza, a fellow Democrat from California, "President Obama projected an arrogant 'I'm right, you're wrong' demeanor that alienated many potential allies."[65]) Mubarak told veteran correspondent Christiane Amanpour that he didn't hold a grudge, however, and believed Obama to be "a good man" who simply "does not understand."[66]

"He's not good with personal relationships; that's not what interests him," said an experienced US diplomat, adding further light to the problem.

"But in the Middle East, those relationships are essential. The lack of them deprives D.C. of the ability to influence leadership decisions."[67]

This observation about Obama's hectoring style was echoed again and again by a wide spectrum of leaders, from Arab diplomats to British prime minister David Cameron and New York City mayor Michael Bloomberg. (The latter two called Obama's stance "arrogant."[68])

In the Cairo speech, Obama assured his listeners that he considered it "part of my responsibility as President of the United States to fight against negative stereotypes of Islam wherever they appear." One thing he may not have understood—but could have learned if he'd listened to Arab diplomats —was that many activist Muslims perceive this good will as dishonest. As we've learned, when a Western leader insists that Islam is a religion of peace, it is seen as a means of pacification, a gun-wielding imperialist trick to cow Muslims into disarmed and non-threatening "Uncle Tom" subservience.

America's senior leadership did not grasp any of this. Despite growing chaos, the administration (through the embassy in Syria) encouraged democracy protesters while Clinton and other top advisers urged the president to increase US support to moderate, secular Syrian rebel groups, as if the situation could be contained and transformed into a 1776-style fight for freedom.

Obviously, that did not happen. Arms quickly fell into the hands of jihadists with an ideology indistinguishable from al-Qaeda's, Iran entered the fray without reserve, and ISIS came to dominate the scene for three bloody years; the current death toll is about 500,000, mainly young people. A measure of the disaster: among the factions that matter, the most moderate belonged to the decidedly immoderate Muslim Brotherhood. The number of fighters who really want a Western-style democracy is small, and they are so ineffective as to be insignificant.

On the opposite end, we have the Kurds who fought valiantly against the Islamic State. At first glance, Syria's Kurdish Democratic Union Party (PYD) is democratic and secular. They have sexual equality—just look at the images of those women soldiers! Progressive and conservative American globalists clung to this group as proof of what might happen if enough military power is lent to the right people. (And they lent heaps to the PYD.) But look more closely: this is not the liberal world at all. It is a Bookchinite socialist Paradise that does not allow rival ideologies and practices forced collectivization. Property is redistributed punitively based on ethnicity and political affiliation. Rivals are suppressed and arrested. My personal experience of this group is that it is totalitarian and mafia-like in the way it enforces the parameters of its Paradise. As for those women "warriors," I had a fourteen-year-old student in a scholarship program who was forcibly recruited with threats to kill her father. She was disfigured in the fighting. This group's socialist dream is one of the most extremely prescribed versions of enforced Paradise outside of North Korea.

I will stop here, although it is possible to go on for many, many pages with example after example from every side. All this is to say that the answer to the terror of history is not to be found in liberal or conservative ideology any more than it is to be found in older religious forms of millenarianism or the original socially constructed cosmology of Mesopotamia. None can force open the exit door from history, none can bring Paradise, and one is just as dangerous to human life as any other. Just ask anyone in Syria, where every shade of the spectrum has played a part in its destruction.

Apocalypse and Paradise

Here we are, as angry as Cain. Alienation and hatred dominate our social intercourse, our screens are filled with furious faces and loud, shouting voices, and our ears are deaf to all others.

We survive by this deafness, dwelling in encampments built to separate us from any rival reality. We hide in information technology, which, despite its proliferation, makes us less informed. Our perception has become more and more psychotic, divorced from natural inputs and relations.

Computer-aided estrangement extends to conventional warfare, where push-button slaughter is routine. Precision-guided missiles launched from ships strike blows without repercussion or flesh-and-blood entanglements. Drone warfare practically defines reified alienation: desk-bound pilots fly the craft, site their pre-judged targets, and kill them with hellfire missiles from the air-conditioned comfort of Las Vegas.[69] At least in ancient Babylon a thug had to put his life in danger, feel the impact of his blade against bone, and live with the reality of what he'd done, stained by his carnage. It was an awful human connection, but a connection nonetheless—real, with emotional recoil. Today, even that is gone.

The possibility of filling that void and reconnecting to something real is one of the appeals of ad hoc militias and terrorist organizations. I know their young recruits well; they grew up in the first generation of full-time, plugged-in kids. They finally feel alive when confronting death face-to-face, with human-to-human conflict.

Their violence seeks apocalypse, a word I've used ambiguously at times as it is commonly a way of talking about ultimate cataclysm. And although

Zoroaster's colorful description of the cleansing fire that will reveal the new world suggests just that, apocalypse does not really mean something like a nuclear holocaust. It simply means to lay bare, to unveil, or reveal something hidden. As it was used around New Testament times, it often meant to reveal the truth of something. For example, we can read it in Plutarch in a non-theological context, where apocalypse specifically means to reveal what has been hidden through deception. That is exactly what Zoroaster meant; for the Persian prophet, apocalypse was about unmasking the Lie to reveal the world as it is meant to be.

When suicide bombers kill themselves and others, their motivation is to rend the veil. They want to touch what is real beneath the mask of illusion and mediation. When my mother wrote in her diary, "I wanted to die, I cried to God to kill me and my boys and take us out of our misery," this was what she hoped to accomplish. I trust you see that this desperate act is futile—it is the same forcing of God's hand we've seen over and over again, a false apocalypse.

There is a true Apocalypse, but it comes, as its name clearly instructs us, as a revelation, an unveiling of what is truly present already. It is Plato's anamnesis. Would-be holy warriors be warned: there is no guarantee of revealing Paradise upon death. Proudly physicalist skeptics should take heed, too. Death, if not a doorway to Paradise, might seem to them at least a termination of suffering. That final exit surely means, at least, an escape from the stress of our histories, personal and otherwise. And I agree: this is a reasonable premise if there is no consciousness beyond material life. But here I urge caution: the concept of termination means the end of the line. What if there is no line?

In truth, the timeless qualities of consciousness, the seeming permanence of identity, do not match with the apparently linear course of aging and death. We all watch ourselves as our material states age and grow frail, and we wonder why—as if another person, a timeless person, sees it. Our souls do not age—are you so certain they will die?

For those seriously committed to the idea of such a simple timeline, I urge the study of physics. The universe that objective science reveals is one where time is relative and states of being are often beyond description and prediction. Our bulky day-to-day experience obscures our view, and even more so in our material-obsessed age.

I suspect that, subjectively, you know this already; you are innately in touch with eternity and the limitations of corporeal existence. Humans grasp eternity easily; consider how our happiness seems unbounded and our despair unending in any given instance. Now consider that final instance of life: if our last breath is terrifying, it may be an eternal moment tantamount to hell. I don't mean a moment stuck in time, frozen—but rather a moment of eternal depth, free of perceived time. As we live in the moment, we will die in it.

So, the coffin is no guarantee of escape. We know this. It's what lies at the root of the fear of death. We don't fear non-existence, or the act of dying per se, but we understand all too well the reality of eternity, the conscious-ness of the womb. We existed before birth in a prenatal universal connection to life beyond ourselves and we will exist beyond death the same way.

The good news is that Apocalypse leading to Paradise can occur in advance of the grave. We can live and die in eternal moments of reconcilia-tion. Zoroaster, Plato, Buddha, Jesus, and the others taught that the eternal answer was immediate; Paradise, or release from *samsara*, however it may be described, is always available. Be born again, awaken, see things as they are. "The kingdom of God cometh not with observation: Neither shall they say, Lo here! or, lo there! for, behold, the kingdom of God is within you."[70] The phase shift of the Apocalypse is a sidelong move across the axis of eternity, it is not an end date on the calendar of history.

How do we get there? It is entered directly through the disciplines prac-ticed by the Axial Age teachers. Buddha taught disciplined observation through a dedicated regime of meditation. Others taught abstaining from false securities and idols. In all these examples, contemplation, generous acts, and compassion are keys to the garden gate.

Zoroaster himself was clear: Paradise is never far away.

> The first step that the soul of the faithful man made, placed him in the Good-Thought Paradise; the second step that the soul of the faithful man made, placed him in the Good-Word Paradise; the third step that the soul of the faithful man made, placed him in the Good-Deed Paradise; the fourth step that the soul of the faithful man made, placed him in the Endless Light.[71]

His eschatology was lateral, not linear.

So, eternal life cannot be "after" life in the sense of forward or further down the line. It is neither the "after" of political revolution nor the "after" of suicidal violence. It is "after" in a different sense—that of the Hebrew word *'aḥărît* ("in back of" or "behind"), which formed the prophetic Hebrew phrase *'aḥărît hayāmîm* ("behind the days"), translated so inelegantly as the

"End Time." We want to get behind and beyond time, not slog our way to the wrongly conceived end of it, or hasten the false end through violence.

I must say, however, that when holy warriors (even Bolshevik ones) utilize the tactic of annihilation, they are not entirely wrong. The annihilation proposed by Zoroaster and his monotheistic cousins in the Apocalypse is the destruction of false universes. They painted the Apocalypse as a burning away of illusions, revealing a universe somehow new, and yet somehow the original creation as it was meant to be. How is that possible? The best way I know to understand this is to remember that the human universe we know is a fiction. We composed and constructed it. The state we remember as Paradise can therefore be recalled just as surely as it was forgotten. It can be revealed by the dissolution of post-civilization's veil of falsehood just as quickly as it was concealed.

I don't mean this to sound easy, and wouldn't claim that entering the consciousness of Paradise precludes ordinary suffering or making damaging choices. I've behaved clumsily in life and often stupidly. I suffer as anyone would and as anyone moderately awake should. It hurt when Jesus was nailed to the cross. He was known to weep, sweat blood, and admit to taking a path that caused him suffering. The Apostle Paul suffered over unstated struggles in his fleshly existence and claimed to be "the worst of sinners."[72] Being awake to truth in the sleeping world of lies can be excruciating. Being partly awake while partly asleep is even more painful. The act of awakening is frightening. Paradise is a dimension, a space, not an avoidance of a passing pain in the material time-bound world. Our present phase, as Buddha made absolutely clear, is one of suffering, and the more one awakens, the more intense that suffering can be.

Awakening reminds us that ours is a volatile existence. At its best, in its materiality, this phase is a pleasant experience, a passing fancy, an exciting ride through time—in fact, it is the ride, the movement, the swing of the clock's pendulum, the beating of the heart, and the orbit of the earth around the sun that alone gives us that sense of time's flow. Physics instructs us that perceived time is movement and decay.

In keeping with the Hebrew notion of *'aḥărît*, we can picture ourselves rowing backwards up a still river—the past unfolding before us as we move—the stuff of memory. The future is behind us, revealed inch by inch, first as the present and finally as the past. But the stream is just there, one totality, the sense of before and after an effect of our movement and limited perception. Depending on what we encounter, the journey is more or less pleasant or fraught, but it is only a journey.

I have a ' friend who simply lives, as far as I can observe, in eternal Paradise, yet he is an atheist and materialist. He did not need to follow my course to enter Paradise. Something about his years in a Turkish prison, including several months of gruesome torture, has killed his Tree of Knowledge ego to an extent that he is practically a model of Christ. Having taken up the cross and chosen, like Jesus, to "forgive those who know not what they do," he has entered Paradise.[73] He bears no grudge against his torturers, to the point that he has sat with them to offer forgiveness.

Any path to Paradise is like his; it's a serious, arduous effort, and a matter of personal responsibility. Reconciliation, peace, love, fulfillment, and satisfaction are evidence of Paradise. A lack of suffering in this material world is no evidence at all.

There are no shortcuts. And because awakening cuts laterally and does not come at the end of a line, it must be refreshed moment by moment. Awakening happens in an instant but staying awake is a continuous linkage of instances; it is not a package, once received and kept as a possession. Jesus said to take up the cross daily and Buddha said to continually maintain awareness, epitomized by the observation of each breath. It is very simple, but extremely difficult.

This, I believe, is the greatest obstacle. Laziness was a precipitating factor in hierarchy's rise. People gave up and surrendered to a fantasy and to the will of myth-makers. Giving responsibility to the imagineers of civilization was a shortcut that provided enough assurance to get through the day, so long as no one looked too closely. It relieved just about everyone from responsibility. Over time, prophets and philosophers understood there was a better way. But to follow it is arduous. At the end of the day, some of us may just be too shiftless to enter Paradise, even if the door is standing wide open.

I can offer practical advice on two levels. One is an appeal to active personal spirituality. For the brave and vigorous: meditation, prayer, community, accountability, humility, and all of the disciplines of the devotional life are gifts to us.

The second part of the advice is relational. How do we live with one another in a world constructed by competing cultures and ideas? All we really need to do is bow equally before the only judge of Good and Evil—to relinquish that desire, as Genesis says, "to be like god." Call the judge what you will: God, Reality, the Universe, Nature, History—it doesn't matter. Be judged together and love each other in compassion, forgiveness, and generosity, as brothers and sisters who lack the knowledge to judge.

In this, Adam and Eve depict our temporal experience. They lived with a choice between reifying knowledge and life, represented by the two trees, which they may consume or not. We live still with this choice every day. Whether it leads to alienation and judgment, or eternal and reconciled life, is up to us at any given instance. It seems that eating from both trees is not possible. We have to choose, and choose continuously.

From my collection: Australian Aboriginal art on stone. It reminds me of my 400 million-year-old *orthoceras* fossil. In the timeless realms of cosmic music, the relationship between them resounds.

The *carcharodontosaurus* (African T. rex) tooth and abstract designs on the Kurdish tribal rug in the background also remind me of the shared fabric of all life.

EPILOGUE

Black Jews

It seems right to finish this story with a return to something biographical, relational, and sweaty—to Muslims and Jews, my friends and brothers at a moment when I didn't understand much at all.

My first real encounter with the Middle East, you will recall, was at the Tel Aviv airport. After a fifteen-hour excursion (New York–Paris–Tel Aviv), we landed in the Promised Land. My tasseled and side-curled Chasidic seatmates had tut-tutted at my impiety. Then I waited at the Tel Aviv airport, which in the early 1980s made me think we had mistakenly landed in Damascus. The smells, the throbbing Eastern music, and the dark-browed countenance of the locals was not the urbane Jewish homeland I expected. Disturbed and confused, I arrived at the Galilee kibbutz to clean pots and pans, and there slowly acclimated to the experience of this skeletal land of promise, which I hoped would grow flesh and be quickened by the Holy Spirit.

I grew to like the god-despising kibbutzniks, and though they thought me a religious fool, they were invariably kind. It was the beginning of a lesson in brotherhood. I've told you about the river greenery and the presence of Jesus it brought on Sabbath walks. Our other respite from the glories of socialist labor was just as enlightening but far more pedestrian: it was the nearby city of Qiryat Shemona.

The whole town looked Middle Eastern in the worst way. It was concrete, ugly, and smelly. The food was Arab. The music sounded Arab. Everyone looked, dare I say it, surly. And yet the city had more Jews of the Bible-believing kind than the kibbutz. I knew this because of their yarmulkes and their synagogues. Why, then, did these people look like those from the airport? How was it that the most Jewish Jews around me were also the most Arab?

The mystery only deepened when one of my saltier workmates tried to make sense of it for me, saying without a hint of chagrin, "They're blacks, what about it...?"

"*Slicha ani lo mevin... shachoorim?*" I asked. ("Pardon, I don't understand... blacks?") I thought it was a misunderstanding of my new vocabulary. He doubled down. "Yes, *habibi*, blacks."

They were in fact Mizrahi Jews from the lands of Morocco, Yemen, Egypt, Syria, and Iraq. As I got to know them, I understood that they were the underclass and latecomers to the Zionist End Time happening. I got to know many of them. They counted themselves Israeli and Jewish, of course. But they were also Arabs. They swore in Arabic and spoke to their mothers in Arabic and blasted the Arabesque hit parade from their cassette players and watched Arabic movies on TV. By most outward signs, then, true-believing Jews (at least around where I lived) were more likely to be culturally Arab than to be the familiar European Jews I grew up with.

Adding to the intrigue, this block of Jews was also more likely to vote for Menachem Begin and the right-wing Likud. Their growing numbers—for they had more children—turned the tide to the political right in the mid-1970s. That's who propelled the heirs of the Jewish terror group Irgun to office and helped Ronald Reagan become president. Arab Jews diverted the course of history.

I learned all this from my friend Yossi as we walked around biblical ruins in Galilee, both of us wearing the same plaid shirts and dripping Muslim prayer beads from our fingers. (An affectation he taught me, to which I remain devoted.) Unlike almost all kibbutzniks, he was a hawk, and although an unbeliever, he stood on the right side of prophecy as far as I was concerned. Yossi wholeheartedly endorsed restoring and securing the biblical territory of Israel.

"I was raised to hate Begin!" Yossi told me this while visiting Jesus' home base at Capernaum. Until the mid-1970s, the prime minister and his kind were gadflies on the Israeli body politic. Begin's roots were not in the dominant ideological bloc, the Labor Zionists, of which the kibbutz movement formed the backbone. Of course, those Labor heroes bore the names that rang in my ears like biblical legends: Moshe Dayan, Yitzhak Rabin, Golda Meir, and founder David Ben-Gurion. They were Zionism to me, but they were of one mind with most kibbutzniks—that is to say, secular, leftist, and humanistic—merely the Messiah's donkey, not real believers, apparently.

Yossi helped me understand the Irgun and Begin. He said that while all Jews in Israel celebrated the United Nations' creation of Israel in 1948, the Irgun rejected its terms, which mandated sharing the land with Arabs. No, no, no! they said. We'd rather fight the Arabs and get all of it! No partition! And not just the land between the Jordan River and the sea; we want Israel to sit astride both banks—East and West! According to biblical boundaries, all the way to the Euphrates! Ben-Gurion's dominant majority considered their stance immoral and impractical.

"But it's my view, too," Yossi said, going completely against the tide of kibbutz culture. "Before '48, the Irgun and Ben-Gurion's Haganah were at war. The only thing that brought them together was Ben-Gurion finally realizing that the Arabs would never let us live in peace—that they rejected partition first. The partition plan failed because the Arabs tried to destroy us. They pounced the minute the UN announced it. Ben-Gurion could bring the Irgun into the fold because we had no choice but to fight the Arabs."

The Irgun's uncompromising vision of Mediterranean-to-Euphrates borders is known as Greater Israel. Naturally, it rang true with me: those were the borders promised by God; where is the argument? Plus, Begin's insistence that Jerusalem become part of Israel as its capital was mandatory and inevitable: the Bible said so—the Temple would have to be rebuilt! It also rang true with Religious Zionists and the Arab Jews.

I was starting to get the picture. Yossi's compatriots impressed upon me the unlikelihood of Begin's election in 1977. "He was anathema to Israel's political elite." Or, if you were a reader of the *New York Times*, a generally Israel-friendly paper in the first part of the twentieth century, he was more than anathema, he was a terrorist. A headline from December 30, 1947, reads, "Irgun Bomb Kills 11 Arabs and 2 Britons."[1] The *Times* repeatedly referred to Begin's group as the "Zionist terrorist organization Irgun."[2] Why not? They killed, kidnapped, and hanged British soldiers, assassinated international dignitaries, and blew up Arab and British civilians.

Begin's election was a turning point as the Likud Party has remained dominant ever since. How did he pull off this unlikely starboard tack in Israel's destiny? In short, the wind in their sails was driven by all those Arab Jews in the yarmulkes. Sure, they were devoted to Arab culture. But these Arab Jews, these Mizrahi, understood Arabs better, and knew that to be successful in the Middle East meant being harshly realistic. "Who do you think really understands the Arab mentality? It's Jews from Arab lands! Just look at the countries they come from! Do you think Assad, Nasser, or Saddam got where they are by being nice? No way! They kicked Jews out, didn't they?! Prime Minister Begin knows how to play by those rules!"

So, in Begin they found a leader who understood what it takes to fulfill God's promises. But Yossi refused to admit any religious motive. My non-religious friend, whose father came from Poland as a socialist, chose to stand shoulder-to-shoulder with Middle Eastern Jews and Religious Zionists and evangelical Christians. This was, it seems, Israel's future: non-religious millenarians.

The Music of the Universe

Yossi's stance was already odd for a kibbutznik, but considering his peculiar passion, it seemed amazingly improbable, miraculous even: he was an Arabist, fluent in the language, and he loved its speakers and their culture. He'd served as an intelligence officer recently in Lebanon, his job to visit and chat with village elders. He relished it. These were his friends and his fascination.

Sparkling with stories of this one and that one and how one very important sheikh presented him with those ivory worry beads always in his hand, he demonstrated to me something of what Isaiah meant when he said the lamb and wolf would lie down together.

It wasn't just that he was a right-wing Israeli Jew living his life in devotion to Arab Islamic culture and claiming Lebanese Shiites as dear friends. It was his being the evangelist of Islam to me, the Christian fundamentalist. He introduced me to Muslims for the first time. I've spent the rest of my life serving Muslims because of this right-wing Israeli spy.

Yossi didn't just talk about it, either. He wanted me to experience his passion. He'd take me on visits with Bedouin who lived close to us, living traditionally in tents like Abraham. The patriarch was Abu Fathi. He greeted us in robes and headgear out of *Lawrence of Arabia* and presented his son, a tracker in the Israeli army, as indeed many Galilee Bedouin were. (They volunteered.) His pretty daughter was there, too, happily subservient, all averted glances and blushes while serving the bearded young American sweet mint tea, followed by giggles when she caught him looking at her. Abu Fathi didn't mind—these were earthy people; everything smelled like the barnyard.

At night, we sat around a fire while Yossi held court, directing conversation like Johnny Carson and pausing to translate for me. For lubrication in these gatherings, we drank the dreaded *mirra* coffee and ate *labneh* on hot flat bread. *Mirra* was circulated by a communion of the ceramic cup and taken in one shot, sourly potent. One was denied a round if the hand reaching for it shook. I was instructed that three rounds was the expectation and the limit, but my hosts liked to make a game of it and were proud of their brew, concocted in a mysterious set of tinned copper pots of varying sizes that sat permanently in the ash of the rock-lined fire pit. To my mind it must have been always burning, a relic of Zoroastrian passersby.

They were Muslims, of course, but somehow it went beyond that. Bedouin were Abrahamic, and though I did not dwell on the thought, I wondered about Islam's origin in the deserts of Abraham and Midian where Moses and Muhammad met the Divine. It would cross my mind that maybe our religions had evolved to such an extent that the original point of it— Abraham's and Moses' nameless God of the desert—was lost to us all. Mesmerized by the coals and high on the *mirra*, I hallucinated Jesus, every bit a nomad, too, sitting around this fire and speaking with my Jewish and Arab friends as one of their own.

Abu Fathi's brother played a flute for us, while the girl swayed nearby in a way I expected to be forbidden, but that was not. Something about the flutist's style reminded me of that other music, those caterwauling violins from the airport and from our neighboring town. Asking Yossi about the connection, I learned that this popular music sounded Arab because it was the effluence of Mizrahi culture, a Mediterranean-Jewish-Arab-Ottoman fusion.

Those same Middle Eastern and North African Jews who thrust right-wing Begin into power produced this increasingly popular music. It was subversive and quietly illicit, frowned upon by the Zionist elite who preferred Russian folk songs and Bach. "Israeli music was the songs of the pioneers," Yossi told me. "This music isn't what we grew up on."

Aficionados circulated it underground on cassettes like some kind of Soviet-era samizdat to be found alongside the pornography and martial arts videos at bus stations and beside the vegetables at open-air markets—places populated by Mizrahi Jews and Arab workers alike.

My nearest city, Qiryat Shemona, was rife with the stuff. It contributed to the feeling of "leaving Israel" when I went to town, that feeling of having gone to Syria. Yossi was again instructive: "You should listen to it on the radio. We broadcast a music show in Arabic—it's the latest stuff."

I asked if it was for propaganda.

"*Betach*, for sure... but it's just making friends. You should listen."

I did. The announcer spoke Arabic, the intended audience within earshot: Israeli Arabs, Palestinians, Lebanese, Syrians, and Egyptians. This was a reminder that the cities of the Levant are too close for comfort; Damascus was closer to us than Jerusalem. The songs featured Mizrahi Jews singing in Hebrew, Arabic, and a little of both. I loved it. So did the Arabs. It was top-of-the-charts stuff all over the Middle East. The same numbers that ricocheted off the concrete walls of nearby Damascus and Beirut echoed from poser boys' cars in Tel Aviv and the grimy markets of Qiryat Shemona.

The radio show's reach was not only broad but deep. The host, Shafiq Salman, received thousands of fan letters from Arabs. In neighboring countries, a black market in Israeli music cassettes boomed; in Egypt, it was so pervasive that it became a political talking point. The government's opponents said its popularity revealed a dilution of Egyptian identity, and it was all the fault of the peace process. In Syria, President Assad was reportedly a listener. The Muslim Brotherhood hated it, of course, but they were none too happy with Assad and the leaders of Egypt to begin with.

Yet the tapes still sold in large numbers, and the cards and letters poured in, facilitated by a special address in Switzerland (there was no mail service, for example, between Syria and Israel).

A letter from two (presumably young) Syrian women asked, "If the Syrian people requested, do you think Israeli singers would come sing for them personally, without the Syrian ruling family stopping it?" They claimed to record each show, having amassed a library of 250 tapes. "We cannot give you our names because we know that many here listen to you, including President Assad's bodyguards."[3]

The Syrian fangirls had a request: "There is a singer who captures with his voice everyone I know, including my father. If the birds in heaven heard him, they would stop singing. He is Moshe Eliyahu. I hope you will interview him. We send greetings of peace." They also wanted to know how Israelis felt "when Syrians write to you."

Another Syrian woman wrote in Hebrew at the top of her letter in a script that appeared to be roughly copied from a Jewish synagogue in Aleppo, *shalom u-vracha*, "Peace and welcome!" She reported that "I am trying to learn Hebrew so I will know what they say in their beautiful songs. I ask God that an agreement will be reached between our two countries so that we will be able to see you."

A man from Mecca wrote that he often listened to the program: "I hope you will regard me as your friend."

A key figure was Yemenite Jewish singer Haim Moshe.[4] His 1983 release, "Linda Linda," was a recasting of a Lebanese song, and evidently accomplished with aplomb. Eventually, it became a hit among Jewish Israelis, but before that, it was massively and affectionately embraced by Arabs all over the Middle East. He was a superstar everywhere.[5]

I thought about him one night, listening to that Bedouin flute player and entranced by the glowing embers. My mind drifted and I smiled, reminded of other nights I watched glowing embers, when the Israel Defence Forces would drop parachute flares over Lebanon or the Golan Heights. They were mesmerizing and made me think of what they illuminated. At the time, Lebanon was less than a mile and half from my home, and the nearest Syrian town 10 miles away. I could ride my bike up the road and look at the lights of Lebanese villages closer to my home than the nearest Israeli city.

Watching the flares cast their light on Arab and Jew alike, it was easy to imagine the young men encamped so nearby—Israeli soldiers, Syrian forces, and Lebanese. I could swear sometimes, when the wind was just right, that I heard their boomboxes as they whiled away the nights, all listening to "Linda, Linda." Returning soldiers said they could hear it in the opposing camps. Why the hell were they killing each other, then?

When I listen to that music now, I still think about that Bedouin girl, my Israeli Jewish friend, and the Arab Muslim patriarch. There was an elixir in it, a love potion, causing us to bed down together. It certainly worked on me. By the end of that year, my passion for Israel grew to include their neighbors. It wasn't that my thinking had changed—that would take time—but my sense of family changed. I could not feel my brothers and sisters as enemies, even if we had different ideas, abilities, outlooks, perspectives, and beliefs: we were family.

Coming to the final few pages of my report, this anecdote seemed important to tell. It is something about the way music reminded this Cain that Abel was his brother—the way this peculiar symphony of Israeli right-wing spy, American millenarian, and Arab tent-dwellers created a Paradise family together with all those radio listeners, who like us, no longer saw the point of enmity.

Songlines

Music is more than music. And that, in the end, is what ties this whole story together. It is not a sentimental thought. This is about the underlying vibrations of the universe, the most fundamentally active principle in all creation—music as the only language immune to the tortured constructions of our discursive minds, and music that we need not even hear.

Music is as much physics as it is poetry. It is the impossibility of complete knowledge; the eternal character of the universe and the relativity of time; the non-dual behavior of the quantum realm. Physicist Michio Kaku talks about it when interpreting string theory, which he describes as "the simple idea that all the four forces of the universe, gravity, the electromagnetic force, the two strong forces, can be viewed as music."[6]

If you could see an electron, he says, you'd see a vibrating thread or string. "If I twang it, it turns into a neutrino. I twang it again, it turns into a quark... If I twang it enough times, I get thousands of subatomic particles that have been catalogued patiently by physicists."

They vibrate in hyperspace, says Kaku, "a dimension beyond physical comprehension." His calculations show eleven dimensions existing in hyperspace, which is a challenge to us, because we only really know three dimensions; there is more beyond our lived piece of the universe than there is in it.

> So string theory says that all subatomic particles of the universe are nothing but musical notes. A, B-flat, C-sharp, correspond to electrons, neutrinos, quarks, and what have you. Therefore, physics is nothing but the laws of harmony of these strings. Chemistry is nothing but the melodies we can play on these strings. The universe is a symphony of strings and the mind of God, the mind of God that Einstein eloquently wrote about for the last 30 years of his life, for the first time in history, we now have a candidate for the mind of God. It is cosmic music resonating through 11 dimensional hyperspace. That is the mind of God.

I understand what Kaku is saying; it rings true with me. I dream about it, I meditate on it: the Bedouin, the vibrations of the cosmic strings, the communal music of Arabs and Jews and the family of the Garden of Eden.

As I listen to the music of awakening, I hear the name YHWH. If spoken, it would sound like a breath, the wisdom of a bare desert wind, all tenses and yet tenseless and atemporal—a metaphor for the entire cosmos. YHWH is a reference to the music of the universe, oneness and wholeness, and just as Moses learned, it is a token, a memento of pre-recursive consciousness.

This is hard for us. Linguistically, we struggle with the name YHWH, trying to read it as a line, the way Mesopotamia taught us to: WAS-BEING

—IS-BEING—WILL-BE-BEING. No wonder the Zoroastrians distrusted writing. They knew that a line has nothing to do with eternity. Thankfully, YHWH resists translation, forcing us to consider it non-discursively in just the way we listen to music.

I've found Henri Bergson's discussion of *la durée* helpful when thinking about all this. He talks about the way music transcends frozen points in time.[7] The minutes and seconds and individual notes do not constitute "music." Although you may hear the pitch and timbre of music one sound at a time, experiencing music one note at a time is to experience no music at all. Music exists in the flow and neurologically overlapping relationship of the sounds. Our experience of music is completely beyond the particulars, only meaningful in the irreducible duration that makes us feel and understand meaning. Beyond the nuts and bolts of music, it is the ineffable duration that makes it what it is. This is even true of a "single note." Any audible tone is composed of fundamentals, harmonics and overtones. There is no note that is single. Each and every note is literally a vibrant relationship.[8] Music is therefore the art that is most like life itself. While there seems to be a written line of music, only the song of its flowing duration means anything.

Music illuminates the nature of time as we perceive it. In a conventional sense, time is a measure of space, based on movement, whether that of an atom or the orbit of the earth around the sun or the turning of a galaxy. These are only markers and utilitarian measurements of vibrations and movement. Useful to be sure, but our experience of it, our apprehension of life, is more than the single clicks or individual film frames that are the ticking of the clock. Here we experience the duration as something unbound to those reified points, just as we do with music.

I give credit to the Australian Aboriginal peoples who, in recent years, between my travels in the Middle East, have brought so much together for me. I sit with their art and music and find a liminal space that is unexpectedly warm and alive. Like Abraham, they are wanderers. For some 75,000 years, until civilization encroached upon them in the 1600s, they never heard Nintur's call to let her "bring them back from their trails... and lay the bricks for the cities." Quite the opposite—their trails lie at the heart of the Aboriginal window upon the cosmos. We call it the "Dreaming," attempting to put a word on a different landscape of consciousness.

In a probably ill-conceived attempt at explaining it, I might say that the Dreaming is before time, a kind of Genesis story. But it is also in the present, or inhabits the present. And yet, it is a mistake to impose time in any sense upon the Dreaming. "I have never been able to discover any aboriginal word for time as an abstract concept," writes pioneering researcher W.E.H. Stanner.[9]

I trust the rarity of a language surviving without a notion of existing in time is clear. I know of only one other example, discovered among an Amazonian people who first had contact with the outside world in the 1980s. This ability to live in timelessness is what we've been talking about so often in these pages, and pre-contact Aboriginal consciousness preserves at least a glimpse of the way our minds perceived existence in the state we recall as a Paradise.

We who are obsessed with ourselves in befores, nows, and afters will not easily experience the Aboriginal consciousness. Helpfully, Stanner elaborates to give some sense of the Dreaming to us whose brains have been altered by millennia of dwelling on notions of linear time: "The Dreaming determines not only what life is but also what it can be," and while it "conjures up the notion of a sacred, heroic time of the indefinitely remote past," it is much more. "Neither 'time' nor 'history' as we understand them is involved in this... One cannot 'fix' the Dreaming in time: it was, and is, *everywhen*." That feels inescapably like YHWH to me: EVERYWHEN.[10]

The Dreaming suggests transdimensional perception. It is this space that a suicide bomber or end-the-world millenarian wants to escape to by violently rending the apocalyptic veil. Modern materialists—socialists and capitalists—scorn such primitive ambitions. Anything metaphysical they judge as not "scientific" or "real," as if someone could possibly see and understand everything. But their quest is essentially the same—as desperate and absurd as a religious extremist's. Staunch materialists would refashion our present familiar dimensions into a perfect physicalist Paradise. It would include the eventual mastery of nature so that there is no sickness and eventually no aging or death. Their premise is that this is "real" because it is material and three-dimensional. But it may as well be another universe, for it's nothing like the natural order—it is so destructive of nature as to constitute its own counterfeit apocalypse, a destructive cleaving of nature that reveals nothing.

The Dreaming is not about these deceptive escapes. It is about true Apocalypse, a revelation. In the Dreaming, higher dimensions are not isolated from us and our phase of life and do not exclude our experience. Just as we operate in the third dimension and therefore also live with lower dimensions, any higher dimensions such as those discussed by Professor Kaku will easily envelope our three; the Dreaming is aware of the full spectrum. Thereby, true Apocalypse rends only veils of darkening blindness—it is an unmasking of deceiving appearances, not annihilation of nature.

What are other dimensions like? It's best to see for yourself, and as we've said, this requires discipline and practice. Of course, it can be understood abstractly with the right skill set; but here, too, the mathematical language required is challenging and not for the lazy or faint of heart. If you are up for it, there is plenty of scholarly literature available.

Even without that, if you are like me, willing to practice spiritual discipline but not well-equipped at math, we can still sketch a verbal picture that is clear and true. On this point, I'll defer to Carl Sagan, whose demonstration on "The Edge of Forever," an episode in his 1980 *Cosmos* television series, will be worth 100 pages of writing to you. There, he very effectively demonstrates the relationship between the third and second dimensions. Once we get a handle on that, the realities of higher dimensions begin to make more sense for non-specialists.[11]

Here's what I can reliably tell you: a being of the fifth dimension could move as easily in time as we do in space, observing not only our existence as we experience it, but any other possible iterations of our world that there may be. It would have an all-encompassing view of our dimensions—including those of space and time—seeing what we perceived as linear time at a single glance, just as we see a two-dimensional line on piece of paper in its totality. Higher dimensions will give even more unfathomable vistas, apprehending every possible permutation of probabilities.[12]

Importantly, these higher dimensions could influence us. We can't "know" for certain anything directly about multiverses or our universe's higher dimensions, just as a hypothetical two-dimensional being could see nothing of our third dimension. We can, however, influence two-dimensional reality. Who's to know to what extent the higher dimensions act upon us?

In recent years, we've seen enough to understand the possibilities of the unseen's effect on our visible, consciously experienced lives. We can't, for example, observe with certainty the weirdly non-dual behaviors of quantum physics in the familiar way we know the conventional physical world. But quantum reality affects our existence, and we can "know" something of it in an unmediated, non-discursive, and absolutely direct way *through its effect*.

Far-fetched? Consider this: not so long ago this unseen world and its effect described atoms and even molecules of which we had absolutely no objective knowledge. Until the 1800s, talk of atoms was only for philosophers and metaphysicians. Of course, it's clear to us now that this invisible level of reality exists and that we are totally dependent upon it in an obvious and direct relationship. Just because higher dimensions or other universes haven't yielded to our direct scientific knowledge (although predicted by scientific theory), can we really conclude realms unseen and yet-to-be understood have no effect upon us now?

I say no, and, in fact, most of us intuit the existence and influence of the beyond, if only in the still of the night or in that rare moment of desperately alert perception. Appreciating that something beyond our familiar world affects us, moves us, and speaks to us is quite common indeed.

Here is where the music of the cosmic strings resonates in our lives as the unity of song across a bridge of hidden dimensions. For Aboriginal people, that correlation with music is explicit. They experience the Dreaming through "Songlines," song cycles that guide them along specific invisible pathways, often over great geographical distances. In the Dreaming, physical features of nature interface with the song in a matrix of spiritual connection that involves the primordial beings, plants, animals, and more—what the Lakota People of the American plains call "all my relations."

You've probably heard the sound of Aboriginal didgeridoo. It rumbles and whistles and resonates with the body. Listen to one now if you can. Feel the vibration. A true didgeridoo is made by termites, which chew intricate pathways in the wood of the eucalyptus tree, making hidden tunnels and networks that correspond to the paths of the Songlines. This is what gives it that unique vibration and incomparable sound. It is the instrument of the Dreaming, which reaches out to us from the Garden of Eden, the song of the universe, coming from just beyond the membrane of mundanity, as all pure music does.

One day, our material reality will dissolve. All that will be left is these vibrations. It's not just that eventually the earth and stars will no longer exist. Material dissolution is imminent for all of us. We will die, or our ability to construct reality will fade through mental decline. So, we would do well to find those harmonics and harmonies now in our everyday lives. It is for our personal harmony with the reality of life and death, and it is for the possibility of realizing the Paradise dream in society. It is the vibration of the strings that frees enemies to lie down together as Isaiah dreamed: wolf and lamb, leopard and kid, calf and lion, Israeli and Syrian. "They shall not hurt nor destroy in all my holy mountain: for the earth shall be full of the knowledge of the Lord, as the waters cover the sea."[13]

Immortally Mortal

I SPENT TIME WORKING ON PARADISE TODAY, AS I OFTEN DO: MEDITATING, watching my breath, observing the stream of thoughts rising and dissipating, and dissipating more to nothingness. In the absence of thoughts and the generation of streams of words and things to do, and as judgments and ideas cease, I see a presence observing it all. It is me, but a me abstracted from this realm. And it's not just me, but me and all else, a universal me. Aware only of the seeing presence, my temporal self briefly understands much more than the constrained dimensions it usually contends with, and I smile, my consciousness lifting away as if to float out of its container.

There's always a return, of course. A reinstatement of the discursive mind, the things to do and say, the body to feed and clothe, and its pains and pleasures to endure. But in those moments of Apocalypse, I am a friend of mortality and immortality at once—I am free.

But why do we have this material phase if it is temporary and confined to cramped dimensions that groan and suffer? Buddhism and the Abrahamic faiths offer suggestions, and with them, I can accept that it is a necessary part of a bigger picture. But because the picture is so large, an answer to "Why?" must be beyond us. It can no more be defined than God can be defined.

Indeed, if one wants to go further into the question of what lies beyond, consider the way quantum reality is expressed most specifically only by relying on what, in our scheme of things, are "unreal" numbers: "A theory obeying the rules of quantum physics needs imaginary numbers to describe the real world," says a recent report on this peculiarity. Another article claims that "physicists may have just shown for the first time that imaginary numbers are, in a sense, real."[14] The former statement is hardly news; the latter more to our point. To be clear, "imaginary numbers" are not numbers we create as an artificial reality in the way we conjure the Cosmic Order; they are rather so real as to be beyond our imaginations, beyond what we can grasp or project. These "Really Real Numbers," which we read as imaginary in our lived experience, are nonetheless essential to even begin to think about fundamental things.

I cite this to say we do not need to be embarrassed by mystery, where the inconceivable is more fundamentally real than the concrete. And we don't need to become physicists or mathematicians to get there. More useful is the idea of humble acceptance. Our material phase is subjected to suffering—we know that. Hope means believing there is more, that there is something beyond material decay, and accepting that our present condition, with its limited and time-bound perspective, serves its purpose in the greater scheme.

Of course, in a loving, caring environment, where wealth is measured by a lack of wants and nature is unmolested, we will suffer only what is natural. It's harder when so much of our pain is unnatural, when it is made of torments that we inflict upon one another in the vanity of circumventing nature, like competing gods trying to transform the universe into something more to our imagined purpose. It is there that we risk missing the point of life. Although I don't know if we can mitigate the grinding misery of the fake and mechanized environment that we call civilization, I think our awakening to its deception is at least a starting point.

It's not easy. I am too often obsessed with the ticking clock, which in truth has little bearing on things, and I'm as attached to the ephemeral bubble of material existence as anyone else. I easily forget how dependent and collateral this passage is. At such times, true hope is fleeting and the false hope of death's finality appeals to me, as it does to so many of those I work with in the Middle East.

However, I've been saved from this logical despair time and again simply by taking note of what is Real, including a true awareness of my condition and remembering to care for others. True hope is simple, after all: it is remembering that there is more to existence than we can grasp, that we cannot preserve the universes we conjure, that there is a more tangible beyond.

"We know in part, and we prophesy in part," writes the Apostle Paul. "But when that which is perfect, is come, then that which is in part shall be abolished... For now we see through a glass darkly: but then shall we see face to face. Now I know in part: but then shall I know even as I am known."[15]

The main theme of the Garden and the Fall finds its way again into Paul's narrative. He writes of knowledge: we know imperfectly—our language is imprecise—but we are "known" by the Divine, by the Beyond. To know as I am known is the condition imparted by the Tree of Life. It is the condition of Paradise. The Tree of Knowledge of Good and Evil is its counterfeit, a condition where we are god and we know without being known, where we feign supremacy and are not submissive to the great Reality.

Paradise is the humble state of subordination to the larger Reality, to the Universe, to Nature, to God. This is a knowledge without alienation, a knowledge of the judged—not the one making judgments. It is a humble response, not a domineering initiative. To be in harmony with the vibration of the strings, to know as God knows us—that's the Apocalypse, the unveiling, when "that which is perfect" comes and "that which is in part shall be abolished."

I also agree with the Apostle when he explains resurrection in these terms. It does not hinge on zombie-like flesh-and-blood resuscitation; it is rather about the "mystery" of eternal consciousness. When the resurrected Jesus appears to the disciples he is not recognized as his corporeal self and performs non-mortal acts, seeming to walk through walls and ascending to heaven, whatever that could possibly mean in three-dimensional terms. To the astute Apostle Paul, it certainly did not mean Jesus floated up into the blue sky.

So, when Paul talks about how resurrection is "a spiritual body," for "flesh and blood cannot inherit the kingdom of God, nor does the perishable inherit the imperishable," he rebukes those obsessed with physicalism. But he also rebukes those who deny resurrection: "How can some of you say that there is no resurrection of the dead? If there is no resurrection of the dead... our preaching is useless and so is your faith... If only for this life we have hope in Christ, we are of all people most to be pitied."[16]

This is the essential point: if all we value is this short and quickly fading existence, limited in dimension and partial, we are truly in a pathetic and a literally hopeless situation. It is our attempt to perfect this truncated material world that so often makes it more painful and unfair, and in consideration of the many valid reasons to believe that there is something beyond what we can see and touch, I must conclude that these desperate and damaging political machinations are not only pitiful, but dangerous and cruel.

It's a mysterious ending to a mysterious story—but that is what Paradise is all about. I hope these thoughts have been helpful.

Love suffereth long: it is bountiful: love envieth not: love doth not boast itself: it is not puffed up:

It doth no uncomely thing: it seeketh not her own thing: it is not provoked to anger: it thinketh no evil:

It rejoiceth not in iniquity, but rejoiceth in the truth:

It suffereth all things: it believeth all things: it hopeth all things: it endureth all things.

Love doth never fall away, though that prophesyings be abolished, or the tongues cease, or knowledge vanish away.

And now abideth faith, hope and love, even these three: but the chiefest of these is love.

472

ILLUSTRATION CREDITS

Cover and interior front: Brooke Fitts, Brookelyn Photography.

Photographic Inserts: **Page 6,** *top:* Public Domain, *bottom:* author. **Page 7**, author. **Page 8**, author. **Page 93,** Zde, CC BY-SA 3.0, via Wikimedia Commons. **Page 94,** *top:* Mehmet Fatih Aslan—Anadolu Ajansı, (used with permission), *bottom:* author. **Page 95,** Public Domain, from the British Library's collections, 2013. **Page 176,** *top:* INTERFOTO/ Alamy Stock Photo, *bottom:* author. **Page 177**, author. **Page 178,** author. **Page 255,** *top:* Bernd81, CC BY-SA 4.0, via Wikimedia Commons, *bottom:* author. **Page 256,** author. **Page 290,** *top:* XV14 - Roma, Museo civiltà romana - Adorazione dei Magi - sec III dC - Foto Giovanni Dall'Orto 12-Apr-2008, CC BY-SA 4.0 via Wikimedia Commons, *bottom:* author. **Pages 325-326,** author. **Page 357,** Reproduced by kind permission of the Syndics of Cambridge University Library. **Page 358,** Courtesy of Buswell Library Archives & Special Collections, Wheaton College, IL. **Page 387**, *top:* New Crusaders, screenshot, Public Domain, Source: Roger Smither (ed.), The Imperial War Museum Film Catalogue, vol. I, The First World War Archive (Trowbridge 1994), item IWM 17, Ministry of Information, *middle:* author, *bottom:* Tristan Fewings/PA Images/Alamy. **Page 388**, *top:* Courtesy Ronald Reagan Library, *bottom:* author. **Page 456**, author.

NOTES

1. MY GENESIS

1. Marcus Olfson and Stephen C. Marcus, "National Patterns in Antidepressant Medication Treatment," *Archives of General Psychiatry* 66, no. 8 (2009): 848–856. doi:10.1001/archgenpsychiatry.2009.81.
2. Damian Thompson, *The End of Time: Faith and Fear in the Shadow of the Millennium* (Hanover, NH: University Press of New England, 1997), 9–10.
3. Albert Einstein, Peter Barker, and Cecil G. Shugart, *After Einstein: Proceedings of the Einstein Centennial Celebration at Memphis State University, 14–16 March, 1979* (Memphis, TN: Memphis State University Press, 1981), 179.
4. Mircea Eliade, "The Yearning for Paradise in Primitive Tradition," *Daedalus* 88, no.2 (1959): 255–267.
5. Mircea Eliade, *A History of Religious Ideas, Volume 1: From the Stone Age to the Eleusinian Mysteries*, trans. Willard R. Trask (Chicago: University of Chicago Press, 1981), 58.
6. Geoffrey Ashe, *Dawn Behind the Dawn: A Search for the Earthly Paradise* (New York: H. Holt, 1992), 1.

2. A MATTER OF PERCEPTION

1. Stefan Anitei, "What's the Origin of Human Languages?" Softpedia News, July 23, 2007, http://news.softpedia.com/news/Which-is-the-Origin-of-the-Human-Languages-60651.shtml.
2. Luke 23:43 (NRSV).
3. Gen. 2:8–9 (NRSV).
4. Gen. 2:8–14 (NRSV).
5. Deut. 11:24 (NRSV).
6. Rev. 16:12 (NRSV).
7. Garry Wills, *Head and Heart American Christianities* (New York: Penguin, 2007), 33–34.
8. Kurt Eichenwald, "How Bush Snared Blair," *Vanity Fair*, October 2012. See also: Andrew Brown, "Bush, Gog and Magog," *Religion* (blog), *The Guardian*, August 10, 2009, http://www.theguardian.com/commentisfree/andrewbrown/2009/aug/10/religion-george-bush.
9. J.B.S. Haldane, *Possible Worlds: And Other Essays*, rev. ed. (1927; repr., London: Chatto and Windus, 1932), 286.
10. Ofer Aderet, "Einstein Promises an Enjoyable Challenge," *Haaretz*, November 27, 2015.
11. Gerhard Heinzmann and David Stump, "Henri Poincaré," The Stanford Encyclopedia of Philosophy (Spring 2014), ed. Edward N. Zalta, http://plato.stanford.edu/archives/spr2014/entries/poincare/.
12. Aage Petersen, "The Philosophy of Niels Bohr," *Bulletin of the Atomic Scientists* 19, no. 7 (September 1963).
13. Robert N. Goldman and Albert Einstein, *Einstein's God: Albert Einstein's Quest as a Scientist and as a Jew to Replace a Forsaken God* (Northvale, NJ: Jason Aronson, 1997), 51.
14. Gen. 2:17 (NRSV).
15. Gen. 1:26 (NRSV).
16. Gen. 3:1–24 (NRSV).

17. Peter L. Berger, and Thomas Luckmann, *The Social Construction of Reality: A Treatise in the Sociology of Knowledge* (Garden City, NY: Doubleday, 1966), 61.
18. Ibid., 116.
19. Gen. 3:9–10 (NRSV).

3. EXILE

1. Andrew Curry, "Gobekli Tepe: The World's First Temple?" *Smithsonian*, November 2008, https://www.smithsonianmag.com/history/gobekli-tepe-the-worlds-first-temple-83613665/.
2. National Geographic Learning, *Archaeology: Cities, Empires, Religion, Migrations of the Past* (Belmont, CA: Wadsworth, Cengage Learning, 2013), 51.
3. Curry, "Gobekli Tepe."
4. Gen. 3:17 (NRSV).
5. National Geographic Learning, *Archaeology*, 50.
6. Jacques Cauvin and Trevor Watkins, *The Birth of the Gods and the Origins of Agriculture* (Cambridge: Cambridge University Press, 2000).
7. Thomas Hobbes, *Of Man, Being the First Part of Leviathan*, Vol. 34, Part 5 (New York: P.F. Collier & Son, 1909–14).
8. Sharon A. Lloyd and Susanne Sreedhar, "Hobbes's Moral and Political Philosophy," The Stanford Encyclopedia of Philosophy (Spring 104), ed. Edward N. Zalta, http://plato.stanford.edu/archives/spr2014/entries/hobbes-moral/.
9. Robert A. Heinlein, *Starship Troopers* (New York: Putnam, 1959).
10. "Thomas Hobbes Biography," Encyclopedia of World Biography, accessed August 2022, http://www.notablebiographies.com/He-Ho/Hobbes-Thomas.html.
11. Lloyd and Sreedhar, "Hobbes's Moral."
12. Hobbes, *Of Man*.
13. Jared M. Diamond, "The Worst Mistake in the History of the Human Race," *Discover* (1987): 64–66.
14. Christopher Ryan and Cacilda Jethá, *Sex at Dawn: The Prehistoric Origins of Modern Sexuality* (New York: Harper, 2010), 11.
15. Marshall Sahlins, *Stone Age Economics* (London: Routledge, 2008), 1.
16. Marshall Sahlins, "The Original Affluent Society," *Ecologist* 4, no. 5 (1974): 181.
17. Sahlins, *Stone Age Economics*, 37–38.
18. Ibid., 4.
19. Jonathan Haas and Matthew Piscitelli, "The Prehistory of Warfare: Misled by Ethnography," in *War, Peace, and Human Nature: The Convergence of Evolutionary and Cultural Views*, ed. Douglas P. Fry (New York: Oxford University Press, 2013), 177–185.
20. R.B. Ferguson, "The Causes and Origins of Primitive Warfare," *Anthropological Quarterly* 73, no. 3 (2000): 159–164.
21. Richard A. Gabriel, *The Culture of War: Invention and Early Development* (New York: Greenwood Press, 1990), 21.
22. Diamond, "The Worst Mistake," 65.
23. Gabriel, *Culture of War*, 19–20.
24. Gen. 3:7–19 (NRSV).
25. Gen. 1:26–27 (KJV).
26. Oxford Dictionaries, s.v. "transpersonal," accessed March 10, 2014, https://en.oxforddictionaries.com/definition/transpersonal
27. Midr. Gen. Rab. 8:1.
28. Midr. Lev. Rab. 14:1.
29. Gal. 3:28 (NRSV).

4. AFTER EDEN

1. Michael Corballis, "The Uniqueness of Human Recursive Thinking," *American Scientist* 95, no. 3 (2007): 240.

2. Julian Jaynes, *The Origin of Consciousness in the Breakdown of the Bicameral Mind* (Boston: Houghton Mifflin, 1976).

3. Daniel B. Smith, *Muses, Madmen, and Prophets: Rethinking the History, Science, and Meaning of Auditory Hallucination* (New York: Penguin, 2007).

4. Peter D. Kramer, "Hearing Voices," *New York Times Book Review*, April 8, 2007.

5. Thomas Metzinger, *The Ego Tunnel: The Science of the Mind and the Myth of the Self* (New York: BasicBooks, 2010), Introduction.

6. Gen. 4:1–16 (NRSV).

7. Is. 1:13–23 (NRSV).

8. 1 Sam. 15:22 (NRSV).

9. "Airpower Summaries," U.S. Air Forces Central, accessed August 2022, http://www.afcent.af.mil/About/Airpower-Summaries.

10. 1 Sam. 13:14 (KJV).

11. 2 Sam. 18:33 (NRSV).

12. Gen. 4:11 (NRSV).

13. Gen. 5:1–2 (TANACH).

14. Gen. 5:28–29 (NRSV).

15. Gen. 5:32 (KJV).

16. Gen. 10:1 (KJV).

17. Gen. 10:8–12 (NRSV).

18. Stephanie Dalley, "Babylon as a Name for Other Cities Including Nineveh," in *Proceedings of the 51st Rencontre Assyriologique Internationale,* ed. Robert D. Biggs, Jennie Myers, and Martha Tobi Roth (Chicago: Oriental Institute of the University of Chicago, 2008), 25, http://oi.uchicago.edu/sites/oi.uchicago.edu/files/uploads/shared/docs/saoc62.pdf.

19. Thorkild Jacobsen, "The Eridu Genesis," *Journal of Biblical Literature* 100, no. 4 (December 1981): 513–529, http://www.jstor.org/stable/3266116.

20. Samuel Noah Kramer, *The Sumerians: Their History, Culture, and Character* (Chicago: University of Chicago Press, 1971), 73, 293.

21. Kramer, *The Sumerians,* 269–270.

22. "Enmerkar and the Lord of Aratta," Electronic Text Corpus of Sumerian Literature, last modified December 12, 2006, http://etcsl.orinst.ox.ac.uk/cgi-bin/etcsl.cgi?text=t.1.8.2.3#.

23. Gen. 11:1–9 (NRSV).

24. Everett Fox, *Genesis and Exodus: A New English Rendition* (New York: Schocken Books, 1990).

25. "The Flood Story," Electronic Text Corpus of Sumerian Literature, last modified December 12, 2006, http://etcsl.orinst.ox.ac.uk/cgi-bin/etcsl.cgi?text=t.1.7.4#.

26. Flavius Josephus, *Antiquities of the Jews*, trans. William Whiston, 1:4, http://penelope.uchicago.edu/josephus/

27. Stanley Diamond, *In Search of the Primitive: A Critique of Civilization* (New Brunswick, NJ: Transaction Books, 1974), 1.

5. ROYALTIES

1. Justin D. Faris, "Wheat Domestication: Key to Agricultural Revolutions Past and Future," in *Genomics of Plant Genetic Resources*, ed. Roberto Tuberosa, Andreas Graner, and E A. Frison (New York: Springer, 2014), 439.

2. Hakan Özkan, Andrea Brandolini, Ralf Schäfer-Pregl, and Francesco Salamini, "AFLP Analysis of a Collection of Tetraploid Wheats Indicates the Origin of Emmer and Hard Wheat Domestication in Southeast Turkey," *Molecular Biology and Evolution*, 19, no. 10

(October 2002): 1797–1801. ("The findings... localize the origin of tetraploid wheat domestication to southeastern Turkey... an extremely small core area in the Near East... in southeastern Turkey near the Tigris and Euphrates rivers...")

3. Ian Hodder, "John Templeton Foundation," Çatalhöyük Research Project, accessed August 2022, http://www.catalhoyuk.com/partners/templeton.

4. Ibid.

5. "Consciousness And Creativity At The Dawn Of Settled Life: The Test-Case Of Çatalhöyük," John Templeton Foundation, accessed August 2022, https://www.templeton.org/grant/consciousness-and-creativity-at-the-dawn-of-settled-life-the-test-case-of-catalhoyuk.

6. Jacques Cauvin, Ian Hodder, Gary O. Rollefson, Ofer Bar-Yosef, and Trevor Watkins, "Review of *The Birth of the Gods and the Origins of Agriculture*, by Jacques Cauvin, translated by Trevor Watkins (New Studies in Archaeology)," *Cambridge Archaeological Journal* 11, no. 1 (2001): 105–121.

7. Douglas Pottenger Fry, ed., *War, Peace, and Human Nature: The Convergence of Evolutionary and Cultural Views* (Oxford: Oxford University Press, 2013), 216.

8. James Mellaart, "Excavations at Hacılar, second Preliminary Report, 1958," *Anatolian Studies* 9, (1959):: 54, doi:10.2307/3642332.

9. Ian Kuijt, "People and Space in Early Agricultural Villages: Exploring Daily Lives, Community Size, and Architecture in the Late Pre-Pottery Neolithic," *Journal of Anthropological Archaeology* 19 (2000),: 75–102.

10. Mircea Eliade, 1955. *The Myth of the Eternal Return* (London: Routledge & Kegan Paul, 1955), 139.

11. Mircea Eliade, *Myth and Reality* (New York: Harper & Row, 1963), 192.

12. Robert N. Bellah, *Religion in Human Evolution: From the Paleolithic to the Axial Age* (Cambridge, MA: Belknap Press of Harvard University Press, 2011), 263.

13. Ibid.

6. ALIEN ORIGINS

1. Eliade, *A History of Religious Ideas*, 47.

2. Peter M.M.G. Akkermans, "Old and New Perspectives on the Origins of the Halaf Culture," in *La Djéziré et l'Euphrate syriens de la Protohistoire à la fin du IIe millé- naire av.J.-C.*, ed. Olivier. Rouault and Markus. Wäfler (Turnhout, Belgium: Brepols, 2000), 43-54, https://www.academia.edu/564231.

3. Hobart M. King, "Obsidian," Geology.com, accessed August 2022, http://geology.com/rocks/obsidian.shtml.

4. Fry, *War, Peace, and Human Nature*, 218–219.

5. Ibid.

6. John Garstang, *Prehistoric Mersin, Yümük Tepe in Southern Turkey: The Neilson Expedition in Cilici* (Oxford: Clarendon Press, 1953), 111–112.

7. Eliade, *A History*, 76.

8. John Noble Wilford, "In Syria, a Prologue for Cities," *New York Times*, April 5, 2010, http://www.nytimes.com/2010/04/06/science/06archeo.html.

9. I.S. Shklovski and Carl Sagan, *Intelligent Life in the Universe* (New York: Dell, 1960), 453–464.

10. Kramer, *The Sumerians*, 36, 135–136.

11. Ibid., 122.

12. Ibid., 116.

13. Stephen Bertman, *Handbook to Life in Ancient Mesopotamia* (New York: Facts on File, 2003), 120.

14. Gwendolyn Leick, *Mesopotamia: The Invention of the City* (London: Penguin, 2001), 59.

15. "A Hymn to Inana," Electronic Text Corpus of Sumerian Literature, last modified December 19, 2006, http://etcsl.orinst.ox.ac.uk/cgi-bin/etcsl.cgi?text=t.4.07.3&display=

Crit&charenc=gcirc&lineid=t4073.p7#t4073.p7.

16. Jeremy A. Black, Anthony Green, and Tessa Rickards, *Gods, Demons, and Symbols of Ancient Mesopotamia: An Illustrated Dictionary* (Austin: University of Texas Press, 1992), 109.

17. "Inana and Enki: translation," Electronic Text Corpus of Sumerian Literature, last modified December 18, 2002, http://etcsl.orinst.ox.ac.uk/section1/tr131.htm.

18. Diane Wolkstein and Samuel Noah Kramer, *Inanna, Queen of Heaven and Earth: Her Stories and Hymns from Sumer* (New York: Harper & Row, 1983), 36–37.

19. Leick, *Mesopotamia*, 35.

20. Ibid., 41.

21. Bellah, *Religion in Human Evolution*, 216.

22. Bertman, *Handbook to Life*, 334.

23. David W. Anthony, *The Horse, the Wheel, and Language: How Bronze-Age Riders from the Eurasian Steppes Shaped the Modern World* (Princeton, NJ: Princeton University Press, 2007), 66.

24. Leick, *Mesopotamia*, 42.

25. Ibid., 46.

26. Eliade, *A History*, 60.

27. Susan Pollock, *Ancient Mesopotamia: The Eden That Never Was* (Cambridge: Cambridge University Press, 2008), 93.

28. Leick, *Mesopotamia*, 46.

29. Denise Schmandt-Besserat, "Two Precursors of Writing: Plain and Complex Tokens," in *The Origins of Writing*, ed. Wayne M. Senner (Lincoln, NE: University of Nebraska Press, 1991), 27–41.

30. Richard A. Gabriel and Karen S. Metz, *A Short History of War: The Evolution of Warfare and Weapons* (Carlisle Barracks, PA: Strategic Studies Institute, 1992), 3.

31. Ibid., 2.

32. Kramer, *The Sumerians*, 79–81.

33. Gabriel and Metz, *A Short History*, 6.

34. Bellah, *Religion in Human Evolution*, 220.

7. COUNTERCULTURE

1. Paul Kriwaczek, *Babylon: Mesopotamia and the Birth of Civilization* (New York: St. Martin's Press, 2013), 110.

2. Gabriel and Metz, *A Short History*, 5–6.

3. Enheduanna, William Wolfgang Hallo, and Johannes Jacobus Adrianus van Dijk, *The Exaltation of Inanna* (New Haven: Yale University Press, 1968), 1.

4. Gabriel and Metz, *A Short History*, 7.

5. Ibid., 7–8, 13.

6. Josh. 24:2 (NRSV).

7. Gen. 11:31 (NRSV).

8. Abraham Malamat, *Mari and the Early Israelite Experience* (London: Oxford University Press, 1992), 27–30.

9. Tad Szluc, "Journey of Faith," *National Geographic*, December 2001, 90.

10. Daniel Lewis, "Tad Szulc, 74, Dies; Times Correspondent Who Uncovered Bay of Pigs Imbroglio," *New York Times*, May 22, 2001.

11. Malamat, *Mari*, 22; see also plate 6.

12. Szulc, "Journey of Faith," 122.

13. Malamat, *Mari*, 23.

14. Gen. 13:2 (NRSV).

15. Berger and Luckmann, *The Social Construction*, 27.

16. Ibid., 85–86.

17. Fox, *Genesis*, 54.

18. Heb. 11:8 (AKJV).
19. Gen. 23:3–5 (NRSV).
20. Bereshit Rabbah 38:13.
21. Rambam, Mishneh Torah, Hilkhot Avodah Zarah 1.
22. Fox, *Genesis*, 54.
23. Nehama Leibowitz and Aryeh Newman, *Studies in Bereshit (Genesis): In The Context of Ancient and Modern Jewish Bible Commentary* (Jerusalem: World Zionist Organization, Dept. for Torah Education and Culture, 1981), 116.
24. Jer. 51:9 (ESV).
25. Deut. 32:7–9 (NRSV).
26. See Heb. 11:10 and Acts 7:5.
27. Gen. 11:31 (NRSV).
28. Kristina Josephson Hesse, "Contacts and Trade at Late Bronze Age Hazor: Aspects of Intercultural Relationships and Identity in the Eastern Mediterranean," PhD diss. (Umeå University, 2008).
29. Heb. 11:10 (NRSV).
30. Acts 7:5 (NRSV).
31. Heb. 11:9 (GNV).
32. Gen. 35:10 (NRSV).
33. Josephus, *Antiquities*, 1:15.
34. Ex. 3:1–6 (NRSV).
35. Ex. 3:13–15 (NRSV).
36. For an introduction to parallel worlds, see: Alexandra Witze, "A Quantum World Arising from Many Ordinary Ones," *Nature* (October 2014).

8. FROM PARABLE TO HISTORY

1. Deut. 33:2; Jud. 5:4–5 (NRSV).
2. Ex. 13:18 (NRSV).
3. Daniel Fleming, *Yahweh before Israel: Glimpses of History in a Divine Name* (Cambridge: Cambridge University Press, 2020), 22. See also: Clyde E. Billington, "The Name YAHWEH in Egyptian Hieroglyphic Texts," Associates for Biblical Research, March 8, 2010, https://biblearchaeology.org/research/exodus-from-egypt/3233-the-name-yahweh-in-egyptian-hieroglyphic-texts
4. Num. 23:8–9 (NRSV).
5. Num. 25:1–18, 31:15–18 (NRSV).
6. Josh. 24:11–13 (NRSV).
7. Josh. 8:24 (NRSV).
8. Israel Finkelstein and Neil Asher Silberman, *The Bible Unearthed: Archaeology's New Vision of Ancient Israel and the Origin of Its Sacred Texts* (New York: Free Press, 2001).
9. Judg. 21:25 (NRSV).
10. 1 Sam. 8:5–20 (NRSV).
11. 1 Sam. 15:23 (NRSV).
12. 1 Sam. 8:10–18 (NRSV).
13. Finkelstein and Silberman, *The Bible Unearthed*, 153.
14. Ibid., 158.
15. Ibid., 159.
16. Richard A. Gabriel, *The Ancient World* (Westport, CT: Greenwood Press, 2006), 41.
17. Is. 2:2–4, 9:1–5 (NRSV).
18. Finkelstein and Silberman, *The Bible Unearthed*, 215.
19. Sennacherib and Daniel David Luckenbill, *The Annals of Sennacherib* (Chicago: The University of Chicago Press, 1924), 32–33.
20. Ibid., 70.

21. Is. 12:2, 31:1 (NRSV).
22. Is. 36:18, 37:11 (NRSV).
23. 2 Kings 21:2 (NRSV).
24. Finkelstein and Silberman, *The Bible Unearthed*, 248.
25. Ibid.
26. Baruch Halpern, *From Gods to God: The Dynamics of Iron Age Cosmologies*, ed. Matthew J. Adams (Tübingen: Mohr Siebeck, 2001), 97.
27. 2 Chron. 34:1–7 (NRSV).
28. 2 Chron. 34:15 (NRSV).
29. Josh. 1:8 (NRSV).
30. 2 Kings 22:13 (NRSV).
31. 2 Kings 23:22 (NRSV).
32. 1 Kings 11:1–4 (NRSV).
33. 1 Kings 11:7; 2 Kings 23:13 (NRSV).

9. AXIAL AGE

1. This biographical detail was preserved by multiple sources and is referenced in the New Testament. See Hebrews 11:37.
2. My account paraphrases from several translations of the Buddhacarita.
3. Aśvaghoṣa, *Buddhacarita: In Praise of Buddha's Acts: (Taishō volume 4, number 192)*, trans. Charles Willemen (Berkeley: Numata Center for Buddhist Translation and Research, 2009).
4. Dvayatānupassanā Sutta, Sn. 3.12, transl. the author.
5. Aśvaghoṣa, *Buddhacarita*.
6. Dhammapada, 153–4, trans. Ven. Thanissaro Bhikkhu.
7. Aśvaghoṣa, *Buddhacarita*, Vol. 14, trans. Edward B. Cowell.
8. Jerry Samet, "The Historical Controversies Surrounding Innateness," The Stanford Encyclopedia of Philosophy (Spring 2014), ed. Edward N. Zalta, http://plato.stanford.edu/archives/fall2008/entries/innateness-history/.
9. Halpern, *From Gods to God*, 99.
10. Jer. 23:24 (NRSV).
11. Jer. 3:16 (NRSV).
12. Jer. 18:15 (NRSV).
13. Jer. 10:1–5 (NRSV).
14. Jer. 17:9 (NRSV).
15. Jer. 26:8 (NIV).
16. 2 Kings 24:13–17 (NRSV).
17. 2 Kings 25:7 (NRSV).
18. Jer. 16:16–21 (NRSV).
19. Jer. 16:12–15 (NRSV).
20. Is. 2:2 (NIV).
21. Is. 2:4 (NRSV).
22. Is. 9:7 (NRSV).
23. Is. 11:6 (NRSV).
24. Jer. 51:11 (NRSV).
25. Is. 9:2–7 (NRSV).
26. Is. 45:1–25 (ESV); Is. 44:8 (ESV).
27. Holy Quran, *Al Kahf* 18:107–108 (Sahih).
28. Talmud, Megilla 9a:2.
29. Mary Boyce, *Zoroastrians: Their Religious Beliefs and Practices* (London: Routledge & Kegan Paul, 1979), 19.
30. Gernot Windfuhr, ed., *The Iranian Languages* (London: Routledge, 2009), 264.
31. Avesta, Yasna 50:11.

32. John 8:8; Rev. 12:9.

33. Herodotus, *Histories*, 1.138, http://data.perseus.org/citations/urn:cts:greekLit:tlg0016.tlg001. perseus-eng1:1.138.

34. F. Max Müller, ed., *The Sacred Books of the East, Volume 23, The Zend-Avesta*, Pt. 2, trans. James Darmesteter (Oxford: Clarendon Press, 1883), 344.

10. GREAT EXPECTATIONS

1. Paul-Alain Beaulieu, *The Reign of Nabonidus, King of Babylon, 556–539 B.C.* (New Haven: Yale University Press, 1989), 233.

2. Psalm 137 (NRSV).

3. Jer. 29:4–11 (NKJV).

4. Jeremiah 52:31; 2 Kings 25:27 (NRSV).

5. Berossus and Stanley Mayer Burstein, *The Babyloniaca of Berossus* (Malibu, CA: Undena Publications, 1980), 28.

6. Beaulieu, *Nabonidus*, 88.

7. Hayim Tadmor, "The Inscriptions of Nabunaid: Historical Arrangement," *Assyriological Studies* 16 (1965): 351–64.

8. Beaulieu, *Nabonidus*, 76.

9. Ibid., 71.

10. Ibid., 57.

11. Ibid., 59–60.

12. Is. 14:12–15 (KJV).

13. Beaulieu, *Nabonidus*, 49. See also: Jeremy Black and Tina Breckwoldt, *A Concise Dictionary of Akkadian* (Wiesbaden, Germany: Harrassowitz, 2012), 70.

14. Dan. 5:1–31 (NRSV).

15. Herodotus, *Histories*, 1:188–191., trans. George Rawlinson.

16. Xenophon, *Cyropaedia*, 7.5.31–34., trans. Henry G. Dakyns, rev. F. M. Stawell.

17. Beaulieu, *Nabonidus*, 225–226, 233.

18. Ibid., 225.

19. Piotr Michalowski, "The Cyrus Cylinder," in *The Ancient Near East: Historical Sources in Translation*, ed. Mark William Chavalas (Malden, MA: Carlton Blackwell, 2008), 428–29.

20. Beaulieu, *Nabonidus*, 225.

21. Herodotus, *Histories*, 1:131.

22. Ibid., 1:136–138.

23. Xenophon, *Cyropaedia*, 8.8.1–9.

24. Excerpts from Darius' royal inscriptions at Persepolis and Naqsh-i-Rustam. See inscriptions DPd 3, DNa 1, and DNb 7–8.

25. Josephus, *Antiquities*, 18:1.

26. Diamond, *In Search of the Primitive*, 3.

27. Herodotus, *Histories*, trans. A.D. Godley, Vol. 4 (Cambridge: Harvard University Press, 1920), 8.98.

28. Boyce, *Zoroastrians*, 76.

29. Ibid., 77.

30. Albert de Jong, *Traditions of the Magi: Zoroastrianism in Greek and Latin Literature* (Leiden, The Netherlands: E.J. Brill, 1997), 163, 327 (quoting Diogenes Laertius).

31. Boyce, *Zoroastrians*, 78–79.

32. Ibid., 98.

33. Dan. 9:1–2 (NRSV).

34. Dan. 9:24 (TANAKH).

35. Lev. 26:18 (TANAKH).

36. See Dan. 7:13–14.

37. Dan. 12:1–14 (TANAKH).

38. Josephus, *Antiquities*, 14:7.

39. Plutarch, *Plutarch's Lives,* trans. Bernadotte Perrin, Vol. 3 (London: William Heinemann, 1916), 387.

40. Ibid.

41. Valerii P. Nikonorov, "The Use of Musical Percussion Instruments in Ancient Eastern Warfare: The Parthian and Middle Asian Evidence," in *Musikarchäologie früher Metallzeiten: Vorträge des 1. Symposiums der International Study Group on Music Archaeology im Kloster Michaelstein, 18.–24 Mai 1998*, ed. Ellen Hickmann, Ingo Laufs, Ricardo Eichmann, and Hans Hickmann, (Rahden, Germany: Verlag Marie Leidorf GmbH, 2000), 71.

42. Philip M. Edge, Jr., and William H. Mayes, "Description of Langley Low-Frequency Noise Facility and Study of Human Response to Noise Frequencies Below 50 CPS" (Washington, DC: National Aeronautics and Space Administration, 1966), 9. See also Vic Tandy and Tony R. Lawrence, "The Ghost in the Machine," *Journal of the Society for Psychical Research* 62, no. 851 (1998): 360–364.

43. Kaufmann Kohler, "Eschatology," in *The Jewish Encyclopedia*, ed. Isidore Singer et al. (New York: Funk & Wagnalls, 1902), 209–218.

44. Rutherford H. Platt, Jr., *The Forgotten Books of Eden*, 1926, http://www.sacred-texts.com/bib/fbe/fbe193.htm.

45. Boyce, *Zoroastrians*, 21–22.

11. THE MESSIAH

1. Mick Brown, "Jesus, Who's Got Time to Keep Up with the Times?" *The Sunday Times*, July 1, 1984.

2. Scott Cohen, "Don't Ask Me Nothin' About Nothin' I Might Just Tell You The Truth," *Spin*, 1, no. 8 (December 1985): 37.

3. Cornelius Tacitus, *Histories*, 5:13, http://penelope.uchicago.edu/Thayer/E/Roman/Texts/Tacitus/Histories/5A*.html.

4. Flavius Josephus, *The War of the Jews*, trans. William Whiston, 6:312, http://penelope.uchicago.edu/josephus/.

5. Josephus, *Antiquities*, 18:1.6.

6. Ekkhard Stegemann and Wolfgang Stegemann, *The Jesus Movement: A Social History of Its First Century* (Edinburgh: T & T Clark, 1999), 119.

7. Josephus, *Antiquities*, 17:271–272.

8. Luke 23:2–5 (ESV).

9. Acts 5:37 (NRSV).

10. Josephus, *The War of the Jews*, 4:131.

11. Ibid., 4:134.

12. Ibid., 2:442.

13. Edward Gibbon, *The History of the Decline and Fall of the Roman Empire: A New Edition, in Four Volumes, Vol. 3* (London: Jones & Company, 1825), 179.

14. Glanville Downey, "Libanius' Oration in Praise of Antioch (Oration XI)," *Proceedings of the American Philosophical Society*, 103, no. 5 (1959): 652–686, http://www.jstor.org/stable/985424.

15. H.V. Morton, *In the Steps of St. Paul* (New York: Dodd, Mead & Company, 1936), 98.

16. Matt. 1:1 (NRSV).

17. Matt. 1:22–24 (ESV).

18. Matt. 1:20 (ESV).

19. Matt. 2:1 (NIV).

20. St. John Chrysostom, *Homilies on the Gospel of Matthew*, 6.4.

21. James A. Kellerman, and Thomas C. Oden, *Incomplete Commentary on Matthew (Opus imperfectum)* (Downers Grove, IL: IVP Academic, 2010), 21.

22. Ibid., 32.

23. Mary Boyce and Frantz Grenet, *A History of Zoroastrianism,* Vol. 3 (Leiden, The Netherlands: E.J. Brill, 1989), 448–451.
24. Ibid.
25. Matt. 4:15–16 (NRSV).
26. Matt. 4:24 (NRSV).
27. Matt. 3:9 (NRSV).
28. At the time, water was used for ritual purification and as part of the Jewish conversion rite for Gentiles. Previously in Jewish thought, the spirit of the LORD gave authority to leaders and revelation to prophets. Only in Zoroastrianism is the Holy Spirit so explicitly associated with fire in this way, where fire famously represents the presence of the Creator Ahura Mazda and where, through the Holy Spirit and fire, creation will be cleansed of the Lie.
29. Matt. 5:21 (NRSV).
30. Matt. 8:4 (NRSV).
31. Matt. 12:1–4 (NRSV).
32. Matt. 8:10–12 (NRSV).
33. Matt. 9:9–13 (NRSV).
34. Gal. 2:15 (YLT).
35. Matt. 15:21–28 (NRSV).
36. Matt. 28:19 (NRSV).
37. Matt. 6:19, 27 (ESV).
38. Matt. 1:18 (NRSV).
39. John 1:1 (NRSV); Eph. 1:21 (NRSV).
40. Matt. 8:20 (ESV).
41. Matt. 28:19 (Geneva). Italics added.
42. Matt. 6:12–25 (NIV).
43. Matt. 7:1–5 (ESV).
44. Luke 7:36–38 (ESV).
45. Joel B. Green, *The Gospel of Luke* (Grand Rapids, MI: Eerdmans, 2014), 310.
46. Talmud, B.Ketubot 72a.
47. Luke 18:9–14 (ESV).
48. Matt. 6:3–4 (NRSV).
49. Matt. 25:31–46 (NRSV).
50. Rev. 12:10 (KJV). See also: 1 Peter 5:8; Zech. 3:1.
51. Josephus, *The War of the Jews*, 1:21.
52. Matt. 16:13–26 (NRSV).
53. Matt. 22:15–22 (ESV).
54. Matt. 16:24–26 (ESV).
55. Plato, *Apology*, 30a–b.
56. *Diamond Sutra*, 3, http://diamond-sutra.com/read-the-diamond-sutra-here/diamond-sutra-chapter-3/.
57. 1 Cor. 15:12, 35–54 (ESV).
58. See Outi Lehtipuu, *Debates over the Resurrection of the Dead: Constructing Early Christian Identity* (Oxford: Oxford University Press, 2015).
59. 1 Cor. 15:51 (ESV).
60. Col. 1:18 (ESV).
61. Gal. 3:28 (NRSV).
62. Matt. 16:27 (NRSV).

12. THE ANTICHRISTS

1. Luke 17:2–12 (KJV).
2. Matt. 13:10–16 (NRSV).

3. Benny Shanon, "Biblical Entheogens: A Speculative Hypothesis," *Time and Mind* 1, no. 1 (2008): 51–74.

4. See Richard J. Miller, "Religion as a Product of Psychotropic Drug Use," *Atlantic Monthly*, December 27, 2013.

5. Ezek. 38:20–22 (ESV).

6. Kaufmann Kohler, "Kingdom of God," in *The Jewish Encyclopedia*, Vol. 7, 502–503.

7. John 18:36 (NRSV).

8. Matt. 24:2 (NRSV).

9. Gershom Gorenberg, *The End of Days: Fundamentalism and the Struggle for the Temple Mount* (Oxford: Oxford University Press, 2002), 228.

10. Dio Cassius, Earnest Cary, and Herbert Baldwin Foster, *Dio's Roman History: In Nine Volumes*, Vol. 8 (London: William Heinemann, 1925), LXIX.14, 451.

11. Richard Gottheil and Samuel Krauss, "Bar Kokba and Bar Kokba War," in *The Jewish Encyclopedia*, Vol. 2, 509–510.

12. Jerome, *Chronicles*, VI.2. http://www.tertullian.org/fathers/jerome_chronicle_06_latin_part2.htm; see also: Daniel Boyarin, "Justin Martyr Invents Judaism," *Church History* 70, no. 3 (2001): 427–61, http://www.jstor.org/stable/3654497.

13. Ariel David, "Before Islam: When Saudi Arabia Was a Jewish Kingdom," *Haaretz*, March 15, 2016.

14. Tertullian, *Adversus Marcionem*, 3.13.

15. Norman Cohn, *The Pursuit of the Millennium: Revolutionary Millenarians and Mystical Anarchists of the Middle Ages* (New York: Oxford University Press, 1969), 29.

16. Origen, *Contra Celsum*, 2.30.

17. Tertullian, *De Corona Militist*, 11–12.

18. Hippolytus Romanus, Henry Chadwick, and Gregory Dix, *The Treatise on the Apostolic Tradition* (London: S.P.C.K., 1968), 26.

19. Irenaeus, *Adversus Haereses*, 5.35:1.

20. Ibid., 5.32:1.

21. Tertullian, *Adversus Marcionem*, 3.25.

22. Gary B. Ferngren, *Medicine and Health Care in Early Christianity* (Baltimore, MD: The Johns Hopkins University Press, 2016), 86.

23. Helmut Koester, "The Great Appeal," Frontline, PBS, accessed August 2022, http://www.pbs.org/wgbh/pages/frontline/shows/religion/why/appeal.html.

24. James Carroll, *Constantine's Sword: The Church and the Jews: A History* (Boston, MA: Houghton Mifflin, 2002), 167.

25. Ibid., 171.

26. John B. Bury, *History of the Later Roman Empire*, Vol. 1 (London: Macmillan, 1923), 366.

27. Paul Veyne, *When Our World Became Christian: 312–394* (Cambridge: Polity Press, 2010), 1.

28. Hippolytus, Chadwick, and Dix, *The Treatise*, 26.

29. Carroll, *Constantine's Sword*, 174.

30. St. John Chrysostom, *Logoi Kata Ioudaiōn*, 1.8.

31. Kaufmann Kohler and Louis Ginzberg, "Chrysostomos, Joannes (generally known as St. Chrysostom)," in *The Jewish Encyclopedia*, Vol. 5, 75–76.

32. Matt. 16:24–26 (KJV).

33. Chrysostom, *Ioudaiōn*, 5.4.

34. Mary Boyce and I.K. Poonawala, "Apocalyptic," in *Encyclopaedia Iranica*, ed. Ehsan Yarshater, Vol. 2 (London: Routledge & Kegan Paul, 1982), 154–160.

35. Ann Byle, "LaHaye, Co-Author of Left Behind Series, Leaves A Lasting Impact," *Publishers Weekly*, July 27, 2016.

36. David Paul Nord, Joan Shelley Rubin, and Michael Schudson, *History of the Book in America, Volume 5: The Enduring Book: Print Culture in Postwar America* (Chapel Hill: University of North Carolina Press, 2009), 376.

37. Ray Walters, "Paperback Talk," *New York Times*, March 12, 1978, 93.

38. Cohn, *The Pursuit*, 30.

39. Ibid., 28.

40. Stephen J. Shoemaker, "The Reign of God Has Come: Eschatology and Empire in Late Antiquity and Early Islam," *Arabica*, 61, no. 5 (2014), 514–558. doi: https://doi.org/10.1163/15700585-12341312.

41. Moshe Gil, *Jews in Islamic Countries in the Middle Ages* (Leiden, The Netherlands: E.J. Brill, 2004), 5.

42. Holy Quran, *An-Najm* 53:36–37 (Yusuf Ali).

43. See Holy Quran, *Al-Ahzab* 33.40.

44. Jacob Neusner, *God's Rule: The Politics of World Religions* (Washington, DC: Georgetown University Press, 2003), 99.

45. Holy Quran, *Muḥammad* 47.18 (Yusuf Ali).

46. W.C. Chittick, "Muslim Eschatology," in *The Oxford Handbook of Eschatology,* ed. J.L. Walls (Oxford: Oxford University Press, 2008), 132.

47. Holy Quran, *Āl ʿImrān* 3.59 (Sahih).

48. Holy Quran, *Al-Anbiyaa* 20:96–97.

49. Sebeos, *History*, Chapter 30.

50. Stephen J. Shoemaker, *The Death of a Prophet: The End of Muhammad's Life and the Beginnings of Islam* (Philadelphia: University of Pennsylvania Press, 2012), 24.

51. Ibid., 18.

52. Ibid., 28.

53. See "Israa' and Mi`raj.. A Miraculous Journey," IslamOnline, accessed August 2022, https://islamonline.net/en/israa-and-miraj-journey.

54. The Supreme Moslem Council, *A Brief Guide to al-Haram al-Sharif* (Jerusalem: Supreme Moslem Council, 1925), 4, https://www.jewishvirtuallibrary.org/jsource/History/supreme_Moslem_Council_Guide_1925.pdf.

55. H. A. R Gibb and J. H Kramers, "Al Kuds," in *Shorter Encyclopaedia of Islam.* Leiden, The Netherlands: E.J. Brill, 1991.

56. Christian Robert Lange, *Paradise and Hell in Islamic Traditions* (New York: Cambridge University Press, 2016), 247.

57. Carolanne Mekeel-Matteson, "The Meaning of the Dome of the Rock," *The Islamic Quarterly*, 43, no. 3 (1999): 149.

58. Holy Quran, *Al Isra* 17:1 (Sahih).

59. Holy Quran, *Al Hajj* 22:26 (Haleem).

13. THE MILLENNIUM

1. Holy Quran, *Maryam* 19.34–35 (Asad).

2. Matthew of Edessa and Ara Edmond Dostourian, *Armenia and the Crusades, Tenth to Twelfth Centuries: The Chronicle of Mathew of Edessa* (Lanham, MD: University Press of America, 1993), 44.

3. R.C. Small. *Crusading Warfare, 1097–1193* (Cambridge: Cambridge University Press, 1967), 78.

4. Rev. 9:1–11 (NRSV).

5. Wulfstan II, *Sermo Lupi ad Anglos.*

6. Cohn, *The Pursuit*, 35.

7. Robert the Monk and August Charles Krey, *The First Crusade: The Accounts of Eye-witnesses and Participants* (Princeton, NJ: Princeton University Press, 1921), 30–33.

8. Steven Runciman, *A History of the Crusades. The First Crusade and the Foundation of the Kingdom of Jerusalem,* Vol. 1 (Cambridge: Cambridge University Press, 1987), 115.

9. Thomas Asbridge, *First Crusade: A New History; The Roots of Conflict Between Christianity and Islam* (New York: Oxford University Press, 2004), 5–6.

10. Ibid., 20.

11. Robert and Krey, *The First Crusade*, 196.

12. Cohn, *The Pursuit*, 75.

13. Martin Luther, *On War Against the Turk* (1529).

14. R.G. Clouse, "Views of the Millennium," in *Evangelical Dictionary of Biblical Theology*, ed. Walter A. Elwel (Grand Rapids, MI: Baker Books, 2001), 771.

15. Gülru Necipoğlu, "The Dome of the Rock as palimpsest: 'Abd al-Malik's grand narrative and Sultan Süleyman's glosses," in *Muqarnas, Volume 25: Frontiers of Islamic Art and Architecture*, ed. Gülru Necipoğlu and Julia Bailey (Leiden, The Netherlands: E.J. Brill, 2009), 17–105.

16. Richard Gottheil and Abraham Danon, "Bajazet II," in *The Jewish Encyclopedia*, Vol. 2, 460.

17. Martin Jacobs, "Exposed to All the Currents of the Mediterranean: A Sixteenth-Century Venetian Rabbi on Muslim History," *AJS Review* 29, no. 1 (2005): 33–36.

18. Mor Altshuler, "He Launched the Age of Jewish Messianism," *Haaretz*, February 9, 2006, https://www.haaretz.com/1.4891320.

19. Alan Mikhail, *God's Shadow: Sultan Selim, His Ottoman Empire, and the Making of the Modern World* (New York: Liveright, 2020), 104–117, 386.

20. Ibid., 2.

21. Ibid., 124–125.

22. "Apocalypticism Explained: Christopher Columbus," Frontline, PBS, accessed August 2022, https://www.pbs.org/wgbh/pages/frontline/shows/apocalypse/explanation/columbus.html.

23. Increase Mather, *The Mystery of Israel's Salvation, Explained and Applyed: or, A Discourse Concerning the General Conversion of the Israelitish Nation* (London: John Allen, 1669), https://quod.lib.umich.edu/e/evans/N00091.0001.001.

24. For an overview of Puritan America, see "Apocalypticism Explained: The Puritans," Frontline, PBS, accessed August 2022, https://www.pbs.org/wgbh/pages/frontline/shows/apocalypse/explanation/puritans.html.

25. Ezek. 37:1.

26. Luke 21:24–32 (KJV).

27. Mather, *The Mystery*, 11.

28. Sir William Whitla and Sir Isaac Newton, *Sir Isaac Newton's Daniel and the Apocalypse* (London: J. Murray, 1922), 305.

29. Rob Iliffe, *Priest of Nature: The Religious Worlds of Isaac Newton* (New York: Oxford University Press, 2017), plate 11.

14. TWENTIETH-CENTURY CRUSADE

1. Isidore Singer and Max Schloessinger, "Kalischer, Zebi Hirsch," in *The Jewish Encyclopedia*, Vol. 7, 421–422.

2. Lucien Wolf, *Notes on the Diplomatic History of the Jewish Question: With Texts of Treaty Stipulations and Other Official Documents* (London: Jewish Historical Society of England, 1919), 121–122.

3. ir Martin Gilbert, "Lawrence of Judea: The Champion of the Arab Cause and His Little-Known Romance with Zionism," *Aish*, July 6, 2011, http://www.aish.com/jw/me/Lawrence_of_Judea.html. See also Cecil Bloom, "T. E. Lawrence and Zionism," *Jewish Historical Studies* 38 (2002): 125–45, http://www.js-tor.org/stable/29780052.

4. Barbara W. Tuchman, *Bible and Sword: England and Palestine from the Bronze Age to Balfour* (New York: Random House, 2011), 174.

5. Ibid., 176.

6. Simon Sebag Montefiore, "How the Balfour Declaration laid the roots of Israel," *The Sunday Times*, October 15, 2017, https://www.thetimes.co.uk/article/how-the-balfour-declaration-laid-the-roots-of-israel-wdnsk2xw2.

7. Arthur James Balfour, "Balfour Declaration 1917," The Avalon Project, Yale Law School, November 2, 1917, http://avalon.law.yale.edu/20th_century/balfour.asp.

8. Donald M. Lewis, *The Origins of Christian Zionism: Lord Shaftesbury and Evangelical Support for a Jewish Homeland* (Cambridge: Cambridge University Press, 2014), 3.

9. For further reading on Scofield's influence, see Ernest R. Sandeen, *The Roots of Fundamentalism: British and American Millenarianism, 1830–1930* (Chicago: University of Chicago Press, 2008); R. Todd Mangum and Mark S. Sweetnam, *The Scofield Bible: Its History and Impact on the Evangelical Church* (Colorado Springs, CO: Paternoster Publishing, 2009).

10. "President Gives Hope to Zionists," *New York Times*, March 3, 1919, A1.

11. Paul C. Merkley, *The Politics of Christian Zionism 1891–1948* (London: Routledge, 2012), 89.

12. Stephen Spector, *Evangelicals and Israel: The Story of American Christian Zionism* (New York: Oxford University Press, 2009), 20–21.

13. Woodrow Wilson and Arthur Stanley Link, *The Papers of Woodrow Wilson* (Princeton, NJ: Princeton University Press, 1977), Vol. 23, 20; Vol. 25, 105.

14. United States Congress, House, Committee On Foreign Affairs, *Establishment of a National Home in Palestine: Hearings before the Committee on Foreign Affairs, House of Representatives*, 67th Congress, 2nd session, April 18–21, 1922, https://lccn.loc.gov/43048503.

15. Robert O. Smith, *More Desired Than Our Owne Salvation: The Roots of Christian Zionism* (New York: Oxford University Press, 2013), 175.

16. *Musnad Ahmad*, 4.273.

17. https://en.wikipedia.org/wiki/Faisal–Weizmann_Agreement.

18. Dr. Talaat Fahmi, "Muslim Brotherhood Marks 100-Year Sykes-Picot, Vowing Victory Despite Wounds, Sacrifices," Ikhwanweb, May 17, 2016, http://www.ikhwanweb.com/article.php?id=32542&ref=search.php.

19. Sayyid Quṭb and A.B. Al-Mehri, *Milestones, Ma'alim fi'l-tareeq* (Birmingham, UK: Maktabah Booksellers and Publishers, 2006), 71, 123.

20. Ibid., 85–86.

15. APOCALYPSE NOW

1. "The World's Muslims: Unity and Diversity," Pew Research Center's Forum on Religion & Public Life, August 9, 2012, https://www.pewresearch.org/religion/2012/08/09/the-worlds-muslims-unity-and-diversity-executive-summary/.

2. Barbara Stowasser, "The End is Near: Minor and Major Signs of the Hour in Islamic Texts and Contexts," in *Apocalypse and Violence*, ed. Abbas Amanat and John J. Collins (New Haven, CT: Yale Center for International and Area Studies, May 2002), 60.

3. Graeme Wood, "What ISIS Really Wants," *Atlantic Monthly*, March 2015, https://www.theatlantic.com/magazine/archive/2015/03/what-isis-really-wants/384980/March 2015.

4. Mariam Karouny, "Apocalyptic Prophecies Drive Both Sides to Syrian Battle for End of Time," *Reuters*, April 2, 2014.

5. Abu Musab al-Suri, *A Call to Global Islamic Resistance* (2004), 1,375.

6. Holy Quran *Al-Anfal* 8:60 (Sahih).

7. Jean-Pierre Filiu, *Apocalypse in Islam* (Berkeley: University of California Press, 2012), 188.

8. Abbas Amanat, "Islam in Iran v. Messianic islam in Iran," *Encyclopaedia Iranica*, ed. Ehsan Yarshater, Vol. 14 (London: Routledge & Kegan Paul, 1982), 130–134.

9. "Address by H.E. Dr. Mahmoud Ahmadinejad, President of the Islamic Republic of Iran, Before the 66th Session of the United Nations General Assembly," New York, September 23, 2011, https://gadebate.un.org/sites/default/files/gastatements/66/IR_en.pdf.

10. "Address by H.E. Dr. Mahmoud Ahmadinejad, President of the Islamic Republic of Iran, Before the 67th Session of the United Nations General Assembly," New York, September 26, 2012, https://gadebate.un.org/sites/default/files/gastatements/67/IR_en.pdf.

11. Tamar Hermann, *The National-Religious Sector in Israel 2014* (n.p.: The Israel Democracy Institute, 2014), https://en.idi.org.il/media/4663/madad-z-english_web.pdf.

12. Chanan Morrison and Abraham Isaac Kook, *Sapphire from the land of Israel: A New Light on the Weekly Torah Portion from the Writings of Rabbi Abraham Isaac HaKohen Kook* (Mitzpeh Yericho: Chanan Morrison, 2013), 124.

13. Paul S. Boyer, *When Time Shall Be No More: Prophecy Belief in Modern American Culture* (Cambridge, MA: Harvard University Press, 2000), 187.

14. "Four Arab Armies Reported on March Toward Palestine: Official Syrian Circles Say Holy Land Will Be Under Attack Tomorrow," *Los Angeles Times,* May 14, 1948.

15. "Israel: A Nation Under Siege," *Time,* June 9, 1967, 39.

16. Samuel Katz, *Battleground—Fact and Fantasy in Palestine* (New York: Bantam Books, 1985), 10–11, 185.

17. "Middle East: The Quickest War," *Time,* June 16, 1967, 22–34.

18. Tim Lister, "Maps, land and history: Why 1967 still matters," CNN, May 24, 2011, http://edition.cnn.com/2011/WORLD/meast/05/24/israel.1967/index.html.

19. Tom Segev, *1967: Israel, the War, and the Year That Transformed the Middle East* (New York: Metropolitan Books, 2007), 138.

20. Ibid., 283.

21. Ibid., 284.

22. Ibid., 287.

23. Ibid., 286.

24. Irving Spiegel, "Church Leaders Ask Aid to Israel," *New York Times*, May 28, 1967, 8.

25. Boyer, *When Time Shall Be No More*, 188.

26. Don F. Neufeld, "Jerusalem Conference on Bible Prophecy," *Advent Review And Sabbath Herald* 148, no. 27 (July 8, 1971): 1.

27. Ibid.

28. Boyer, *Time Shall Be No More*, 188.

29. Benjamin Glatt, "Christian Film 'In Our Hands' Brings Six Day War To The Big Screen," *Jerusalem Post*, May 17, 2017.

30. "The Quickest War," *Time*, 22.

31. "The Foreign Relations: Hot-Line Diplomacy," *Time*, June 16, 1967, 15–34.

32. Seth S. King, "20–Year Division of Jerusalem Seems Ended by Israeli Troops," *New York Times*, June 7, 1967, 18.

33. "The Future of Jerusalem," *New York Times*, June 28, 1967, 44.

34. Segev, *1967*, 380–381.

35. "The Western Wall: History and Overview," Jewish Virtual Library, accessed August 2022, http://www.jewishvirtuallibrary.org/history-and-overirew-of-the-western-wall.

36. Micah Goodman, "Redemption and Crisis of Religious Zionism," *Haaretz*, September 22, 2015.

37. "Judaism: Should the Temple Be Rebuilt?" *Time*, June 30, 1967, 56.

38. "The Quickest War," *Time*, 32.

39. Patrick Cockburn, "West Bank Sealed Off After Two Israelis Are Shot Dead," *Jerusalem Post*, July 26, 1996.

40. Jonathan Lis, Nadav Shragai, and Yuval Yoaz, "Yatom: Jews Nearly Succeeded in 1984 Temple Mt. Bomb Plot," *Haaretz*, July 24, 2004.

41. The Temple Institute, https://www.templeinstitute.org.

42. "Time to Wake Up: Make the Dream a Reality!" The Temple Institute, July 21, 2017, https://youtu.be/tAZ8zdMCiuQ.

43. Ed Adamczyk, "Yitzhak Rabin's Legacy 20 Years Later: A Pliable History," *UPI*, November 4, 2015.

44. Michael I. Karpin and Ina Friedman, *Murder in the Name of God: The Plot to Kill Yitzhak Rabin* (New York: Metropolitan Books, 1998).

45. Seffi Rachlevsky, *Ḥamwrw šel mašiyaḥ* (Tel-'Abiyb: Ydiy'wt 'aharwnwt, 1998).

46. "77% of Israelis See Removal of Temple Mount Metal Detectors as Capitulation," i24 News Israel, July 26, 2017, https://www.i24news.tv/en/news/israel/151359-170726-77-of-israelis-see-removal-of-temple-mount-metal-detectors-as-capitulation. Hillel Fendel, "49% Want Holy Temple Rebuilt," Arutz Sheva, Israel National News, July 18, 2010, http://www.israelnationalnews.com/News/News.aspx/138655.

47. Jeffrey Goldberg, "The Iranian Regime on Israel's Right to Exist," *Atlantic Monthly*, March 9, 2015.

48. All Erdoğan official statements referenced can be found through the Office of the President of the Turkish Republic. See also: Ferdi Turkten, Baris Gundogan, Kemal Karadağ, "Cumhurbaşkanı Erdoğan: 24 Temmuz Cuma günü cuma namazı ile birlikte Ayasofya'yı ibadete açmayı planlıyoruz," Anadolu Ajansi, October 7, 2020, https://www.aa.com.tr/tr/ayasofya-camii/cumhurbaskani-erdogan-24-temmuz-cuma-gunu-cuma-namazi-ile-birlikte-ayasofyayi-ibadete-acmayi-planliyoruz/1906430; Recep Tayyip Erdoğan, "TBMM 27. Dönem 4. Yasama Yılı Açılış Konuşmaları," transcript of speech delivered to the Turkish Grand National Assembly, the 4th Legislative Year, October 1, 2020, https://www.tccb.gov.tr/konusmalar/353/122222/tbmm-27-donem-4-yasama-yili-acilis-konusmalari.

49. Recep Tayyip Erdoğan, speaking to AKP party group in Turkish parliament, Ankara, June 13, 2017.

50. "Turkey Could Cut Diplomatic Ties with Israel," *Daily Sabah*, December 5, 2017.

51. *Sahih Muslim*, 41.6985.

52. At the time of writing, the sermons were available online.

53. Kate Mather, "Riverside Imam Draws Criticism for Fiery Sermon," *Los Angeles Times*, July 31, 2017.

54. "Principles of One Community," David Joint Unified School Distict, accessed August 2022, https://www.djusd.net/services/climate/principles_of_one_community.

55. "Müslümanlar ile Yahudilerin Son Savaşı," *İslam ve İhsan*, July 17, 2017.

56. James Walsh, "Killing for God," *Time*, December 4, 1995.

16. NEW WORLD ORDER

1. Joseph Kraft, "Is America Ready for a Christian President from the South?" *Washington Post*, March 18, 1976. A19.

2. Michael Novak, "The Hidden Religious Majority," *Washington Post*, April 4, 1976, C1, C5.

3. "The Evangelicals," *Newsweek*, October 25, 1976.

4. "Religion: Counting Souls," *Time*, October 4, 1976.

5. J. Brooks Flippen, *Jimmy Carter, the Politics of Family, and the Rise of the Religious Right* (Athens: The University of Georgia Press, 2011), 192.

6. Ibid.

7. Ibid., 266.

8. Jimmy Carter, *White House Diary* (New York: Farrar, Straus and Giroux, 2010), 57.

9. United States Department of State, "Department of State Bulletin," November 7, 1977, 639.

10. Ronald Reagan, "Remarks at Liberty State Park," speech, Jersey City, New Jersey, September 1, 1980.

11. Kathy Sawler and Robert G. Kaiser, "Evangelicals Flock to GOP Standard Feeling They Have a Friend in Reagan," *Washington Post*, July 16, 1980, A15.

12. Ibid.

13. Ibid.

14. Bill Peterson, "Iowa Caucuses: Ready to Put the Political Trusts to the Test," *Washington Post*, January 20, 1980, A1.

15. John Herbers, "Ultraconservative Evangelicals A Surging New Force in Politics," *New York Times*, August 17, 1980, A1.

16. Ronald Reagan, Kiron K. Skinner, Annelise Graebner Anderson, and Martin Anderson, *Reagan: A Life in Letters*, (London: Simon & Schuster, 1980), 654.

17. John Herbers, "Religious Leaders Tell of Worry on Armageddon View Ascribed to Reagan," *New York Times*, October 21, 1984, 32.

18. See: *Jerusalem Post*, October 28, 1982.

19. William Rose, "The Reagans and Their Pastor," *Christian Life*, May 30, 1968, 43–44.

20. Antiochian Orthodox Christian Diocese of North America, *The Word*, June 1983.

21. "Scripture Lesson," *New York Times*, October 28, 1981, A21.

22. *Public Papers of the Presidents of the United States: Ronald W. Reagan, Book II (1983)* (Washington, DC: US Government Printing Office, 1985), 1708–1713.

23. James Mills, "The Serious Implications of a 1971 Conversation with Ronald Reagan," *San Diego Magazine*, August 1985, 140–141.

24. Nicholas Dawidoff, "The Riddle of Jimmy Carter," *Rolling Stone*, February 3, 2011.

25. Pat Robertson, "Biblical Prophecy Fulfilled? Pat Interprets a Biblical Prophecy Concerning Iraq, Syria, Egypt and Israel and Calls for Its Fulfillment," PatRobertson.com, accessed August 2022, http://www.patrobertson.com/Teaching/patprophecy.asp.

26. Administration of Jimmy Carter, Statement by the White House Press Secretary, August 8, 1978.

27. Daniel Schorr, "Reagan Recants: His Path from Armageddon to Detente," *Los Angeles Times*, January 3, 1988.

28. Pat Robertson and Bob Slosser, *The Secret Kingdom: A Promise of Hope and Freedom in a World of Turmoil* (Nashville, TN: T. Nelson, 1982).

29. "Haçlı seferleri öyle 9 asır geçmişte değil!" Anadolu Agency, September 8, 2013, https://www.aa.com.tr/tr/turkiye/hedefi-baris-olan-surece-en-ideal- katkiyi-veririz/220074.

30. Taha Aykol, "The 'Crusader-Zionist alliance' saga," *Hürriyet*, December 21, 2017.

31. "Text: Osama bin Laden's 1998 Interview," *The Guardian*, October 8, 2001, https://www.theguardian.com/world/2001/oct/08/afghanistan.terrorism15.

32. "Remarks by the President Upon Arrival" (transcript of remarks delivered in Washington, DC, September 16, 2001), https://georgewbush-whitehouse.archives.gov/news/releases/2001/09/20010916-2.html.

33. Ibid.

34. Ewen MacAskill, "George Bush: 'God Told Me to End the Tyranny in Iraq,'" *The Guardian*, October 7, 2005.

35. Robert Draper, "Rumsfeld and Iraq: And He Shall Be Judged," *GQ*, May 18, 2009.

36. "Pentagon Briefings No Longer Quote Bible: Under Bush Cover Pages of Daily Intelligence Report Included Verses," *Associated Press*, May 18, 2009.

37. Gustav Niebuhr, "Muslim Group Seeks to Meet Billy Graham's Son," *New York Times*, November 20, 2001, B5.

38. Richard M. Nixon, *The Memoirs of Richard Nixon*, Vol. 1 (New York: Warner Communications, 1979), 615.

39. Samuel P. Huntington, *The Clash of Civilizations and the Remaking of World Order* (New York: Touchstone, 1997).

40. Charles Colson, "Bloody Borders: Islam Hijacked?" *Breakpoint*, Commentary #011214 (2001).

41. Bernard Lewis, "The Roots of Muslim Rage: Why So Many Muslims Deeply Resent the West, and Why Their Bitterness Will Not Easily Be Mollified," *Atlantic Monthly*, September 1990.

42. Brian Montopoli, "Conservatives Fight 'Homosexual Extremist Movement,'" CBS News, September 28, 2009, https://www.cbsnews.com/news/conservatives-fight-homosexual-extremist-movement/.

43. Richard Lei, "Christian Soldier," *Washington Post*, November 6, 2003.

44. Jeremy Scahill, *Dirty Wars: The World Is a Battlefield* (New York: Nation Books, 2014), 110.

45. Nicholas Schmidle, "In the Crosshairs," *The New Yorker*, June 3, 2013.

46. "From Hypocrisy to Apostasy: The Extinction of the Grayzone," *Dabiq*, No. 7, 54.

47. "Islam is the Religion of the Sword Not Pacifism," *Dabiq*, No. 7, 22.

48. Barack Obama, "A Politics of Conscience," speech, Hartford, Connecticut, June 23, 2007.

49. Reinhold Niebuhr, *The Children of Light and the Children of Darkness: A Vindication of Democracy and a Critique of Its Traditional Defense* (Chicago: The University of Chicago Press, 2011), 118.

50. David Brooks, "Obama, Gospel and Verse," *New York Times*, April 26, 2007, A25.

51. Laura Barton, "Hope—The Image That is Already an American Classic," *The Guardian*, November 10, 2008.

52. 1 Cor. 15:52 (KJV).

53. Peter Hamby, "Obama: GOP Doesn't Own Faith Issue," CNN Politics, October 8, 2007, http://edition.cnn.com/2007/POLITICS/10/08/obama.faith/index.html.

54. "The Obama Cult: If Barack Obama Disappoints His Supporters, They Will Have Only Themselves to Blame," *The Economist*, July 23, 2009.

55. Sandro Magister, "There's a Strange Prophet in the White House," *L'Espresso*, August 23, 2010, http://chiesa.espresso.repubblica.it/articolo/1344430bdc4.html?eng=y.

56. Morton Keller, *Obama's Time: A History* (New York: Oxford University Press, 2015), 1.

57. Matt Patches, "Shepard Fairey on the Future of Political Art and Whether Obama Lived Up to His 'Hope' Poster," *Esquire*, May 29, 2015.

58. James Atlas, "What Is Fukuyama Saying? And to Whom Is He Saying It?" *New York Times Magazine*, October 22, 1989.

59. *Authorization for Use of Military Force Against Iraq Resolution of 2002*, Public Law 107–243, *U.S. Statutes at Large* 116 (2002): 1498.

60. *The Congressional Record*, 107th Congress, 2nd Session, Vol. 148, No. 133 (October 10, 2002): S10288, https://www.congress.gov/107/crec/2002/10/10/CREC-2002-10-10.pdf.

61. Francis Fukuyama, "After Neoconservatism," *New York Times Magazine*, February 19, 2006.

62. Barack Obama, "Obama's Speech Against The Iraq War," transcript of speech delivered in Chicago, October 2, 2002, https://www.npr.org/templates/story/story.php?storyId=99591469.

63. "Remarks at the Paul H. Nitze School of Advanced International Studies and a Question-and-Answer Session," The American Presidency Project, April 10, 2006, https://www.presidency.ucsb.edu/documents/remarks-the-paul-h-nitze-school-advanced-international-studies-and-question-and-answer.

64. Helene Cooper and Robert F. Worth, "In Arab Spring, Obama Finds a Sharp Test," *New York Times*, September 24, 2012.

65. Rep. Dennis Cardoza, "Dem Lawmaker Blasts 'Professor Obama' As Arrogant, Alienating," *The Hill*, December 13, 2011.

66. Ewan MacAskill, "Mubarak Claims Obama 'Does Not Understand Egyptian Culture,'" *The Guardian*, February 4, 2011.

67. Cooper and Worth, "In Arab Spring."

68. Paul Wright, "Barack Obama's Arrogance to Blame For ISIS, Claims David Cameron's Ex-Aide," *Newsweek*, January 9, 2018. See also: Mark Davis, "Murdoch Reveals 'Arrogant' Obama," *Sydney Morning Herald*, November 6, 2010.

69. Creech Air Force Base, Nevada, is one of dozens of major drone operation centers.

70. Luke 17:20–21 (KJV).

71. Vishtasp Yasht, F. Max Müller, and James Darmesteter, *The Sacred Books of the East, Volume 23, The Zend-Avesta, Pt. 2* (Oxford: Clarendon Press, 1883), 344.

72. 1 Tim. 1:15–16 (NIV).

73. Luke 23:34 (KJV).

EPILOGUE

1. "Irgun Denounces Partition Support," *New York Times*, September 8, 1947, 7.

2. "Irgun Bomb Kills 11 Arabs, 2 Britons," *New York Times*, December 30, 1947, 1.

3. Thomas L. Friedman, "Using Songs, Israelis Touch Arab Feelings," *New York Times*, May 3, 1987, 1,44.

4. Dan Petreanu, "The Thursday Interview: Haim Moshe. A musician, not a political crusader," *The Jerusalem Post*, February 2, 1989.

5. Amy Horowitz, "Israeli Mediterranean Music: Straddling Disputed Territories," *Journal of American Folklore* 112, no. 445 (Summer 1999): 459.

6. "A Universe in a nutshell: The physics of everything, with Michio Kaku," Big Think, accessed August 2022, https://bigthink.com/videos/universe-in-a-nutshell-the-physics-of-everything-with-michio-kaku/. See also: Michio Kaku, "Reading the Mind of God," *Subtle Energies & Energy Medicine* 17, no. 1 (2006).

7. Henri Bergson, *Time and Free Will: An Essay on the Immediate Data of Consciousness*, transl. F.l. Pogson (London: Allen & Unwin, 1959).

8. Further reading: Caitlin Dawson, Daniel Aalto, Juraj Simko, and Martti Vainio, "The influence of fundamental frequency on perceived duration in spectrally comparable sounds," *PeerJ* 5, no. e3734 (September 2017), doi:10.7717/peerj.3734. Also: "Fundamental and Harmonic Frequencies," https://www.teachmeaudio.com/recording/sound-reproduction/fundamental-harmonic-frequencies.

9. W.E.H. Stanner, *White Man Got No Dreaming: Essays, 1938–1973* (Canberra: Australian National University Press, 1979), 23.

10. Ibid., 24, 29.

11. This is often streaming on YouTube. For episode details, see: IMDb, *Cosmos*, Season 1, Episode 10, "The Edge of Forever." https://www.imdb.com/title/tt0760462/?ref_=adv_li_tt.

12. See Rick Groleau, "Imagining Other Dimensions," PBS, October 28, 2003, https://www.pbs.org/wgbh/nova/article/imagining-other-dimensions/. See also Joachim I. Krueger, "The Didge and You," Psychology Today, May 18, 2007, https://www.psychologytoday.com/nz/blog/one-among-many/201705/the-didge-and-you.

13. Isaiah 11:8-10 (KJV).

14. Charlie Wood, "Imaginary Numbers May Be Essential for Describing Reality," Wired, March 7, 2021, https://www.wired.com/story/imaginary-numbers-may-be-essential-for-describing-reality/; Emily Conover, "Quantum Physics Requires Imaginary Numbers to Explain Reality," ScienceNews, December 15, 2021, https://www.sciencenews.org/article/quantum-physics-imaginary-numbers-math-reality/.

15. 1 Cor. 13:11-13 (Geneva).

16. 1 Cor. 15:19 (NRSV).

INDEX

Edison, Thomas, 138
Edom (Edomites), 179, 183, 25, 320
Egypt, Moses and 172-173; the Shasu
    and, 180; first mention of Israel,
    182; Merneptah Stele, 187; biblical
    Judah and, 192, 195-197, 209-210;
    Ptolemaic dynasty of, 242, 247;
    Muslim Brotherhood and,
    383-385, 390; secularism and, 395;
    Soviet relations with, 396; Six-day
    war and, 397-400; Jimmie Carter
    and, 420, 427; Barack Obama and,
    447-449, Arab Spring and,
    447-448
Eichmann, Adolph, 398-399
Einstein, Albert, 22, 32-36
El, 183-184, 188-190, 199-200, 202
Eldad, Israel, 405
Eliade, Mircea, 22, 114, 118-119, 122,
    141
Elohim, 35
En, 141-143
Encke (comet), 153
End Time(s), idea's origin and
    meaning, 223-224, 237-240, 244,
    452-453; Jewish expectations of,
    252, 273; Byzantine Empire and,
    311; Muhammad and, 316-317,
    320-323; Crusades and, 339;
    Columbus and 351-352; Luther
    and, 343-347; modern-day Islam
    and, 382, 389-392, 411-412, 431;
    American politics and, 370-371,
    417-418, 420-428; Jewish terror
    and, 408; rebirth of Israel and,
    360-361, 396-400; secular use of
    30, 444; Bob Dylan and, 263
Enheduanna, 150-151, 153, 155, 158
Enki, 125-130
Enlil, 87, 229
Enmerkar, 87, 140, 142
Erdoğan, Recep Tayyip, 409-411,
    431-432, 387
Erech, 83-84, 127
Eridu, as biblical Babel, 83; claim of
    first kingship, 85, 89-91; ziggurat
    of, 122; template for civilization,
    123, 125-132; origin of hierarchy
    and, 133, 141; alien hypothesis and,
    124
Eridu Genesis, 85-86
Essenes, 251-252, 264
Etzion, Yehuda, 406

Euphrates River, 28-30, 46, 91, 103;
    Turkish dam on,123; Abraham
    and,154; conquest of Babylon and,
    232; as Israel's border, 459
Evangelicalism (American), 367, 372,
    394
Exile (Israel to Assyria), 200; (Judah
    to Babylon), 211, 226, 238, 245, 254
Ezekiel, 223, 245, 253, 293, 318, 401;
    Ronald Reagan and, 426
Ezra, 241

Faisal, Prince, 383
Falwell, Jerry, 367, 418, 422-424, 429,
    388, **396**
Feniger, Ofer, 398
Ferguson, R. Brian 57
Ferngren, Gary, 303
Finkelstein, Prof. Israel, 183,
    186-187, 198
First World War, 244, 363-368, 372,
    382, 409, 431, 387
Flavius Josephus, 90, 122, 172,
    264-267, 284
Fourth Philosophy, 264-266,
    285-286
Fox, Everett, 88
Frashokereti, 230
Fry, Douglas, 108, 121-122
Fukuyama, Francis, 30, 442-445

Gabriel, Richard A, 57, 59, 144, 152
Gallipoli, 431
Garden of Eden, 12, 19-20, 25, 27, 39,
    42, 76, 149, 157, 217, 278,
    280-281; real-world analogues of,
    46, 49, 56, 60; historicity of, 31-32;
    psychological analogues of, 67-68,
    74; civilization as return to, 115;
    Jewish Temple metaphor of, 211;
    Islam and, 317, 323; Dome of the
    Rock and, 333
Garstang, John, 121
Georges-Picot, François, 383
Ginsberg, H.I., 307
Global War on Terror, 433-436
Göbekli Tepe, 46-49, 53-54, 56,
    59-60, 65, 75, 79, 89, 91, 99-103,
    105, 131, 203, 94
Gog/Magog, 253-254; religious
    violence and, 293; Byzantine
    Christians and, 310; early Islam
    and 318; Turks as, 334-339;

Martin Luther and, 345; Christian
Zionism and, 363, 420; Ronald
Reagan and, 426, 429; Pat
Robertson and 309, 430
Golden Age, 20, 23
Gorbachev, Mikhail S, 427-428
Gorenberg, Gershom, 295
Goy (goyim), 163, 275
Graham, Billy, 152, 260, 367,
415-416, 422, 425
Graham, Franklin, 435, 437
Great Schism, 335
Green, Keith, 262-263, 376
Gymnasia (Greek), 242

Hacilar (Hacılar), 109-111, 117, 119,
123, 155
Hagia Sophia, 312, 343, 347, 380,
409-410
Halafians, 118-122
Haldane, J.B.S, 34
Halevi, Yehuda, 164
Hallucinogens, 293
Halpern, Baruch, 198, 207
Hamas, 385, 411, 413
Hammurabi, 158
Harding, Warren G, 371-372
Harmoush, Mahmoud, 411
Hannukah, 248, **255**
Harran (City of Moon God Sin),
153-157, 166-167, 169, 228, 229, 231,
335, 176
Harran (Brother of Abraham), 155
Hasidim (Hasidim), 252, 290, 295,
299
Hate speech, 412
Hazor, 155, 160, 166-168
Health, in prehistory, 52-54, 57-58
Heaven (early conceptions of), 27,
49, 85-89, 101, 112, 125, 127, 131-133
Hellfire missile, 80, 450
Heraclius, Emperor, 308, 312-314,
316, 318, 430, 325
Herod the Great, 251, 264, 285, 295,
256
Herodotus, 224, 232-233, 235, 237,
270
Herzl, Theodore, 361, 364
Heylel, 230
Hezekiah, 192-198, 330-331, **178**
Hippolytus, 300, 306
Hitler, 11, 70, 80, 143, 372, 399, 446;
paradise dream of, 215
Hobbes, Thomas, 50-60, 85, 91,
107-108

Hodder, Ian, 49, 104-106
Holocaust, 66, 121, 360, 396-199
House of War (*Dar al-Harb*), 381
Huntington, Samuel, 435-436
Hussein, King, 402, 407, 413
Hussein, Saddam, 3, 80, 227, 391,
438, 443-445, 447, 460

Iliad, 70
Impalement, 181
Inanna, 127-130, 138, 150-151, 181
Indra, 254
Interest (compound); invention of,
139-140, 144, 145; Zoroastrian
abhorrence of, 235
Inventions, 129
Iran, 26, 31, 385, 389, 392-393,
408-409, 411, 424, 430, 431, 437,
445, 449; in antiquity, 215,
216-218, 236, 252; 429-30
Iraq, Iraqis, 30, 80, 84-85, 123,
154-155, 226-227, 383, 389-393, 395,
433-434, 437, 443-445, 447, 458
Irenaeus, 300-301, 310
Isaiah, 77-78, 191, 194-196, 203-206,
215, national security and, 209; as
YHWH proponent, 196; sawn in
two, 203; universal appeal of, 211;
relation to Marxism, 213; as
archetype of progressivism, 212;
concept of messiah and, 214; End
Time concept and, 223; Lucifer
and, 229-230, Zoroastrianism and,
252-253, 271; Jesus fulfills
prophecies of, 269-270; recent
fulfilled prophecies of, 401, 404,
427; metaphysical interpretation
of, 460, 468
Ishmael, 156, 172, 314-315, 318, 320
Isimud, 129-130
ISIS (Islamic State), 16-17, 26, 28-31,
79-81, 157, 216, 293, 385-386, 390,
393, 432, 437-438, 449
Islam, 158, 163, 172, 183, 198, 245,
297, 308, 334, 339, 381-386,
431-438, 448-449, 460; Martin
Luther and, 343-344; early history
of 313-324; Columbus and, 351
Israel, (Kingdom of), 183, 186-194,
198; (State of), 26, 161, 267, 366,
37, 395-396, 406
Istanbul, 150, 193, 343, 349, 350,
376-380, 432

BLESSING

יְבָרֶכְךָ יְהוָה וְיִשְׁמְרֶךָ
יָאֵר יְהוָה פָּנָיו אֵלֶיךָ וִיחֻנֶּךָּ
יִשָּׂא יְהוָה פָּנָיו אֵלֶיךָ וְיָשֵׂם לְךָ שָׁלוֹם

The LORD bless you and keep you;
the LORD make his face to shine upon you, and be gracious to you;
the LORD lift up his countenance upon you, and give you peace.